COST ACCOUNTING
Analysis and Control

THE WILLARD J. GRAHAM SERIES IN ACCOUNTING

CONSULTING EDITOR   ROBERT N. ANTHONY   *Harvard University*

COST ACCOUNTING
Analysis and Control

GORDON SHILLINGLAW

Professor of Accounting
Graduate School of Business
Columbia University

 THIRD EDITION · 1972

RICHARD D. IRWIN, INC. *Homewood, Illinois 60430*

IRWIN-DORSEY INTERNATIONAL *London, England WC2H 9NJ*

IRWIN-DORSEY LIMITED *Georgetown, Ontario L7G 4B3*

Third Edition

First Printing, April 1972
Second Printing, June 1973
Third Printing, April 1974
Fourth Printing, November 1974

Library of Congress Catalog Card No. 78–183254
Printed in the United States of America

To
BARBARA
JAMES
and
LAURA

Preface

Cost Accounting deals with the internal financial details of individual business firms and other organizations. Cost accounting systems are necessary in the first instance to help management plan and control the organization's operations. In addition, some cost accounting data are used in the preparation of financial statements for the organization as a whole, and some are required by the organization's relationships with other organizations or groups, such as government agencies or creditors.

The Approach

My aim in this book is to provide a comprehensive introduction to the field of cost accounting, with primary emphasis on the ways in which it can serve management. Other questions—such as what costs are to be reported as the cost of balance sheet assets, and what costs are to be taken to the income statement as current expenses—although not ignored, are not my dominant concern. My primary interest is in what managers want or need to know and how best to provide this information.

Furthermore, I prefer to emphasize *meaning* rather than technique. Mastery of cost accounting techniques unaccompanied by an understanding of what they are designed to achieve is no mastery at all. Most of the problems, exercises, and cases are designed to implement this approach.

In writing this book I have tried to keep two groups clearly in mind—those preparing for accounting careers and those who are, or plan to be, consumers of accounting information and accounting services. I have tried to give the accounting professional the deep coverage that he needs, while organizing the material so that those not interested in careers in accounting or financial management can focus on the fundamental issues which concern them. Although the accounting specialist probably should proceed at a slower pace and work more of the problems than the non-financial student will find appropriate, the overall approach and basic objectives should be the same for both. The accountant must understand why management needs information so that he can provide it; the operating executive must be able to understand the information that the accountant provides. Both should be keenly aware of the limitations of this information.

I have tried to write each chapter so that the average student will be able to understand the concepts and also apply them to practical problems. The student should realize, however, that he cannot read this book, or any accounting book for that matter, as he would a detective story or novel. For best results, he should copy key figures from the numerical illustrations on notepaper and make sure that he can trace the relationships among these figures as they are unfolded in the text.

Outline

The book is divided into four parts of unequal length. Part I, consisting of the first three chapters, has two objectives. First, it is designed to identify and describe the management processes of planning and control and the demands placed by these processes on the accounting system. Second, it is used to introduce a set of elementary concepts from managerial economics, decision theory, and statistical analysis that provide the foundation on which the current practice of cost accounting is built.

The core of the book is in Parts II and III. Part II explores the methods that might be used to measure the costs of individual products, projects, services, or other segments of the organization's operations, primarily for use in managerial decision making. It also examines the more technical accounting question of how factory costs can be divided between balance sheet and income statement for public financial reporting. Part III deals with periodic financial planning and control reporting at all organizational levels from first-line supervision to top management. Particular attention is paid to the multiproduct, divisionalized corporation.

Part IV is in a sense an appendix to Part II. It introduces a number of models that can be used for several kinds of management decisions—evaluating capital expenditure proposals, product pricing, rationing available capacity, and establishing inventory order quantities and re-order points. My primary objective in each case is to examine the kinds of data that the model requires, a question that the model builder often assumes away.

The Revision

The third edition is structurally quite different from its predecessors. My goal in reorganizing the material has been to emphasize the universality of cost accounting concepts. Cost accounting originated in the factory and is often viewed as a factory-centered system. While I have given factory operations ample attention, I hope that I have been successful in placing factory cost measurement and reporting systems in their proper perspective, as essential but nondominant elements of cost accounting systems. In line with this, I have selected the illustrations for the first few chapters almost exclusively from nonmanufacturing situations and have used nonmanufacturing illustrations, cases, and problems extensively in other parts of the book.

In substantive terms, the major changes have been the introduction of a new chapter dealing with the behavioral aspects of budgetary planning and reporting systems and a major expansion of the coverage of short-run optimization models. Although a cost accounting text is an inappropriate and inefficient vehicle for an exploration of these topics in depth, they cannot be ignored. I have tried to duplicate the material available in more specialized texts as little as possible, going only far enough to provide the background essential to an understanding of how this material relates to cost accounting.

Using the Book

This text can be the basis for a one-term survey course, a two-term comprehensive course, or two separate courses in cost measurement and financial planning and control systems. The reorganization of Parts II and III arose in part out of an effort to implement the last of these alternatives.

If the book is used for a one-semester survey course, a number of chapters will have to be omitted if the coverage of each is to be adequate. Choice of the chapters to be omitted will of course depend on the preferences and interests of the individual instructor and on the coverage of complementary courses in controllership, budgeting, finance, business economics, and quantitative methods. My own outline for such a course would cover chapters 1–5, 9–11, 12 (first part), 14, 15, 17, 18, and 21–23, with as much additional material as the time available would permit.

The problem material for this edition has been revised extensively and many new problems have been added. The number of case studies has been increased substantially. As in the preceding edition, solutions to a set of representative problems and exercises are provided in Appendix B, for those students who have the time to work problems other than those assigned by their instructors. These selected problems are intended mainly to provide exercise in the rudiments of problem solving and for this reason have fairly definite numerical solutions. The more difficult problems are not well represented in Appendix B because they generally contain qualitative elements that can be worked out properly only through class discussion.

Acknowledgments

I owe much to many for the help and encouragement they have provided as this book has gone through three editions. I am grateful to Myron J. Gordon for his advice in the preparation of the first edition and for permitting me to use a number of problems originally prepared for our joint work, *Accounting: A Management Approach.* Thomas M. Hill, Zenon S. Zannetos, and Carl Devine were also very helpful to me in the writing of the first edition, as was the late Willard J. Graham.

In revising the book I have benefited greatly from a host of comments made by users of the first two editions and by my colleagues at Columbia University. Harvey Babiak, Lawrence J. Benninger, Gary A. Fox, William Gruber, Kenneth W. Lemke, J. Leslie Livingstone, Earl Spiller, Jr., and Stephen A. Zeff all made useful comments on the text and problems in the previous edition, and the list would be longer if my memory were as strong as my gratitude.

I relied heavily on Carl L. Nelson and Russell A. Taussig in writing the previous edition; both were a continent away while the present edition took its final form, but their comments on portions of the manuscript were insightful and unarguable.

Eric L. Flamholtz reviewed the new behavioral chapter and helped me avoid a number of gaps and errors in the coverage. Gerard von Dohlen wore down more than one blue pencil as he read drafts of several chapters, and these chapters are immeasurably better as a result.

None of these friendly critics is responsible for defects that survive in this edition, of course. The gaps that remain between their perceptions and my execution are beyond their control; I can only hope that I have been skillful enough to take advantage of most of the help that has been offered me.

John C. Burton, Carl Nelson, David Solomons, Russell Taussig, Lawrence Benninger, and Harvey Babiak have been most generous in letting me use or modify problems or cases they have written. I am also grateful to Luigi Dusmet de Smours, director of the IMEDE Management Development Institute in Lausanne, Switzerland, for his permission to use cases that I wrote while serving on the IMEDE faculty.

Finally, I wish to thank Yatinder Aggarwal for undertaking the tedious job of checking the solutions to the problems accompanying all but two of the chapters and for carrying out this task faithfully, cheerfully, and promptly. Dennis Frolin and Shahid Ansari provided the basic solutions to the problems and cases accompanying Chapter 18, while Thomas Huff checked the solutions for Chapter 28. I am grateful to them all for their help.

March 1972   GORDON SHILLINGLAW

Contents

xiii

PART II. COST MEASUREMENT

Accounts in Perspective. Revenue Classification: *Routine Coding of Revenues. Incorporation into the Accounts. The Use of Sampling to Cut Systems Cost. The Nonclassification Alternative. Recording Non-transactions. Indirect Revenue Effects.* Classification of Operating Costs: *Organizational Classification Bases. Descriptive Classification. Product or Project Classification. The Problem of Common Costs. Other Costing Bases.* Nonmonetary Data.

Applicability of Job Order Costing. Job Costing in the Service Organization: *Direct versus Overhead Costs. Predetermined Burden Rates. Departmental Burden Rates. Treatment of Other Overhead Costs. The Variability of Overhead Cost.* Factory Job Order Costing: *Classification of Materials Costs. Classification of Labor Costs. The Job Cost Sheet. Development and Use of Unit Costs.*

Identification of Direct Labor Time: *Setup Time. Rework Time.* Treatment of Wage Supplements: *Overtime Premiums. Average versus Marginal Overtime Premium. Shift Differentials. Incentive Pay. Fringe Benefits. Wage Guarantees.* Classifying Materials Costs: *Pricing Materials Quantities. Defective and Lost Units. Scrap.*

Accounts for Job Order Costing: *Recording the Purchase and Use of Materials. Using Control Accounts and Subsidiary Ledgers. Recording Labor Costs. Recording Overhead Cost Absorption. Recording Job Completions. Recording the Cost of Goods Sold. The Statement of Manufacturing Costs. Summary of the Cost Flows.* Explaining the Overhead Variance: *Sources of the Overhead Variances. Determining Spending Variances. Computing Volume Variances. Summarizing the Overhead Variance Analysis.* Disposing of Overhead Variances: *Approximating Average Historical Cost. Taking All Variances to Income. Assigning All Variances to the Balance Sheet. Industry Practice.*

Calculating Unit Cost: *Identifying the Process Centers. Measuring Costs. Measuring Output. Computing Unit Cost. Computing Product Cost. The Need for Additional Cost Divisors. Departures from Output Homogeneity. Inventory Shrinkage or Growth.* Control Uses of Process Costing. Accounting for Interdepartmental Transfers: *Why Special Calculations Are Needed. First-In, First-Out Method. Moving Average Method.*

The Nature of Variable Costing: *Application to Job Order Costing. Application to Process Costing. Handling Semivariable Costs. Handling Step Functions. Terminology: Variable Costing versus Direct Costing.*

The Case for Variable Costing: *Relevance of Average Variable Cost. Easier Cost Estimation. Better Focus on Profit Variability.* Arguments against Variable Costing: *Relevance to "Long-Run" Decisions. The Concept of Attributable Cost. Suboptimization under Variable Costing.* Variable Costing and External Reporting: *Effects on Reported Income. Pros and Cons of Variable Costing Financial Statements. Reconciling Internal and External Statements.* Overhead Variance Analysis under Variable Costing.

Manufacturing Cost Differentials. Other Applications: *Bank Service Charges. Vending Machine Profitability.*

terion. Monetary Measurements. Behavioral Problems in System Administration: *Insensitivity of the Budgeting Staff. Budgets as Pressure Devices.*

Part I

Cost Accounting and Its Setting

chapter **1**

The Role of Cost Accounting

The origins of accounting can be traced back into prehistory. Accounting records of a sort have been found in Minoan palaces, Egyptian tombs, and Assyrian temples dating from more than two millenia before the age of Rome. Judging from the fragmentary evidence that has survived, these early records were mainly to help the royal or temple steward keep track of the funds that he was responsible for. This kind of stewardship accounting still has an important place in the modern accounting system, but the emphasis of cost accounting is far different. Mainly a 20th-century development, its role is to provide and process information about the organization's various products, services, and other activities.

Because this kind of information is primarily for management's use, any study of cost accounting must be preceded by some understanding of the management processes which require its output. Accordingly, the purpose of this chapter is to provide a quick description of these management processes and of the other determinants of cost accounting structure.

THE MANAGEMENT CONTROL PROCESS

The managerial process which concern cost accounting most directly are those which center on planning for the future and controlling current operations. These may be characterized broadly as processes of management control, utilizing four separate though interrelated techniques:

1. Control through planning.
2. Control through direction and supervision.
3. Control by feedback response.
4. Control by appraisal.

3

Control through Planning

Control always begins at the planning stage. No other technique controls the firm's destiny as planning does, and the difference between effective and ineffective planning can be so great as to overshadow the effect of all other control techniques combined.

Planning is the process of deciding on a course of action, of finding and choosing among the alternatives available. It takes three forms: (1) *policy formulation*—establishment of the major ground rules that determine the basic direction and shape of the enterprise, the limits within which management is free to exercise its discretion; (2) *decision making* —the choice among alternative solutions to specific operating or financial problems within the prescribed policy limits; and (3) *budgeting*—the

Exhibit 1–1

MANAGEMENT PLANNING PROCESSES

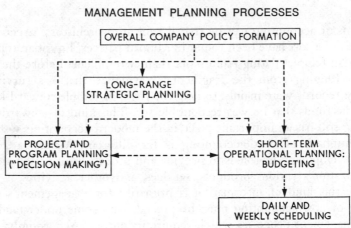

preparation of comprehensive operating and financial plans for specific intervals of time.

Exhibit 1–1 represents an attempt to diagram the relationships among these three types of planning. In general, the progression moves from the top of the chart toward the bottom. Policies and strategic plans tend to act as tight or loose constraints on the shorter term processes, although this is not wholly rigid. Policies are always subject to review as conditions change or more information becomes available; long-range plans are also modified for the same reason.

The relationship between project and program planning and short-term operational planning is more complex. For example, the establishment of a marketing program ordinarily takes place as part of the periodic operational planning process. Similarly, a decision to promote one product more actively than another is likely to be part of operational planning—and will certainly affect the resulting operating plan. Both of these kinds of decisions may also be made later, however, when changing conditions give evidence that this part of the operating plan can no longer be carried out effectively or can be improved upon.

Scheduling, shown at the bottom of the chart, is really part of operational planning. It is the process of determining in detail what needs to be done to carry out the planned program; establishing timetables for the performance of these tasks; and seeing to it that men, materials, facilities, and funds are available in the necessary quantities at the necessary times and places to carry out the plan.

Control through Direction and Supervision

The second control mechanism consists of the interrelated processes of direction, coordination, and supervision. These are the means by which plans are executed and results achieved. They consist of seeing to it that customer orders are obtained, that production and delivery schedules are met, that prescribed procedures are followed, and that expenditures are kept consistent with the established plans.

This mechanism, which might be called direct control or concurrent control, relies upon the leadership and human relations abilities of management to achieve its ends. It requires a capacity to anticipate potential trouble spots and to take action before trouble arises. It also presumes an ability to see when things are going wrong, without waiting for the more formal indications provided by specifically designed feedback linkages, and in this it shades imperceptibly into the third control process.

Control by Feedback Response

The third link in the chain of control techniques is responsive control, the actions taken on the basis of the observation and analysis of performance. The two elements in this process are the signal or *feedback* that action is necessary and the *response* to that signal. The feedback usually takes the form of observed differences or deviations between actual and planned performance. Routine weekly or monthly reports of the kind illustrated in Exhibit 1–2, for example, are *attention directing* in that they emphasize deviations from plans and signal the presence of conditions or problems that should be investigated.

Responses to feedback data are of two types: corrective and adaptive. The response should be a corrective action if direct control has been inadequate, and an adaptive action if the deviation was due to an inhospitable environment. Adaptive action is a kind of replanning, and this takes us back where we started.

It should be emphasized that performance reports or other information feedback mechanisms are not the control device. Control is accomplished

Exhibit 1–2
ILLUSTRATIVE CONTROL REPORT

			General Accounting Expense Analysis Actual versus Budget			
	June				January–June	
Actual	Variance			Actual	Variance	
Amount	Amount	Percent		Amount	Amount	Percent
			Payroll			
$ 2,520	$(100)		Salaries—General	$15,620	$ (850)	
5,635	535		" —Accts. P & R	34,930	5,095	
5,067	342		" —Tabulating	31,415	1,962	
7	79		Overtime	300	80	
$13,229	$ 856	6.1	Total	$82,265	$6,287	7.6
$ 886	$ 14	1.6	Payroll Overhead	$ 4,800	$ 120	2.5
			Other Controllable Expenses			
$ 1,056	$ 43		Stationery	$ 6,547	$ (877)	
155	(12)		Telephone & Telegraph	961	(60)	
6	(6)		Traveling Expenses	150	(15)	
2	28		Overtime Meals	120	30	
2	—		Books & Periodicals	25	2	
—	—		Sundry Expense	15	1	
$ 1,221	$ 53	4.2	Total	$ 7,818	$ (919)	(11.8)
$15,336	$ 923	6.0	Total Controllable	$94,883	$5,488	5.8

Source: Clarence C. Benedict, "An Integrated System of Variance Analysis for Operating-Control Reports," in American Management Association, Special Report No. 25, *Reporting Financial Data to Top Management* (New York: American Management Association, 1957), p. 158.

by direct action, and all the reports in the world won't bring a deteriorating situation back under control unless they trigger some sort of action. Feedback, in other words, has an intermediate purpose—to improve the quality of the actions taken by management and to increase management's confidence that its actions are the right ones.

Control by Appraisal

The feedback mechanism serves another purpose—that of performance appraisal. The gap between actual and satisfactory performance helps management distribute rewards and penalties among its subordinates. Periodic performance reports thus serve a *scorecard* function for higher management in addition to the attention-directing function for management at the direct control level.

Appraisal performs three kinds of control tasks. First, the monetary and nonmonetary rewards accompanying consistent good performance and the penalties for poor performance inevitably affect the motivation of the affected personnel. If the reward structure is well conceived, this motivation should work positively to stimulate progress toward company goals.

Second, a soundly based appraisal system will lead to the promotion of the more effective managers to positions of greater scope and responsibility. This once again should contribute to company strength and profitability.

Third, the mere presence of an appraisal system can have a salutary effect on performance. People often behave differently—sometimes better, sometimes worse—if they know that their performance is being monitored.[1] Acceptance of the appraisal system is likely to improve performance, and management's task is to secure this acceptance.

The big problem here is that performance has many dimensions, many of them extremely difficult if not impossible to quantify. The things that can be easily measured may not be the most important aspects of performance, and emphasis on these aspects may direct performance into the wrong channels. When this happens, the blame is usually placed on the measurement system, but in truth the fault lies with management for misusing the measures that are available. Nevertheless, those who operate the feedback reporting system have an obligation to point out the shortcomings of their measures as well as to try to find ways of extending the scope of quantification.

Interrelationships among the Processes

The interrelationships among these processes are illustrated in Exhibit 1–3. Decisions and plans are made on the basis of information from various sources. These decisions are translated into action by the operating executives. Information on the results of these actions is recorded and compared with the planned results, and these comparisons then provide a basis either for corrective action (responsive control) or for adaptive action (replanning). They also serve in the appraisal of personnel.

Other Classification Systems

The few pages devoted here to the management control process can do no more than introduce the subject. A better understanding of the process requires both experience and exposure to the rather extensive literature that has developed over the years.

Various writers have chosen different ways of describing the structure of management controls. Anthony, for example, uses a three-way breakdown—strategic planning, management control, and operational control—distinguishing largely on the basis of the scope of the decisions taken

---

[1] Some interesting evidence bearing on this point is provided by Neil C. Churchill, William W. Cooper, and Trevor Sainsbury, "Laboratory and Field Studies of the Behavioral Effects of Audits" in Charles P. Bonini, Robert K. Jaedicke, and Harvey M. Wagner, *Management Controls: New Directions in Basic Research* (New York: McGraw-Hill Book Co., 1964), pp. 253–67.

Exhibit 1–3

BASIC PLANNING AND CONTROL LOOPS

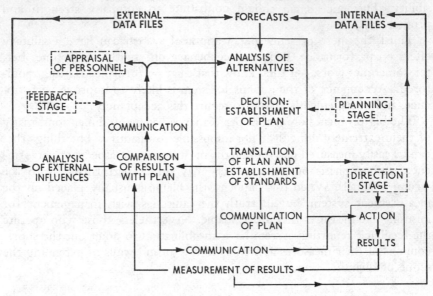

and their susceptibility to routinization.[2] Strategic planning concerns decisions with the largest scope and greatest potential impact (expansion into new markets), while at the other extreme operational control deals with actions that are narrow in focus and have short time horizons (eliminating excess inventories).

The choice of a classification scheme depends on its purpose, and our decision to describe management control in terms of a four-way classification of control mechanisms does not imply that other classification schemes are wrong—they just do not provide as good a background for the chapters that follow. For example, the principles underlying strategic planning decisions are the same as those that must be applied in periodic budgeting, even though the impact of decisions of the former type may be potentially much greater than those of the latter. The accountant must provide the same kinds of data for both, and thus it will pay him to try to identify the elements common to both kinds of decisions.

ACCOUNTING'S ROLE IN MANAGEMENT CONTROL

Accounting's contribution to management control processes is the province of *managerial accounting*. An integral part of the company's

[2] Robert N. Anthony, *Planning and Control Systems: A Framework for Analysis* (Boston: Harvard Graduate School of Business Administration, Division of Research, 1965).

management information system, managerial accounting serves management in several ways. First, it serves as a vital *source of data* for management planning. The accounts and document files are a repository of a vast quantity of details about the past progress of the enterprise, without which forecasts of the future can scarcely be made.

Second, it provides a cadre of *trained personnel* to assist management in the analysis of alternatives and in the preparation of plans. This analysis is not exclusively, or necessarily even predominantly, an accounting function, but attempting to plan without at least some participation by knowledgeable accounting personnel is a hazardous undertaking in most cases. In fact, the chief accounting officer or controller is an active and influential member of the top management group in many companies, but he becomes so because of his personal qualities and the relevance of his experience. The title of controller does not necessarily carry with it direct control responsibilities except within the accounting organization.

Third, managerial accounting provides a *means of communicating* management plans upward, downward, and outward through the organization. At early stages in planning, this means identifying the feasibility and consistency of the various segments of the plan. At later stages it keeps all parties informed of the plans that have been agreed upon and their roles in these plans.

Fourth, it supplies *feedback reports*, for both attention-getting and scorecard-keeping purposes. This is often the most visible contribution of managerial accounting within the firm and perhaps for this reason gets the most attention.

Finally, managerial accounting has a role to play in the *interpretation of results*. Response to feedback data typically requires identification of the likely cause or causes of departures from plan and location of the responsibility for follow-up action. Within certain limits, this too can be an accounting function.

In short, managerial accounting is an important part of the company's management information system. It must consider management's needs at all levels, and it should also provide a unified means of data accumulation and feedback.

OTHER FUNCTIONS OF ACCOUNTING

The accounting organization performs many functions other than those of managerial accounting. These may be classified for convenience into three groups:

1. *External reporting functions:* preparation of financial and statistical reports to shareholders, taxing authorities, and other interested parties.
2. *Internal control functions:* administration of systems to safeguard assets, maintain the accuracy of accounts, and review adherence to prescribed policies and procedures.

3. *Routine service functions:* maintenance of data and document files, preparation of invoices and payrolls, etc.

External Reporting

The external reporting functions are the province of *financial accounting*, designed to satisfy the information requirements of those whose focus of interest is the company as a whole. Its scope is largely limited to the development of historical reports summarizing the company's financial history and current financial position.

This contrasts sharply with managerial accounting, which tends to focus on segments of the company, such as product lines or divisions or branch territories. This is not to imply that management has no interest in financial accounting. On the contrary, management often uses data drawn from company income statements, funds statements, and balance sheets in making decisions on such matters as dividend distributions and new financing; but the dominant purpose of such statements is external rather than managerial, and the basic ground rules for external financial reporting are established by outsiders.

The breakdown of accounting information into internal and external categories is not always rigid. Sometimes the same figures are needed for both; sometimes internal figures that management does not use for decision making nevertheless need to be reported to outside groups to help justify the decisions that management has made.

For example, management would find cost data indispensable in preparing a bid for a special contract to supply a government agency with, say, 100,000 door latches. If the bid were accepted, the company might then need to use these same data in obtaining a bank loan to finance the project, and would probably use its records of actual costs incurred to convince the government's accountants that the contract price was reasonable.

Despite all these apparent inconsistencies, it remains useful to regard financial and managerial accounting as two separate components of the accounting program. This will help keep accounting methods and accounting purposes in clear relation to each other.

Internal Control

Internal control has been defined as "the plan of organization and all of the coordinate methods and measures adopted within a business to safeguard its assets, check the accuracy and reliability of its accounting data, promote operational efficiency, and encourage adherence to prescribed managerial policies."[3]

The asset-protection aspects of internal control constitute the system

---

[3] Committee on Auditing Procedure, American Institute of (Certified Public) Accountants, *Internal Control* (New York: AICPA, 1949), p. 6.

of *property control*. To help safeguard the company's cash balances, for example, only a limited number of persons should be granted the authority to approve the expenditure of company funds. In large or medium-sized companies and even in many small ones, these procedures generally also provide for the separation of the actual handling of cash and signing of checks from the authorization and approval process.

The accountant's responsibility for property control is pervasive, and references will be made throughout this book to procedures designed to perform this function. The main emphasis, however, is on the information functions of cost accounting, and the treatment of property control systems will be subordinated to this purpose.

Routine Services

Little need be said about the routine services provided by the accounting staff. It must maintain document files for evidentiary purposes and sometimes for later internal analysis as well. It must prepare a variety of command documents, such as employee payrolls and customer invoices.

All of these are important functions, and care must be exercised to insure that the system design is effective and economical. Typically the data input to the information system is produced in the document-preparation operation, which means that both objectives must be recognized in system design.

THE PLACE OF COST ACCOUNTING

With all this as background, we may at last be in a position to try to indicate what cost accounting is. Perhaps the most logical way to begin is with a definition of cost. *Cost represents the resources that have been or must be sacrificed to attain a particular objective.* For example, the objective may be to acquire a plot of land, and cost is measured by the amount of cash that will have to be paid to acquire the land. Other objectives may require different methods of measuring cost, as we shall see in Chapter 2, but the definition is universal.

Cost accounting, then, deals with the measurement of resource sacrifices. By itself, however, this definition is more pedantic than useful. A better approach is to ask what a company's cost accounting department is likely to do. It is typically concerned primarily with four activities, often though not exclusively in connection with factory operations:

1. *Cost finding:* measurement or estimation of the costs of individual products, departments, or other segments of the firm's operations.
2. *Cost analysis:* estimation of the relationships between costs and various determinants of costs.

3. *Cost recording:* classification and distribution of costs among the various ledger accounts.
4. *Cost reporting:* communication of cost data to various interested parties.

These four activities are the nucleus of cost accounting, no matter how much more broadly we may find it convenient to define the field.

Cost accounting's main contribution to financial accounting is in providing the data used to distinguish between those factory costs that are to be charged against current revenues as expenses[4] and those that are to be assigned to the company-produced goods and services in end-of-period inventories. This is primarily a matter of cost finding, and we shall begin to examine this aspect of cost accounting in Chapter 4.

Cost accounting's role in managerial accounting is much more diffused and hence more difficult to pin down. For managerial purposes, cost data are often of limited usefulness by themselves, but need to be weighed in conjunction with revenue and investment data as well. Furthermore, the principles governing the processing and analysis of cost data for management cannot really be separated from those governing the recording, reporting, and analysis of other kinds of data. For these reasons the cost-finding, cost analysis, cost-recording, and cost-reporting activities of managerial accounting cannot be developed or discussed in isolation but must be fully integrated into the planning and control framework into which they must fit.

Reflecting this view, cost accounting is defined here more broadly as *the body of concepts, methods, and procedures used to measure, analyze, or estimate the costs, profitability, and performance of individual products, departments, and other segments of a company's operations, for either internal or external use or both, and to report on these questions to the interested parties.*

Thus defined, cost accounting encompasses all of managerial accounting and the factory cost finding aspects of financial accounting as well. To objections that this is too broad a definition, the only reply is that it is intended primarily to delineate an area that must be studied as an interrelated whole. Narrower definitions would not succeed in narrowing the scope of the inquiry. Thus in a sense it doesn't matter how the subject is defined, as long as narrower definitions are accompanied by an appropriately wider selection of contributory material.

SUMMARY

Accounting is first and foremost a service function, centering on the provision of information. Financial accounting consists of providing

---

[4] An expense is a cost that has been used up, directly or indirectly, in the creation of the revenues of a specific period. Expenses appear on the income statement; costs that have not yet become expenses are shown on the balance sheet.

companywide information, primarily to outsiders, while managerial accounting is devoted to supplying information to management on segments of the firm's operations, for use in the various processes of management control.

This chapter has distinguished four control techniques: planning, direction and supervision, feedback response, and appraisal. All of these require accounting data to some extent, and a major portion of the task of supplying such data is in the domain of cost accounting. Narrowly defined, cost accounting consists of the activities of cost finding, cost analysis, cost recording, and cost reporting, primarily in factory operations. These activities must be so closely integrated with the rest of managerial accounting, however, that the study of cost accounting requires a full understanding of the entire managerial accounting structure.

Cost accounting also serves financial accounting by deriving product unit cost data for use in pricing end-of-period inventory balances and determining the cost of goods sold. One task of the following chapters will be to examine the methods used for this purpose in terms of their applicability to managerial problems.

EXERCISES AND PROBLEMS

1. Describe each of the items in Exhibit 1–3 as it might be applied to you in your role as a student or to some business operation you are very familiar with.

For example, under "Analysis of Alternatives," you might list the major alternatives available to you in planning your program, how the costs and benefits associated with each alternative might be measured, what kinds of data you would want, and what criteria you might use in choosing among the alternatives.

2.† "Well, I seem to manage, somehow," Derek Steele said, "But I'll have to think about it a bit before I can tell you just how I do it."

Mr. Steele was the proprietor of a small grocery store in Panbridge, England. He sold several hundred different items of packaged foods, bread, wines, and household supplies, as well as a line of fresh dairy produce—milk, cheese, butter, etc. Mr. Steele's son-in-law, a recent graduate in management studies, had asked him how he planned and controlled the inventories of the items that he offered for sale in his store.

Mr. Steele decided to make a few notes about the process. Bread and dairy produce, he noted, were delivered daily. Except for unusual items ordered for specific customers, he never placed an order for these items. Instead, he told the delivery man each day what he thought he would need until the next day's delivery. Any unsold bread could be returned the next day to the delivery man, but at a reduced price. Milk could be kept in the

---

† Copyright 1968 by l'Institut pour l'Etude des Méthodes de Direction de l'Entreprise (IMEDE), Lausanne, Switzerland. Reproduced by permission.

store for two days, and Mr. Steele was always careful to sell any milk left over from the previous day before placing the current day's delivery in the display case. Butter, cheese, and similar items could be kept a good deal longer, and Mr. Steele ordinarily ordered several days' requirements at a time.

Most other items were ordered either by telephone or from wholesalers' or manufacturers' representatives who called at the store. Three or four of these representatives would stop at Mr. Steele's store in a typical day. For some items ordered in this way, delivery was made the following day; for others, the delay was longer, sometimes as long as two weeks.

Mr. Steele knew that he could obtain lower purchase prices on some items if he would buy larger quantities in each order. To do this, however, he would have to order much farther ahead of the desired delivery date, and he would also have to prepare additional storage space behind his store. When his son-in-law asked him how much he could save by making purchases in larger quantities, Mr. Steele had to reply that he didn't know, but he was happy doing business as he was.

Most of Mr. Steele's customers bought only a few items at a time, things that they had forgotten during their last visit to the chain store or things that would not justify a trip to the chain store on the high street. Mr. Steele's prices were a little higher than chain store prices, but he did not feel that he would get any more business of this sort if he reduced his prices to the chain store level.

"I don't know how you'd describe my system," he said, "but I watch my shelves fairly closely. When I see that I'm running low on an item, I order it. If I buy something and it doesn't sell well, I notice that too, and the next time the salesman asks me to order it I tell him no. If he comes in with something new, I try to decide whether my customers will like it and how much shelf space it will take. Some things come in several sizes and colors, and I might have to push several items aside to make room for one new one. That new line of toilet soap, for example, comes in three sizes and each size comes in three colors. I had to drop one brand of laundry detergent to make room for all that variety, but my customers like the soap and I think I made the right choice.

"Actually, my biggest problem comes from the daily deliveries. If I order too little, my stock is exhausted before the end of the afternoon. Over-ordering is not as serious a mistake, because I can adjust the next day's order on everything but bread.

"Most of this I do myself. My clerk is a pleasant young fellow, but he's not very bright. He can follow instructions, but I have to make it quite clear what he is expected to do."

a) Describe the planning portion of the process used by Mr. Steele to plan and control his inventories. What kinds of data might he find useful at this point? Where might he expect to find these data?

b) Describe the feedback portion of the process. What kinds of data would be useful and where would they come from?

c) To what extent is this a decision-making process? How much of the work could Mr. Steele safely delegate to his clerk?

chapter **2**

Basic Concepts for
Short-Term Decisions

Accounting systems provide much of the data used by management in planning or decision-making processes. If these data are to be revealing rather than misleading, they should be based on concepts similar to those implicit in management decision models. In this chapter we shall describe the decision process in some detail and then explore the basic economic concepts underlying most management decision models.

THE STRUCTURE OF DECISIONS

People in organizations reach decisions by many different routes, but at least seven different elements seem to be common to all:

1. Problem diagnosis.
2. Goal selection.
3. Identification of constraints.
4. Identification of alternatives.
5. Environmental forecasting.
6. Prediction of outcomes and payoffs.
7. Selection and application of decision rules.

Problem Diagnosis

Decisions become necessary whenever management becomes aware of the existence of problems or opportunities. A problem has been defined as a gap between an existing or forecasted condition or result and a desired condition or result. Thus if an automobile fails to start in the morning, it might seem that the problem is to get it started. Alternatively, the problem might be stated as the discrepancy between the need to get to the office at nine o'clock and the present inability to use the car to accomplish this. The solution may be to get someone to start the car, or it may even be to abandon the car and get to the office by some other means. This process of problem formulation is known as diagnosis.[1]

Little purpose would be served by emphasizing the distinction between opportunities and problems. An opportunity, too, can be thought of as a gap between an anticipated result and a better result. Both are in a certain sense problems that must be solved by a decision-making process. Once recognized, they require exactly the same analytical apparatus. The only difference is that problems are often more likely to be brought to management's attention than opportunities. If an activity is achieving satisfactory results, the system ordinarily generates less pressure to search for opportunities to make it better.

Goal Selection

The definition of a problem as a gap between a desired result and a present or anticipated result indicates the importance of objectives. Without a goal there can be no gap, and thus no need for a decision as to how to close the gap.

It is usually accepted that one of the objectives of a business enterprise is profit. Profit, in turn, is merely a means toward the goal of company survival, which in turn is a means toward other more fundamental goals. Survival and other more basic goals are too vague to provide much guidance to the decision maker, however, and this requires the expression of more immediate or operational goals to provide such guidance. Increased profit is an example of an operational goal.

Identification of Constraints

Management's freedom of choice is always limited to some extent. Sometimes the boundaries are established by law or regulatory action, sometimes they reflect the moral values of the community or of management itself, and sometimes they are imposed by other decisions that management has already made. Another kind of constraint is imposed by the lack of certain kinds of resources. The firm's capacity may be measured in units of time or money or space or knowledge, and one or more of these may be inadequate to absorb all of the activities management has in mind.

---

[1] William H. Newman, Charles E. Summer, Jr., and E. Kirby Warren, *The Process of Management* (3d ed.; Englewood Cliffs, N.J.: Prentice-Hall, 1972), chaps. 11 and 12.

Moral, legal, informational, and prior-decision constraints are qualitative and therefore are expressed, if at all, as company policies. Many of these are unwritten; many are neither formally stated nor consciously held. They pose questions that management is expected to answer with a yes or a no.

Constraints imposed by limited supplies of time, space, or money, on the other hand, are likely to be stated as numerical quantities. When applied to a particular proposal, they require answers in the form of how much of the scarce capacity the proposal will use up; the yes or no answer is not absolute but depends on how good the other possible uses of the scarce resource seem to be.

Identification of Alternatives

Once the problem or opportunity has been identified, the next step is to list the alternative actions that might be taken. Alternatives are not always obvious but must be sought out. Successful business management is often a matter of finding and exploiting opportunities that others have overlooked.

For example, Mr. B. T. Ersman, president of Peerless Spring Company, recently faced the need to decide whether to add a newly designed window catch to his company's product line. Peerless Spring manufactures a line of spring-closing devices and other household and industrial hardware products. It has a strong distribution organization, but intensified competition in recent years has cut into its sales volume, leaving the company with substantial idle productive capacity and a small annual operating loss.

The new window catch was developed and patented by an independent inventor who offered Peerless Spring an exclusive license to manufacture and market this device in return for a royalty of 10 cents for each unit sold. Mr. Ersman wanted to take this offer if it seemed to promise a reasonable chance of success.

In this case management had no difficulty in identifying the problem or opportunity. It had expensive idle capacity and a chance to do something with it. Similarly, Mr. Ersman's operational goal was quite clear— to increase the company's profitability. The constraints on his freedom of choice in this affair were also simple: (1) the company's policy of selling only products that it manufactured or assembled itself; and (2) the inability of the local labor market to supply workers for more than one working shift. The first of these ruled out any alternatives that would call for subcontracting production of this new product; the second would cause rejection of any alternative that would push total factory production beyond the maximum limits of single-shift capacity.

In the end, Mr. Ersman and his staff decided to recognize only two alternatives: (1) using the company's regular sales organization to offer the new product to Peerless Spring's present customers; and (2) total rejection of the inventor's offer.

This limited range of alternatives illustrates one important fact: people do not search until they have found all the alternatives available. In fact, it is doubtful that anyone can ever be sure that he has identified all alternative courses of action open to him. Furthermore, the search cannot be allowed to take so much time that action is unduly delayed.

There is some evidence that people search only until they find at least one alternative that promises a satisfactory solution of the problem. The term *satisficing* has been coined to describe this behavior.[2] It might have been possible, for example, for the Peerless Spring Company's engineers to design a better product or to obtain a better product from some other source. Mr. Ersman, however, was content to exclude these other possibilities, at least until he found out whether the window catch proposal seemed good enough to meet his minimum standards.

Environmental Forecasting

Environmental conditions, sometimes called *events* or *states of nature*, are usually more difficult to describe precisely than alternatives. Environmental conditions represent the uncontrollable variables bearing on the decision.

Mr. Ersman knew that the number of possible states of nature was very large, but he had no way of including them all in his analysis. Instead, he asked his sales manager to give him three sales forecasts—the most likely volume and upper and lower limits. The number of recognized combinations of alternatives and states of nature was thus six, three for each alternative, represented by the boxes in the following diagram:

Alternative \ Event	Good Market 1	Anticipated Market 2	Poor Market 3
Accept proposal A	A–1	A–2	A–3
Reject proposal R	R–1	R–2	R–3

The existence of more than one possible state of nature is one of the main dimensions of *uncertainty*. Uncertainty may or may not be recognized explicitly in decision making, but it is always present to some degree.

[2] James G. March and Herbert A. Simon, *Organizations* (New York: John Wiley & Sons, 1958), pp. 140–41.

Outcomes and Payoffs

The table above is not very useful as it stands. What it lacks is some measure of the results to be expected under each possible combination of actions and states of nature.

Results can be stated in two ways: first, as the outcomes expected for each action/state of nature combination; and second, as the payoffs stemming from these outcomes. The outcomes here were measured in added sales dollars; the payoffs were measured in dollars of added profit.

To get these estimates, Mr. Ersman referred the window catch proposal to his sales and production managers for their estimates of sales and costs. Both were enthusiastic. The sales manager recognized immediately that the safety catch could be sold to the company's present customers with only a slight expansion of the sales force. Furthermore, the market could be realized almost immediately, without a long period of costly promotional outlays. After discussions with his salesmen, he decided that a price of $1.50 would be competitive. At this price, a sales forecast of 300,000 units a year seemed reasonable, assuming the following annual increases in total company selling and administrative costs:

Sales salaries and commissions	$33,000
Travel and entertainment	24,000
Secretarial and clerical salaries	4,000
Office supplies	500
Promotional aids and samples	3,500
Advertising	5,000
Total	$70,000

The production manager looked very favorably upon this new product as a means of taking up some of the idle capacity in one of his two factories. Working closely with the factory controller, he estimated that factory costs would be increased by the following amounts per year:

Production materials	$150,000
Payrolls (including payroll taxes)	120,000
Power	9,000
Equipment maintenance	15,000
Factory supplies	6,000
Total	$300,000

These estimates were summarized as follows for presentation to Mr. Ersman:

Sales		$450,000
Expenses:		
Factory	$300,000	
Selling and administrative	70,000	
Royalties	30,000	400,000
Added yearly profit before taxes		$ 50,000

The sales manager felt that the 300,000-unit figure was reasonable in the light of the overall size of the market and the prices and quality of competing products, but agreed that optimistic and pessimistic forecasts would also be useful. After talking to several of his key men, he concluded that the worst he could do would be 200,000 units a year; at the very best, sales might go as high as 400,000 units.

Mr. Ersman had always been able to rely on the sales manager's estimates of the range within which sales were likely to fall, and he accepted them this time, even though the product was a new one to the Peerless Spring Company. The production and accounting people then came up with alternative cost figures at the higher and lower sales volumes, as follows:

	200,000 Units	400,000 Units
Sales..	$300,000	$600,000
Expenses:		
Factory cost of goods sold................	$240,000	$360,000
Selling and administrative................	60,000	80,000
Royalties..............................	20,000	40,000
Total expenses......................	$320,000	$480,000
Added profit (loss).......................	$(20,000)	$120,000

Turning to the other alternative, rejection of the inventor's offer, Mr. Ersman was concerned that some competitor might get hold of it and use it to make inroads in the market for Peerless Spring's other window catches. According to the sales manager, however, this was highly unlikely. The only manufacturers whose lines and distributive organizations would enable them to market this window catch effectively did not offer the kind of product selection that Peerless Spring's customers insisted upon. He felt highly confident in predicting that rejection of the offer would not harm the company's position in any way.

Once he had all of this information, Mr. Ersman put it all together in the following payoff table:

Alternative \ Event	Good Market	Anticipated Market	Poor Market
Accept proposal	+$120,000	+$50,000	−$20,000
Reject proposal	0	0	0

In this case, the bottom line could have been eliminated, because it shows zero values for each state of nature; but this is far from being always the case.

Selection and Application of Decision Rules

Once the payoff table has been constructed, the decision maker must apply a decision rule—a set of instructions for choosing a course of action that will meet the company's objectives. Mr. Ersman's decision rule was not very clearly stated. He wanted to pick the alternative that seemed most likely to yield the larger profit, so long as that alternative would not expose him to "too great" a risk of loss if the state of nature proved unfavorable. This risk-profit relationship was not expressed mathematically, however.

It should be clear that profit maximization is a meaningless decision rule under conditions of uncertainty. If the market was poor, then rejection of the proposal would have been the profit-maximizing alternative; the reverse would be true for a good or average market. To apply this kind of decision rule, therefore, some means must be found to reduce the payoffs under each alternative to a single figure.

One possibility is to weight the possible payoffs according to the relative probabilities that the various states of nature will occur. The resultant weighted payoff is called the *expected value* of the alternative.

Suppose, for example, that Mr. Ersman decided that the $120,000 gain had a 30 percent chance of happening, the $50,000 payoff, a 50 percent chance, and the $20,000 loss, a 20 percent chance. In technical language, the three states of nature had probabilities of 0.3, 0.5, and 0.2, the total being 1.0. The expected value of the outcome for each alternative is found by multiplying each possible payoff by its probability and adding the products, as follows:

Probability	0.3	0.5	0.2	
Event / Alternative	Good Market	Anticipated Market	Poor Market	Expected Value
Accept proposal	0.3 × 120,000 = +36,000	0.5 × 50,000 = +25,000	0.2 × −20,000 = −4,000	+57,000
Reject proposal	0.3 × 0 = 0	0.5 × 0 = 0	0.2 × 0 = 0	0

In this case the expected value is slightly in excess of the $50,000 forecast payoff because the probabilities are not symmetrically distributed.

The decision rule implicit in the expected value calculation is maximization of the expected value of the payoffs. This is not necessarily the decision rule that Mr. Ersman would have used if he had calculated the probabilities explicitly. For example, if a $20,000 loss on this project would have put the company in bankruptcy and Mr. Ersman out of a job, he might have been much more cautious, weighting the possible loss by a factor much larger than its relative probability.

This is not the place to discuss different decision rules or the profit maximization assumption. In what follows, the emphasis will be on the derivation of data relevant to decisions rather than on the decision rules applied to them. It is always assumed, however, that for any given state of nature, the decision maker is interested in knowing which alternative seems to promise the greatest profit. How he then weighs the outcomes associated with the various states of nature is left largely to more specialized works on decision making.

Application to Not-for-Profit Organizations

This same structure applies just as well to the decisions of the managers of not-for-profit organizations as to those of private enterprises. The objectives of the organization may differ, and this will affect both the decision rule and the choice of a scale by which to measure payoffs or results; but these are substitutions, not deletions. The seven-element package is still there in full.

One peculiarity is that measures that the private businessman thinks of as measures of payoff may become measures of capacity utilization in a not-for-profit organization, to be compared with constraints. Conversely, the constraints of private business may turn out to be the decision variables in other forms of organization. For example, a profit-seeking company might reasonably choose the alternative that seems to be the most profitable, subject to the constraint that adequate protection against water pollution must be provided. A foundation-supported job training school, however, is likely to try to choose those teaching programs that will maximize a figure such as the number of people added to the skilled labor force. In this case, the net direct profit or loss may merely be a figure representing the program's absorption of capacity, represented by the amount of funds available to support all programs in total. Failure to distinguish clearly between decision rules and constraints can lead to decisions that are very inconsistent with the goals of the organization.

INCREMENTAL ANALYSIS

The comparisons in the previous example were based on the incremental principle: that data for decisions should represent the differences between alternative courses of action. In other words, the concept that is relevant in quantitative analysis for decision making is the concept of *incremental profit*: the difference in profit for the company as a whole that is expected to result from choosing one alternative instead of another.

Profit versus Income

Notice that this definition uses the term "profit" rather than "income." Incremental profit is an economic concept and is not necessarily identical to incremental income, which is an accounting concept. Incremental profit is defined as the effect of the choice between alternatives on the company's *net cash flow*—the margin between receipts and outlays of cash or equivalent liquid assets. Because measurement of accounting net income often requires the recognition of expense and revenue in periods other than the period of receipt or expenditure of cash, it may differ significantly from cash flow in any given time period. It is cash flow, however, not income flow, that represents the resources made available to management by the outcome of a particular course of action. It is thus more relevant to decision making.

Many internal accounting systems use the term profit to refer to the accounting income reported or budgeted for individual segments of the company's business, and we shall not make a point of avoiding this usage of the term. When discussing incremental profit, however, or incremental revenue or incremental costs, we shall always be referring to differences in cash flows rather than differences in reported income.

Incremental versus Absolute Profit

The income summaries in periodic accounting statements are useful in decision making, but they generally must be adjusted to make them fully relevant. The income budgeted or reported for a particular product line or other business segment is not necessarily the portion of the company's income that can be attributed to that segment.

For example, let us assume that a company's management is examining the profitability of its sales branches. The income statement for the Baltimore branch for the previous year showed an income contribution of $50,000, as follows:

Sales...	$1,000,000
Cost of sales..................................	600,000
Gross margin..................................	$ 400,000
Branch expenses..............................	350,000
Branch income contribution before taxes..............	$ 50,000

Assuming that the future will be like the past, and that sales, cost of sales, and branch expenses all represented current cash flows, it would seem that closing this branch would reduce company profit by $50,000 a year before taxes. Upon investigation, however, it is discovered that other sales branches in neighboring territories could service the Baltimore territory by adding only $270,000 a year to their branch expenses, without any loss in Baltimore sales volume. This is $80,000 less than the annual cash operating expenses of the Baltimore branch. In incremental terms, therefore, the Baltimore branch is actually losing $80,000 a year instead of earning a $50,000 profit.

The absolute profit figures for a given segment of a company's business operations are relevant to decision making only if—

1. The choice is between continuing the operation as it is or discontinuing it entirely, with no other alternatives possible.
2. The costs and revenues recorded for this operation are those that would have been avoided or lost if the operation had not taken place.
3. The recorded costs and revenues are a reasonable approximation of the future costs and revenues that would be avoided or lost by discontinuing the operation.

These conditions are seldom met, and the problem, therefore, is to decide how much the historical figures must be adjusted to make them useful for decision making.

Incremental Revenues

Alternatives often differ in the amount of sales revenues that they will yield. Revenue effects of a choice between alternatives may be of three types:

1. Direct effects.
2. Complementary effects.
3. Substitution effects.

A direct effect would be a change in the revenues of the business operation itself. In the above example, the direct effect of abandoning the Baltimore territory completely would be to lose revenues of $1 million. Because other branch offices could serve the Baltimore territory with no loss in sales, however, the net direct effect can be said to be zero.

Complementary and substitution effects are changes in the revenues of other company operations. A complementary change moves in the same direction as the direct change (an increase in toothbrush sales resulting from a campaign to sell more toothpaste, for example); a substitution effect is a change in one operation that partially offsets the change in another. The increase in sales of neighboring branches could be construed as a substitution effect.

Whether an effect is direct, complementary, or substitution is of course unimportant. What is important is that all such changes be reflected in the estimates of incremental profit.

Incremental versus Sunk Cost

The increments most completely within the domain of cost accounting are cost increments. Incremental or *differential* cost is the difference in total cost that will result from selecting one alternative instead of another.

For example, the engineering department of a company has made a suggestion that substantial savings can be realized by purchasing a higher quality of castings to be used in one of the company's products. The higher cost of materials would be more than offset by the savings in machining time, electricity, and other costs. Estimated monthly costs under the two alternatives are:

	Current Castings	Better Castings
Materials..........................	$140,000	$170,000
Labor.............................	80,000	55,000
Supervision.......................	15,000	15,000
Taxes.............................	14,000	14,000
Depreciation and insurance.........	32,000	32,000
Other factory costs................	63,000	53,000
Total.............................	$344,000	$339,000

The incremental cost is thus $344,000 minus $339,000, or $5,000 a month. In this case incremental cost is negative, indicating a saving rather than an addition to total cost.

The term incremental cost is often used in another sense, to refer to the *elements* of cost that will change as the result of the decision rather than to the net difference between two sets of cost totals. For example, in the illustration, the only costs affected by the decision are those recorded in the accounts for materials, labor, and other factory costs. These are the incremental costs as far as this analysis is concerned, and we may shorten the analysis by filtering out as irrelevant all of the other costs that will not be affected by the decision. Thus the above table reduces to the following comparison:

	Current Castings	Better Castings	Increment
Direct materials..........	$140,000	$170,000	+$30,000
Machining labor..........	80,000	55,000	− 25,000
Other factory costs.......	63,000	53,000	− 10,000
Total..................	$283,000	$278,000	−$ 5,000

The net increment remains the same, $5,000, but attention is focused sharply on the items that are important.

The complement of incremental cost is *sunk cost*, defined as any cost that will not be different if one alternative is chosen instead of another. The definition, therefore, depends on the specific problem being analyzed; what is incremental with respect to one decision may be sunk with respect to another. In the preceding illustration, three of the cost elements were treated as sunk costs for that particular analysis:

	Current Castings	Better Castings
Supervision........................	$15,000	$15,000
Taxes............................	14,000	14,000
Depreciation and insurance........	32,000	32,000
Total............................	$61,000	$61,000

The shift to a different grade of castings would leave all of these cost elements unchanged. Therefore, these sunk costs are irrelevant to that decision and can safely be left out of the analysis.

Separate Costs for Separate Purposes

It should be clear from these definitions that the magnitude of incremental cost (and of incremental profit) depends on the decision to be made and the alternatives being compared. For example, the plant manager's salary is a sunk cost if the problem is to decide whether to install additional materials-handling equipment; but it is presumably an incremental cost if abandonment of the plant is in question, and it may be partly incremental if the question is whether to double the plant's capacity.

Avoidable Costs

A term frequently used to refer to incremental cost is avoidable cost. This term is used when the choice is between continuing and discontinuing one of the company's operations or activities, or between keeping and disposing of certain of its facilities. Studies of plant abandonment, discontinuation of a product line, or withdrawal from a geographical market area all call for the application of the concept of avoidable cost. The complement of avoidable cost, unavoidable cost, refers to the sunk costs in this kind of analysis.

Opportunity Cost

Another term that crops up in discussions of incremental analysis is the concept of opportunity cost. In its broadest sense, opportunity cost is the net cash inflow that is lost by the diversion of an input factor from one use to another. It is the value of an opportunity forgone. The opportunity cost of the time that a salesman spends in an air-conditioned theater on a hot summer's day is the incremental profit that would have been obtained on the sales that he lost by not calling on customers. From the salesman's point of view, the opportunity cost is the amount of commission that he loses by not making sales.

The concept of opportunity cost is implicit in any comparison of alternatives. The merits of any particular course of action are relative merits, the difference between this action and some other. Opportunity cost is thus more an expression of a method of approach than a definition of cost.

The explicit introduction of opportunity cost figures into profitability calculations is often helpful, however, when one or more of the inputs required by one of the alternatives is already in the possession of the company. No current outlay of cash must be made to get these inputs, but they may nevertheless have a cost. This cost is measured by what has to be given up in order to make them available for the current proposal— their value in their best alternative use. This is their opportunity cost.

For example, a variety chain paid $100,000 for a plot of land in 1955 for the construction of a shopping center. Uncertainty as to the highway relocation plans of state public works officials led to a postponement of the shopping center project, and the land has lain idle ever since. The route of the new highway has now been established, and the company is again considering the possibility of using the tract as a shopping center site. Only two alternatives are under consideration: either to build the shopping center or to sell the land. The value of the shopping center is derived from the stream of future net cash receipts that can be obtained from rentals to other tenants and from the sale of merchandise in a new company store in the center. The value of the second alternative is the net amount that could be realized from the sale of the land. The net advantage of the shopping center is the difference between these two values.

Suppose that the land can be sold now for a price that will yield the company $800,000 after deducting all commissions, fees, and taxes, and that the value of the future cash flows from the shopping center is $1,200,000. (The derivation of this latter amount is the subject of a later chapter.) The comparison is:

Alternative	Expected Receipts
Build shopping center...............	$1,200,000
Sell land...........................	800,000
Incremental profit..................	$ 400,000

An alternative way of reaching the same result is to charge the opportunity cost of the land as an explicit cost of the shopping center proposal:

Value of center.....................	$1,200,000
Less: Cost of land.................	800,000
Incremental profit..................	$ 400,000

The company could obtain $800,000 in liquid resources by selling the land, and thus this is the amount it invests by not selling the land. The price paid in the past is irrelevant.

This alternative approach is useful because the owned resources to be incorporated into a particular project are often a small part of the total project, and there may be several such resources. This makes it inconvenient to set up a full set of alternatives, one for each possible combination of resource uses. The better procedure is to compute an opportunity cost for each resource and insert it into the calculation.

SUMMARY

Decisions are the choices that people make among the alternatives available to them. Given a set of objectives, the decision maker will try to select the alternative that he thinks will be most consistent with these objectives, provided that it violates none of the constraints imposed by the firm's capacity or by limiting influences outside the firm.

The result of each alternative is measured by its payoff. Because payoffs depend not only on the action selected but also on external environmental conditions, it may be necessary to prepare more than one payoff estimate for each alternative. The decision maker must then decide what weight to give to each possible outcome—in other words, he must choose a decision rule.

Accountants provide much of the data and do much of the analytical work underlying managerial decisions. In all cases, the data must reflect the incremental principle that only differences between alternatives are relevant.

From this basic principle have come the concepts of incremental profit and incremental and sunk costs, together with a number of secondary concepts such as avoidable cost and opportunity cost. The task of the accountant or any other analyst is to translate the available data into incremental terms.

EXERCISES AND PROBLEMS

1. A motorist has computed that he can save money by leaving his car at home and flying from Boston to New York. Air fare and taxis, round trip, amount to $41. The motorist has found that it costs an average of 8 cents a mile to own and operate his car. The round trip requires him to drive 420 miles. Highway tolls and New York garage fees for a typical three-day trip amount to $9. Do you agree with the motorist's conclusions? Assume that he places no value on any time he might save by flying.

2. Your automobile battery is very old, and you are afraid that it will go dead during the coming winter if you don't replace it now. If you buy a new battery now, you can buy it at a price of $20. If you wait and the battery dies, you will have to pay $25 for a replacement.

Cold weather is approaching, and you believe that the probability of the battery dying during the winter is 70 percent.

a) Construct a payoff table.
b) Describe the decision rule that you would apply in this situation and indicate what decision you would make.

3.* An outlay of $10,000 is proposed. Incremental cash receipts resulting from this outlay could be anywhere from zero to $25,000. The probabilities are:

Receipts	Probability
$ 0	0.1
5,000	0.2
10,000	0.4
15,000	0.2
20,000	0.05
25,000	0.05

a) Construct a payoff table.
b) Compute expected value for each alternative action.

4.* The Rice Company makes bumper jacks, and last year it sold 50,000 at a price of $3 and produced them at an average cost of $2.25. The sales manager states that at a price of $2.50 he could sell 75,000 units. The factory manager estimates that 75,000 could be produced at an average cost of $2 each. What are the incremental revenue, the incremental cost, and the incremental profit on reducing the price to $2.50 each?

5. Franklin Enterprises can ship product A to a customer for $40. Shipping charges for product B are $30. If both products are packed together, the total shipping cost is $50. Only one unit of product B may be packed with each unit of product A.

a) The customer now buys product A but not product B. What cost would you use in evaluating the desirability of getting the customer to buy product B?
b) Franklin Enterprises ships equal quantities of both products to its warehouses near the customer at the $50 combined shipping cost. The customer buys only product B, product A being sold to other nearby customers. The customer has found a use for product A and asks for a price quotation. What shipping cost would you use in calculating the profitability of any given price?

6. A factory's costs can be estimated accurately from the following schedule of average hourly cost:

Hours	Cost
4,000	$6.25
4,500	6.11
5,000	6.00
5,500	5.91

---

* Solutions to problems marked with an asterisk can be found in Appendix B.

The company has a chance to bid on a new job that would add 500 hours a month for two months to the factory's volume. Efficient workers for this job can be obtained without difficulty or loss of efficiency. The job would have no effect on nonfactory costs.

Without this job, the factory would operate at a monthly volume of 4,000 hours. When built, the plant was expected to operate 5,000 hours a month, on the average.

What is the minimum price the company could afford to quote for this job without being worse off?

7. An oil company has paid a foreign government $4 million for the rights to explore for oil. If oil is found, the agreement calls for the oil company to pay the government $1 for every barrel produced.

The company has spent $3 million on the drilling operation and has just struck oil. Management estimates that it will be able to recover 10 million barrels of oil from this field. This oil can be sold for $2.50 a barrel and it will cost 50 cents a barrel to get it out of the ground.

Yesterday, however, the government imposed an additional fee of 60 cents a barrel, to pay for insurance against damages caused by oil spills that might take place in the future.

Should the company begin producing oil? Prepare an analysis to support your recommendation.

8. The Downtown Business Institute has two classrooms for which it pays a monthly rental of $400 each. These classrooms are adequate for the three courses that the institute now offers to its students. These three courses make the following monthly profits:

Course	Profit
Bookkeeping	$800
Typing	650
Shorthand	480

Classroom rentals and top management expenses have not been charged to these courses.

Management is thinking of offering a course in computer programming. This could be done in the existing classroom, but only if one of the three current courses were to be discontinued. Additional classroom space is available in the institute's present building, however, and management is trying to decide whether to rent this space and offer the new course.

The additional space can be rented for $550 a month. The expected monthly profit from the new programming course is as follows:

Tuition and fees		$2,500
Expenses:		
Teaching salaries	$700	
Equipment rental	200	
Telephone charges	150	
Books and supplies	300	
Other	100	
Total expenses		1,450
Profit		$1,050

What should the institute do? Cite figures to support your conclusions.

9. During 19x3 and early 19x4, the management of the Irvington Corporation became increasingly concerned about the declining profitability of one of its products. Data relating to this product for the first quarter of 19x4 and the three full years preceding are as follows:

	19x1	19x2	19x3	1st Qtr. 19x4
Units sold............................	100,000	110,000	80,000	20,000
Net revenue from sales.................	$495,000	$540,000	$474,000	$115,000
Manufacturing cost of goods sold:				
Materials...........................	$ 59,400	$ 67,350	$ 54,500	$ 13,800
Labor..............................	136,300	155,000	123,900	31,000
Other manufacturing costs............	121,500	149,800	146,300	39,700
Freight and delivery costs..............	25,200	30,600	31,000	8,200
Sales salaries and commissions..........	34,750	37,000	33,700	8,550
Other selling and office expenses........	26,400	31,400	37,600	9,650
Total direct product expenses.......	$403,550	$471,150	$427,000	$110,900
Product profit........................	$ 91,450	$ 68,850	$ 47,000	$ 4,100
Share of the market:				
Units sold..........................	15%	12%	8%	7.5%
Dollar sales........................	18	16	15	14.5

Analyze these data and prepare a report that will help management decide where the major problems might lie or what course of action to take.

10. A direct mail company would charge you $2,000 to print and mail to a list of 10,000 selected executives a brochure describing your new "exec-o-mat" desk calendar. You buy these from a manufacturer for $15 and sell them for $30. An incremental cost of $1 is incurred to pack and ship each exec-o-mat. Your annual profit from other sources is $3,000, and your bank balance is now $2,500.

Your previous experience with mailings of this kind has indicated that any sales made in response to the mailing will be made in the three months immediately following the mailing. Your experience also leads you to expect a 3 percent response to the mailing (in this case, 300 units sold). The probabilities that you assign to the various possible outcomes are:

Percent Response		Probability
Range	Average	
0.51–1.5..............	1.0	0.10
1.51–2.5..............	2.0	0.25
2.51–3.5..............	3.0	0.50
3.51–4.5..............	4.0	0.10
4.51 or more..........	5.0	0.05

If you decide to undertake the mailing, you will increase your inventory and hire an additional stock boy, so as to be prepared for any orders that come in. The stock boy's wages and added inventory carrying costs on the additional inventory would amount to $500 a month. Costs of carrying the current levels of inventory and operating the stock room total $3,000 a month.

The carrying cost figures included in the estimates quoted in the preceding paragraph apply only if sales made in response to the mailing total at least 300 units. In addition to these, extra incremental carrying costs of $0.50 would be incurred for each unit sold less than 300. (For example, if 200 units were sold, the extra carrying costs resulting from the failure to meet the 300-unit minimum would total $0.50 \times (300 - 200) = $50. This figure covers the entire three-month period—it is not a cost per month.)

a) Prepare a profitability estimate on the basis of the forecasted 3 percent response.
b) Prepare a payoff table, with five states of nature.
c) Compute the expected value under each alternative management action.
d) Is this a situation in which the decision maker would be likely to use a decision rule that departs materially from maximum expected value? Comment.

11. The Jones Company has 2,000 yards of a plastic material on hand; 1,000 yards were purchased at an invoice price of $2 a yard and 1,000 yards were purchased later at an invoice price of $2.20 a yard.

This material deteriorates in storage and if the company does not use or sell its present inventories within the next six weeks they will become worthless.

Some of the inventory could be used to make product A. Each unit of product A requires one yard of the plastic material plus $3 in other incremental costs. A maximum of 500 units of product A could be sold at a price of $5.25 a unit.

The company is also thinking of manufacturing product B. Each unit of B requires one yard of the plastic material plus $4 in other incremental costs.

The Jones Company could sell any quantity of the plastic material for $1.80 a yard. It could also buy additional quantities of this material for $2.40 a yard.

a) What unit cost would you use in considering a proposal to produce and sell 500 units of product B during the next six weeks? 1,000 units? 1,500 units? 2,000 units? 2,500 units?
b) In addition to the above possibilities, the company has one chance in three of receiving an order for 300 units of product D within the coming two weeks. Product D sells for $9, requires one yard of the plastic material, and has other costs of $2. Prepare a revised set of cost estimates for product B under these circumstances.

12. In March, 1969 Alvin Cranshaw was trying to decide what to do. Mr. Cranshaw was the owner-president of Cranshaw Packaging Services, Inc., a small firm located in Bethlehem, Pennsylvania. The Cranshaw firm advised its clients with ideas about how to package their products, worked with clients' personnel to keep packaging equipment operating efficiently, and even supplied men and equipment from time to time to do small specialty packaging jobs that clients were not equipped to do themselves.

Mr. Cranshaw's immediate concern was whether to take a job for one of his packaging machines, the AX-40. This machine had been developed by Mr. Cranshaw and one of his engineers several years earlier to provide the company with capacity to wrap regularly packed products in special gift wrappings. It had proved so successful that it was always fully booked during the months of August through mid-November, as clients prepared for the annual holiday trade. It often remained partly idle during the rest of the year, however, because few local companies needed special packaging work in the off season.

Mr. Cranshaw had worked untiringly to find more off-season jobs for the AX-40, but his efforts had been only partly successful. Now two local manufacturers who had never before been Cranshaw clients had expressed an interest in using the machine during the spring months, but only at prices lower than Cranshaw Packaging usually charged. One of these, Maurer Products, Inc., offered to pay $30,000 for the use of the equipment for a period of 35 days. The work would be done by Cranshaw employees in the Cranshaw shop. The other prospect, Franklin Packing Company, wished to use the equipment in its own plant, with its own employees. The contract would be for a 60-day period, including shipping and installation time. Franklin Packing would pay $10,000 plus all costs of transportation and installation, including transport insurance.

No other potential users were in sight, and Mr. Cranshaw thought that if he took on one of these jobs he might make some money and gain a steady customer to boot. Before going ahead, however, he asked Robert Underwood, his assistant, to work up the costs for the two proposals. Mr. Underwood returned with the following figures:

	Maurer	Franklin
No. of days required	35	60
Proposed contract price	$30,000	$10,000
Estimated costs:		
Labor	$17,500	$ 100
Supplies	2,000	. . .
Maintenance	500	750
Depreciation ($20/day)	700	1,200
Amortization of development costs ($100/day)	3,500	6,000
Power	2,100	. . .
Insurance	100	250
Administrative expenses (5 percent of sales)	1,500	500
Total costs	$27,900	$ 8,800
Profit margin	$ 2,100	$ 1,200

Mr. Underwood reminded Mr. Cranshaw that the costs of developing and building the AX-40 had not yet been completely amortized. For this reason, this machine would remain fairly costly to operate for about two more years. Although the profit margins on both proposals were very slim, he felt that one of them should be accepted.

Only one of these two proposals could be accepted because both customers wanted to use the machine at about the same time. What would you have recommended?

chapter 3

Cost-Volume-Profit
Relationships

The costs of operating a business firm or any other organization depend on a large number of factors, such as the size and quality of the local labor supply, the age of its facilities, the volume of activity, and the effectiveness of the cost control system.

One of these, operating volume, is almost invariably singled out for special attention, probably because it is the most volatile. Changes in the volume level tend to occur more frequently than changes in other factors, and can have a highly magnified impact on net income. The purpose of this chapter is to see how operating costs may be related to volume and how management might use information on these relationships.

COST-VOLUME RELATIONSHIPS

The operating costs of any organization are likely to respond in some way to changes in the volume of activity. The best way to study the possible structure of these responses is to start with some ideas from economics and then see how these have been used and adapted in accounting.

The Economist's View of Cost Behavior

Economists have developed theoretical descriptions of the relationship between cost and volume in the short run—that is, a period long enough to permit a change in the quantity of goods or services produced but too short to permit a change in the organization's operating capacity.

Capacity limitations may take any of three forms: *physical* capacity,

35

provided by buildings, machinery, furniture, etc; *organizational* capacity, provided by management, supervisory, and staff personnel; and *financial* capacity, provided by working capital and other financial resources. All of these are likely to be fixed in the short run. It takes time to conceive of the need for new facilities; arrange for financing; build, buy, or rent the facilities; provide the necessary personnel; and put all of these resources to work. Capacity reductions also take time. This means that during any short period, the firm must operate with a relatively constant stock of productive resources, including organizational and financial resources.

Fixed Costs. The costs of providing an organization's basic operating capacity are its fixed or capacity costs. As economists define them, these are costs that are entirely unaffected by changes in the volume of activity during the short run. This assumption is represented by the straight horizontal line in the left-hand panel of Exhibit 3–1: the total fixed cost is the same at all feasible operating volumes.[1]

Exhibit 3–1

BEHAVIOR OF FIXED COSTS

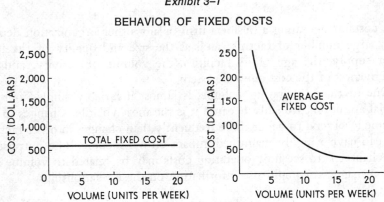

If this is a good description of the behavior of fixed costs, then average fixed costs will vary with volume in the way shown in the right-hand panel of the exhibit. Average fixed cost, represented by the height of the curved line in this panel, will decline steadily as volume increases. For example, if total fixed costs amount to $600 a week, the average will be $600 if output amounts to one unit, $300 at the two-unit level, $150 at four units, and so on.

Variable Costs. Although some organizations have only fixed costs, total cost will ordinarily increase as volume increases. One possible pattern of variation is shown in Exhibit 3–2. Estimates of operating costs

---

[1] Volume is a *flow* concept—that is, it measures the rate at which the organization or a part of it works during a given period of time. No interpretation of volume figures is possible unless the time period is specified.

have been prepared for each of a number of possible operating volumes from zero to 30 units a week. These estimates are represented by the dots in the exhibit. The curved line that has been drawn through these dots can be used to forecast costs of operating at other possible volumes.

In the language of economics, all costs in excess of those necessary to operate at the zero level are known as variable costs, the costs incurred by the use of the organization's capacity. For example, we can read from the diagram that the total cost of operating at a volume of 1,500 units a week is about $1,500. Since fixed costs are $600 a week, the remaining $900 are variable costs.

Exhibit 3–2

ECONOMISTS' VIEW OF THE COST-VOLUME PATTERN

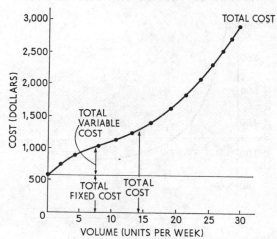

The rate of cost variation at any given volume level—that is, the price that the company must pay to expand its output to the next level—is indicated by the slope of the total cost line at that volume. If the line is climbing sharply, this means that total cost is increasing rapidly for a small increase in output; if the line is relatively flat, added volume is relatively cheap.

The assumed relationship between variable costs and volume in Exhibit 3–2 is only one possibility among many, but it is familiar to any student of economics. In this pattern, total costs rise steeply as the firm moves up through the bottom part of the volume range at the left of the exhibit, reflecting the difficulties of operating efficiently in a plant that was designed for much larger volumes.

The gentler slope of the cost curve in the middle of the volume range reflects the plant's ability to operate normally, with adequate specialization of the work force, normal production runs, and smooth production schedules. Unfortunately, this happy state does not last forever, and in the upper portion of the volume range the total cost line rises more and more steeply as diminishing productivity sets in. Bottlenecks develop, production scheduling becomes more complex, production delays become more frequent, and the control process is subject to increasing strain. If the diagram were extended far enough to the right, the total cost line would eventually climb right off the top of the page as further increases in output become infinitely expensive.

Average Cost. Expressed in terms of cost per unit, the total cost curve of Exhibit 3–2 becomes the unit cost curve of Exhibit 3–3. Average

Exhibit 3–3

EFFECT OF VOLUME ON AVERAGE COST

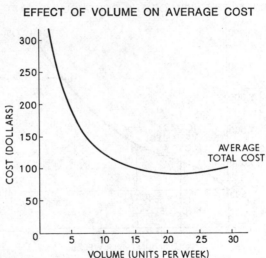

unit cost is high when volume is low because total fixed costs are spread over a relatively few units of product and because economies of mass production are not available to reduce variable costs per unit. As volume increases within the limits of constant capacity, average unit cost decreases, reflecting both a decrease in the average fixed cost and reductions in average variable cost due to economies of mass production. Later, diseconomies begin to set in and average variable cost starts to rise. At some point, this increase just offsets the decline in average fixed costs, and the average total cost curve turns upward, as in Exhibit 3–3.

Marginal Cost. Changes in average variable cost per unit are the result of changes in marginal cost. Marginal cost is defined as the added cost that results from increasing the rate of output by a single unit.[2]

---

[2] A strict definition would equate marginal cost with the rate of increase of cost relative to the increase in volume. If the cost curves are continuous, as in the diagrams in this chapter, marginal cost can be obtained by measuring the mathematical

Exhibit 3–4 illustrates the relationships among marginal cost, average variable cost, and average total cost. The marginal cost curve is more sensitive to changes in volume than the average variable cost curve because averages reflect changes more slowly than individual observations. Even after marginal cost begins to rise, reflecting the onset of diminishing marginal productivity, average variable cost continues to fall because the increment or addition to cost is still lower than the average. This means that the marginal cost and the average variable cost curves must cross at the low point of the average variable cost curve.

Exhibit 3–4

MARGINAL COST, AVERAGE VARIABLE COST,
AND AVERAGE TOTAL COST

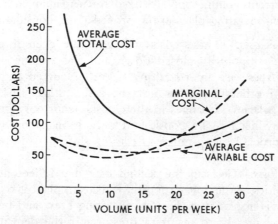

The same relationship holds true between marginal cost and average total cost. As long as the additions to cost resulting from additions to volume are less than average total cost, the average total cost curve will continue to fall; but when marginal cost goes above the average, the average must rise.

Types of Fixed Costs

Few businessmen are likely to use the economist's definitions of fixed and variable costs. All that the word "fixed" means to the businessman is that the total amount of the cost will not be affected by small changes in volume; if volume changes are large or if other influences are felt, the total amount can change. To cite one minor example, heating and air-

---

derivative or slope of the total cost line at any point. Alternatively, total cost can be obtained by adding or integrating marginal costs for all volumes up to a given volume, including the costs that will be incurred if the facilities are not operated at all.

conditioning costs are generally fixed with respect to volume changes, and yet they obviously vary from season to season and can be influenced by a wide variety of other factors as well.

In planning and decision making, it is useful to recognize three categories of fixed costs:

1. *Committed costs:* Costs that result solely from the existence of the organization's basic operating capacity, the consequence of decisions made in previous periods (e.g., depreciation).
2. *Enabling costs:* Costs necessary to provide operating capacity within certain volume ranges but subject to change if volume is expected to be outside the given volume range (e.g., supervision).
3. *Discretionary costs:* Costs which have no cause-and-effect relationship to current volume but are fixed by management decisions, usually when operating plans are approved (e.g., consultants' fees).

Committed Costs.   These costs will continue even if all company operations are temporarily closed down and the volume of activity is zero. Some of these are amortizations of costs incurred in prior periods (depreciation); others represent current cash outlays (property taxes and executive salaries). Changes in these costs occur only gradually, and in general they need to be considered only if management wishes to examine the probable long-range effects of shifting to a new level of operating capacity.

Enabling Costs.   Costs in the second category reflect discontinuities and indivisibilities in the cost structure. If a steam plant is to provide any steam at all, it is necessary to hire an operating crew and burn a certain amount of fuel merely to maintain pressure. If the demand for steam is increased beyond a certain point, another boiler must be fired up. This introduces "steps" into the fixed cost function—steps that are in addition to the variable costs associated with the generation of varying amounts of steam within stated volume ranges. For example, a department's cost budget might show the following totals:

	Units of Output per Month			
	10,000	12,000	14,000	16,000
Variable costs ($1 per unit)	$10,000	$12,000	$14,000	$16,000
Fixed costs.	5,000	5,000	6,000	6,000
Total costs.	$15,000	$17,000	$20,000	$22,000

In this case, a step of $1,000 per month in the fixed costs is required whenever volume is to be increased from 12,000 to 14,000 units a month.

If the steps are sufficiently close together they may be averaged out and treated as part of the variable costs.

Discretionary Costs. A substantial number of cost elements fall into the third category, discretionary fixed costs. In a sense, all fixed costs are the result of management decisions made at some time. Unlike enabling fixed costs, however, discretionary costs bear no technological relationship to current volume levels. They are established by management as part of its overall operating plan for the period. Many of them are incurred to obtain future sales—e.g., some kinds of advertising, research, and product development. Others are incurred to maintain a current position or to facilitate current managerial activity—e.g., legal services, market research, etc. Some do in fact vary with the volume of activity because management appropriates funds to these activities on the basis of anticipated sales volume, but this does not constitute cost variability for decision-making purposes.

Variable Costs

Since the businessman's definition of fixed cost is likely to differ from the economist's, his definition of variable cost must differ as well. To the businessman, variable costs are those that change as a necessary response to small changes in volume. When called upon to draw a line representing total variable costs at various volumes, most businessmen would probably draw a straight line, as in Exhibit 3–5. This implies that average variable cost will be constant for all volumes of activity up to full capacity, and that marginal cost is also constant and equal to average variable cost.

This does not necessarily mean that the businessman is unaware of the diseconomies that may accompany the increased use of capacity or that

Exhibit 3–5

LINEAR COST VARIABILITY

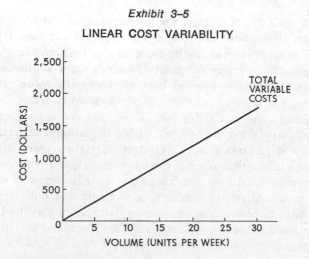

he is blind to the limitations of the straight-line assumption. It merely means that he believes that a straight line may be a reasonable approximation to the true cost-volume relationship within a fairly wide volume range.

The cost curve in Exhibit 3–6 is fully consistent with this conclusion. To begin with, no figures are provided for volumes less than seven units a week because the organization never operates in this range. Next, the total cost line rises in steps, as additional fixed costs come on the line to provide adequate support to more intensive rates of utilization. Within

Exhibit 3–6

ACCOUNTANT'S VIEW OF THE COST FUNCTION

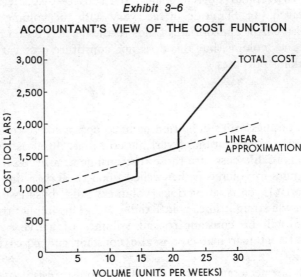

the limits of each of these steps, the line is straight, reflecting a constant marginal cost throughout the range. The slope of the line, representing the rate of increase in cost, is the same in the first two ranges, but increases at volumes in excess of about 23 units a week as the use of overtime and nonpreferred equipment becomes more and more pronounced.

In drawing a cost curve for this organization, many accountants would draw the dashed line in Exhibit 3–6. Their purpose is to emphasize the rate of variability (slope of the line) within the anticipated volume range between 14 and 22 units a week. To dramatize their point, they extend the line to the left until it reaches the edge; its height at this point is then identified as total fixed cost even though it is far in excess of the amount the company would actually incur if it went on a standby or caretaker basis. This kind of representation does no harm as long as the portions of the line outside the relevant volume range are not taken literally.

Whether the stepped increments in total cost should be treated as fixed or as variable costs is a matter of some dispute. Beyer, for example, treats these as variable costs,[3] whereas many other accountants view them as fixed. The distinction in many cases will have little practical significance; but when it does, a reasonable compromise is to include the stepped increments with the variable costs if the steps occur at fairly frequent intervals, and as fixed costs if the steps are fairly broad.

Semivariable Costs

Some costs do not fall precisely into either the fixed or the variable category but contain elements of both. These are generally referred to as semivariable costs. A typical example is the cost of electric power: Some power consumption is independent of operating volume, while another component is likely to vary directly with volume.

Fixed Costs and Sunk Costs

Whenever two alternatives differ in the rate of utilization of the existing facilities and organization, knowledge of cost variability is essential to the estimation of incremental cost. Confusion often arises, however, because it is often assumed that fixed costs are always sunk costs and that variable costs are always incremental. This is not always true. Fixed costs are those that do not change with relatively small changes of volume within the limits of existing capacity. Sunk costs are those that are unaffected by a choice between alternatives. Sunk cost is much the broader term of the two and may apply either to the fixed or to the variable costs.

For example, in most instances property taxes are fixed costs of plant operations. They will not be increased if the company is able to obtain additional volume to utilize plant capacity more fully. For a plant utilization decision, therefore, property taxes are not only fixed but also sunk costs. In studying the desirability of expanding the plant's operating capacity, however, these fixed costs are no longer entirely sunk because a larger plant will presumably carry a greater assessed valuation and therefore greater property taxes.

Similarly, when the problem is to compare the costs of operating at two different levels of output within the normal operating range, the only incremental costs may be the variable costs. A variable cost can also be a sunk cost under some circumstances, however. For example, if the company is considering whether to rent or own its manufacturing plant, total variable manufacturing costs are unlikely to be affected by the choice. Therefore, they may be treated as sunk costs for the purpose of reaching this specific decision.

---

[3] Robert Beyer, *Profitability Accounting for Planning and Control* (New York: Ronald Press, 1964), chap. 7.

BREAK-EVEN AND PROFIT-VOLUME CHARTS

Management can use information on cost behavior for many purposes. For example, by providing standards of what costs ought to be at different volume levels, it can help management judge whether costs are being kept under control.

By far its biggest impact, however, is in incremental analysis and profit forecasting. To illustrate the value of cost-volume information in this application, let us examine a set of commonly used devices known as *profit graphs*—that is, pictorial representations of relationships among costs, volume, and profits.

Break-Even Charts and Break-Even Points

One form of profit graph is the break-even chart, illustrated in Exhibit 3-7. The volume of sales is measured along the horizontal axis, and total costs and total revenues for each sales volume are represented by the vertical distances above the base line. The vertical distance between the total revenue and total cost lines at any volume represents the expected profit or loss at that volume.

As we have already seen, the cost line in this diagram is only representative within a relatively small portion of the output range. The profit spreads to the left and right of this range have little meaning and are introduced only to facilitate the explanation of the nature of fixed costs.

Exhibit 3-7

BREAK-EVEN CHART

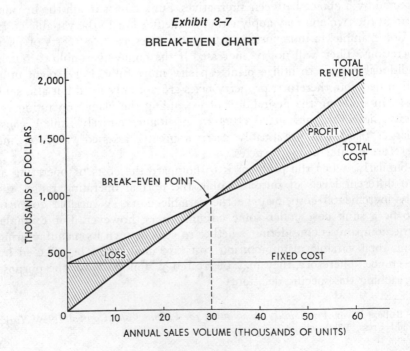

The fixed costs shown in Exhibit 3–7, for example, are the fixed costs associated with sales volume of, say, 20,000 to 40,000 units.

The volume at which the total revenue and total cost lines intersect is known as the break-even point. The break-even point may also be calculated algebraically if the cost and revenue functions are assumed to be linear, as they are in Exhibit 3–7, by using the following formula:

$$\text{Break-even volume} = \frac{\text{Fixed costs}}{\dfrac{\text{Revenues} - \text{variable costs}}{\text{Sales volume}}}$$

For example, assume that fixed costs total $420,000, the price of the product is $30 a unit, and the variable cost is $16 a unit. This means that each unit sold contributes $14 toward absorbing the company's fixed costs. This $14 is the product's *variable profit*, also known as marginal income or P/V income. At this rate it will take sales of 30,000 units to absorb fully the $420,000 in fixed costs associated with operations within the normal volume range. This answer .can also be obtained by substituting in the formula:

$$\text{Break-even volume} = \frac{\$420,000}{\dfrac{\$30 - \$16}{1}} = \frac{\$420,000}{\$14} = 30,000 \text{ units}$$

Charting Minimum Profit Requirements

The break-even chart can be modified in various ways. One of the most common modifications is to redefine fixed costs to include a provision for the company's annual dividend requirements or for a specified profit target. Exhibit 3–8 illustrates this possibility, using $140,000 as the annual dividend figure. In this diagram, the amount of fixed charges (fixed cost plus dividends) is represented by the vertical distances between the top and bottom parallel lines. Total variable profit is represented by the vertical distances between the total revenue and total variable cost lines. The vertical distances in the shaded areas then measure the expected deviations from the indicated profit target of $140,000 a year.

Two break-even points can now be calculated, the original one and a new one reflecting the dividend as an additional fixed charge:

$$\text{Break-even volume} = \frac{\$420,000 + \$140,000}{\$14} = 40,000 \text{ units}$$

Notice that the fixed charges in this diagram have been placed on top of the variable costs rather than underneath. The advantage of this kind of presentation is that it permits a direct view of the total variable profit and its relationship to the total of the fixed charges.

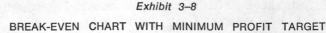

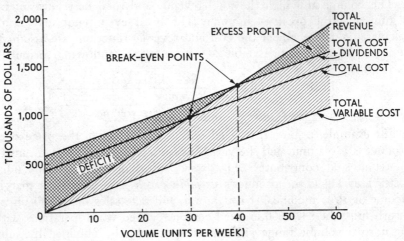

Significance of the Break-Even Point

The point at which the company or a segment of the company breaks even provides neither a standard for performance nor a guide for managerial decisions. Of considerably greater interest are the underlying relationships among volume, costs, and profit on which the break-even chart is based.

Many managers seem to find the break-even point useful, however, as a partial measure of the risks a particular course of action is likely to entail. A decision that will raise the break-even point is often presumed to be riskier than other decisions. This notion is often implemented by the calculation of the *margin of safety* or spread between anticipated volume and the break-even volume.

For example, if sales are expected to amount to 45,000 units, the margin of safety is 15,000 units, or one third of the expected volume. The margin of safety over the dividend-covering level is 5,000 units, or one ninth of the expected sales.

The Shape of the Revenue Line

The total revenue line in each of the previous exhibits was drawn as a straight line, implying that price will be the same at all possible operating volumes. In contrast, the revenue line in most of the models used by economists is curved rather than straight. The argument is that reductions in price are necessary to secure additional volume, and therefore that changes in total revenue will be less than proportionate to changes in volume.

One explanation for the use of the straight line is that firms in many industries do not reduce prices in the short run as a means of getting additional sales. When this is the case, the increasing difficulty of increasing sales volume will show up in a rising total cost curve rather than in a nonlinear total revenue line.

While this may be valid, a second explanation is more fundamental. The typical profit graph includes neither a downward curving revenue line nor an upward curving cost line because the graph is designed to show the effects on profit of variations in the *effectiveness* of marketing effort, other things being equal, rather than the effects of variations in the *amount* of effort expended. In other words, the only cost variations shown on the chart are those that result from changes in volume. If the response to the marketing effort is good, the profit will be high; if not, it will be low. Cost variations designed to produce volume variations do not appear in the chart.

Measuring Volume in Dollars

Few operations are so homogeneous that total sales volume can be measured adequately in physical units. Instead, dollar volume is used. When this is done, the break-even formula in the earlier illustration becomes:

$$\frac{\$420,000}{\dfrac{\$30 - \$16}{\$30}} = \frac{\$420,000}{46.7\%} = \$900,000$$

The denominator of this fraction is the ratio of variable profit to sales, known as the *variable profit ratio* or P/V ratio.

Whenever volume is not homogeneous, the profit-volume relationship depends on the product mix—that is, the relative proportions in which the various products are sold. The reason is that some products are likely to have higher P/V ratios than others. If the mix is a rich one, the spread between the cost and revenue lines will be wide; if low-margin products predominate, the spread will be narrow.

With volume measured in dollars, the revenue line must be drawn as a straight line and must be drawn at a 45-degree angle to the base if the vertical and horizontal scales are the same. This creates no difficulties unless management wishes to use the chart to contrast two different pricing structures. Contemplated changes in product prices can be reflected in the chart only by adjusting the cost line: an increase in prices requires a downward adjustment of the cost line and vice versa.

The only way to avoid this is to measure volume in terms of a schedule of fixed product prices. If this is done, a change in price can be diagrammed by changing the slope of the revenue line. The cost line can be left undisturbed.

Profit-Volume Charts

Another kind of profit graph is the profit-volume chart, illustrated in Exhibit 3–9. Separate lines for costs and revenues are eliminated in this type of presentation by plotting the profit difference only. Volume is again measured along the horizontal axis, and profit or loss is repre-

Exhibit 3–9

PROFIT-VOLUME CHART

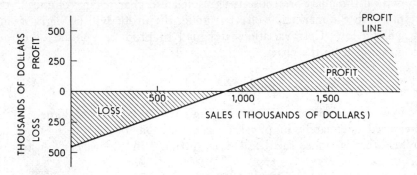

sented by the vertical spread between the profit line and the zero-profit base line. The point at which this line crosses the base line is the break-even point.

This kind of chart is generally simpler than the break-even chart, although what it gains in simplicity it may lose in ease of explanation. It has one advantage over the break-even chart, however, in that either actual or standard sales dollars may be used as the index of volume. Only the *net* effect of price changes or cost changes is reflected in the profit line.

It should be noted that both kinds of profit graphs assume that sales and production volumes are identical and that beginning and ending inventories are costed at the same prices. In using these charts for forecasting reported net income, changes in these variables will need to be allowed for.

Uses of Profit Graphs

Profit graphs are useful primarily as a means of visual presentation of information on profit variability. For example, suppose that a company markets the following three products:

Product	P/V Ratio	Current Sales	Variable Profit
A.....................	20%	$ 6,000,000	$1,200,000
B.....................	40	3,000,000	1,200,000
C.....................	60	1,000,000	600,000
Total.................		$10,000,000	$3,000,000

Deduction of fixed costs of $1.6 million leaves a net profit before taxes of $1.4 million per year.

Individual salesmen handle all three lines, but they tend to emphasize product A because its lower price makes it easier to sell. If the product mix could be altered so that the three products were sold in the proportions of 40%–40%–20%, variable profit from $10 million annual sales would be $800,000 from product A, $1.6 million from product B, and $1.2 million from product C, for a total of $3.6 million.

Using these calculations, Exhibit 3–10 was drawn for presentation at a sales force meeting. Two separate product mixes were presented, the current 60%–30%–10% mix and a target of 40%–40%–20%. Referring to the chart, the sales manager pointed out that profits would be increased by $600,000 a year if sales volume could be maintained at current dollar

Exhibit 3–10

EFFECT OF PRODUCT MIX ON PROFIT

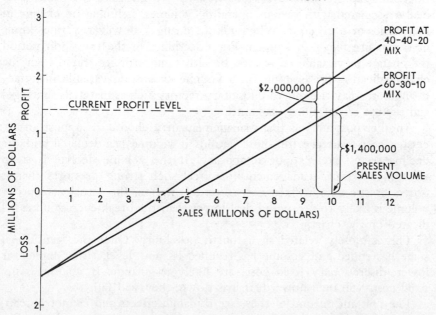

levels but with products selling in the target proportions. Even if dollar sales were to fall by as much as $1 million a year, total profit would still rise if the target proportions could be achieved.

One shortcoming of this kind of presentation is that it does not reflect the costs that might be necessary to accomplish the change. Existing product mix is the result of a combination of circumstances, including prices, competitive conditions, and the market conditions faced by the company's customers. Although it may be possible to disturb this balance simply by instructing the sales force to emphasize certain products at the expense of others, more positive action is frequently necessary, and this costs money. Changes in the fixed costs of distribution or in relative product prices or in the method of compensating salesmen are frequently necessary to secure the desired change in product mix.

For example, product C's high P/V ratio doesn't necessarily make it the most profitable product, nor does it necessarily call for devoting more promotional effort to this product. If total sales volume remains at $10 million while the mix goes to a 40–40–20 basis, total variable profit will go up from $1.4 to $2 million, an increase of $600,000. But suppose that the company would have to spend an extra $1 million a year to get its customers to change their buying patterns in this way. In this case, the added effort would have to bring total sales up to $11,111,111 to produce the same net profit as before.

Dynamic Effects

Profit graphs are static devices, designed to illustrate the profit normally associated with various operating volumes, assuming no change in P/V ratios or fixed costs. When volume changes, however, various kinds of things are likely to happen. For one thing, in the transition period the change in variable costs may be either more or less rapid than the chart indicates—for example, in a volume expansion, variable manufacturing costs may rise due to temporary factors such as materials shortages and the use of untrained personnel.

Another possibility is that management may choose to support an excessive cost structure for short periods if volume has declined and the decline seems likely to be temporary. If the volume decline is steep enough, however, management may feel such strong pressures that it orders drastic cuts in fixed costs. For this reason, the actual zero-profit volume is likely to be a good deal lower than the break-even volume indicated on the chart.

This is closely related to a fourth possibility. Once the transitional stage has ended and volume has reached its new level, either higher or lower, discretionary fixed costs are likely to change. If volume is up, fixed costs will inch upward; if it is down, they will fall.

The first and second of these are dynamic effects and cannot be captured effectively in a static diagram. The fourth is not a necessary result of changes in volume and probably should not be charted. This leaves only the third kind of effect—emergency cost reductions. This one can be reflected in the profit graph if management wants to diagram its probable response to sharply reduced volume. In most cases, however, the focus of attention is on the immediate vicinity of the anticipated volume and this added refinement is unimportant.

Dealing with Uncertainty

If risk is measured by the margin of safety, any two situations or proposals with identical margins of safety will appear to be equally risky. They may differ widely, however, in the degree of certainty attached to the profit estimates or in the sensitivity of profit to changes in volume.

One way of reflecting these differences is to accompany the profit graph with a probability distribution.[4] The first step is to estimate the probabilities of achieving different possible volumes. These estimates are difficult to make and are highly subjective, but they provide a highly useful additional dimension to the decision-making process.

For simplicity let us assume that only five volumes are possible, with the probabilities shown in the second column of Exhibit 3–11. Let us

Exhibit 3–11

PROBABILITY-RATED PROFIT FORECASTS

Weekly Volume (units)	Probability	Profit or (Loss)
10,000....................	15%	$(20,000)
20,000....................	24	(5,000)
30,000....................	42	10,000
40,000....................	14	25,000
50,000....................	5	40,000
Total....................	100%	xxx

assume further that the figures in the third column are the anticipated profits and losses shown on the company's profit graph. These figures can be presented in a diagram like the one in the left-hand panel of Exhibit 3–12. The probabilities of losses are indicated by the lengths of the shaded bars; the clear bars represent the probabilities of profitable operations.

This same information is shown in cumulative form in the right-hand

---

[4] This technique was first developed by Robert K. Jaedicke and Alexander A. Robichek, "Cost-Volume-Profit Analysis under Conditions of Uncertainty," *Accounting Review*, October 1964, pp. 917–26.

Exhibit 3–12

PROBABILITY-ADJUSTED PROFIT GRAPHS
In Thousands of Dollars

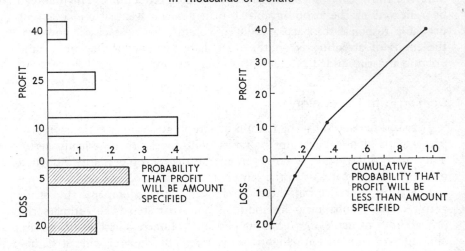

panel of the exhibit. The horizontal distances from the left-hand edge show the probabilities that actual profit will be less than the amount indicated on the left-hand scale. A flat slope indicates a fairly conservative situation with modest rewards and modest penalties; a steep slope like the one illustrated is more risky, with rich opportunities and costly penalties.

These are no longer profit-volume diagrams, although the second one has the same general shape as the diagrams we discussed earlier. Even so, this may be a better way of presenting profit-volume information than the conventional break-even or profit chart whenever management is more interested in risk factors than in the profit function itself. For an impression of the sensitivity of profit to volume fluctuations, on the other hand, one of the more conventional formats is preferable.

STATISTICAL REGRESSION ANALYSIS

The most highly developed method of estimating cost-volume relationships is statistical regression analysis. This consists of finding a formula that seems to provide the best description of the relationship that *has existed* between cost and volume during some specific period of time in the past.

The Method of Least Squares

A good way to begin is to plot the historical cost observations on a scatter chart like the one shown in Exhibit 3–13. This provides a visual impression of the pattern of relationship and should help identify observations that reflect highly abnormal conditions. Each point on the chart represents the cost of maintenance labor used and the volume achieved in the factory grinding department in one of the past twelve months. Wage rates and operating methods remained constant during this period, so that all of the observations are roughly comparable.

The straight line drawn in Exhibit 3–13 was positioned by eye. The method most widely used in practice, however, is the method of least

Exhibit 3–13

SCATTER CHART AND REGRESSION LINE

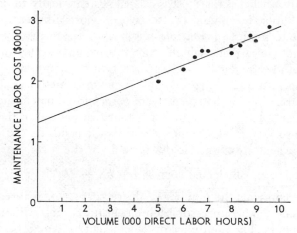

squares, which gets its name from an attribute of the line of relationship it produces: The sum of the squares of the vertical deviations of the actual observations from the line identified by this method will be less than the sum of the squares of the vertical deviations from any other line that might be drawn on the chart.

If the relationship between cost and volume is linear, it can be described by the equation for a straight line:

$$C = f + kV$$

in which

V = volume,
C = total cost at that volume,
f = total fixed cost per period at zero volume,
k = average variable cost per unit of volume.[5]

[5] Widely available computer programs can be used to derive the least-squares equation quickly and easily. For a basic explanation of the method, see a standard statistics text such as Samuel B. Richmond, *Statistical Analysis* (2d ed.; New York: The Ronald Press Company, 1964), chap. 19; for an advanced treatment, see E. Malinvaud, *Statistical Methods of Econometrics* (Chicago: Rand McNally and Company, 1966), chaps. 3, 5, 6, 7, 11, 13, 14.

The relationship between volume and maintenance labor cost represented by the straight line in Exhibit 3–13 can be described by the following equation:

Maintenance labor cost = $1,218 a month + $.17 a direct labor hour

This equation can be used to provide an estimate of cost for any known or estimated level of volume.

Multiple Regression Analysis

If the analyst believes that cost is related systematically to one or more factors in addition to volume (or to two or more different measures of volume), the technique of *multiple regression analysis* may prove useful.

For example, in a plant which generates its own steam and uses this steam for both heating and motive power, two of the important variables may be temperature (or "degree-days") and machine-hours. In order to discover the relationship between steam costs and volume as indicated by the number of machine-hours, it is necessary to neutralize the effects of temperature variations which impose varying demands on the steam plant for heat. The analysis might yield a formula of the form:

$$\text{Budgeted cost} = a + bX + cZ$$

in which X represents the number of degree-days (65° Fahrenheit minus average outside temperature for each day) and Z represents the number of machine-hours. The multiplier or "coefficient" c would be the average amount of cost variation per machine-hour.

The relationships can also be nonlinear. For example, a study of newspaper composing room costs some years ago revealed that a line based on the logarithms of the observations provided a much better fit than a line based on the raw data.[6] The relationship took the following form:

$$\log C = a + b \log X + c \log Z$$

in which

      C = composing room time
      X = the number of "assembly units" (a measure of the
            difficulty of the job)
      Z = the amount of newspaper space used.

In other words, the analysts identified linear relationships between the logarithm of cost and the logarithms of the other variables. This represents a nonlinear relationship in terms of the raw data, but because the relationship was linear in terms of the logarithms the statistical problems

---

[6] Sidney Davidson and Robert H. Roy, "A Case Study in Newspaper Operations," in Robert H. Roy (ed.), *Operations Research and Systems Engineering* (Baltimore, Md.: Johns Hopkins University Press, 1960).

were no greater than those the investigators would have encountered in fitting a linear equation to the raw data themselves.

Reliability of the Estimates

The reliability of the estimating equation can be tested by well-known statistical techniques. One of the most commonly used measures of reliability is the *standard error of estimate*, a measure of how far the observations are from the regression line. If all of the observations fall on the line the standard error of estimate is zero. The wider the scatter around the line, the bigger the standard error of estimate will be.

The standard error figures are useful in that they permit the cost analyst to calculate the range within which cost will probably lie, together with the percentage probability that it will be within this range. If the standard error is relatively large, the usefulness of the estimating equation will be relatively small.

The overall reliability of the estimating equation is measured by the *coefficient of determination*, the proportion of the total variation in cost that the regression equation is able to account for. (Statisticians measure the total variation by adding the squares of the differences between actual cost and average cost for the entire observation period. The amount of variation that is not accounted for by the regression line is measured by the sum of the squares of the differences between actual costs and the cost values indicated by the equation.)

Limitations of the Data

Regression analysis is predicated on the assumption that the available data meet a number of conditions laid down by the statistician. To cite just one example, multiple regression analysis reflects the assumption that the cost-determining factors are not related to each other in any systematic way. If interrelationships exist, then the individual coefficients cannot be meaningful. If the number of assembly units in the newspaper study referred to above had been correlated with the amount of newspaper space used, then the coefficient would not have indicated the full effect of variations in the number of assembly units. The total equation would have remained useful, but the individual coefficients would have lost their significance.[7]

Even if the individual observations can satisfy the definitional conditions laid down by the statistician, the cost analyst seldom can obtain

---

[7] For a good review of the usefulness of multiple regression analysis in cost estimation and of the technical difficulties to be overcome, see George J. Benston, "Multiple Regression Analysis of Cost Behavior," *The Accounting Review*, October 1966, pp. 657–72.

as many observations as he would like. Other things being equal, more observations mean more confidence in the line of relationship. In most cases, however, the only way to get more observations is to use data from a longer time period. Since conditions change, observations made even a year or two ago may not be directly usable for identifying current relationships.

Two methods can be used to cope with this latter problem. First, the observations for periods that can be classified as highly abnormal can be excluded from the analysis entirely. Abnormality is a matter of opinion, of course, and exclusions on this score ordinarily have to be based on clearly identifiable events such as strikes or natural disasters.

For the remaining observations a second technique should be considered. This consists of adjusting the data for the measurable effects of changes that are known to have taken place in factors other than volume. If wage rates have gone up by 10 percent, for example, all labor cost figures for periods before the increase can be raised by 10 percent.

This kind of adjustment assumes that changes in one factor will not induce changes in another. For example, it assumes that the quantity of labor used for a specified operating volume will be the same after the wage increase as it was before. This may not be strictly true, but in general the induced change is gradual enough to keep the analytical error to a minimum as long as only relatively recent data are used.

Limitations of the Equations

Even if great care is exercised to secure data comparability, the regression line remains a description of the past. If the past has been inefficient, the lines of relationship will reflect these inefficiencies. In other cases, goods or services are not consumed during the periods in which their costs are charged to operations, again making it difficult to identify the underlying relationships.

Furthermore, regression analysis will not identify behavior patterns that cannot be described by fairly simple mathematical formulas. Although most of the illustrations in this textbook assume straight-line relationships, step functions or other discontinuities are also possible. These cannot be picked out by least-squares regression analysis.[8]

Mere satisfaction of a mathematical formula, in other words, does not guarantee that the cost-volume equation will be reasonable. Cost estimates should be based on the best estimates of future relationships, and

---

[8] Few empirical studies of cost behavior have identified clearly defined, nonlinear relationships, but this is not surprising, mainly because nonlinearities are most likely to exist in portions of the volume range not covered by the observations. For a review of empirical cost-volume studies, see J. Johnston, *Statistical Cost Analysis* (New York: McGraw-Hill Book Company, Inc., 1960).

these may or may not coincide with the relationships indicated by mathematical equations derived from historical data.

SUMMARY

For many decisions, management needs to estimate how costs are likely to respond to changes in operating volume. It must distinguish between fixed and variable costs, and between discretionary fixed costs and those providing essential support to current operations. It must also look for steps in fixed costs and for nonlinearities in the variable costs.

One common use of the distinction between fixed and variable cost is in the calculation of P/V ratios and profit graphs. The P/V ratio provides ready-made estimates of variable costs and revenues when these can be assumed to vary in proportion to volume. Increments in fixed costs, on the other hand, must be estimated separately as differences in total cost for each time period.

Profit graphs permit management to visualize the risks and opportunities arising from uncertainties in sales forecasts. Pictures are often easier to understand than tables of numbers. The focal point in these charts is short-run profit variability in response to externally produced changes in volume, and only within a relatively small portion of the total possible output range. Break-even points can also be identified on these charts, but they serve mainly as rough indicators of risk and should not be overemphasized.

Mathematical equations representing cost-volume relationships can be derived by statistical means. Statistical techniques are not always appropriate, partly because they are relatively expensive and partly because the relationships between cost and volume are not expressable in simple mathematical terms, but they should be considered whenever the need for accuracy is great enough.

EXERCISES AND PROBLEMS

1. The following letter was received from a cost accounting student:

Dear Sir:

In your book you say that fixed costs may be affected by changes in the volume of activity. I have had three economics instructors, all of whom have their doctoral degrees, tell me that this definition is incorrect. They argue that if a cost is fixed it does not change. Would you please explain to me this difference of opinion?

Sincerely,

How would you answer this letter?

2. From the following estimates of hourly cost at different hourly volumes, compute (*a*) average total cost, (*b*) average fixed cost, (*c*) average variable cost, and (d) marginal cost for each volume of activity. (Note: For this problem assume that fixed cost is the same at all volumes.)

Units	Cost
0	$100
1	200
2	250
3	290
4	330
5	370
6	410
7	450
8	500
9	570
10	670

3.* From the following estimates of cost per hour at different volumes, compute (a) average total cost, (b) average fixed cost, (c) average variable cost, and (d) marginal cost for each volume of activity. (Note: For this problem assume that fixed cost is the same at all volumes.)

Units	Cost
0	$10
1	11
2	12
3	13
4	14
5	15
6	16
7	17
8	18
9	20
10	23

4.* The Cranby Company sells a single product for which the following data are available:

Current selling price	$4.90 per unit
Expected sales volume	200,000 units
Budgeted fixed costs	$1.60 per unit
Budgeted variable costs	$2.20 per unit

The company is contemplating an increase in the selling price of its product to $5.40 per unit.

a) What would be the new break-even point?
b) How many units would have to be sold at the new price to produce a 10 percent increase in total profit before taxes?

5.* The Carillo Company sells two products, A and B, with P/V ratios of 40 and 30 percent and selling prices of $5 and $2.50 per unit, respectively. Fixed costs amount to $100,000 a month. Assuming that each product accounts for one half of the company's dollar sales, how many units of each product must be sold to obtain a profit of $40,000 a month?

* Solutions to problems marked with an asterisk can be found in Appendix B.

6. A company is considering a proposal to change the price of its product. The following data are available:

	Present	Proposed
Selling price......................	$ 15.00	$ 13.50
Monthly sales (in units).............	10,000	12,000
Variable costs per unit...............	$ 9.00	$ 9.00
Monthly fixed costs..................	$40,000	$42,000

The increase in fixed costs would be necessary if the factory were to increase its production volume to the new level. Selling costs would be unaffected by the proposed price change.

a) Would the price reduction be profitable? Show your calculations.
b) What would be effect of the proposed price change on the break-even point? How might knowledge of the effect on the break-even point affect the pricing decision?

7. The figures in the table below are the hourly volume and materials cost totals for department X during the 12 most recent months:

Hours	Cost
3,000..........................	$3,300
2,130..........................	2,070
2,700..........................	2,730
2,610..........................	2,550
2,880..........................	2,760
2,670..........................	2,400
2,820..........................	2,820
2,640..........................	2,070
2,850..........................	2,400
2,730..........................	2,340
2,670..........................	2,430
2,700..........................	2,370

Using any method that seems suitable, develop a line of relationship between hourly volume and materials cost.

8. A study of the costs of the Paltec Company's Pittsford factory produced the following estimates of costs per hour at various levels of output per hour:

Output	Costs
13............................	$136
12............................	124
11............................	113
10............................	102
9............................	82
8............................	73
7............................	65
6............................	58
5............................	52
4............................	46
3............................	40

The analyst who prepared these estimates stated that the cost figures for all output rates in excess of nine units per hour included a provision for $10 per hour in additional fixed costs that need not be incurred at output rates of nine units an hour or less. (Note: Assume that the cost function is linear in the volume range of zero to six units an hour.)

a) Compute average total cost, average variable cost, and marginal cost for each output rate and plot the resultant figures on a single sheet of graph paper.

b) Discuss the problem you encountered in computing marginal cost for an output rate of 10 units an hour, and defend your solution of this problem.

9. As a result of an expansion program, Pasabache Industries has excess capacity which is expected to be absorbed by the domestic market in a few years. Twenty-five thousand machine-hours are available for the next year.

It has received inquiries from two firms located abroad. One offers to buy two million units of product A at 3.8 cents a unit; the second offers to buy three million units of product B at 5 cents a unit. Management has made the following estimates:

	Product A	Product B
Unit costs:		
Variable costs...............	$0.029	$0.042
Fixed costs..................	0.009	0.012
Total costs..................	$0.038	$0.054
Machine hours per thousand units....	6	8

One of the two orders will be accepted. Which should it be? Why?

10.* A company is considering the advisability of converting a machine from production of product A to production of product B. The following facts are available:

(1) Product A now sells at a price of $3, and annual sales amount to 100,000 units.

(2) Product B would sell for $5, and annual sales would amount to 120,000 units.

(3) Unit production costs are:

	Product A	Product B
Variable costs..................	$1.78	$2.65
Fixed costs.....................	0.32	0.85
Total costs.....................	$2.10	$3.50

(4) Introduction of product B would require the sales department to spend an additional $95,000 a year for maintenance work in customers' factories and offices.

(5) No other changes in selling and administrative costs would result from the change of products.

(6) The company must choose between the products—that is, the machine would be fully utilized with either product and could not manufacture both. Sales of the company's other products would be unaffected by this decision.

Assuming that the estimates are reliable, which product should be manufactured and sold? (Show your calculations.)

11.* The Powwow Flour Milling Company is currently operating its mill six days a week, 24 hours a day, on three shifts. It could easily obtain a sufficient volume of sales at current prices to take the entire output of a seventh day of operations each week. The mill's practical capacity is 6,000 hundredweight of flour per day.

Flour sells for $5.70 a hundredweight (cwt.), and the price of wheat is $2.17 a bushel. Approximately 2.35 bushels of wheat are required per cwt. of flour. Fixed costs now average $2,100 a day, or $0.35 per cwt. The average variable cost of mill operation, almost entirely wages, is $0.17 per cwt.

Sunday operation would require the payment of double wages for Sunday work, which would bring the variable cost of Sunday operation to $0.33 per cwt. Total fixed costs per week would increase by $210 if the mill were to operate on Sunday.

a) Compute the average total cost per cwt. for six-day operation. What is the net profit margin before taxes, per cwt.?
b) Compute the average fixed cost per cwt. for seven-day operation. Would it be profitable for the mill to operate on Sundays?

12.* Monthly power cost and machine-hour data for the Shelby Company for the 12 months of 19x0 were as follows:

Month	Machine-Hours	Cost
January.....................	3,500	$1,000
February....................	4,200	1,100
March......................	4,900	1,300
April.......................	4,400	1,200
May........................	4,300	1,200
June........................	3,800	1,100
July........................	3,300	1,090
August......................	4,100	1,280
September...................	4,700	1,400
October.....................	3,800	1,210
November...................	3,000	1,080
December...................	4,000	1,230

Power costs during 19x0 were affected by a 10 percent increase in power rates (prices paid for power). This rate increase was effective on July 1, 19x0. No further increase is expected during 19x1.

a) Using any method you deem appropriate, develop a line of relationship between power cost and machine-hours.
b) Using this relationship, how much power cost would you expect at volumes of 2,500 and 5,500 machine-hours? Would you have as much confidence in these estimates as you would have in estimates of cost at, say, 3,500, 4,500, or 6,500 machine-hours? Explain.

13. A manufacturing plant operates on a single-shift, five-day week. It can produce up to 8,000 units of output per week without the use of overtime or extra-shift operation. Fixed costs for single-shift operation amount to $30,000 per week. Average variable cost is a constant $10 per unit at all output rates up to 8,000 units per week. The plant's output can be increased to 12,000 units a week by going on overtime or adding Saturday operations or both. This entails no increase in fixed costs, but the variable cost is $12 per unit for any output in excess of 8,000 units per week up to the 12,000-unit capacity.

The plant also operates a second shift if sales volume warrants, and if second-shift operation is more efficient than overtime or Saturday operation. The maximum capacity of the second shift is 7,000 units per week. The variable cost on the second shift is $10.50 per unit, and operation of a second shift entails additional fixed costs of $4,500 per week.

a) At what operating volume does it become economical to operate a second shift? (Assume that the product cannot be inventoried in any substantial quantities.)

b) Prepare a schedule of marginal cost for output rates ranging from 5,000 units per week to 17,000 units per week, in 1,000-unit intervals, assuming that any overtime or Saturday operations are performed by the first shift.

14. The Mossback Company manufactures and sells five products for which the following data are pertinent (all dollar figures are per unit):

	Prod. A	Prod. B	Prod. C	Prod. D	Prod. E
Annual sales (units)	200,000	1,000,000	500,000	400,000	800,000
Returns and allowances.	$0.05	$0.03	$0.12	$0.16	$0.10
Variable costs.	1.42	0.84	2.81	3.12	5.22
Fixed costs.	0.84	0.46	1.95	2.42	1.46
Unit price.	2.50	1.50	3.95	5.70	8.00

The company's productive facilities are general-purpose facilities, and all products require operations to be performed in every department of the factory.

a) Compute the break-even volume for each product.

b) Compute the break-even volume for the company as a whole at the present product mix. Explain any difference between your figure and the total of the figures derived in (a).

c) Prepare a profit forecast under the assumption that the product mix were to change to the following:

Product	Unit Sales
A.	150,000
B.	800,000
C.	400,000
D.	500,000
E.	1,000,000

d) If fixed selling expenses had to be increased by $400,000 a year to effect the shift in product mix, would you recommend taking this action?

15. The Penn Yan factory of the Marlman Products Company operates on a five-day week. For cost accumulation and reporting purposes, the year is

divided into 13 "months" of four weeks each. You are given the following information about this factory:

(1) Property taxes, insurance, depreciation, salaries, and miscellaneous costs amount to $12,600 a month when the plant is shut down.

(2) Salaries and the costs of telephone, electricity, steam, and heat are $6,300 a month greater when the plant is operating than when it is shut down, no matter what rate of output is achieved.

(3) Whenever production rates equal or exceed 120 units a day, management authorizes expenditures of $2,500 a month for employee recreation, window washing, and community services. If the production rate equals or exceeds 160 units a day, management authorizes additional expenditures of $3,780 a month for adult education and related activities.

(4) Labor and materials costs amount to $10 a unit.

(5) The costs per month of other items not previously mentioned above, for various daily volumes, are:

Units	Costs
80	$ 5,600
90	6,300
100	7,000
110	7,700
120	8,400
130	9,100
140	9,800
150	10,800
160	12,160
170	13,940
180	16,200
190	19,000
200	22,400

a) From the preceding information, compute for each operating volume from 80 units a day to 200 units a day the following figures: (1) total cost per month, (2) total fixed cost per month, (3) total variable cost per month, (4) average total cost per unit, (5) average fixed cost per unit, (6) average variable cost per unit, and (7) marginal cost per unit.

b) Plot the figures obtained in (a) on graph paper, using separate graphs for total costs and for unit costs.

c) The plant is now operating at a rate of 150 units a day. What is the incremental cost of increasing the output rate to 160 units a day?

d) The company can sell as many units as it can produce at a price of $24.10 per unit, after deducting selling and administrative costs. What is the most profitable rate of daily output? What if the net price is $14.10?

16. The Wyman Company has been working for several months on the development of cost estimates for its Rutherford factory. One department's principal labor cost is the cost of processing labor. All other labor costs are classified as "indirect" labor.

Operating volume in this department is measured by the number of processing labor hours. Processing labor hours and indirect labor costs for the past two years were:

| Month | 19x1 | | 19x2 | |
	Processing Labor Hours	Indirect Labor Costs	Processing Labor Hours	Indirect Labor Costs
January...............	9,000	$12,820	12,000	$18,800
February..............	8,000	11,290	10,000	14,730
March................	6,000	12,400	11,000	17,050
April.................	7,000	13,100	10,000	15,220
May..................	8,000	11,540	11,000	16,350
June.................	7,000	10,600	12,000	17,900
July.................	8,000	11,580	12,000	15,700
August...............	9,000	12,600	9,000	11,860
September............	7,000	9,820	10,000	13,050
October..............	6,000	8,800	8,000	10,120
November.............	7,000	9,680	6,000	7,960
December.............	9,000	12,430	7,000	9,180

Additional information:

(1) Rearrangement of the department's machines on July 1, 19x2, made it possible to reduce materials handling time. The factory's industrial engineer estimates that this reduction has led to a saving in indirect labor costs of approximately 20 cents a processing labor hour every month since that time. The rearrangement has had no effect on the amount of overtime worked.

(2) Employees are paid a premium of 50 percent of their regular hourly wage rate for each hour of overtime work. Overtime premiums paid on processing labor and indirect labor time have been included in the indirect labor cost figures given above. Analysis of payroll documents shows that overtime premiums were as follows during the two years:

Month	19x1	19x2
January.........................	$520	$2,400
February.......................	290	930
March..........................	0	1,750
April...........................	0	920
May............................	340	1,250
June............................	100	1,800
July............................	280	1,500
August.........................	600	560
September......................	120	1,150
October........................	0	320
November.......................	80	0
December.......................	630	80

(3) Wage rates were 5 percent higher in 19x2 than in 19x1. Wage rates will remain at their 19x2 level throughout the current year.

(4) A fire destroyed a machine in March, 19x1. Employees whose wages would otherwise have been identified as processing labor costs were assigned to other tasks classified as indirect labor until the replacement machine was ready for operation on April 10, 19x1.

Separate overtime premiums from other components of indirect labor costs, make any other adjustments that seem appropriate, and prepare separate estimating equations for overtime premiums and for the other components of indirect labor cost. You should use either least-squares regression analysis or graphic curve fitting.

17. The PDQ Company manufactures a line of high-quality office furniture which it sells to dealers in the Middle Atlantic and New England states. Its sales force is divided into two divisions: one covering the five northern New England states and the northern half of Connecticut; and the other covering the District of Columbia, Delaware, Maryland, Pennsylvania, New Jersey, New York, and southern Connecticut. Estimated sales and expenses for the next year are as follows (in thousands of dollars):

	New England Division	Mid-Atlantic Division	Total Company
Sales...............................	$1,200	$900	$2,100
Costs:			
Variable costs:			
Manufacturing....................	$ 700	$525	$1,225
Sales commissions................	60	45	105
Sales brochures...................	120	90	210
Fixed costs:			
Directly traceable................	120	120	240
Indirect—allocated..............	40	30	70
Total costs.....................	$1,040	$810	$1,850
Income before taxes..................	$ 160	$ 90	$ 250
Taxes at 50 percent................	80	45	125
Net Income........................	$ 80	$ 45	$ 125

The directly traceable costs include depreciation of $20,000 for the New England division and $30,000 for the Mid-Atlantic division. Sales commissions are equal to 5 percent of sales. The indirect fixed costs are head office costs, necessary to enable the company to operate in either region or in both. They have been allocated to the divisions in proportion to sales.

a) The manager of the Mid-Atlantic division, which is the newer of the two divisions, has proposed that sales promotion in his territory be increased materially by adding a merchandising manager and two more salesmen to his staff and additional newspaper advertising, the annual fixed cost of these additional efforts amounting to $20,000. He expects that sales would increase 10 percent if this were done, with no change in selling prices. Would you support his proposal? Give reasons for your answer.

b) As an alternative proposal, the manager of the Mid-Atlantic division suggests that prices be reduced by 5 percent (this price reduction would be effective in both divisions). If this were done, physical sales volume in the Mid-Atlantic territory could be increased by 25 percent without incurring the additional sales promotion costs proposed in (a) above. Physical sales volume in the New England division would not be changed as a result of this price reduction. Evaluate the profitability of this proposal.

c) If, instead of accepting either of the above proposals, the company decided to abandon the Mid-Atlantic territory, what effect would this have on annual cash flows before taxes?

18. The Stafford Company makes cleaning fluid. It is sold to wholesale distributors at a price of $2 a gallon.

The company's marketing vice president estimates that sales for the coming year will total eight million gallons. When questioned, he says that he believes the probabilities that sales will be in various ranges are (in millions of gallons):

Probability	Range
.10	10–11
.15	9–10
.25	8– 9
.25	7– 8
.15	6– 7
.10	5– 6

This table can be converted into the following table of the cumulative probability that sales will exceed specified levels (in millions of gallons):

Probability	Sales Exceed
.00	11
.10	10
.25	9
.50	8
.75	7
.90	6
1.00	5

Management has made the following estimates of operating costs (in millions of dollars) at various volumes (millions of gallons):

Volume	Cost
5	$11.7
6	12.5
7	13.3
8	14.2
9	15.5
10	17.5
11	20.5
12	24.5

Estimates of cost at volumes between the levels shown in this table can be derived by linear interpolations.

a) Prepare a profit-volume diagram reflecting the estimated probabilities. Indicate how management might use it.

b) The marketing vice president believes that by spending an additional $200,000 he can increase the cumulative probability by 0.1 at each volume level from 6 million to 11 million gallons. (Add 0.1 to each probability figure in the second table above.) Prepare a revised profit-volume diagram, and indicate how, if at all, it would help management decide whether to make the additional expenditure.

Part II

Cost Measurement

chapter 4

Structure of the

Accounting Data Bank

The accounting system provides data for management's use by analyzing and recording the flows of resources into, within, and out of the organization. These flows are measured in monetary terms.

To accomplish this, the accountant must provide a set of accounts that will accumulate data in a form that fits management's needs. These call for two kinds of data: (1) data for use in decision making or planning future operations, and (2) data for use in monitoring current operations. The purpose of this chapter is to see how these two kinds of needs affect the structure of that section of the accounting data bank that provides operating cost and revenue data for management. Although the chapter focuses on the accumulation of historical data, it should be remembered that the same structure also can be used for cost and revenue estimates.

ACCOUNTS IN PERSPECTIVE

It is all too easy for an accountant to impute to the accounting system a universality it does not deserve. To counter this tendency, let us start with four simple observations.

First, the accounts are not management's only source of data for planning and control reporting. For one thing, the organization's data bank ordinarily includes a good deal of information expressed in physical units, such as total output, man-hours, yield ratios, employee turnover percentages, and so forth. Furthermore, data on external conditions often occupy a vital section of the managerial data bank.

Second, the accounting data bank often suffers from a confusion of purposes. The stewardship and property control functions of accounting typically require fairly complete records of resource acquisition and use. The addition of management's needs to these investor-oriented requirements often leads to a parallel demand for complete classification of all operating costs and revenues. In many cases, however, classification of sample data may be sufficient; sometimes classification may serve no managerial purpose at all.

Third, accounting systems often measure resources at unit prices that have no relevance to current management decisions. The data recorded in the accounting data bank should be regarded solely as a point of departure, as a set of indicators rather than as gospel truth.

Finally, all data-gathering and classification schemes are subject to the law of diminishing productivity—that is, beyond some point successive increments of data have progressively smaller managerial payoffs. Ideally, the amount of data provided should be determined from the application of a cost-benefit model, comparing the value of information with its cost. Although formal efforts to apply such models are scarce, they are always implicit in the system. Every system represents a set of decisions as to how much and what kinds of information will be productive.

With these reservations in mind, we can proceed to a discussion of the operating account structure, first for the organization's revenues and then for its costs.

REVENUE CLASSIFICATION

Management's revenue-determining decisions focus on segments of the firm's business, not on the totality. This means that revenue information ought to be classified by segment—e.g., by product or by geographical area.

Routine Coding of Revenues

The accountant's traditional approach is to decide in advance what classifications are most likely to be useful to management and then to code the data from each sale transaction accordingly. For example, Exhibit 4–1 shows the coding structure used by the Apex Lighting Company, a regional electrical contractor. Apex Lighting's management recognizes the three distinct types of business shown in the left-hand column of Exhibit 4–1: (1) installation of industrial and commercial lighting systems; (2) highway lighting installations; and (3) repair services, mostly rewiring of older offices and apartment buildings. Each of these has its own code number, shown at the far left.

Apex Lighting's revenues are also coded to indicate which of the company's three sales districts they come from. These code numbers are shown in the column headings of Exhibit 4–1, and a full identification of a revenue item requires both a business-type code and a district code. For example, the code 4400.91 would be used to identify the revenue from an industrial installation job in the western sales district.

The amounts shown in each cell in Exhibit 4–1 indicate the total revenue from the specified line of business in the specified district. Adding the figures vertically gives total sales for each district; the same numbers can be added horizontally if line-of-business totals are wanted. Total company sales figures can be obtained by adding the amounts in all nine cells.

In large companies, revenues are customarily classified on more than two bases.[1] Revenue codes for individual salesmen, customer industries, or channels of distribution are not at all uncommon. Addition of new

Exhibit 4–1

APEX LIGHTING COMPANY
Revenue Account Structure

	4200 Eastern District	4300 Central District	4400 Western District
91—Industrial installation	$142,640	$218,815	$73,448
92—Highway installation	83,173	192,061	76,905
93—Repair services	66,543	61,008	25,497

classification bases does not add accounts, however—it multiplies them. For example, suppose that Apex Lighting wants to be able to find out how much business it has gotten directly from customers and how much it has obtained on a subcontracting basis, both groups divided into contracts obtained by Apex's own sales force and contracts obtained through independent agents. To obtain these breakdowns, the accountant would add a new code number to the identifier for each transaction, and this would automatically require four cells in place of each of the 9 cells in the exhibit, or 36 in all.

The impact of this may be apparent. Each additional classification basis increases the flexibility of the data base, but it also increases both the cost of data processing and the probability that classification errors

---

[1] An idea of the possibilities can be derived from an examination of National Industrial Conference Board, *Sales Analysis*, Studies in Business Policy, No. 113 (New York: NICB, 1965).

will occur. One revenue account is easy to code, but every classification basis beyond this adds to the amount of time the coding will take and increases the number of mistakes that will be made. The operational problem is to decide how much the additional detail is worth.

Incorporation into the Accounts

The full revenue classification scheme is not always reflected in the formal ledger accounts. The accountant always has the option of storing the coded information in some other way. For example, a keypunch operator may be instructed to enter industry and channel of distribution codes on the punched card record of each transaction, even though only the regional and product classifications are reflected in the formal account structure.

This procedure has two main advantages. First, it reduces the number of individual figures that must be transcribed into the formal accounting records. This reduces costs and saves time, particularly in less highly mechanized systems. Second, it reduces the amount of storage capacity occupied by the ledger. Active storage capacity is expensive, particularly in electronic systems.

The disadvantage of excluding certain classifications from the ledger is that management must wait longer for the classified information once it decides to call for it. Cards or tape or even the original sales documents themselves must be handled, scanned, and made to yield up their contents, and all this takes time. To overcome this problem, the accountant often prepares frequently requested analytical summaries before they are asked for and keeps them in files that are more accessible and more compact than the raw data files themselves.

The Use of Sampling to Cut Systems Cost

Selection of either of these first two alternatives requires the coding of each revenue transaction. A second possibility is to code and classify only a representative sample of the transactions. A good sample, drawn on the basis of a carefully prepared sampling plan, can provide essentially the same information as full classification systems, and at a fraction of the cost. For example, the sampling plan might call for coding and keypunching the data from 2,000 transactions instead of the full 40,000 transactions of the period. The result will be a set of percentage distributions which can then be multiplied by the total sales for the period to provide estimates of the sales in any one category.[2]

---

[2] For an introductory discussion of sampling procedures, see Clifford H. Springer, Robert E. Herlihy, Robert T. Mall, and Robert I. Beggs, *Statistical Inference*, Mathematics for Management Series, Vol. 3 (Homewood, Ill.: Richard D. Irwin, 1966), chap. 5.

The Nonclassification Alternative

Carrying the sampling concept one step further, the company might even choose to eliminate transaction coding completely and instead store the original sale documents or a sample of them until such time as someone calls for a particular kind of data. At that time a sample could be extracted, coded, and processed. This has one clear advantage over the methods discussed previously—the accountant does not have to decide in advance what classification bases are most likely to be useful. Instead, he can wait until the data are called for and then build a classification scheme appropriate to the demand. This may very well be different from anything he would have thought of earlier.

This last alternative is ordinarily unsatisfactory. First, the costs of prolonged storage of the original documents are likely to be prohibitive. Second, processing costs are likely to be greater if the documents have to be processed twice or more than if they are processed only once. Third, since some classification bases are generally in constant demand, the documents will always be processed at least once anyway, thus leading to storage of both the original documents and some processed data. Finally, considerable delays are likely to be encountered once a demand for data is registered. Unless the demand is for data that the routine classification system would not have provided, this delay will be considerably greater than it would be under any of the other alternatives discussed here.

Recording Nontransactions

This scheme can also be expanded to include data about nontransactions, which may be even more important than transactions data. Nontransactions data are seldom recorded in the formal ledger accounts, but a good accounting system will provide some means for recording them. For example, orders received have to be logged in some form to provide management with the information necessary to plan ahead. This information may also be better for appraising the performance of the sales force than current revenues, which are most often recorded at the time goods are shipped. This date may be very much later than the date of the order.

Another kind of nontransaction is a nonsale. The reasons why a salesman loses a potential order may be just as significant as the fact that he was able to obtain others. Another kind of nonsale information is *stockout* information—that is, sales that were not made because the company could not deliver the desired products. This kind of information is needed for most inventory control models, in which the likely losses from stockouts must be compared with the costs of carrying extra inventories to guard against such losses.

Indirect Revenue Effects

Revenues can always be traced directly to one business segment or another. The revenue from a segment is not always the same as that directly traceable to it, however. For example, a study of the revenues recorded in the accounts of a meat packing plant revealed that almost 90 percent of these revenues could have been obtained even if that plant had not been in operation.

This is an example of a *substitution* relationship between business segments, as withdrawal from or entry into a particular segment results in shifts of revenues from one segment to another. The interrelationship can also be of another kind, however—a *complementary* relationship. A razor blade manufacturer, for instance, finds that the revenues attributable to the sale of the company's razors include not only the sale price of the razors themselves but also the sale prices of a certain number of blades that razor owners will buy later on.

Routine revenue accumulation seldom can cope with indirect revenue effects. Instead, these effects must be estimated by statistical or other analytical methods. The important point, when using recorded revenue data, is to recognize the possibility that complementary or substitution relationships may exist.

CLASSIFICATION OF OPERATING COSTS

Operating costs are the costs of the resources used during a period to carry on the organization's activities, that is, the objectives to be achieved by the costs. The main task of most cost accountants is *cost finding*—measuring or estimating the relationships between operating costs and the organization's "cost objectives" (or "costing units").

The typical set of cost accounts is three-dimensional; that is, an effort is made to classify each cost in three ways:

1. By organizational unit.
2. By descriptive element.
3. By product, project, program, or service.

The control reporting need is paramount in the first of these, while planning requirements dictate the structure of the third. Descriptive classifications may be designed to serve either or both of these needs.

Organizational Classification Bases

One object of cost finding is to measure or estimate the cost of each *responsibility center* within the organization. A responsibility center may be defined as an organization unit headed by a single person, answerable

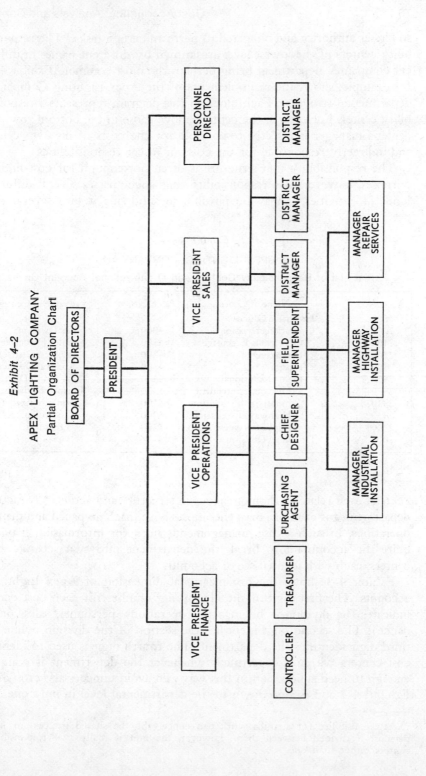

Exhibit 4-2

APEX LIGHTING COMPANY

Partial Organization Chart

to higher authority and obligated to perform certain tasks.[3] The responsibility centers of the lowest level are known by different names in different companies, department being perhaps the most common. Exhibit 4–2, for example, shows the main elements of the Apex Lighting Company's departmental structure. Each block in this diagram represents a responsibility center. For each of the centers above those in the bottom row, the center's manager is directly responsible for the costs of his own center and indirectly responsible for the costs of lower responsibilities.

The responsibility unit structure is often not enough for cost-finding purposes, however. If a responsibility unit encompasses several different kinds of activities, it may be possible to subdivide it into several *cost*

Exhibit 4–3

APEX LIGHTING COMPANY

Partial List of Responsibility Centers and Organizational Account Codes

Acct. No.	Name of Center	Acct. No.	Name of Center
1000........	Executive Office		
2000........	Operations Division:	4000........	Sales Division:
2100........	Operations Executive	4100........	Sales Executive
2200........	Purchasing	4200........	Eastern District
2300........	Design	4300........	Central District
2400........	Field Operations:	4400........	Western District
2410........	Field Superintendent	5000........	Finance Division:
2420........	Industrial Installation	5100........	Finance Executive
2430........	Highway Installation	5200........	Controller
2440........	Repair Services	5300........	Treasurer
3000........	Personnel Division		

centers, each relatively homogeneous in structure and activity. A factory department, for example, may encompass both machine-paced and manual operations. In such a case, management's need for information may require the accountant to break the department into two separate cost centers, each with its own set of accounts.

Exhibit 4–3 shows the organizational dimension of Apex Lighting's accounts. The first digit of the identifying number for each cost center indicates the division it belongs to (operations, personnel, sales, or finance). The second digit identifies the section of the division, while the third digit identifies the department. The fourth digit is used to identify cost centers within a department whenever the department is complex enough to need subdivision in this way. To avoid unnecessary crowding, Exhibits 4–2 and 4–3 go down to the departmental level in only one sec-

---

[3] Responsibility for a unit's work can conceivably be shared by two or more persons; if divided between them, however, the unit is really two responsibility centers rather than one.

tion, field operations; the more detailed breakdown into cost centers is omitted entirely.

Descriptive Classification

For management purposes, the data in each account should be *homogeneous*. This means that the costs assigned to a particular account should exhibit the same pattern of response to the various determinents of cost behavior.

The main reason for this requirement lies in the need for data for planning. Cost estimation ordinarily proceeds from estimates of cost determinants to estimates of cost via some estimated relationship. The more heterogeneous the account, the more difficult it will be to estimate cost relationships. For example, if lubricating oil costs vary with the number of machine hours and the costs of cleaning supplies vary with the number of labor hours, putting them in the same account would be likely to obscure the underlying relationships.

Homogeneity also has a control reporting objective. The manager can control cost only by acting on the determinants of cost, and if an account includes items with different determinants, the manager can never be clear as to where his efforts should be directed.

To provide data of greater homogeneity, each cost center's costs are typically classified by "natural elements" such as salaries, supplies, power costs, and so on. For example, Exhibit 4–4 shows the coding system used by the Apex Lighting Company to classify the costs charged to each of the cost centers in the company's field operations division. This gives the chart of accounts its second dimension: when a cost is incurred, it must be classified both by cost center and by the nature of the goods or services consumed. Thus if John Jones works a full eight hours in the repair service department at an hourly rate of $3, the account 2440.01 (Repair Services—Productive Labor) will be charged with $24.

Even with this many accounts, the data contained in any one account are unlikely to be completely homogeneous. For one thing, perfect homogeneity is probably unattainable. Costs are determined by the interaction of a myriad of forces, most of them either unknown or imperfectly understood. Since the company's knowledge of cost behavior is imperfect, its ability to classify costs on a behavioral basis is also limited. Second, more accounts mean higher clerical and storage costs, slower access time, and added opportunities for error; and at some point any further trade-off of cost for homogeneity becomes unprofitable.

As a result, management must compromise. It must try to predict which classifications will prove most useful in the future and most difficult to apply later if they are not applied to the data now. On these grounds, it is likely that the cost of the outside consulting services used by a division would be recorded separately from, say, the costs of manu-

Exhibit 4–4

APEX LIGHTING COMPANY

Chart of Cost Accounts: Field Operations Departments

Department \\ Element	2410 Field Superintendent	2420 Industrial Installation	2430 Highway Installation	2440 Repair Services
01 Productive labor	2410.01	2420.01	2430.01	2440.01
11 Supervision	2410.11	2420.11	2430.11	2440.11
12 Labor—travel time	2410.12	2420.12	2430.12	2440.12
13 Labor—idle time	2410.13	2420.13	2430.13	2440.13
14 Clerical labor	2410.14	2420.14	2430.14	2440.14
15 Other labor	2410.15	2420.15	2430.15	2440.15
21 Overtime premium	2410.21	2420.21	2430.21	2440.21
22 Vacation and holiday pay	2410.22	2420.22	2430.22	2440.22
23 Payroll taxes	2410.23	2420.23	2430.23	2440.23
24 Pensions	2410.24	2420.24	2430.24	2440.24
31 Travel allowances	2410.31	2420.31	2430.31	2440.31
41 Productive materials	2410.41	2420.41	2430.41	2440.41
51 Tools	2410.51	2420.51	2430.51	2440.51
52 Supplies	2410.52	2420.52	2430.52	2440.52
53 Equipment rental	2410.53	2420.53	2430.53	2440.53
54 Depreciation	2410.54	2420.54	2430.54	2440.54
61 Insurance	2410.61	2420.61	2430.61	2440.61
71 Other expense	2410.71	2420.71	2430.71	2440.71

factured parts that have been purchased from outside subcontractors. It would be most unusual, however, to use separate office supplies accounts for each of the company's suppliers of this kind of goods. The determinants of office supplies costs are unlikely to be very different from supplier to supplier, and the chance that separate cost information might someday be useful to management is likely to be far too small to justify the added effort required to record the data separately.

Product or Project Classification

Many cost accounting systems go beyond the two-dimensional organizational-descriptive account structure and use a three-dimensional cost classification scheme. The third dimension serves to identify the project, program, product, or service that the cost has contributed directly to.

For example, Apex Lighting finds it useful to measure the costs of fulfilling each of its installation and repair contracts. Its management can then use this information in judging whether the contract was as profitable as expected or in preparing estimates for similar contracts in the future.

In other cases, the cost data may be the basis for charges to customers. Automobile repair garages, for example, ordinarily keep a record of the amount of time spent and the number of repair parts used on each repair job. It is then a simple matter to figure out the customer's bill by multiplying these quantities by the prices shown in the company's regular price list.

Still another use of this third dimension is in the preparation of cost figures for projects or services destined for use within the company itself. New product development projects or product advertising programs are good examples of this kind of costing object.

This third classification basis differs from the other two in that the individual categories are constantly changing. When Apex Lighting finishes work on a contract, the code number for that contract is no longer part of the active classification scheme; a new number will be created for each new contract. Aside from this difference, the third dimension is identical in structure to the other two.

The Problem of Common Costs

Unfortunately, cost classification is far more difficult than the preceding discussion would imply. The problem is that many costs cannot be traced uniquely to individual products or cost centers. For example, the sales manager's work presumably benefits all of the company's product lines to some extent, but there is no way of saying how much of his salary is incurred for any one. Such a cost is known as a common cost—one that provides or supports the organization's capacity to achieve two or more cost objectives.

Whether a particular cost is traceable or common depends on which cost objective or costing unit is referred to. Although all costs are traceable to *some* cost center, many of them may be common with respect to the particular cost center management is interested in at the moment. Thus the sales manager's salary is traceable to the sales division but common to the individual sales branches as well as to the various product lines.

The accountant usually refers to a traceable cost as a *direct* cost of the costing unit to which it can be traced—that is, a direct cost is any cost that is specifically traceable to a particular costing unit. All costs that are common to two or more costing units are referred to as *indirect* costs of those units.

The illustration in Exhibit 4–5 may help to clarify this distinction. All of the costs of the field operations headquarters, industrial installation, highway installation, and repair services departments are direct costs of Apex Lighting's field operations division. The divisional headquarters costs are indirect, however, when the costing unit is one of the three operating departments within the division.

The next step is even more complicated. Investigation reveals that the legal fees included in divisional headquarters costs, although indirect to the highway installation department, are clearly traceable to the company's highway installation business. In addition, of course, all of the

Exhibit 4–5

APEX LIGHTING COMPANY

Partial Diagram of Relationships between Direct and Indirect Costs

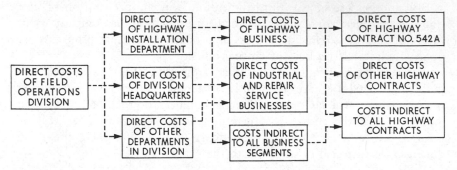

direct costs of the highway installation department are also direct costs of the highway installation business. Finally, most of the direct costs of the highway installation business are also direct costs of one highway installation contract or another, but a few are not traceable to any one contract and therefore are indirect to them all.

The commonness of costs is a problem because management needs information for decisions relating to individual products or other cost objectives for which the company must incur costs in addition to those that are strictly traceable to that objective. For example, a large highway installation contract may increase the work load of the controller's staff and increase the costs of the controller's department. These added costs cannot be labeled as highway installation costs when they are incurred because they are indistinguishable from other costs of the controller's department, but they are costs attributable to fulfilling the contract nevertheless.

To provide a more complete record of the costs attributable to the operation of individual cost centers or to the creation of individual products or services, the accountant is often called upon to analyze the indirect costs and find some basis for assigning all or part of them to individual departments or products or services. This task is one of the most difficult and most controversial aspects of the cost accountant's work. To do justice to the complexity of the task, we shall have to devote a major part of each of the remaining chapters in this part of the book to a description and evaluation of the methods that the accountant can use to perform it.

Other Costing Bases

At one time or another, management is likely to need estimates of the costs of costing units other than cost centers or product lines. Other possibilities are the costs of serving individual groups of customers, the costs of processing small orders, or the costs of different methods of delivering the company's products.

The cost accumulation scheme seldom provides for routine accumulation of costs on bases such as these. The main reason is that few costs are specifically traceable to individual costing units in these categories. The specific cost of processing a small order is very small and would be very expensive to isolate in the accounts. As a result, when this kind of cost breakdown is needed, it must be provided by other means. This problem is discussed in Chapter 13.

NONMONETARY DATA

The data bank is not limited to revenue and operating cost data or derivatives of these. Another part consists of nonfinancial data of various sorts. Examples include output statistics, the number of customer calls made by salesmen to various kinds of customers, the amount of time lost due to accidents, and the percentage of defective units in various production lots.

Nonmonetary data to some extent are substitutes or surrogates for monetary data. For example, the amount of lost time is usually important because lost time means financial loss. This financial loss may be difficult to understand, however, and in these circumstances the physical statistic may serve management's needs as well as or better than its monetary translation.

Nonmonetary data are similar to monetary data in another respect. They are classified data—classified by department, machine, delivery route, product, or some other segment of the firm's activities. Generally speaking, however, the problem of commonness of cost is avoided because physical statistics are usually collected for a specific purpose related to the activity to which the statistics relate. The problem of commonness must be faced only if management wants to translate the physical fact into monetary terms.

Needs for physical data vary so widely from company to company that generalizations are difficult. Furthermore, accumulation of such data creates no conceptual problems that are not also encountered in the classification and accumulation of data measured in monetary terms. For these reasons, most of the discussion in the chapters that follow will relate to monetary data only.

SUMMARY

Management needs a wide variety of historical data, both for use in reviewing past operating performance and for use in forward planning. These data are processed and then stored in a sort of data bank until they are needed or discarded as no longer relevant. This data bank can consist of (a) original documents or other records of events that have taken place, (b) selected data from these documents in encoded form, (c) summaries of these data, in the form of account totals, or (d) various combinations of these.

Although the managerial accountant is often concerned with those portions of the data bank that contain physical unit data, most of his work centers on data expressed in monetary or financial terms. He is particularly interested in the classification and accumulation of data on the operating costs and revenues of previous periods. This chapter has attempted to sketch the main structural elements of this section of the data bank, thereby laying the foundation for the chapters that follow.

From the analyst's point of view, the ideal account structure is one in which each account contains only homogeneous information—that is, every amount entered in a particular account is the result of the same set of determinants as every other amount in this account. Thus the patterns of relationship between the amounts in the account and their determinants would be obscured only by random variations.

Most systems represent compromises between this ideal and the constraints imposed by the costs of achieving homogeneity and by the difficulty of identifying the underlying relationships. Thus, although revenues are usually classified by product line and by organization segment, further classification by customer group or channel of distribution may be dispensed with or reduced in detail.

Similarly, operating costs are ordinarily classified on either two or three bases—by cost center; by descriptive element; and possibly by the product, project, or service to which they can be traced. Unfortunately, however, many costs cannot be classified without ambiguity on all three of these bases because they are common costs, relating not just to one but to two or more cost objectives. At least some of these common costs can be reassigned later, if this seems desirable, but the cost assignment processes discussed in this chapter are based solely on the accountant's ability to trace costs unequivocably to particular cost objectives. This is and must be the basis on which the initial classification and recording of costs takes place.

EXERCISES AND PROBLEMS

1. Using any coding system that seems appropriate, sketch out the rough outlines of a chart of accounts for a company which has the following characteristics:

Balance Sheet:
    Three major asset categories, with 100 possible subcategories in each.
    Two major liability categories, with 50 possible subcategories in each.
    Ten ownership equity accounts.

Factory Costs:
  One factory.
  Twelve departments in the factory.
  Twenty cost elements in each department (e.g., salaries).
Administration Costs:
  One department.
  Ten cost elements.
Marketing:
  Three products.
  Two branch territories and home office.
  Ten cost elements.

2. The Montagu Company was originally established to distribute a new type of waterproof, heat-resistant glue to shoe manufacturers. The glue was produced under contract by a large chemical company, and product sales were made by a field sales force of four salesmen who contacted shoe manufacturers directly. These salesmen were all chemical engineers and had the responsibility of training their customers' personnel in the proper method of applying the glue. The revenues and expenses of the company have been recorded in a fairly simple set of accounts:

Sales	Office Supplies
Sales Returns and Allowances	Rent
Cost of Goods Sold	Printing and Postage
Sales Salaries	Telephone and Telegraph
Sales Commissions	Retirement Expense
Travel Expenses	Insurance Expense
Office Salaries	Miscellaneous Expenses

The president of the company has just decided to expand operations in two ways: first by taking on the distribution of a line of shoe findings (miscellaneous small items used in shoe manufacture), and second by marketing the company's glue to furniture manufacturers. Two salesmen are to be added to the shoe trade sales force. The furniture trade sales force will consist initially of three new salesmen to be hired for that purpose. The president, who heretofore has also acted as sales manager and controller, has decided to promote his senior salesman to the position of sales manager. The present office manager will become controller and office manager, with a new assistant to be hired.

a) What changes, if any, will the company need to make in its accounting system to meet the income measurement objective? To meet other management objectives?
b) What problems do you foresee in the measurement of income for individual product lines?

3. The Harrell School is a nonprofit educational institution. It has both day students and boarding students enrolled in a college preparatory high school program.

The school also conducts an evening program for older children and young adults who have dropped out of high school but are now working to earn their high school diplomas on a part-time basis.

The school also sponsors various noncredit adult education courses in a variety of subjects ranging from foreign languages to home repair techniques.

Athletic fields, a dormitory, and a classroom and office building are all located on the school's campus, far from the downtown area of a medium-sized city. The dormitory contains kitchen and dining facilities, as well as rooms for the boarding students. Boarding students take all of their meals in the dining room, seven days a week; day students may either bring their lunch or eat in the dining room with the boarding students upon payment of a weekly fee. No dining service is provided to the students and faculty of the evening programs.

The school's administrative staff consists of a headmaster (who also teaches one course in the day program), an admissions director, a director of the evening programs, a guidance counselor, an administrative assistant, a bookkeeper, and two secretaries.

The dormitory staff consists of a director, a dietician, a head cook, two "residents," and a number of people who do the cooking, serving, and cleaning. Three men take care of the buildings and grounds on a full-time basis, bringing in part-time help as needed for special or evening work.

The school has a full-time faculty for the day program. The evening programs are staffed on a part-time basis, with fees negotiated separately for each course. The buildings and grounds staff are paid extra for evening work.

A small endowment fund is invested in long-term securities. The income from these investments supplements the revenues from tuition and fees and the annual gifts from foundations and alumni and friends of the school.

Textbooks are provided free to students in the evening high school program. Students in the day program and in the adult education courses buy their books from the school. All book sales are handled by the administrative assistant.

a) Design a chart of accounts that you think would provide management with the kinds of accounting information it needs. Indicate how you think management would use these data. (You need not develop a system of numerical codes for your accounts.)

b) Indicate what criteria you used in designing the account structure. You should be able to explain why each account is necessary.

c) What problems, if any, would you expect to encounter in identifying operating data with the accounts that you have set up?

4. The Ace Maintenance Company provides routine equipment maintenance service and performs equipment repairs for a large number of industrial users in the New York metropolitan area. The company will service or repair almost any factory equipment and has built a reputation for prompt, efficient service.

Ace Maintenance was founded 10 years ago by Paul Mace, a highly gifted salesman and administrator. Mr. Mace is still president of the company, doing most of the direct selling himself. His vice president, Don Wynant, is responsibile for hiring all service personnel and for the day-to-day operation of the service end of the business.

The company has no other top executives. Robert Bradford, the controller, is responsible solely for billing, payrolls, and other routine accounting and bookkeeping operations. Ralph Petrillo, the only other man reporting to Mr. Mace, has the title of sales manager but serves primarily as an administrative assistant.

The company's operating cost accounts for a typical month show the following balances:

	Executive Office	Accounting	Operations
Salaries and wages..............	$10,000	$3,000	$26,000
Overtime premiums.............	...	...	1,100
Materials and supplies...........	500	450	1,000
Repair parts...................	...	...	14,000
Utilities......................	1,200	...	...
Payroll taxes..................	300	120	1,200
Pension plan...................	700	150	1,300
Travel........................	100	...	2,100
Advertising....................	200	...	...
Insurance.....................	800	...	...
Taxes.........................	900	...	...
Rent..........................	2,500	...	...
Miscellaneous..................	400	30	600
Total.........................	$17,600	$3,750	$47,300

a) In what ways do you think that the account structure probably ought to be changed? Give reasons for each of your suggestions.

b) What problems would you be likely to encounter in trying to carry out your suggestions?

chapter 5

Product or Project Costing:
Job Order Production

The most important cost objectives are to perform services, manufacture products, or carry out programs or projects. The purpose of this chapter is to study the basic features of job order costing, a method that accountants often use to measure the costs of reaching these kinds of cost objectives.

APPLICABILITY OF JOB ORDER COSTING

Job order costing can be used whenever two or more products, services, projects or programs are produced independently of each other but with the use of the same facilities, provided that the job is clearly distinguishable from its fellows all the while it is in process. A university can use this costing technique to identify the costs of a concert or lecture series, for example, or the costs of an experimental adult education program. A business firm may use job costing techniques to measure the costs of various research projects in the company's laboratories, the costs of particular advertising campaigns, or the manufacturing costs of individual products. For convenience, we shall refer to all of these situations as job order production.

Factories or service businesses operate on a job order basis whenever the sales of individual products or services are too small to justify devoting facilities exclusively to any one of them for any significant length of time. Most production to individual customer specifications falls into this category (e.g., automotive repair shops, job printing plants, and management consulting firms).

Job order production is also the rule whenever the production cycle is particularly long, so that many time periods elapse before finished output can be measured. Examples here include shipbuilding, building construction, and most industrial research projects.

JOB COSTING IN THE SERVICE ORGANIZATION

Service organizations account for an ever-increasing percentage of overall economic activity. Job costing can be used in a wide variety of service organizations. It seems appropriate, therefore, to begin with an illustration from the service sector, the job costing system used by the Apex Lighting Company, the lighting systems contractor referred to in Chapter 4.

Direct versus Overhead Costs

The costs that are traced directly to individual jobs or contracts are known as *direct costs* of those jobs. They include items such as the costs of employees' time spent on the job (referred to in this company as "productive labor"); amounts charged by outside contractors for work on the job; the costs of materials, parts, and supplies used on the job; and rental charges for equipment rented for use on the job.

Apex Lighting's field operations and design departments also incur many costs that cannot be traced to any one contract. These are called the *overhead costs* of these departments. They are distinguished from direct job costs in that they are incurred either jointly for the benefit of more than one job or in units that are individually too small to be traced readily to specific jobs. Depreciation of drafting tables and other design department equipment is an example of the first kind of overhead; the cost of pencils used by operating foremen is an illustration of the second. The first cannot be traced to individual contracts; the second is not traced to specific contracts because it would be inconvenient to do so. The real costing problem is to decide how and to what extent these overhead costs should be charged to individual jobs or contracts.

Because most overhead costs cannot be traced to specific jobs, the only way of including them in job cost is to use some kind of average rate. Such an average is known as a *burden rate* or overhead costing rate.

One possibility would be to divide the actual overhead costs for each period by some measure of the total operating volume of that period. For example, suppose that the overhead costs in Apex Lighting's operations division amounted to $209,000 during November, on an operating volume of 19,000 productive labor hours. This averages $11 per productive labor hour:

$$\frac{\text{Actual overhead cost}}{\text{Actual volume}} = \frac{\$209,000}{19,000 \text{ hours}} = \$11 \text{ an hour}$$

If this rate were used in contract costing, $11,000 in overhead costs would be assigned to a contract on which 1,000 productive labor hours were used during the month.

Predetermined Burden Rates

Apex Lighting actually used this kind of burden rate for many years. The system was changed, however, because management found that it produced confusing information about the profitability of individual contracts. For example, Apex Lighting did three virtually identical jobs for Ace Realty, Inc. at six-month intervals, using about 1,500 productive labor hours on each one. The first returned a profit margin of $7,155, while $5,380 was reported for the second and only $2,655 for the third. The cost figures showed the following breakdown:

	Job 1	Job 2	Job 3
Contract price..........	$32,000	$32,000	$32,000
Costs:			
Direct........	$ 9,200	$ 9,140	$ 8,960
Overhead.....	15,645	17,480	20,385
Total.........	$24,845	$26,620	$29,345
Profit margin........	$ 7,155	$ 5,380	$ 2,655

Thus while the direct costs remained virtually constant, the amounts charged as overhead went up alarmingly. The reason was that the burden rate rose from $10.50 an hour for the first job to $11.50 an hour for the second and $13.50 an hour for the third. These increases, in turn, were due to reduced overall volume. Although variable overhead costs amounted to $1.50 an hour in each period, average fixed costs went from $9 an hour in the first period to $10 in the second and $12 in the third. The explanation was that while total fixed cost remained at $180,000 a month, overall volume dropped from 20,000 hours in the first month to 18,000 in the second and 15,000 in the third:

	Period 1	Period 2	Period 3
Total fixed cost................	$180,000	$180,000	$180,000
Total volume (no. of productive hours).......	20,000	18,000	15,000
Average fixed cost.............	$9/hr.	$10/hr.	$12/hr.

Management felt that these changes were the result of changes in the level of business generally and had no bearing on the profitability of individual contracts. In fact, the sales manager even went so far as to say that the contract was even more profitable when overall volume was low because the company needed the business more then than in better times.

The company's solution was to adopt a predetermined burden rate—that is, the rate was not to be the average overhead cost of each individual period, but rather the average of a "normal" or typical period:

$$\text{Burden rate} = \frac{\text{Estimated overhead costs in a normal month}}{\text{Total volume in a normal month}}$$

Normal volume for this purpose was defined as the percentage of capacity that was regarded by management as essential for efficient, competitive operation. This is consistent with the criteria used in deciding the size of newly constructed plants, which must include some provision for periods of partial idleness. For Apex Lighting, a volume of 21,000 productive labor hours was regarded as normal. With new labor-saving equipment in place, management estimated that monthly overhead costs would total $210,000 at this volume ($180,600 in fixed costs plus $1.40 an hour). On this basis, the burden rate was set at:

$$\frac{\$210,000}{21,000} = \$10 \text{ per productive labor hour}$$

Using this rate, the accountant would assign $10,000 in overhead costs to a contract using 1,000 productive labor hours.

The predetermined rate also serves to simplify and speed clerical operations—that is, overhead can be applied to jobs as the work is performed, without awaiting the calculation of actual cost and actual volume at the end of the month. The rate is not affected by month-to-month changes in average overhead costs.

Departmental Burden Rates

Apex Lighting's costing structure is slightly more complicated than this discussion would imply. Each of the three field operations departments—industrial installation, highway installation, and repair services—has its own burden rate; the design department has its own costing rate.

The reason for this added complexity is to obtain more accurate cost estimates. The design department, for example, has a much higher burden rate than any of the field operating departments, $25 per labor hour. It is argued that costing accuracy requires that design department overhead costs be divided among the jobs in proportion to the amount of design work required, rather than in proportion to the amount of work done by the personnel of all four departments in total.

The data in Exhibit 5–1 can be used to illustrate the effect of using departmental overhead rates instead of a single rate for all kinds of work. Notice that the single rate of $10 an hour has been replaced by four rates ranging from $7.50 to $25 an hour. The difference shows up quite

Exhibit 5–1

APEX LIGHTING COMPANY

Departmental Burden Rates

Department	Overhead Cost at Normal Volume	Direct Labor Hours at Normal Volume	Overhead Rate per Direct Labor Hour
Design.........................	$ 25,000	1,000	$25.00
Industrial installation...............	86,000	10,000	8.60
Highway installation................	39,000	5,200	7.50
Repair services....................	60,000	4,800	12.50
Total..........................	$210,000	21,000	....

clearly when these new rates are applied to three different jobs, each requiring 1,000 labor hours, as shown in Exhibit 5–2. With a companywide burden rate, each of these jobs would have been assigned 1,000 × $10 = $10,000 in overhead costs.

One reason for this difference is that many costs that can be classified as direct costs in the industrial installation and highway installation departments are overhead costs in repair service. For example, the highway installation department has no equipment of its own. It rents whatever equipment it needs for individual contracts, and the rental costs are recorded as direct contract costs. All repair equipment is company-owned, however, and depreciation on this is included in repair service department overhead. Use of a single overhead rate for all departments would result

Exhibit 5–2

APEX LIGHTING COMPANY

Application of Departmental Burden Rates

	Hours Spent in Department	Departmental Overhead Rate	Total Overhead Cost Applied
Industrial system contract A47:			
Design department...............	100	$25.00	$ 2,500
Industrial installation department.....	900	8.60	7,740
Total......................	1,000		$10,240
Highway lighting contract TX4:			
Design department...............	200	$25.00	$ 5,000
Highway installation department.....	800	7.50	6,000
Total......................	1,000		$11,000
Repair contract 2A66:			
Repair service department..........	1,000	$12.50	$12,500

in charging a highway contract with its own equipment rental costs and a portion of repair service equipment depreciation as well.

Treatment of Other Overhead Costs

The Apex Lighting Company assigns only the costs of the design department and the three field operating departments to individual jobs. Costs of other departments are almost never traceable to specific jobs, and no satisfactory averaging basis has yet been found. As the company's president puts it, an average would be useful only if it showed how costs are affected by the job. That is, a useful average would have to be one that would give a good approximation of the incremental cost of taking on each job. So far, Apex Lighting has found no average that would do this. This being the case, management prefers to treat these costs as charges against company operations generally, without trying to assign them to individual contracts.

The Variability of Overhead Cost

The assumption underlying the assignment of overhead to individual jobs is that it measures the amount of overhead attributable to those jobs. For many decisions, however, a narrower focus is necessary. The incremental overhead cost associated with a particular job often consists of the short-run variable costs only. When this is the case, the burden rates described above will overstate the incremental effects of management's decisions.

Accounting systems that provide information on the variable costs of individual products are known as variable costing or direct costing systems, and we shall use Chapter 9 to give them a thorough examination.

FACTORY JOB ORDER COSTING

Job costing has had its most complete development in the factory, and our second illustration will examine some of the terms and methods likely to be encountered in a factory job costing system. Here the costing unit is a batch of products that can be identified easily as it passes through the production process.

Classification of Materials Costs

Accounting for job lot production begins with the issue of a production order. This contains instructions as to the specifications of the items to be produced, the number of units required, a list of materials to be used, the operations to be performed, the equipment to be used, and the required delivery date.

The first step in production is the transfer of *direct materials* from a storeroom to a production center. Direct materials are all materials, parts, and subassemblies that are used in one particular job order. *Indirect materials* or supplies, on the other hand, are issued for general factory use and not for the specific benefit of any one job.

These definitions are based on the traceability of the costs and not necessarily on the physical incorporation of the specific input into the end-product. Thus direct material costs of a large order for precision-ground lenses would include the costs of grinding materials that are used directly on the job, even though they are not physically incorporated in the finished product. They should be treated as overhead only if they cost too little to justify the clerical expense of tracing them to jobs.

In most cases, production departments obtain materials and supplies from the storeroom by submitting *materials requisitions*. Each requisition shows the items required and the quantities of each. For direct materials, the requisition shows the job order number, while for indirect materials it shows the number of the cost center and an account number indicating how the materials were used (e.g., lubricating materials, cleaning supplies, packing materials, etc.).

Finally, if a production foreman finds that he has requisitioned more materials than he needs, he returns the excess to the storeroom, noting the quantity on a *returned materials card*.

Classification of Labor Costs

Departmental labor costs are also classified on much the same basis as materials costs. *Direct labor* cost is any labor cost specifically traceable to one particular job. *Indirect labor* is labor expended on tasks such as machine repair, lubrication, cleaning, or other tasks not related directly to a particular production order.

The counterpart of the materials requisition is the labor *time ticket*. When a worker begins work on a particular job, the job number is entered on a time ticket which is then stamped with the date and hour. At the end of the day or of the work to be done, or at the time the worker is taken off the job, whichever comes first, the time ticket is again stamped with the time. (For indirect labor, the time ticket shows the number of the cost center in which the work was done, together with a number denoting the kind of work.) The hours shown on the time tickets are then multiplied by the appropriate hourly rates to derive the amounts to be charged to individual jobs or overhead accounts.

The Job Cost Sheet

When the job order is issued, the accounting department is notified and a job cost sheet is prepared. Exhibit 5–3 shows a simple job cost sheet that might be used by a small manufacturer of vacuum cleaners and parts.

Exhibit 5–3

JOB ORDER COST SHEET

Description: Canister No. 278
Date Ordered: 5/1/—
Quantity Ordered: 2,000

Job Order No.: 1234
Date Completed: 5/12/—
Quantity Completed: 2,000

Materials Cost					Cost Summary:
Date	Item	Quantity	Price	Amount	Materials... $ 901.50
					Labor...... 71.40
5/3	Shell No. 14	2,000	$0.32	$640.00	Overhead... 126.00
5/4	Shell No. 14	50	0.32	16.00	Total...... $1,098.90
5/5	Handle No. 142	2,000	0.12	240.00	
5/10	Paint	2	2.75	5.50	Unit cost..... $ 0.549 each
	Total			$901.50	

Labor Cost						Overhead	
Date	Cost Center	Opera-tion	Hours	Rate	Amount	Rate	Amount
5/4	2	22	6.5	$2.20	$14.30	$6.00	$ 39.00
5/6	3	31	10.0	2.10	21.00	5.00	50.00
5/10	4	42	14.5	1.80	26.10	2.00	29.00
5/11	4	44	4.0	2.50	10.00	2.00	8.00
	Total				$71.40		$126.00

This lists the job number, the number of units to be produced, and delivery information, as well as the costs of direct labor and materials. In some cases, as in the Apex Lighting Company, space has to be provided for equipment rentals and other kinds of costs that can be charged directly to individual jobs.

Overhead costs are also entered on the job cost sheet, in this case in the lower right-hand corner. These entries are usually made when the job is completed, by applying predetermined departmental burden rates to the number of activity units used on the job. Thus if activity is measured in machine-hours, the amount charged to a job will be determined by multiplying the burden rate by the number of machine-hours used on that job. This amount is often referred to as the *overhead applied* or *overhead absorbed*, to distinguish it from the various overhead costs actually incurred in the factory during the period.

The burden rates used in Exhibit 5–3 were based on direct labor hours. Because the job order factory manufactures so many products of different size and complexity, production volume almost never can be measured satisfactorily by the total number of units of product manufactured. Instead, volume is measured by some index of productive input such as direct labor hours or machine-hours or pounds of materials. In practice, different cost centers often use different indexes of volume, but this added complexity can be left to another chapter.

Development and Use of Unit Costs

In the Apex Lighting Company, each job yields a single unit of output, the completed job, and the costing focus is on the job as a whole and to a lesser extent on the individual tasks required by the job. In factory production, however, a typical production lot is likely to consist of a number of identical units of a given product. When the job is finished, the total cost assigned to it is generally divided by the number of product units in the batch or lot to determine the unit cost of the job.

These unit cost figures may be asked to serve three purposes. First, they can be used to measure the costs of the units in this lot until they are either used in production or sold to outside customers. Second, management may use them in estimating the costs of future lots of the same product, for pricing and other decisions. Third, they may be compared with the estimated costs of the job as a means of monitoring operating performance.

Inventory Costing. As an example of the first of these, the canisters covered by Exhibit 5–3 are component parts for several of the company's vacuum cleaner models. When this job was finished, the canisters were moved to a parts storeroom near the assembly department. At that time, the cost figure of $0.549 a unit was recorded on the stock card for this part. Later on, when some or all of these canisters are issued into finished products, they will become direct materials of the assembly job order at a cost of $0.549 a unit. (Alternatively, the cost of this lot may be added to the costs of any canisters already in the storeroom so that a new average can be computed, applicable to the new units and the old. This is the *moving average* basis of inventory costing.)

Decision Making. The $0.549 cost figure might also be used to estimate the costs of the canisters to be incorporated in a new vacuum cleaner model. It must be remembered, however, that the unit cost figures that emerge from job order costing are *average* costs. The decision maker needs estimates of the *incremental* costs of each decision, and these are seldom equal to the average costs recorded in the past. Even if all other conditions remain constant, an unlikely assumption in itself, operating volume is likely to change. It may even be affected by the decision itself.

Even if the value of the unit cost figures is in doubt, however, the job cost sheets themselves are undeniably an invaluable source of data on direct product costs. To make them even more useful, the costs charged to the job cost sheet are often coded to indicate the type of materials used, the operations performed, and so forth.

Control Reporting. Management sometimes compares job cost data with the cost estimates that were made before the job was placed in production. This has some usefulness as a means of checking the accuracy of the estimates, but it is much less useful as a check on the effectiveness of factory cost control. Control reporting is departmental, following responsibility lines, and it is difficult to adapt job cost data to this basis. At best, unit costs can be identified as higher or lower than the advance estimates and investigation can reveal the cost centers responsible for most of the deviation. It is generally impractical, however, to derive departmental totals of these deviations when there are many cost centers and many jobs. Development of cost data for use in cost control will be discussed later, beginning in Chapter 15.

SUMMARY

Job order costing is the method that accountants use to measure the costs of individual construction contracts, research projects, and factory job orders. It can be used whenever two or more products, services, projects, or programs are produced independently of each other but with the use of the same facilities. Under job order costing, the accountant assigns to each job or project all of the costs that can be traced readily to that job or project, and then adds a provision for the average cost of nontraceable costs, or overhead.

Overhead cost averages used for this purpose are known as burden rates. They are usually predetermined rates, and each department or cost center ordinarily has its own rate, used for costing the work done in that particular cost center.

The burden rate may represent all of the cost center's costs (full costing systems) or the variable costs only (variable costing systems). Even in so-called full costing systems, however, some costs are usually excluded from the burden rates. In manufacturing companies, for example, the accountant usually includes in the burden rate only those costs that are readily traceable to the manufacturing divisions of the company.

Unit cost figures that result from job order costing procedures are subject to all of the weaknesses of any average. They provide raw data on which estimates of incremental cost can be based, but the analyst should not fall into the trap of assuming that the increment will always be equal to the average. We shall elaborate on this point in later chapters.

EXERCISES AND PROBLEMS

1.* The following data have been collected in connection with job No. 7863, manufactured by the Belmont Machine Works:

(1) Materials issued:

August 4	$3,800
August 9	1,700
August 20	800

---

* Solutions to problems marked with an asterisk can be found in Appendix B.

(2) Direct labor:

	Hours	Cost
Week of August 2	200	$520
Week of August 9	300	800
Week of August 16	250	550
Week of August 23	100	220

(3) Manufacturing overhead applied at a rate of $1.50 per direct labor hour.
(4) Order completed (100 units), August 25.

Prepare a job order cost sheet for this job, enter the appropriate information, and compute the cost per unit.

2.* Chailly, Inc., uses a job order costing system in its factory with a predetermined burden rate based on direct labor hours. You are given the following information:

(1) Job No. 423 was started on March 3, finished on March 28.
(2) Other data:

	Job No. 523	All Jobs (in March)	Budgeted for Entire Year
Direct labor hours	60	10,000	100,000
Direct labor cost	$200	$ 40,000	$ 350,000
Direct materials cost	$800	$150,000	$1,300,000

(3) Factory overhead budgeted for the entire year was $900,000; actual overhead for the month of March was $106,000.

Compute the cost of job No. 423.

3. The burden rate of a factory is $3 a machine-hour, based on estimated costs at a normal operating volume of 10,000 machine-hours a month. Operating volume is now running at a rate of 9,000 machine-hours a month and overhead costs at this volume total $28,800, an average of $3.20 an hour. No change in cost or volume is in sight unless management accepts the order described in the next paragraph.

A customer has offered to buy all of its requirements of a machined part for the next year. This order would add 1,000 machine-hours a month to the factory's volume. The price received would exceed the cost of direct labor and direct materials by $2,900 a month.

Would you use $3.20, $3, or some other figure to estimate overhead cost for the purpose of deciding whether to accept this order? Give your reasons. Would you accept the order?

4. The Robertson Company has been using a single plantwide overhead rate in its factory. The controller has proposed using department overhead rates instead. You have the following information:

(1) Three products (A, B, C) are produced in three departments (1, 2, 3).
(2) Labor hours required for each unit of product are:

Product	Department			Total
	1	2	3	
A....................	2	1	1	4
B....................	0	2	2	4
C....................	2	3	3	8

(3) Product produced in a normal year: A, 40,000 units; B, 40,000 units; and C, 10,000 units.

(4) Overhead incurred in a normal year: department 1, $400,000; department 2, $300,000; and department 3, $100,000.

(5) Sales this year: A, 20,000 units; B, 40,000 units; and C, 10,000 units.

(6) The company's inventories are listed on a full cost Lifo basis, and the year-end inventories of product A were 10,000 units greater than the year-beginning quantities.

a) Estimate the effects of changing to departmental overhead rates based on direct labor hours.

b) Explain the arguments for and against making this change.

5. Franklin Associates is a management consulting firm. It charges costs to its various contracts in the following way:

(1) Professional and secretarial staff: direct time—actual time spent times actual salary rate; indirect time—through burden rate.

(2) Art work and printing: direct work—from supplier invoices; indirect work—through burden rate.

(3) On-premises copying: project-related work—5 cents a copy; other work —through burden rate.

(4) Travel: from expense vouchers.

(5) All other costs: through burden rate.

Budgeted time and costs for the year and actual time and costs for February were as follows:

	Annual Budget		February	
	Hours	Cost	Hours	Cost
Direct costs:				
Professional staff............	25,000	$200,000	2,000	$15,000
Secretarial staff..............	6,000	24,000	550	2,300
Art work and printing........		7,000		800
Copying.....................		2,000		200
Travel......................		35,000		2,700
Indirect costs:				
Professional staff............	5,000	40,000	600	5,200
Secretarial staff.............	12,000	48,000	800	3,300
Art work and printing........		3,000		300
Copying.....................		1,000		100
Travel......................		8,000		400
Other......................		56,000		4,700

a) Prepare a predetermined hourly rate for indirect costs.

b) The following direct cost data were recorded during February for one of the company's contracts. How much cost was assigned to this contract during February?

> Professional staff (70 hours)........................ $630
> Secretarial staff (10 hours)......................... 45
> Art work and printing............................ 60
> Copying... 10
> Travel... 280

6. The Frantic Products Company manufactures a variety of fabricated metal products and sells metal castings in a variety of sizes, shapes, and specifications. The casting shop is the biggest department in the factory, and each casting order is costed separately on a job order basis.

Management is now setting an overhead costing rate for the coming year. The following data have been estimated:

	Capacity Production	Normal Volume	Anticipated Current Volume
Output (pounds)........................	10,000,000	7,000,000	6,000,000
Furnace hours..........................	90,000	63,000	54,000
Direct labor hours......................	45,000	31,500	27,000
Costs:			
Direct labor.........................	$225,000	$157,500	$135,000
Indirect labor........................	90,000	70,000	68,000
Other overhead costs..................	60,000	55,000	54,000

The normal volume figures represent the designed capacity of the plant—that is, the plant was designed so that operations at this volume would be at a competitive average unit cost.

The casting crews can tend several furnaces at a time, the exact number depending on the kinds of products being cast. For simple flat castings, the crew can handle as many as six furnaces, while for rods and extrusions only one or two furnaces can be handled by a single crew.

The ratio of master casters to helpers also varies from product to product, but not nearly as widely.

a) Compute burden rates for this department on four different bases: (1) pounds, (2) furnace hours, (3) direct labor hours, and (4) direct labor costs.

b) Using each of these burden rates in turn, compute the amount of overhead that would be assigned to two jobs with the following characteristics:

	Job No. 1	Job No. 2
Pounds............................	10,000	10,000
Furnace hours.......................	90	120
Labor hours........................	45	50
Labor dollars.......................	$225	$200

c) What criteria would you use in deciding which of these four rates to use?

7. One of the jobs in the factory of the Gentry Company during June was job No. 422, calling for the manufacture of 100 Flister Blidgets, Polished, Large. The factory accountant had to record the following events, among others, during June:

June		
	1	Issued 200 pounds of material X for job No. 422 at $0.75 a pound.
	4	Issued 50 pounds of material Z for job No. 422 at $3.20 a pound.
	5	Expended labor during week on job No. 422—76 hours in department A at $4 an hour.
	8	Issued lubricants and cleaning compounds to department A, $100.
	11	Returned 10 pounds of material Z to storeroom—quality not up to specification for job No. 422.
	11	Issued 15 pounds of material Z for job No. 422, at $3.30 a pound.
	12	Expended labor during week on job No. 422—33 hours in department A at $4, and 10 hours in department B at $3.50 an hour.
	15	Discovered defects in five Flister Blidgets, which were then sent back to department A for reworking.
	16	Issued 20 pounds of material P to department B for job No. 422, at $2 a pound.
	17	Damaged five pounds of material P originally issued for job No. 422, and transferred them to scrap bin.
	18	Finished job No. 422.
	19	Expended labor during week on job No. 422—3 hours in department A (reworking defective units) at $4 an hour, and 30 hours in department B at $3.50 an hour.
1–19		Burden rates for production departments: department A, $2 a direct labor hour; department B, $5 a direct labor hour.
	30	Collected the month's scrap from both departments, 100 pounds with scrap value of 10 cents a pound (total materials processed by both departments during the month, 10,000 pounds).

a) Prepare a job order cost sheet, enter all the pertinent costs, and compute unit costs, by element, for job No. 422. (Note: Some of the items may not be reflected directly in the job order cost sheet.)

b) How would you use the unit cost obtained in (*a*)? Explain.

8. The Corgut Company uses a job order costing system in its factories. Predetermined burden rates are used in all departments.

Three jobs were in production in the machine shop of the Akron plant during the first week of March. Cost estimates for these three jobs were as follows:

	No. 1273	No. 1276	No. 1280
Materials......................	$ 450	$ 500	$ 700
Labor........................	1,400	900	1,000
Overhead.....................	800	500	600
Total........................	$2,650	$1,900	$2,300

Jobs No. 1273 and 1276 were completed during the week and transferred to the finished goods stock room. The following data relating to the machine shop were recorded during the week:

	No. 1273	No. 1276	No. 1280	Total
Work in process, March 2:				
Materials..........................	$200	$420	...	$ 620
Labor.............................	650	400	...	1,050
Overhead..........................	380	220	...	600
Direct materials issued................	300	100	$800	1,400
Direct labor.........................	900	600	500	2,550
Overhead applied to jobs..............	520	350	290	1,160
Materials purchases...................				1,800
Actual overhead cost.................				1,390

It is estimated that all the materials required for job No. 1280 had been issued prior to the end of the week and that 40 percent of the labor required to complete this job had been performed.

a) Prepare job order cost sheets for the three jobs and enter the amounts indicated by the data above.

b) Indicate how management might use the data on the job cost sheets. What problems would you encounter in trying to use these data for these purposes?

chapter 6

Classifying Labor and
Materials Costs

The distinction between direct and indirect costs is not always obvious. Some costs that are apparently traceable to certain jobs may in fact turn out to be attributable to others or even to influences totally unrelated to individual jobs. The purpose of this chapter is to see how these questions can arise and what can be done to resolve them.

IDENTIFICATION OF DIRECT LABOR TIME

Under certain circumstances, management may choose to classify some labor hours as indirect even though they can be traced quite easily to specific jobs or projects. For example, setup time and rework labor time may be handled in this way. A brief look at each of these should be useful.

Setup Time

The arguments for charging the cost of setup labor to individual job orders are relatively straightforward. Such costs can be traced, in most instances, to specific job orders. Including them in the direct labor charge will produce a more precise record of historical product cost than can be obtained by including them with manufacturing overhead. Treating setup cost as overhead means that the charge to any one job will be based on average relationships which are unlikely to hold true for any one specific job.

There are counterarguments, however. If lot size varies, the average setup time per unit is likely to vary inversely with the size of the batch. Under these conditions, classifying setup cost as direct labor destroys the proportionality between direct labor cost and units produced, an assumption that is particularly valuable in cost analysis for planning and decision making. Secondly, if setup labor is charged directly to jobs, variations in unit cost resulting from differences in lot size tend to be buried with variations due to all other causes. This reduces the usefulness of unit cost information for cost control purposes.

The best solution here is a compromise. Setup time should be classified as direct labor but with a distinctive coding that permits segregation of the setup charges and their accumulation in cost center accounts either on a routine basis or by special reruns of the cost cards.

Rework Time

Another element of labor cost that might be classified either as direct labor or as overhead is the cost of rework labor. Not all units of product are completed in satisfactory condition. Some are spoiled and must be discarded or scrapped; some are spoiled but can be placed in salable condition by reperforming certain operations; and still others are spoiled but can be sold as seconds or irregulars. The cost of the labor expended to correct defects in workmanship in job order production is generally referred to as rework cost.

Rework labor may be process-related, product-related, or both. Rework is product-related whenever the anticipated amount of rework labor varies from product to product. It is said to be process-related whenever it depends on such factors as the effectiveness of departmental supervisors and the quality of the materials, equipment, and labor used.

Rework labor time in job order production should be classified as direct labor if rework labor is product-related, because the amount of rework cost experienced on the job is truly a cost of that job. If rework is process-related, however, the amount required by any one job will depend on chance; that is, it will depend on how good the process happens to be when this particular job is performed. Under these conditions the amount of rework actually performed on a job is not a good measure of the amount of rework labor attributable to that job. A better measure will be the company's average rework experience on all jobs combined, and this is obtained by classifying rework labor as an overhead cost, getting it into product cost by including a provision for it in the departmental burden rate.

A second argument for classifying rework labor as overhead is that this is the simplest way of getting departmental totals for cost control reporting. The result is that measurable amounts of rework costs are usually classified as overhead unless they are strongly product-related. In the latter case, they should be classified as direct labor, but the cost records should be coded in such a way as to permit the derivation of departmental totals routinely or upon request.

TREATMENT OF WAGE SUPPLEMENTS

The cost of employment includes a good deal more than the basic wage or salary rate. Five supplemental elements deserve discussion at this point:

1. Overtime premiums.
2. Shift differentials.
3. Incentive pay.
4. Fringe benefits.
5. Wage guarantees.

Overtime Premiums

A virtually universal feature of hourly wage or incentive pay plans is the overtime premium, the amount added to the base rate for hours worked in excess of some specified number each day or each week. For example, if the basic or straight-time wage rate is $4 an hour and the over-time rate is $6, the overtime premium is $2 an hour. Overtime hours are charged to jobs or to indirect labor accounts in just the same way as regular-time hours; the only issue is whether these hours should be charged at the straight-time rate ($4) or at the full overtime rate ($6).

Overtime premiums are not and should not be charged directly to the specific jobs processed in overtime hours. First, the jobs processed on overtime are not necessarily the ones responsible for the overtime. In some cases a direct charge to a job can be justified, as in the case of a rush order for a specific customer, but in general the overtime results from a *total* demand on the production facilities in excess of single-shift capacity. All production shares equally in the responsibility for the overtime.

The second argument for treating overtime premiums as overhead is that cost control efforts as well as many decisions focus on the cost center rather than on the product. For these purposes it is desirable to accumulate wage premium payments departmentally rather than by individual product units. For example, the need for second-shift operation may be evidenced by mounting overtime premium costs. Even though production requirements are now being met satisfactorily through the use of overtime, it may be more economical to replace the costly overtime operations with a partial second shift or expanded first-shift work force.

Average versus Marginal Overtime Premium

Classification of overtime premiums as overhead serves a control reporting objective and also has the negative advantage of excluding spurious elements from the direct labor charge, but it still leaves one question unanswered: how much overtime premium should be included in product cost?

Like other overhead items, overtime premiums enter product costs through the burden rate. Ordinarily the burden rate includes provision for average wage premiums at normal volume. Decisions as to the profitability of individual segments of the business, however, call for information on incremental cost. If overtime premiums are substantial, it can be argued that every job should be costed at the full overtime rate, on the grounds that elimination of any job would lead to savings at this rate.

The relevance of this argument will depend on the facts in any particular situation. If an increase or decrease in output will lead straight time and overtime to change by identical percentages, then the average is appropriate. If an output change will affect only the overtime hours, then the full overtime rate should be used. In other cases, some intermediate assumption will best fit the facts. The point of this discussion is not to recommend a doctrinaire solution but to point out once more that average cost may approximate incremental cost poorly. It should not be used unless it seems to fit the case at hand.

Shift Differentials

Shift differentials—wage premiums paid for work on second and third shifts—are very similar to overtime premiums. For decisions relating to the utilization of capacity, a strong argument can be made for charging all products with the *maximum* shift differential that will have to be paid. The average shift differential is relevant to this purpose only if the production technology requires round-the-clock operation, so that the marginal wage rate is a composite wage rate from all three shifts.

Most companies classify shift differentials as overhead and include a provision for an average differential in the burden rate. Segregation of shift differentials permits the measurement of the aggregate amount of these costs and thus presumably facilitates control comparisons, even though the average differential may not be a good measure of opportunity cost and thus may be less relevant to decision making.

Incentive Pay

Employee compensation systems in which the employee's earnings depend at least in part on his output are called incentive pay plans.[1] We shall discuss only one of these, the straight piecework system.

The earnings of an employee on piecework are computed for each

---

[1] Other types of incentive plans are based not on individual output but on group output or company profit. The latter are more properly referred to as profit-sharing plans. For an exposition of a group incentive plan, see Frederick G. Lesieur (ed.), *The Scanlon Plan* (New York: John Wiley & Sons, 1958). For brief, simple descriptions of a number of other incentive plans, see Robert I. Dickey (ed.), *Accountants' Cost Handbook* (2d ed.; New York: Ronald Press, 1961), Sec. 6, pp. 27–32, and Sec. 15, pp. 26–28.

payroll period by multiplying the agreed rate per piece times the number of good pieces produced. This is usually accompanied by a minimum day-work rate, so that if an employee's production falls below the day-work minimum, he will be paid at the day rate rather than the piecework rate for that period. For example, if John Jones is paid on the basis of $0.10 a piece with a $2 an hour guarantee and he works 38 hours during the week, his minimum wage for the week is $76 (38 × $2) even though his week's output might be only 600 pieces, which would entitle him to only $60 on a piecework basis.

Straight piecework systems pose only two simple kinds of cost classification problems:

1. Time spent on work for which no piece rate has been established (nonrated or hourly-rated work).
2. Output rates that are lower than the minimum daily guarantee.

Time spent on nonrated work can be charged to jobs or cost center accounts at the applicable hourly rates, just as it would be if the company had no piece-rate system. In contrast, the difference between the guaranteed minimum wage ($76 in the example above) and the piece-rate total ($60) is invariably classified as overhead. The main reason is that the failure to achieve the prescribed output level is ordinarily due to process-related factors rather than to product-related causes. In other words, the extra wage payment (usually called *make-good pay* or *day-rate differential*) results from the inexperience or incompetence of the employee or from defects in operating conditions rather than from difficulties inherent in individual products. Only if the piece rates have been incorrectly calculated does it make any sense to try to treat make-good pay as a component of direct labor cost.

Fringe Benefits

Indirect forms of employee compensation, popularly referred to as fringe benefits,[2] are accounting for an increasingly large fraction of total employment costs. Examples include paid vacations, paid holidays, company-sponsored recreation and education programs, company contributions to pension plans, medical insurance, and supplemental unemployment benefit plans.

Most companies record the manufacturing portion of the costs of these items in factory overhead accounts, charged directly or allocated to departments and then assigned to product cost by inclusion in factory burden rates. To illustrate, let us assume that a company pays five supplemental wage costs: (1) federal old-age insurance (FICA) taxes at a rate

[2] For a more extensive review of this topic, see the National Association of Accountants, *Accounting for Labor-Related Costs, Research Series No. 32* (New York: NAA, 1957).

of 5 percent of gross wages; (2) unemployment compensation taxes at an average rate of 3 percent of gross wages; (3) pension accruals at 5 percent of gross wages; (4) vacation and holiday pay at 6 percent of gross wages; and (5) college tuition payments for children of employees averaging 50 cents a week for each employee.[3]

One alternative is to classify all of these costs as overhead. In this case, a direct labor hour would be charged to the job at the worker's hourly base rate or incentive pay rate. Fringe benefit costs would enter the job cost sheet by way of the burden rate.

Two objections could be raised to this treatment. First, the department head can control these fringe benefits only through his control of labor utilization in his department, and thus reporting them separately serves no purpose. Second, the base wage rate understates the cost of each labor application. The use of an hour of labor time costs more than the base rate, and the job cost sheet should reflect this.

This suggests a second possibility: to charge all labor time to jobs or cost center indirect labor accounts at a labor *charging rate* which includes a provision for fringe benefits as well as the base wage rate.

In the example above, the costs of the first four fringe benefits vary with the employee's gross pay and total 19 percent of the base wage rate. The college tuition program costs vary only slightly with the number of employees and not at all with the number of labor hours worked in any year. Because their behavioral pattern is unique, they should probably be excluded from the charging rate. On this basis, the charging rate for an employee with a $3 hourly base rate would be:

Base rate	$3.00
FICA tax	0.15
Unemployment	0.09
Pension	0.15
Vacation and holiday pay	0.18
Charging rate per hour	$3.57

This rate would then be used to charge an hour of direct labor time to a job cost sheet or an hour of indirect labor time to a cost center over-head cost account. For a $4-an-hour man, the charging rate would be 119 percent of $4, or $4.76, and so on.

This will not change the amount charged to individual jobs if the burden rate is based on direct labor cost. For example, if the burden rate would otherwise have been 80 percent of direct labor cost, it will now be 61 percent, with the other 19 percent going in through the direct labor charge itself. Most burden rates are based on labor hours, machine hours, or materials consumption, and in these cases the switch to a charging rate will produce more accurate job cost figures.

---

[3] Payroll tax rates are changed from time to time. To simplify the illustrations, arbitrary round-number rates have been assumed.

Wage Guarantees

Direct labor costs are ordinarily assumed to be proportionately variable with volume. This assumption is weakened whenever production facilities are designed to be operated by balanced crews. The adoption of a guaranteed wage plan or a salary plan for former hourly workers has a similar effect.

Even with these rigidities in the cost structure, direct labor hours should be treated as direct costs rather than as overhead, except in limiting cases. Any difficulty in seeing this point may stem from a confusion between a guaranteed wage per man and a stabilized total payroll. Labor cost adjustments under stabilized wage plans take the form of adjusting the size of the permanent work force rather than the number of hours worked by individual employees. Some of this adjustment can be made painlessly by not hiring workers to replace workers who leave as part of the normal turnover, for retirement or new jobs in other companies. Transfer of employees to other duties within the company is also possible in many cases. When these outlets are inadequate to meet the requirements for adjustment of the labor force, layoffs of workers become necessary. The separate accumulation of idle time costs in overhead accounts provides the necessary information foundation for appraising the effects of continued employment of excess labor as opposed to the costs that the company would incur as a result of discharging employees.

In other words, salary costs of direct production workers are variable except in a very short-run sense, and failure to recognize this can lead to highly misleading accounting information. Rising labor costs are just as serious in the salary-only plant as they are when the employment contract calls for hourly wages.

CLASSIFYING MATERIALS COSTS

The term "materials" in manufacturing applies to raw commodities, fabricated parts, and subassemblies. Although materials are generally acquired from outside vendors, parts and subassemblies that are manufactured in the company's plants and placed in inventory storage are also generally classified as materials.

Pricing Materials Quantities

Most cost accounting information is stored and reported in monetary terms. For this purpose, the quantities of materials received, issued, and on hand must be assigned dollar prices.

The relevant price for decision making is the opportunity cost of the materials. This will be expected replacement cost if materials stocks are to be replenished, or resale market value if replenishment is not contemplated and sale is the most profitable alternative to the proposed use of the materials. Historical cost is not relevant in any case, unless of course it happens to coincide with opportunity cost.

Opportunity cost, unfortunately, is an extremely difficult concept to apply in routine cost bookkeeping, and most systems do not attempt even a partial application of the concept. Instead, materials are priced either at an outlay cost or, in standard costing systems, at predetermined or standard prices. For the moment, two issues arising when outlay costs are used need to be discussed:

1. Should cost be defined as purchase price or as net delivered cost?
2. In what sequence should costs be transferred from materials inventory accounts?

Inclusiveness of Cost. Vendor prices are sometimes net delivered prices, sometimes factory prices before adding freight and subtracting discounts. The issue is essentially the same as for labor fringe benefits— what does the input actually cost? Once again it seems clear that any cost that is dependent upon the acquisition of the materials is as much a part of the price of the materials as the amount payable to the vendor. Net delivered cost is thus the preferred basis for inventory unit costing.

The only questions are questions of materially and convenience: are freight charges and discounts large enough to affect unit cost materially, and is it convenient to match them with purchases on an item-by-item basis? If they are immaterial, then freight costs and discounts can be recorded separately and closed out directly to the income statement, without passing through the inventory accounts. If they are material in amount, it may still be inconvenient to try to obtain net delivered cost invoice by invoice and item by item, and in this case some predetermined average amount may be added to or subtracted from gross invoice prices to get an approximation of net delivered cost.

For example, suppose that six different items are included in a single shipment and covered by a single invoice. Dividing the actual freight bill among these items is time-consuming and expensive. Charging freight to purchase cost on the basis of a predetermined average is undoubtedly less accurate, but it may be close enough to guide management in materials usage decisions under most circumstances.

Sequence of Cost Releases. The second problem is to choose a method of costing the materials issued from inventory. Most historical costing systems (that is, those that do not use standard prices) follow either the Fifo or moving average method.[4] Either of these will lead to departures of recorded materials cost from current replacement cost at the time of issuance. If inventory turnover is rapid, these departures will ordinarily be small. Otherwise, some thought should be given to departing from

---

[4] For a discussion of these and other methods, see Myron J. Gordon and Gordon Shillinglaw, *Accounting: A Management Approach* (4th ed.; Homewood, Ill.: Richard D. Irwin, 1969), chap. 12.

historical cost altogether for internal cost tranfers, using an approximation of current replacement cost. Adoption of such a plan would require a relatively simple end-of-year adjustment to restore an outlay cost basis for external financial reporting. The adjustment would be similar to that discussed in Chapter 16 for standard costing systems.

Defective and Lost Units

Few problems are encountered in assigning the costs of issued materials to operating accounts. Indirect materials are seldom subdivided into many categories, and the main question is what to do with costs that were originally charged as direct materials but turn out to have been unproductive or wasted.

For example, upon completion of a job lot of 100 units of product, it is found that 5 units are defective and must be sold as seconds. The total cost of the job was $3,900 or $39 a unit. One way of looking at this is to say that some of the costs expended on the defective units were nonproductive and should be removed from the product cost accounts. Suppose that it is decided to assign a value of $15 a unit to the seconds, indicating a loss of $24 a unit. The $3,900 recorded on the job cost sheet would then be divided as follows:

Cost of first-quality units, 95 units @ $39	$3,705
Cost of second-quality units, 5 units @ $15	75
Loss from product defects, 5 units @ $24	120
Total	$3,900

The loss on rejects may be further classified by causes if a basis for such a classification exists and if the amounts are large enough.

A roughly equivalent procedure is to transfer to a special loss account the average unit cost of materials and possibly of labor as well. This account can also be charged for overhead and credited with the salvage value of the rejected units. The basic idea is the same as that described in the preceding paragraph.

A second alternative is to credit the job with the recoverable value of the rejected units, leaving the good units to bear the net cost of the job. For example, if $20 is the total net resale value of the seconds, unit cost for the 95 good units would be:

Total cost	$3,900
Less: Value of seconds	100
Net cost	$3,800
Unit cost ($3,800 ÷ 95)	$ 40

The argument for the first alternative is that it gives factory management a means of observing changes in overall rejection rates from period to period. Provision for *normal* rejection experience can then be built into the burden rate structure. This will be entirely satisfactory if the rejection rate is entirely process-related. In fact, whenever losses are a function of the machine or operation rather than of the particular job or product, assigning rejection losses to those jobs on which they happen to occur results in less accurate rather than more accurate costing. The better procedure for planning purposes, therefore, is to accumulate such losses departmentally and include in product cost through the burden rate a provision for normal losses only.

The second alternative should be used only if the rejection rates are product-related—that is, if the rejection rate is determined primarily by the characteristics and specification of the product. In these circumstances, the job cost sheet will not provide fully informative cost data unless all of the costs of achieving actual output yield are included.

Scrap

Scrap poses a somewhat different problem. Most scrap is traceable to departments but not to individual job orders except at prohibitive cost. The cost of scrapped materials is seldom segregated by departments or cost centers, however. Instead, the net market value of scrap recovered is typically credited to a cost center overhead account.

The result is to overstate the cost of direct materials and understate average overhead costs. As long as materials costs and scrap recoveries are identified by cost center, however, an adequate basis for control reporting is available, and the inaccuracy in product cost is likely to be immaterial.

SUMMARY

The distinction between what is traceable to a job (a direct cost) and what is to be classified as overhead (an indirect cost) is not always clear. In deciding what to do with such items as the cost of setup time and overtime premiums, for example, the accountant should ask whether the cost is job-related or process-related. Job-related costs are determined by the characteristics of the job and should be classified as direct; process-related costs should be classified as overhead even if a basis for tracing them to individual jobs is available.

The accountant should also distinguish between costs that are always present and those that apply only to work done in some time periods. Costs that are seasonal or irregular in timing should be separated from those that are present at all times. Unless timing is job-determined, as in certain kinds of seasonal work, seasonal or irregular cost elements should be either classified as overhead or coded distinctly in the job cost sheets.

EXERCISES AND PROBLEMS

`1. The workweek of employees in the foundry department of the ABC Company ranges between 42 and 50 hours, with all hours in excess of 40 per week being paid at a rate of one and one-half times the basic hourly wage rate of $3.60 an hour. On the average, each worker works 45 hours a week.

a) What is the foundry labor cost per hour that should be included in product unit cost for public financial reporting? How much of this should be shown as direct labor? Explain your answer.

b) Management is trying to decide whether certain products are profitable enough to continue manufacturing. From this point of view, what is the foundry labor cost of a product that requires 10 hours of foundry labor? Explain.

2. The Burns Machinery Company manufactures a wide variety of machined parts and a small number of specialized assemblies. In manufacturing a certain part, it has the option of using machine A, which requires three hours for initial setup and adjustment, or machine B, which requires only one hour of initial setup. Once the setup is completed, machine A can turn out approximately 50 parts an hour, whereas machine B's output is at an average rate of 30 parts an hour.

a) How large a production lot would be necessary to justify the use of machine A, assuming that wage rates are the same for setup and operating labor on both machines?

b) Should the cost of setup labor be classified as direct labor or as indirect labor? Support your answer.

3.* The Plane Company uses a job order costing system. Metal scrap is collected weekly from each department and stored in a bin near the loading dock. A scrap dealer empties the scrap bin once a month and makes payment on the basis of the current market price of scrap.

During March, 200 pounds of scrap were collected from department X and 1,000 pounds of scrap were collected from all departments combined. The price paid by the scrap dealer was 10 cents a pound. During March, department X worked on three jobs, weighing 10,000, 5,000 and 1,000 pounds, respectively. The costs of materials used on these jobs totaled $30,000, $5,000 and $2,500, respectively.

Indicate how you would account for scrap in this situation.

4. In a job order for 500 piece parts, 80 parts are damaged beyond repair in the production operation and must be junked.

Should the costs of these parts be removed from the job order cost sheet? Indicate the criteria by which you judged this question and the reasons why application of these criteria led to the course of action you have chosen.

5. Carson, Inc. manufactures a number of products. Past records indicate that about 5 percent of the units will be defective and will have to be reworked. This is true of all products. Rework labor time averages 8 percent of the amount of productive direct labor (productive time excludes rework time).

---

* Solutions to problems marked with an asterisk can be found in Appendix B.

Job No. 563 consisted of 200 sole plates, of which 20 were defective. Productive direct labor on this job amounted to $500, and rework labor to correct the defects cost $65.

Would you charge the cost of rework labor cost to the job order cost sheet in this case? If not, how would you record it? Give your reasons.

6. All work in the Hudson Company's factory is on a job order basis. An incentive wage plan is in use, based on the number of "points" earned each week. Each job is rated as to its difficulty and the workers earn more points per unit for difficult jobs than for simpler work. The total number of points earned is referred to as the output for the week.

The incentive plan is accompanied by a guaranteed minimum wage. The amount of the guarantee depends on the worker's seniority.

Five men are employed in the stamping department. During the week of August 15, each man worked a full 40-hour week, with no overtime. Their wage guarantees and output were as follows:

Name	Guaranteed Hourly Minimum	Points Earned
Brackett, S. J.	$3.50	1,840
Emery, P. L.	3.75	1,900
Evans, E. C.	3.50	1,960
Forest, T. A.	4.00	2,050
Simmons, F.	3.50	1,650

a) Compute the gross earnings of each worker, assuming that wages are paid on a piecework basis at 8 cents a point, subject to the guaranteed hourly minimum. How much of the total gross earnings would be charged to job cost sheets, and how much would be classified as overhead?

b) Compute the gross earnings of each worker assuming that a group incentive plan is in operation. Each member of the group receives his guaranteed hourly minimum if total production is equal to or less than 7,300 points a week. Whenever production exceeds this minimum, the hourly rate for each worker is increased by one half of 1 percent for each 100 points in excess of 7,300. How would you reflect the incentive bonus in charges to individual job orders?

7.* John Taft is paid a straight-time wage rate of $4 an hour. Excluding vacation periods and holidays, the factory normally operates 250 day a year. Seven of these days are Saturdays. The factory operates an eight-hour day, with occasional overtime. A worker in Mr. Taft's job classification will ordinarily work 50 hours of overtime in addition to the Saturday work. Overtime and Saturday work are paid at 150 percent of the straight-time wage rate.

In addition to direct wages for time spent on the job, the company is responsible for the following labor-related costs:

(1) A two-week paid vacation; this is provided to any employee who is employed throughout the year; vacation pay for other employees is in proportion to the period worked. Vacation pay is computed on the basis of 40-

hour week at straight-time pay. All employees take their vacations at the same time, during August, when the factory is closed for two weeks.

(2) Eight paid holidays a year, at straight-time wage rates; these holidays are provided to employees on the payroll at the time of each holiday. The factory does not operate on holidays.

(3) A maximum of five days' sick leave during a year; the average employee takes three days' sick leave during a year. Employees who are not employed for a full year are eligible for sick leave in proportion to their number of weeks on the payroll.

(4) The portion of payroll taxes (FICA, etc.) to be paid by the employer is 8 percent of the first $7,200 of each employee's gross pay.

(5) Private pension contributions equal to 3 percent of gross pay, including overtime and Saturday work premium and holiday, vacation, and sick pay.

(6) An employee recreation program, which averages $10 per employee per year; most of this goes to pay for equipment and to pay the salaries of coaches and athletic instructors.

(7) A cafeteria subsidy; the prices of meals in the factory cafeteria are adequate to cover the cost of the food served and to pay the wages of cafeteria personnel. The company supplies space and equipment and pays the salaries of a dietitian and a bookkeeper, at a combined cost which averages $15 per employee per year.

a) Compute the number of hours Mr. Taft would be expected to work during a normal year.

b) Compute a labor charging rate for Mr. Taft, based on the working hours calculated in (*a*) and including any of the labor-related costs you feel should be included.

c) Give your reasons for including or excluding each item.

8. The firm of Rundell Associates does a number of kinds of drafting, lettering, and commercial artwork for outside clients. A system of requisitions and time sheets is used to accumulate the costs of materials and personal services consumed on individual job orders.

Although a few jobs are accepted on a flat fee basis, most jobs are priced to customers on a cost-plus-time basis. On these jobs, the customer's bill includes four elements:

Costs of materials used.
Personal service fees (at predetermined hourly rates, including markup over hourly cost).
Overtime premiums paid for work on specific jobs.
Miscellaneous out-of-pocket costs incurred on specific jobs.

Materials costs on some jobs are substantial, and occasionally a customer will complain that he is being charged for too many spoiled materials. In general, however, materials costs amount to less than 10 percent of the gross amount of the customer invoice.

Customers complain frequently about the size of the personal service fee, but this appears to be part of a bargaining strategy to impress on Rundell Associates the need to watch costs carefully on subsequent orders. Complaints about the overtime premiums are considerably stronger and often lead to downward revision of the invoices. During recent months these downward revisions have been large enough to cut the firm's net profit in half and the managing partners are worried.

Indicate any changes that you would make in the company's cost accounting and billing procedures, giving reasons for your changes. If you wish to leave any or all of the present system unchanged, indicate briefly why you think no improvement is called for.

9. Department X performs a variety of machining operations, using eight machines of various capabilities and work speeds. The machines are generally interchangeable, but variations from machine to machine in setup and operating times are substantial.

The foreman of department X is responsible for assigning specific jobs to specific machines, for the control of departmental costs, for maintaining product quality, and for meeting delivery schedules. Scheduled completion dates for each department are ordinarily set by the production scheduling department after consultation with the department foreman. To maintain quality standards, department X's output is subjected to either sampling or 100 percent inspection and defective units are returned immediately for rectification (rework).

Department X employs six men regularly and operates a single shift. Four of the six are paid on piece rates, subject to an hourly minimum rate; the other two are paid a straight hourly wage. All workers are paid a premium for overtime work (in excess of 40 hours a week) of 50 percent of the minimum or base hourly rate. The amount of this premium is not affected in any way by the amount of piecework earnings.

Piece rate earnings for a trained worker are expected to average 125 percent of the minimum hourly rate, and piece rate workers are also paid 125 percent of the minimum hourly rate when they are required to work on orders for which no piece rates have been established (nonrated work); when they are idle for 15 consecutive minutes or longer because work is temporarily unavailable; or when they are assigned to maintenance, cleanup, or other auxiliary tasks. No compensation is paid for rework labor time.

Five categories of departmental labor time are recognized in the accounts. The hours shown are normal weekly hours:

	Hours
Piece-rated production	150
Nonrated production	16
Work flow and cleanup	64
Setup	20
Waiting	10
Total	260

All setup labor is performed by one of the hourly paid workers. T. F. Jones, and no overtime premium is budgeted for this operation. Mr. Jones devotes the rest of his time to routine maintenance, materials handling, and so forth (described by the company as "work flow and cleanup labor"), along with the other hourly paid worker, R. J. Selden. No overtime hours are budgeted for either of these workers.

Piece rates are established on the basis of the machines with the shortest operating cycle that can be adapted to the particular product. When a piece rate worker is forced to use slower machines, he is given a premium in addition to the regular piece rate, based on the amount necessary to equalize earnings per hour under normal conditions. This "substitute equipment premium" is expected to average 2 percent of the regular piece rate earnings during a normal month.

The daily hourly minimum for piece rate production is computed only on the hours spent on piecework, including rework labor hours—in other words, total hours minus hours spent on setup, waiting time, and all other kinds of nonrated work except rework time. The total, called net piecework hours, is multiplied by the man's hourly base rate to find the guaranteed minimum piecework earnings. If this is more than the man's actual piecework earnings, including premiums for use of nonpreferred equipment, he is paid the guaranteed minimum. The make-good differential is expected to average 2 percent of regular piecework earnings plus substitute equipment premiums.

Employer payroll taxes average 8 percent of gross pay, vacation and holiday pay approximate 4 percent, and company pension contributions amount to 5 percent. Health insurance premiums paid by the company total 10 cents an hour up to 40 hours per man per week. Workmen's compensation insurance premiums amount to 1 percent of gross payrolls other than the overtime premium portion of the payrolls. Overtime premiums are expected to average 10 percent of the minimum hourly pay rates.

The following data relate to the operation of department X for the week ending January 28:

| Worker | Base Rate | Hours | | | | | Regular Piecework Earnings | Substitute Equipment Premium |
		Actual	Non-rated	Work Flow & Cleanup	Setup	Wait Time		
Adams.........	$3	44	5	..	..	..	$120	$20
Jones..........	6	40	..	8	30	2	...	..
Marron........	3	46	..	2	..	1	169	..
Peters.........	3	42	14	..	..	6	68	5
Selden.........	3	32	..	32	..	..	..	..
Terrill.........	3	40	5	..	..	..	96	..
Total..........		244	24	42	30	9	$453	$25

a) Compute the total gross payroll for the week of January 28, exclusive of employer payroll taxes and other fringe benefit costs.

b) List the costs that you would charge to individual job orders. State your reasons for your treatment of each component of the gross payroll. In addition, indicate how you would handle the fringe benefits, giving your reasons for the treatment you have selected.

10. More than two years ago, several eastern railroads agreed to adopt a uniform system of track control signals. This decision led to an abrupt decline

in the sales volume of one of Valley Manufacturing Company's largest industrial customers, who then canceled or reduced the size of his orders for several Valley Manufacturing products. Since that time, Valley Manufacturing has been unable to keep its factory operating at normal volumes, despite a vigorous sales promotion program.

Yesterday morning, Bob Pettifogg, the company's sales manager, handed Tom Pruitt, the marketing vice president, a customer order for 12,000 foot wrinklers, to be made and delivered within the next six months. To get this order, Mr. Pettifogg had quoted a price less than the standard catalog price, which meant that Mr. Pruitt's approval was necessary.

Although the factory would have to put a number of workers on overtime for the next six months to meet the required delivery schedule, Mr. Pettifogg is convinced that the order should be accepted. "First," he said, "all of the work would be done in department 27, which we can't seem to keep busy no matter how hard we try. If we don't take this order, we'll be running only 7,000 machine-hours a month in that department, against a normal monthly volume of 10,000 machine-hours. This order will bring in 1,000 machine-hours of work each month for six months, and that's a big difference.

"Second, while I'll admit that the margin is slim, the price I have quoted is greater than our cost, even after allowing for the abnormal amount of overtime. The price is $2.50 a unit and the cost is $2.40. That gives us a margin of about 4 percent of sales. That isn't much, but it's better than nothing."

Mr. Pettifogg then handed Mr. Pruitt the following cost and profit summary to back up his recommendation:

Cost per unit:	
Direct materials...	$0.57
Direct labor (0.4 hour × $3.50)......................	1.40
Factory overhead:	
Normal (0.5 mach.-hr. × $.80......................	0.40
Overtime premium adjustment......................	0.03
Total cost per unit............................	$2.40
Selling price..	2.50
Profit margin per unit................................	$0.10

"The provision for factory overhead," Mr. Pettifogg continued, "is based on the department's normal burden rate of 80 cents for each machine-hour used, plus an allowance for extra overtime premiums that would have to be paid to get this job out on time. Normal overheads are shown in this second table, together with a monthly overhead cost forecast for the next six months at a monthly volume of 7,000 machine-hours:

	Forecast at 7,000 Hours	Normal at 10,000 Hours
Indirect labor............................	$3,100	$4,000
Overtime premium........................	...	800
Supplies..................................	840	1,200
Depreciation..............................	1,100	1,100
Other.....................................	750	900
Total................................	$5,790	$8,000
Average per machine-hour..............	$0.827	$0.80

"The cost accountant tells me that except for the overtime premium adjustment, we can get a reasonably good estimate of overhead cost at any volume between 7,000 and 10,000 machine-hours per month by interpolating between the figures given in this table."

"I understand the normal overhead charge," Mr. Pruitt replied, "but what is this overtime premium adjustment? I thought they didn't have enough to keep busy down there and yet they're charging us for extra overtime."

Mr. Pettifogg was ready for this question. "It's true that they have plenty of idle capacity," he said, "but it's idle machine time, not idle labor. They could increase the size of the work force by hiring people, but they won't do that unless they can see good prospects for keeping them busy for a lot longer than six months. They figure that it would be cheaper to go on overtime than to train new workers, use them, and let them go six months from now.

"This means that we have to adjust the burden rate to allow for the unusual amount of overtime. I made the overtime premium adjustment myself, on the basis of estimates prepared by the factory scheduling department. These show that overtime premiums for department 27 as a whole would probably average 14 cents a machine-hour until this order was finished. The burden rate already includes 8 cents for overtime premiums, so I added another 6 cents an hour, or 3 cents a unit, to allow for this factor."

Acceptance of this order would have no effect on total selling and administrative expenses, but the average ratio of selling and administrative expense to total sales would be reduced by about one fifth of one percent.

Mr. Pruitt sees no reason why acceptance of this order would lead to reductions in the prices the company would be able to get in the future for this or other products; his sole concern is whether the quoted price is a profitable one. What would you tell him?

CASE 6–1: TIPOGRAFIA STANCA, S.p.A.†

Mr. Giulio Cattani, founder and president of Tipografia Stanca, S.p.A., was worried. The company was doing more business than ever before—sales were at an annual rate of about L125 million a year‡—but net income had decreased slightly during recent months and the ratio of income to sales had dropped sharply. Mr. Cattani wondered what had gone wrong and what he could do about it. He called in his chief (and only) accountant, Mr. Gaetano Pareto, and asked him to find out what was happening.

Tipografia Stanca was an Italian corporation located in Milan and doing a general printing business on a customer order basis. Mr. Cattani set the price to be charged for each job. When possible, he waited until the work was done and then quoted a price equal to 140 percent of the cost

† Copyright 1968 by l'Institut pour l'Etude des Méthodes de Direction de l'Entreprise (IMEDE), Lausanne, Switzerland. Published by permission.

‡ When this case was written, the Italian lira could be exchanged at the rate of approximately L620 to the United States dollar.

of the paper stock used, plus L2,500 for each labor hour. Straight-time wage rates in the past, adjusted for recent wage rate increases, had averaged about L800 an hour, and this formula seemed to provide an adequate margin to cover overhead costs and provide a good profit.

Most of Tipografia Stanca's work was due on the basis of predetermined contract prices. In bidding on these jobs, Mr. Cattani applied his standard pricing formula to his own estimates of the amount of labor and paper stock the job would require. He prided himself on his ability to make these estimates, but he sometimes quoted a price that was higher or lower than the formula price, depending on his judgment of the market situation.

Stanca's production procedures were fairly simple. When a customer's order was received, it was assigned a production order number and a production order was issued. The material to be printed, known as the customer's copy, was given to a copy editor who indicated on the copy the sizes and styles of type that should be used. The editor sometimes made changes in the copy, usually after telephoning the customer to discuss the changes.

Once the customer's material had been copy-edited, it was sent to the composing room, where it was set in type. A proof copy was printed by hand and returned to the copy editor, who checked the printed copy against the original. Any errors in the proof were indicated in the margin and the marked proof was sent to the customer for approval. At this point the customer might decide to make changes in the copy, and these changes, as well as corrections of type-setting errors, were made as soon as the corrected proof was returned to the composing room.

In some cases a second proof was sent to the customer for his approval, but at Tipografia Stanca most orders were sent to the pressroom as soon as the customer's corrections had been made and the second proof had been approved by the copy editor.

At this point, the order was ready for production on one of the presses in the pressroom. Printing instructions were contained in the production order, which specified the particular press to be used; the number of copies to be printed; the color, size, style, weight and finish of the stock or paper to be used; and similar details. Copies were then printed, bound, and packaged for delivery to the customer.

An order could take as little as one day in the copy-editing and composing-room stages or as long as several weeks. Printing, binding, and packaging seldom took more than two days except on very large production runs of multipage booklets.

For many years the shop had had enough work to keep it busy steadily throughout the year, without serious seasonal slack. As a result, Tipografia Stanca's before-tax profit had fluctuated between 13 and 15 percent of net sales. The interim profit report for the first half of 1968 therefore came as a great shock to Mr. Cattani. Although volume was slightly greater than in the first half of 1967, profit was down to 8.8 percent of sales, an all-time low. The comparison, with all figures expressed as percentages of net sales, was as follows:

	1968	1967
Net sales	100.0%	100.0%
Production costs	77.6	72.3
Selling and administrative costs	13.6	13.9
Profit	8.8	13.8

Mr. Pareto knew that the company's problem must be either low prices or excessive costs. Unfortunately, the cost data already available told him little about the cost-price relationship for individual jobs. Tipografia Stanca's operating costs were classified routinely into 20 categories, such as salaries, pressroom wages, production materials, depreciation, and so forth. Individual job cost sheets were not used and the cost of goods in process was estimated only once a year, at the end of the fiscal year.

Detailed data were available on only two kinds of items: paper stock issued and labor time. When stock was issued, a requisition form was filled out, showing the kind of stock issued, the quantity, the unit cost, and the production order number. Similar details were reported when unused stock was returned to the stockroom.

As for labor, each employee directly engaged in working on production orders filled in a time sheet each day, on which he recorded the time he started on a given task, the time he finished it or moved on to other work, and (in the case of time spent directly on a specific production order) the order number. His department number and pay grade were recorded on the time sheet by the payroll clerk.

Mr. Pareto's first step was to establish some overall cost relationships. Employees, for example, fell into three different pay grades, with the following regular hourly wage rates:

Grade	Rate
1	L1,200
2	800
3	600

These rates applied to a regular work week of 44 hours a week. For work in excess of this number of hours, employees were paid an overtime premium of 50 percent of their regular hourly wage. Overtime premiums were negligible when the work load was light, but in a normal year they averaged about 5 percent of the total amount of hourly wages computed at the regular hourly wage rate. In a normal year this was approximately L40 per direct labor hour.

In addition to their wages, the employees also received various kinds of benefits, including vacation pay, health insurance, and old-age pensions. The cost of these benefits to Tipografia Stanca amounted to about 70 percent of the total payroll. Mr. Pareto estimated that all other shop overhead costs—that is, all copy department, composing room and pressroom costs other than direct materials, direct labor, overtime premiums, and employee benefits on direct labor payrolls—would average L400 per direct labor hour in a normal year.

Armed with these estimates of general relationships, Mr. Pareto then proceeded to determine the costs of several recent production orders. One of these was order A–467. This was received for copy editing on Monday, October 5 and delivered to the customer on Friday, October 9. Mr. Cattani had quoted a price of L180,000 on this job in advance, on the basis of an estimate of L48,000 for paper stock costs and 45 direct labor hours. All requisitions and time records relating to order A–467 are in-

Table 1

PARTIAL LIST OF MATERIALS REQUISITIONS

For the Week of October 5–9

Req. No.	Job No.	Amount*
4058..........................	A-467	L30,000
R162..........................	A-469	(2,000)
4059..........................	A-467	6,000
4060..........................	A-442	600
R163..........................	A-455	(900)
R164..........................	A-472	(800)
4060..........................	A-467	3,600
R165..........................	A-465	(1,200)
4062..........................	A-467	9,600
4063..........................	A-471	32,000
4064..........................	A-473	26,400
4065..........................	A-458	2,200
R166..........................	A-467	(3,300)
4066..........................	A-481	17,600

* Amounts in parentheses are returned materials.

cluded in the lists in Tables 1 and 2. (To save space, some of the details shown on the requisitions and time tickets have been omitted from these exhibits.)

a) Develop a costing rate or rates for labor costs, to be used to charge a job cost sheet or factory overhead account for an hour of labor time. You must decide whether to use a single rate for all pay grades or a separate rate for each. You must also decide whether to include various kinds of fringe benefit costs in the labor costing rates or to regard these as overhead. Also develop a burden rate for use in charging shop overhead costs to individual job orders. For this purpose, overtime premiums and the cost of employee benefits accruing as a result of overtime premiums should be regarded as shop overhead.

Table 2

PARTIAL SUMMARY OF LABOR TIME SHEETS

For the Week of October 5–9

Employee No.	Pay Grade	Dept.	Job No.*	Hours
14.....................	2	Copy	A-463	6.6
14.....................	2	Copy	A-467	1.4
15.....................	1	Copy	A-467	3.3
15.....................	1	Copy	—	2.7
15.....................	1	Copy	A-467	8.8
18.....................	3	Press	A-467	4.0
18.....................	3	Press	A-472	4.6
22.....................	1	Composing	A-455	3.8
22.....................	1	Composing	A-467	8.4†
22.....................	1	Composing	—	1.5
23.....................	2	Press	A-458	3.4
23.....................	2	Press	A-467	4.7
23.....................	2	Press	—	1.1
23.....................	2	Press	A-459	2.5†
24.....................	2	Copy	A-470	7.4
28.....................	1	Press	A-467	7.0
28.....................	1	Press	A-458	1.0
31.....................	3	Press	—	8.0
33.....................	1	Composing	A-471	7.6
33.....................	1	Composing	A-472	4.2
40.....................	2	Press	A-469	3.6
40.....................	2	Press	A-467	4.9
40.....................	2	Press	—	0.2
43.....................	1	Press	A-467	3.5
43.....................	1	Press	A-481	5.8

  * A dash indicates time spent on general work in the department and not on any one job.
  † Employee No. 22 worked 6 hours of overtime during the week, none of them on job A-467, while employee No. 23 worked 8 hours of overtime, including 4 hours spent on job A-467.

b)   Prepare a job order cost sheet for production order A–467, and enter the costs that would be assigned to this order, using the costing rates you developed in the answer to (*a*) above.

c)   What conclusions might Mr. Pareto have reached on the basis of his analysis of this order? What suggestions would you make to Mr. Cattani?

d)   What would be the advantages of developing product unit costs routinely for every job? Do you think that these advantages would be great enough to persuade Mr. Cattani to hire an additional clerk for this purpose at an annual cost of about L2 million?

e)   What method or methods other than the one used in (*a*) and (*b*) above might be used to charge overtime premiums to individual job orders? Which method would best meet Mr. Cattani's needs?

chapter 7

Product Costs for
Company Financial Statements

Factory job order costing can be used solely to provide management with cost information, but in most cases unit costs derived from job order costing also play an important role in determining net income and in measuring inventories for companywide financial reporting. The usual way to do this is to make the factory job cost sheets a part of the formal account structure. The purpose of this chapter is to see how this can be accomplished.

ACCOUNTS FOR JOB ORDER COSTING

Costs enter the factory accounts with the acquisition of raw materials, facilities, and other goods and services. They leave only when the finished products are transferred to finished goods storerooms or are shipped to customers. Five aspects of the procedures used to account for factory costs require discussion at this point:

1. Recording the purchase and use of materials.
2. Using control accounts and subsidiary ledgers.
3. Recording labor costs.
4. Recording overhead cost absorption.
5. Recording job completions.

Recording the Purchase and Use of Materials

Materials accounting begins with the issue of a *purchase requisition* or its equivalent—a request to the purchasing department to acquire certain items from outside vendors. Once a vendor is selected, a purchase order is prepared detailing the amounts and specifications of the materials desired, usually together with a requested delivery date.

When the goods are shipped, the vendor sends an *invoice* to the purchasing department, together with other shipping documents. The invoice lists the actual quantities shipped, the prices charged, and the total amount of the payment due. When the goods are received, they are inspected and counted and a *receiving report* is prepared. At this point the accountant usually makes an entry to record the receipt of the materials and the company's liability to the vendor.

For example, suppose that a company purchased materials during May at a cost of $30,000 and placed them in the factory storeroom. Payment for these materials was to be made within 30 days. In summary form, the entry to record these purchases would be:

```
Materials Inventory..........................................  30,000
    Accounts Payable.......................................            30,000
```

That is, the purchases increased both the asset total and the company's liabilities by $30,000. (Other companies may use other account titles or follow somewhat different bookkeeping procedures. For example, purchases may be debited initially to a purchases account.)

Materials costing $22,675 were withdrawn from the storeroom during the month and issued to factory departments. Of this sum, $22,145 represented the cost of materials issued specifically for individual jobs, to be charged as direct material on those jobs. The remaining $530 was the cost of supplies for general use in the factory, not traceable to any specific job or jobs. It was thus chargeable to a factory overhead account.

The entries to record these materials issues can be summarized in the following single entry:

```
                                      (1)
Work in Process..........................................  22,145
Factory Overhead.........................................     530
    Materials Inventory....................................            22,675
```

This entry records the transfer of these costs from one asset account (Materials Inventory) to another asset account (Work in Process) and to an operating cost account (Factory Overhead). Factory Overhead is like an asset account in that it accumulates costs that have not yet been transferred to the income statement as expense. It differs from an inventory account, however, in ways that we shall study in a moment.

Using Control Accounts and Subsidiary Ledgers

The Materials Inventory, Work in Process, and Factory Overhead accounts in this illustration appear in the company's general ledger or main file of accounts and are known as *summary* or *control* accounts.

Exhibit 7–1

STORES LEDGER CARD

PART NO. 1623 D									
DESCRIPTION: Bearing Pin, Brass						UNIT: Dozen			
	In			Out			Balance		
Date	Quan-tity	Price	Amount	Quan-tity	Price	Amount	Quan-tity	Price	Amount
May 1							106	$2.14	$226.84
4				70	$2.14	$149.80	36	2.14	77.04
10	200	$2.20	$440.00				236	2.19	517.04

This means that the balances in these accounts correspond in total to the amounts shown in more detailed subsidiary ledgers or cost files.

For example, the detail underlying the Materials Inventory account balance is provided in the individual stock cards in the subsidiary ledger known as the stores ledger. One of these stores ledger cards is shown in Exhibit 7–1. Similarly, the balance in the Work in Process account should agree with the total of all the costs shown on the job cost sheets for jobs still in process, and the Factory Overhead control account balance should correspond to the total of the amounts shown in the detailed overhead accounts for the individual factory cost centers.

The main purposes of these summary or control accounts and their accompanying subsidiary files are (1) to reduce the bulk of the general ledger, and (2) to facilitate access to portions of the account file without temporarily immobilizing other portions of the file. The detailed accounts have been left out of this illustration for simplification only.

Recording Labor Costs

Payroll accounting has two sides: the first dealing with the *liability-payment* aspects of the transactions and the second having to do with the identification of the cost with various segments of activity, usually referred to as the *distribution* of labor cost.

Payroll Accrual. The liability-payment aspects of payroll accounting are not part of cost accounting, and only the briefest summary of procedures is necessary here. Wage and salary liabilities are accrued on the basis of information from two sources: personnel records and attendance or production records. For each employee, a master personnel record is maintained, showing his employment history with the company, job classification, title, current rate of pay, and authorized deductions for hospitalization insurance, pension plans, savings plans, union dues, and so forth.

The attendance record is usually provided by an in-and-out clock card from which it is possible to compute the total elapsed time the employee has been in the plant and ready for work during the payroll period. Elapsed time is classified between regular time and overtime, and the clock card identifies the shift worked if the company operates more than one shift.

For salaried employees, the payroll liability is ordinarily taken directly from the master personnel record. Attendance cards may be checked for excessive absences or for paid overtime if the salary plan adjusts for these. For hourly employees, wage liability for the payroll period is computed by multiplying the rate shown on the personnel record by the number of hours worked, as shown on the clock card. If a shift differential is paid for workers on second and third shifts, the basic

Exhibit 7–2

LABOR COST DISTRIBUTION SHEET

DATE: May 11, 19—   PAYROLL GROUP M14
WEEK NO. 19

Employee No.		Name	Hours	Base Rate	Account No.	Job No.	Amount
Dept.	Serial						
1	316	J. C. Abrams	3.0	1.75	0301	1762	5.25
1	316	J. C. Abrams	1.0	1.75	0301	1762	1.75
1	316	J. C. Abrams	5.0	1.75	0301	1762	8.75
1	423	A. B. Allen	8.0	2.00	1412		16.00
1	437	T. P. Andrews	6.0	1.80	0301	1879	10.80
1	437	T. P. Andrews	2.0	1.80	1417		3.60

rate is adjusted to provide for this differential. Overtime hours are paid for at the overtime rate applicable to the particular employee and shift.

Labor Cost Distribution. Labor cost distributions in job order production are usually based on the individual time tickets described in Chapter 5. Because these time tickets are prepared as work is performed, the company has the option of distributing wage costs directly from the time tickets without waiting for reconciliation with the attendance records.[1] For example, Exhibit 7–2 shows a daily cost distribution sheet with a separate line for each time ticket. This sheet, or the card file underlying it, provides the basis for entries in the control accounts on the individual job cost sheets and in the subsidiary cost ledger.

As we indicated in Chapter 4, each cost center may have several indirect labor accounts. Some of these, bearing titles such as Waiting for

---

[1] Payroll accrual and cost distribution can be performed simultaneously if the payroll period and cost reporting period coincide. The procedure described here is useful if cost reports are needed more frequently or if different clerical personnel process the payrolls and distribute the costs.

Materials, Waiting for Repairs, and Rework Labor, are used to accumulate the costs of various kinds of nonproductive or down time. Use of such an account is justified whenever a particular event is likely to happen often enough and with a large enough effect to require routine feedback. For example, if machine breakdowns are likely to cause 10 hours of idle time a year in a 10-man cost center, management probably doesn't need precise data on breakdown time.

In our example, the factory payrolls for May totaled $19,330. This amount included $14,225 for the portion of production workers' time that could be traced to individual jobs (the direct labor), and $5,105 for various types of indirect labor. A summary entry to record these payrolls could be:

(2)

Work in Process..	14,225	
Factory Overhead..	5,105	
Payrolls Payable..		19,330

The direct labor costs were thus treated as part of the cost of the asset Work in Process; indirect labor costs were placed temporarily in an operating cost summary account, Factory Overhead; and both were financed temporarily by an increase in the company's liabilities.[2] The direct labor costs were also entered on the individual job cost sheets, while the indirect labor costs were recorded in the various cost center overhead accounts.

Recording Overhead Cost Absorption

In addition to materials and payroll costs, the factory incurred other costs during the month of May. These costs, which totaled $6,425, could not be traced to specific jobs, so they too were classified as factory overhead. Some of these, such as electric power and telephone charges, represented services purchased and used during the month. These totaled $4,655. Others represented amortizations of the costs of plant and equipment ($1,220) and factory property insurance ($550) purchased in previous months and years.

Entries were made in detailed cost center operating cost accounts (Supervision, Depreciation, etc.), but for our purposes all of these can be represented by a single summary entry:

(3)

Factory Overhead...	6,425	
Accumulated Depreciation...............................		1,220
Prepaid Insurance...		550
Accounts Payable...		4,655

---

[2] This liability, or most of it, was extinguished almost immediately by the payment of cash. When and how liabilities are liquidated has no bearing on cost accounting, however, and payment transactions therefore can be ignored in this illustration.

This shows that the $1,220 and $550 were merely transferred from one asset category to another, while the remaining $4,655 was financed by a temporary increase in the company's liabilities.

Factory overhead costs made their way into the Work in Process inventory account by the procedure known as *overhead absorption* or overhead application. This procedure consists of multiplying each cost center's burden rate by the total volume of activity in that cost center. For example, suppose that the factory uses a single plantwide burden rate of $3 a direct labor hour. In all, 3,500 direct labor hours were recorded during the month. At this volume, a total of $10,500 ($3 × 3,500) was assigned to jobs in process and entered in the job cost sheets. This total was also charged to the Work in Process control account by the following entry:

(4)

Work in Process... 10,500
    Factory Overhead......................................   10,500

This entry transferred a number of the costs that were initially recorded in Factory Overhead to the asset account, Work in Process. The Factory Overhead account thus served only briefly as an asset account.[3] Viewing this account diagramatically, we can see that actual costs came in at the left and the amounts absorbed went out at the right:

Factory Overhead

→(1)	530	(4)	10,500→
→(2)	5,105		
→(3)	6,425		
	12,060		
Bal. 1,560			

We shall return in a moment to look at the $1,560 difference between the amount that came in and the amount that went out.

Recording Job Completions

The final step in job costing is to transfer the costs of completed jobs from the in-process inventory account. In the typical case, many job orders would be in production each month. To keep the illustration simple, however, let us assume that our factory had only four jobs in process

---

[3] In practice, two overhead summary accounts are used for each cost center instead of the one illustrated here. One of these (Overhead Cost Summary) summarizes the balances in the operating cost accounts and has a debit balance); the other (Overhead Cost Absorbed) accumulates the amounts absorbed by production and has a credit balance. This refinement has been ignored in this illustration to provide a clearer picture of the absorption process.

during May. The job cost sheets for these four jobs showed the following totals after the above transactions had been recorded:

Job	Direct Materials	Direct Labor	Overhead Applied	Total
1........................	$ 5,840	$ 3,200	$ 2,400	$11,440
2........................	11,235	4,855	3,510	19,600
3........................	3,465	5,140	3,840	12,445
4........................	1,605	1,030	750	3,385
Total..................	$22,145	$14,225	$10,500	$46,870

The first two of these jobs were completed during May, and the finished products were turned over to the sales division. The job order cost sheets for these two jobs were removed from the in-process file, and an entry was made to transfer the costs accumulated on these two jobs to the Finished Goods Inventory account (another control account):

Finished Goods Inventory.................................. 31,040
    Work in Process..   31,040

At the same time, entries were made in a subsidiary finished goods ledger to record the number of units finished and the cost per unit. For example, job 1 was the manufacture of 1,100 water pumps. A filing card was prepared for water pumps, and an entry was made to record the completion of 1,100 water pumps at a unit cost of $10.40. A second card was prepared for job 2, consisting of 500 oil burners at a unit cost of $39.20. (Once again, remember that the typical production lot is ordinarily much smaller than these, at least as a percentage of total factory output. In addition, it should be remembered that some job orders cover the manufacture of parts rather than finished products; the costs of such jobs would be transferred to Materials Inventory rather than to Finished Goods Inventory.)

Recording the Cost of Goods Sold

The cost of manufactured goods finally becomes an expense when the goods are sold. In this case all of the water pumps and 425 of the oil burners were sold during May, for a total cost of goods sold of $28,100:

Product	Number Sold	Unit Cost	Total Cost
Pumps......................	1,100	$10.40	$11,440
Burners....................	425	39.20	16,660
Total......................			$28,100

These amounts were subtracted from the finished goods ledger cards for these two products, and an entry was made to transfer the cost to the Cost of Goods Sold account:

Cost of Goods Sold.. 28,100
    Finished Goods Inventory.............................   28,100

This shows the decrease in the company's assets and in the owners' equity in the business that results from the transfer of finished goods to the company's customers. This must then be compared with the amount by which the proceeds from these sales increased the company's assets and the owners' equity.

The Statement of Manufacturing Costs

A summary statement of manufacturing costs is often useful in connection with overall income reporting. A statement of this kind is shown in Exhibit 7–3. To facilitate reconciliation of the income statement with the balance sheets, this statement shows the beginning and ending inventory figures as well as the costs for the month. These inventory balances were not introduced earlier in the illustration because the costs of items transferred from materials inventory or from the factory to the finished goods storerooms were derived directly from perpetual inventory records.

The upper part of this statement shows the costs charged to the factory during the month. The amount charged to jobs differs from this

Exhibit 7–3

STATEMENT OF MANUFACTURING COSTS

Direct materials:		
Materials and supplies inventory, May 1..............		$52,485
Purchases.......................................		30,000
		$82,485
Less: Supplies used...............................	$ 530	
Materials and supplies inventory, May 31.........	59,810	60,340
Direct materials used.............................		$22,145
Direct labor.....................................		14,225
Factory overhead:		
Indirect labor...................................	$ 5,105	
Supplies.......................................	530	
Depreciation...................................	1,220	
Insurance......................................	550	
Other overhead.................................	4,655	
Total overhead..............................	$12,060	
Less: Overhead unabsorbed.....................	1,560	
Overhead applied to production...................		10,500
Total product cost...............................		$46,870
Add: Work in process, May 1.....................		...
		$46,870
Less: Work in process, May 31...................		15,830
Cost of Goods Finished...........................		$31,040

total by the amount of overhead unabsorbed. Adding the cost of the beginning in-process inventory, zero in this case, yields the total cost in process during the month, $46,870. The cost of goods finished is then obtained by subtracting the costs assigned to the jobs still in process at the end of the month (jobs 3 and 4).

This statement can be converted into a statement of the cost of goods sold by adding or subtracting the change in the finished goods inventory.

Summary of the Cost Flows

The complete cycle is summarized schematically in Exhibit 7–4. Costs enter the factory accounts at the left of the diagram. Some are stored temporarily in inventory, fixed asset, or prepayment accounts which appear on the company's balance sheet. Others (direct labor) go directly to work in process, while others go temporarily into factory overhead accounts. As materials are issued and work is performed, costs move out of the accounts at the left and into work in process, either directly or by way of the factory overhead accounts. Factory overhead is charged to work in process by means of predetermined burden rates.

As jobs are completed, the costs are transferred from work in process to the finished goods inventory account. Despite all this motion, they are still shown on the balance sheet. Finally, as the revenues from particular goods are recognized, the costs leave the·balance sheet and go to the income statement under the heading "Cost of goods sold." Some costs, in other words, go through three kinds of balance sheet accounts before being recognized as expense. (Factory overhead is often called

Exhibit 7–4

COST FLOWS FOR INCOME DETERMINATION IN MANUFACTURING

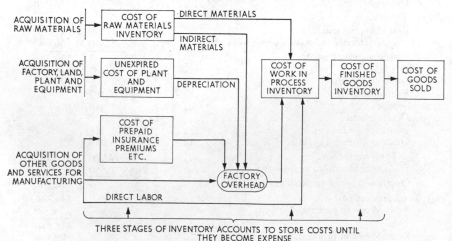

THREE STAGES OF INVENTORY ACCOUNTS TO STORE COSTS UNTIL
THEY BECOME EXPENSE

manufacturing expense, but we prefer to restrict the term expense to describe costs deducted from revenue, as defined in Chapter 1.)

EXPLAINING THE OVERHEAD VARIANCE

The cost flows described in the preceding section can be summarized in still another way, as a series of productive inputs and outputs. In the example, the company's cost accounting procedures were designed both to measure unit cost and to distribute the costs of the various productive

Exhibit 7–5

ORIGIN AND DISTRIBUTION OF FACTORY COSTS

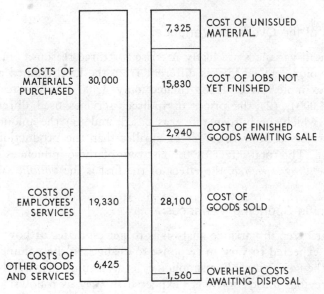

inputs (labor, materials, etc.) among the various outputs of the period, as shown in Exhibit 7–5. Notice that the two bars in this diagram are of the same height, corresponding to a total cost of $55,755. Inputs and outputs must be equal because the cost accounting system defines output in terms of the inputs used to produce them. Inputs and outputs are thus merely two ways of describing the same total.

The only difficulty with this approach is that one of the so-called outputs, "overhead costs awaiting disposal," was fictitious. The $1,560 assigned to this fictitious output was merely the balance remaining in the Factory Overhead account, the difference between the overhead costs recorded for the month and the amount absorbed (the amount charged to jobs through the predetermined burden rate).

This $1,560 is called the *overhead variance*. If the overhead costs have exceeded the amount absorbed, as in this case, overhead is said to be underabsorbed and the variance is referred to as *unfavorable*. Whenever the amount absorbed is greater than the amount of cost charged to the overhead accounts, on the other hand, overhead is said to be overabsorbed and the variance is *favorable*.

The presence of these variances in a company's factory cost accounts raises two questions:

1. Why did they arise?
2. Where should they appear on the company's financial statements?

This section deals with the first of these questions; the second will be taken up in the next section.

Sources of the Overhead Variance

Overhead variances are likely to arise for three reasons: (1) the production volume achieved was different from the level defined as normal (in the example, direct labor totaled only 3,500 hours instead of the normal 4,000); (2) the prices of indirect services used differed from those on which the burden rate was based; and (3) the amounts of indirect services used were larger or smaller than the production volume warranted. The total effect of the last two of these influences is known as the *spending variance;* the effect of the first is the *volume variance*.

Determining Spending Variances

The first step in variance analysis is to get estimates of how overhead costs are expected to vary in response to changes in the volume of work done in the cost center. For simplicity, let us assume that overhead costs in the previous illustration were expected to vary as follows:[4]

Total overhead = \$7,400 a month + \$1.15 × actual direct labor hours

It was noted earlier that normal volume in this factory was 4,000 direct labor hours a month. From the formula, we can calculate that factory overhead costs were expected to total \$12,000 a month at this volume:

Total overhead = \$7,400 + \$1.15 × 4,000 = \$12,000

This is the basis on which the company set the burden rate at \$3 per direct labor hour:

$$\text{Burden rate} = \frac{\$12,000}{4,000} = \$3 \text{ per direct labor hour}$$

---

[4] In practice, each cost center is likely to have its own burden rate. Introduction of multiple burden rates in this illustration would serve only to make the discussion more difficult to follow.

Actual volume during May, however, required only 3,500 hours of direct labor. The overhead cost appropriate to this volume totaled only $11,425:

$$\text{Total overhead} = \$7,400 + \$1.15 \times 3,500 = \$11,425$$

The difference between this amount and the actual overhead cost for the month ($12,060) is the spending variance:

Actual overhead cost..........................	$12,060
Expected overhead cost at actual volume........	11,425
Overhead spending variance...................	$ (635)

This shows that actual spending was $635 greater than management would normally expect to spend at this volume, and was therefore unfavorable. (By convention, unfavorable variances are either printed in red or enclosed in parentheses, as above.)

The spending variance is actually a combined variance, in that it may include the effects of differences between actual and expected prices of overhead cost elements as well as differences between actual and expected quantities of indirect services used. The spending variance can be separated into these two components by the techniques that we shall describe in Chapter 15.

Computing Volume Variances

The spending variance accounts for only $635 of the $1,560 total overhead variance in the illustration. The remaining $925 is known as the volume variance. This arose because actual volume was less than the volume on which the burden rate was based. If the burden rate had been based on a direct labor volume of 3,500 hours instead of 4,000 hours a month, the burden rate would have been:

$$\frac{\$7,400 + \$1.15 \times 3,500}{3,500} = \$3.2643 \text{ per direct labor hour}$$

The amount absorbed by production volume at this rate would have been:

$$\$3.2643 \times 3,500 = \$11,425$$

The total variance therefore would have been the same as the spending variance; the volume variance would have been zero.

The volume variance arises only when the burden rate is used to absorb costs that do not vary in direct proportion to variations in overall operating volume. Depreciation on the factory building, for example, will be the same whether operating volume is 3,000 or 4,000 direct labor hours a month, but the total amount charged to job orders (absorbed) by the predetermined rate will vary with production. When production levels are low. fixed overhead will be underabsorbed, and vice versa.

The volume variance in the illustration above arose because $7,400 of the overhead costs included in the burden rate calculation were fixed. These accounted for $1.85 of the burden rate:

$$\text{Absorption rate for fixed costs} = \frac{\$7,400}{4,000} = \$1.85 \text{ per direct labor hour}$$

Actual absorption amounted to $6,475:

$$\$1.85 \times 3,500 = \$6,475$$

The $925 difference between this and the $7,400 in expected fixed costs was the volume variance for the period.

The volume variance must be interpreted carefully. It does not mean that costs were $925 greater than expected because volume was lower than normal. It merely says that no production was available to absorb $925 of the costs that were expected to occur. Expressed differently, $925 was spent to provide production capacity that the company did not use.

The volume variance in this illustration, like the spending variance, was unfavorable—that is, actual production volume was too small to absorb all of the expected overhead costs at this volume. The volume variance can also be favorable, because "normal" volume is usually less than maximum volume and actual volume is sometimes greater than normal. Under these circumstances, production volume will absorb more fixed costs than the company expects to incur.

Summarizing the Overhead Variance Analysis

The overall variance computation may be summarized in the following manner:

(1)	Actual costs charged..........................	$12,060	
(2)	Budgeted costs for actual volume..................	11,425	
	Spending variance (1)—(2)...................		$(635)
(3)	Costs absorbed by actual volume.................	10,500	
	Volume variance (2)—(3)....................		(925)
	Total variance (1)—(3)....................		$(1,560)

Exhibit 7–6 presents this same information in graphic form. The line labeled "Absorbed" represents the amount absorbed at various volumes. This amount is directly proportional to volume, $3 for each direct labor hour, and thus appears as a straight line on the chart, starting at the double zero at the lower left-hand corner of the chart.

The "Expected" line represents the total cost expected at various volumes. Because some of the cost center's costs are fixed, this line has a gentler slope than the "Absorbed" line. Cost variability in this case is proportional to volume—$1.15 in budgeted variable costs for each direct labor hour—and thus is shown as a straight line.

The two lines cross at a volume of 4,000 direct labor hours, the normal operating volume of the cost center. The vertical distance between the "Expected" and "Absorbed" lines at any volume represents the volume variance at that volume level and arises solely because actual volume departs from the volume on which the burden rate has been based. Volume variances at volumes in excess of normal volume, such as that marked *b* in Exhibit 7–6, represent overabsorption and are classified as

Exhibit 7–6

OVERHEAD COST VARIANCES ILLUSTRATED

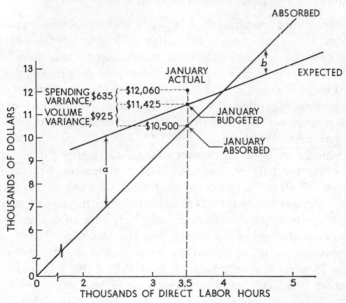

favorable. Volume variances at volumes lower than normal, in the zone to the left of the intersection of the lines in the exhibit, represent underutilization of capacity and are referred to as unfavorable. Both the $925 volume variance arising from the illustration and the one marked *a* are in this category.

Exhibit 7–6 also shows the aggregate spending variance. Actual costs are superimposed on this chart as a single point, located directly above the actual volume achieved. The spending variance is then represented by the vertical distance between the actual cost for the period and the point on the budget line corresponding to actual volume, in this case 3,500 direct labor hours.

DISPOSING OF OVERHEAD VARIANCES

Another question is how the overhead variances should be reflected in companywide financial statements. The accountant has three alternatives:

1. To transfer the entire overhead variance to the income statement.
2. To leave the entire amount on the balance sheet, as a deferred charge or credit to the operations of future periods.
3. To divide the variance between inventory and cost of goods sold in some way that will make these figures approximate average historical cost.

Approximating Average Historical Cost

The choice of disposal method is partly a question of materiality and expediency, but it is or should be mainly dependent on the costing precepts of financial accounting theory. According to one point of view, the use of burden rates is an expedient to facilitate data processing. Actual historical costs, according to this point of view, are still essential for inventory costing, regardless of whether these costs are high or low or what the reasons were for the departure of actual historical costs from predetermined averages or standards.

The logical conclusion of this argument is to require a division of cost variances between balance sheet and income statement. For example, in the illustration, all of the units in job 1 were sold and the overhead absorbed by that job would therefore be included in the cost of goods sold. Of the 500 units in job 2, however, only 425 were sold, leaving 75 still in inventory at the end of the period. For this job, 425/500 (85 percent) of the applicable overhead should go to the income statement, leaving the remaining 15 percent on the balance sheet. All of the overhead absorbed by the other two jobs should remain on the balance sheet, because both jobs were still in process at the end of the month. Using these percentages, the amount of overhead absorbed by the burden rate can be divided as follows:

Job	Income Statement	Balance Sheet	Total
1	$2,400.00		$ 2,400.00
2	2,983.50	$ 526.50	3,510.00
3	....	3,840.00	3,840.00
4	....	750.00	750.00
Total	$5,383.50	$5,116.50	$10,500.00

This shows that the overhead absorbed by the goods sold amounted to 51.3 percent of the total amount absorbed during the month. To approximate average historical cost, therefore, 51.3 percent of the overhead variance, or $800, would have to be transferred to the income statement, leaving the remaining $760 on the balance sheet as an adjustment to the cost of inventories. An entry to accomplish this would be:

Cost of Goods Sold.. 800
Inventory Adjustment.. 760
    Factory Overhead... 1,560

This would reduce the balance in the Factory Overhead account to zero. The balance in the inventory adjustment account would be included in the inventory figure shown on the end-of-period balance sheet.[5]

Taking All Variances to Income

A second school of thought holds that the predetermined burden rate provides a better measure of product cost than average historical cost, on the ground that variances result from departures of actual conditions from normal conditions.[6] The justification for leaving any cost on the balance sheet as a representation of an asset is a presumption that the present value to the company of future cash flows attributable to this cost is at least equal to the cost. Management's commitment to incur a cost, in other words, presumes that value is not less than cost. If actual costs exceed the amount upon which the commitment was based so that cost exceeds value, then part or all of the excess will have been proven unproductive. An up-to-date estimate of normal cost is ordinarily a better measure than average historical cost of the commitment implicit in management's decision to manufacture the product. If this proposition is accepted, then departures from normal cost should not be inventoried on the balance sheet.

The argument for this approach is perhaps best seen in connection with overhead volume variances. If volume variances are averaged over current production, inventoried unit cost will rise when volume declines and fall when volume expands, as shown in Exhibit 7–7. Because a decline in volume usually occurs in response to a generally unfavorable economic outlook for the factory's output, the use of average actual cost will ordinarily lead to high unit cost in poor times when products are difficult to sell and low unit cost in good times. This is a strange result. Asset balances reflect cost, not value, but it is difficult to justify an inventory costing method that yields unit cost figures that move inversely with movements in product value.

---

[5] For an argument that is generally favorable to costing inventories at average historical cost, see L. J. Benninger, "Accounting Theory and Cost Accounting," *Accounting Review*, July 1965, pp. 547–57.

[6] Many manufacturing companies determine all elements of product cost in advance through the use of standard costs. This leads to variances in direct labor and direct materials as well as overhead variances. Because standard costing has not yet been discussed, however, the arguments are presented here as if they related only to overhead variances.

The predetermined burden rate was developed at least partly to avoid this paradoxical result. This presumes that the fixed costs from which volume variances stem are costs of providing capacity. The amount absorbed indicates the cost of that portion of capacity used by specific products; the amount unabsorbed is attributable not to the products produced but to those that were not produced. Following this reasoning, none of the cost of idle capacity should be assigned to product inventories.

Clearing favorable volume variances to the income statement is harder to justify. Once again the argument is that each product should be assigned its full share of the costs of providing capacity. Overutilization of capacity is due to currently favorable conditions which change the profitability of the company's products rather than their costs. Just as

Exhibit 7–7

EFFECT OF VOLUME ON AVERAGE FIXED COST

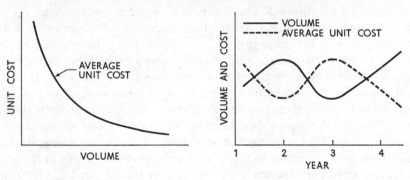

the costs of idle capacity are assignable to products not produced, so the benefits from supernormal output accrue to the extra products rather than to the normal output.

The main drawback of this latter position is that the volume variance that accompanies supernormal production volume could provide a misleading indicator of income if the production represented a speculative buildup of inventory. This has led some accountants to favor the expensing of unfavorable variances but the spreading of favorable variances over total production for the period.

Assigning All Variances to the Balance Sheet

The third possible approach also accepts normal cost as the appropriate measure of product cost but maintains that departures from normal are temporary and will cancel themselves out if a long enough time period is permitted. Therefore, all variances should remain on the balance sheet until offset in later periods by variances in the opposite direction.

This viewpoint would be valid if variances could all be regarded as the result of random forces. Random fluctuations affect totals during a short period, but the longer the reporting period the greater is the likelihood that residual variances are nonrandom. The presumption that 12 months is a long enough time for random variances other than volume variances to cancel each other, together with uncertainty as to the length and average level of business fluctuations, has generally ruled out any extensive support for this third alternative in annual reporting.

Industry Practice

Statements issued by the American Institute of Certified Public Accountants imply that inventory costs should ordinarily approximate average actual costs and that any significant variances, including volume variances, therefore should be split between income statement and balance sheet accounts.[7] Industry practice, however, does not seem to conform to this pattern. A survey carried out two decades ago, for example, found that an overwhelming majority of the companies surveyed used the normal cost approach to the disposition of variances. Out of 127 companies responding to a questionnaire, 114, or approximately 90 percent, credited overabsorbed overhead variances either to the cost of goods sold or to profit and loss, and 112 charged underabsorbed overhead in the same manner.[8] Another survey 12 years later came to substantially the same conclusions.[9]

SUMMARY

Unit cost data from job order cost sheets are often used to measure the cost of goods in inventory and the cost of products sold. If half of the units in a production order are sold, half of the costs shown on the job cost sheet will be transferred to the income statement as the cost of goods sold; the other half will remain on the balance sheet as the cost of the units still in inventory.

This procedure serves to take care of all of the costs that have been entered on the job cost sheets, but actual cost will always differ from this amount whenever predetermined burden rates are used. This difference is known as the overhead variance or over- or underabsorbed overhead, and it raises two questions:

1. Should it appear on the income statement or the balance sheet?
2. How did it arise?

---

[7] American Institute of Certified Public Accountants, *Accounting Research and Terminology Bulletins, Final Edition* (New York, 1961), p. 29 and p. 30n; see also Paul Grady, "Inventory of General Accepted Accounting Principles." *Accounting Research Study No. 7* (New York: AICPA, 1965), p. 102.

[8] National Association of (Cost) Accountants, "Costs Included in Inventories, Research Series No. 10," *N.A.(C.)A. Bulletin*, August 15, 1947, pp. 1577–1608.

[9] Osamu Nisizawa, "Inventory Cost Allocation Practices and Concepts," *N.A.(C.)A. Bulletin*, December 1959, pp. 81–93.

The accountant generally answers the first question by carrying the entire variance to the income statement for the year in which it arises. His answer to the second is generally more complicated, but he begins by subdividing the variance into two main parts: (*a*) the spending variance, representing the effects of variations in input quantities and prices; and (*b*) the volume variance, representing the effects of volume variation on total cost absorption. Later chapters will examine these questions in more detail.

EXERCISES AND PROBLEMS

1.* The Basic Foundry prepares metal castings for specific orders, using a job order costing system. The following information about job No. 103 is available:

(1) Materials issued: 21,000 pounds at $0.66 a pound.
(2) Labor hours: 2,000 at $2.15 an hour.
(3) Factory overhead charged to jobs: $4 a direct labor hour.
(4) Unused material returned to storeroom: 800 pounds.
(5) Castings started: 10,000.
(6) Castings completed: 9,800.

a) Compute unit cost of production to the nearest cent.
b) Prepare journal entries to record these transactions.

2. Job order X150 was placed in production in December 19x1. During December, materials costing $800 were issued for use on this job, and 60 direct labor hours were expended at an average rate of $2.20 an hour. The burden rate in 19x1 was $4 a direct labor *dollar*.

The company's new fiscal year began on January 1, 19x2. Job order X150 was finished in January with the additional expenditure of 90 direct labor hours at an average wage rate of $2.30 an hour, and additional direct materials amounting to $250 were issued for use in this job. The burden rate in 19x2 was set at $9 a direct labor *hour*.

The job consisted of 500 product units, but 20 of these units were spoiled and were discarded as trash. The remaining 480 units were placed in the finished goods stockroom on January 28, 19x2. The next day 100 of these units were sold and shipped to customers.

a) Compute unit cost to the nearest cent. Explain your method of accounting for the spoiled units.
b) Prepare journal entries to record these transactions.

3.* The estimated monthly fixed overhead cost for one department is $8,000 and the estimated variable overhead cost is $1.20 per dollar of direct labor cost. The estimated average monthly direct labor cost is $10,000.

During the month of August direct labor cost amounted to $9,000. Manu-

---

* Solutions to problems marked with an asterisk can be found in Appendix B.

facturing overhead was $21,700. Account for the manufacturing overhead, using T accounts, and develop the relevant variances.

4. A company uses a job order costing system with a predetermined burden rate based on normal volume. Overhead costs are budgeted at $10,000 a month plus $2 for each direct labor hour. Normal volume is 10,000 direct labor hours. Actual volume for August was 9,000 direct labor hours, and actual overhead cost totaled $28,700. Job No. 423 was started on August 6 and completed on August 20, with the expenditure of 400 direct labor hours.

a) How much overhead was charged to job No. 423?
b) How much overhead was charged to all jobs during August?
c) What was the total factory overhead variance for August?
d) Break this variance into two parts and explain what each part means.
e) Which of these two parts would probably be further subdivided or shown in greater detail? Indicate the nature of this subdivision.

5. The predetermined burden rate for 19x1 was $2 a machine-hour. The total overhead cost of goods manufactured and sold, based on this rate, was $100,000. This left $20,000 in unabsorbed overhead, which was deducted from revenues on the 19x1 income statement.

The overhead cost component of the inventory on December 31, 19x0 amounted to $30,000. Actual overhead cost in 19x1 equaled the amount absorbed by production in that year.

a) What effect did the use of a predetermined burden rate in 19x1 instead of actual overhead cost have on reported profit for 19x1 and 19x2, assuming that inventory cost flows follow the Fifo principle?
b) How would your answer differ if Lifo were in use, assuming that physical inventories were the same at the end of 19x1 as at the beginning?

6. The trial balances of the Andrews Company included the following balances at the beginning and end of the year:

	January 1	December 31
Sales revenue		$1,500,000
Labor cost of goods sold		200,000
Materials cost of goods sold		600,000
Overhead cost of goods sold		400,000
Overhead in process	$ 50,000	80,000
Overhead in finished goods	100,000	120,000
Manufacturing overhead (debit)		218,000
Operating expenses		250,000
Variances in inventory		

The company's inventories were costed on a Fifo basis. The burden rate had not been changed for two years, and there was no under- or overabsorbed overhead in the previous year. The burden rate was based on normal volume.

a) Compute reported income before taxes for the year, on the assumption that the cost of inventories to be reported on the year-end balance sheet is to approximate actual cost rather than normal cost.

b) Perform the operations called for in (*a*) with the same underlying assumptions but based on the Lifo method of inventory costing.

7.* The Gray Company capitalizes all freight charges relating to materials purchased and deducts all discounts in computing the amounts to be entered in the stores ledger. A perpetual inventory is maintained. On April 1, the company had 200 units of material No. 1476A in inventory at a cost of 50 cents each. The following transactions in material No. 1476A occurred during April:

April 2   Received 500 units from Alpha Company at a price of 55 cents each, delivered; terms, net 30 days.

      4   Issued 50 units for use in job No. N1346.

      8   Issued 200 units for use in job No. N1402.

    12   Received 500 units from Beta Company at a price of 48 cents each, f.o.b. Cleveland; freight charges, $20; terms, 2 percent, 10 days, net 30 days.

    16   Issued 400 units for use in job No. N1481.

    18   Issued 50 units for use in job No. N1346.

    25   Issued 250 units for use in job No. N1417.

    28   Received 1,000 units from Beta Company at a price of 47 cents each, f.o.b. Cleveland; freight charges, $40; terms, 2 percent, 10 days, net 30 days.

a) Prepare a stores ledger card for material No. 1476A and make the necessary entries, using a moving average method of inventory measurement.

b) Repeat this procedure using a Fifo inventory measurement method.

8.* The Zebra Company used an estimated overhead rate of $2.50 per direct labor hour for 1966. At the end of 1966, after having worked 125,000 labor hours, the company had an underabsorbed overhead of $46,750. It apportioned this in proportion to the labor hours in work-in-process and finished goods inventories and in cost of goods sold. The labor hours in each of these were:

Work in process	15,000
Finished goods	25,000
Cost of goods sold	85,000
Total	125,000

While auditing the records of the Zebra Company, you find:

(1) A machine costing $10,000 was charged to Manufacturing Overhead; a fixed asset record card for this machine was prepared correctly, however, and depreciation on the machine was correctly charged to manufacturing overhead during the year.

(2) The salary of the president for July ($3,000) was incorrectly charged to Manufacturing Overhead.

(3) Job No. 389 was charged with overhead of $250 which should have been charged to Job No. 298. Both jobs have been completed and sold.

Prepare any necessary adjustments and apportion any under- or overabsorbed overhead resulting from those adjustments.

9. The Collins Company costs its raw materials inventories by the moving average method. Freight-in is distributed to materials purchased in proportion to purchase prices. The stores ledger cards show the following balances at the beginning of March:

> Material A, 700 pounds at $0.252.................... $176.40
> Material B, 400 pounds at $0.165..................... 66.00
> Material C, 26,000 feet at $0.03..................... 780.00
> Material D, 5,000 feet at $0.125..................... 625.00

The following events occurred during March:

March 2   Issued: 200 pounds material A, 5,000 feet material C.
    5   Received: 20,000 feet material C at $0.03 a foot, 10,000 feet material D at $0.12 a foot. Freight for both items, $180.
    9   Issued: 300 pounds material A, 150 pounds material B, 8,000 feet material C, 5,000 feet material D.
   16   Received: 1,000 pounds material A at $0.24, 500 pounds material B at $0.16. Freight for both items, $64.
   22   Issued: 700 pounds material A, 400 pounds material B, 20,000 feet material C, 3,000 feet material D.

a) Prepare stores ledger cards for these four materials and make the necessary entries.
b) Prepare summary journal entries to record the above transactions.

10. The Tinpot Company's factory has a job order costing system. It uses predetermined full cost burden rates. It classifies its manufacturing overhead cost accounts into two categories: class A (wholly fixed), and class B (partly fixed and partly variable). The following data are available:

(1)   Normal volume, 20,000 direct labor hours.
(2)   Class A costs:
    (*a*)   Budget at normal volume, $20,000.
    (*b*)   Variable costs, none.
    (*c*)   Actual costs for July, $21,100.
    (*d*)   Volume variance for July, $1,400, favorable.
(3)   Class B costs:
    (*a*)   Budget at normal volume, $30,000.
    (*b*)   Variable costs included in (*a*), $1.10 per direct labor hour.
    (*c*)   Actual costs for July, $34,000.

a) What was the actual operating volume for July?
b) How much of the cost in each class was assigned to products during the month?
c) Prepare a variance summary for the month, in as much detail as you can derive.

11.* The Ace Appliance Company had the following inventories on October 1:

Raw material and stores.................... $12,650
Work in process........................   8,320
Finished goods...........................   11,100

The following transactions took place during the month:

(1) Purchased material at a cost of $4,500.
(2) Issued direct material, $6,320; indirect material, $930.
(3) Payroll: direct labor, $3,300; indirect labor, $1,880; selling and administrative salaries, $2,600.
(4) Miscellaneous manufacturing overhead, $2,700.
(5) Applied manufacturing overhead at 150 percent of direct labor cost.
(6) Goods completed during month cost $12,650.
(7) Miscellaneous selling and administrative expenses, $1,835.
(8) Ending inventory, finished goods, $9,250.
(9) Sales revenue from goods sold, $19,350.

a) Account for the above transactions, using T accounts, and establish the closing balances in the inventory accounts.
b) Prepare an income statement for the month, with a supporting schedule of the cost of goods manufactured and sold. (Overhead over- or under-absorbed is to be included in the cost of goods sold.)

12. The records of the Simmons Company showed the following information for 19x0:

Inventories, January 1:
  Materials.. $ 50,000
  Work in process...................................   12,000
  Finished goods....................................   63,000
Inventories, December 31:
  Materials..   43,000
  Work in process....................................   16,000
  Finished goods.....................................   61,000
Operating cost accounts (from December 31 trial balance):
  Purchases of materials (for direct and indirect use)..........   169,000
  Purchases returns and allowances........................   (2,000)
  Direct labor..   80,000
  Indirect labor..   7,000
  Indirect material (from materials inventories)...............   6,000
  Power and light.......................................   3,000
  Heat...   4,000
  Depreciation—buildings................................   5,000
  Depreciation—equipment...............................   8,000
  Miscellaneous factory costs............................   1,000
  Overhead absorbed....................................   (32,000)

a) Set up the necessary operating cost and inventory accounts, enter the January 1 balances given above, and make entries to record the year's transactions, including the cost of goods sold.
b) Prepare a statement of the cost of goods manufactured.

13. The April 1 balances of the Apex Company's inventory and overhead accounts were:

Raw material..	$35,000
Work in process.......................................	8,000
Finished goods..	26,000
Overhead (under-) or overabsorbed.....................	(3,000)

The following additional information is available.

(1) The following costs were incurred during the month:

Raw materials purchased...............................	$23,000
Direct labor..	14,000
Indirect labor..	8,000
Power...	1,500
Depreciation..	1,500
Supplies..	2,000
Other manufacturing costs.............................	5,000
Selling and office expense............................	9,000

(2) Raw material costing $31,000 was put into process during April.

(3) At the close of the month the production orders still in process, all of which had been started during the month, had been charged with the following costs: direct material, $4,000; direct labor, $1,500.

(4) Overhead is charged on the basis of 140 percent of direct labor cost.

(5) Finished goods inventory as of April 30 amounted to $18,000.

a) Present journal entries to cover the transactions indicated by the above information.

b) List the balances in the inventory accounts and the amount of the over- or underabsorbed overhead as of April 30.

14. A factory uses a job order costing system. A careless bookkeeper has lost the file of job order cost sheets covering the work done last week, but the underlying documents are still available. You have the following data.

(1) Direct labor hours and direct materials used were:

Job Order	Materials	Labor
498........	$1,500	116
506........	960	16
507........	415	18
508........	345	42
509........	652	24
511........	308	10
512........	835	30
Total......	$5,015	256

(2) The direct labor wage rate is $4 an hour.

(3) The burden rate is $5 a direct labor hour.

(4) Actual overhead costs for the week were $1,480.

(5) Jobs No. 498, 506, and 509 were completed.

(6) Fixed overhead costs are expected to amount to $1,000 a week; variable overhead costs should average $1 per direct labor hour.

(7) The factory had no work in process at the beginning of the week.

a) Prepare a summary table that will show the total cost assigned to each job.

b) Compute and analyze the amount of overhead over- or underabsorbed during the week.

15. The Sandrex Company uses a job order cost accounting system. Direct labor costs are charged daily to Work in Process and credited to Accrued Wages Payable on the basis of time tickets. Direct materials costs are charged to Work in Process and credited to Materials Inventory. Factory overhead costs are charged initially to a Factory Overhead account.

Overhead costs are charged to the Work in Process account by means of a predetermined burden rate of $2 per direct labor hour. The accompanying credit is to a separate account titled Factory Overhead Absorbed. The costs of goods finished are transferred from Work in Process to a Finished Goods account at the time each job is completed. A perpetual inventory system is used for both materials and finished goods.

Prepare journal entries to record the facts described below. Each of these events should be regarded as independent of the others, and it should be assumed in each case that any pertinent prior recordings have been made correctly unless it is stated otherwise. If no entry is required, explain why.

a) Goods manufactured at a cost of $8,000 are sold for $14,000. Manufacture of these products was completed in the preceding accounting period. The job cost records show that the total manufacturing cost of $8,000 includes $2,000 of materials, $3,000 of direct labor, and $3,000 of overhead.

b) Factory overhead is charged to a job on which 480 direct labor hours have been recorded during this period.

c) It is discovered prior to the end of the period that an error has resulted in treating 500 hours of direct labor at $2.50 an hour as indirect labor (i.e., the charge was made to Factory Overhead). The job on which this labor was used has been finished but not yet sold.

d) Materials costing $5,000 and supplies costing $500 are issued from the factory storeroom. Of the materials, $1,000 is for use in constructing new display cases in the salesroom. The display cases are completed and placed in use this period. The remaining materials are issued to the factory for specific job orders. Of the supplies, $100 is for the immediate use of the sales office. The remainder are for factory use.

e) Prior to the end of the period, it is discovered that $1,000 of direct materials have been charged to the wrong job. At the time this error is discovered, both jobs have been completed but not yet sold.

f) Prior to the end of the period, it is discovered that an error was made in adding up the direct labor hours on a certain job which has now been completed and sold. The dollar amount of direct labor was added correctly, but the hours were overstated by 100.

16. The Subway Car Company manufactures railway and subway cars to customer orders. Revenues are recognized at the time finished products are shipped to customers. A predetermined burden rate of $3 per direct labor hour is used in the company's factory.

On March 1, $120,000 in materials and supplies were on hand. The company maintains no inventory of finished goods, but it had three jobs in process in its factory on March 1, consisting of the number of cars and the costs accumulated in prior months as shown below.

Job No.	Cars	Costs
6456....................	1	$ 43,000
6457....................	4	134,000
6459....................	3	27,000

The following transactions affecting manufacturing costs occurred during the month of March:

(1) A new job order, No. 6460, was placed in production.

(2) Materials, supplies, and parts in the amount of $97,000 were purchased on account.

(3) Materials, supplies, and parts were issued to production departments as follows:

Job 6456...	$ 2,000
Job 6457...	20,000
Job 6459...	35,000
Job 6460...	5,000
General factory use..................................	18,000

(4) Labor time tickets showed the following totals:

Job 6456.............................	1,200 hours, $ 6,000
Job 6457.............................	8,000 hours, $50,000
Job 6459.............................	10,000 hours, $36,000
Job 6460.............................	800 hours, $ 4,000
Indirect labor.......................	3,000 hours, $ 7,400

(5) Factory depreciation for the month was $10,000.

(6) Other factory operating costs amounted to $35,000 (credit Accounts Payable).

(7) Job 6456 was finished and shipped to the customer on March 18.

(8) Two cars in job 6457 were finished and shipped to the customer on March 28. The remaining two cars in the job were one half completed on March 31.

a) Record the above information in appropriately titled T accounts. Direct labor and direct materials costs are charged directly to a single Work in Process account. All manufacturing overhead costs are charged, when incurred, to a Manufacturing Overhead account. Factory overhead absorbed is credited to this Manufacturing Overhead account.

b) Prepare a statement of the cost of goods manufactured and sold.

17. The Farquar Corporation uses job order costing in its factory. The inventory accounts showed the following balances as of February 1:

Materials and Supplies.......................	40,000
Jobs in Process.............................	57,000
Finished Goods.............................	73,000

The job cost file showed the following details at that time:

	Materials	Labor	Overhead	Total
No. D1762...	$ 600	$ 1,900	$ 2,850	$ 5,350
No. D1783...	2,900	3,200	4,800	10,900
No. E0004...	4,000	1,400	2,100	7,500
No. E0010...	6,500	1,000	1,500	9,000
No. E0011...	14,000	2,000	3,000	19,000
No. E0013...	4,000	500	750	5,250
Total......	$32,000	$10,000	$15,000	$57,000

The following transactions were recorded during February:

(1) Materials and supplies received in the factory storeroom, $62,000.

(2) Materials and supplies issued by the storeroom to factory departments:

Job No. E0004...................................	$ 500
Job No. E0010...................................	1,000
Job No. E0013...................................	2,500
Job No. E0015...................................	8,000
Job No. E0016...................................	11,000
Job No. E0017...................................	6,000
Job No. E0018...................................	9,000
Indirect materials...............................	7,500
Total..	$45,500

(3) Labor performed in factory departments:

Job No. D1762...................................	$ 200
Job No. D1783...................................	700
Job No. E0004...................................	7,200
Job No. E0010...................................	8,700
Job No. E0011...................................	12,000
Job No. E0013...................................	7,800
Job No. E0015...................................	3,600
Job No. E0016...................................	9,000
Job No. E0017...................................	15,000
Job No. E0018...................................	3,000
Indirect labor..................................	31,500
Total..	$98,700

(4) Other overhead costs charged to the factory:

Supervision.....................................	$22,500
Maintenance....................................	8,800
Heat, light, and power...........................	4,600
Payroll taxes and pensions........................	20,300
Depreciation....................................	9,500
Miscellaneous...................................	1,200
Total..	$66,900

(5) A predetermined burden rate of $1.50 a direct labor dollar was used during the month.

(6) Jobs completed and transferred to finished goods: Nos. D1762, D1783, E0004, E0010, E0013, E0017.

(7) Cost of finished goods sold, $138,000.

The fixed costs in this factory were expected to amount to $50,000 in February. Variable overhead costs were expected to average 75 percent of direct labor cost.

a)   Enter the February 1 balances in the inventory accounts and record the month's transactions.
b)   Prepare a statement of the cost of goods manufactured and sold.
c)   Compute and analyze the amount of the under- or overabsorbed overhead.

chapter 8

Product Costing:

Process Production

When a particular product or service is needed in large enough volumes to require the full-time use of production or service facilities for considerable periods of time, the production operation is referred to as process production and the method used to measure or estimate unit cost is known as *process costing*.

Although something like process costing can be applied in service industries such as telecommunications and banking, the technique was developed initially and has had its widest application in manufacturing industries such as oil refining, steel making, and food processing. The purpose of this chapter is to outline the most important features of factory process costing systems.

CALCULATING UNIT COST

Process costing techniques can be applied either in cost estimation before production takes place or in cost measurement after the fact. In either case, the accountant measures or estimates the costs and output of each *process center* for a specified period of time such as a month. (A process center is a cost center that is engaged directly in product processing.) Each process center's costs are then divided by its output to obtain an average unit cost of that profit center's output. The total unit cost of a finished product is the sum of the unit costs of all of the process centers that perform productive operations on that product.

In sum, the procedure for calculating or estimating unit cost in process costing consists of five steps:

1. Identify the process center.
2. Accumulate or estimate each process center's operating costs for a specified period of time.
3. Measure or estimate each process center's output for this same time period.
4. Divide cost by output to obtain average unit cost.
5. Add the unit costs of various process centers to obtain the unit cost of individual products.

Identifying the Process Centers

Because unit cost is to be obtained by dividing cost by a single output figure, each process center's output must be homogeneous—that is, each unit of output must be enough like every other unit to permit finished production to be measured by a simple unit count. A cost center which produces a variety of highly dissimilar products independently of each

Exhibit 8–1

PRODUCT FLOWS IN STRAIGHT SEQUENTIAL PROCESSING

other cannot be treated as a process center without introducing serious inaccuracies into the calculation of product cost.

A production process may be split up into two or more process centers, all processing the same product, if they perform different kinds of operations on that product. This is typical of straight sequential processes like the one illustrated in Exhibit 8–1. Here the physical flows move steadily from left to right, but the work done consists of three separate operations, each requiring the exclusive use of a specific portion of the company's productive facilities. (For simplicity, the terms process center and department will be used interchangeably in this discussion.)

Recognition of separate process centers in situations like this permits management to see where costs are going up, where they are going down, and which operations are the most costly. In general, the decision of how many process centers to recognize in a given production sequence can be made on the basis of the criteria set forth in Chapter 4 for the identification of cost centers.

Production need not always flow in a single, straight-line sequence through the factory. Sequences such as those shown in Exhibit 8–2 are also fully adaptable to process costing. In the topmost panel, the output

Exhibit 8-2

PRODUCT FLOWS IN PARALLEL PROCESSING

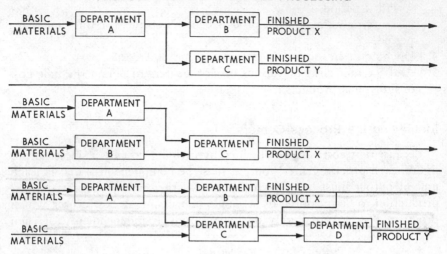

of one process center is split between two subsequent process centers for separate processing into two different products. Thus, even though the factory's output is not homogeneous, consisting of two products rather than one, the output of each of the three departments is homogeneous and process costing can be used.

In the center panel, the outputs of two separate proceessing operations are combined in a third to yield a single product, while in the bottom panel part of the output of department B goes to department D for further processing (e.g., assembly) while the rest goes into the finished stockroom (e.g., replacement parts). Process costing is applicable in all three situations; the only requirement is that output at each stage must be homogeneous.

Measuring Costs

The measurement of product cost in process costing is simpler than in job order costing. Costs need to be identified by process center only; since each process center's output is homogeneous, this serves to identify them by product as well.

Notice that the direct materials–direct labor–overhead breakdown used in job order costing is not appropriate here. Because the product costing unit in process costing is the process center's output for a period of time, *any* cost traced to the process center can be referred to as a direct cost. The line is thus no longer between direct and indirect materials but between different classes of direct materials.

Process costing has one cost measurement problem that is not met in job order costing. Costs are transferred from process center to process center, following the flow of semifinished products through the factory. This means that the process center manager cannot know the cost of his basic materials until the costs of prior process centers are measured at the end of each period.

For example, a small factory has only two process centers, department A and department B. Department A processes raw materials and transfers its output to department B for finishing. Costs of these two departments

Exhibit 8–3

SUMMARY OF DEPARTMENTAL COSTS

	Department A	Department B
Raw materials..........................	$60,000	$ ...
Materials from dept. A....................	....	??
Productive labor.......................	20,700	8,700
Nonproductive labor......................	1,800	870
Overtime premiums......................	900	870
Supplies............................	2,700	3,480
Other costs...........................	9,900	7,830
Total..............................	$96,000	$??

for the month of June are summarized in Exhibit 8–3. The question marks in the right-hand column can be replaced with numbers only after department A's costs have been computed. To do this, we must first decide how to measure department A's output.

Measuring Output

The purpose of computing output is to get a figure that can be divided into the costs of the resources put into a process center during a particular measurement period. It should represent, therefore, the results achieved by these inputs.

If the process center has no work in process either at the beginning or at the end of the measurement period, all inputs (and therefore all costs) relate to the units *completed* during the period. Output is thus measured by the number of units completed.

If the process center has units in process at the end of a period, however, some of the inputs relate to these units, and the output figure should reflect both completed and uncompleted units. By a similar line of reasoning, if the process center started the measurement period with work already in process, the amount of work done on these units in the previous period must be subtracted from the number of units completed to get an output figure that is comparable to the costs of the period's inputs. In other words, output consists of all of the work done, and this may be greater or less than the number of units completed during the period.

For example, a fisherman who fills half of his basket has definitely accomplished something—half as much as if he had filled it to the top. In fact, he has had a good deal more success than his neighbor who came home with a full basket of fish, most of them bought on the pier from other fishermen.

Our two-department factory example can make this more specific. Department A started the month of June with no inventory in process. During the month it completed operations on 85,000 pounds of product and transferred this quantity to department B. In addition, it had 15,000 pounds of product in process at the end of the month. At first glance, the calculation of output seems easy:

Units completed......................................	85,000
Units still in process, end of month.....................	15,000
Total...	100,000

Unfortunately, this is incorrect. The units in process are not fully equivalent to completed units because some costs will still have to be incurred to complete them in the next period. Uncompleted units, in other words, should be counted only in proportion to the percentage of the required inputs that have already been expended on them.

In this case, department A had already applied all of the materials necessary to finish the uncompleted units, but only one third of the processing work had been done. Therefore:

1. With respect to *materials costs*, each pound of work in process at the end of the month was fully equivalent to a pound of finished product.
2. With respect to *processing costs*, each pound of work in process was equivalent to one third of a pound of finished product.

The cost divisor for materials costs, therefore, was 100,000 pounds, as calculated above, but the correct divisor for labor and other processing costs was only 90,000 pounds:

Units completed (pounds)..................................	85,000
Equivalent units in ending inventory (⅓ of 15,000 pounds)......	5,000
Unit cost divisor (pounds).................................	90,000

This 90,000-pound figure is also known as *equivalent production.*

The output calculation for department B is more complicated. This department completed work on 89,000 pounds of product during the month and transferred this amount to the finished goods warehouse. It also had 6,000 pounds of half-completed product in process at the end of the month. Unlike department A, however, department B began the month with an inventory of 10,000 pounds of product, half-processed in this department.

The divisor for materials costs is easy to calculate. Because "materials" in department B consist of the semifinished output of department A, units in process are always complete as to materials; that is, all of the basic materials that are necessary to a unit of finished product have already been applied in department A. The cost divisor is obtained by adding the number of units still in process at the end of the month to the number of units completed during the month and subtracting the number of units in beginning inventory:

Units completed (pounds)... 89,000
Units in ending inventory (pounds).............................. 6,000
                                                                 95,000
   Less: Units in beginning inventory (pounds)...................... 10,000
Materials cost divisor (pounds)................................... 85,000

The divisor for processing costs (including the costs of any processing materials added gradually during the production process in department B) is calculated in the same way, except that the inventory figures must be converted to their equivalent in finished units:

Units completed (pounds)... 89,000
Equivalent units in ending inventory ($\frac{1}{2}$ of 6,000 pounds)............. 3,000
                                                                 92,000
   Less: Equivalent of work done in prior period on beginning inventory
     ($\frac{1}{2}$ of 10,000 pounds)....................................... 5,000
Equivalent production (pounds).................................. 87,000

This is actually less than the number of units completed during the month because the amount of work in process decreased between the beginning and the end of the month. Another way of stating the same thing is that equivalent production equals the number of units completed plus or minus the change in work in process.

The rationale for this calculation is diagrammed in Exhibit 8–4. Of the 89,000 pounds completed during the month (upper block in the diagram), the equivalent of 5,000 pounds was actually produced during the previous month, and thus must be subtracted (unshaded area at the left of the block). This indicates that the work actually done during June on the units completed during the month was the equivalent of complete processing of 84,000 pounds of finished product (shaded area in the upper block). To this must be added the 3,000-pound equivalent

Exhibit 8–4

CALCULATION OF EQUIVALENT PRODUCTION

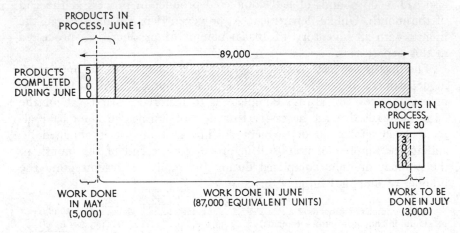

PRODUCTS IN PROCESS, JUNE 1

89,000

PRODUCTS COMPLETED DURING JUNE | 5000

PRODUCTS IN PROCESS, JUNE 30 | 3000

WORK DONE IN MAY (5,000)

WORK DONE IN JUNE (87,000 EQUIVALENT UNITS)

WORK TO BE DONE IN JULY (3,000)

of the inventory still in process at the end of the month, represented by the shaded area in the lower block of the exhibit. The total of these figures is equivalent production.

Computing Unit Cost

Calculating unit cost is a simple matter once the cost divisors have been computed. For example, department A's costs (from Exhibit 8–3) need only be divided by the divisors computed above:

	Total Cost	Divisor	Unit Cost
Raw materials.....................	$60,000	100,000	$0.60
Productive labor.................	20,700	90,000	0.23
Nonproductive labor..............	1,800	90,000	0.02
Overtime premiums.............	900	90,000	0.01
Supplies........................	2,700	90,000	0.03
Other costs.....................	9,900	90,000	0.11
Total.........................	$96,000		$1.00

The unit cost computation in department B is just as simple. This company charges department B at the full unit cost of $1 a pound for all products transferred to it. Once this has been done, unit costs in department B can be determined:

	Total Cost	Divisor	Unit Cost
Materials from dept. A............	$ 85,000	85,000	$1.00
Productive labor.................	8,700	87,000	0.10
Nonproductive labor.............	870	87,000	0.01
Overtime premiums..............	870	87,000	0.01
Supplies.......................	3,480	87,000	0.04
Other costs....................	7,830	87,000	0.09
Total.........................	$106,750		$1.25

Notice that materials, labor, and other processing costs of department A are merged in a single figure in department B. To department B's manager, these are just like the costs of any other materials he uses. If he spoils a unit, he loses the entire cost of that unit, and he doesn't care whether prior departments' labor costs amounted to 10 percent or 90 percent of the total.

This possibility of loss is the main reason for charging department B with the cost of materials received from prior departments. If department B had lost half of the units received from department A, for example, the unit cost on the top line of department B's cost summary would have gone up from $1 to $2 a pound:

$$\frac{\$85,000}{50 \text{ percent} \times 85,000 \text{ lbs.}} = \$2$$

The most accurate way to reflect this kind of shrinkage in unit cost is to transfer costs from process center to process center and recognize the loss in the process center in which it occurs.

Computing Product Cost

The procedure outlined in the preceding section is fully appropriate whenever the factory manufactures a single product which passes in a rigid sequence from one process center to another. Minor modifications are necessary, however, whenever individual process centers process more than one product, as in the bottom panel of Exhibit 8–2 above. This is possible as long as the center performs the same operation on each of the products that pass through it, even though the products themselves may differ widely in other respects.

In such cases, a separate line should be provided for the prior depart-

ment costs of each product. In this way, all products will enter into the
calculation of the average processing cost, but each product will retain
its own identity and its own unit cost. For example, if 50,000 units of
product X and 40,000 units of product Y are processed in department C
and then sent on their separate ways, department C's costs might be summarized in the following way:

	Total Cost	Unit Cost	
		Product X	Product Y
Costs from prior departments:			
Product X........	$ 80,000	$1.60	...
Product Y........	96,000	...	$2.40
Labor........................	72,000	0.80	0.80
Other processing costs...........	108,000	1.20	1.20
Total........................	$356,000	$3.60	$4.40

Processing cost is the same for each product, but total unit cost differs
because the unit costs of prior departments' work were different.

The Need for Additional Cost Divisors

This illustration has assumed that two cost divisors would suffice for
each department. This was based on two assumptions:

1. All the materials required for a unit of departmental output were
   placed in process at the same time, in this case at the beginning of
   processing in each department.
2. All departmental processing costs made their contribution to production in proportion to departmental labor, so that a single measure of
   degree of completion could be applied to all.

These assumptions are not always valid. For example, materials such
as containers may be added at the end of processing rather than at the
beginning. Furthermore, some processes have two or more processing
determinants. In processes in which products must age, for example, a
distinction must be made between those costs that relate to the amount
of physical work done on the products and those that relate to the
amount of time they have spent aging in the department. A separate de-
gree-of-completion figure can then be applied to each of these categories.

Lest all these calculations seem unduly formidable, it should be noted
that in many processes inventories are sufficiently stable to justify using
the number of units completed during the month as an approximate

measure of departmental ouput. This simplifies matters considerably in that it makes it unnecessary to calculate separate cost divisors for different cost elements. Care should be taken, however, to insure that the assumption is not applied when the number of equivalent units in inventory changes materially from one month to the next.

Departures from Output Homogeneity

Although process costing is strictly applicable only when departmental output is homogeneous with respect to departmental operations, it is nevertheless often applied when this condition is not met. For example, process costing would probably be used in a process center which is engaged in filling pint, quart, and gallon containers with three different types of liquids. The output in this case is not homogeneous, but it is close enough to it to justify the simplifying assumption that it is. Output can be measured either in gallons or in numbers of containers filled, depending on whether costs are more likely to be related to gallons or to the container count.

Whether the homogeneity assumption can be applied is of course a matter of judgment, and the tolerable limit of heterogeneity cannot be specified precisely. The main criterion is whether management loses significant information by not computing separate unit costs for separate products, information which cannot be obtained more cheaply in other ways. For the container-filling operation, for example, an inexpensive engineering study could probably provide adequate estimates of the differences in cost per gallon resulting from different container sizes or different liquid inputs. In other cases, subdivision of the process center into smaller, more homogeneous cost centers will be the answer. Job order costing should be adopted only as a last resort, because of its higher clerical cost and more complicated paper work.

Inventory Shrinkage or Growth

Until now we have assumed that in-process inventories could be measured in the same units as finished goods. Sometimes, however, inventories are subject to normal processing losses or shrinkage, so that a gallon of inventory will yield less than a gallon of finished product. Conversely, a gallon of work in process may yield two gallons of finished product through the later addition of water or other materials. Finally, finished products may be measured by weight or unit count while in-process units are measured by volume. Any of these situations requires the conversion of the inventory quantities to their normal equivalent in finished units.

For example, suppose that a process center finishes work on 120,000 gallons of product during the month and has 40,000 gallons of semiprocessed product in process at the end of the month. Under normal circumstances, inventory at this stage is expected to shrink by 25 percent before processing is completed. The appropriate figure to enter into the output calculation is thus 75 percent of 40,000 or 30,000 finished gallons. If the company figures that half of the department's work has been done on these in-process inventories, only 15,000 equivalent gallons should enter into the divisor for processing costs. In summary, assuming no beginning inventory, the cost divisors would be:

	Actual Gallons	Equivalent Materials	Equivalent Processing
Units completed...............	120,000	120,000	120,000
Units in process...............	40,000	30,000	15,000
Total......................	160,000	150,000	135,000

CONTROL USES OF PROCESS COSTING

Unit cost figures obtained by process costing techniques have the same application in inventory costing and decision making as those coming from job order costing. Because product cost in process costing is also

Exhibit 8–5

DEPARTMENTAL COST REPORT: PROCESS PRODUCTION

Cost Center: 5116—Coke Batteries					Month: October	
	Current Month, 44,000 Tons		Last Month, 40,000 Tons	Year Ago, 43,000 Tons	Year to Date	
Cost Item					This Year	Last Year
	Cost	Per Unit	Per Unit	Per Unit	Per Unit	Per Unit
Direct materials...........	$981,200	$22.30	$22.38	$21.98	$22.54	$21.65
Recoveries..............	(230,121)	(5.23)	(5.22)	(5.26)	5.58	5.41
Net direct materials........	$751,079	$17.07	$17.16	$16.72	$16.96	$16.24
Indirect materials..........	1,463	0.03	0.03	0.03	0.03	0.03
Fuels...................	79,538	1.81	1.77	1.75	1.76	1.68
Labor...................	13,251	0.30	0.31	0.26	0.31	0.27
Utilities.................	2,604	0.06	0.06	0.07	0.06	0.06
Services.................	41,623	0.95	1.05	0.88	1.03	0.85
Maintenance.............	5,190	0.12	0.13	0.16	0.11	0.12
Administrative...........	8,095	0.18	0.22	0.17	0.19	0.17
Total...................	$902,843	$20.52	$20.73	$20.04	$20.45	$19.42

departmental cost, however, unit product cost is often used to provide departmental information in ways that are not possible under job order costing.

An example of a process center control report is shown in Exhibit 8–5. In this exhibit, departmental costs are classified into several descriptive categories and a unit cost is computed for each. Extra columns are provided to show last-month, year-to-date, and prior-year figures. Space is usually added for explanations of important changes in the figures.

Such reports are an attention-getting device that may lead immediately to corrective action or eventually to decisions on changes in methods, equipment used, and so forth. They have a number of shortcomings, however. For one thing, the cost comparisons shown are entirely with the past, not with what is expected or what should have happened. This is not good control reporting unless it can be presumed that the prior-period figures represent a satisfactory level of cost performance for the current period.

Second, because many process center costs contain fixed elements, unit cost will fluctuate inversely with fluctuations in volume. These fluctuations in unit cost are not relevant to the process center manager because volume fluctuations are not ordinarily within his control.

Third, unit cost can change due to changes in the unit prices of productive inputs charged to the process center. These price changes can arise in three ways:

1. Changes in current purchase prices and wage rates.
2. Changes in the cost performance of prior process centers—an increase in unit materials cost, for example, may merely reflect an increase in the unit cost in a prior center rather than a poor materials yield in the process center being studied.
3. Changes due to the methods used to cost materials inventories—charges for materials costed on a Fifo basis, for example, can change from period to period even though purchase prices are currently stable.

Some means must be found for isolating the influences of these changes either from the accounts themselves or from the reports issued for control purposes. Various possibilities for accomplishing one or the other of these will be considered in later chapters.

ACCOUNTING FOR INTERDEPARTMENTAL TRANSFERS

The unit costing procedures described above can be applied either to historical costs or to estimates of future costs. Slightly different procedures may be used, however, to assign costs to units transferred from department to department, to finished goods inventory, and to the cost of goods sold accounts.

Why Special Calculations Are Needed

The reason why the above procedures may be modified for this purpose can be seen from a simple example. Suppose that department B's 10,000-pound opening inventory had a total materials cost of $10,500, based on the department's cost experience during the previous month. The total cost in this department's materials account would thus be as follows:

Costs of opening inventory	$10,500
Costs transferred from department A	85,000
Total cost to be accounted for	$95,500

If the $1 a pound cost computed for the month of June were to be applied both to the ending inventory and to the units finished during the month, only $95,000 would be accounted for:

Units finished (at $1 each)	$89,000
Units in ending inventory (at $1 each)	6,000
Total cost accounted for	$95,000

The $500 discrepancy between these two figures arises because the cost of the opening inventory was ignored in the unit cost calculation for June; yet these costs entered into the cost pool that had to be distributed.

The accountant has three main alternatives: (1) transfer the $500 difference to a nondepartmental expense account; (2) use a method of inventory bookkeeping that does take the beginning inventory into consideration; or (3) depart from historical costing entirely and cost both inventories and goods transferred at standard costs. The under- or over-absorbed balances that result from using the first of these alternatives are likely to be very small; therefore it can be adopted if it is more convenient than the others. To see why it might be more convenient, however, let us look briefly at two methods that do take opening inventory costs into consideration—the Fifo and moving average methods. We shall discuss the standard cost alternative in Chapter 15.

First-In, First-Out Method

Under Fifo inventory costing, beginning-of-month inventory cost balances are transferred to the next department as part of the cost of the first units completed during the month. For example, the cost of the

10,000-pound initial inventory in department B was $11,600, made up as follows.

	Per Unit	Total Cost
Materials*.....................	$1.05	$10,500
Processing....................	0.11	1,100
Total........................	$1.16	$11,600

* The correct title here would be "Semiprocessed Products Received from Department A," but because these semiprocessed products are really department B's materials, we shall use the simpler account title.

Completion of these units in June added another $1,250 to this total (the 10,000 pounds were half processed at June's average cost of $0.25 a pound). Thus under Fifo the first 10,000 units completed would lead to a transfer of $11,600 plus $1,250, or $12,850, to the finished goods inventory account.

The other 79,000 units completed would then be costed at the average cost for the month, or $1.25. The total cost of output transferred to finished goods therefore would be:

	First 10,000	Next 79,000	Total
Materials..............	$10,500	$79,000	$ 89,500
Processing............	2,350	19,750	22,100
Total................	$12,850	$98,750	$111,600

For convenience, no distinction would be made in finished goods inventories between the first 10,000 and the next 79,000 pounds of product. They would all be entered at an average cost of approximately $1.254 a pound ($111,600 divided by 89,000). This simplification would also be made if the work were transferred to another department rather than to finished inventories.

The inventory remaining in department B on June 30 would then be Fifo-costed at average cost for the month:

Materials: 6,000 lbs. at $1........................ $6,000
Processing: 6,000 lbs., half processed, at $0.125...... 750
Total..................................... $6,750

The cost distribution of department B could then be summarized as in Exhibit 8–6.

Exhibit 8-6

DISTRIBUTION OF PROCESS COSTS: FIFO METHOD

Costs of Department B

	Total Amount	Per Equivalent Pound
Costs in department:		
Materials:		
In process, 6/1...................	$ 10,500	$1.05
Received........................	85,000	1.00
Total.........................	$ 95,500	xxx
Processing costs:		
In process, 6/1...................	$ 1,100	$0.22
Labor...........................	8,700	0.10
Other...........................	13,050	0.15
Total.........................	$ 22,850	xxx
Total departmental cost...............	$118,350	xxx
Cost distribution:		
To finished products:		
Materials......................	$ 89,500	$1.006
Processing.....................	22,100	0.248
Total finished products..........	$111,600	$1.254
In process, 6/30:		
Materials......................	$ 6,000	$1.000
Processing.....................	750	0.125
Total in process, 6/30..........	$ 6,750	$1.125
Total cost distributed...............	$118,350	xxx

Moving Average Method

The calculation procedure can be simplified slightly by use of a single average (referred to below as a moving average) to apply to all products in a department during the month. For example, the total cost of materials in process in department B during June was $95,500 (opening balance plus $85,000 for materials received from department A during the month). Under the moving average method, this would be distributed evenly over the 95,000 pounds completed and still in process at the end of the month, at an average rate of $1.005 a pound:

Transferred, 89,000 pounds at $1.005.................	$89,445
In process, 6/30, 6,000 pounds at $1.005.............	6,030
Total...	$95,475

Due to the rounding error, this total is $25 less than the actual materials cost charged to the department. This could be eliminated by carrying the unit cost calculation to more decimal places or by adding or subtracting the rounding error in the amount transferred out or the amount remaining in process at month-end.

Similarly, the $22,850 in processing costs in department B's accounts would be divided between the 89,000 pounds transferred and the 6,000 pounds remaining in process. The unit cost divisor in this case would be 92,000 pounds, because the ending inventory was only half processed (89,000 pounds of fully completed products plus the equivalent of 3,000 pounds in the ending inventory). Average cost would be $0.248.

The processing cost to be transferred would thus be $22,072 (89,000 pounds × $0.248), leaving $778 as the cost of the ending inventory in process. These calculations are summarized in Exhibit 8–7.

Exhibit 8–7

DISTRIBUTION OF PROCESS COSTS: MOVING AVERAGE METHOD

Costs of Department B

	Total	Per Pound
Costs in department:		
Materials:		
In process, 6/1...............	$ 10,500	$1.05
Received................	85,000	1.00
Total................	$ 95,500	$1.005
Processing costs:		
In process, 6/1...............	$ 1,100	$0.22
Labor................	8,700	0.10
Other................	13,050	0.15
Total................	$ 22,850	$0.248
Total Department Cost...............	$118,350	$1.253
Cost distribution:		
To finished products:		
Materials................	$ 89,445	$1.005
Processing................	22,072	0.248
Total finished products..........	$111,517	$1.253
In process, 6/30:		
Materials................	$ 6,055	$1.005
Processing................	778	0.124
Total in process, 6/30..........	$ 6,833	$1.129
Total Cost Distributed...............	$118,350	xxx

The unit cost divisor under the moving average approach differs from equivalent production by the number of equivalent units in the opening inventory:

	Materials	Processing
Units completed during period	89,000	89,000
Plus: In process, end of period	6,000	3,000
Cost divisor, moving average	95,000	92,000
Less: In process, start of period	10,000	5,000
Equivalent production	85,000	87,000

The peculiarity of the average cost calculation is that the sum of the number of units finished and still in process at the *end* of the period is divided into the sum of the costs incurred during the period and the costs in process at the *beginning* of the period. The reason for this is that the latter sum reflects all of the costs while the former sum represents all of the units available to absorb these costs. Equivalent production, on the other hand, is used as a divisor for the current month's costs only, and this requires the subtraction of the opening inventory.

The differences between the moving average and Fifo methods should not be overstressed. The resultant unit costs will not depart materially from each other unless the production cycle is particularly long and monthly cost per unit of equivalent production changes rapidly. For this reason, the choice between the two ordinarily can be made on the basis of convenience. In any case, equivalent production is the only legitimate divisor in calculating current unit cost because it is the only one that measures the amount of work done, the amount for which the current period's costs were incurred.

SUMMARY

Whenever the output of a production center is sufficiently homogeneous to be measured in physical product units, unit cost can be determined by the process costing method. In process costing, unit cost is determined by dividing each cost center's costs by its output for a specified period of time.

The only difficult question is how to calculate output for this purpose. The solution is to group resource inputs into classes selected so that inputs in each class are applied at approximately the same stage of the production process. For each class, output is equal to the number of units finished by the process center during the period plus or minus the change in the number of equivalent finished units in process. If in-process inventories increase, then output is greater than the number of units finished, and vice versa.

The process costing procedure can also be used to prepare forecasts of unit costs for decision making. As we pointed out in Chapter 3, however, fixed costs may be wholly or partially sunk with respect to some decisions. Furthermore, the variable costs may not change in direct proportion to changes in volume, and average cost therefore may not be a very good measure of incremental cost.

EXERCISES AND PROBLEMS

1. Department A finished work on 50,000 units during April and transferred them to department B. On April 1, department A's inventory consisted of 15,000 units complete as to materials but only one-third processed. During April it received 58,000 unprocessed units from the storeroom, and on April 30, it had 24,000 units still in process, complete as to materials but only one-half processed.

Compute equivalent production figures for the month for materials and for processing costs.

2.* In a particular process, all materials are placed in production at the beginning of the process. The following data relate to the month of May:

```
Inventory in process, May 1..............   1,000 pounds, 40% complete
Placed in process.......................  10,000 pounds
Completed............................   9,000 pounds
Inventory in process, May 31.............    800 pounds, 60% complete
```

a) Compute unit cost divisors for the month for materials and for processing costs, in a form suitable for the application of Fifo inventory costing.

b) Make similar computations in a form suitable for the application of moving average inventory costing.

3.* The Stanley Chemical Company uses a process costing system of unit cost determination. The company's factory consists of two departments: raw materials are first mixed in the mixing department and then transferred to the refining department for completion. Units of product still in process in a department at the end of a month are assumed to be 100 percent complete as to materials and 50 percent complete as to processing costs in that department. The costs of units lost in production are to be spread evenly over equivalent good production in that department. You are given the following data for the month of January:

	Mixing	Refining
Quantities:		
In process, January 1...................	0	0
Transferred in......................	100,000	92,000
Transferred out.....................	92,000	80,000
In process, January 31.................	7,000	10,000
Lost in process.....................	1,000	2,000
Costs charged to department:		
Materials..........................	$ 49,500	$ 0
Labor.............................	57,300	42,500
Other processing costs...............	38,200	38,250
Total.......................	$145,000	$80,750

* Solutions to problems marked with an asterisk can be found in Appendix B.

Prepare a production cost summary and distribution sheet with two columns for each department, one for total costs and the other for unit costs. The upper part of the sheet should show the costs to be accounted for; the lower portion should show the division of these costs between the ending departmental inventories and the units transferred out during the month.

4. The Tawny Company's Albany factory has two departments, mixing and curing. Costs are accumulated in departmental accounts, and at the end of each month the goods transferred from mixing to curing and from curing to finished goods are costed at average cost for the month. The following information is available for the month of July:

	Mixing	Curing
Pounds of materials received:		
From storeroom (at $0.50 a pound)........	40,000	...
From mixing department...............	...	35,000
Pounds of product transferred out...........	35,000	25,000
Pounds of product in process, July 31........	5,000	10,000
Processing costs.........................	$15,500	$ 9,150

The ending inventory in the mixing department was three-quarters processed; the ending inventory in curing was half processed. Neither department had inventory in process on July 1.

a) Compute (1) materials cost per unit and (2) processing costs per unit for each department.
b) Prepare a table showing the costs to be accounted for in each department and how you would distribute these costs between the work completed and the work still in process at the end of the month.
c) Prepare a journal entry to record the transfer of costs from the mixing department to the curing department. Each department has two work-in-process accounts, one for materials and the other for processing costs.

5. The following costs were charged to process 2 of the H Company during July:

Costs transferred from process 1.........................$184,000
Materials added in process 2........................... 34,000
Processing costs...................................... 104,000

Production figures for the month for process 2 were:

Work in process, July 1...................... 2,000 pounds, 60% completed
Finished during July.........................20,000 pounds
Work in process, July 31.................... 5,000 pounds, 40% completed

Process 2 materials are not added to the semifinished product received from process 1 until the very end of processing in process 2. The work in process in process 2 on July 1 had a cost of $22,500.

a) Compute the number of equivalent units for the month, giving separate figures for materials and for processing costs.

b) Compute the July 31 cost of work in process and the cost of units transferred out of the process during July, using the first-in, first-out method.

6. Department X receives semiprocessed material from department W, processes it, and transfers its output to department Y for further processing. The materials received from department W are first subjected to heat, which reduces the moisture content. Weight losses during subsequent processing steps in this department are insignificant.

October 19x3 operations in department X are summarized by the following data:

Work in process, October 1, 19x3...................	None
Material received from department W...............	60,000 lbs. @ $1
Processing costs for the month:	
Processing materials............................	$13,500
Processing labor...............................	$40,500
Supervision...................................	$ 6,750
Other processing costs.........................	$15,750
Goods transferred to department Y..................	40,000 lbs.
Partially processed goods still in process, October 31, 19x3.......................................	10,000 lbs.

The goods still in process in department X on October 31 were approximately one-half processed in this department. (Note: All anticipated shrinkage due to weight loss had already occurred.)

a) Compute the unit cost to be assigned to goods transferred to department Y during the month.

b) Processing costs per unit in department X for selected prior months were as follows:

	Costs
September 19x3.........................	$1.78
August 19x3............................	1.74
July 19x3..............................	1.75
June 19x3..............................	1.68
October 19x2...........................	1.65
October 19x1...........................	1.55

What conclusions, if any, can you reach from these data as to the effectiveness of cost control in department X during October 19x3? What additional information, if any, would you like to have in using these unit cost figures for this purpose? Give your reasons.

7.* The Butts Company has a two-process factory in which all materials are placed in process in department A at the start of processing and semifinished products are transferred to department B for completion. No additional materials are introduced in department B. The following data relate to the month of June:

Department A:
  Beginning inventory (50 units, one-fourth completed): materials, $50; processing costs, $50.

Raw materials received during month (100 units), $100.
Processing costs incurred during month, $390.
Ending inventory: 60 units, one-third completed.

Department B:
   Beginning inventory (40 units, one-half completed): materials, $213;
      processing costs, $150.
   Processing costs incurred during month, $540.
   Ending inventory: 45 units, two-thirds completed.

No product units were lost in either department during the month.

a) Compute unit costs in each department for the month of June on a
   moving average basis.
b) Using these unit costs, determine the cost of the work still in process
   on June 30 and the cost of goods transferred out of each department
   during the month.

8. Materials are received in department A, processed, and then transferred
to department B, where final processing takes place. The following data relate
to the operations of department A for December:

	Quantity	Cost
Inventory in process, December 1:		
Materials.....................................	95 {	$ 228
Processing costs..............................		72
Materials added from stockroom..................	520	1,242
Processing costs...............................	...	528
Units completed and transferred to department B.....	310	?
Inventory in process, December 31:		
Materials.....................................	190 {	?
Processing costs..............................		?

All materials are placed in process at the start of processing—thus all work
in process is complete as to materials. A total shrinkage of 10 percent is regarded as normal in department A, however, and it is assumed that half of
the expected shrinkage has already taken place in the inventory in process at
any time.
   Inventory in process is assumed to be half processed in the department,
and the costs of lost units are to be spread over all equivalent good units
produced.

a) What is equivalent production for the month with respect to (1)
   materials and (2) processing costs?
b) Compute the unit costs that you would report to management to reflect
   the efficiency of the department's operations for the month.
c) Using the moving average method, compute the costs to be transferred
   to department B and the costs of work still in process in department A
   at the end of December.

9. The Andrews Metals Company operates two refining units of equal size, with identical equipment, paying identical wage rates. The following data relate to the operations of these two units during the month of September:

	Selby Mill	Franklin Mill
Quantities:		
Pounds in process, Sept. 1 (half completed)	9,800	8,400
Pounds received	78,000	52,000
Pounds refined, completed	60,000	37,500
Pounds in process, Sept. 30 (half completed)	7,700	9,800
Costs:		
Materials in process, Sept. 1	$ 8,000	$ 6,400
Processing costs in process, Sept. 1	7,000	5,600
Materials	75,311	49,536
Supervision	5,965	5,805
Operating labor	60,843	36,765
Depreciation	31,018	30,960
Scrap credit	(1,779)	(1,161)

A certain amount of shrinkage is expected in the refining process, inasmuch as the refined metal weighs less than the ore concentrate from which it is refined. This weight loss takes place continuously during processing and is assumed to be proportionate to the percentage of completion. For the purpose of costing materials in process, it is assumed that the refined metal constitutes 75 percent of the ore concentrate, by weight.

Prepare an analysis that will assist management in comparing the relative efficiency of the two plant managers in controlling operating costs. Indicate what additional information you would like to have, if any.

10. Factory department 67 makes an industrial chemical known as Monite. Monite's standard cost is $12 a gallon ($5.25 for materials, $4.25 for labor, and $2.50 for other processing costs), but these figures are obsolete and must be changed. The reason is that department 67 was recently closed down to permit the installation of new equipment which was expected to reduce costs substantially.

The new equipment was put into operation on a trial basis two months ago, but last month was the first full month under normal working conditions. Management is anxious to find out whether the anticipated reduction in operating costs was achieved. The following information is available:

(1) Inventory in process, beginning of month: 2,000 gallons, complete as to materials, half of processing work completed. Materials cost was $11,400; labor cost, $3,300; and other variable processing costs, $5,600.

(2) Operating costs charged to department 67 during the month: materials, $130,000; labor, $48,300; and other processing costs, $73,600.

(3) Amount of Monite finished during the month: 20,000 gallons.

(4) Inventory in process, end of month: 8,000 gallons, complete as to materials but only half of processing work completed.

a) If last month's costs were typical, did the introduction of the new equipment lead to lower unit cost? Compute unit cost for each group of costs to document your answer.

b) One of the company's cost analysts believes that this month's unit cost will be less than last month's. What good reasons can you advance to support this belief?

11.† Dashing Dachshund Dippers are made in two sequential processes, bristle toning and assembly. The bristle toning department manufactures bristle sets, while the assembly department assembles the final product. The data are:

Bristle toning department:
   Opening inventory: 400 units, 100 percent complete as to materials ($1,900) and 50 percent complete as to processing costs ($1,860).
   Units started during month: 3,150.
   Bristle sets completed and transferred to assembly: 3,000.
   Units spoiled: 50. This is considered normal; scrap recovery of $75 is credited against current period material cost.
   Closing inventory: 100 percent complete as to materials, 40 percent complete as to processing costs.
   Costs for the current period: materials, $9,375 (before credit for scrap recovery); labor, $6,000; other processing costs (variable), $4,500; other processing costs (fixed), $3,000.
   Unit costs are determined by the moving average method.

Assembly department:
   Opening inventory: 200 units, 100 percent complete as to materials ($5,300) and 25 percent complete as to processing costs ($975).
   Materials required in this process (per finished unit): two bristle sets from bristle toning; one bristle holder, at $3 (required at start of process).
   Units started: 1,500.
   Units transferred to finished goods: 1,500.
   Units spoiled: none.
   Closing inventory: 100 percent complete as to materials, 75 percent complete as to processing costs.
   Costs for the current period: materials, to be computed from data given above; labor, $8,000; other processing costs (variable), $6,400; other processing costs (fixed), $4,800.
   Ending inventories and transfers to finished goods are costed on a Fifo basis.

a) Prepare a production cost summary and distribution sheet for each department.

b) What unit costs should be reported to management as the costs of operations for the month? Should any distinction be made between fixed and variable costs in such calculations?

---

† Adapted from a problem by John C. Burton.

c) What are the shortcomings of these unit cost figures for managerial decision making?

12. In recent months, the Vyberg Company has been unable to satisfy all of its customers' demands for Vylac, an industrial chemical manufactured in the company's Rochester plant. To meet these demands, a second set of Vylac processing facilities is now under construction at the company's Chicago factory, and these facilities are expected to go on stream in six or seven months.

The new facilities will give the company more production capacity than Vylac's present users can possibly take. In fact, management's decision to build the new facilities was predicated on the marketing director's assurance that he could find and develop additional profitable markets for this product. He has now come up with several suggestions, and you have been asked to assist management by estimating Vylac's unit cost.

Vylac is now manufactured in department 423 in the Rochester plant. Production facilities in this department are used exclusively for the manufacture of this product. Vylac is produced by mixing three materials (designated A, B, and C for easy reference here), heating the mixture under pressure in the presence of a catalyst, cooling it, and filtering out impurities. The finished product is then pumped into storage tanks for later packaging or shipment in bulk containers.

You have begun your investigation by collecting cost and output data from the Rochester plant records. Because the several steps in the manufacturing process take place in a continuous sequence, the process has always been treated as a single operation for product costing purposes. The following information on last month's operations has been made available to you:

Costs charged to department:
Material A, 10,000 pounds	$ 20,800	⎫
Material B, 1,000 gallons	5,200	⎬ 53,300
Material C, 4,000 gallons	27,300	⎭
Labor and other processing costs	48,000	
Total input costs	$101,300	

Quantities (gallons of Vylac):
In process, beginning of month	4,000
Finished and pumped into storage tanks	48,000
In process, end of month	8,000

Because processing starts when the raw materials are put into the mixing tanks, no additional materials are ever needed to complete the units that are in process in this department at any time. You also find that approximately half of the processing work had already been performed on the units in process in this department at the beginning and end of last month. Finally, a check of the accounts reveals that the work in process in this department at the beginning of last month was carried at a total materials cost of $4,000 and a total processing cost of $1,800.

The facilities at Chicago will be almost identical to those at Rochester, and the engineers see no reason why costs in the two plants should be very far apart once the new plant has gone through the shakedown stage, as long as production volumes are comparable.

a) Compute unit cost for last month.

b) Indicate how you think management might use these unit cost figures. Identify any additional information that you think would make the unit cost figures more useful. How, if at all, would you change the unit cost calculations?

13. A process takes basic raw materials, heats them under pressure, and then combines them with a bonding material to produce a heavy-duty adhesive. One half pound of raw material and one half pound of bonding material are necessary for every pound of finished adhesive.

The entire process takes three hours. The materials neither gain nor lose weight during the first two hours. At the end of that time the bonding material is added. No further weight gain or loss takes place after the addition of the bonding material. This means that if the flow of work is uniform, one third of the units in process at any time will be full-weight units and two thirds will be half-weight units.

The following data apply to the month of August.

Quantities:

Work in process, August 1........................	3,000 pounds
Finished during the month.....................	12,000 pounds
Work in process, August 31...................	6,000 pounds

Costs:

Work in process, August 1:	
Raw materials.............................	$ 9,630
Bonding material.........................	3,900
Processing costs..........................	1,755
Materials received during the month:	
Raw materials.............................	33,000
Bonding material.........................	40,500
Processing costs for the month................	14,250

a) Compute the divisors that you would use in determining average operating cost for the month for each of the three cost components. Unit costs are to be average costs per unit of finished product. The flow of work was uniform throughout the month.

b) Prepare a cost summary and cost distribution sheet for the month. The moving average method is used to account for in-process inventories and units transferred to the finished goods stockroom.

14.† The King Process Company manufactures one product, putting it through two processes—No. 1 and No. 2.

For each pound of process No. 1 output, two units of raw material X are put in at the start of processing. For each gallon of process No. 2 output, three cans of raw material Y are put in at the end of processing. Two pounds of process No. 1 output are placed at the start of process No. 2 for each gallon of finished goods started. Spoilage generally occurs in process No. 2 when processing is approximately 50 percent complete, and the costs of the

---

† Adapted from a uniform CPA examination.

spoiled units are assigned to the good units produced during the period. The recovery value of spoiled units is deducted from prior department costs.

The company uses Fifo for inventory costing for process No. 1 and finished goods, and moving average cost for inventory costing for process No. 2. Separate accounts are maintained for each process for (1) raw materials, (2) processing costs, and (3) prior department costs (costs of semiprocessed products received by process No. 2 from process No. 1).

Data for March:

(1) Units transferred:
      From process No. 1 to process No. 2: 2,200 pounds.
      From Process No. 2 to finished goods: 900 gallons.
      From finished goods to cost of goods sold: 600 gallons.
(2) Raw material unit costs: X, $1.51 per unit; Y, $2 per can.
(3) Processing costs: process No. 1, $3,344; process No. 2, $4,010.
(4) Spoilage recovery, $100.
(5) Inventory data:

	Process No. 1		Process No. 2		Finished Goods	
	Initial	Final	Initial	Final	Initial	Final
Units of product.........	200 lbs.	300 lbs.	200 gal.	300 gal.	700 gal.	1,000 gal.
Fraction complete, processing costs......	½	⅓	½	⅔		
Cost:					$13,300	
Materials.............	$560		0			
Processing costs.......	$108		$ 390			
Prior department costs............	0		$2,200			

a) Compute unit cost, element by element, for each process.
b) Compute the cost of the March 31 inventory in each process and in finished goods.
c) Compute the effect of spoilage on unit cost in process No. 2. Do you agree with the company's practice of including the cost of spoiled units in the cost of the good units produced? Give your reasons.
d) Compute the amount of cost to be transferred from process No. 1 to process No. 2 and from process No. 2 to finished goods. Prepare journal entries to record these transfers.

chapter **9**

Product Costing:
The Variable Costing Concept

Product cost can be measured on either a full costing or a variable costing basis. The measurements in the preceding chapters reflected the full costing or absorption costing concept—that is, product cost included provisions for all elements of factory cost. Variable costing systems, in contrast, include some factory costs in measures of product cost and exclude others. The purpose of this chapter is to study the advantages and disadvantages of variable costing relative to the older full costing concept.

THE NATURE OF VARIABLE COSTING

Product cost measured on a variable costing basis includes only those factory costs that vary in response to short-run changes in the rate of production. Fixed manufacturing costs are ordinarily excluded from product cost completely, although in some dual systems both variable cost and full cost are computed.

Application to Job Order Costing

Variable costing differs from full costing in job order costing only in the treatment of overhead. Direct labor and direct materials are typically assumed to be fully variable with volume and therefore are assigned to product units in the manner described in Chapter 5. In fact, some costs that could be treated as direct labor or direct materials are often transferred to overhead at least partly because they are not proportionally variable. Extra pay for second- and third-shift work is a case in point.

Thus direct labor and direct materials are often proportionally variable, by definition as well as by assumption. Factory overhead is then included in product cost by means of burden rates that cover only the variable components of the overhead cost elements.

For example, suppose that departmental volume is measured in machine-hours and departmental overhead costs are expected to vary as follows:

	Fixed per Month	Variable per Machine-Hour
Supervision....................	$1,400	....
Indirect labor...................	.....	$0.10
Indirect materials...............	.....	0.05
Maintenance....................	100	0.08
Power........................	.....	0.02
Total........................	$1,500	$0.25

In this case the burden rate would be 25 cents a machine-hour. A job order requiring 10 machine-hours in this department would be charged $2.50 (10 hours × $0.25) for variable overhead, and no charge would be made for any portion of the $1,500 in fixed cost.

Notice the treatment of maintenance costs. Maintenance costs in this case are semivariable, with a minimum monthly expenditure of $100 plus increments of $0.08 a machine hour in response to the use of the department's equipment. The variable and fixed components cannot be recorded separately because the accountant has no way of labeling a particular maintenance expenditure as fixed or variable. Fortunately, this is no barrier to variable costing. Since the burden rate is predetermined, the only requirement is that a rate of variability can be calculated for each cost element, in this case $0.08 for maintenance cost.

Application to Process Costing

One way of applying the variable costing concept to process production is to divide each production center's cost elements into two groups—fixed and variable—and compute unit cost only for the variable elements. This is probably the most common method of application.

To illustrate, Exhibit 9–1 shows the calculation of unit cost in the mixing and grinding department of a cement mill. Eight cost elements are classified as variable, and an average unit cost is computed for each element each month. The fixed costs, however, are not averaged over the units produced.

The output figures used in this kind of calculation are measured in the

Exhibit 9–1

DEPARTMENTAL COST REPORT: VARIABLE COSTING BASIS

DEPT.   Mixing and Grinding
PRODUCTION   201,000 Bbls.   MONTH OF   November

	This Month		Prior Period Unit Cost	
	Total Cost	Unit Cost	Last Month	Last Year
Variable costs:				
Direct labor............	$ 6,541	$0.0327	$0.0329	$0.0304
Indirect labor*.........	303	0.0015	0.0024	0.0018
Payroll charges........	1,298	0.0065	0.0066	0.0056
Fuel and water.........	2,527	0.0126	0.0119	0.0115
Light and power.......	9,806	0.0490	0.0486	0.0487
Grinding supplies........	953	0.0048	0.0049	0.0046
Dust collector.........	427	0.0021	0.0011	0.0015
Total variable........	$21,855	$0.109	$0.108	$0.104
Fixed costs:				
Supervision.............	$ 712			
Maintenance labor.......	2,299			
Maintenance materials....	1,956			
Total fixed..........	$ 4,967			

* All labor is traceable to the department and thus is direct labor, as that term has been defined here. This company uses the term to identify those classes of work performed directly in production, while indirect labor is identified as the costs of miscellaneous departmental chores such as cleaning and messenger work.

way described in the last chapter. The only difference is that the cost divisors are applied solely to the variable cost elements.

Handling Semivariable Costs

The main defect with the method just described is that it doesn't provide for semivariable costs. When these are material in amount, the correct approach is to use a predetermined burden rate, at least for those components of cost that cannot reasonably be assumed to be completely and proportionately variable. Exhibit 9–2 illustrates how this change might affect unit costing in the cement mill's mixing and grinding department. One item previously classified as variable has now been reclassified as semivariable on the ground that it includes a fixed cost component, while two items not previously included in product cost have been moved from the fixed to the semivariable category. For each element, actual costs for the month are shown for the information of the department head, but the unit cost figures shown in this section of the exhibit are predetermined and represent the variable component only. They do not reflect the current month's cost experience in any way.

Exhibit 9–2

VARIABLE UNIT REPORT USING PREDETERMINED
RATES FOR SEMIVARIABLE COST ELEMENTS

DEPT. Mixing and Grinding PRODUCTION 201,000 Bbls.			MONTH OF November	
	This Month		Prior Period Unit Cost	
	Total Cost	Unit Cost	Last Month	Last Year
Variable costs:				
Direct labor............	$ 6,541	$0.0327	$0.0329	$0.0304
Indirect labor...........	303	0.0015	0.0024	0.0018
Payroll charges.........	1,298	0.0065	0.0066	0.0056
Fuel and water..........	2,527	0.0126	0.0119	0.0115
Grinding supplies........	953	0.0048	0.0049	0.0046
Dust collector..........	427	0.0021	0.0011	0.0015
Total variable........	$12,049	$0.060	$0.059	$0.055
Semivariable costs:				
Light and power........	$ 9,806	$0.042*		
Maintenance labor.......	2,299	0.005*		
Maintenance materials....	1,956	0.009*		
Total semivariable.....	$14,061	$0.056*		
Total product cost........	xxx	$0.116		
Fixed costs:				
Supervision.............	$ 712			

* Predetermined rates for variable component only.

The unit cost figure of $0.116 a barrel is a hybrid: partly predetermined and partly based on cost performance for the month. This makes it very similar to unit cost under job order costing, in which actual direct labor and materials costs are mingled with overhead applied on the basis of predetermined burden rates.

Handling Step Functions

Cost functions are seldom as simple as the previous illustrations have implied, although often we don't know enough about them to specify more complex relationships with any confidence.

Suppose, however, that a department's overhead costs are expected to vary as shown in the upper portion of Exhibit 9–3. This is a form of step function, in which some elements of cost vary discontinuously with volume, going up in irregular steps. Most authorities would agree that these steps should be reflected in the variable cost burden rate, and this

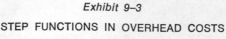

Exhibit 9–3

STEP FUNCTIONS IN OVERHEAD COSTS

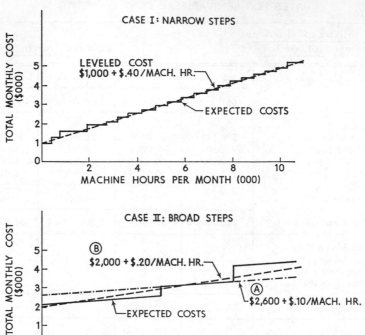

is shown as a dashed line in the exhibit. The slope of this line represents the average rate of variability within the normal limits of volume variation—in other words, the variable overhead cost burden rate. In this case the burden rate is 40 cents a machine-hour.

The situation represented in the lower half of Exhibit 9–3 is not as clear-cut. For fairly large ranges of volume variation, the rate of cost variability is represented by the slope of line *A*. If the entire volume span from zero to capacity is included, however, the leveled cost line would be the one labeled *B* and the rate of cost variability would be twice as high, 20 cents a machine-hour instead of 10 cents.

Most advocates of variable costing would probably use line *A* in a case of this sort, on the grounds that average variable cost figures are typically applied to decisions encompassing fairly small increments in operating volume, and that averaging the step functions would cloud the meaning of unit cost when the steps are this large.

Terminology: Variable Costing versus Direct Costing

Product costing systems of the kind just described are generally referred to as *direct costing* systems. This is unfortunate. By definition, a direct cost is a traceable cost, and the term direct costing therefore should be reserved for systems which base product cost on the costs that are traceable to the production centers that the product passes through.

Some direct costing systems do in fact equate product cost with the costs specifically traceable to production centers, and the term direct costing is appropriate. Others, however, do try to include provisions for variable overheads that are not specifically traceable to direct production centers and exclude traceable fixed costs. These are true variable costing systems, and should be described as such.

THE CASE FOR VARIABLE COSTING

The proponents of variable costing generally rest their case on three main premises:

1. Average variable cost is the relevant measure of incremental cost for most short-run decision models.
2. Incremental cost estimates are easier to derive under variable costing than under full costing even when average variable cost is not the relevant cost figure.
3. Variable costing makes for easier, clearer cost and profit forecasting.

Relevance of Average Variable Cost

Many types of managerial decisions require comparisons of the profitability of different methods of utilizing existing capacity. These are known as short-run decisions. Most short-run decision models are based on the presumption that the only relevant costs are the variable costs. In fact, economic theory defines fixed costs as those that do not change at all in response to short-run changes in the level of activity as long as physical capacity remains unchanged.

Most decision models go one step further and presume that average variable cost for each product is constant, that is, that total variable cost varies proportionately with variations in physical volume. Variable costing provides cost data in a form that matches this assumption; full costing does not. Under absorption costing, the only way to get the data upon which to base such estimates is to go back to the data from which unit costs were prepared and try to extract the fixed components.

The importance of this point became painfully evident to the manager of the machinery products division of a well-known company some years ago. He had a chance to manufacture two prototype units of a new kind of heavy-duty gearbox that one of his customers was experimenting with. He was told that he could have the order if he would quote a price of $8,000 a unit, or $16,000 in total. He made the following cost calculation for the two units combined:

Materials and purchased parts	$ 3,300
Setup labor	800
Production labor	4,680
Factory overhead	9,140
Total cost	$17,920
Minimum profit margin	1,792
Minimum price	$19,712

He told the customer that he would take on the job, but only if the price could be raised to $9,856 a unit, or $19,712 for the two. The customer rejected this offer and had the prototype units manufactured elsewhere.

Variable costing figures would have provided better guidance in this situation. After this incident, the division's accountants were put to work dividing the departmental burden rates into fixed and variable components. Using just the variable components, the revised cost estimate for the prototype units was as follows:

Materials and purchased parts	$ 3,300
Setup labor	800
Production labor	4,680
Variable factory overhead	3,890
Total cost	$12,670

The division's factory had ample capacity to take on this small order and the fixed costs would have been unaffected by it. The company's incentive to accept this order therefore would have been clearly indicated by a comparison between the offered price and the variable costs:

$$\text{Incremental profit} = \$16,000 - \$12,670 = \$3,330$$

Easier Cost Estimation

The second argument for variable costing is that it serves as a clearer, less ambiguous base on which to build estimates of incremental costs when fixed costs are likely to change. In other words, it makes the simplifying assumption that average variable cost is an acceptable approximation of incremental variable cost, but it forces the analyst to make specific, explicit assumptions in each case about the impact of the decision on fixed costs.

For example, suppose that product X is expected to have the following costs at a normal volume of 100,000 units a month:

	Total Amount	Unit Cost
Variable costs:		
Manufacturing..........................	$40,000	$0.40
Selling and administrative................	5,000	0.05
Total variable.......................	$45,000	$0.45
Fixed costs:		
Manufacturing..........................	10,000	0.10
Selling and administrative................	10,000	0.10
Total cost............................	$65,000	$0.65

The product sells for $1, and therefore the difference between price and variable cost is $0.55 a unit. This is the *variable profit* or *P/V income* (P/V stands for profit/volume).

Because a 55 percent variable profit ratio is quite high, management has asked for an analysis of the profitability of efforts to expand sales volume. Marketing management feels that it would be feasible to increase its selling effort substantially, increasing fixed selling and administrative costs to $18,000 a month. This would increase sales by 30 percent, to 130,000 units a month, with no reduction in selling price. Factory management says that although a 30 percent increase in volume is feasible without additional investment in production facilities, factory fixed costs would go up by $1,000 a month.

If the company uses variable costing, the anticipated effect of this decision can be shown directly, without confusion:

	Present Effort	Expanded Effort	Change
Sales.........................	$100,000	$130,000	+$30,000
Variable expenses...............	45,000	58,500	+ 13,500
Variable profit....................	$ 55,000	$ 71,500	+$16,500
Fixed costs.....................	20,000	29,000	+ 9,000
Product profit....................	$ 35,000	$ 42,500	+$ 7,500

In absorption costing, in contrast, this increment would be derived by first obtaining net product margin and then adjusting this for differences in under- or overabsorption of fixed costs. Absorption costing works with full cost averages, and the derivation of increments from such data can be extremely difficult.

Variable costing makes for greater clarity in still another way. Suppose, for example, that product X is a component part of a number of the company's other products. The cost assigned to product X will thus become part of the direct materials costs of these other products. If product costing is on a full costing basis, then materials costs will be measured at 50 cents a unit—40 cents for the variable component and 10 cents for the fixed. As direct materials, however, the entire 50 cents will be thought of as a variable cost of the ultimate end-product. In other words, by a touch of the pen, the accountant has performed the modest miracle of converting 10 cents of fixed costs into variable costs. Variable costing avoids this kind of error and the confusion it can lead to.

Better Focus on Profit Variability

The third argument for variable costing is that it gives management a clearer view of the effect of changes in volume on the company's profits. Take product X, for example. Under variable costing, profit forecasts at three different volumes would take the following form:

	60,000 Units	100,000 Units	120,000 Units
Sales revenues..............................	$60,000	$100,000	$120,000
Variable expenses (45 percent)..............	27,000	45,000	54,000
Variable profit.............................	$33,000	$ 55,000	$ 66,000
Fixed costs...............................	20,000	20,000	20,000
Product profit.............................	$13,000	$ 35,000	$ 46,000

Unlike the previous illustrations, this table does not represent the effects of three alternative company decisions; instead, it permits an examination of the implications of the uncertainty inherent in sales volume forecasts for a given set of marketing and pricing policies.

The same results could be achieved under full costing, but at the price of accepting some technical jargon:

	60,000 Units	100,000 Units	120,000 Units
Sales.....................................	$60,000	$100,000	$120,000
Less:			
Manufacturing cost (50%)...............	$30,000	$ 50,000	$ 60,000
Selling and administrative expense ($10,000 @ 5%)...........................	13,000	15,000	16,000
Under(over)absorbed factory overhead.....	4,000	....	(2,000)
Total expense.......................	$47,000	$ 65,000	$ 74,000
Product profit............................	$13,000	$ 35,000	$ 46,000

The under(over)absorbed factory overhead item is a hard one to compute when each factory produces many different products, and is even harder to explain to nonaccountants.

One point should be emphasized at this point. Even though variable costing does not assign fixed costs to products, it does not ignore them. In fact, variable costing can be said to give more prominence to the fixed costs than absorption costing systems. Profit forecasts under variable costing show the total amount of fixed cost that must be covered. This serves not only to dramatize the relative significance of fixed costs but also to point out the effects of decisions which establish them. In absorption costing they are buried.

ARGUMENTS AGAINST VARIABLE COSTING

While there are those who maintain that cost estimates for short-run decisions should reflect the full costing concept, most of the opposition to variable costing focuses on two arguments:

1. Average full cost is a better measure of the amount of resources consumed in manufacturing the product, and thus is more relevant to decisions that have relatively long time horizons, particularly product pricing, marketing policy, and capacity expansion or contraction problems.
2. The use of variable cost figures will lead to product selling prices that are lower than their profit-maximizing level.

Relevance to "Long-Run" Decisions

Average variable cost is ordinarily a poor measure of the long-run cost effect of adding or dropping a product or of expanding or contracting its volume by large percentages. This leads some to conclude that full cost figures should be used instead. The idea is that, given a large enough change in volume and enough time to adjust to the new situation, total cost will vary in direct proportion to changes in operating volumes and average cost will remain constant.

Two factors stand in the way of this happy solution. The first of these is cost *indivisibility*, stemming from the availability of certain resources in large aggregates only. In one company's maintenance shop, for example, a reduction of 90 percent in the work load would not have permitted the disposal of a single piece of equipment—each piece had to be available to do its own specialized work whenever an emergency arose. The cost of keeping these machines in working order was thus an indivisible cost.

Indivisibilities lead to lower average costs for higher rates of utilization of the indivisible elements and incremental costs that are less than average costs—the more highly indivisible the fixed cost, the farther the increment will be from the average. For example, if average fixed cost amounts to $10 and none of the fixed costs is divisible, then the average will be a very poor approximation of incremental cost; incremental fixed cost will be zero, not $10. If 90 percent of the fixed costs are proportionately divisible, however, average fixed cost will only overstate the increment by $1.

The second factor that leads incremental cost away from average cost is that changes in capacity change not only the total but the structure of the fixed costs. Average fixed costs will decline as capacity increases, at least up to a point, not only because the indivisible cost elements are spread over larger and larger volumes but also because larger volumes permit the company to change the technology being employed. Adding machines give way to bookkeeping machines and bookkeeping machines to computers.

Economists have speculated for many decades on the effect on average cost of changes in capacity. They have assumed that this average cost will decrease as capacity increases up to some point, after which it will tend to increase. Some empirical studies have tended to support this assumption; none has disproved it.[1] If the assumption is valid, then, the *long-run marginal cost*—the change in total cost resulting from a change in the scale of operations—is not constant.

Full cost, in other words, is useful for decision making only if it approximates long-run marginal cost, and most evidence seems to indicate that the long-run cost curve is not sufficiently linear to justify this assumption.

These two difficulties are compounded by the difficulty of measuring average fixed cost. For one thing, not all of the fixed costs that are assigned to individual production centers can be traced unequivocably to those centers. We shall deal with this problem at length in the next chapter, but we might as well admit right here that allocations of non-traceable fixed costs are seldom meaningful and always suspect.

Even if departmental fixed cost could be measured precisely, average cost would still be imprecise. An average always represents conditions at one particular activity level, and it is difficult to identify the activity level at which average cost is equal to long-run marginal cost. In fact, it is highly unlikely that many accountants try. Thus even if the firm is operating in a volume range in which long-run marginal cost is approximately constant, full cost cannot be assumed to be equal to long-run marginal cost.

---

[1] Two summaries of empirical studies in this area are to be found in P. J. D. Wiles, *Price, Cost, and Output* (Oxford: Basil Blackwell & Mott, Ltd, 1956), chap. 12, Appendixes A and B; and J. Johnston, *Statistical Cost Analysis* (New York: McGraw-Hill Book Co., 1960), chap. 5.

The Concept of Attributable Cost

Ideally, for the reasons outlined earlier, incremental fixed cost ought to be estimated explicitly for each decision. Time is often too short, however, to permit the analyst to examine every cost element in every cost center; a ready-made figure is useful to have around. In fact, this is exactly how full costing was born and why it has stayed around for so long.

Probably the major defect of full cost for this purpose is its slavish and totally unnecessary adherence to the concept of *complete cost distribution*, which means that every factory cost should be assigned to one product or another. A better approach is to substitute another concept, the concept of attributable cost.[2] Attributable cost is the amount of cost that could be eliminated if the company were to discontinue a given cost center, activity, or product, given enough time to make the transition from the present level of activity to zero.

The original notion of full cost was probably something like this before someone decided that it also had to lead to a 100 percent distribution of factory costs. That is, full cost ought to measure the amount of cost that the company would not have incurred if the product had never been part of the company's cost structure. Thus a cost center's burden rate would show, on the average, how much of the factory's overhead costs were incurred because that cost center was there—and would not have been incurred if the cost center had never been part of the operation.

Application of this concept is likely to lead to burden rates that, taken together, are inadequate to absorb all factory overhead at normal volume. The reason is that most factories enjoy some of the benefits of economies of scale, so that additional activities can be introduced without a proportional increase in key capacity-producing costs.

Basically, the cost elements that create the possibility of economies of scale are the indivisible fixed costs. They are charges against all of the factory's operations as a group, but not against any single operation. To implement the attributable costing concept, therefore, the company should include in the burden rate not only the short-run variable costs but also those fixed costs that are significantly divisible; in other words, those that rise in steps in the manner illustrated in the lower half of Exhibit 9–3.

For example, assume that a department with a normal operating volume of 10,000 machine-hours has the following budgeted costs at normal volume:

---

[2] For a lengthier discussion of this concept, see Gordon Shillinglaw, "The Concept of Attributable Cost," *Journal of Accounting Research*, Spring 1963, pp. 73–85.

	Total Cost per Month	Normal Cost per Hour
Variable costs.........................	$3,000	$0.30
Divisible fixed costs.....................	2,000	0.20
Indivisible fixed costs...................	1,000	0.10

A full cost burden rate would be 60 cents a machine-hour, while a rate based on attributable cost would be 50 cents and a rate for the variable costs would be only 30 cents.

Attributable cost is not necessarily a good measure of long-run marginal cost, but it is likely to be closer to measuring the cost impact of certain classes of decisions than either full cost or average variable cost. For example, the quality control staff may be entirely salaried, and the program's cost may be regarded as entirely fixed, but a significant change in production volume will almost unquestionably lead to a change in total quality control costs as the size of the inspection force is increased or decreased.

Once again, attributable cost should not be regarded as an all-purpose measure of incremental cost. If the decision is important enough to warrant a full-scale investigation of cost effects, the assumption that divisible fixed costs will vary roughly in proportion to volume needs to be questioned. For other decisions, however, it can be used as an approximation that is accurate enough in the circumstances.

Suboptimization under Variable Costing

At the beginning of this section we noted that the opponents of variable costing advance two main arguments in support of their position. The second of these is that variable costing will encourage management to reduce prices in order to expand volume, and that they will carry this to such a point that company profits will suffer—that is, unit margins will not be offset by a great enough increment in total sales volume.

We are in no position to evaluate this claim. We do know that it is accepted as gospel truth by many intelligent executives, but no survey or experiment has ever been made to authenticate it in the general case. Even if the claim is true, however, it would seem that the fault lies in the company's pricing system rather than in the costing base. The accountant's job is to give management the best cost data within his means; management must then decide how best to use these data in pricing.

We do not intend to dodge the issue of how costs should be used in product pricing. In fact, the issue is so important that one entire chapter is devoted to it. To avoid duplication, therefore, we shall put this argument aside for the moment and finish it when we get to Chapter 27.

VARIABLE COSTING AND EXTERNAL REPORTING

The objective of variable costing is to provide product unit costs for use by management. It was not designed to provide data for public financial reporting and in fact has been specifically rejected for this purpose by the bulk of the accounting profession. The following statement of a committee of the American Accounting Association is representative: ". . . the cost of a manufactured product is the sum of the acquisition costs reasonably traceable to that product and should include both direct and indirect factors. *The omission of any element of manufacturing cost is not acceptable.*"[3] Variable costing for public financial reporting does have its supporters, however, and this section will be devoted to examining the implications of this possibility.

Effects on Reported Income

Variable costing income can differ from absorption costing income for a number of reasons. The only factor that is likely to cause a material difference, however, is a disparity between production and sales.

To begin with, let us assume that a company manufactures only one product. Normal production volume is 50,000 units a year at an average fixed cost of 25 cents a unit. Variable costs are a constant 75 cents a unit. The cost figures at normal volume are:

	Total	Per Unit
Variable manufacturing costs................	$37,500	$0.75
Fixed manufacturing costs..................	12,500	0.25
Total.....................................	$50,000	$1.00

Let us also assume that this formula applies at all volumes; that is, the company's factory cost total can always be determined from the following formula:

$$\text{Total factory cost} = \$12,500 + \$0.75 \times \text{units manufactured}$$

The following production and sales figures were recorded during three successive periods:

---

[3] Committee on Accounting Concepts and Standards, "Accounting and Reporting Standards for Corporate Financial Statements: 1957 Revision," *Accounting Review,* Vol. 32 (October 1957), p. 539 (italics added). Two members of the committee dissented from this portion of the statement.

	Units Manufactured	Units Sold
Period 1......	50,000	50,000
Period 2......	55,000	47,000
Period 3......	44,000	52,000

Period 1: Production Equals Sales. Under absorption costing, the cost of goods sold is determined by multiplying sales volume by the full unit cost at normal volume. In this case, during period 1:

$$\text{Cost of goods sold} = 50,000 \times \$1 = \$50,000$$

The amount of cost absorbed by production is determined by multiplying production volume by full unit cost at normal volume, in this case $1. At this rate the production volume of 50,000 units would have just absorbed the $50,000 in factory cost that was normal at this volume.

Under variable costing, all fixed factory overhead costs are treated as period costs; they are taken directly to the corporate income statement as expenses of the current period, without passing through product inventory accounts. Thus the income statement for period 1 would show the following manufacturing costs:

Variable cost of goods sold (50,000 × $0.75)...................	$37,500
Fixed factory costs..	12,500
Total costs shown as expense...............................	$50,000

In other words, $50,000 of manufacturing costs would appear on the income statement under either system. Assuming a selling price of $1.20 a unit and no selling and administrative expenses at all, revenues would be $60,000 and net income in both cases would be $10,000.

Period 2: Production Exceeds Sales. In period 2, production of 55,000 units exceeded sales by 8,000 units, and these excess units were in the finished goods inventory at the end of the period. Production costs were at the levels anticipated for this volume of production:

$$\text{Total factory cost} = \$12,500 + 55,000 \times \$0.75 = \$53,750$$

Production absorbed $41,250 in variable costs (55,000 × $0.75) and $13,750 in fixed costs (55,000 × $0.25). Under absorption costing, in other words, fixed costs would be overabsorbed by $1,250:

Absorbed fixed costs................................	$13,750
Actual fixed costs..................................	12,500
Overabsorbed fixed costs............................	$ 1,250

Again assuming a selling price of $1.20 and no selling and administrative expenses, the absorption costing income statement for period 2 would show the following:

Sales (47,000 units @ $1.20)...................................		$56,400
Cost of goods sold:		
Cost of goods manufactured:		
Variable costs @ $0.75..................................	$41,250	
Fixed costs @ $0.25....................................	13,750	
	$55,000	
Less: Ending inventory (8,000 units @ $1).................	8,000	
Cost of goods sold....................................		47,000
Gross margin...		$ 9,400
Add: Fixed factory costs overabsorbed...........................		1,250
Net Income before Taxes.....................................		$10,650

Thus despite a 3,000-unit reduction in sales volume, absorption costing would produce a $650 increase in reported income.[4]

An income statement prepared on a variable costing basis would show $47,750 in manufacturing costs and net income of $8,650:

Sales (47,000 units).......................................		$56,400
Cost of goods sold:		
Cost of goods manufactured @ $0.75.........................	$41,250	
Less: Ending inventory (8,000 units @ $0.75)................	6,000	
Cost of goods sold....................................		35,250
Variable profit margin......................................		$21,150
Fixed factory costs..		12,500
Net Income before Taxes.....................................		$ 8,650

This is $1,350 less than the variable costing income for period 1, reflecting the 3,000-unit sales reduction multiplied by the 45-cent variable profit per unit ($1.20 selling price minus $0.75 variable cost).

The $2,000 difference between the two income figures for period 2 lies entirely in the amount of fixed cost assigned to the end-of-period inventory. Whereas variable costing would have charged the entire $12,500 to period 2 expense, absorption costing would have assigned $2,000 of this to the 8,000-unit addition to inventories (at the 25-cent burden rate), leaving only $10,500 for the income statement:

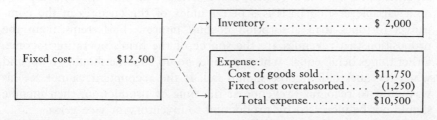

____

[4] The same effect would be observed if a postdetermined burden rate were used. Assuming a zero opening inventory, the fixed costs assigned to the units sold would be 47/55 of $12,500, or $10,680. Net income would be $10,470, but this would still be greater than the period 1 figure.

Exhibit 9–4

COMPARATIVE INCOME STATEMENTS
Sales Exceed Production

	Absorption Costing	Variable Costing
Sales (52,000 units)...................	$62,400	$62,400
Cost of goods sold:		
Cost of goods manufactured (44,000 units):		
Variable costs @ $0.75.............	$33,000	$33,000
Fixed costs @ $0.25...............	11,000	....
	$44,000	$33,000
Cost of beginning inventory (8,000 units) .	8,000	6,000
Cost of goods sold...............	52,000	39,000
Product margin.......................	$10,400	$23,400
Unabsorbed factory fixed cost...........	1,500*	12,500
Net Income before Taxes................	$ 8,900	$10,900

* Actual, $12,500, less absorbed, $11,000.

Period 3: Sales Exceed Production. Production in period 3 was cut back to 44,000 units while sales went up to 52,000, completely eliminating the inventory of finished units. The income statement for the period would show the figures in Exhibit 9–4. Net income under variable costing would be $2,250 greater than in period 2 on a sales increase of 5,000 units. The absorption costing figure, however, would go down by $1,750, the result of charging all of period 3's fixed costs plus $2,000 of period 2's.

Over a number of years, the two methods will produce virtually identical cumulative net income totals, but in any one year the difference can be substantial.

Pros and Cons of Variable Costing Financial Statements

The case for variable costing in public financial reporting rests on two arguments. First is the argument that a series of income figures computed on a variable costing basis is a better index of the changes in the company's fortunes than absorption costing figures. This stems from the proposition that revenues are the source of the firm's operating income. Other things being equal, when revenues go up, income should go up; and when revenues fall, income should fall. If the accountant cannot see his way clear to recognize revenue at the time of production, then income should not be increased by production to inventory or vice versa.

This is true under variable costing, but not under absorption costing. Absorption costing income can be influenced significantly by the level of production, and management's decisions on the rate of production can smooth or accentuate period-to-period income fluctuations that are caused by changes in the level of sales revenues.[5] This is why absorption costing income in our example was almost constant despite large fluctuations in revenues. The potential amount of smoothing varies inversely with the rate of inventory turnover and with the length of the reporting period. In other words, monthly financial statements are more vulnerable to this effect than annual statements; statements of companies with slow-moving inventories are more vulnerable than those of high-turnover firms.

The second argument of the variable costers is that inventories ought to reflect only those costs that are optional in timing, the so-called relevant costs.[6] In other words, the goods in inventory could have been produced by expenditures either in the period just ended or in future periods. By producing them now, the company has enabled itself to avoid future expenditures. The amount of the costs thus avoided is the measure of "relevant" cost. Those fixed costs that will not be avoided in the future because production has already taken place in the past, it is argued, should not be treated as product costs and therefore should be taken directly to the income statement as expenses of the period.

This is not precisely an argument for variable costing in financial statements, because some fixed costs could be avoided if no production at all took place and thus should be included in "relevant" cost. Variable cost is ordinarily closer than full cost to the cost avoidability criterion, however, and the argument has been used to support variable costing for public financial reporting.

The arguments against variable costing for corporate financial reporting are also doctrinaire rather than pragmatic. The full costers argue that all factory costs are necessary to production and that therefore every fixed cost should be reflected in one burden rate or another for inclusion in product cost.

The difficulty with this argument is that it cannot be tested. Because some overhead costs are truly common costs, not traceable to any one product, any allocation contains an inescapably arbitrary element. This means that it is impossible to cite any figure as an unequivocal measure of unit cost, and the variable cost–full cost argument can never be resolved on doctrinaire grounds. The real question is what difference it makes to the user of the financial statements, and no evidence on this point is yet available.

It is worth repeating, however, that the most important distinction

---

[5] This problem disappears if revenue is always recognized at the time of production, but the accountant seldom feels that he has enough information to recognize revenue on a production basis.

[6] For a discussion of these issues, see David Green, "A Moral to the Direct Costing Controversy?" *Journal of Business,* July 1960, pp. 218–26; Charles T. Horngren and George H. Sorter, " 'Direct' Costing for External Reporting," *Accounting Review,* January 1961, pp. 84–93; and George J. Staubus, "Direct, Relevant, or Absorption Costing?" *Accounting Review,* January 1963, pp. 64–74.

between variable costing and absorption costing is not that they lead to different measures of periodic income but that they provide different measures of the relative profitability of individual products, territories, or other segments of the company's business. This point was admirably expressed in a report issued by the National Association of Accountants: "Direct costing has sometimes been described as a plan for eliminating fixed costs from inventories. This description stresses an incidental feature rather than the prime objective of the plan, which is provision of information about cost-volume-profit relationships."[7]

Reconciling Internal and External Statements

Whenever variable costing is used for internal costing but external financial statements reflect the full costing principle, some means must be found for bridging the gap between the two.[8]

One possibility is to maintain a dual system, with product cost records showing both variable cost and full cost figures. This is clerically expensive and can only be justified if the full cost figures have commensurate managerial significance, or if they are needed for cost-plus contracts.

An alternative is to maintain product cost records on a variable cost basis only, with a supplemental account to reflect some average aggregate amount of fixed overhead appropriate to the level of inventory on hand. The balance in this account can be updated periodically by applying some formula to the variable costs in inventory as of the statement date. This can be done economically, and the resultant inventory cost totals will ordinarily serve the purposes of external financial reporting as well as carefully worked out, fully allocated unit cost figures.

OVERHEAD VARIANCE ANALYSIS UNDER VARIABLE COSTING

Factory overhead variances arise whether absorption costing or variable costing is adopted. In Chapter 7 we broke the total overhead variance down into two components:

1. A spending variance, representing the difference between the actual costs and the costs that management would ordinarily expect to incur at the actual level of production.
2. A volume variance, representing the difference between these anticipated costs and the amounts charged to products.

A similar breakdown can be made under variable costing, but if variable costs vary in a linear way, the volume variance will be zero.

---

[7] "Direct Costing, Research Series No. 23," *N.A.C.A. Bulletin,* Vol. 34 (April 1953), p. 1080.

[8] For some evidence on this point, see *Current Application of Direct Costing, Research Report No. 37* (New York: National Association of Accountants, 1961).

For example, in the last illustration variable cost was assumed to amount to 75 cents a unit. Let us assume that 55 cents of this was for direct labor and direct materials, so that the overhead formula is as follows:

$$\text{Total factory overhead} = \$12,500 + \$0.20 \times \text{units produced}$$

In period 3, therefore, when 44,000 units were produced, total overhead cost should have been $12,500 + $0.20 × 44,000 = $21,300. Now suppose that actual costs were:

Variable overhead..........................	$ 8,400
Fixed overhead............................	12,800
Total overhead............................	$21,200

The difference between these two sets of figures are the spending variances:

	Actual Costs	Anticipated Costs	Spending Variance
Variable overhead..................	$ 8,400	$ 8,800	$400
Fixed overhead....................	12,800	12,500	(300)
Total...........................	$21,200	$21,300	$100

The volume variance in this case would be zero, because the entire $8,800 anticipated at a 44,000-unit volume was assigned to production (44,000 × $0.20 a unit). Because fixed costs were not absorbed in product costs, no volume variance in fixed costs can arise.

A volume variance can arise under variable costing, however, if the cost function is nonlinear. For example, suppose that variable overhead costs are expected to vary according to the following formula:

$$\text{Total variable cost} = \$0.10\, V + \$3 \left(\frac{V}{1,000}\right)^2$$

in which V is the number of units produced.

This is represented graphically by the curved line in Exhibit 9–5. If the accountant is to use a single predetermined rate for product costing, he must use a rate that is accurate at only one level of activity. If normal volume is 50,000 units, variable overhead costs at that level are:

$$\$0.10 \times 50,000 + \$3 \times (50)^2 = \$12,500$$

and the variable costing burden rate is:

$$\frac{\$12,500}{50,000} = \$0.25 \text{ per unit}$$

Exhibit 9–5

VOLUME VARIANCE FROM NONLINEAR COST FUNCTION

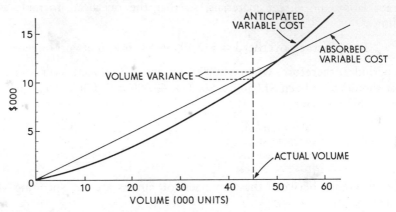

Using this rate, the amount absorbed at various volumes is represented by the straight line in Exhibit 9–5. The vertical distance between the "Anticipated" and "Absorbed" lines arises, as in the absorption costing case, because the burden rate is based on a volume different from actual volume. Thus it represents a volume variance. At a volume of 44,000 units, the amount absorbed would be 44,000 × $0.25 = $11,000. The anticipated amount, taken from the curved line, would be $10,208. The volume variance would be $792, the difference between these two figures. This is the vertical distance between the two lines at the 44,000-unit level.

The volume variance in this case measures the error inherent in the use of a straight line to approximate a nonlinear function. In fact, if management knows this much about the shape of the cost function and if it is this far from linear, then the linear approximation probably should not be used at all. Variable costing always assumes linearity, and it is useful to management only when it is a reasonable approximation of the known facts.

SUMMARY

Variable costing is an alternative to the full costing basis for developing factory unit cost for manufactured products and services. It defines product cost as the average variable cost of producing the goods or services.

The main argument for variable costing is that it provides information that is more readily useful for decision-making purposes. Although incremental cost with respect to a particular decision may not be equal to either variable cost or full cost, it is easier to move from variable cost to incremental cost than to take full cost figures and convert them into estimates of incremental cost. Furthermore, estimates of short-run variability often can be taken directly from a variable costing data bank, whereas special studies are necessary to obtain these data if absorption costing is used. Finally, because variable costing forces the analyst to deal explicitly with fixed costs, these items are much less likely to be overlooked.

When management decisions have a time horizon longer than the very short run, variable cost is likely to understate incremental cost quite seriously. To provide for such cases and reduce the need for special studies of longer term incremental cost, the accountant may decide to develop unit costs routinely on an attributable costing basis. Attributable cost includes a provision for fixed costs that are likely to be affected by large, permanent changes in total production volume. These attributable cost figures can be incorporated in the ledger accounts as substitutes for full costs. Alternatively, they can be kept only in the unit cost files, apart from the ledger accounts.

Variable costing is not now generally acceptable for public financial reporting. Arguments have been advanced both for and against such acceptance, but they are largely irrelevant to the question of the desirability of variable costing. Variable costing must stand or fall on its managerial advantages. It is possible to use variable costing for routine recording of transactions while at the same time using absorption costing for public financial statements. The adjustment of inventory figures for changes in the inventoried portion of fixed costs is a relatively simple task, and the need to report income on an absorption costing basis should not preclude the use of variable costing if management finds it more useful for internal purposes.

EXERCISES AND PROBLEMS

1. The company uses a process costing system. Variable costs in process X totaled $20,000 last month; fixed costs amounted to $5,000. Process output totaled 64,000 pounds.

a) What was unit cost under variable costing?
b) Suppose that output would have been 80,000 pounds if a trainee had not forgotten to close a drain valve. This sort of accident or error occurs very seldom. How, if at all, does this change your answer to (*a*)?

2. The company used a factory overhead burden rate of $2.50 a machine-hour, both in 19x4 and in 19x5, based on full costing. Under- or overabsorbed factory overhead cost is closed out to the income statement at the end of each year.

In 19x5 the company recorded a total of 100,000 machine-hours. Actual overhead amounted to $275,000. Overhead costs included in inventories totaled $50,000 on January 1, 19x5 and $75,000 on December 31, 19x5, using the method followed by the company.

Budgeted variable factory overhead costs averaged $1 a machine-hour both in 19x4 and 19x5. Reported income for 19x5 was $100,000.

What would reported income have been if the company had reported income on a variable costing basis? (Ignore income taxes.)

3.* The company has four products, with direct costs and selling prices as follows:

Product	Selling Price	Direct Costs per Unit	
		Materials	Labor
A.....................	$20	$7	$2
B.....................	19	5	3
C.....................	18	3	4
D.....................	17	1	5

The burden rate is 200 percent of direct labor—50 percent for variable costs and 150 percent for fixed costs.

a) Compute a profit margin for each product, per unit and as a percentage of selling price, using full cost absorption.

b) Perform the same computations, using variable costing.

4.* The Adams Plastics Company recorded the following data for the years 19x1 and 19x2:

	19x1	19x2
Production—pounds.....................	5,000,000	6,000,000
Sales—pounds..........................	5,000,000	5,100,000
Direct labor...........................	$ 50,000	$ 60,000
Direct materials.......................	100,000	120,000
Fixed factory overhead.................	60,000	60,000
Variable factory overhead.............	40,000	48,000

Assuming that five million pounds is the normal production volume and that all under- or overabsorbed overhead is closed at the end of the year to cost of goods sold, compute the amount of factory cost charged against revenue for each year, using (a) full costing, and (b) variable costing. You may assume that the company had no inventory at the beginning of 19x1.

5. Factory overhead costs for three product groups are expected to vary with monthly output as shown in the following table:

---

* Solutions to problems marked with an asterisk can be found in Appendix B.

Output (in Units)	Group A	Group B	Group C
5,000 or less...................	$1,000	$ 500	$2,000
5,500..........................	1,100	600	2,000
6,000..........................	1,200	600	2,000
6,500..........................	1,300	700	2,000
7,000..........................	1,400	700	2,000
7,500..........................	1,500	800	2,000
8,000..........................	1,600	800	2,000
8,500..........................	1,700	900	2,700
9,000..........................	1,800	900	2,700
9,500..........................	1,900	1,000	2,700
10,000..........................	2,000	1,000	2,700
10,500..........................	2,100	1,100	2,700
11,000..........................	2,200	1,100	2,700
11,500..........................	2,300	1,200	2,700
12,000..........................	2,400	1,200	3,400

Production need not be in multiples of 500 units but can be any volume from zero to 12,000 units a month.

a) Assuming that volume ordinarily fluctuates between 8,500 and 11,000 units a month, what figure would you use to represent the variable cost per unit? Explain your reasoning for each group of costs.

b) How, if at all, would your answer differ if you were asked to supply attributable cost per unit?

6. A company owns two factories: factory No. 1 and factory No. 2. Costs for an output of 14,000 units of product X in factory No. 1 are:

Materials................................	$35,000
Labor....................................	14,000
Variable overhead.........................	12,600
Fixed overhead...........................	8,400
Total....................................	$70,000

The raw materials cost in this table is the amount charged to factory No. 1 for product A, which is manufactured in factory No. 2. Each unit of product X requires two units of produt A as a raw material.

Factory No. 2 sells part of its output to factory No. 1 and part to outside customers. Its normal monthly volume is 50,000 units of product A, and the costs of producing this volume are:

Materials................................	$10,000
Labor....................................	5,000
Variable overhead.........................	2,500
Fixed overhead...........................	45,000
Total....................................	$62,500

Factory No. 1 uses variable costing; factory No. 2 follows the full costing concept in product costing. Personnel in one factory have no access to the other factory's cost records.

a) You are the factory controller for factory No. 1. Compute the variable unit cost of product X.

b) How would your answer to (*a*) have differered if both factories had used variable costing?

7. The sales manager of Tortilla Flatware, Inc. has recommended the addition of a new deluxe model to the company's product line. He is confident that he can sell 20,000 units a month at a unit price of $20. Most of these would be sold to customers who would otherwise buy competitors' products; sales of Tortilla's regular model would be reduced by only 1,000 units a month.

The company uses variable costing with supplemental rates to cover average fixed costs. Cost estimates for the regular model and the new deluxe model show the following:

	Regular	Deluxe
Unit cost:		
Direct materials.....................	$ 6	$ 9
Direct labor..........................	2	7
Variable overhead....................	1	2
Total variable cost...................	$ 9	$18
Fixed cost............................	3	4
Total cost...........................	$12	$22
Selling price per unit.................	15	20
Profit (loss) per unit.................	$ 3	$(2)

Adequate physical capacity is available to manufacture the new model, but a new assembly line would have to be manned, with additional supervisors, inspectors, and other personnel. The additional fixed costs of operating this line would amount to $38,000 a month. The fixed cost of manufacturing the regular model would not be affected by a reduction of 1,000 units a month, and the sales manager is confident that he could handle the new model with no increase in selling costs.

a) Should the new model be introduced if management accepts the sales manager's estimates? Show figures to support your conclusion.
b) To what extent did the company's variable costing system make your analysis easier or more difficult? Should it be replaced either by a full costing system or by attributable costing?

8. A company used a job order costing system with a factorywide predetermined burden rate based on estimated costs at a normal volume of operations. Factory overhead costs were classified into three categories:

(1) Fixed: unaffected by month-to-month changes in production volume.
(2) Semivariable: affected by changes in volume, but less than proportionally.
(3) Variable: proportional to volume.

Factory volume was measured by the number of direct labor hours. You are given the cost and volume expected during a normal month and actual data for the month of May:

	Normal	May
Factory overhead costs:		
Fixed............................	$ 50,000	$ 49,500
Semivariable......................	30,000	32,000
Variable.........................	20,000	23,500
Total...........................	$100,000	$105,000
Factory volume (no. of direct labor hours).........................	50,000	50,000

Costs in the semivariable category are expected to vary at a rate of 50 cents a direct labor hour.

a) Prepare a predetermined burden rate based on the variable costing concept.

b) Assuming that product costing was based on the variable costing concept, compute unit cost for a job lot of 1,000 units requiring a total of $1,000 in direct materials and 500 direct labor hours at an average wage rate of $4 an hour.

c) How much factory overhead was charged to all jobs combined during May: (1) if product costing was based on variable costing? (2) if product costing was based on full costing?

9. The Leininger Corporation uses the variable costing concept in job order costing. The following transactions occurred in the factory during the month of July:

(1) Purchased materials on account, $22,500.
(2) Issued direct materials, $18,000; factory supplies, $3,500.
(3) Accrued hourly payrolls for four weeks, $40,000.
(4) Accrued salary payrolls for the month, $10,000.
(5) Distributed labor costs: direct labor, $36,000; supervision and clerical, $10,000; indirect labor, $7,000.
(6) Incurred other factory overhead, $70,000.
(7) Applied variable overhead to work in process: $0.75 per direct labor dollar.
(8) Transferred finished goods to inventory. There was no work in process at either the end or the beginning of the month.

a) Compute the unabsorbed overhead for the month. Why does this arise?
b) No distinction between fixed and variable overhead costs was made in items (1) through (6). How is it possible to operate a variable costing system without making such distinctions?
c) Prepare journal entries to record these transactions.

10.* Sales and profits of the Feaster Manufacturing Company for the first two quarters of the year were as follows:

	First	Second
Sales.......................	$300,000	$450,000
Net profit..................	55,000	57,000

The directors are concerned that a 50 percent increase in sales has resulted in only a small increase in profit. The chief cost accountant explains that unabsorbed overhead was charged to second-quarter operations. His statement is based on the following data:

	First Quarter	Second Quarter
Sales—units..................................	20,000	30,000
Production—units.............................	30,000	24,000
Ending inventory—units.......................	10,000	4,000
Selling price per unit.........................	$ 15	$ 15
Variable manufacturing cost per unit.............	5	5
Fixed manufacturing overhead costs..............	180,000	180,000
Fixed overhead per unit (burden rate)...........	6	6
Selling and administrative expenses..............	25,000	27,000

The company uses a first-in, first-out (Fifo) method for costing inventory. All underabsorbed or overabsorbed manufacturing costs are closed out to Cost of Goods Sold at the close of each period.

a) Prepare income statements for the two periods, using the method now employed by the Feaster Manufacturing Company. Indicate the book value of the ending inventory for each quarter.

b) Prepare similar statements using the variable costing method.

c) What would second-quarter net profit have been under each method if production in that period had been 30,000 units?

11. A company has three multiproduct factories for which the following data are available:

	Factory 1	Factory 2	Factory 3
Normal monthly volume.............	50,000	30,000	100,000 lbs.
	Labor hours	Machine-hours	
Expected overhead costs at normal volume:			
Variable........................	$75,000	$30,000	$20,000
Fixed...........................	25,000	90,000	80,000

All three factories use predetermined burden rates for product unit costing.

Factory 1 makes product X, with the following input requirements per unit: materials—two and a half pounds of material A from factory 3, two units of material B from factory 2, one unit of material C from an outside vendor at $5; direct labor—three hours at $4.50 an hour.

Direct labor and materials costs in factory 3 average 70 cents a pound. A unit of material B has a direct labor and direct materials cost in factory 2 of $2 a unit and requires one and a half hours of machine time in factory 2.

a) Compute the unit cost of product X following the full costing principle.

b) Compute the unit cost of product X following the variable costing principle.

c) The manager of factory 1 is also in charge of a small sales force which has the responsibility of bringing in orders to keep the factory busy. Business has been very slack lately throughout the industry and, being anxious to secure additional business, the manager of factory 1 has authorized his salesmen to quote prices only slightly higher than the costs of his labor, materials, and variable overhead. His products are of recognizably competitive quality, but the low price quotations have not been low enough to get the orders. Can you offer any suggestions as to why this may be the case?

12. The Dowd Company operates one small factory in which it manufactures a single product for sale to customers in the chemical and plastics industries. The company's costing system is based on the full costing concept. The following results were reported for the years 19x1 and 19x2:

	19x1	19x2
Sales—units....................................	25,000	37,500
Beginning inventory—units....................	5,000	15,000
Ending inventory—units.......................	15,000	7,500
Production—units............................	35,000	30,000
Fixed factory overhead costs....................	$280,000	$290,000
Selling and administrative expenses..............	30,000	36,000

Although materials prices and wage rates increased during these years, the company was able to offset these increases to a large extent by a vigorous program of cost reduction. Accordingly, variable cost remained unchanged at $7 a unit during these two years. The selling price of the product also remained constant, at $20 a unit. Factory fixed costs were assigned to products in both years on the basis of a burden rate of $8 a unit.

All underabsorbed or overabsorbed factory costs were taken to the income statement for the year in which they arose.

a) Compute reported income for the two years by (1) full costing and (2) variable costing.
b) What would the company's reported income have been in 19x2 if production had been 37,500 units under (1) full costing? (2) variable costing? Assume that total fixed costs would have been as stated above and that the same burden rates were used in both years.

13. The Jonas Good Company uses the variable costing principle for internal cost accounting but reports inventories and income to the public on a full cost Fifo basis. It uses a predetermined burden rate for variable overhead costs.

For convenience, the inventory accounts are maintained on a cost element basis rather than a stage-of-completion basis. That is, the balance in the Materials in Inventory account represents the cost of raw materials, the cost of the direct materials content of work in process, and the cost of the direct materials content of finished goods inventory. Three such accounts are maintained for the variable costs: Materials in Inventory, Labor in Inventory, and Variable Overhead in Inventory.

A fourth inventory account—Fixed Overhead in Inventory—is maintained for fixed overhead costs, to permit full cost public reporting. No entries are made in this account during the year; thus the January 1 balance remains in the account until the year-end adjustments are made. At the end of the year, the fixed costs applicable to the year-end inventories are determined by using a predetermined burden rate, based on that year's budgeted ratio of fixed cost to direct labor cost at normal volume. A year-end adjustment is then made to bring the balance in the Fixed Overhead in Inventory account up to date.

For public reporting purposes, any under- or overabsorbed overhead remaining after inventory accounts have been adjusted to their correct year-end balances is carried directly to the income statement as an adjustment to the cost of goods sold.

The following data are available (all figures are in thousands of dollars):

		19x1	19x2
(1)	January 1 inventory:		
	Materials in inventory	$ 70	$130
	Labor in inventory	60	180
	Variable overhead in inventory	30	?
	Fixed overhead in inventory	45	?
(2)	Actual costs for the year:		
	Materials purchased	180	100
	Direct labor employed	210	60
	Factory overhead costs	220	150
(3)	Revenue from sales	400	600
(4)	Operating expenses	50	55
(5)	December 31 inventory:		
	Materials in inventory	130	30
	Labor in inventory	180	90

(6) Budgeted variable overhead during each of these two years amounted to 40 percent of direct labor cost. At normal volume, budgeted fixed overhead was equal to 150 percent of variable overhead in 19x1 and 160 percent of variable overhead in 19x2.

(7) Production volume was normal in 19x1, but production schedules in 19x2 were cut back drastically to permit the company to correct a serious overstocking of inventory.

a) Compute the variable and fixed overhead cost components of year-end inventories for both years.

b) Prepare income statements for each year according to (1) variable costing and (2) full costing.

c) Assuming that financial statements are to reflect the full costing concept, what adjusting entry must be made as of December 31, 19x1 to correct the balance in the Fixed Overhead in Inventory account? What entry should be made as of December 31, 19x2?

d) The company pays an executive bonus equal to a fixed percentage of the net income reported to the public and to the stockholders of the Jonas Good Company. Do you believe that the bonus would be more equitable if it were based on the income reported internally to management on a variable costing basis? Give your reasons.

14. The Buongusto Company manufactures four products—A, B, C, and D—in its factory. Current data relating to these products show the following:

	A	B	C	D
Unit cost:				
Direct materials....................	$ 5	$ 8	$ 6	$10
Direct labor.......................	15	20	18	16
Factory overhead..................	11	19	18	22
Total unit cost...................	$31	$47	$42	$48
Unit price.........................	45	60	50	44
Unit margin (loss)...................	$14	$13	$ 8	$(4)
Number of units sold.................	1,400	700	1,000	500

All sales are made to manufacturers' representatives at the prices cited above. The company's selling and administrative expenses are totally fixed and amount to $25,000. Production and sales volumes are identical, and unabsorbed factory overhead amounts to $8,680.

The factory consists of three production departments. Departmental burden rates based on the full costing concept are used to charge factory overhead costs to individual products. The following cost estimates are available for departments 1, 2, and 3:

	Dept. 1	Dept. 2	Dept. 3
Measuring unit for departmental volume.....................	Pounds	Machine-Hours	Direct Labor Hours
Overhead costs at various volumes:			
0 units......................	$ 4,000	$20,000	$ 2,000
7,000 units.....................	9,400	37,000	17,000
8,000 units.....................	9,600	38,000	18,000
9,000 units.....................	9,800	39,000	19,000
10,000 units.....................	10,000	40,000	20,000
11,000 units.....................	10,200	41,000	21,000
12,000 units.....................	10,400	42,000	22,000
13,000 units.....................	10,800	44,000	24,000
Burden rate (based in each department on 10,000 volume units).......	$1/lb.	$4/mach.-hr.	$2/DLH

Cost estimates are not available for volumes between zero and 7,000 units because the factory has never operated in this range, although it has gotten close many times. When pressed, the factory manager says that some reduction in fixed costs would be possible if volume went below 7,000 units, but that the reduction would be very small because most fixed costs are highly indivisible. At the other end of the scale, volume has gone as high as 13,000 units, but only occasionally. Operating volume ordinarily ranges between 8,000 and 12,000 units in each department.

The departmental requirements imposed by the four products are as follows:

	A	B	C	D
Weight of components from dept. 1 (lbs. unit)......	3	1	2	4
Machine-hours in dept. 2 (mach.-hrs./unit)..........	1	2	3	4
Direct labor hours in dept. 3 (DLH/unit)............	2	5	2	1

The company's treasurer feels that product D should be dropped from the line. "We're losing money on it now," he says, "and if we were to spread that unabsorbed overhead back over the four products we'd be losing even more."

"If you drop this one," the sales manager says, "we'll just have to assign more overhead to the others. That would probably wipe out the profit on product C. We'd have to raise the price of product C and I know our representatives wouldn't like that."

a) Explain, insofar as possible, the $8,680 underabsorption of factory overhead costs.
b) Compute departmental burden rates on a variable costing basis.
c) Prepare an estimate of the effects of dropping product D. Do your figures indicate that it should be dropped at this time? If not, when should it be dropped?
d) Prepare a brief reply to the points made by the treasurer and sales manager.
e) Would variable costing, attributable costing, or full costing provide the best basis for decision making in this kind of situation?

15. The Upson Company manufactures four products in a single factory. Factory volume is considerably lower than normal, and substantial unfavorable overhead variances have resulted. Sales, cost, and expense data for the four products are as follows:

	Product A	Product B	Product C	Product D	Total
Sales................	$2,000,000	$2,500,000	$1,000,000	$500,000	$6,000,000
Cost of goods sold:					
Materials...........	$ 300,000	$ 400,000	$ 200,000	$ 40,000	$ 940,000
Labor...............	500,000	600,000	400,000	100,000	1,600,000
Overhead............	600,000	800,000	500,000	100,000	2,000,000
Total cost of goods sold...........	$1,400,000	$1,800,000	$1,100,000	$240,000	$4,540,000
Gross margin..........	$ 600,000	$ 700,000	$ (100,000)	$260,000	$1,460,000
Selling and administrative expenses (15% of sales)...........	300,000	375,000	150,000	75,000	900,000
Unadjusted net profit.....	$ 300,000	$ 325,000	$ (250,000)	$185,000	$ 560,000
Underabsorbed overhead..					300,000
Net Income before Taxes.............					$ 260,000

Factory overhead is approximately 40 percent variable at normal operating volumes. Variable selling and administrative expenses amount to approximately 5 percent of sales.

The substantial losses reported for product C have led management to consider discontinuing its manufacture, but the company's controller has opposed any such action, saying that company profits would be even lower without product C than with it.

a) Prepare a report that would support the controller's position and provide a better indicator of the relative profitability of each of the company's products.

b) The president of the company agrees with your figures but says that as soon as practical product C should be dropped. "In the long run," he says, "we cannot afford to retain any product that does not cover its costs." At what time would you consider it "practical" to drop product C? What information would you find useful in making such a decision?

c) Is it conceivable that even in the long run it might be profitable to keep product C in the line? Under what conditions?

d) A copy of your report is brought to the attention of the manager of the market research department, who calls you in and tells you that you have overlooked the following relevant facts:

(1) Fifty percent of the sales of product C are for applications in which product D can also be used. If product C were not available, sales of product D could be increased by $400,000 a year without any substantial change in fixed selling expenses.

(2) Twenty percent of the sales of product C are sold in conjunction with product A. These customers would not be able to substitute product D and would seek other sources of supply of product A. It is estimated that sales of product A would decline by 10 percent if product C were withdrawn from the company's line.

(3) The company's controller has also estimated that a complete abandonment of product C would permit a reduction of fixed factory, selling, and administrative costs in the amount of $100,000 a year. If product C were kept in the line only as a service to product A customers, receiving no direct selling effort or advertising, the reduction in fixed costs would amount to only $40,000 a year.

In view of this additional information, prepare a report indicating whether sales of product C should be continued, or discontinued entirely, or continued only as a service to the small group of product A customers whose business would be lost if product C were not available.

chapter **10**

Interdepartmental Allocations
for Product or Project Costing

Every operating cost is traceable to some cost center, but not all of these cost centers work directly on the products or projects for which management wishes to accumulate costs.

For example, Exhibit 10–1 shows a partial organization chart for a medium-sized company. The company has two main operating divisions, a commercial products division and a research division. Each of the 18 blocks in the diagram represents a cost center. The shaded cost centers work directly on commercial products; the cross-hatched blocks represent cost centers that work directly on research projects. All other cost centers are indirect. Some are service centers, providing measurable services to other cost centers; others are support centers, providing either capacity or administrative support to two or more cost centers. They all have one feature in common, however: they do not work directly on individual products or research projects.

Most accountants argue that product or project costs should include a provision for all or some of the costs of indirect cost centers. The objectives are:

1. To obtain more accurate product or project costs for management decisions.
2. To provide data for cost-based contract prices.
3. To obtain more accurate product or project costs for external financial reporting.

The purpose of this chapter is to examine various methods of cost reassignment to see which of them, if any, are likely to achieve these objectives.

208

Exhibit 10–1

DIRECT VERSUS INDIRECT COST CENTERS

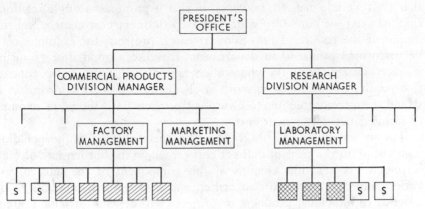

APPROACHES TO COST REASSIGNMENT

The simplest method of taking the costs of indirect cost centers into product or project cost accounts is to add them up, take an average, and multiply this average by some indicator of the size of each job order or project.

For example, suppose that the costs of all of the unshaded blocks in the research division portion of Exhibit 10–1 amounted to $200,000, while research labor costs totaled $1 million. (Research labor costs are part of the direct costs of the cross-hatched cost centers in the lower right-hand corner of Exhibit 10–1.) For reasons that we shall examine in a moment, management has decided to divide the costs of the indirect cost centers among the company's research projects in proportion to the amount of research labor cost assigned to each project. These costs averaged 20 percent of research labor cost in this period ($200,000 divided by $1 million), and the distribution was as follows:

	Research Labor Cost	Costs Absorbed @ 20%
Project A	$ 500,000	$100,000
Project B	300,000	60,000
Project C	200,000	40,000
Total	$1,000,000	$200,000

This method is used by many companies to determine the indirect cost of work performed on jobs or contracts for government agencies. It is a very crude method, however, in that it presumes a single relationship between the costs of a wide variety of indirect cost centers and the output of the research labor. Some research projects, for example, may be performed primarily in departments that use a good deal of maintenance department work, while others take place mainly in departments that require no maintenance work at all. In the face of this diversity, it would seem reasonable not to charge all projects with the same amounts of maintenance department cost.

The second approach tries to allow for these differences by including a provision for the costs of indirect cost centers in the burden rate of each direct cost center. The amount of this component of the burden rate varies from cost center to cost center, and therefore the amounts to be assigned to individual products or projects will depend on which direct cost centers they pass through.

The key element in this second approach is the assignment of the costs of indirect cost centers to the direct cost centers, a process known as cost *allocation* or cost *redistribution*. The question is whether methods of allocation can be found that will produce better product or project costs than the first approach.

ALTERNATIVE ALLOCATION METHODS

The costs of indirect cost centers are assigned to other cost centers by means of *charging rates*. Four kinds of charging rates need examination:

1. Transfer prices.
2. Activity charges.
3. Capacity charges.
4. Ability-to-pay charges.

The first of these is applicable to service centers; the other three are or can be used to allocate the costs of support centers.

Transfer Prices

Probably the most obvious base for a service department charging rate is a measure of usage—the number of units of service performed by the service department. Typical usage or consumption indexes are:

Department	Usage Index
Electric power	Kilowatt-hours
Maintenance	Maintenance labor hours
Stock room	Requisitions

A charging rate expressed as an amount per unit of service performed is known as a transfer price.

Activity Charges

If a reliable index of usage is unavailable, and if service department costs are variable, the correct approach is to find a measure of the volume of activity in departments receiving or creating the need for the service. The measure selected should be one that seems to correlate well with variations in service department costs. For example, if some costs of the payroll department vary with the total number of labor hours in the factory, it would be appropriate to use a charging rate of so much per factory labor hour. A charging rate of this sort is known as an activity charge.

Capacity Charges

Unlike the variable costs, the fixed costs of a service department are incurred to provide service capacity rather than the service themselves. Examples include the costs of providing floor space, heat and light, and plant management. In such cases, the cost to be allocated to a given department should be based on its relative share of the total service load during peak load periods, if this can be ascertained or estimated.

Because in most cases the service facilities are provided jointly for the joint use of a number of departments, it is difficult to determine with any precision just what percentage of capacity each department is responsible for. The problem, in other words, is to obtain an index of total service capacity and then to obtain some measure of each department's occupancy of that capacity. Thus the charging rate in this case can be called an occupancy charge, capacity charge, or possibly a potential-activity charge, and it is based on a measure of the facilities provided rather than facilities used.

Ability-to-Pay Charges

The lack of a reasonable index of use or of any clearly defined pattern of cost variability leaves a gap in the cost allocation structure. This gap is filled, whenever possible, by measures of relative occupancy of the facilities provided. Occupancy indexes are often difficult to find, however, and in situations of this sort the capacity of the service department is often assumed to correlate with the size of the other departments or with their ability to absorb service department charges.

The ability-to-pay criterion is often justified on the grounds that each department and each product must bear its "fair share" of all costs and that if no other basis can be found for allocation, the ability-to-pay criterion is better than nothing. Unfortunately, this begs the question. If it is impossible to find a reliable index of usage, occupancy, or variability, then the overhead cost must be truly a common cost of the various departments and any allocation is bound to be arbitrary and potentially misleading. Under these circumstances the use of the ability-to-pay charging rate lends to the allocation an aura of precision and objectivity that is completely unjustified. Either no allocation should be made or some basis should be chosen that will be instantly recognizable as arbitrary and of no managerial significance.

AN ALLOCATION PLAN

Allocations using these methods are used in all kinds of organizations, from industrial research laboratories to advertising agencies. They can be applied to budgeted data to get predetermined burden rates, or to historical data to get after-the-fact average costs. Furthermore, the allocation system may be designed to get full cost, attributable cost, or average variable cost figures.

To illustrate the approach, let us look at a system that is used to derive predetermined, full-cost burden rates in the factory of the Standoff Company, a small metal products company. This factory is divided into three service and three production departments, plus two artificial cost centers that have been established to receive two kinds of centrally administered cost elements—electricity and building ownership.

Primary Cost Distributions

Because predetermined burden rates are to be used, allocations are based on budget data. Budget and statistical data for a normal month are shown in Exhibit 10–2.

The first step is to distribute the costs that will be recorded in special factorywide accounts: electric power and building ownership costs. For electric power, a transfer price is clearly appropriate. These costs are incurred to provide a service, readily measurable in kilowatt-hours. Power consumption estimates are available for five cost centers, as shown in the fifth line of the exhibit. The Standoff Company purchases electricity at a flat rate of two cents a kilowatt-hour (kwh), and at this rate the budgeted power cost distribution is:

Department	Kwh Used	Amount Charged
Building operation.........................	10,000	$ 200
Factory administration.....................	.....	.....
Equipment maintenance....................	5,000	100
Machining.................................	45,000	900
Welding and plating.......................	12,500	250
Assembly.................................	7,500	150
Total.....................................	80,000	$1,600

Exhibit 10–2

STANDOFF COMPANY: DATA FOR BUDGETED ALLOCATIONS

	Total	Service Departments			Production Departments		
		Building Operation	Factory Administration	Equipment Maintenance	Machining	Welding and Plating	Assembly
Budgeted operating statistics:							
Floor space (sq. ft.)	50,000	.....	5,000	3,000	20,000	7,000	15,000
Direct labor hours	22,000	.....	.....	2,000	6,000	2,000	12,000
Total labor hours	32,900	900	.....	2,000	10,000	4,000	16,000
Machine-hours	8,000	.....	.....	.....	8,000	.....	.....
Power consumed (kwh)	80,000	10,000	.....	5,000	45,000	12,500	7,500
Maintenance hours used	2,000	.....	.....	.....	1,500	300	200
Departmental overhead:							
Supervision and clerical help	$14,400	$ 1,000	$ 8,100	$ 1,000	$ 1,600	$ 900	$ 1,800
Indirect labor	31,500	1,900	.....	8,000	9,200	5,000	7,400
Operating supplies	4,000	600	1,400	600	600	500	300
Equipment depreciation	2,200	100	200	300	1,000	400	200
Miscellaneous	3,100	200	1,500	440	400	170	390
Total	$55,200	$ 3,800	$11,200	$10,340	$12,800	$ 6,970	$10,090
Unassigned overhead:							
Electric power	1,600						
Building depreciation, taxes, and insurance	2,000						
Total Factory Overhead	$58,800						

The amount assigned to the building operation department covers the estimated cost of lighting the factory and factory office; it also includes the electric costs of operating a few simple pieces of office equipment. In principle, the latter should be separated and allocated to the factory administration department, but in this case they are such a small part of the total that the company's accountants feel that the effort is not justified.

The costs of building ownership are a different matter. They are incurred to provide operating capacity, not a measurable service. They are common costs of the entire building, and are unaffected by the intensity at which the building is used. In this case the appropriate allocation method is a capacity charge, based on an index of facilities provided. Using the floor space occupancy figures from Exhibit 10–2, the budgeted allocations of building ownership costs are:

Department	Floor Space		Cost Allocated
	Amount	Percent	
Building operation......................	.....	...	.....
Factory administration................	5,000	10	$ 200
Equipment maintenance................	3,000	6	120
Machining	20,000	40	800
Welding and plating..................	7,000	14	280
Assembly............................	15,000	30	600
Total.............................	50,000	100	$2,000

These two allocations are often referred to as *primary* distributions because they do not require the transfer of costs from one department to another and can be made in any sequence as long as they are made before any secondary distributions are made.

Redistribution by Sequential Allocation

Since service and support centers often provide services or capacity to each other as well as to production centers, the costs of one depend on the costs of each of the others. In principle, this means that the allocations should be made simultaneously, using a set of interlocking mathematical equations. The Standoff Company has chosen to use a sequential method, however. Under sequential allocation, the service and support centers are ranked in terms of the relative amounts of services or facilities they provide to each other. Costs of the center providing the most universally used services or facilities are distributed first, and so on.

This method is illustrated schematically in Exhibit 10–3. In this case, department P uses department X's services, which in turn require the services of department Y. When costs are allocated sequentially, department P's burden rate includes a provision for the costs of department X.

Exhibit 10–3

ILLUSTRATIVE COST ALLOCATION SEQUENCE

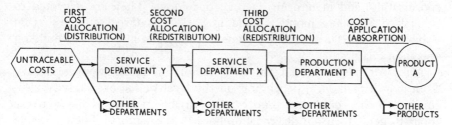

The charging rate for department X, however, includes a provision for a portion of the budgeted cost of department Y, and this includes a provision for a portion of the costs that are common to all departments.

In the Standoff Company scheme, building operation department costs are distributed first, to all five other departments. Factory administration costs, including the costs received in the building operation department allocation, come next, and are spread among the equipment maintenance and factory production departments only—no further charges are made to the building operation department accounts. Finally, equipment maintenance costs, both direct and allocated, are charged to the three production departments.

Building Operation Department Allocation. The function of the building operation department is to maintain and protect the building and its electrical and plumbing systems. In other words, it provides the other departments with the capacity to do business rather than with measurable services. Budgeted costs for this department total $4,000 a month, including $200 for electric power, and these are almost entirely fixed for the volume ranges within which the company expects to operate.

Under these conditions, the controller has decided to allocate building operating costs by means of capacity charges, measuring capacity by the amount of usable floor space. The average budgeted cost per square foot of floor space is eight cents a month ($4,000 divided by 50,000 square feet), and the resulting budgeted allocation is:

Department	Floor Space	Cost Allocated
Factory administration..................	10%	$ 400
Equipment maintenance.................	6	240
Machining............................	40	1,600
Welding and plating...................	14	560
Assembly.............................	30	1,200
Total.............................	100%	$4,000

Factory Administration Department Allocation. Factory administration costs are incurred by the factory manager and his staff in directing, coordinating, and monitoring factory operations. They are expected to amount to $11,800 a month, including $11,200 in direct charges (from Exhibit 10–2), $200 in building ownership charges, and $400 in building operation charges.

A few of the Standoff Company's factory administration costs vary from month to month, depending on the level of factory activity. According to the controller's figures, the variable portion is likely to be about 10 cents for each direct labor hour in the factory. These variable costs do not produce a measurable service, and therefore an activity charge rather than a transfer price must be used, in this case 10 cents per budgeted direct labor hour. (Because variable factory administration costs seem to vary with the number of maintenance labor hours as well as with direct labor hours in the three production centers, direct labor is redefined to include the maintenance labor hours for this calculation.) The allocation is as follows:

	Direct Labor Hours	Variable Cost Allocated
Equipment maintenance..................	2,000	$ 200
Machining...........................	6,000	600
Welding and plating...................	2,000	200
Assembly............................	12,000	1,200
Total...............................	22,000	$2,200

This accounts for only a small percentage of the budgeted factory administration costs, however. The remaining $9,600 of costs are fixed, incurred to provide administrative capacity or support to the other factory departments. For these, a capacity charge is appropriate. Although administrative capacity is very difficult to measure, the controller believes that it consists mainly of an ability to handle the greatest number of problems that are likely to arise. Since he also feels that the number of problems is likely to be proportional to the number of people employed in the factory, he has decided to measure each department's occupancy of the factory's administrative capacity by its budgeted total labor hours. The three production centers and equipment maintenance are budgeting a total of 32,000 labor hours among them (from Exhibit 10–2). The budgeted average fixed cost of factory administration thus averages 30 cents a budgeted labor hour. At this rate the budgeted allocation is:

	Total Labor Hours	Fixed Cost Allocated
Equipment maintenance..................	2,000	$ 600
Machining...........................	10,000	3,000
Welding and plating..................	4,000	1,200
Assembly............................	16,000	4,800
Total...............................	32,000	$9,600

Equipment Maintenance Department Allocation. The equipment maintenance department provides a service, in this case measurable by a single indicator, maintenance labor hours. Thus a transfer price is the appropriate charging rate.

Strictly speaking, the fixed costs of operating the maintenance department should be allocated on the basis of service consumption during peak service periods, because this is the measure of required capacity. In this case, however, the controller believes that budgeted consumption is an adequate index of the amount of capacity required, and therefore can be used for both the fixed and the variable portions of maintenance department cost.

The costs budgeted for maintenance are divided into fixed and variable components as follows:

	Fixed	Variable	Total
Direct charges (Exhibit 10–2)..............	$1,340	$9,000	$10,340
Allocations:			
Electric power........................	20	80	100
Building ownership.....................	120	....	120
Building operation.....................	240	....	240
Factory administration.................	600	200	800
Total..................................	$2,320	$9,280	$11,600

This is for a budgeted volume of 2,000 maintenance labor hours. Therefore, the charging rates are $1.16 an hour for fixed costs and $4.64 an hour for variable costs, a total of $5.80 an hour.

Completed Allocation Sheet. The completed factory cost budget is shown in Exhibit 10–4. The sequential or step-down procedure shows clearly in this exhibit, and at the end of the process all budgeted factory costs[1] have been reassigned to one or another of the three production

---

[1] Although this should represent the normal monthly costs of operating the department rather than the costs budgeted for a particular year, the two figures have been assumed equal here to simplify the illustration.

Exhibit 10–4

STANDOFF COMPANY: BUDGETED OVERHEAD DISTRIBUTION SHEET USING SEQUENTIAL ALLOCATIONS

	Total	Service Departments			Production Departments		
		Building Operation	Factory Administration	Equipment Maintenance	Machining*	Welding and Plating†	Assembly†
Direct overhead:							
Supervision and clerical help	$14,400	$1,000	$ 8,100	$ 1,000	$ 1,600	$ 900	$ 1,800
Indirect labor	31,500	1,900	.....	8,000	9,200	5,000	7,400
Operating supplies	4,000	600	1,400	600	600	500	300
Equipment depreciation	2,200	100	200	300	1,000	400	200
Miscellaneous	3,100	200	1,500	440	400	170	390
Total	$55,200	$3,800	$11,200	$10,340	$12,800	$ 6,970	$10,090
Primary distributions:							
Electric power	1,600	200	.....	100	900	250	150
Building depreciation, taxes, insurance	2,000	....	200	120	800	280	600
Total factory overhead	$58,800	$4,000	$11,400	$10,560	$14,500	$ 7,500	$10,840
Secondary distributions:							
Building operation		(4,000)	400	240	1,600	560	1,200
			$11,800				
Factory administration:							
Variable			(2,200)	200	600	200	1,200
Fixed			(9,600)	600	3,000	1,200	4,800
				$11,600			
Equipment maintenance:							
Variable				(9,280)	6,960	1,392	928
Fixed				(2,320)	1,740	348	232
Allocated totals					$28,400	$11,200	$19,200
Normal volume					8,000	2,000	12,000
Burden rate					$3.55	$5.60	$1.60

* Volume in machine-hours, burden rate per machine-hour

† Volume in direct labor hours, burden rate per direct labor hour.

departments. The production department totals are then used to establish departmental burden rates for the year.

In the machining department, the burden rate is based on a normal production volume of 8,000 machine-hours. The full-cost burden rate, shown on the bottom line of Exhibit 10–4, is thus $3.55 per machine-hour. The burden rates in the other two departments are computed in the same way, but based on direct labor hours instead of machine-hours.

The Standoff Company actually goes one step beyond this; it divides the burden rates into fixed and variable components. This process should be familiar by now, but one aspect is new. If a production center's consumption of a service center's services is fixed, then the variable cost of providing these services becomes a fixed cost of the production center.

For example, Standoff's machining department uses 1,500 hours of maintenance labor at its normal monthly volume of 6,000 direct labor hours. Of this, 300 hours is routine periodic or preventive maintenance, leaving only 1,200 hours to vary with production volume. The average rate of variation is thus 1,200 divided by 6,000, or 0.2 maintenance labor hours for each direct labor hour in machining. The average variable cost of maintenance labor is $4.64 per hour, so the variable costing burden rate includes $0.2 \times \$4.64 = \$0.93$ for the variable costs of variable maintenance services.

Redistribution by Simultaneous Allocation

Before the electronic computer was developed, the accountant was limited to sequential allocations or other mathematically simple allocation procedures. Most companies now have access to electronic computers, however, and can at least consider setting up a set of allocation equations that can be solved simultaneously.

This approach derives from the mutual interdependence of the various service centers. They do provide services or facilities to each other and thus, it is argued, each should be charged with a portion of the costs of each of the others. Such allocations can be referred to as *cross-allocations*. The result should be more accurate cost center charging rates and product costing rates.

The simultaneous allocation approach is easy to apply to the Standoff Company example. The only service departments that provide service or support to each other are the building operation and factory administration departments. Therefore only two equations are necessary, and we don't need a computer to perform the arithmetic.

Once again the first step is to allocate the costs of electric power and building ownership. These allocations are the same as in the earlier procedure, and lead to the totals shown on the "Total factory overhead" line of Exhibit 10–4.

The next step is to set up the allocation equations. The building operation department has a total labor budget of 900 hours, or 9/329 of the factory grand total of 32,900 hours. Using this as the measure of this department's occupancy of factory administrative capacity, the full budget of the building operation department would be:

$$\text{Building operation budget} = \$4,000 + 9/329 \times \text{budgeted fixed costs,}$$
$$\text{factory administration}$$

This equation has two unknowns, the total building operation department budget and the total amount of budgeted fixed cost in the factory administration department. The latter quantity, in turn, depends in part on the budgeted fixed costs of the building operation department. The reason is that factory administration occupies 5,000 square feet, or 10 percent, of the factory's floor space. This obliges this department to absorb 10 percent of the budgeted fixed costs of operating the building. All building operation costs are fixed in this case, and the budget formula for factory administration is:

$$\text{Budgeted fixed costs, factory administration} = \$9,200 + 0.1 \times \text{building}$$
$$\text{operation budget}$$

With two equations and two unknown quantities, it is a simple matter to determine the budgeted fixed cost for these two departments:

Building operation.................................... $4,263
Factory administration............................... 9,626

In other words, $263 in factory administration costs are allocated to the building operation budget, and $426 in building operation costs are allocated to factory administration.

Given these allocations, the charging rates for fixed costs are as follows:

	Budgeted Fixed Costs	Capacity	Charging Rate
Building operation.............	$4,263	50,000 sq. ft.	$85.26/M sq. ft.
Factory administration.........	9,626	32,900 lab. hrs.	$ 0.2926/lab. hr.

When these rates are used, the equipment maintenance department budget becomes:

Direct charges... $10,340
Electric power ($0.02 × 5,000 kwh)...................................... 100
Building ownership (6 percent of $2,000)............................... 120
Building operation (3,000 sq. ft. × $0.08526)......................... 256
Factory administration:
   Variable (2,000 labor hours × $0.10).............................. 200
   Fixed (2,000 labor hours × $0.2926).............................. 585
Total... $11,601

The revised charging rate for equipment maintenance is thus $11,601 divided by 2,000, or $5.8005 per maintenance labor hour ($1.16 for the variable costs of maintenance and $4.6405 for the fixed costs).

The final allocations under this method are shown in Exhibit 10–5. Two things should be noted in this exhibit. First, the budgeted costs of each service or support department are exactly equal to the amounts allocated to other centers. Second, the burden rates for the three production centers are not very different from those in Exhibit 10–4. The first of these is inherent in the method; the second is peculiar to this simple illustration. With more service departments and more interrelationships between service departments, the effect could be material in amount.

EVALUATION OF ALLOCATIONS

Controversy about cost allocations does not center on the choice between simultaneous and sequential allocations. The real issue is whether these allocations provide better product or project cost figures.

From a managerial point of view, this is simply an extension of the variable costing controversy. The Standoff Company's management recognizes the importance of variable cost data to the extent of requiring a segregation of the fixed and variable components of service center charging rates, but its system is otherwise a full costing system.

In our opinion, full cost allocations are likely to be misleading. Management is likely to believe that they indicate the amount of service center or support center costs that could be avoided in the long run if a particular cost center's demand for service or support were to be permanently discontinued. This calls for the use of the attributable cost concept that we developed in the previous chapter, not full cost.

Most full-cost allocation systems start with the idea that the amount to be allocated to a cost center ought to represent the amount attributable to that center's operations. The problem is that the concept of attributability is not necessarily compatible with the concept of complete cost distribution. Attributable cost is likely to lead to a less-than-complete allocation of service and support center costs because some of these costs are bound to be indivisible, incurred to provide the service or support center with its basic capacity. These indivisible costs are unavoidable as long as the center remains in being.

This means that the totals to be allocated under a full-costing system are not relevant to any decision except perhaps the discontinuation of the service or support activity itself. Thus the added accuracy that is gained by switching to cross-allocations is a spurious gain, and accountants would do better to spend their time deciding what to allocate.

As to the choice between attributable cost and variable cost allocations, we must leave this in abeyance. Chapter 13 will try to demonstrate that attributable cost figures may be of some help to management in some situations. If these situations are important enough, attributable cost allo-

Exhibit 10–5

BUDGETED OVERHEAD DISTRIBUTION SHEET USING CROSS-ALLOCATIONS

	Service Departments			Production Departments		
	Building Operation	Factory Administration	Equipment Maintenance	Machining	Welding and Plating	Assembly
Direct overhead	$3,800	$11,200	$10,340	$12,800	$6,970	$10,090
Primary distributions	200	200	220	1,700	530	750
Total factory overhead	$4,000	$11,400	$10,560	$14,500	$7,500	$10,840
Secondary distributions:						
Building operation	(4,263)	426	256	1,705	597	1,279
Factory administration:						
Variable	.....	(2,200)	200	600	200	1,200
Fixed	263	(9,626)	585	2,926	1,170	4,682
Equipment maintenance:						
Variable	.....	.....	(9,280)	6,960	1,392	928
Fixed	.....	.....	(2,321)	1,741	348	232
Allocated totals	.....	.....	.....	$28,432	$11,207	$19,161
Normal volume:						
Machine hours				8,000	.....	.....
Direct labor hours				.....	2,000	12,000
Burden rate				$3.554	$5.6035	$1.59675

cations will be worthwhile; otherwise, the far simpler variable costing system should be used.

The only valid reason for omitting allocations altogether from product unit costing procedures is on the grounds of immateriality—either overhead costs are entirely fixed or the variability is so small that it can be ignored, at a consequent saving in bookkeeping costs. It should be clear from the preceding chapter that adoption of the variable costing principle is not an argument for excluding *all* factory overhead costs from product cost. Variable overhead costs are just as much a part of variable cost as direct labor and materials.

No matter which of these alternatives is selected, costs above the factory level are almost never allocated to factory cost centers. The same is true when the costing unit is the research project or the advertising program—that is, costs incurred at higher management levels are not included in project or program cost.

In general, the relationship between these costs and individual departmental operations is so difficult to establish that the effort is usually abandoned. These costs are likely to be assigned to jobs only when sales contracts specify that prices are to be based on actual costs, and even then crude divisionwide or companywide averages are more likely to be used than interdepartmental allocations.

SUMMARY

The underlying objective of departmentalizing the burden rate is to produce product costs that are more nearly representative of the total short-run and long-run costs necessary to manufacture each product. This usually leads the accountant to develop a scheme of interdepartmental cost allocations, so that costs that are not traceable to direct production or research centers can be included in the burden rates of these centers.

Ideally, the fixed costs of service and support centers should be allocated by means of capacity charges; the variable costs should be allocated by means of transfer prices or activity charges. If the service is measurable, a transfer price is appropriate; if not, an activity charge is the only possibility. Capacity charges for the fixed costs should be based on potential usage, that is, usage during periods of peak service department operation.

It might seem that the accuracy of product or project costs can be improved by multiplying the number of cost centers, each of them consisting of a single operation or series of related operations. From the discussion in this chapter, however, it should be apparent that this added accuracy may be more apparent than real. The narrower the segment of plant operations, the greater is the proportion of allocated costs. Because many of these allocations must be made in a highly arbitrary fashion, the gain from a greater homogeneity of operations may be largely offset by the lessened significance of the cost center cost totals.

This is not to imply that burden rates are more accurate for larger cost centers. It simply means that further subdivision of a responsibility unit into smaller cost centers for product costing may not add to the accuracy of product costs while misleading some people into believing that it does.

EXERCISES AND PROBLEMS

1.* The Hubbard Woods Company applies factory overhead to all orders by use of departmental burden rates. The divisions of the factory for this purpose are (1) melting and pouring, (2) molding, (3) core making, and (4) cleaning and grinding. From the data shown below, prepare an overhead distribution sheet showing in detail the manufacturing overhead chargeable to each department under an absorption costing system.

Normal manufacturing costs per month are:

```
Indirect labor:
    Melting and pouring.............................. $1,000
    Molding.........................................    300
    Core making.....................................    100
    Cleaning and grinding...........................    300
Supplies used:
    Melting and pouring.............................     50
    Molding.........................................     50
    Core making.....................................    200
    Cleaning and grinding...........................    100
Taxes (equipment $12, building $24)..................     36
Compensation insurance...............................     65
Power................................................     50
Heat and light.......................................     80
Depreciation—building................................     64
Depreciation—equipment...............................     60
        Total........................................ $2,455
```

Department	Floor Space (Sq. Ft.)	Cost of Equipment	Direct Labor	Compensation Insurance†	Horsepower Rating
Melting and pouring.......	500	$2,000	....	$2.00	10
Molding.................	2,000	500	$1,200	1.00	..
Core making............	500	1,500	500	1.00	10
Cleaning and grinding......	1,000	2,000	1,300	1.50	30
Total..................	4,000	$6,000	$3,000	...	50

† Rate per $100 of payroll.

2.* A factory has four direct production departments and three service departments. One of these service departments, department S, has costs of $2,000 a month plus $0.20 for each unit of department S service provided to other departments.

Monthly service unit consumption and volume of production activity in the factory's four direct production departments are normally as follows:

* Solutions to problems marked with an asterisk can be found in Appendix B.

Department	Service Units	Production Volume
1........................	1,000	10,000 direct labor hours
2........................	5,000	8,000 direct labor hours
3........................	8,000	20,000 machine-hours
4........................	6,000	15,000 direct labor hours
Total....................	20,000	

Service consumption is wholly fixed in department 1 and proportionally variable with volume in the other three departments.

Each batch of 1,000 units of product A requires 10 direct labor hours in department 1, 20 direct labor hours in department 2, 100 machine-hours in department 3, and 5 direct labor hours in department 4. Overhead is charged to products on the basis of predetermined departmental burden rates, including provisions for service department costs.

a) How much department S cost would be included in the cost of a batch of product A if costing is on a full costing basis?

b) How much department S cost should be included in the cost of a batch of product A if costing is on a variable costing basis?

3. The Calnan Company's Elmira factory has seven production and four service departments. One of the service departments, department S, has the following monthly budget at its normal monthly volume of 1,400 service hours:

Service labor...........................	$4,200
Supervision............................	700
Supplies...............................	280
Depreciation...........................	1,750
Other costs............................	70
Total................................	$7,000

All of these except supervision and depreciation are proportionately variable with volume. Supervision costs represent the salary of the department head. Depreciation is the straight-line amortization of the cost of the equipment used in department S (seven identical service machines).

Raw materials for product X are processed in department 1 and then transferred to department 2 for finishing. Product X is only one of the many products that these two production departments work on every month.

Normal monthly operating statistics for these two departments are as follows:

	Department 1	Department 2
Normal monthly operating volume....	25,000 pounds of output	10,000 direct labor hours
Normal monthly consumption of department S services.............	300 service hours	200 service hours

Consumption of department S services in these two departments varies in direct proportion to changes in operating volume.

One unit of product X weighs 10 pounds and requires five direct labor hours in department 2.

a) How much department S cost should be included in the cost of a unit of product X on a full cost basis?

b) How much department S cost should be included in the cost of a unit of product X on a variable costing basis?

c) How much department S cost should be included in the cost of a unit of product X on an attributable costing basis?

4. Department 3 in the Calnan Company's Elmira factory (see the preceding problem) uses a good deal of department S service. Under normal conditions, it will use 100 hours of service each month for routine work plus one service hour for every 100 direct labor hours in department 3.

Normal volume in department 3 is 10,000 direct labor hours a month, and a departmental burden rate is computed on that basis.

a) How large a provision for the costs of department S should be included in a variable costing burden rate for department 3?

b) How large a provision for the costs of department S should be included in an attributable costing burden rate for department 3?

c) Department 3 employs an outside company, Factory Services, Inc., to do some work that Calnan's own service departments are not equipped to do. Factory Services has offered to do the work now done by department S in department S under an annual contract at a flat fee of $500 a month. The decision on this proposal is to be made by the manager of the Elmira factory. Analyze the proposal and recommend a course of action.

5. The Langdon Company has two producing and two service departments. Estimated monthly cost and operating data in a normal year are as follows.

Direct departmental costs are:

	Department			
	Producing Able	Producing Baker	Maintenance	General Plant
Direct labor cost....................	$15,000	$20,000	...	...
Maintenance labor cost...............	...	...	$6,000	...
Other indirect labor.................	8,000	14,000	1,000	$13,500
Total labor cost....................	$23,000	$34,000	$7,000	$13,500
Maintenance materials...............	...	...	900	...
Other indirect materials.............	600	7,000	...	1,500
Miscellaneous costs.................	2,600	4,000	1,900	1,000
Total costs........................	$26,200	$45,000	$9,800	$16,000
Maintenance hours..................	900	600	xxx	xxx

The fixed component of the indirect labor cost in each producing department is: Able, $2,000; Baker, $4,000.

Indirect materials are completely variable in both producing departments. Miscellaneous costs are completely fixed in both producing departments.

Each producing department requires some maintenance hours for routine maintenance, no matter what the level of production. In addition, Able department requires one maintenance hour for every $20 of direct labor cost in Able department and Baker department requires one maintenance hour for every $40 in Baker department direct labor cost.

In the maintenance department, maintenance labor cost and maintenance materials are considered variable with maintenance hours. Indirect labor and miscellaneous costs are fixed.

General plant costs are entirely fixed. It is assumed that the other three departments benefit from general plant services in proportion to their budgeted total labor cost.

a) Develop full cost burden rates for the two producing departments, including provisions for absorption of budgeted service department costs. Use direct labor cost as your index of volume.

b) Prepare departmental burden rates on a variable costing basis.

6. A company's factory has three producing departments, a maintenance department, and a steam electric power plant. Because the company produces a variety of products, some of them highly seasonal, and because some of the products do not require work in all departments, a considerable variation occurs from month to month in the proportion of power consumed by the various departments.

The following statistics taken from the company's annual budget show the horsepower of motors in each department, annual power consumption in kilowatt-hours, and annual direct labor costs:

	Horse-power	Power Consumption	Labor Costs
Maintenance department...........	20	30,000	......
Producing department A...........	200	480,000	$250,000
Producing department B...........	300	540,000	200,000
Producing department C...........	80	150,000	500,000
Total.........................	600	1,200,000	$950,000

Departmental burden rates are used for product costing in the three producing departments.

The annual budget for the power plant shows the following:

Fixed costs.........................	$50,400
Variable costs.......................	21,600
Total.............................	$72,000

a) What provision for electric power costs should be made in the budget of each of the four power-consuming departments if the company follows the variable costing principle in product costing? Explain.

b) How would your answer to (a) differ if the company were to use full absorption costing but still wanted variable cost information available? Show your calculations and state your reasons.

7. The Premier Company's factory has four production departments and four service departments—office, buildings, maintenance, and shipping room. All cost accounting, scheduling, and storage functions are performed in the office department. The buildings department is responsible for heating, lighting, and maintaining the factory building and grounds. The maintenance department handles repairs of all equipment except office equipment, the latter being serviced on contract by an outside firm. Shipping handles all incoming shipments and packs finished products for distribution to the company's customers and sales branches.

The annual budgets of the direct charges of the service departments, reduced to a monthly basis, are as follows:

	Office	Buildings	Mainte- nance	Shipping Room
Supervision..........................	$ 2,000	$ 500	$ 900	$ 400
Salaries.............................	12,000	.....	....	....
Indirect labor.......................	.....	3,500	6,200	1,500
Supplies............................	4,500	1,000	920	1,900
Depreciation—building...............	.....	2,500	....	....
Depreciation—equipment..............	100	100	210	....
Heat and light.......................	.....	6,000	....	....
Other direct charges.................	17,920	3,400	1,700	540
Total direct charges.................	$36,520	$17,000	$9,930	$4,340

Budgeted or normal operating data for the year, also on an average monthly basis, are:

	Floor Space (Square Feet)	Total Employees	Maintenance Labor Hours	Machine- Hours
Department 101...........	18,000	50	560	8,000
Department 102...........	16,000	40	610	12,000
Department 103...........	33,000	100	930	16,000
Department 104..........	20,000	60	500	10,000
Office....................	10,000	34	...	.....
Buildings.................	1,000	11	...	.....
Maintenance..............	1,000	17	...	.....
Shipping room............	2,000	6	...	.....
Total...................	101,000	318	2,600	46,000

Prepare a cost distribution sheet, allocating service department costs sequentially in the following sequence and on the following bases: (a) buildings

—floor space; (b) office—number of employees; (c) maintenance—maintenance labor hours; and (d) shipping room—machine-hours.

8. Elliot Associates is a medium-sized management consulting firm with headquarters in New York and a number of branch offices. All costs are traceable to the direct consulting offices except the costs of two headquarters service departments. Data on these two departments and on the Cleveland branch office are as follows:

	Service Dept. X	Service Dept. Y	Cleveland Branch	Entire Company
Normal volume..............	20,000 service units	8,000 service units	2,000 consulting hours	xxx
Direct costs at normal volume:†				
Variable costs.............	$30,000	$61,000	$40,700	xxx
Fixed costs..............	20,000	16,000	31,800	xxx
Total direct costs........	$50,000	$77,000	$72,500	xxx
Service consumption at normal volume (in units):				
Dept. X services (all consumption is variable)....	0	2,000	3,000	20,000
Dept. Y services:				
Variable portion.........	0	0	600	6,000
Fixed portion...........	0	0	400	2,000

† The costs shown for the service departments are the total direct costs of those departments. The costs shown for the Cleveland office are the direct overhead costs of that office and do not include the salaries of the consulting staff or items that are billed directly to clients.

All service department fixed costs are totally indivisible. All Cleveland fixed costs are proportionally divisible.

a) Prepare an overhead costing rate for the Cleveland office on an attributable costing basis.

b) Indicate briefly how this rate might be used. Do you think that a variable costing rate or a full costing rate would be better for these purposes than an attributable costing rate?

9.* The Tisket Tasket Casket Company, manufacturers of burial caskets and morticians' equipment, has three service departments and eight production departments. The company has decided to use predetermined rates as the basis for service department cost allocation. The budgeted direct departmental charges for the three service departments for the current year are as follows:

Department A................ $12,000 per month
Department B................ 18,000 per month
Department C................ 20,000 per month

The estimated numbers of service units budgeted for this year are as follows:

| Service | Budgeted Monthly Service Consumption by Departments | | | | |
Department	A	B	C	Production	Total
A...................	....	1,200	800	6,000	8,000
B...................	600	....	1,400	8,000	10,000
C...................	2,000	1,000	....	12,000	15,000

This table should be read as follows: service department A provides 1,200 units of service to service department B, 800 units of service to service department C, and 6,000 units of service to the various production departments.

a) Compute, for each of the three service departments, a charging rate per service unit that covers only the costs directly traceable to that department (direct departmental charges). In other words, the charging rate will not include any provision for the costs of other service departments, nor will service departments be charged for their use of other service departments' services.

b) Compute charging rates by sequential allocation, taking the service departments in alphabetical order.

c) Compute charging rates which give full recognition to the interdependence of the three service departments, using cross-allocations. Three equations must be solved simultaneously, one for each service department. The equation for department A is:

$$\text{Charging rate } A = \frac{\$12,000 + 600 \times \text{charging rate } B + 2,000 \times \text{charging rate } C}{8,000 \text{ total service units consumed}}$$

10. A manufacturing firm has four departments, two of which are producing departments (A and B) and two of which are service departments (C and D). Volume in each producing department is measured in direct labor hours. Costs are shown in the following table (DLH is direct labor hours):

| Department | Traceable Fixed Overhead Costs | Traceable Variable Overhead Costs | | Units of C's Services Required | Units of D's Services Required |
		Per DLH	Per Unit of Service		
A........	$50,000	$2.00	...	0.010 per DLH	....
B........	30,000	1.50	...	0.035 per DLH	0.0475 per DLH
C........	19,350	...	$2.00	.. ᴺᵀᴰ.ᴾ......	0.050 per unit of C's services
D........	9,780	...	3.00	0.010 per unit of D's services	....

Each line in this table shows the inputs required by one department. The line for department A, for example, shows that the traceable fixed costs of this department are $50,000, direct variable overhead costs are $2 per direct labor hour, and 0.01 of a unit of service provided by department C is needed for each direct labor hour in department A.

Expected production volume is 29,000 direct labor hours in department A and 20,000 direct labor hours in department B.

a) Compute a full cost burden rate for each producing department to the nearest tenth of a cent. (Note: This requires cross-allocations.)
b) Compute burden rates for use in a variable costing system.

11. M. Lebec has a small factory consisting of two production departments, a machinery maintenance department (serving the machines of the two production departments), a methods and scheduling department, and a small factory office. The building is rented at a monthly rental that covers the cost of heat, light, building maintenance, etc. For a typical month, the costs of general factory overhead and of the service departments are as follows:

Plant manager's salary	$1,560
Rent	2,400
Direct departmental costs—service departments:	
Factory office	1,260
Methods and schedules department	1,530
Maintenance department	1,800

All of these costs are regarded as wholly fixed and indivisible except those of the factory office and the maintenance department. The factory office costs include the salaries of the factory accountant and the bookkeeper ($1,140 a month) and forms, paper supplies, etc. ($120 in an average month—$30 fixed and $90 variable with factory direct labor hours).

Of the direct maintenance department costs, $800 represents the salary of the maintenance supervisor, depreciation on shop equipment, and other costs of providing maintenance capacity. The remaining $1,000 represents the wages of the maintenance men and the costs of maintenance supplies required for a maintenance volume of 200 maintenance labor hours a month. This $1,000 is regarded as a variable cost in that, in periods of low maintenance requirements, the maintenance men are assigned to other productive work in the factory.

The overhead costs traceable to the two production departments, A and B, are as follows:

	A	B
Fixed	$ 7,600	$1,880
Variable	4,260	1,920
Total	$11,860	$3,800

Physical statistics for a typical month are:

	Factory Office	Methods and Schedules	Maintenance	Production Dept. A	Production Dept. B
Direct labor hours	. . .	. . .	. . . .	4,000	6,000
Employees	2	2	3	18	27
Machine-hours	. . .	. . .	. . . .	6,000	3,000
Maintenance hours	. . .	. . .	. . . .	120	80
Floor space (sq. ft.)	900	300	1,200	6,400	3,200

Routine maintenance amounts to 30 hours a month in production department A and 50 hours in production department B. The remainder is variable with machine-hours.

a) Compute a full cost burden rate for each production department, first distributing the plant manager's salary and factory rent among the five departments, and then redistributing service department costs sequentially, in the left-to-right sequence shown in the table above. The allocation bases are:

> Plant manager's salary........................ Employees
> Rent.. Floor space
> Factory office.............................. Employees
> Methods and schedules....................... Machine-hours
> Maintenance................................. Maintenance hours

A machine-hour burden rate should be used in production department A; the burden rate for department B should be based on direct labor hours.

b) M. Lebec is considering whether to accept an order for 100 units of product X at a reduced price for delivery six months from now. Adequate capacity will be available to handle this order, and fixed costs will be essentially the same whether the order is accepted or rejected. Each unit of product X requires one hour of department A labor, one hour of department B labor, three machine-hours in department A and half a machine-hour in department B. How much overhead cost should be allocated to each unit of product X for purposes of this decision? You need not necessarily use the burden rates developed in (a) above, but you should explain briefly your reasons either for using these rates without adjustment or for using different figures.

chapter **11**

Costing Joint Products

When the processing of a single input or set of inputs yields two or more products, these products are referred to as joint products. Gasoline and fuel oil are joint products. So are beefsteaks and cowhides.

Joint costs are the costs of those input factors that are necessary for the manufacture and separation of all the joint products as a group and not specifically for any one of them alone. For example, livestock purchase prices and slaughtering costs are true joint costs of all of the products that the meat packer derives from cattle or hogs. The cost of curing ham, however, is not a joint cost of ham and lard but is specific to the ham—that is, it is a *separable* cost specifically traceable to one product alone.

Joint costs pose two questions for the accountant. First, how should they be treated for decision making? Second, how are they to be allocated among the individual joint products for inventory measurement? This chapter will examine these two questions.

JOINT COSTS IN DECISION MAKING

Managerial decisions that must be made in connection with joint products are essentially of two types:

1. Decisions relating to the joint products as a group—e.g., discontinue total production or expand total production.
2. Decisions relating to the depth of additional processing to be applied to individual joint products—e.g., sell the product as it stands or process it further before sale.

Joint Products as a Group

For the group of joint products as a whole, the question is whether the total revenue to be derived from the sale of all joint products, less any processing and distribution costs necessary to place these products in marketable form, is adequate to cover the incremental costs of the joint inputs. For example, the decision to work a mine which produces ore containing gold, zinc, and lead must be based on consideration of the market prices of all three metals. Inasmuch as the price of gold is fixed by law, some marginal mines are worked only when zinc and lead prices are high. The amount of newly mined gold flowing into the U.S. Treasury fluctuates with the prices of other metals that are mined jointly with gold.

A related problem is to determine the maximum price that the company can afford to pay for joint inputs of a given grade or specification. For example, in buying raw materials that vary in quality, the price that can be paid will be higher on grades that yield a greater proportion of high-value products. The maximum purchase price is a function of the total value of all the joint products less all the joint costs of processing or conversion.

Individual Joint Products

Once it has been determined that joint production is profitable, the next question is how far to process each of the joint products. For example, should cowhides be tanned or should they be sold on the market untanned? For this kind of decision, the question is whether the sale value of the product can be increased by more than the incremental separable costs.

The cost of the steer no longer has any meaning for this decision. What is relevant is opportunity cost, in this case the amount that could be realized from the sale of the untanned hides. If hides can be sold untanned for 30 cents a pound, then 30 cents a pound is the opportunity cost of any hides that are retained for further processing. (Not selling the hides at 30 cents requires the same economic sacrifice as buying hides at 30 cents; this is the meaning of opportunity cost.) The relevant comparison is:

Market value of tanned hides...............................		$0.40
Less: Market value of untanned hides.....................	$0.30	
Incremental separate processing cost.................	0.08	0.38
Incremental processing profit.............................		$0.02

The stage of production at which the joint products are separated for further independent processing or sale is commonly referred to as the *split-off point*. Exhibit 11–1 shows a process with two split-off points. Raw materials are first cooked, after which three separate products are split off: grease, a glue and water mixture, and a residue. Both the glue-water mixture and the residue are subjected to separate processing. Processing the mixture yields one product only: glue. Processing the residue, on the other hand, yields two products: grease and tankage stock. The latter is then cooked once again to yield fertilizer tankage.

Exhibit 11–1

SPLIT-OFF POINTS IN JOINT PRODUCTION

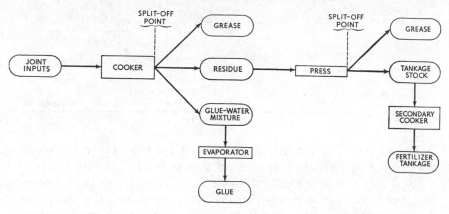

The costs of operating the primary cooker are joint costs of all the outputs. The costs of operating the evaporator, on the other hand, are separable costs of the glue and have no connection with the grease and tankage outputs. Conversely, the cost of operating the press is a joint cost of grease and tankage stock but cannot be regarded as a cost of the glue.

This illustration should demonstrate that a split-off point can be identified even if no outside markets exist for the individual products at this point. The absence of a market for one of the joint products merely means that opportunity cost for that product is zero. The desirability of processing this product further, therefore, can be determined by comparing the costs of further processing with the net market proceeds from the product after processing. No allocation of the joint costs will assist in this decision.

Separable Costs and Joint Production Decisions

The separable costs of further processing and distribution of individual products may in some cases have a bearing on the decision as to whether to manufacture the joint products as a group. In making this decision, the incremental profit from further processing should be considered but processing losses should be ignored.

For example, suppose that processing a certain material will yield 2,000 tons of product A and 500 tons of product B a week at a total joint cost of $60,000 a week. Product A can be sold for $40 a ton, but product B is unsalable without further processing. After further processing, product B can be sold for $15 a ton, but incremental separable processing costs total $6,000 a week. The decision to continue joint production should be based on the following comparison:

	A	B	Total
Sales.......................................	$80,000	$7,500	$87,500
Incremental separable processing cost.........	....	6,000	6,000
Product contribution.........................	$80,000	$1,500	$81,500
Joint processing cost......................			60,000
Joint profit................................			$21,500

But suppose that product B can be sold for only $10 a ton, or total revenues of only $5,000. Unprocessed units of product B must be trucked away at a cost of $1 a ton. In this case further processing of B cannot be justified, and the joint production decision must be based on the revenue for product A alone. Product B will be obtained along with A, but management is under no compulsion to process it further. In this case the comparison might take the following form:

Sales, product A.....................................		$80,000
Less: Joint processing costs.........................	$60,000	
Removal costs, product B......................	500	60,500
Joint profit...		$19,500

Any costs of disposing of the unwanted by-product must be charged against product A revenues, but any losses that would occur if the by-product were processed further can be disregarded.

COSTING JOINT-PRODUCT INVENTORIES

For external financial reporting, the accountant seeks to measure inventories by the amount of resources sacrificed to obtain them. This amount cannot be measured for individual joint products, however, because the joint costs apply only to the group as a whole; it can only be approximated by an allocation procedure. Three bases of allocation deserve discussion:

1. Physical unit basis.
2. Market price basis.
3. Net realization basis.

Physical Unit Basis of Allocation

The simplest method of allocation is to count the number of units of each of the joint products, add these figures together, and then divide the total number of units into the total joint cost to get an average unit cost. Under this method, all products have the same unit cost.

For example, suppose that it costs a lumber mill $5,000 to produce

100,000 board feet of lumber. This lumber is inspected and divided into five different quality grades, in the following proportions:

Grade	Board Feet
Clear	10,000
Industrial	20,000
No. 1	40,000
No. 2	20,000
No. 3	10,000
Total	100,000

In this case the average cost of $5,000 divided by 100,000, or $50 per thousand board feet, would be used to measure the cost of each of the five grades of lumber.

The main defect of this method is that it ignores the cost-value relationship implicit in accounting measurements of nonmonetary assets. The purpose of costs is to create values. The use of cost to measure assets is based on the assumption that a prudent manager will not incur costs unless the value created is likely to exceed the costs. If the value of the group is greater than the cost of producing it, then no portion of the joint cost can be said to be unproductive and no joint product can be assigned costs in excess of the value of that product.

Suppose, for instance, that the various grades of lumber can be sold at the following prices per thousand feet:

Grade	Price
Clear	$120
Industrial	90
No. 1	75
No. 2	60
No. 3	30

Use of the $50 figure for all grades implies that some of the joint costs are more productive than others, an economic impossibility. When applied to the poorest grade of lumber, it produces an even more absurd result—an apparent loss on production. If this were true, the company could avoid the loss by not producing No. 3 lumber; since this can't be done without sacrificing the other grades as well, the cost figure must be wrong.

Support for this conclusion can be found in another quarter as well. Clear evidence that outputs are not equally costly is provided by the premiums that ordinarily must be paid for higher quality inputs. For example, if a given stand of timber is expected to yield a high proportion of the higher valued grades of lumber, the timber rights will command a higher price than if the lower grades predominate. Therefore, since output value affects input cost, it would seem reasonable to reflect value differences in the cost allocation.

Market Price Basis of Allocation

A second method uses product selling prices to measure the relative values of the various joint products. This method is illustrated in

Exhibit 11-2. The prices in column (2) are the market prices of the joint products at the split-off point. Based on these prices, the market value of the joint outputs totals $7,500, as shown at the bottom of column (3). Each product's percentage of this total is then multiplied by the $5,000 total joint cost to yield the cost allocations in column (5).

Thus clear lumber has 16 percent of the total market value and therefore gets 16 percent of the joint costs, or $800. Dividing this by the output figure in column (1) yields a unit cost of $80 per thousand board feet. (The unit cost figures can also be determined by multiplying the market prices in column (2) by the cost-value ratio: $5,000/$7,500 = 2/3.)

This method does succeed in allocating all of the joint costs. Further-

Exhibit 11-2

JOINT COST ALLOCATED ON RELATIVE MARKET VALUE BASIS

Grade	(1) M Feet Pro- duced	(2) Price per M Feet	(3) Market Value (1) × (2)	(4) % of Total Market Value	(5) Total Cost Allocated (4) × $5,000	(6) Allocated Cost per M Feet (5) ÷ (1)
Clear........	10	$120	$1,200	16%	$ 800	$80
Industrial....	20	90	1,800	24	1,200	60
No. 1.......	40	75	3,000	40	2,000	50
No. 2.......	20	60	1,200	16	800	40
No. 3.......	10	30	300	4	200	20
Total........	100	xxx	$7,500	100%	$5,000	xxx

more, unit cost can never be greater than market price unless market prices are too low to cover the joint costs in total. Paradoxically, however, the method doesn't necessarily insure that the allocated cost will always be less than market value, nor that cost figures will be proportional to value. The reason is that price is not always a good measure of value. Some products that have no market price at the split-off point may be very valuable when fully processed; others with high prices may be very costly to market and distribute, so that their value is much less than their price. When either of these conditions prevails, another method must be found.

Net Realization Basis of Allocation

The merits of the market price basis can be salvaged and its defects avoided if market value is defined as net realization at the split-off point rather than market price. Net realization is defined as the selling price of the *end product* less any costs necessary to process it after the split-off point, sell it, and distribute it.

For example, suppose that our lumber company markets its output of

Exhibit 11–3

CALCULATION OF NET REALIZATION

Grade	(1) M Feet Produced	(2) End-Product Selling Price	(3) End-Product Sales Value (1) × (2)	(4) Separate Processing and Marketing Costs	(5) Net Realization (3) − (4)
Clear...........	10	$120	$1,200	....	$1,200
Industrial........	20	90	1,800	$ 40	1,760
No. 1...........	40	95	3,800	600	3,200
No. 2...........	20	80	1,600	320	1,280
No. 3...........	10	75	750	190	560
Total..........	100	xxx	$9,150	$1,150	$8,000

clear and industrial grades without further processing, but sells the other three grades only after processing each of them separately. Clear lumber can be sold without any additional marketing costs, and industrial grade lumber requires very little marketing effort. The products made from the other three grades are costly to produce and distribute, but the net realization is greater than the unprocessed lumber would generate if sold without processing.

The necessary data are shown in Exhibit 11–3. The selling prices of the finished products are shown in column (2). Column (4) shows the separate costs of processing and marketing the various products, and column (5) shows the net realization from each.

Cost allocations can now be based on these net realization figures, as in Exhibit 11–4. Each product's percentage of the total net realization of all five products combined, from column (3), is applied to the total joint cost of $5,000 to determine the amount to be allocated to each, shown in column (4). These amounts are then divided by the outputs of the various

Exhibit 11–4

COST ALLOCATION ON A NET REALIZATION BASIS

Grade	(1) M Feet Produced	(2) Net Realization	(3) Percent of Total Net Realization	(4) Joint Cost Allocated (3) × $5,000	(5) Allocated Unit Cost (4) ÷ (1)
Clear.............	10	$1,200	15	$ 750	$75
Industrial........	20	1,760	22	1,100	55
No. 1............	40	3,200	40	2,000	50
No. 2............	20	1,280	16	800	40
No. 3............	10	560	7	350	35
Total...........	100	$8,000	100	$5,000	xxx

joint products to derive the unit cost figures in column (5). Thus clear lumber provides 15 percent of the net realization and is allocated 15 percent of the joint cost, or $750. This amounts to $75 for each thousand board feet.

Using the Unit Cost Figures

The net realization method is widely used because it provides unit costs for inventory measurement that are less than the net realizable value of the units in inventory. For example, inventories of lumber in the illustration would be measured by the unit cost figures in column (5). Inventories of processed lumber would be measured by these amounts plus the average separable costs of processing the lumber. If the separable costs of No. 3 lumber are $10 for processing and $5 for marketing, inventories of the processed product will be measured at $35, their share of the joint costs, plus $10 (marketing costs are not included in the cost of unmarketed inventories).

Unit costs also enter into profit calculations. Product profit margins under the uniform net realization method are proportional to net realization, however, and no product will show a loss as long as all products as a group are profitable. It should be apparent that unit costs and profit margins determined in this way have no relevance to management decision making. The decision maker needs measures of the sacrifices that the company must make to secure units of the individual products. No method designed to allocate all of the joint costs to the various joint products will provide this information.

By the same token, the unit costs of individual joint products should not be used in depth-of-processing decisions. For example, suppose that the clear lumber can be converted into cabinets at an incremental cost of $50 per thousand square feet. The cabinets can be sold at a price of $150. If the lumber is charged against this proposal at the $75 unit cost derived in Exhibit 11–4, the proposal will look quite profitable:

Revenue..		$150
Less: Joint processing cost........................	$75	
Separable processing cost.....................	50	125
Operating margin....................................		$ 25

In view of the opportunity costs, however, the proposal is clearly unprofitable:

Incremental revenue:	
Revenue from sale of cabinets...........................	$150
Less: Revenue from sale of lumber.....................	120
Incremental revenue...............................	$ 30
Separable costs...	50
Processing loss...	$(20)

Since the total joint cost will be $5,000 whether the lumber is processed or sold "as is," the accountant's unit cost is a sunk cost and irrelevant to this decision.

THE COSTING OF BY-PRODUCTS

Cost accounting systems generally distinguish between two classes of joint products—(1) coproducts or main products and (2) by-products. The distinction is important in accounting for only one reason: co-products are costed by some variant of one of the methods described above, while by-products are costed on a different basis.

Defining By-Products

Although the distinction between the two types of products is inevitably imprecise, a reasonable working definition is that a by-product is a joint product for which the market value is an immaterial proportion of the total market value of all the joint products.

Any distinction between joint products and by-products must be regarded as strictly temporary, to be reconsidered as conditions change. Gasoline, for example, was originally thought of as a by-product in the manufacture of kerosene. With the growth of the automobile and electric lighting, kerosene became the by-product; but the jet airliner brought kerosene back into the picture as a major product once more.

Illustration of By-Product Costing

The costing method known as the by-product method consists of subtracting the net realizable value of the by-products from the total of the joint costs. The residual is then divided among the main products.

For example, suppose that a process yields three products, A, B, and C. Product C is to be treated as a by-product, A and B as main products. The total cost of processing a 1,000-pound batch of products is $934. Yield and market value data are as follows:

Product	Yield (Pounds)	Market Value per Pound	Total Market Value
A........................	200	$1.90	$ 380
B........................	500	1.50	750
C........................	300	0.10	30
Total.................	1,000	xxx	$1,160

The first step in the by-product method is to subtract the market value of the by-product from the total joint cost:

Joint cost.............................	$934
Less: Value of by-product..............	30
Cost assigned to main product............	$904

The remainder of the joint cost is then apportioned between the main products by one of the methods described earlier. A relative market value distribution is as follows:

Product	Percent of Total Market Value	Total Cost Allocated	Allocated Cost per Pound
A......................	33.6	$304	$1.52
B......................	66.4	600	1.20
Total....................	100.0	$904	xxx

This method assigns to the by-product a cost equal to its anticipated value. In the example, joint cost amounts to $934, but only $904 of this is assigned to the main products. The remaining $30 goes to product C, which then shows neither a profit nor a loss.

Timing of By-Product Recognition

By-product revenues may be recognized in the accounts either at the time of split-off or at the time the by-products are sold. Deferral until point of sale has the advantage of avoiding the need to estimate sale value. It has the disadvantage of introducing into the accounts irregularities that have nothing to do with the production operations in the periods in which the by-products are sold. Unless the total value of all of the by-products is immaterial, by-product values should be recognized in the periods in which they are produced.

Inventory Measurement of By-Products

The selection of the time for recognizing the value of by-products carries with it an implicit assumption as to the method of measuring by-product inventories. Delay in recognition to the time of sale implies that by-products will be carried as memorandum quantities only. Recognition of value at the time of split-off implies measurement at market value. This violates the cost basis for inventory measurement in general, but the effect on net income is likely to be immaterial.

JOINT PRODUCTS IN VARIABLE PROPORTIONS

Until now, we have assumed implicitly that all joint products are the output of fixed-yield processes, in which each product's percentage of the total physical output is fixed by formula, as in certain chemical reactions. Now we shall turn briefly to two kinds of variable proportions situations:

1. *Materials-determined yields:* the percentage yield of each of the joint products depends on the quality or composition of the joint materials inputs.
2. *Processing-determined yields:* the relative yields of the various joint products can be varied by alterations in the processing methods employed.

Unit costs for inventory measurement are obtained in the variable proportions case by applying the net realization method described earlier. Once relative yields are free to vary, however, measures of incremental cost can also be calculated.

Measuring Incremental Costs

Measuring incremental cost is relatively simple when the yield depends on the kind of materials used. To illustrate, suppose that materials costing $100 can be processed for $50 to yield 20 units of X and 50 units of Y. Suppose further that if higher quality materials costing $120 are used instead, the output of X will go up to 25 units without any reduction in the output of Y. The marginal cost of product X is thus $20 (the addition to cost) divided by five units (the addition to output), or $4.

The same idea can be applied to more complex situations in which yields can be influenced by the processing methods used. For example, assume that a department produces two products, X and Y, from a single process. Product X sells for $5 a pound; product Y is priced at $2 a pound. Production of these two products is currently in the ratio of 40 percent product X and 60 percent product Y, but by varying production techniques the yield of X can be increased to a maximum of 60 percent if conditions warrant.

This may be treated as a problem in the desirability of further processing. First, let us assume that the increased yield of product X results from subjecting product Y to an additional processing operation (as in subjecting gas-oil distillates to catalytic cracking to increase the gasoline yield). If 60 pounds of product Y can be processed further to yield 20 additional pounds of product X, at an incremental processing cost of $0.75 per pound, we get the following comparison:

Revenues after processing:		
Product X, 20 pounds at $5................................		$100
Product Y, 40 pounds at $2................................		80
Total..		$180
Less: Processing cost, 60 pounds at $0.75.................	$ 45	
Market value of Y processing......................	120	165
Incremental profit..		$ 15

Phrasing this in another way, the incremental cost of another 20 pounds of product X is the sum of $45 processing cost and $40 in lost revenues from the sale of 20 pounds of product Y, or $85. The incremental cost of product X is thus $4.25 a pound.

A similar set of calculations can be prepared if the increased yield results, not from further processing of one of the original joint products, but from modifications in the basic processing techniques themselves. The incremental cost of increasing the yield of any product is still the sum of incremental processing costs plus the sale value of the other joint products lost by the shift in product mix.

Measurement Difficulties

Two major difficulties hamper efforts to apply this approach in practice. First, incremental cost is not a constant but varies, depending on relative yields. If the crude run is yielding 35 percent gasoline, the cost of increasing the yield to 36 percent will probably be less than it would be to increase the yield from 40 to 41 percent. This requires the development of a schedule or table of incremental costs, one for each assumed product mix.

Second, the opportunity cost of products sacrificed to increase the yield of others is the net revenue lost by this sacrifice. This is not necessarily equal to the product price. For example, if existing market prices are rigid and increased output of product Y will merely result in increased inventories of product Y, then the opportunity cost component of the incremental cost of product X is zero. (It may even be negative to allow for inventory carrying costs.) Even if market prices are flexible, if the company's share of the market is so large that increases in sales volume can be achieved only by price reductions or greater promotional effort or both, the opportunity cost of product Y will almost certainly be less than its market price.

Incremental Cost Figures for Public Financial Reporting

Despite these difficulties, this sort of calculation is made routinely in industries such as oil refining. It is not generally available for public financial reporting, however, for two reasons. First, the incremental cost calculation is not applicable to joint production in which relative product proportions are fixed. No amount of manufacturing can increase the amount of beefsteak recoverable from any given steer, and the cattle market is not sensitive enough to provide measures of incremental cost from changes in materials specifications.

Second, when this method is used, the total costs of all of the joint products are highly unlikely to equal total joint cost. As long as outlay cost continues to be the basis for inventory costing for public financial reporting, this method cannot be used for this purpose.

CONTROL OF JOINT PRODUCT INVENTORIES

Stocks of individual joint products are likely to get out of balance unless continuing efforts are exerted to keep them in line. Increased sales of one joint product lead to increases in inventories of others; this can continue for a long time unless direct action is taken.

This problem might be solved by adjusting product prices, but this is not always feasible. Price cuts, for example, may be ruled out temporarily on the ground that the company wishes to maintain a stable price structure. Price increases in the products with greater demands may be ruled out for the same reason.

In the absence of price changes, management has three alternatives. First, it can allow the inventories to grow in the expectation that demand will pick up later on. If carrying costs are relatively modest, this may be an attractive solution.

Second, management can cut production of all products far enough to ensure that production of the slow-moving items no longer exceeds sales. This is a drastic solution and is seldom profitable. The question of operating versus not operating is, as we have pointed out, a problem in total costs and total revenues and not a matter of the profitability of any one item alone.

Finally, management can devote more selling effort to the overstocked products. Cost allocations should not affect the decision to do this, but they often do. Unless the margin between selling price and allocated cost is big enough to cover the additional marketing costs, the additional effort will appear to be unprofitable and will not be made.

Recalculation of the joint cost allocations in this situation may help, but they still will not tell the manager how much he can afford to spend to move his surplus stocks. For this purpose, the only relevant figure is opportunity cost, and this may even be negative. To avoid misunderstandings, joint cost allocations should not be reported to executives who make decisions on individual joint products unless they measure opportunity costs.

SUMMARY

When products are produced independently, a large number of costs can be attributed clearly to one product or another by the methods described in the preceding chapters. When two or more products are produced jointly from a single set of inputs, however, no such identification is possible. Unit costs can be computed by methods outlined in this chapter, but they have no relevance in decision making and should be ignored for that purpose. The sole purpose of joint cost allocation is for public financial reporting, or to find "reasonable" solutions for such purposes as price determination under cost-plus pricing contracts or value estimation for insurance or tax purposes.

EXERCISES AND PROBLEMS

1. The Emilia Company allocates joint costs between first-quality and second-quality products on the basis of their relative market value at the split-off point.

Selling prices and allocated unit costs are as follows:

	Price	Cost
Firsts	$1.75	$1.50
Seconds	1.40	1.20

The seconds are reworked at a cost of 33 cents a unit. They are then sold as first-quality products. What unit cost would you assign to any of these reworked units that remain in the inventory at the end of the period?

2. The Omar Meat Company is a "breaker." It inspects meat carcasses in packing houses to find top prime grade carcasses which it cuts and either sells immediately or cures. All cuts except ribs and loins are sold to the chains and retail meat market at cost or below. The ribs and loins are cured from two to four weeks at 33 degrees and kept free of mold, and are then sold as "Omar's vintage beef." The cured boneless prime loin strip sold in November for $2.33 a pound in 100-pound minimum lots to restaurants and clubs. The price for smaller lots was $4 a pound, dry-iced and prepaid. The Omar Meat Company's profits run $75,000 on a gross of $2,500,000.

a) What kind of cost calculation would result in the statement "sold to the chains and retail meat markets at cost or below?"
b) Comment on the usefulness of the calculation described in (a) for (1) guiding management in pricing the other cuts to chains and retail meat markets, and (2) costing any inventory of such other cuts on hand as of a balance sheet date.

3. During the past year the Atom Chemical Company converted raw materials into 500,000 pounds of material A and one million gallons of liquid B. The total joint cost of production was $388,000. After separation, material A was further processed and converted into material C at an additional cost of 3 cents a pound. The sales price of material C was 40 cents a pound and that of liquid B 30 cents a gallon.

a) Prepare a physical flow diagram of these processes. Enter cost, quantity, and price data on this diagram.
b) Compute the unit cost that you would use to measure each of these products for public financial reporting.

4.* The total cost of processing 100,000 barrels of crude petroleum—including raw material, labor, and overhead—is $440,000. Expected yields and market values of products are as shown below. Compute unit product costs for inventory costing purposes.

Product	Barrel Yield	Estimated Market Values	
		Per Barrel	Total
Aviation gasoline...............	8,000	$ 6.25	$ 50,000
Motor gasoline.................	42,000	5.00	210,000
Kerosene......................	10,000	4.40	44,000
Distillate fuels.................	20,000	4.00	80,000
Lubricants.....................	5,000	10.00	50,000
Residual fuels..................	10,000	2.60	26,000
Gases and loss.................	5,000	...	.....
Total........................	100,000	xxx	$460,000

5. The Jensen Chemical Company has a plant which produces two chemicals, borine and selinate, in a single joint process. The total cost incurred to the split-off point is $864,000 a month. Monthly production is two million gallons of borine and 300,000 pounds of selinate.

Borine is processed further to make one of the company's branded products, Tri-Bor. The net realization from sales of Tri-Bor, after deducting separate processing costs, is equivalent to 45 cents a gallon of borine. The average selling price of selinate is 20 cents a pound.

a) Compute the total cost and unit cost of borine on the assumption that selinate is a coproduct.
b) Compute the total cost and unit cost of borine on the assumption that selinate is a by-product.

6.* The General Chemical Company makes a broad range of chemicals. In one of its processing units two materials are combined to make three joint products. The relative market value method is used to allocate the joint costs among the products, and the relevant cost, price, and quantity information is given below.

* Solutions to problems marked with an asterisk can be found in Appendix B.

Input	Quantity	Cost per Unit
Material A............................	100 lbs.	$0.12
Material B............................	50 gals.	0.15
Direct labor..........................	3 hrs.	2.00
Manufacturing overhead................	3 hrs.	3.50

Output	Quantity	Price per Unit
Product I............................	30 lbs.	$0.60
Product II...........................	60 lbs.	0.40
Product III..........................	20 gals.	0.30

What is the unit cost of each product, using the company's method?

7. A process yields two products, Nix and Pox. Ten pounds of raw materials cost $42 and yield 7 pounds of Nix and 3 pounds of Pox. Costs of processing the materials average $22 for each 10 pounds of materials. Nix sells at a price of $9 a pound. Pox sells for $4 a pound, but only after the company spends $1 a pound to process it into salable form.

The process is now operating at its maximum physical capacity. Total output of Nix and Pox cannot be increased.

a) Using the net realization basis, compute a unit cost for each of the two products.
b) A new proposal has just been made to use 10,000 pounds of Nix to manufacture 10,000 pounds of a new product each month. The new product would yield $15 a pound in revenues; incremental costs to produce and sell the new product would average $6.25 a pound, excluding the cost of Nix. Should the proposal be accepted?
c) Should the proposal described in (b) be accepted if the total output of Nix and Pox can be increased at approximately the same average costs as for existing production? You may assume that sales of the new product would not affect outside sales of Nix. Specify any additional information you would need before making this decision.

8. A company processes soybeans. The initial process separates soybean oil and leaves a cakelike residue. The cake is then ground and moisturized to form soybean meal.

Last week the company processed 10,000 bushels of soybeans to yield 90,000 pounds of soybean oil and 450,000 pounds of cake. Further processing of the cake yielded 500,000 pounds (250 tons) of meal, the increase in weight resulting from added moisture.

The cost of the beans was $2.40 a bushel, the costs of joint processing were $5,760, and the costs of processing the cake into meal amounted to $1,000. The market price of meal was $60 a ton, and the market price of oil was 20 cents a pound.

a) Compute unit costs for the week using the net realization method of cost allocation.
b) Compute unit costs allocating joint costs on a physical unit basis.
c) The company has an opportunity to sell 50,000 pounds of cake. What figure would you use as the cost of cake for the purpose of deciding whether to take advantage of this opportunity?

9. The Andrews Creamery Company receives bulk from farmers. The largest portion of this milk is pumped into holding tanks for subsequent pasteurization, homogenization, and bottling. The remainder is fed into cream separators, in which the cream is separated from skim milk. Some of the cream is then pasteurized and bottled for sale. The remainder is churned into butter. Skim milk is sold to a local cheese facotry.

During January the Andrews Creamery received 20,384 hundredweight (cwt.) of bulk milk, with a butterfat content of 820 cwt., for which it paid farmers $75,625. The output of the creamery for the month was as follows:

	Total Cwt.	Butterfat Content Cwt.
Whole milk......................	13,580	522
Cream for sale....................	569	228
Cream for butter.................	167	67
Skim milk.......................	5,968	...
Losses..........................	100	3
Total.........................	20,384	820

The estimated market value of the creamery's output for the month was $1.01 per cwt. plus $78 per cwt. of butterfat content. Processing costs for the month amounted to $4,484.

a) Compute the cost per cwt. for each class of the creamery's products on a relative market value basis and prepare a summary showing the total costs allocated to each product class. No cost is to be assigned to lost product.

b) How would you cost product losses in a management report for the month?

10. Products A, B, and C are joint products. Products A and B are treated as main products; product C is treated as a by-product, its market value of $20 a pound being subtracted from joint costs at the time of split-off. The remaining joint costs are allocated between the main products on the basis of relative market values less completion costs.

During July, joint product costs amounted to $85,000 and costs of separate processing of product B totaled $10,000. The month's production was as follows:

> Product A............................ 30,000 lbs.
> Product B............................ 10,000 lbs.
> Product C............................   200 lbs.

Product A sells at a net price of $2 a pound; product B is sold at a price of $4 a pound.

a) How much of the joint cost is assigned to each unit of product C?

b) How much of the joint cost is assigned to each unit of product A?

c) In view of its high price per pound, do you agree with the company's decision to treat product C as a by-product? Explain briefly.

d)   A proposal has been made to cost inventories of product A at $2 a pound and unprocessed product B at zero, on the ground that these figures represent their opportunity costs. Comment briefly on this proposal.

11.* A department processes materials to yield two joint products, A and B. The following data relate to the month of May:

(1)   Materials issued to the department, $7,920.
(2)   Departmental processing costs, $9,240.
(3)   Finished production: 10,000 gallons of A (market value, $8,000); 5,000 gallons of B (market value, $12,000).
(4)   Work in process, May 1: none.
(5)   Work in process, May 31: 2,000 gallons, complete as to materials and half processed in the department (each gallon is assumed to yield one-half gallon of A and one-fourth gallon of B—the other one-fourth gallon of materials is lost through evaporation).

Compute unit costs by the relative market value method. (Note: You will need to compute equivalent production in dollars of market value.)

12. Product X and material Y are produced at a joint cost of $105,000 a month. Material Y is then processed further at a cost of $20,000 a month to become product Z.

Both X and Z are sold outright to a chain of grocery stores and the company incurs no selling expenses on these products. Material Y cannot be sold without further processing and cannot be obtained from other sources outside the company.

In a normal month, output consists of the following quantities and prices:

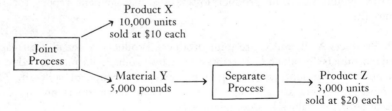

a)   How much profit does the company earn on sales of product Z?
b)   This company has 100 units of product X in its inventory. Given only the information above, at what amount would you expect the company to report this inventory on its balance sheet? Explain your calculations and your reasons for selecting the method you used.

13.† The Stendahl Company has used the net realization method to allocate joint costs between two products. Product A has a sales value of $10 a unit, while product B has no sales value without further processing. After separate processing, product B is sold for $6 a pound.

The company has just hired a new chief accountant, who feels that the net realization method assigns too much cost to product B. "We need both

---

† Based on a suggestion by Professor Lawrence Benninger.

of these products to make the process pay," he said recently. "This means that every dollar we spend processing product B makes just as great a contribution to earnings as a dollar spent on the main process."

Production in a typical month amounts to 5,000 units of product A and 10,000 units of product B. The costs of the joint process amount to $67,000 and separate processing of product B costs $10,000. The chief accountant's proposal is to place all costs in a single pool and allocate them on the basis of the relative sales value of the two products. The ratio is:

$$\frac{\text{Cost}}{\text{Sales value}} = \frac{\$67,000 + \$10,000}{5,000 \times \$10 + 10,000 \times \$6} = 70 \text{ percent}$$

a) What unit costs would emerge if the chief accountant's proposal were adopted?

b) What unit costs would be derived from the net realization method?

c) Which allocation method would you support? Give the reasons for your choice.

14. The Umbrage Hosiery Company sells its entire output of hosiery to several large chain store organizations, which market them under the chain stores' own brand names. During June, the hosiery mill's output and costs were as follows:

Production (pairs):
Firsts...................................... 8,000
Seconds.................................... 800
Rejects.................................... 200

Costs:
Joint materials and processing costs.............. $11,790
Packing and trademarking, firsts.................. 400
Packing, seconds............................. 16

Prices (per pair):
Firsts...................................... $1.55
Seconds.................................... 1.02
Rejects.................................... 0.20
Scrap recovery............................. $230

All firsts and seconds were sold. The company could have sold at least 20 percent more firsts at the same prices if the products had been available.

a) Compute unit cost using the net realization method and treating firsts and seconds as coproducts and rejects as by-products.

b) The factory accountant has been asked to compute the losses on seconds and rejects and report them to management. He has decided to measure these losses as the difference between average unit cost and the sales value of seconds and rejects at the split-off point. (1) Compute average unit cost for this purpose and measure the losses. (2) How much cost would you assign to firsts under this approach? (3) State your reasons for agreeing or disagreeing with this method of measuring losses on seconds and rejects.

15. The Wilde Corporation operates a factory with two production departments. Materials first pass through department I, where a substantial loss

in weight takes place at the start of processing. The semiprocessed materials pass on to department II, where they are processed further to form two separate products, Elong and Ulong, together with a waste material known as "tailings." The following data refer to the month of April:

	Department I	Department II
Quantities (pounds):		
Materials received........................	100,000	80,000 (from Dept. I)
Work in process, April 1 (materials 100% complete, one half processed in department)......	20,000	None
Work completed...........................	80,000	{20,000 Elong / 50,000 Ulong / 8,000 tailings}
Work in process, April 30 (materials 100% complete, one third processed in department).....	15,000	None
Costs:		
Costs in process, April 1:		
Materials.............................	$ 8,100	None
Processing costs........................	6,000	None
Materials received........................	28,000	?
Processing costs incurred.................	46,700	$31,050

Sales and selling costs during April were as follows:

	Elong	Ulong	Tailings
Selling price per pound.....................	$ 3.00	$ 2.00	$0.10
Units sold (pounds)........................	18,000	70,000	8,000
Traceable costs of packing and delivery........	$2,700	$14,000	0

The traceable costs of packing and delivery were wholly variable with the number of pounds sold. In addition, fixed selling and administrative costs, not traceable to any product, amounted to $40,000 for the month.

The company uses the moving average method of inventory costing. Joint cost is allocated on the basis of the net realization method. Tailings are to be treated as a by-product.

a) Compute the total cost and cost per unit of department I inventory in process on April 30.
b) Compute the unit costs that would be used in recording the transfer to finished goods inventory of Elong, Ulong, and tailings, respectively.
c) Prepare unit cost figures for department I that can be used by management as rough indicators of departmental efficiency during the month of April.
d) Inventories of Elong have been increasing during recent months, and it is now believed that it will not be possible to sell more than 18,000 pounds a month in the foreseeable future. Sales of Ulong are expected to average 50,000 pounds a month. Two pounds of Elong are produced for every five pounds of Ulong, and these proportions cannot be altered.

The production manager has recently figured out a way of treating Elong to make it acceptable to a few customers who use a competing product. Approximately 2,000 pounds of treated Elong can be sold each month to these customers, at a price of $2.50 a pound. The costs of treatment would be $0.50 a pound, and the costs of selling the product would be $0.20 a pound. Should the 2,000 pounds of Elong be treated in this way? Support your conclusion with figures from this problem and a concise statement of your reasoning.

16. The management of Lincoln Products Company is considering a customer's request for a monthly shipment of 10,000 pounds of Awlcon, an industrial chemical, at a mill price of 70 cents a pound. This is considerably less than its current list price of 90 cents, but higher than its standard manufacturing cost (66 cents). Management would like to accept this contract, but only if it will increase the company's profits.

Awlcon is a specialty product, not available from other manufacturers. It is used as a processing chemical in several industries; the largest present user buys about 5,000 pounds a month. The proposed contract would be the company's first breakthrough into the rubber products industry. Because the end uses are so different, management has little fear that lower prices to the rubber manufacturers would spread to its other customers. In any case, management is convinced that it will never penetrate this industry without some price concessions.

Awlcon is manufactured in two stages. In the first stage, raw materials are processed to produce two intermediates, in fixed proportions. One of these intermediates is then processed further to yield a product called Tincon; the other intermediate is converted into Awlcon in a separate finishing operation.

The Awlcon finishing process yields both finished Awlcon and a waste material. This waste material has no market value, but the company is able to convert it into a salable product called Griscon. The company can sell as much Griscon as it can produce, at a price of 30 cents a pound.

The relationships between these production processes can be seen in the following diagram:

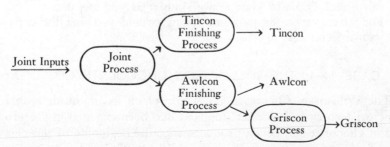

The company has a standard costing system which yields the following total standard cost per pound for each product, based on the net realization method:

Tincon	$0.38
Awlcon	0.66
Griscon	0.30

Volume, costs, and prices are expected to be at normal levels for the next year. Production quantity, market price per pound, and sales volume are as follows in a normal month:

	Quantity (Pounds)	Market Price	Market Value
Tincon.................	400,000	variable	$194,000
Awlcon.................	100,000	$0.90	90,000
Griscon.................	10,000	0.30	3,000
Total.................			$287,000

At these normal volumes, materials and processing costs are expected to total as follows:

	Basic Process	Separate Finishing Processes		
		Tincon	Awlcon	Griscon
Materials........................	$ 64,000	$22,000	$ 3,000	$ 200
Labor...........................	30,000	45,000	18,000	1,100
Variable overhead.................	6,000	10,000	5,000	100
Fixed overhead...................	10,000	5,000	1,000	600
Total...........................	$110,000	$82,000	$27,000	$2,000

Output can be increased or decreased fairly easily by as much as 25 percent of normal volume. Any larger increase would require an expansion of plant capacity. Within these limits, materials, labor, and variable overhead costs tend to vary directly and proportionately with volume, while fixed costs remain fairly stable. Selling and administrative costs are entirely fixed and none of them can be traced to any of the three products.

a) Under what conditions, if any, would you recommend acceptance of this order? Quantify your answer insofar as you are able.

b) For what purpose or purposes, if any, would you find the company's standard unit cost figures useful?

CASE 11–1: THE WILLIAMSON CHOCOLATE CO., LTD.†

The Williamson Chocolate Co., Ltd., which has its headquarters and principal factory in Leicester, England, has been engaged in the production of chocolate and cocoa products since the beginning of this century. Subsidiary companies have been established in Canada, Australia, and South Africa, and each of the subsidiaries manufactures the more important of the company's products and markets them in its home market.

† This case was written by Professor David Solomons. Copyright 1964 by l'Institut pour l' Etude des Méthodes de Direction de l' Entreprise (IMEDE), Lausanne, Switzerland. Reproduced by permission. Places and dates have been disguised.

The Australian company is located in Melbourne, where all of its manu-facturing activities take place, and warehouses for local distribution are also maintained in Sydney, Adelaide, and Perth. The main output at the factory is chocolate in bars. Cocoa beans, the principal raw material for the manufacture of chocolate, are imported from abroad. As a rule, the beans are cleaned, roasted, ground, and then passed through a press. In the press, cocoa butter is separated from cocoa powder, which comes out of the press in the form of cocoa cake. The cocoa butter leaves the press in liquid form because of the heat that is generated during the press opera-tion. The cocoa butter is then stored in large tanks, ready for use in the current production of chocolate.

The Melbourne factory was a net user of cocoa butter, i.e., its chocolate production called for more cocoa butter than could be obtained from the pressing of cocoa beans for powder manufacture. This extra cocoa butter could have been imported but it was subject to a heavy import duty, and the local management believed that it was cheaper to import beans and extract the cocoa butter from them. As a result of implementing this policy the factory found itself with a steadily mounting stock of cocoa powder.

The following figures show how the stock of cocoa powder (in pounds) increased during the period 1968–70:

1968:		
Stock at January 1, 1968..........................		30,500
Output of press.................................		416,975
		447,475
Less: Usage in 1968...........................		324,500
Stock at December 31, 1968.....................		122,975
1969:		
Output of press.................................		638,750
		761,725
Less: Usage in 1969...........................	506,420	
Sales in 1969...............................	35,500	541,920
Stock at December 31, 1969.....................		219,805
1970:		
Output of press.................................		792,125
		1,011,930
Less: Usage in 1970...........................	641,600	
Sales in 1970...............................	43,385	684,985
Stock of cocoa powder, December 31, 1970..........		326,945

These large stocks of cocoa powder held at the factory caused a serious storage problem, and the local management made continuous efforts to find profitable outlets for the excess cocoa powder. However, the sale of this powder on the Australian market raised a question as to its proper valuation. In accordance with accounting instructions issued by the head office in London some time before the last war, the cost of the cocoa beans purchased together with the labor and overhead costs of the pressing process had to be allocated between the cocoa butter and the cocoa cake on the basis of the fat content remaining in these two products after the pressing operations. This gave a cost for cocoa powder of about $0.23 a pound or about 50% above its current market price at the end of 1970. The company was therefore unable to dispose of its excess stock of cocoa cake without incurring a considerable loss. For balance sheet purposes, however, the company made a provision in its accounts in order to bring the book value of its stock of cocoa down to the market value.

During 1971, cocoa prices fell further and the subsidiary was unable to sell any large quantities of its excess stocks, because its costs were too high. There was practically no internal market for cocoa cake. It did succeed, however, in exchanging 13,000 pounds of cake against 2,000 pounds of cocoa butter with another manufacturer.

In the middle of 1971, Mr. Cannon, the marketing manager, brought forward a scheme to market a new cocoa preparation for making a hot chocolate drink. The marketing prospects seemed good so long as the selling price could be kept low enough. This new product offered a promising means of disposing of the excess stocks of cocoa powder but only if they were costed out at substantially less than the cost allocated to them in the books.

The production manager, Mr. Parker, supported this proposal with enthusiasm. He had repeatedly drawn the attention of the subsidiary's managing director, Mr. Woodstock, to the storage problem created by the cocoa stocks, and he welcomed the possibility which now opened up of dealing with this problem once for all. Besides, he said, he had never been able to see the logic of basing the cost of cocoa powder on its fat content. It was its flavor which was important, and fat content had little to do with flavor.

Both Cannon and Parker were surprised to find that Mr. Woodstock was not unreservedly enthusiastic about Cannon's proposal. He pointed out that if cocoa powder were charged to the new product at present cost levels, the product would never show a profit; and without a drop in the price of cocoa beans greater than anyone could at present foresee, the only way to reduce the cost of cocoa powder would be to change the basis of cost allocation between cocoa powder and cocoa butter. This could not be done without permission from London and he was by no means certain that such permission would be given unless some basis of cost allocation which was clearly better than the present one could be proposed. It was all very well to attack the present basis of allocation, as Mr. Parker had done. But unless he or somebody else could suggest a better one, why should London agree to a change?

Mr. Woodstock went on to point out that there was another aspect of the matter which made him reluctant to approach London. If the allocation of costs to cocoa powder were reduced, with a consequent increase in the cost of cocoa butter, the calculation which had been supplied to

London in 1967 to support the expenditure of $40,000 on a new cocoa press would be completely undermined. Only on the basis of the present cost of producing cocoa butter as compared with the cost of importing it could investment in the press be justified. If more cost were to be allocated to cocoa butter, it might be shown that it ought to be imported after all, and the investment in the press would be shown to have been misguided.

a)   What alternative methods of eliminating the surplus cocoa power are available to Mr. Woodstock? What figures would he want to consider?

b)   What should Mr. Woodstock tell London? Should he recommend a change in the allocation method?

chapter **12**

Standard Product Costs
for Management Decisions

Useful though historical product cost data often are, many companies supplement them or even replace them entirely with standard costs. Standard product costs are developed in the first instance to permit management to judge whether costs are higher than they should be—in other words, their main purpose is to provide information for use in cost control.

The role of standard costs in cost control will be discussed in depth in later chapters. The purpose of this chapter is to explain what standard costs are and how they should be used in the development of cost estimates for managerial decision making.

STANDARD COST FILES

The standard cost files in job order production contain three kinds of information:

1. *Standard prices:* the standard price for each type of material, each component part, and each category of factory labor, together with the standard overhead rate for each production center.

2. *Standard operations costs:* the standard input quantities required to perform each production operation within the factory's capability, multiplied by their standard prices or rates.

3. *Standard product costs:* for each product, a list of the standard input quantities that are deemed necessary for the manufacture of one product unit, multiplied by standard input prices.

Data in the first two categories are combined into standard product costs by means of three kinds of documents:

1. The standard bill of materials.
2. The standard operations flow sheet.
3. The standard cost sheet.

Bill of Materials

Materials quantity standards start from product specifications as to size, shape, appearance, desired performance characteristics, and permissible tolerance limits. These are reflected in the bill of materials, which describes and indicates the quantity required of each of the various materials and parts that will go into the creation of the finished product. A sample bill of materials, for a product known as a base plate, is shown in Exhibit 12–1.

Exhibit 12–1

BILL OF MATERIALS

STANDARD MATERIALS REQUIREMENTS

ITEM Base Plate No. 423

STANDARD QUANTITY 1,000

DRAWING NO. 9463

DATE 11/14/—

MATERIALS			REMARKS
No.	Description	Required for Standard Lot	
176	Steel plate	4,200 lbs.	

PARTS

Part No.	Description	Specs. per Unit	Required for Lot	Part No.	Description	Specs. per Unit	Required for Lot
201	Anchor	1	1,010				
217	Brace	2	2,080				

Operations Flow Sheet

Labor quantity standards also start from product specifications, which determine the factory operations necessary to manufacture the product.

Exhibit 12–2

OPERATIONS ROUTING SHEET

	STANDARD OPERATIONS LIST				
ITEM Base Plate No. 423				DRAWING NO. 9463	
STANDARD QUANTITY 1,000				DATE 11/14/—	

Dept.	Operations		Job Class	Hours Allowed	Remarks
	No.	Description			
P	1731	Setup	1	2.0	
M	2146	Cut	2	5.5	
M	2172	Drill	2	21.0	
M	2175	Bevel	3	6.0	
M	2304	Polish	3	14.5	
A	2903	Press	5	2.5	
A	2905	Slip	5	2.5	

These operations are summarized on a flow sheet such as the one shown in Exhibit 12–2. This flow sheet specifies the operations to be performed and the labor quantities required for each. The column headed "Job Class" specifies the kind of employee who normally should be assigned to each operation. The form may also specify the equipment to be used and the amount of machine time required.[1]

Standard Cost Sheet

Standard product costs are computed by entering the data from the standard bill of materials and the standard flow sheet, together with standard materials prices and wage rates obtained from the standard cost files, on a standard product cost sheet such as that shown in Exhibit 12–3. This shows the operations, materials, and costs deemed reasonably necessary for a lot of 1,000 units of the product. The first column specifies the types

---

[1] Typical bills of materials and operations flow sheets contain more detail than is appropriate here. For more realistic illustrations, see Robert I. Dickey (ed.), *Accountants' Cost Handbook* (2d ed.; New York: Ronald Press, 1960), sec. 15, pp. 8–19.

Exhibit 12–3

STANDARD COST SHEET

Description: Base Plate No. 423
Batch Quantity: 1,000 pieces

Standard Cost per Batch: $915.60
Standard Cost per Unit: $0.9156

STANDARD COST SHEET

Operation or Item	Dept.	Materials			Labor			Overhead			
		Quantity	Price	Cost	Hours	Rate	Cost	Base	Quantity	Rate	Cost
Setup	P				2.0	3.50	7.00	LH	2.0	4.00	8.00
Steel plate	M	4,200	0.06	252.00							
Cut	M				5.5	3.00	16.50	MH	5.5	2.40	13.20
Drill	M				21.0	3.00	63.00	MH	32.0	2.40	76.80
Bevel	M				6.0	3.00	18.00	MH	5.0	2.40	12.00
Polish	M				14.5	3.00	43.50	MH	41.5	2.40	99.60
Anchor	A	1,010	0.14	141.40							
Press	A				2.5	2.00	5.00	LH	2.5	1.80	4.50
Brace	A	2,080	0.07	145.60							
Slip	A				2.5	2.00	5.00	LH	2.5	1.80	4.50
Total		..	..	539.00	..	..	158.00	..	..	..	218.60

of materials required and the operations to be performed, while the second identifies the departments responsible. The next six columns list the quantities and costs of these various standard inputs.

The first column under "Overhead" identifies the input on which overhead charges are based. (LH stands for direct labor hours and MH stands for machine-hours.) The next column indicates how many of these input units are to be used. Multiplying the amounts in this column by the appropriate burden rates yields the standard overhead cost, in this case totalling $218.60. The column totals are then added together and the total is entered in the top right-hand corner of the form.

Standard Overhead Cost

The concepts underlying standard overhead costs are virtually identical with the concepts underlying the application of overhead to products through the use of burden rates, except that the overhead assigned to a product depends on some standard input quantity required to make the product rather than on the actual input quantity. For example, if the burden rate is $3 per direct labor hour and the product cost standard calls for 1.5 assembly labor hours, the standard assembly overhead cost is $4.50 per unit, no matter whether the actual assembly hours average 1.0 or 2.0 per unit.

SETTING PRICE STANDARDS

The two major elements in any standard cost are (1) the physical inputs required to produce a given physical output and (2) the unit prices of the input factors. Different criteria underlie the selection of these two elements, and separate discussion is therefore necessary.

Setting Labor Rate Standards

The derivation of standard labor costs requires the multiplication of standard labor time by the applicable standard wage rate. For planning purposes, the rate standard presumably should be the average rate expected to prevail during the planning period. For administrative convenience, this is usually defined as the fiscal year; but for some decisions affecting longer (or shorter) periods, current-year standards have to be adjusted.

Pay rates of individual factory employees are likely to differ widely depending on such factors as the amount of the operator's skill or experience and the conditions under which he is required to work. Even so, management has a choice when setting standard wage rates: it can use a single standard wage rate for all operations performed in a given cost center, or different rates for different operations.

The single rate is simpler and can be used without substantial loss of accuracy in any of three situations:

1. Wage rates of all workers in the cost center fall within a narrow range.
2. The employees work as a balanced team consisting of predetermined numbers of workers from each pay grade.
3. Differences in wage rates are not related to the nature of individual operations or of the equipment on which they are performed.

Multiple rates should be used whenever none of these conditions prevails. For example, suppose that a cost center has 10 employees who are normally engaged in direct labor operations:

1 setup man........................	$5 an hour
7 operators........................	3 an hour
2 handlers.........................	2 an hour

The average wage rate of the 10 employees is thus $3 an hour. Suppose further that two operations require 20 labor hours each, as follows:

	Operation 1	Operation 2
Setup hours....................	1	4
Operator hours.................	14	15
Handler hours.................	5	1
Total hours....................	20	20

The only way that standard cost can reflect differences in the labor mix required by these two operations is to use multiple rates. If a single rate is used, standard labor cost will be $20 \times \$3 = \$60$ for each operation. Multiple rates will yield the following standard labor costs:

	Operation 1	Operation 2
Setup........................	$ 5	$20
Operator.....................	42	45
Handler......................	10	2
Total........................	$57	$67

On the other hand, if all jobs use the three kinds of labor in a 1:7:2 ratio, then multiple rates will yield the same cost total. The added complexity will add nothing to the accuracy of the standard cost figures. Similarly, if wage rate differences result solely from differences in the employee's length of service and seniority is not the basis on which workers are assigned to particular operations, the average rate is the only rate that should be used for each operation. Multiple rates would serve no purpose.

Setting Materials Price Standards

Standard materials prices are generally built up from supplier price lists, catalogues, and the like, utilizing any information available as to probable future changes in these prices. The standard presumably should include some provision for freight-in and variable handling costs, less expected discounts from gross purchase prices. For example, the standard price of a metal stamping might be determined as follows:

Purchase price, in 500-piece quantities.......	$3.45
Freight from supplier's plant..............	0.04
Less: Purchase discounts................	(0.07)
Standard materials price..................	$3.42

If fluctuations tend to be frequent, with no discernible trend either upward or downward, the normal price concept is appropriate. If the direction of future price changes can be predicted with reasonable assurance, however, a strong argument can be made for using the average price predicted for the period in which the standard costs will be used.

SETTING QUANTITY STANDARDS

Setting materials and labor quantity standards is more than a problem of applying scientific methods to determine the underlying physical laws of relationship between input and output. For one thing, the relationships are almost never rigid, and thus management has some power of choice. Second, both the level of the standard and the method of establishing it may influence the motivation and performance of affected personnel. We shall deal only with the first of these in this chapter; motivational questions arise because standard costs are used in operating control systems, and will be discussed as part of our discussion of these systems.

Specifying Standard Yield Levels

In most processes, actual costs will be exactly equal to standard solely by chance. No matter how well standardized the operation or how simple the product, some variation in operating time or materials consumption is inevitable.

For example, under normal conditions 100 typical 12-ton batches of material may be expected to yield the quantities shown in Exhibit 12–4. In this case the average yield is 9.6 tons per batch and the modal yield is 10 tons. Setting the standard on the basis of either the mean or the mode— 1.25 or 1.20 tons of materials for a ton of product—does not imply that variations can be eliminated. Any standard set somewhere within the probable performance range will be exceeded some of the time and not met some of the time. The question is where in this range the standard should be set.

Three possible measurement rules illustrate the choices available: average past performance, anticipated future performance, and attainable good performance. Average past performance is generally rejected, particularly in the initial development of standards, on the ground that past experience fails to measure either what costs ought to be or what they will be. The choice is generally made between the other two possibilities.

Standards may be based on estimated future performance if data for decision making is the main objective or if outsiders require the measurement of product cost at amounts that are very close to actual average cost. Standards that are designed primarily for use in cost control, on the other hand, are most likely to reflect the concept of *attainable good performance*. They represent a level of performance that is reasonably attainable

Exhibit 12–4

EXPECTED DISPERSION IN MATERIALS YIELDS

Tons of Good Product per Batch	Percentage of Batches	Total Yield (Tons)
12	5	60
11	20	220
10	40	400
9	15	135
8	10	80
7	6	42
6	3	18
5	1	5
Total	100	960

by an average experienced worker under standardized conditions. Such a standard includes allowances for normal waste and other normal, recurring departures from perfection.

For example, under ideal conditions a production lot of 500 table lamps would use 500 on-off switches, but the cost standard would probably be based on some greater number, such as 510 or 520 switches for each 500 lamps. Reasonably attainable performance may be in excess of expected future performance, however, if the latter includes the output of poorer workers or if the work is performed under nonstandardized conditions.

Methods of Setting Standards

Standard product costs can be set either by engineering methods or by an analysis of historical data.

Engineering Methods. Engineered standards are based on a careful analysis of the technological characteristics of the work to be performed. This analysis can be performed either on preexisting data or on the results of special data collection routines.

Sometimes the "data" simply represent the accumulated experience of engineers or other technical personnel. For example, an experienced garment cutter usually can estimate quite accurately the number of men's suits that can be cut from a given quantity of cloth because he has done this kind of job so many times before. In other cases, the estimators can synthesize data from commercially available tables of time standards for individual work elements of specific operations (Methods Time Measurement).

When neither past experience nor element time tables are adequate, the estimator can obtain data by observing a series of test runs (time studies and yield studies). The workers assigned to a test run are usually seasoned operators who know the equipment and will work at a steady pace. Even with these precautions, the time study man usually has to use his judgment in deciding whether the observed running times or materials yields reflect abnormal conditions. If not, he will adjust the data or exclude the observations altogether. Once this has been done, the data presumably reflect normal or random variations only.

The next step is to convert these data into standard costs. So-called ideal or perfection standards can be obtained from the engineering data by some such device as averaging the best 10 percent of the observations or selecting the observation representing some high percentile such as the 90th.[2]

The starting point for a reasonably attainable standard is ordinarily the arithmetic average of the observations, but further adjustment is still necessary. The time study observations typically include no provision for nonproductive time except for small amounts inherent in the workers' operating methods. The next step, therefore, is to add a provision for the amount of nonproductive time—waiting for work, attending to personal needs, etc.—that is ordinarily inevitable. Similar allowances for the effects of worker fatigue also may be introduced. These allowances may be based (a) on statistical studies of the past incidence of nonproductive time and the effect of fatigue, (b) on work sampling observations,[3] or (c) on supervisory judgment.

Analysis of Historical Data. An alternative to the use of engineering methods is to derive quantity standards initially by analyzing the quantity data shown on job costing or departmental process costing records of the past. Standards determined in this way are regarded as less accurate than engineered standards, but they can be developed much more rapidly and much more cheaply. For these reasons, controlled test runs are seldom undertaken except to meet other objectives, such as work standardization

---

[2] Some companies use these ideal standards to measure departures from perfection. Ideal standards have no relevance for decision making, however, and their use for control purposes requires a great deal of sophistication.

[3] Work sampling techniques are described briefly in Chapter 13.

and methods improvement. When studies are made for these purposes, accurate usage standards can be obtained as a by-product at little additional cost. When a company is first introducing standard costing, however, it may very well get an adequate set of initial standards by historical analysis.

Reflecting Experience Patterns

Standards that are valid at one moment in time may become progressively more out of date with the passage of time due to systematic and predictable experience patterns.

The best documented experience pattern is the *learning curve*, first used by aircraft manufacturers during the 1939–45 war. They discovered that unit cost declined as a function of the cumulative number of units produced, and that this decline could be predicted fairly accurately. These patterns were reflected in learning curves, showing the percentage decline in unit cost that could be expected from a given percentage increase in cumulative output.

For example, an 80 percent learning curve is one in which doubling cumulative output will reduce cumulative average unit cost by 20 percent. If the first 1,000 units cost a total of $10,000 to produce, or $10 a unit, the average cost of the first 2,000 units will be expected to be $8. (To achieve this, of course, the cost of the second 1,000 units will have to be only $6,000, or $6 each. Learning curve improvement ratios are usually stated as percentage reductions in cumulative unit average cost).[4] An 80 percent learning curve is illustrated in Exhibit 12–5.

Because the rate of decrease is constant, the curve in Exhibit 12–5 would appear as a straight line if the observations were plotted on double logarithmic paper. The descriptive formula is:

$$Y = KX^s$$

in which Y is the cumulative average variable cost, K the variable cost of the first unit, X the cumulative production, and s the ratio of the logarithm of the learning rate or "improvement ratio" to the logarithm of the number two. Converted to logarithmic form, this formula becomes:

$$\log Y = \log K + s \log X$$

which is identical in form to the general formula for a straight line.

Total variable cost for any volume can be obtained easily by multiplying the cumulative average cost by total production:

$$XY = X(KX^s) = KX^{s+1}$$

---

[4] The improvement ratio can also be defined as the percentage reduction in incremental unit cost, but formulas based on improvements in the cumulative average are slightly easier to work with.

Whenever significant improvement patterns prevail, the learning curve can be an essential input to the decision process. Cost overestimation can have just as serious effects as cost underestimation, and the learning curve can be used to reduce the chance of both. This means that the standard costs that are used to represent the cost of inventories on hand at the end of a period should not be placed in the data bank unless accompanied by other data from which cost forecasts for different periods and different production runs can be computed—that is, the single quantity standard

Exhibit 12–5

AN 80 PERCENT LEARNING CURVE

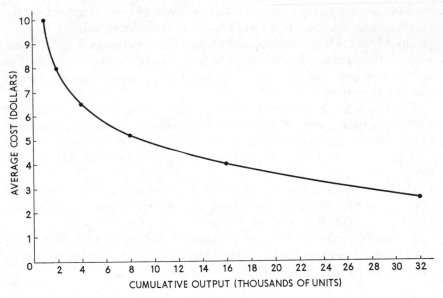

has to be replaced by a set of quantity standards: those embodied in the learning curve.

Suppose, for example, that a company is asked to bid on an order for 4,000 units of a product which has already had a run of 4,000 units at an average variable cost of $64 and an 80 percent improvement curve. The incremental variable cost of the next 4,000 units can then be computed as follows:

New average cost: 80 percent of $64..........		$51.20
New total cost: 8,000 × $51.20...............	$409,600	
Old total cost: 4,000 × $64.................	256,000	
Total incremental cost......................	$153,600	
Average incremental cost: $153,600/4,000......		$38.40

An ability to forecast this cost reduction may make the difference between landing and losing a profitable order.

Although most processes improve as the company gains experience with them, learning curves can be observed mainly in processes that can be thought of as new. Most of them are based on companies' experiences with new products or new models, but the same pattern can be found in new plants as well. All that is necessary is repetitive production over an extended period of time.

It should be emphasized that learning curves are not theoretical abstractions. They are based on observations of actual events. When a historical record exists, the relationship between cost and experience can be estimated by applying regression analysis to the historical observations. In new situations, for which historical data are few or nonexistent, the curves for previous products or processes with known improvement factors can be used if management can identify similarities with the new situations. Estimates prepared in this way are subject to error, but they are likely to be better than estimates predicated on a zero improvement factor. Ironically, the shape of the improvement function may be much more accurately predictable than the cost of the initial units, and it is these that most cost estimation techniques focus on.[5]

Standards under Incentive Wage Plans

Standard wage rates and standard labor quantities can be set independently whenever wage rates are not affected by the amount of work that the employee performs each hour. This is true when hourly wage rates are in effect. It also applies in straight piecework plans or whenever the worker's pay is proportional to earned standard hours, which is really another way of measuring piecework production. (In such cases, standard cost is determined by the piece rate, and the amounts paid in certain circumstances to bring piecework wages up to the hourly minimum are charged to overhead.)

The situation is somewhat different whenever pay is not proportional to output. For example, suppose that for each 40 hours devoted to incentive-rated work, an employee's weekly pay is $3.50 for each earned standard hour plus $1.50 for each earned standard hour in excess of 35. Rest time and personal time are included in elapsed time for this purpose; waiting time in excess of 15 minutes and time spent on nonrated work are paid at a straight hourly rate of $4 and are thus excluded from the elapsed time total. A worker who records 42 earned standard hours plus 3 hours of nonrated work in a 40-hour workweek would be paid as follows:

---

[5] Two informative articles on the learning curve are F. J. Andress, "The Learning Curve as a Production Tool," *Harvard Business Review*, January–February 1954, pp. 87–97; and Patrick Conley, "Experience Curves as a Planning Tool," *IEEE Spectrum*, June 1970, pp. 63–68.

Incentive pay:
(1) Gross elapsed time.......................... 40   hours
(2) Less: Nonrated time....................... 3   hours

(3) Net elapsed time (1) − (2)................. 37   hours
(4) Base output (3) × 35/40.................... 32.375 hours
(5) Earned standard hours...................... 42   hours

(6) Base incentive pay (5) × $3.50............... $147.00
(7) Bonus pay [(5) − (4)] × $1.50............... 14.44

(8) Total incentive pay........................ ..$161.44
Hourly pay:
(9) Nonrated time (2) × $4..................... 12.00
Total gross pay (8) + (9)........................... $173.44

If this worker's output represents standard efficiency then the standard wage rate for incentive work is $161.44 ÷ 42 = $3.84 for each earned standard hour.

REVISION OF STANDARD COSTS

Quantity standards for materials yield and labor performance are changed less frequently than price and wage rate standards. Changes in quantity standards are made only in the case of changes in specifications or methods. For example, the introduction of a new and faster type of machinery would result in a change in methods, whereas the breakdown of equipment requiring the use of substitute equipment for extended periods of time would be regarded as a temporary change. Similarly, a permanent increase in materials prices would be the cause of revisions of standards, whereas a strike in a supplier's plant which forced a temporary diversion of purchases to other suppliers would not result in revision of standards.

Changes in standards may also be made because the existing standards are incorrect. Persistent, unexplained variances, coupled with continuing complaints by the foreman that particular standards are too tight, presumably should be studied, either by engineering methods, by temporary reinstatement of job costing procedures, or by analysis of work documents if these permit indentification of products or operations. The usual outcome of these studies is change either in the work methods or in the standards.

The real question to be answered in connection with revision of standards is not whether they will be revised, but when. Since planning and decision making require up-to-date standards, prompt and frequent revisions would seem desirable. File maintenance is an expensive operation, however. Furthermore, it may be necessary to deny access to the files while changes are being made. For these reasons, the typical solution is to accumulate revisions in a subsidiary file, without immediate reflection in the main file that is used in the accounting routine. After some specified period, usually a year but sometimes more or less than a year, the revisions can be incorporated into the main file.

STANDARD VS. HISTORICAL COSTS FOR DECISIONS

The only role of the cost files in decision making is to provide raw material for use in developing cost estimates. The issue, therefore, is whether standard costs offer any advantages over historical costs for this purpose. This depends on the answers to four partially interdependent questions:

1. Which is more flexible?
2. Which produces faster estimates?
3. Which is cheaper to maintain?
4. Which is more immune to irrational variations?

Flexibility

To estimate future costs from any figure in the cost files, the accountant must identify the conditions in which that cost figure is or was appropriate, forecast the conditions under which future costs are likely to be incurred, and then forecast the cost effects of the changes in conditions.

For example, suppose that 4 hours of setup time and 10 hours of running time are necessary to manufacture 100 units of product X. If management needs an estimate for a run of 500 units, setup time and running time must be estimated separately. Assuming a wage rate of $4 an hour, fixed setup time and proportionately variable running time, the new estimate should reflect the figures shown in the second line of the table below:

	Labor Hours			Labor Cost	Labor Cost per Unit
Lot Size	Setup	Run	Total	Cost	
100................	4	10	14	$ 56	$0.560
500................	4	50	54	216	0.432

The usefulness of historical cost files will be increased if they include a description of the conditions under which production took place. A good job order cost sheet will show the lot size, the date, and perhaps the equipment used. If setup time is large, it should be recorded separately from running time. To facilitate analysis, the job cost sheets should show physical input quantities as well as costs. Even if all of these steps are taken, however, few systems record such facts as the operating condition of the equipment used, the qualifications of the operators, the quality of the materials, the time of day, atmospheric conditions, or the amount of supervisory attention, and each of these may have a significant impact on cost.

A related problem is that the historical cost files may include little information on operations that the company performs infrequently. This means that the available data may be atypical. The quantity of input factors consumed during a particular time period or on a particular job may be unusually high or low due to special and temporary circumstances. For example, the most recent run of product X had a rejection rate of 1 percent. A forecast based on this figure is likely to be less accurate than one derived from a number of observations or a well-constructed standard.

Historical cost data may also be distorted by the methods used to cost materials inventories. Materials issued in one month are generally charged to production at the prices paid months earlier. These prices may be close to current prices or far off, and the size of the error in any particular case cannot be measured without extensive analysis.

The advantage of the standard cost files here is not that they provide an automatic means of adaptation to any given set of conditions but rather that at least some of the assumptions underlying the cost figures are fairly explicit. Both input price and input quality are specified, thereby simplifying the task of adjustment to nonstandard conditions. In some cases, alternative standards may be derived for use when specific, well-defined departures from standard conditions occur, as in the use of standby equipment or substitute materials. Even when this is not the case, however, the clarity of the assumptions underlying the standard cost figures is an aid to their use in cost estimation.

Speed

An even greater advantage of standard cost files is that they provide faster access to pertinent cost data. Historical job order cost sheets are filed by job rather than by product or type of material or operation performed. If an estimate is needed for a product that has been made before, the entire file must be sifted to find the job sheets for previous lots of this product. This can be very time-consuming.

The situation is much worse if the product is a new one. New products generally require the same kinds of operations and materials as old products, but in different combinations. Assembling all or a meaningful sample of past experience, operation by operation, may call for extraction of data from hundreds of cost sheets and the examination of many more. Unless the entries on the job cost sheets are fully coded to identify the types of materials or operations performed, it may even be impossible.

A well-constructed standard cost file, on the other hand, will contain cost standards for almost every operation the factory is equipped to perform. This means that once the operations and materials have been specified, the standard cost for a new product usually can be assembled in short order.

Finally, standard costs may permit faster cost estimation because they are more up to date than historical costs. Standard costs are generally revised annually or at least every other year, with piecemeal interim revisions whenever major changes in specifications or methods take place. The more recent the standard, the more likely that it will correspond to antici- pated experience and thus the more likely that it can be used without adjustment.

Economy

Standard costing systems are likely to be more costly to set up than historical costing systems because of the time and effort required to de- velop the standards. Once set up, however, they need be no more expen- sive to run than historical job order costing, and may even be cheaper.

Few companies have developed standard costs as an economy measure, but economies are possible. A standard cost file rules out the need for job order cost sheets and unit cost figures in the inventory ledgers. Detailed inventory records can be kept in physical quantities only, because dollar totals can always be obtained by multiplying by standard unit cost.

Normality

The first three arguments say that standard cost files may provide better or cheaper estimates of actual costs. For some purposes, however, the estimator may wish to produce estimates that are less than or greater than expected actual costs. The main reason for this deliberate bias is that conditions are expected to be abnormal and the costs not representative of "competitive parity." For example, a company's need to use abnormal amounts of overtime if it undertakes a particular job is certainly relevant to the decision to accept that job, but it may be inappropriate if a long series of repeat orders is likely to ensue, giving the firm an opportunity to eliminate the unusual overtime.

The concept of normality may also apply to measures of average fixed cost. Although average fixed cost is irrelevant to short-term decisions, it may be useful information if the scope of the decision is broad enough. The appropriate measure in these circumstances is attributable cost at normal volume. In fact, one of the worst misuses of accounting data is to raise prices because falling volume or poor cost control has led to a rise in average unit cost. Except in very unusual circumstances, the higher prices will cause volume to shrink even more, leading to a further increase in average cost. Carried to its logical extreme, this approach could lead the firm to price itself completely out of the market.

SUMMARY

Standard costs are widely used as management's main source of de- cision-oriented information on individual operations and products. Stan- dard prices ordinarily should reflect all dimensions of price that depend solely on time worked or output achieved. On these grounds employer pension contributions could ordinarily be subsumed in the standard wage rate, while overtime premiums could not. Standard prices also should be established at the levels expected to prevail during the planning period, to permit the standard cost to be used for cost estimates and the relative importance of individual cost elements to be readily apparent.

Quantity standards that are to be used in the data bank should represent the results of efficient operations during the planning period. If actual results are expected to depart from these levels, the anticipated deviations from standard should also be made available in the data bank. Similarly, if performance is expected to correlate with the number of times the job has been performed, multiple standards should be placed in the data bank, one for each possible level of cumulative output.

Standard costs for control reporting may not meet these requirements in all instances, for reasons that we shall explore in later chapters. Whenever such differences are material, the data bank should contain both sets of standards. In most cases, however, a single set of standards will suffice.

EXERCISES AND PROBLEMS

1. You have been asked to prepare a standard container cost per unit for a certain product, given the following data:

(1) Each unit of product requires one container.
(2) Average performance last year: 1,050 containers used per 1,000 units of product.
(3) Average performance of engineering department test run using average experienced workers: 1,030 containers used per 1,000 units of product.
(4) Best performance found by engineering department: 1,015 containers used per 1,000 units of product.

Select a standard performance level for use in computing standard cost and indicate the reasons for your choice.

2. A steel rolling mill processes steel ingots with a standard price of $40 a ton. Scrap losses are expected to average 18 percent, by weight, of ingots received in the mill. This scrap is entirely recoverable and is valued at $30 a ton. What is the standard ingot cost per ton of rolled product?

3.* The Egbert Company buys a raw material in powdered form, dissolves it in water, concentrates the solution by boiling, adds sugar, and then packages the final product in one-pint jars. In the initial mix, one pound of raw material added to 0.95 gallons of water yields one gallon of mix. In the boiling operation, a 25 percent reduction in volume takes place.

Addition of one-half pound of sugar per gallon of concentrate completes the blending operation, and the mixture is allowed to cool. The addition of sugar and the cooling operation do not affect the total liquid volume. A loss

---

* Solutions to problems marked with an asterisk can be found in Appendix B.

of 2 percent of volume is expected during the filling operation due to spilling, evaporation, overfilling of some jars, and residue left in the blending kettles. The raw material costs 80 cents a pound, and sugar has a standard price of 8 cents a pound.

Compute the standard materials cost per one-pint jar of finished product to the nearest 10th of a cent.

4.* A customer has asked you to prepare a bid on supplying 800 units of a new product. Production will be in batches of 100 units. You estimate that production costs for the first batch of 100 units will total $100 a unit. You also expect that a 90 percent learning curve will apply to the cumulative production labor costs on this contract.

a) Prepare an estimate of the labor costs of fulfilling this contract.
b) Estimate the incremental labor cost of extending the production run to produce an additional 800 units.
c) Estimate the incremental labor cost of extending the production run from 800 to 900 units. (Note: you may use either the formula or a graph to derive this estimate.)

5. The manufacture of a certain product requires the cutting of doughnut-shaped rings from a rectangular strip of material. The material is bought in strips of four-foot length, each weighing two pounds. The strip of material is fed into a machine which cuts the rings, leaving circular disks (like the holes in doughnuts) and a perforated strip of material or "skeleton" (what is left of the material after the rings and disks have been removed). Six rings and six disks are cut from each strip of material. Each ring weighs two ounces, and each disk weighs 1.2 ounces.

The standard price of the material is 64 cents a foot. The skeletons remaining after the rings and disks have been removed are sold as scrap at 20 cents a pound. Rings can be purchased from outside vendors at a price of 36 cents each; disks would cost 24 cents apiece if bought outside. Standard costs are necessary for cost control reporting.

a) Assuming that both the disks and the rings are useful in production and that no damage occurs in cutting, compute standard materials costs for rings and for disks. Explain the basis of your calculations and indicate why you chose this method in place of others that you might have considered.
b) Repeat the calculation described in (a) but assume that 10 percent of the disks and rings will be improperly cut and must be sold as scrap.
c) Repeat the calculation described in (b) assuming a 10 percent cutting loss and also assuming that the company has no use for the disks and that they, too, will be sold as scrap at 20 cents a pound.
d) Assuming that the company has been operating under the conditions specified in (c) and that it has now found a way to utilize half of the disks in the manufacture of a new product, what would you recommend be established as the standard materials cost of the disks? Explain.

6.* Many operations or processes are based on labor crews rather than individuals performing separate operations. The Daily Foods Company, which prepares frozen precooked dinners, has organized its kitchen on a crew basis, each crew normally consisting of one head cook, two assistant cooks, and three helpers. Variations in crew size and composition are frequent, however, depending on the items being processed and the size of the batch. Furthermore, the company's wage structure provides for seniority pay differentials within each job classification. Thus, although the base pay for an assistant cook is $3 an hour, some assistant cooks are paid at a rate of $3.25 an hour. The average straight-time pay rates for the three job classifications are, per hour:

$$\begin{array}{ll}\text{Head cooks} & \$3.80 \\ \text{Assistant cooks} & 3.15 \\ \text{Helpers} & 1.80 \end{array}$$

To prepare standard labor costs for the operation of breading chicken breasts, the company maintained a record of actual operating hours during a test period, averaging as follows:

	Items Processed in Batch			
	1,000	1,500	2,000	2,500
Man-hours and wage rates:				
Head cooks	2.3 at $3.50	2.6 at $3.60	3.0 at $3.70	3.7 at $3.90
Assistant cooks	2.3 at 3.20	5.7 at 3.10	6.0 at 3.25	7.4 at 3.15
Helpers	4.6 at 1.60	5.2 at 1.80	9.0 at 1.75	11.1 at 1.80

Prepare a standard cost per item for the breading operation using the portions of the above data that seem most appropriate and assuming that most lots will consist of between 1,800 and 2,200 items.

7. Technologics, Inc. manufactures products that incorporate very advanced technological features. Each new product is virtually unique, and the effect of learning on cost is very pronounced.

A customer has asked for a price quotation on an order for 512 sensometers. They would be produced in series, one at a time. Technologics' engineers estimate that the initial setup costs would total $10,000, production labor costs of the first unit would amount to $4,000, and an 80 percent cumulative learning curve would apply to production labor costs. Production would be spread over an eight-month period.

a) Using the formula provided in the chapter, estimate the labor cost of the entire order.

b) The customer feels that the bid based on your estimate in (a) is too high. You are unwilling to lower your bid for this quantity, but the customer has suggested that you rebid on the basis of a total production run of 750 units, spread over 12 months. Prepare a new cost estimate.

c) The customer changed his mind and accepted your original bid for the 512-unit contract. Midway through that contract he asks you to bid on extending the contract to cover an additional 238 units. Prepare an estimate of labor costs that would be useful to management in the evaluation of this possibility.

8. Historical job order cost records show the following labor hours and costs per unit for product A:

Production Date	Hours	Cost
June 19x2.....................	1.8	$6.50
January 19x3..................	1.5	6.15
April 19x3....................	2.1	7.87
October 19x3..................	1.9	7.20
February 19x4.................	1.6	6.80
June 19x4.....................	2.3	9.70
August 19x4...................	1.8	8.20
February 19x5.................	1.7	8.00
May 19x5......................	2.0	9.20
September 19x5................	1.9	8.75

No change in work methods took place during this time.

Employees are paid on an hourly basis, with seniority differentials based on length of service. Studies have indicated that output per man-hour does not correlate significantly with length of service, although of course not all workers are equally productive. The wage rate agreed on for 19x6 is $5 an hour plus 10 cents for every five years of service. The employees' length of service will be distributed as follows during 19x6:

Years of Service	% of Employees
0–4.........................	15
5–9.........................	40
10–14.......................	25
15–19.......................	15
20–24.......................	5

As part of the preparation for the company's adoption of standard costing, an industrial engineer timed three of the work crews selected by the department foreman as average experienced workers. Each of these crews processed five of the September 19x5 batches of 100 units each, with the following results:

	Total Man-Hours per Batch		
	Crew 1	Crew 2	Crew 3
Batch 1....................	165	150	160
Batch 2....................	170	175	185
Batch 3....................	150	170	180
Batch 4....................	155	180	170
Batch 5....................	170	185	185
Total.....................	810	860	880

a) What standard labor cost would you recommend in this case? Give reasons for your recommendation.

b) The standard that you developed in (*a*) was probably based on staff work of a quantitative nature. In a practical case, would you expect to have to consider any variables that are difficult to express in numerical terms? How would you deal with any such variables?

9. The Amdur Company recently completed development work on a new product and commenced production on a limited scale. The product has found favor with the company's customers, and the company intends to expand production to a rate of 1,000 units a week.

Labor costs for the first 2,000 units have totaled $20,000. Judging from past experience, the company's industrial engineers have estimated that a 90 percent learning curve will be applicable to this product.

a) Compute cumulative total labor cost and cumulative average labor cost for the first 128,000 units.

b) On a sheet of graph paper, prepare a diagram showing cumulative total cost for various cumulative volumes between 2,000 and 128,000 units.

c) From the diagram in (*b*), prepare a schedule showing the additional labor costs of producing each additional 4,000 units of product from zero to 128,000 cumulative units.

d) Much of the company's business consists of providing customers with specially selected combinations of the company's products. Each customer's package is different from the others, and competition is very keen. Cost estimates for each package are prepared by combining the product cost figures shown in the standard cost file. What labor cost standard would you establish for the first year for use in this way?

10. The Peermore Products Company is developing standard costs. Employees in department 231 are classified in the following categories with their corresponding base pay rates:

General foreman..................	$280 a week
Foremen.........................	$220 a week
Assistant foremen................	$190 a week
Operators—grade 1..............	$4.20 an hour
Operators—grade 2..............	$3.90 an hour
Helpers.........................	$3.00 an hour
Cleanup men....................	$2.75 an hour

All department employees get time and a half for work in excess of 40 hours per week. A differential of 10 cents an hour is awarded to workers operating a second shift if this is needed.

Operations are of the continuous-process type, but equipment may be shut down overnight and started up again the next day without additional start-up cost or damage to equipment or product. Men work in crews, the normal crew consisting of one assistant foreman, two grade 1 operators, four grade 2 operators, three helpers, and one cleanup man. The general foreman works the day shift only, but one foreman is on duty in the department for each shift worked. Although the available equipment permits a maximum of five crews in any one shift, the department frequently operates with only four crews and in some cases with only three crews. A second shift is never operated with fewer than three crews.

In preparing for the change-over to standard costs, the methods department has accumulated output data, by crew, for the past four weeks. Each crew worked 40 hours in each week. These data are as follows:

	Pounds Produced in Week Ending—				
	4/7	4/14	4/21	4/28	Total
Day crew A................	24,106	26,095	21,734	23,052	94,987
Day crew B................	18,641	25,348	24,219	23,830	92,038
Day crew C................	25,214	20,900	22,462	20,585	89,161
Day crew D................	27,116	24,238	25,003	23,812	100,169
Day crew E................	21,306	19,681	22,146	19,046	82,179
Night crew F..............	22,862	20,193	22,712	17,571	83,338
Night crew G..............	16,796	20,523	18,618	21,222	77,159
Night crew H..............	20,000	17,982	22,105	18,890	78,977
Night crew I..............	23,148	24,267	19,473	21,049	87,937

a) Develop a standard labor cost per pound.
b) Defend your method of deriving (1) standard output per crew hour and (2) standard labor cost per crew hour.

11.† Elise Toiletries, Inc., is introducing a new product, known as Lano-Lov Skin Lotion, to be sold in four-ounce bottles. Cost and engineering studies have produced the following estimates:

Item No.	Description	Cost	Quantity Used per 125-Gallon Batch
2147............	4-ounce bottle	$5.50 per gross	102% of minimum
315............	Label	$3.30 per 1,000	103% of minimum
4247............	Compound 34A	$40 per 100 lbs.	70.0 lbs.
3126............	Alcohol and glycerine	$40 per 100 lbs.	76.0 lbs.
4136B...........	Perfume oil	Manufactured	3.5 lbs.

The product is reshipped in the bottle cases, so no cartons are required. To allow for normal overfilling, waste, and breakage, standard materials cost (excluding containers and labels) is to be established on the basis of materials consumption at a rate of 104 percent of the quantities indicated in the table above. Waste allowances for the containers and labels are included in the percentage figures given in the right-hand column of the table.

Standard direct labor per gross is to be based on the following estimates: compounding, 0.12 hours at $5 an hour; filling and packing, one hour at $4.

Manufacturing overhead is to be included in standard cost at the following rates: compounding, $3 per standard labor hour; filling and packing, $1.50 per standard labor hour plus $0.90 per gross.

Perfume oil is mixed by the company according to its secret formula. The

---

† Adapted from a uniform CPA examination.

standard cost of a 90-pound batch of 4136B perfume oil is as follows: ingredients, $2,169.95; direct labor, 4.4 hours at $5.28 an hour; manufacturing overhead, $7.50 per batch plus $1.95 per standard labor hour.

Prepare a standard cost sheet for one gross of bottles of this product. Calculations should be made to the nearest cent per gross. (One gallon contains 128 fluid ounces; a gross is 144 bottles.)

12. Pierre Malin was adamant. "I know the competition is rough, he said, "but if we can't get enough out of this to cover our costs then we have no business going in."

"I couldn't agree more," George Riley replied, "but you're measuring costs the wrong way."

Pierre was the general manager and George was the controller of the Sanders Company, a small manufacturer of molded plastics products. At issue was the price to be quoted in a sealed bid that the company was submitting for a large order of drinking cups to be supplied to a local school board.

The company's molding department consists of a group of injection molding machines with interchangeable dies. Each die has a number of openings or "cavities" in the shape of the product to be molded. The molding operation consists of closing the machine, whereupon melted polystyrene is forced under pressure into the die. There it is cooled into solid form by the circulation of cold water until it reaches a predetermined temperature, at which point the die opens and the molded products are ejected. The operator then closes the machine, and the process is repeated.

The drinking cups were a relatively new product for the Sanders Company, but orders for this product had been coming in at a fairly steady rate. The reason for Mr. Riley's enthusiasm was that this was the first opportunity to penetrate the large institutional market in the area. The initial contract was for 500 gross (6,000 dozen), but the potential market was many times this amount every year.

Standard product cost was based on engineering studies of physical input requirements and cost estimates prepared by the accounting department. Standard cost in cents per dozen cups was as follows:

Materials	12.0
Labor	3.3
Overhead	2.2
Total standard cost	17.5

The standard cost of the plastic powder used as raw material is $9 per thousand cups, reflecting normal wastage. Standard materials cost also includes $1 a thousand to amortize the cost of the dies used.

The labor cost of the molding operation is a function of (1) the number of cavities per die, (2) the length of the molding cycle (interval between closings), and (3) the number and compensation of operators tending each machine. The number of cavities per die is determined largely by the size and shape of the molded product, although the number of cavities actually in use may be reduced by blocking off one or more cavities that have developed defects that would lead to the rejection of finished products. Because of the high costs of die removal and setup, a die may be kept in operation with a fairly substantial number of its cavities blocked off.

The length of the molding cycle depends on how quickly the operator responds to the opening of the die. While the die is closed, he is engaged in inspecting the molded products and separating them from the plastic framework to which they are attached when ejected, and he may delay clearing and closing the machine if he is busy with these tasks when the machine opens.

The Sanders Company typically assigns one worker to a machine, with a relief man for each 10 machines. This relief man also keeps the machines supplied with raw material. The machine operators and relief men are paid at the rate of $4.35 an hour, with time and a half for overtime. Each man is entitled to a 15-minute rest period each morning and afternoon and a half-hour lunch period, as part of a normal eight-hour shift. His machine is operated by the relief man during the smoking period, but it remains idle during the lunch period. A study of recent experience revealed that each operator was idle for an average of 15 minutes a day while minor repairs or adjustments were being made to his machine. This idle time is not recorded separately on a routine basis. If a machine is to be out of operation for a half-hour or more, the operator is assigned to other tasks, such as correcting minor defects in rejected products.

The standard labor cost of an hour of machine time is $5.28, computed as follows:

Machine-hours per day: 10 machines at 7.25 hours each
    (total time less lunch and normal waiting time) 72.5

Daily labor cost for 10 machines:
    10 operators, 8 hours at $4.35 an hour $348.00
    1 relief man, 8 hours at $4.35 an hour 34.80
Total $382.80
Labor cost per machine-hour . . . . $ 5.28

If the operator acts immediately, the complete cycle time is 25 seconds, but standards reflect an average cycle time of 30 seconds. The dies for the cups contain 20 cavities, but standard cost reflects the assumption that 20 percent of the cavities will be blocked. This would indicate a standard production rate of 1,920 cups an hour, and a standard labor cost of 3.30 cents a dozen.

Overhead cost was based on full absorption costing at normal volume. Variable costs account for approximately 30 percent of overhead cost at normal volume. The variation is in proportion to changes in labor cost.

Mr. Malin felt that standard cost was a poor basis for cost estimation in this case. "Our work force is very green," he said, "and I expect that cycle time will be one-third longer than standard. Overall volume is down, too, and this means that we can't take advantage of quantity discounts on our purchases. This will add 11 percent to the purchase prices of plastic powder. Besides, the lower volume means that we'll probably have to add 10 percent to our standard overhead cost to carry the cost of idle capacity. All of these things bring our costs up close to 20 cents a dozen, without any allowance for profit. I don't think we can win the contract on that basis."

"You're probably right on that score," George answered. "My guess is that we'll have to put in a bid of 19 cents a dozen if we really want this order. With standard cost at 17.5 cents a dozen, this shaves the margin pretty thin, but I think we ought to go ahead. This is a big market, and I think that standard cost gives us a better guideline than your expected actual cost figure. We can't expect our customers to pay for our inefficiencies."

Would you use standard costs, expected actual costs, or some other cost figure in this situation? Explain your reasoning.

chapter **13**

Distribution Cost Analysis

Most marketing policy or strategy decisions—which products to emphasize, what distribution channels to use, what kinds of customers to approach, what discount structure to adopt, etc.—require careful analysis
of the company's nonmanufacturing costs. This is generally referred to,
somewhat inaccurately, as distribution cost analysis.[1]

CLASSIFICATION OF NONMANUFACTURING ACTIVITIES

The term nonmanufacturing activities covers a multitude of sins, from
research and development through marketing and product distribution
to finance, accounting, and administrative activities. For discussion, these
can be classified into three groups:

1. Repetitive service activities.
2. Diversified service activities.
3. Independent program activities.

This classification is based on the nature and measurability of the relationships between functional inputs (costs) and outputs (invoices prepared,
orders taken, etc.).

Repetitive Service Activities

Repetitive service activities are a close counterpart of direct factory
production operations. In this category can be classified all those activities or functions for which relatively homogeneous units of output or

---

[1] For an extended discussion of these methods, see Donald R. Longman and
Michael Schiff, *Practical Distribution Cost Analysis* (Homewood, Ill.: Richard D.
Irwin, 1955), chaps. 8–14.

work units can be clearly identified. Examples include shipping, billing, warehousing, and payroll preparation.

The work load in a repetitive service activity is ordinarily almost entirely a function of factors outside the control of the activity manager—that is, the number of units of service performed depends strictly on the demands imposed by other activities. Because the tasks performed are relatively homogeneous, it is at least theoretically possible to establish standard relationships between output (number of work units) and input (in either physical units or costs).

Selection of work units is not always simple. The output of an activity often can be measured in many different ways, which means that the accountant or other analyst has to decide which unit of measure best suits his particular purpose. For example, in payroll preparation the work unit could be either the number of paychecks, the number of employees, or the number of payrolls drawn up each month.

Ideally, the measuring unit should measure the factors that cause the organization to incur the costs in question. When more than one potential measure passes this test, the nod should go to the one that correlates most closely with variations in the required inputs.

Diversified Service Activities

Diversified service activities are similar to repetitive service activities in that the services provided are determined largely by the requirements of other activities; but they differ in that the units of output are many, nonstandardized, and constantly changing. Examples include the duties of a good part of the executive force, office management, secretarial work, telephone switchboard operation, and similar tasks. Secretarial output could possibly be measured in terms of the number of telephone calls made, number of letters typed, number of visitors received, and so forth, but there is so little homogeneity within any one of these measures that they offer very little promise for standardization.

It may be apparent that diversified service activities have their counterparts in manufacturing, too. Factory supervision, for example, clearly falls into this category.

Independent Program Activities

Independent program activities have few counterparts in manufacturing. Whereas the scope of the activities of the first two categories is determined in large measure by the actual or anticipated service demand, independent program activities in a sense are self-justifying. The reason is that independent program activities are defined as those that are undertaken to obtain results that are deemed desirable in themselves and not because they are required by other activities. For example, whereas invoice typing is made necessary by the shipment of goods, advertising campaigns and direct selling activities can only be justified by the desirability of the results achieved. In other words, output cannot be measured in terms of physical work units but must be measured more qualitatively in terms of the benefits derived from the work done.

Examples of independent program activities are research and development, advertising, and direct selling. Research and advertising typically consist of a number of semi-independent projects or programs moving along on separate time schedules, each with its own particular objective and generally with its own individual budget. Direct selling, on the other hand, might even be recognized as a separate category, on the ground that it consists largely of repetitive, continuous activities rather than discontinuous projects. All three of these are alike, however, in that they are all characterized by an inverse relationship between cost and results—that is, the level of cost is justified by the qualitative desirability of the results of the expenditure rather than by a technological need to supply certain inputs to meet a service demand.

Broad versus Narrow Classification

Functions or activities can be classified either broadly or narrowly. A broad classification identifies an activity with a certain end result or service and includes in the definition all of the inputs necessary to accomplish that end result. A narrower classification scheme insists on homogeneity within the activity.

For example, repetitive service and independent program work, defined broadly, includes some supervision, which is in itself a diversified service activity. Furthermore, many independent programs will require repetitive services—e.g., advertising departments ordinarily require a good deal of reproduction work and photo developing and printing. It is better to accept this dual classification, however, than to take the pedantic point of view that the sales manager's job is a diversified service activity and not a part of the independent program of direct selling. A place can be found for both kinds of distinctions.

THE GENERAL APPROACH

The focus of interest in distribution cost analysis is the *revenue segment*, such as a product line, a group of customers, a sales territory, or a particular class of orders.

The first task is to identify the costs that can be traced directly to the segment or segments in question. The costs of a fleet of delivery trucks, for example, can often be traced entirely to retail sales or wholesale sales, or to one region or another, if those are the revenue segments management is interested in.

For costs that cannot be traced to the segments being studied, the two-stage analysis diagrammed in Exhibit 13–1 becomes necessary. First, it is necessary to develop unit costs for the "products" of these indirect activities—i.e., unit costs for individual activities or functions such as invoice writing, credit reveiw, payroll preparation, and customer delivery. Second, the analyst needs to estimate the number of units of functional service required by each revenue segment. The costs can then be assigned to each segment by multiplying the unit cost by the number of functional units required.

The process described here is not entirely unfamiliar to anyone who has mastered the principles of accounting for manufacturing costs. Before factory service department costs can be assigned to individual products they normally must be analyzed to determine how much service

Exhibit 13–1

ASSIGNMENT OF NONTRACEABLE COSTS TO REVENUE SEGMENTS

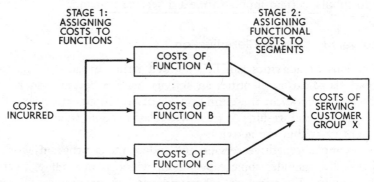

is provided to each of the factory production departments through which the products flow. Substitute "production department" for "function" and "product" for "customer group" in Exhibit 13–1 and the similarity becomes apparent.

DEVELOPING FUNCTIONAL UNIT COSTS

Meaningful functional unit costs can be developed only for repetitive service activities and, in some cases, diversified service activities. Unit costs imply a linear relationship between inputs and outputs, and these are very unlikely to occur in independent program activities—e.g., doubling advertising expenditures is unlikely to double sales volume. The process consists of three steps:

1. Define activities or functions.
2. Select work units or governing factors.
3. Estimate cost-volume relationships for each activity.

Defining Activities or Functions

The typical repetitive service department must perform a series of related functions for economy in administration, and this requires a careful definition of the various tasks that are assigned to the unit. For example, a study of the operations of a billing and order processing department might reveal the following separate processes:

1. Order recording.
2. Credit reviewing.
3. Invoicing—headings.
4. Invoicing—line items.
5. Order file maintenance.
6. Correspondence.

It may be apparent that this first step can be carried out in varying amounts of detail. For example, the function of invoice typing may be divided into two parts: (*a*) typing the customer's address and other general information; and (*b*) typing the individual invoice lines for the goods shipped. For most purposes, the provision of greater detail is subject to the laws of diminishing returns and increasing errors. It is easier to identify the cost of invoice typing than the costs of typing the separate parts of the invoice, and the added refinement may not be worthwhile anyway. The basic criterion should be homogeneity of the task, but it is usually neither possible nor necessary to attempt to apply this criterion rigidly.

Selecting the Work Units

Once the activity or function has been identified, the next step is to select an appropriate work unit. For the order processing department, the work units might be:

Task	*Work Unit*
Order recording	Total orders received
Credit reviewing	Charge orders received
Invoicing—headings	Invoices ⎫ or line items
Invoicing—line items	Line items ⎭
Order file maintenance	Total orders received
Correspondence	Letters written

Different work units might be appropriate for different expense elements if they have different variability patterns. For example, in the truck delivery department:

Element	*Work Unit*
Loading labor	Total pounds loaded
Gas, oil, and maintenance	Miles
Bulk delivery labor	Miles
Route delivery labor	Deliveries
Bulk unloading labor	Deliveries

Even here, the work unit is not entirely homogeneous—for example, bulk delivery labor costs will vary with traffic conditions as well as with miles traveled—but the unit selected is a fairly reliable index of the output requirement.

Service volume for diversified service activities has to be measured indirectly, in units of some governing factor or factors. The governing factor should be one that correlates closely with the cost of carrying out the functional activity. For example, the governing factor for an employee recreation function might well be the number of company employees.

Selection of such units is ordinarily not very difficult, the only practical problem being that so many different factors may be selected for the various functions that obtaining statistics would become a massive job. The typical solution is to try to reduce the number of measuring rods so that one index will serve a number of functions.

Estimating Cost-Volume Relationships

Most costs of repetitive service and diversified service activities are fixed in the short run. Salaries and equipment rental or depreciation often account for 80 percent or more of the total, and these seldom vary with normal fluctuations in service volume. Most of them are relatively divisible, however, and this provides the basis for estimates of attributable cost. The usefulness of distribution cost analysis, therefore, depends on the ability of attributable cost to approximate incremental cost for the alternatives being evaluated. The rule throughout this chapter will be to include in functional unit cost only those cost elements that seem sufficiently divisible to justify the assumption of proportionate change in response to substantial changes in the total volume of functional activity.

Four different methods of obtaining estimates of attributable unit cost deserve discussion:

1. Recorded experience.
2. Supervisors' approximation.
3. Engineered standards.
4. Sampling.

Recorded Experience. It is perhaps natural that some accountants and even some executives feel that the best way to find the cost of various functions is to take a page from the factory's book and set up a system of timecards, supplies requisitions, and perhaps even job orders. Unfortunately, the analogy with factory operations is often unjustified. Time tickets can be used in factory job order production because the amounts per job order are relatively large and because the conditions of production make it relatively easy to identify certain costs with individual jobs. When these conditions are not met, job time tickets are not prepared. For example, effort is never made to assign the salaries of bookkeepers to individual job orders, nor is there much interest in keeping time tickets for work done on continuous assembly lines, even if the products being assembled are not entirely homogeneous. In other words, job costing is expensive and an alert management will avoid using it if it does not produce data worth their cost or if acceptable data can be obtained by less expensive means.

Furthermore, it is even possible that the accuracy produced by timecards and the like is spurious, particularly with respect to salary and wage costs. Unless each task represents a relatively large commitment of resources, the personnel engaged in carrying out the function may find it extremely difficult to identify the time spent. For example, a secretary seldom can be expected to keep an accurate record of time spent answering telephones, typing letters, filing, and so forth.

Supervisors' Approximation. Asking a supervisor to allocate the various elements of his department's costs among the functions performed is the fastest, cheapest, and probably least accurate method. It may be accurate enough for many purposes, however, and should not be rejected without weighing the costs of other methods and the degree of accuracy necessary.

Engineered Standards. Engineered standards are at the other extreme and call for very careful and minute investigation of the input requirements for each function. The engineering method most commonly used today is some variant of the Methods Time Measurement (MTM) technique rather than the older stopwatch approach. Under this approach, the operations are first studied to identify the major tasks to be performed. Standard time allowances for each task are then obtained from commercially available tables.[2]

Sampling. The fourth approach relies on performance observations, too, but obtains these observations by sampling rather than by complete enumeration. One form of sampling is to collect functional cost data during a test period and then set standards on the basis of the period averages. This approach is applicable only if inputs can be identified with individual activities as they are used.

Another sampling method with more general applicability is called *work sampling*.[3] Its immediate objective is to provide a reliable estimate

---

[2] For a good illustration of this technique, see Thomas G. Eshelman, "How Hanes Hosiery Uses Clerical Work Measurement," *Management Services*, March-April 1966, pp. 37–43.

[3] Work sampling techniques are described in depth by Ralph M. Barnes, *Work Sampling* (rev. ed.; New York: John Wiley & Sons, 1957).

of the amount of time spent in various types of productive and non-productive activities. The method consists largely of recording what people are doing at particular instants of time, selected at random, during some longer time period. For example, the sampling plan may require the recording of the activities being performed by each clerk in the office at 9:12, 10:34, etc. From a number of such samples taken at various times, a percentage time distribution can be obtained, and the estimated times to perform the various repetitive service activities can be derived from this.

The work sampling and engineering methods of deriving cost standards are applicable primarily or exclusively to labor costs. Work sampling has both the advantage and the disadvantage of indicating what the costs are rather than what they should be. The disadvantage in this approach is that it gives management little assurance that its costs are reasonable. The advantage is that it provides management with information as to what its money is buying. Furthermore, these studies can indicate trends in functional cost if they are carried out periodically.

These methods are expensive and they ordinarily cannot be justified except as a by-product of a program of work simplification and methods improvement. In other words, the added accuracy of the data derived from engineered standards is ordinarily insufficient by itself to justify the cost and disruption entailed in developing the standards.

PRODUCT-LINE ANALYSIS

Many marketing decisions focus on the profitability of individual product lines. Product profitability analysis therefore provides a logical vehicle by which to illustrate methods of distribution cost analysis. Suppose that a company wishes to decide which of its three product lines deserves the most short-run promotional effort, as well as which of them appear to have weaknesses that if not corrected will endanger their long-run survival. Estimated sales volume and factory costs for the coming year are as follows:

	Line A	Line B	Line C
Gross sales..................	$1,000,000	$800,000	$750,000
Variable factory cost........	500,000	450,000	350,000
Variable factory margin......	$ 500,000	$350,000	$400,000
Attributable fixed factory cost........	50,000	30,000	.....
Attributable factory margin..........	$ 450,000	$320,000	$400,000

Traceable Costs

The first step in an analysis of this kind is to identify marketing, research, and administrative costs that are traceable to the individual product lines. In this case, two groups of cost elements—product management expenses and the costs of samples and product sales brochures—are completely traceable to individual product lines and thus require no allocations. These are expected to be as follows:

	Line A	Line B	Line C
Product management..................	$23,000	$21,000	$22,000
Samples and brochures................	8,000	7,000	10,500

Product-Related Service Costs

The next step is to classify each of the remaining nonmanufacturing activities as either product-related or customer-related. The following functional cost estimates have been prepared for product-related activities (the number of functions has been reduced to simplify the presentation):

	Variable Costs	Attributable Fixed Costs
Sales commissions.........	$0.01 × gross sales	....
Product handling..........	$0.02 × pounds of product	$0.0075 × pounds of product
Storage value.............	....	$0.0230 per year × average inventory cost
Storage space.............	....	$1.40 per year × square feet required
Inspection...............	$3.60 × inspection hours	....

The following statistics have been collected to permit the assignment of the costs of these activities to the various product groups:

	Line A	Line B	Line C
Average inventory...........................	$ 300,000	$182,000	$160,000
Product weight (lbs.)........................	2,000,000	400,000	300,000
Warehouse space required (sq. ft.).............	50,000	6,500	5,000
Inspection hours............................	20,000	2,000	2,500

The allocations based on these statistics and the unit costs given above are:

	Line A	Line B	Line C
Variable product costs:			
Sales commissions	$ 10,000	$ 8,000	$ 7,500
Product handling	40,000	8,000	6,000
Inspection	72,000	7,200	9,000
Total variable product cost	$122,000	$23,200	$22,500
Attributable fixed costs:			
Product handling	$ 15,000	$ 3,000	$ 2,250
Storage value	6,900	4,186	3,680
Storage space	70,000	9,100	7,000
Total attributable fixed cost	$ 91,900	$16,286	$12,930

Customer-Related Service Costs

The remaining service functions are all customer-related; that is, the amount of the cost is determined by such customer characteristics as the number of orders per year or the customer's location. Five of these, together with their cost-governing factors, are:

Order processing	$3.60 per order
Credit review	5.00 per customer
Cashier	0.30 per customer
General accounting	0.25 per customer
Accounts receivable	0.50 per order

These can be incorporated into product line analysis if different kinds of customers buy different product lines. For example, if product line A is sold to 20 customers and product line C is sold to 2,000, then product line C is clearly responsible for more credit review, cashier, and general accounting costs than product line A. In this case, it is estimated that the product lines are responsible for the following numbers of orders each year:

Line	Orders
A	2,000
B	1,000
C	500

That is, the company receives 2,000 orders each year only because it sells product line A, 1,000 only because it sells product line B, and 500 only because it sells product line C. All other orders cover two or more product lines and the costs of processing these are not attributable to any one product line. Using the unit costs listed above, the order cost allocations are:

Line	Allocation
A	$7,200
B	3,600
C	1,800

The Profitability Estimates

Application of the unit cost factors to these estimates yields the product-line profit forecasts shown in Exhibit 13–2. Notice how the ranking of product line A has been changed by the introduction of non-manufacturing costs into the analysis. Just looking at manufacturing costs would give the impression that product line A would have a variable profit ratio of 50 percent of sales and an attributable profit ratio of 45 per-

Exhibit 13–2

PRODUCT-LINE PROFIT FORECASTS

	Product Line A		Product Line B		Product Line C	
	Amount	%	Amount	%	Amount	%
Gross sales	$1,000,000	100.0	$800,000	100.0	$750,000	100.0
Variable product costs:						
Factory	$ 500,000	50.0	$450,000	56.2	$350,000	46.7
Sales commissions	10,000	1.0	8,000	1.0	7,500	1.0
Product handling	40,000	4.0	8,000	1.0	6,000	0.8
Inspection	72,000	7.2	7,200	0.9	9,000	1.2
Total variable product cost	$ 622,000	62.2	$473,200	59.1	$372,500	49.7
Variable profit	$ 378,000	37.8	$326,800	40.9	$377,500	50.3
Attributable fixed costs:						
Factory	$ 50,000		$ 30,000		. . . . . .	
Product management	23,000		21,000		$ 22,000	
Samples and brochures	8,000		7,000		10,500	
Product handling	15,000		3,000		2,250	
Storage value	6,900		4,186		3,680	
Storage space	70,000		9,100		7,000	
Order processing	7,200		3,600		1,800	
Total attributable fixed cost	$ 180,100	18.0	$ 77,886	9.7	$ 47,230	6.3
Product margin	$ 197,900	19.8	$248,914	31.2	$330,270	44.0

cent. Comparable ratios for product line B would be 43.8 and 40 percent. Product line A is a heavy consumer of nonmanufacturing services, however, and recognition of these shows that product line A's variable profit ratio is slightly lower than that of product line B, and its attributable profit or product margin is substantially lower.

Treatment of Independent Program Costs

In this illustration, the only costs of independent program activities to be allocated to product lines were sales commissions, product management costs, and the costs of samples and brochures. The main reason for excluding other costs, mainly those of field selling activities, is that no ready basis was available for assigning them. Most direct selling costs are common costs, not traceable to any one of the product lines in the salesman's book. Salesmen's time reports are not of much assistance in making cost allocations to products, and not only because the salesman finds it difficult to estimate the time spent in promoting any particular product line. The main problem is that direct selling time is a relatively small portion of the salesman's average day. Most of his time he spends waiting in customers' waiting rooms, traveling, listening to the prospect's tale of woe, and performing other necessary but more or less unproductive tasks.

In most cases, subtracting one product line from the salesman's order book will not permit him to make a single additional call per day unless the product line is defined so broadly that it makes up a substantial proportion of his stock in trade. Even if product lines are defined this broadly, however, the proportion of time spent promoting any one line does not provide much information that could not be provided by product margin figures.

The only legitimate allocation is one that would measure the amount of promotional expenditure that could be eliminated if the product line were to be discontinued. Simple allocation formulas almost never meet this specification.

Treatment of Space Costs

In the example, a charge of $1.40 a year was made for each square foot of warehouse space required for any given product line. It should be emphasized that this did not represent the average internal cost of the company's warehouses. The concept of opportunity cost is relevant here, and this may be as low as zero or as high as the market value of comparable quantities of warehouse space. Average internal cost is highly unlikely to measure the opportunity cost of the space occupied and almost never should be used.

Treatment of Depreciation

Depreciation charges on existing equipment are allocations of sunk costs and therefore should not be assigned to revenue segments for short-term decision making. Assignment of this cost to revenue segments is justified only if it approximates the incremental cash flow attributable to a major expansion or contraction of the segment. Divisibility of the depreciable property is a necessary condition, but even here current annual replacement expenditures ordinarily measure the incremental cash flow better than average historical cost.

Consistency with Incremental Approach

If carried out as described here, product cost analysis is in no sense inconsistent with the incremental approach to decision making advocated in preceding chapters. The methods outlined in this chapter are designed to get better data on cost increments. The introduction of attributable cost figures is intended to serve the purposes for which many accountants have computed full cost in the past, without falling prey to the defects of full cost.[4]

No one should pretend that this approach contains the magic formula that will automatically produce the right cost for every situation. In fact, distribution cost analysis is always a substitute for a detailed item-by-item estimate of incremental cost, and is almost inevitably inferior to the latter.

The advantage of the attributable cost figures is that they can be prepared in advance and at less cost than custom-tailored estimates. In a medium-sized office with 20 cost centers and 10 cost elements in each, for example, 200 separate estimates would have to be made for each decision, and this would be prohibitively expensive. What distribution cost analysis does is provide a reasonable approximation to incremental cost. As long as the analyst avoids the full cost fallacy, this can be accurate enough for the purpose.

Revenue Differences

Although the focus of this chapter is on the behavior of distribution costs, the other side of the picture should not be overlooked. Data on revenue responses to a particular decision are often obtained by experimentation. For example, most large food manufacturing companies test-market new products in a limited number of cities before placing them in general distribution, to gauge consumer response and the profitability of different marketing techniques. One test market may be saturated with local advertising, while sales promotion in another area may use point-of-sale displays only. Differences between sales in the two areas may help to indicate the profitability of specific local advertising campaigns.

This kind of experimentation cannot be discussed adequately here, but it ought to be noted that the crucial determinant of incremental profit is more likely to be the impact of the decision on sales volume and mix than its impact on the cost of servicing this incremental volume and

---

[4] For a discussion of the pros and cons of full costs in product cost analysis, see Martin Mellman, "Marketing Cost Analysis—Its Relationship to Factory Costing Methods," *N.A.A. Bulletin*, January 1962, pp. 25–33; and Robert K. Jaedicke, "Marketing Cost Analysis—A Reply," *N.A.A. Bulletin*, July 1962, pp. 57–61.

mix. Any serious student of accounting should attempt to familiarize himself with these methods.[5]

COST ANALYSIS BY SIZE OF ORDER

A product-line classification was chosen as the first illustration of distribution cost analysis because product-line analysis was already familiar from earlier chapters. In a sense, it was a poor starting point, however, because most problems calling for distribution cost analysis relate to some dimension of the customer mix.

One important form of customer-related analysis is the estimation of the costs of handling orders of different sizes. This "unit of sale" analysis can be used by management in such matters as setting minimum order sizes, establishing a quantity discount structure, or altering methods of promoting and distributing products to small-order customers.

Basic Method

Estimates of the costs of handling orders of different sizes can be obtained from the functional cost totals, derived by the methods described earlier. Every functional cost element which has a governing factor that depends on the number, size, or other dimension of customer orders is germane to the analysis. Other items should be rigorously excluded. The cost of writing a customer invoice, for example, is clearly an order-related cost; the salary of the marketing vice president just as clearly is not.

A thorough example would have so many cost elements that a whole chapter would be required to discuss it.[6] To illustrate the method, however, let us assume that functional cost analyses have revealed the following unit cost totals:

Governing Factor	Unit Cost
Number of orders..................................	$1.00 per order
Value of orders....................................	0.001 per dollar
Number of product units ordered....................	0.03 per unit
Number of order lines.............................	0.01 per line

This table, of course, represents the summation of all of the functional cost elements governed by each of the factors listed; a full example would have to list each function separately.

The next step is to find out how many units of each of these governing factors are associated with orders of various sizes. For example, a sample of orders might yield the following statistics:

---

[5] An interesting discussion of the objectives of these studies and the results of a number of them is in Charles H. Sevin, *Marketing Productivity Analysis* (New York: McGraw-Hill Book Co., 1965), especially chaps. 4–8.

[6] For example, see Longman and Schiff, op. cit., chap. 11.

Order Size	Number of Governing Factor Units			
	Orders	Order Value	Product Units	Order Lines
$ 1–$ 99...............	50,000	$ 1,000,000	200,000	100,000
100– 199...............	20,000	2,600,000	500,000	60,000
200– 499...............	20,000	5,600,000	1,100,000	80,000
500 and up.............	10,000	6,000,000	1,200,000	50,000
Total..................	100,000	$15,200,000	3,000,000	290,000

Because the question in this case is how much it costs to obtain and service an order, these statistics next should be restated as averages, as follows:

Order Size	Average Number of Governing Factor Units per Order			
	Orders	Order Value	Product Units	Order Lines
$ 1–$ 99.................	1	$ 20	4	2.0
100– 199.................	1	130	25	3.0
200– 499.................	1	280	55	4.0
500 and up...............	1	600	120	5.0
Average..................	1	$152	30	2.9

The final step is to multiply these statistics by the unit cost figures cited earlier. The end result is the unit cost of an order, as summarized below:

Order Size	Costs Attributed to—				
	Each Order	Value of the Order	Number of Units in Order	Number of Order Lines	Total Cost per Order
$ 1–$ 99......	$1.00	$0.02	$0.12	$0.02	$1.16
100– 199......	1.00	0.13	0.75	0.03	1.91
200– 499......	1.00	0.28	1.65	0.04	2.97
500 and up....	1.00	0.60	3.60	0.05	5.25
Average........	$1.00	$0.152	$0.90	$0.029	$2.08

Orders that contribute less product profit contribution (variable profit or attributable profit) than the amounts shown in the right-hand column are not covering their costs.

In practice, this analysis could be further simplified by consolidating two or more governing factors that are highly correlated. In this example, for instance, the number of units in each order correlated very closely with the value of the order. This can be checked by computing average value per unit, which in this case is virtually constant. Another simplification would be to omit insignificant variables, in this case the number of order lines.

A variant on this approach is to derive, by statistical correlation or regression analysis, mathematical relationships between size of order as the independent variable and the various governing factors as dependent variables. This would avoid the obvious error of saying that a $99 order costs $1.16 while a $100 order costs $1.91. Unfortunately, the correlation is unlikely to be good enough to use, and in most cases the method described here is the only possibility.

The Quantity Discount Problem

The preceding analysis could serve as a basis for the establishment of a quantity discount schedule. From an economic point of view, the quantity discount structure is a means of discriminating among different segments of the market to obtain a greater total revenue from a given physical sales volume than could be derived from a one-price policy. This form of price discrimination has long been accepted practice in the regulated electric power industry. Outside the public utility field, however, public policy has been to discourage systematic discrimination of this sort, principally through the provisions of the Robinson-Patman Act. One way to justify quantity discounts in Robinson-Patman proceedings is to show that they do not exceed demonstrable cost differentials.

Few attempts at cost justification of quantity discounts have been successful, but this does not mean that they could not be successful if the discount structure itself were established on a cost basis.[7] Most cost studies designed to defend a company's discount structure have been conducted after the Federal Trade Commission filed its complaint, and thus it is not surprising that discounts and cost differentials have failed to coincide.

To illustrate briefly how cost data might be used in justifying quantity discounts, suppose that the company in the previous illustration has offered quantity discounts as follows:

Size of Order	Discount
$ 1–$ 99	None
100– 199	3%
200– 499	5
200– 499	5
500 and up	7

If this structure is to be justified, the cost differential per dollar of order value must be at least as great as the percentages indicated. In other

___
[7] For an exhaustive study of this question, see Herbert F. Taggart, *Cost Justification, Michigan Business Studies, Vol. XIV, No. 3* (Ann Arbor: Bureau of Business Research, University of Michigan, 1959).

words, it it costs 10 percent less per order dollar to process a $600 order than to process a $20 order, then any discount of 10 percent or less is justifiable on a cost basis. The computed cost differentials in this example are:

Order Size	(1) Average Order Value	(2) Average Cost per Order	(3) Average Cost per Order Dollar (2) ÷ (1)	(4) Cost Differential from Base Class $0.0580 − (3)
$ 1–$ 99..................	$ 20	$1.16	$0.0580	......
100– 199..................	130	1.91	0.0147	$0.0433
200– 499..................	280	2.97	0.0106	0.0474
500 and up................	600	5.25	0.0088	0.0492

This table shows that the 3 percent discount offered to customers purchasing in $100–$199 quantities is more than justified by the cost savings attributable to these larger orders (0.0580 − 0.0147 = 4.33 percent). The discounts offered to customers buying in larger quantities cannot be justified in this way, however. The 5 percent discount offered to the third class of invoices is 0.26 of a percentage point greater than the cost differential (0.0580 − 0.0106 = 4.74 percent), and the gap is even wider in the case of the top discount category.

A moment's reflection will indicate that these cost differentials per order dollar are not created by those functional cost elements that vary directly with order dollars. These average 60 cents for a $600 order and 2 cents for a $20 order, or ⅒ cent per order dollar in both cases. In more general terms, the costs that are relevant to the quantity discount structure are those that are order-related but do not vary proportionately with the size of the order. When order size is measured in dollars, the relevant costs are those that do not vary in proportion to the dollar value of the individual order but do vary with the number of orders or order elements.

Attributable Cost versus Full Cost

Most authorities on cost justification for Robinson-Patman Act cases prefer to use full cost figures for that purpose. One reason may be that they believe that full cost figures are conceptually preferable. Another is that the Federal Trade Commission accountants are accustomed to working on a full cost basis, and this will make it easier to come to an agreement on technical matters. Another may be that differentials in full cost are likely to be larger than differentials in attributable cost, and thus a larger proportion of the discount structure can be justified.

The foregoing illustration, in contrast, employed the attributable cost concept throughout. Variable cost was rejected on the ground that most decisions to be based on unit costs for different order sizes have a longer time horizon and a broader scope than would be appropriate to variable cost figures. Full cost, on the other hand, was rejected for reasons that have been cited repeatedly in this and previous chapters—it has no clear analytical meaning.

Exclusion of Manufacturing Cost Differentials

No mention has been made thus far of possible differentials in manufacturing costs for orders of different sizes. The reason is that in most cases manufacturing cost per unit is a function of the total volume of production rather than of the volume generated by any one order.

For example, suppose that the company has two orders for the same product, one for 100 units and the other for 1,000 units. Manufacturing costs attributable to production of these units are:

Volume (Units)	Total Cost	Unit Cost
100	$10,000	$100
1,000	80,000	80
1,100	86,900	79

In this case the incremental cost of the 100-unit order could be either $100 or $69 a unit, depending on whether the larger order was also in the shop at the same time. (The $69 figure is the average cost of increasing production from 1,000 units to 1,100 units.) Similarly, the incremental cost of the 1,000-unit order could be either $80 or $76.90. In other words, cost differentials between orders of different sizes do not include differentials in manufacturing costs unless circumstances require that each order be produced separately or else different versions of the product are sold to the customers in the various order-size brackets.

This indeterminacy of cost does not necessarily mean that production cost differentials should not be reflected in price differentials if the Robinson-Patman Act is not applicable. If the 100-unit customer's business can be taken for granted and if the large order cannot be obtained without giving the customer a $20 discount, the cost figures will support this discount. The basic decision factors, however, are marketing factors, namely, the sensitivity of unit sales to price in individual segments of the market.

OTHER APPLICATIONS

The variety of problems that call for distribution cost analysis is very large. In each case the appropriate method of analysis will be very similar to the methods outlined in this chapter, and no purpose would be served by expanding the list of illustrations. It is merely necessary to describe a pair of highly disparate applications to show the universality of the method.

Bank Service Charges

Commercial banks render a variety of services for their demand depositors. Many of these services, such as lines of credit and safe deposit boxes, are provided under separate agreements with the depositor; others are provided automatically as long as the depositor has a balance in his account.

Although most banks have some degree of monopoly power and some banks have a good deal of insulation from direct competition, banking in general is a highly competitive business and fees that are out of line with competitive practice can lead to a substantial loss of business. A bank in a competitive environment is seldom free to raise its service charges far above a compensatory level.

Data on the cost of servicing customers' accounts provide the bank's management with guidance in its pricing policies. If costs exceed service prices by a significant margin, the time may be ripe for an upward adjustment of the price structure. Alternatively, management may wish to question its service policies and operating methods to see if costs can be reduced.

Once again the appropriate approach is to develop estimated or standard costs of performing various functions, and then use these rates to determine the costs of various services. For example, a committee of the New York Clearing House Association several years ago published a pamphlet in which three classes of account-related costs were recognized:[8]

Fixed maintenance costs.
Variable maintenance costs.
Activity costs.

Fixed maintenance costs are the costs of "maintaining depositors' account records, regardless of size of account balances or degree of account activity," and they include the costs of such activities as opening and closing accounts and maintaining signature card files. The pamphlet also sees fit to include in this category the costs of rendering services that benefit all depositors as a group, a category that would not fit in under the attributable cost doctrine.

The *variable maintenance costs* are those, like deposit insurance, which

---

[8] The New York Clearing House Association, Committee on Accounting Procedures, *Bank Cost Accounting Principles and Procedures* (New York, 1961). The references in this chapter are mainly to chap. 7, pp. 40–50.

tend to vary with the size of depositors' account balances. Once again it is unfortunate that the category was expanded to include activities presumed to be of benefit to depositors in proportion to the size of account balances, and most of the illustrations in the pamphlet fell into this latter group. Acceptance of attributable cost as a guiding concept makes this second group superfluous, as all costs that vary with the size of the depositor's account can be treated as *activity costs*, the costs of performing varying amounts of specific banking services for the depositor.

The Clearing House pamphlet identified 30 separate activities likely to be undertaken in servicing regular demand deposit accounts. Repetition of this list here is unnecessary, but the main items were:

Paying checks drawn on the depositor's account.
Cashing checks drawn on other banks.
Processing checks submitted for deposit.
Accepting currency for deposit.
Supplying wrapped currency.
Issuing account transcripts.

By identifying the amount of each of these kinds of activities required by a given class of customers, the bank's management can identify cost-price relationships that are out of line and take whatever action it deems appropriate under current circumstances.

Vending Machine Profitability

As one final example of distribution cost analysis, a company engaged in the sale, supply, and servicing of vending machines recently undertook a study to determine the costs associated with four of its most important types of equipment. The machines were further grouped by type of location—e.g., offices, light industrial factories, heavy industrial factories, supervised public locations, and unsupervised public locations. The company's study recognized eight major classes of activities:

Selling.
Delivery and installation.
Financing.
Field maintenance.
Shop maintenance.
Repainting and reconditioning.
Bookkeeping.
Repossession.

Using some sample data and some data drawn from the routine historical accounting records, the company developed unit costs for activities in each of these classes, as well as records of functional consumption for each of the 20 machine-type–location combinations (Type A—Offices, Type B—Offices, Type A—Light Industrial Factories, etc.).

This analysis provided the company's management with information on which to base its machine rental charges. (The company's objective was to break even on the machine, relying for its profits on products sold in the machine.) Such a study might also reveal that certain types of equipment are more suitable than others in given kinds of locations or that some kinds of locations are so hard on the machines that the profitable course of action is to withdraw from those locations altogether.

SUMMARY

Many problems in marketing management call for estimates of the profitability of specific segments of the company's revenues. Most of these problems call for the analysis of distribution costs.

The first step in distribution cost analysis is the estimation of the costs attributable to the performance of individual nonmanufacturing functions. The next step is to assign to revenue segments any costs that are directly traceable to those segments.

If feasible, nontraceable independent program costs can be allocated to revenue segments on the basis of estimates of the amount of cost that could be eliminated by abandoning those segments. Otherwise, no further allocation of independent program costs should be made.

For service activities, however, the process can be extended further. For these, selection of the governing factor or factors for permits the derivation of functional unit costs. The costs assignable to the revenue segments are then obtained by multiplying the unit costs by estimates of the number of each governing factor associated with each segment.

Some of these analyses focus on individual products, but most of them deal with some dimension of the customer mix—size of order, channel of distribution, location, industry, etc. It is in analyses of this sort that the concept of attributable cost is most needed. Variable cost is too narrow to fit the scope of the decisions to be made, while joint costs are ordinarily so numerous that full cost has no analytical meaning whatsoever.

In reaction to years of neglect in this area, enthusiasts for distribution cost analysis may overstate their case. This kind of analysis is expensive, and it is easy to undertake it too often or carry it to too fine a degree of detail. Means are justified only by the ends to be served, and the analysis should be carried only as far as the application seems to require.

EXERCISES AND PROBLEMS

1.* The management of the Manley Joyce Company has asked one of the company's accountants to prepare estimates of the cost of processing orders for small quantities of the company's merchandise. The accountant prepared the following estimates of the average cost of order processing per order:

---

* Solutions to problems marked with an asterisk can be found in Appendix B.

Credit investigation......................................	$0.30
Warehousing..	0.16
Shipping..	0.25
Billing...	0.46
Accounts receivable department.........................	0.15
Cashier...	0.18
Total per order.......................................	$1.50

Most of the company's products are priced at a markup of 40 percent over standard manufacturing cost.

a) Using $1.50 as the cost of processing an order, what is the smallest order that the company should accept?

b) To what extent do you believe the above cost estimates provide an adequate basis for deciding on minimum order quantities?

2. The Angel Meat Company has studied its selling and administrative expenses to determine the costs attributable to different segments of the company's business. It has found that some of these expenses are fixed, but the bulk of the expenses can be related to one of the following three indicators of sales volume: (1) number of orders, (2) number of items, and (3) number of hundredweights. Classification of expenses on these bases yields the following totals:

	Selling	Packing	Delivery	Administr.	Total
Fixed per month............	$20,000	$1,000	$ 3,000	$15,000	$ 39,000
Variable according to:					
Number of orders.........	46,200	1,200	4,000	23,400	74,800
Number of items.........	21,600	1,400	5,000	11,600	39,600
Number of cwts.........	4,200	2,400	10,000	6,800	23,400
Total....................	$92,000	$6,000	$22,000	$56,800	$176,800

Analysis of orders received during the analysis period shows the following data:

Size of Order	Orders	Items	Total Cwt.
Less than 50 lbs....................	56,000	81,800	14,000
50–199 lbs.......................	58,000	168,200	52,200
200–499 lbs.....................	12,000	45,600	37,200
500–999 lbs.....................	8,000	48,000	56,000
1,000 lbs. and over...............	2,000	16,400	20,600
All orders......................	136,000	360,000	180,000

Compute the cost per hundredweight for each order size, to the nearest 100th of a cent. Defend your method of dealing with fixed costs.

3.* The delivery department of the Egbert Company operates under a departmental budget which recognizes three separate functions: (1) loading

and unloading, (2) truck operation, and (3) truck repairs. Costs directly traceable to each of these functions are charged to functional accounts. All other
fixed charges, mainly supervision of the department's operation and rent on
the garage and truck repair shop, are charged to general department accounts
and not to specific functions.

The departmental budget for the current year is based on the following
data:

	Loading and Unloading	Truck Operation	Truck Repairs	Undistributed Fixed Charges
Normal monthly volume	380 man-hrs.	11,000 miles	11,000 miles	...
Variable cost per unit:				
Labor...............	$2.40	$0.310	$0.050	...
Supplies and parts.....	...	0.150	0.020	...
Outside repairs.......	...	...	0.040	...
Employee benefits.....	0.24	0.031	0.005	...
Total variable......	$2.64	$0.491	$0.115	...
Fixed costs per month:				
Labor...............	...	...	...	$ 900
Rent................	...	...	...	400
Depreciation..........	$ 20	$ 500	$ 100	...
Insurance............	5	125	45	20
Taxes...............	1	20	80	...
Employee benefits.....	...	...	...	90
Total fixed........	$ 26	$ 645	$ 225	$1,410

The loading platform occupies 10 percent of the rented space, the repair
shop occupies 15 percent, and the remaining 75 percent is used as a garage.
Normal driving speed is 15 miles per road hour, not including unloading time.

During the month of May the department's trucks logged 12,000 miles in
820 hours of road time exclusive of unloading time. Loading and unloading
operations consumed 400 man-hours. The department's accounts showed the
following costs for the month:

	Loading and Unloading	Truck Operation	Truck Repairs	Undistributed Fixed Charges
Labor...............	$ 940	$3,690	$ 450	$ 920
Overtime premium.....	...	...	10	240
Supplies and parts......	...	1,710	160	...
Outside repairs.......	...	...	310	...
Employee benefits......	94	369	46	116
Rent................	...	...	...	400
Depreciation..........	20	522	100	...
Insurance............	5	130	45	24
Taxes...............	1	20	80	...
Total................	$1,060	$6,441	$1,201	$1,700

Bulk deliveries during the month accounted for 9,000 miles, 500 hours of road time, and 200 hours of loading and unloading time. Express deliveries accounted for the remaining mileage and time. Prepare an analysis showing the cost to be distributed to these two segments of the company's business. Be prepared to defend your treatment of fixed costs.

4. As part of the preparation for its defense in a Robinson-Patman case, C. E. Niehoff & Company conducted a series of time and motion studies of order-processing operations. Seventeen orders of varying sizes were selected for study, and the processing times were obtained for each of these by a time-study engineer. The engineer then added 25 percent to these observed times to allow for personal needs and fatigue. The total processing times, priced at standard wage rates for individual operations, are listed in the table below:

Order No.	No. of Items	No. of Packages	Net Billing	Processing Cost	Cost per Dollar
44524	1	2	$ 12.00	$ 1.1909	9.92¢
44525	6	23	37.66	1.3141	3.49
44576	20	29	45.14	1.9457	4.31
44575	8	49	56.51	2.0506	3.66
45968	33	69	125.20	2.6529	2.11
44572	25	116	134.47	3.2335	2.33
46162	37	171	206.79	3.6094	1.74
44577	36	86	208.64	3.3236	1.59
44573	63	163	223.76	4.7155	2.11
45969	49	110	259.80	3.8108	1.47
45945	56	163	305.01	5.4135	1.77
46161	49	236	341.79	4.4516	1.30
44991	68	391	496.98	7.1486	1.44
45078	81	334	523.22	8.6659	1.66
45301	101	623	785.80	10.7736	1.36
45079	94	598	811.57	11.4696	1.41
44993	89	469	846.66	10.3696	1.23

Source: Herbert F. Taggart, *Cost Justification* (Ann Arbor: University of Michigan, Graduate School of Business Administration, Bureau of Business Research, 1959), p. 408.

a) On a sheet of graph paper, plot processing costs per dollar of net billing against size of order (measured by net billings) and draw a line of relationship freehand, as accurately as you can.

b) Assuming that these are the best data available, indicate how you would use these figures in: (1) setting a minimum order size; (2) estimating the profitability of different customer groups.

c) Comment on the methods used to obtain the data and their adequacy for the purposes outlined in (*b*).

5. The Henlo Company has separate sales divisions for each of its product lines. The company's factories are not specialized by product lines but serve all divisions to varying degrees.

The Hardy Products Division is one of the company's oldest sales divisions. Its products are marketed through a network of 900 retail stores. Of these, 400 are served directly and the remaining 500 are served by 25 wholesalers.

This divided distribution network was not really planned. Hardy Products originally distributed its products in a relatively small geographical region, close to the company's main factories. No wholesalers were used in this region. When management decided to expand into other areas, it decided that wholesalers would provide the fastest and most effective means of penetrating those areas.

Retailers in the areas served by the wholesalers are very similar to those in the company's older areas, but their average gross sales are slightly lower. This disparity has led management to consider the possibility of hiring additional salesmen so that all retailers could be dealt with directly, replacing the wholesalers entirely.

The following data can be regarded as typical of a full year's activity in the Hardy Products Division:

	Wholesale	Retail
Revenue from sales......................	$500,000	$700,000
Cost of goods sold........................	$420,000	$420,000
Number of salesmen's calls................	500	4,500
Number of invoice lines...................	45,000	255,000

Wholesalers pay lower prices than retailers to compensate them for warehousing and other sales-related functions that Hardy Products performs in connection with its directly served retail customers.

The division's six salesmen are all on salary. When adjusted for changes in salary rates and outside price levels, the cost of sales solicitation per salesman (salaries, travel, and samples) has remained roughly constant from year to year. The number of salesmen has been increased from three to six in the past few years as Henlo's business volume has expanded. The solicitation costs of obtaining the sales listed in the preceding table total $84,000 a year.

A call on a wholesaler takes approximately one and a half times as long as a call on a retailer. Wholesalers are also farther apart than retailers, and in an experiment conducted two years ago, the company found that a salesman assigned full time to wholesale accounts made calls at an average annual rate of 450 calls a year, whereas a salesman working full time on retail accounts made calls at the rate of 900 calls a year.

Costs of inventory record keeping, order receiving and filling, invoicing, accounts receivable bookkeeping, and collecting total $138,000 a year. These are regarded as fixed but have increased from year to year in parallel with the increase in the number of invoice lines.

Advertising expenditures amount to $62,000 a year, covering advertisements aimed at the ultimate consumers of the company's products.

Inventory storage costs which are incurred exclusively to service retailers amount to $24,000 a year. Storage costs consist entirely of warehouse rent, based on the amount of space used. These costs tend to increase from year to year, roughly in proportion to increases in the standard cost of goods sold.

The cost of goods sold is approximately 30 percent fixed and 70 percent variable. The fixed costs are largely indivisible.

Management's objective is to use the channel of distribution that will maximize the profit of the company as a whole.

a) Prepare an analysis of the relative profitability of the two channels used
by the Hardy Products Division. List any assumptions that you felt were
necessary to perform this analysis.

b) What recommendations would you make to management as a result of
your analysis?

6. The mimeograph room in the head office of David Metrics, Inc. was a
busy place. David Metrics was a large management consulting firm with
headquarters in New York and branch offices in 14 other cities in various
parts of the United States. Using several high-speed mimeograph machines, a
high-speed copying machine, and a small copier, the mimeograph room staff
reproduced a large volume of internal memoranda, working drafts, and reports
to the company's clients, and did a significant amount of work for other
tenants of the office building in which the company's headquarters were located. No typing was done in the mimeograph room; all mimeograph stencils
and master copies for the copying machines were prepared by the departments or outside customers from whom the work orders were received.

Jonathan David, the firm's administrative vice president and brother of the
president, felt that the mimeograph room's costs were getting out of hand.
"This doesn't tell me much," he said, pointing to the department's cost summary for the preceding month. "I know we've been doing a lot more copying
work since we put in the high-speed copier, but I can't believe that one new
machine has been responsible for the big cost increases we have had in this
department."

Bill Rogers, the office manager in the New York headquarters, agreed to
pull together some better figures for Mr. David. With the help of one of the
firm's consulting engineers, Mr. Rogers carried out a quick work sampling
study of the mimeograph room's machine operators. This study showed that
the operators' time was divided in the following proportions:

Operating mimeograph machines	20 percent
Operating copying machines	29
Out of room	10
Telephoning	5
Writing	2
Collating mimeograph work	17
Collating copying work	8
Waiting	6
Wrapping	3

The routine cost report for the mimeograph room during this same period
showed the following breakdown:

Supervisor's salary	$ 1,000
Clerical salaries	4,200
Paper and supplies	2,464
Maintenance, mimeograph machines	80
Rentals, copying machines	2,900
Depreciation, mimeograph machines	60
Space charge	240
Total	$10,944

The work load during this period was:

	Mimeograph	*Copying*
Number of work orders............................	5,000	20,000
Number of stencils processed........................	25,000	n.a.
Number of copies made............................	500,000	58,000

Mr. Rogers pointed out that most writing and telephoning was in connection with inquiries about the status of individual work orders. Virtually all wrapping time was spent on mimeographing work. Wrapping time is a function of the number of copies in the order.

After observing a number of representative operations, Mr. Rogers estimated that paper and supplies for copying work cost about twice as much per copy as the paper and supplies for mimeograph work. Copying machine rentals are based on the number of copies made.

a) Assuming that these data are typical, prepare cost estimates for each of the two classes of work done in this department. Be prepared to explain how you derived these estimates.

b) Stencils cost approximately 15 cents each. Adding these costs to those of the mimeograph room itself, calculate the cost of a 50-copy run of a 40-page report (1) by mimeograph machine, and (2) by copier. In either case the finished copies would be wrapped for delivery.

c) How else might Mr. David use the figures derived in (a)?

7. The Lucky Products Company manufactures and sells a line of electronics components to government contractors, telephone companies, and manufacturers of radio and television receivers and transmitters. Sales for the current year are expected to total $5 million, distributed as follows:

	Government	*Telephone*	*Radio-TV*
Sales......................................	$1,200,000	$3,000,000	$800,000
Standard cost of goods sold................	1,000,000	2,400,000	500,000
Gross margin...........................	$ 200,000	$ 600,000	$300,000

Concerned by the low margin on its government business, management has initiated a study of the profitability of the three classes of its business. The following information has been collected.

Standard cost is based on the full costing principle. Supplementary variable cost figures indicate the following ratios of variable cost to full cost at standard volume:

Government........................	70 percent
Telephone..........................	75
Radio-television.....................	80

No factory department is devoted solely to any one class of business.

The following amounts of out-of-pocket fixed factory costs could be eliminated each year if one class of business were to be dropped, the others remaining in service:

Government........................	$100,000
Telephone..........................	500,000
Radio-television.....................	200,000

Bookkeeping costs—that is, the costs of inventory record keeping, order receiving and filling, invoicing, accounts receivable bookkeeping, and collecting—total $150,000 a year. These are regarded as fixed, but have increased from year to year in parallel with the increase in the number of invoice lines. A sample of the invoices prepared this year indicates the following numbers of invoice lines for the three classes of business:

Government	4,500
Telephone	5,500
Radio-television	20,000

Warehousing costs amount to $50,000 a year, almost entirely in wages and salaries of warehouse and storeroom personnel. Warehouse costs tend to vary from year to year, roughly in proportion to the standard cost of goods sold to telephone companies and radio-television manufacturers. Government products are transferred immediately to government supply depots and do not enter the Lucky Products warehouse space.

The costs of central administration, including executive salaries, amount to $200,000 a year. These are almost completely unaffected by the volume of business done.

The company's research and development department has operating costs of $100,000 a year. The department consists of two research engineers, three technicians, and a variety of test equipment. The two engineers specialize in different fields, and both fields provide essential support for all three classes of business.

The costs of field selling total $250,000 a year. None of this is accepted by the government as a cost of the government products, but it includes $50,000 a year to cover the salary and expenses of a sales engineer to work full-time on identifying sales opportunities and preparing bids and proposals in this market. The only other information on these costs is the number of calls made by the other salesmen in the course of a year: 500 on telephone companies and 2,500 on radio-television manufacturers. The sales manager estimates that a call at a telephone company is likely to take about three times as long as a call on a radio-television manufacturer. All salesmen are paid on a straight salary basis, with no commissions.

Advertising accounts for $100,000 a year. Of this, $70,000 is directed specifically to manufacturers of radio-television equipment and $30,000 is for advertisements in engineering journals read by engineers in all industries.

All of the company's operations are contained in a single building. Fixed costs of providing this space amount to $200,000 a year and costs of providing space are included in factory overhead cost—that is, no space costs are allocated to other company divisions. Space occupancy is as follows:

Executive offices	10 percent
Factory	68
Sales	5
Warehouse	10
Bookkeeping	5
Research and development	2

The location and layout of the building make it virtually impossible to sublet any space that might become idle.

a) Prepare a revised estimate of profitability for each class of business and explain the methods and assumptions that you used in the process. (Suggestion: start by listing the total cost in each category; then decide how much to allocate to each class of business.)

b) What course(s) of action or further investigation would you suggest on the basis of this information?

8.† The Western Appliances, Ltd. income statement for the year ended December 31, 19x1 appears below:

Sales (1,900,000 units)			$3,800,000
Cost of sales			2,280,000
Gross profit			$1,520,000
Packing and shipping:			
Shipping containers	$ 91,750		
Packing and shipping labor expenses	221,250		
Freight-out	375,750	$688,750	
Selling expenses (excluding advertising):			
Sales manager's salary	$ 15,200		
Salesmen's salaries	32,000		
Salesmen's commissions	24,000		
Agency commissions	30,000		
Bad debts	11,500	112,700	
Advertising:			
Local newspapers	$ 43,500		
National magazines	57,000	100,500	
Administrative expenses (fixed)		64,750	966,700
Net Operating Profit			$ 533,300

The company manufactures a single product in a variety of colors. The selling price is $2 a unit.

The product is distributed in four market areas—A, B, C, and D.

District A is the district in which the manufacturing plant and offices are located. No salesmen are employed. Orders are received through the mail and by telephone, and customers send their trucks to the plant to pick up their orders when ready.

District B is located 100 miles from the plant. The company employs four salesmen in this area, each on a commission basis. The company also places a quarter-page advertisement once each week in the local newspaper.

District C is located 200 miles from the plant. The company employs eight salesmen in the area, each on a salary basis. The company takes one quarter of a page three times a week in the local paper in district C; the cost per insertion is twice as much as that in district B.

District D is an agency. It is 400 miles distant from the plant. The company shares with the agency the cost of a quarter-page weekly advertisement in the local paper on a 1:3 ratio, the space cost being the same as in district B.

The product is packaged in containers of three different sizes: namely, 16's (small), 32's (medium), and 48's (large), and shipments are made in case lots only. It is assumed that each order calls for one case.

† Adapted from an examination prepared by the Society of Industrial and Cost Accountants of Canada.

Sales commissions are paid on a flat percentage of sales basis. The following unit costs per case have been determined:

	Small	Medium	Large
Container......................	$1	$1.50	$2
Packing and shipping labor			
expenses....................	3	3.50	4
Freight-out (cost per 100 miles)...	2	3.50	5

A statistical analysis of the marketing operation during 19x1 shows the following, in total and by districts:

	Total	A	B	C	D
Number of orders:					
Small cases..............	22,500	2,500	....	20,000	....
Medium cases.............	30,500	5,000	7,500	15,000	3,000
Large cases..............	11,750	....	7,500	.....	4,250
Provision for bad debts—					
% of sales.............		¼ of 1%	⅛ of 1%	⅜ of 1%	½ of 1%

a) Prepare a set of statements showing the profitability of each sales district. Describe and defend the basis on which costs were assigned to each district.

b) Prepare a set of statements showing the profitability of each case size. Describe and defend the basis on which costs were assigned to each size group.

c) It has been proposed that an additional $50,000 a year be spent on local advertising in district C. By how much must the sales volume of the district increase to warrant such an expenditure?

CASE 13–1: ROBSON, LTD.‡

"Sorry to be late, John," Alan Thurston said. "I had a customer in my office and I just couldn't get rid of him."

"That's okay, Alan. I just got here myself. I hope you made a big sale."

"No such luck. I'll bet this customer has never done more than $100 worth of business with us and yet he sat in my office asking questions for an hour. We have too many customers like him."

Mr. Thurston was the sales manager of Robson, Ltd., a small Australian manufacturer of industrial supplies. He made the statement quoted above as he sat down to lunch with Mr. John Axelson, the company's controller. After they had ordered their lunch, Mr. Thurston returned to the subject. "I know how my sales stack up," he said, "but I have no idea how much money we make on the big customers or how much we lose on the little ones. Could you put some figures together for me on this?"

"I can't get at it myself right now," said Mr. Axelson, "but why don't we put Peter on it? It would be good experience for him and I don't have anything else important for him to do at the moment." Peter Halford was Mr. Thurston's nephew and was working at Robson, Ltd. during his summer holidays from the university. This was his second summer with Robson, and Mr. Axelson felt that he knew enough about the company to be able to get the figures that Mr. Thurston wanted.

Table 1

ROBSON, LTD.

Customer Statistics

	Group					
	A	B	C	D	E	F
Annual sales to each customer	$10,000 or more	$2,000–$9,999	$1,000–$1,999	$200–$999	$1–$199	$0
Number of customers	46	117	234	420	2,521	1,872
Total annual sales	$800,000	$500,000	$300,000	$200,000	$200,000	. . .
Total gross margin	160,000	110,000	75,000	48,000	49,000	. . .
Total variable manufacturing profit	280,000	190,000	120,000	79,000	81,000	. . .
Salesmen's calls per year	230	585	940	1,680	4,575	3,740
Customer orders per year	700	800	1,000	2,000	5,000	. . .
Average sales per customer	$17,391	$4,274	$1,282	$476	$79	. . .
Average sales per order	1,143	625	300	100	40	. . .

Mr. Halford first collected the statistics shown in Table 1. He started by classifying all the company's customers and active prospects on the basis of the total amount of business they had done with Robson in the last complete fiscal year. At one extreme, he found that 46 customers had bought more than $10,000 each during the previous year, while 1,872 customers and prospects (all referred to by the company as "customers") had bought absolutely nothing.

Fortunately for Mr. Halford, the company's sales records were quite complete, and he was able to identify the gross margin (sales minus the cost of goods sold) for each customer. As a result of some work he had been doing that summer, he was also able to make an estimate of the variable component of the cost of goods sold, and this permitted him to assemble the set of figures identified in Table 1 as "total variable manufacturing profit" (sales minus variable manufacturing cost of goods sold). The profit-sales ratios varied slightly from group to group, mainly because of differences in the discounts granted to different customers.

The statistics on salesmen's calls and customer orders were readily available in the files, although Mr. Halford had to work fairly hard to dig them out.

Next Mr. Halford turned to the task of identifying the cost of serving individual customers. At his request, Mr. Thurston got all of his salesmen to keep a record of their time for one week. This showed the following breakdown:

Call time (waiting for and talking to customers).....	50 percent
Travel time......................................	30
Office time (preparing reports, following up on orders, etc.)..................................	20
Total..	100 percent

The 10-man sales force was organized regionally, each man having his own sales territory. Some territories were relatively compact, while others required a good deal of traveling. Each salesman was responsible for promoting all of the company's products.

Mr. Halford summarized the annual costs of the sales department and computed the average cost per sales call, as follows:

	Amount	Per Call
Sales supervision......................	$ 18,800	$ 1.60
Salesmen's salaries and benefits..........	122,200	10.40
Clerical salaries......................	8,460	0.72
Salesmen's travel......................	79,900	6.80
Customer entertainment................	14,100	1.20
Samples.............................	7,050	0.60
Rent................................	2,350	0.20
Other...............................	2,820	0.24
Total..............................	$255,680	$21.76

This was the estimated cost of the sales department for the current year. The only omission was $4,230 of clerical salaries which Mr. Halford excluded from the total above on the basis of Mr. Thurston's estimate that the office staff devoted only two thirds of its time to matters related to salesmen (typing expense accounts, preparing payrolls, etc.). The remaining one third of office clerical time was spent processing customer orders and thus should not be included in the cost per call figures. Instead, Mr. Halford included this amount in a rough estimate of the clerical cost of processing an order. Orders came both through the salesmen and directly from the customers, by mail or telephone. The office procedure was the same in either case and Mr. Halford estimated that the total cost of clerical salaries and benefits averaged about $2.40 an order. He thought that he could get a more accurate figure if he tried, but he

didn't have enough time to study the costs of other items such as depreciation on office equipment, office supplies, and office rent.

On the basis of these figures, Mr. Halford prepared the analysis of
customer profitability shown in Table 2. "This will really make Uncle
Alan sit up and take notice," he said. "Even on the most favorable calculation, we still lose $30,000 a year on our small customers and pour

Table 2

ROBSON, LTD.

Statement of Customer Profitability

	Group					
	A	B	C	D	E	F
Selling costs (no. calls × $21.76)	$ 5,005	$ 12,730	$20,454	$36,557	$ 99,552	$ 81,382
Order-filling costs (no. orders × $2.40)	1,680	1,920	2,400	4,800	12,000	...
Total expense...............	$ 6,685	$ 14,650	$22,854	$41,357	$111,552	$ 81,382
Excess of gross margin over expense..................	$153,315	$ 95,350	$52,146	$ 6,643	$(62,552)	$(81,382)
Excess of variable manufacturing profit over expense........	273,315	175,350	97,146	37,643	(30,552)	(81,382)

more than $80,000 down the drain on customers who don't buy anything
at all. I'll bet he changes his sales policy now." He walked confidently
toward Mr. Axelson's office to show him the results of the analysis.

Do these data mean that Robson, Ltd. would be able to increase its
profits by discontinuing salesmen's calls on the customers in groups E
and F? Indicate how you would interpret the data. Also describe any
changes in analytical method that you would recommend. Remember
that this is a small company and that Mr. Halford had only a few weeks,
at most, to study this problem.

Part III

Budgetary
Planning and
Reporting Systems

chapter 14

Budgetary Planning

Much management planning effort is expended in isolated decision making, dealing with specific choices among competing projects or actions. For want of a better term, this can be referred to as project planning. Another form of planning, at least equally important and potentially more powerful, is periodic planning—that is, the process by which management decides what it expects to accomplish during a specific period of time and how it will accomplish this. The purpose of this chapter is to examine the objectives and structure of the periodic planning process as it relates to accounting.

THE PLANNING PROCESS

Periodic planning has both short-term and long-term dimensions. The long-range plan summarizes management's vision of the company's future during the next three to five years, sometimes even longer. Short-term planning, or budgeting, typically deals with the next year only, and the annual budget is the first year's segment of the long-range plan. Both emerge from the same kind of process, and they differ primarily in the amount of detail provided and in the degree of commitment they represent.

The Structure of the Annual Budget

Most people probably think of budgets as limits on the amounts of money they can spend. Although most government budgets and some components of business budgets do take this form, the underlying idea is much broader. In this view, the annual budget is the quantitative expression of management's immediate objectives and its plans for operating and financing the organization during the year. This definition can be applied to any kind of organization—a school, a symphony orchestra, an industrial corporation, or even a government department fighting for a share of the tax dollar.

One way to describe the budget is to list its component parts, as in Exhibit 14–1. The left-hand column of this exhibit lists the major physical elements that the management of a manufacturing company must deal with. These are translated in the next two columns into monetary terms as budgeted operating costs, revenues, and expenses. Finally, these cost and profit budgets are brought together with planned capital expenditures and plans for financing the entire package to form the finance budgets shown at the right.

The budget also has an organizational dimension. Each unit has its own portion of the overall plan, and bringing organizational units together may be even more difficult than coordinating production and sales in the

Exhibit 14–1

BUDGET COMPONENTS

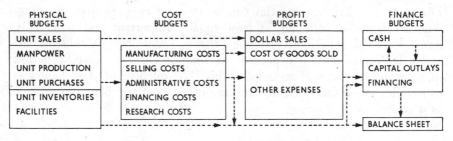

aggregate. At low organization levels, the department head is likely to deal with only a few of the budget components shown in Exhibit 14–1. At higher levels, however, the plan is likely to include the same components as the budget of the organization as a whole.

The Objectives of Budgeting

The annual budgetary planning process has at least four major objectives:

1. To force management to reexamine its objectives, its methods, and its costs.
2. To encourage executives to quantify their plans and to test them against objective standards of desirability and feasibility.
3. To give management a chance to anticipate environmental changes, thereby increasing its ability to shape the organization's future.
4. To develop a formal statement of ends and means that can serve both

as a continuing reminder for the guidance of day-to-day management and as a bench mark against which to measure actual performance.

The first three of these are advantages of the process of budgeting; the fourth can be realized only if the budget documents are continually and constructively used.

The Budgeting Sequence

Given an understanding of the organization's basic purposes and its overriding strategy, the planner can follow a number of routes.[1] In some organizations, the top executives initiate the process by formulating a series of overall goals for the organization as a whole and its major operating segments. These broad goals—such as a specified rate of return on investment or a specified level of service activity—are then transmitted to subordinate executives for translation into workable plans.

In other organizations top management enters the process at a later stage. Exhibit 14–2, for example, shows the planning sequence followed by a large manufacturing company. It begins with the development of basic economic forecasts by headquarters staff departments. The managers of the company's various operating divisions use these forecasts in formulating long-range plans and objectives for their own operations. Headquarters staff groups provide assistance in this process, and the final long-range objectives are approved by top management.

While this is going on, division and product managers are also working on tentative operating plans for the coming year. After the approval of the long-range objectives, these operating plans are formalized and transmitted to headquarters for review, coordination and approval.

Once this process has been completed, the divisional plans are transmitted to the headquarters staff for consolidation and final approval. The overall corporate financing plan and cash budget are also put in final form at this stage.

Two points must be emphasized at this juncture. First, periodic planning is no less a decision process than the intermittent, one-of-a-kind choices that management makes when it decides on new products or sets product prices. Second, periodic planning is an iterative process, in which budget proposals move haltingly, level by level, up through the organization to the top. Budget proposals are prepared, submitted to the next management level, sent back for revision or further evidence, resubmitted, approved and passed up to the next level, reviewed there and sent back down, revised again and resubmitted, and so on.

---

[1] Discussion of the processes by which organizational objectives and strategies are formed is not necessary for an understanding of the content of this section. For an introductory survey, see William H. Newman, Charles Summer, and E. Kirby Warren, *The Process of Management* (3d ed.; Englewood Cliffs, N.J.: Prentice-Hall, 1972).

Exhibit 14–2

PLANNING SEQUENCE AND COORDINATION CHART

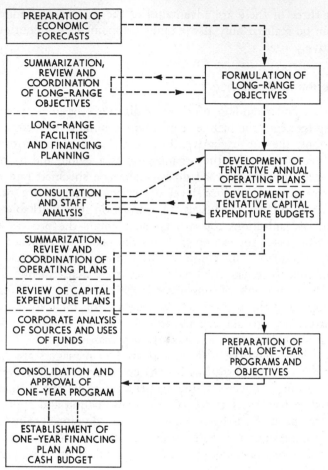

Responsibility for Budgeting

As the foregoing would imply, the development of the annual budget is a responsibility of line management. The task of pulling together all the elements of a profit plan, however, ordinarily falls to the lot of the budget director or controller. The amount of detail and the number of interrelationships among components of the plan in a large corporation can be enormous, and the budget director has no easy task.

The budget director or controller is also responsible for designing and securing support for the procedural aspects of periodic planning, mainly the questions of what is to be budgeted, when, and by whom. The final installation is likely to be summarized in a budget manual spelling out deadlines for various budget components, assigning responsibilities for budget preparation, prescribing forms, and describing the overall budget pattern.

Even if budget components have been reviewed carefully and critically all the way up the line within a given segment of the organization, the corporate controller or budget director often has the authority to subject the proposals to his own tests of feasibility and profitability. He is always free to seek clarification or question whether other alternatives have been investigated, and in some cases he even has the power to ask individual managers to revise their programs.[2] It must be emphasized, however, that in taking any actions of this sort the controller is acting as the agent of line management and is applying tests that line executives would apply. He has no line authority of his own.

Program Budgeting

In organization-based budgeting, primary responsibility for planning is vested in line executives who supervise the personnel who will implement the plan. In program budgeting, on the other hand, the focus is on individual product lines or customer groups, with a separate plan for each. The budget component for a given organization unit is determined jointly by the various programs that affect that unit.

Program budgeting is typically encountered in private business when the organization structure provides for one or more program executives, particularly those known as *product managers*. The position of product manager has arisen in companies in which a completely product-based organization structure would be inefficient, so that individual product programs have to share in the resources of factories or other organization units. In many such companies, management has come to believe that the line organization structure is not conducive to aggressive and coherent product program development, and has superimposed a set of product managers on the conventional line organization.

The product manager is typically responsible for both product and profit planning. He has at least advisory responsibility for selecting channels and methods of distribution and for selecting advertising and promotional material for his product line. He often acts as liaison man between the production and sales departments, but he seldom has any direct authority over either. A meat-packer, for example, has a beef de-

---

[2] For further discussion of these points, see Neil W. Chamberlain, *The Firm: Micro-Economic Planning and Action* (New York: McGraw-Hill Book Co., 1962), chap. 11.

partment, a pork department, a lamb department, and others, each with its own manager, even though most of the production and selling activity is conducted in multiprogram operating units.[3]

Because the product manager has no troops of his own, program budgeting can be a very delicate affair.[4] The line managers, particularly in marketing, have to reconcile the often conflicting demands of the various product managers. Because the line managers will have ultimate responsibility for the implementation of the various programs, and often for their results as well, they must work simultaneously with the various product managers to make sure that their commitments are mutually consistent. With more people to satisfy at one time, the difficulty of planning becomes multiplied.

PREPARING THE ANNUAL BUDGET

The development of a formal budgetary plan requires a careful examination of the interrelationships among its various components. Although the complexity of this process cannot be conveyed effectively in a few pages, a very simple example may at least identify the problems.

The Marketing Plan and Sales Budget

Preparation of the annual operating plan for the Caldwell Company starts with the development of a tentative marketing plan. Caldwell is a small manufacturer of hand drills, marketing a narrow line of products through a regional network of company-owned branches. The company has three products, known as the Drillmaster, the Superba, and the Handyman.

To begin the process, Bob Lloyd, the company's marketing vice president, asked each of his branch sales managers to submit proposed manpower and expense budgets for the coming year, together with estimates of the levels of sales they would expect to get from these expenditures. Each manager was told that national advertising expenses would be approximately the same as the current year's.

Taken together, the initial branch proposals and forecasts added up to the following totals:

---

[3] A concise tabulation of a typical product manager's responsibilities is to be found in Michael Schiff and Martin Mellman, *Financial Management of the Marketing Function* (New York: Financial Executives Research Foundation, 1962), pp. 28–31.

[4] The structure of government agencies often makes program budgeting particularly difficult, but this is one of the most interesting developments in governmental budgeting to come along in recent years. See David Novick, *Program Budgeting* (2d ed.; New York: Holt, Rinehart & Winston, 1969).

	Units	Manufacturer's Price	Amounts
Estimated sales:			
Drillmaster.................	120,000	$35	$4,200,000
Superba....................	50,000	25	1,250,000
Handyman..................	100,000	15	1,500,000
Total....................			$6,950,000
Discounts and allowances.........			278,000
Net sales.....................			$6,672,000
Estimated marketing expenses:			
Branch expense..............			$ 575,000
National advertising...........			125,000
Headquarters expenses........			75,000
Total marketing expense.....			$ 775,000

Before going any farther, Mr. Lloyd checked with Dave Wright, the production manager, to make sure that the company had enough factory capacity to service this level of orders. Reassured, he and his staff assistant began to evaluate the various branch proposals.

First, Mr. Lloyd knew that sales figures alone were not a good measure of the productivity of branch expenses. Unit for unit and dollar for dollar, Drillmaster sales were the most profitable and Handyman sales were the least profitable. A marketing expenditure that brought in Drillmaster orders therefore was a more productive plan than one that brought in an equal volume of orders for the Superba or Handyman models.

This led Mr. Lloyd to ask Bill Frank, the company's controller, for production cost figures. Because the cost estimates were to be used to help decide how to use existing capacity, and fixed factory costs were unlikely to be affected by these marketing decisions, Mr. Frank supplied Mr. Lloyd with estimates of variable manufacturing costs only:

$$\begin{array}{ll} \text{Drillmaster.................} & \text{\$18/unit} \\ \text{Superba.....................} & \text{15/unit} \\ \text{Handyman..................} & \text{10/unit} \end{array}$$

With discounts and allowances at 4 percent of sales, the variable profit rates were as follows:

	Drillmaster	Superba	Handyman
Selling price....................	$35.00	$25.00	$15.00
Discounts and allowances........	$ 1.40	$ 1.00	$ 0.60
Variable product cost...........	18.00	15.00	10.00
	$19.40	$16.00	$10.60
Variable profit.................	$15.60	$ 9.00	$ 4.40
Percent of sales.................	44.6	36.0	29.3

Now Mr. Lloyd was ready to tackle the branch proposals. Each branch's marketing plan was broken down by territory and by channel of distribution. For each channel in each territory, Mr. Lloyd studied the promotional methods to be used, the amounts to be spent, and the anticipated sales volume and mix. He tested these tentative plans against each other, against past figures, and against his own assessment of the market.

He noted, for example, that the Louisville branch manager expected to spend almost 6 percent more to operate his branch, mainly due to salary increases. Sales were expected to rise by about 3.5 percent, but the branch's profit contribution was down slightly, as shown in Exhibit 14–3.

Since the same figures were used for unit manufacturing costs in the two years, the increase in product cost relative to the increase in revenues had to be due to deterioration in the quality of the product mix as larger

Exhibit 14–3

CALDWELL COMPANY

Proposed Profit Plan for Louisville Branch

	Drillmaster	Superba	Handyman	Total	% Change
Current year:					
Unit sales.....................	12,000	6,000	8,000	26,000	
Sales revenues.................	$420,000	$150,000	$120,000	$690,000	
Discounts and allowances.......	$ 16,800	$ 6,000	$ 4,800	$ 27,600	
Variable product costs.........	216,000	90,000	80,000	386,000	
	$232,800	$ 96,000	$ 84,800	$413,600	
Product margin................	$187,200	$ 54,000	$ 35,200	$276,400	
Branch expenses..............				68,000	
Profit contribution..............				$208,400	
Proposed, next year:					
Unit sales.....................	11,000	6,000	12,000	29,000	11.5%
Sales revenues.................	$385,000	$150,000	$180,000	$715,000	3.6
Discounts and allowances.......	$ 15,400	$ 6,000	$ 7,200	$ 28,600	3.6
Variable product costs.........	198,000	90,000	120,000	408,000	5.7
	$213,400	$ 96,000	$127,200	$436,600	
Product margin................	$171,600	$ 54,000	$ 52,800	$278,400	0.7
Branch expenses..............				72,000	5.9
Profit contribution..............				$206,400	0.9

jibe

numbers of the less profitable Handyman were sold and sales of Drill-masters declined. This did not seem to gibe with the forecasts of consumer income in the Louisville area, as supplied by the company's bank. These forecasts indicated both a growth in the size of the market and an ability to move up to more expensive items.

The Louisville manager explained that his sales force could not cover the growing suburban markets effectively without neglecting their old customers in the inner city, and he was reluctant to do that. At Mr. Lloyd's suggestion, however, he drew up a new plan calling for the hir-

Exhibit 14–4

CALDWELL COMPANY
Tentative Sales and Selling Expense Budget

	Units	Amounts
Estimated sales:		
Drillmaster.....................	130,000	$4,550,000
Superba.......................	48,000	1,200,000
Handyman.....................	120,000	1,800,000
Total.....................		$7,550,000
Discounts and allowances...........		302,000
Net sales........................		$7,248,000
Estimated marketing expenses:		
Branch expense..................		$ 620,000
National advertising.............		125,000
Headquarters expenses...........		78,000
Marketing expenses...............		$ 823,000

ing of an additional salesman, and this pushed his estimated profit contribution up to $250,000.

The initial proposal from the Dallas branch led to action of a different sort. Three months ago the Dallas manager put the Handyman model into local supermarkets. The initial results were so encouraging that he built a spectacular 25 percent increase in sales into his proposed sales plan. Mr. Lloyd could find no evidence to shake the manager's confidence in his forecast, and on this basis he instructed all the other branch managers to look into the possibility of tapping this channel of distribution in their areas.

After this process was completed, Mr. Lloyd sent the figures shown in Exhibit 14–4 to Mr. Wright and to Mr. Frank. As a result of the interaction between Mr. Lloyd and the branch managers, budgeted sales went up by a healthy $600,000. Part of this was accomplished by cost increases, like those at Louisville, but these increases were partly offset by cutbacks in other branches and the overall budget for branch expenses increased by only $45,000.

Mr. Lloyd also decided that his original estimate of headquarters expenses was too low, and his final figure was $3,000 greater than the original. This brought his budgeted marketing expenses up from $775,000 to $823,000, a very modest increase in the light of the increase in budgeted sales.

Originating the Sales Forecasts

Companies tend to approach sales forecasting from two possible viewpoints. Under one approach, the aggregative method, all data are gathered and analyzed centrally, generally by a marketing research staff independent of the controller's organization. The alternative, or grass-roots, approach is to have the line selling organization prepare its own sales forecasts for subsequent reviews and consolidation into overall sales budgets.

If forecasting is done centrally, there is good reason to suggest that the field sales force be assigned a greater role than mere collection of statistical data to be processed by the market research staff. At some point the sales forecasts must be broken down by territory, and the current experience of the field sales force can provide an additional dimension to information derived in a more aggregative way. At a minimum, each salesman should be asked to prepare a rough forecast of sales to each of his most important customers. This often reveals developments that are too specific to get into the aggregate data on which market research forecasts are often based.

If the basic forecasts are made in the field, however, both the market research and the budget staffs can be of material assistance. The market research organization, for example, can conduct qualitative research to reveal market potentialities, environmental trends, and competitive activities. It can engage in quantitative research to estimate how much can be sold, by product and by territory or by other major categories of the company's business. These estimates can be checked against the field estimates to reveal any wide discrepancies that can then be traced further. Market research can also perform a service function to the field sales force, analyzing data supplied from the field and advising sales managers in reviewing sales forecasts made by individual salesmen.

No matter which of these approaches is used, most companies will find it impossible to prepare a separate forecast for each product as the Caldwell Company was able to do. Resources simply cannot be spared for this detailed an analysis. Instead, products are classified into closely related groups and forecasts are made for each group as a whole. Typically, this means dollar forecasts or forecasts of some common denominator such as tonnage.

Production Plans

Mr. Wright, Caldwell's plant manager, was not totally idle while Mr. Lloyd was wrestling with his marketing plan. Beginning with Mr. Lloyd's first rough sales forecast, he asked each foreman and department head to examine the adequacy of his current facilities and manpower and to submit suggestions for new facilities, methods, or personnel to meet the anticipated production load more adequately or more cheaply.

These proposals were discussed, modified, and either rejected or approved tentatively. Mr. Wright worked closely with his department heads on estimates of their costs, giving particular attention to departments with large cost increases and those in which costs had consistently

Exhibit 14–5

CALDWELL COMPANY
Production and Manpower Budget

	Drillmaster	Superba	Handyman	Total
Unit sales..........................	130,000	48,000	120,000	
Inventory change....................	5,000	—	6,000	
Total production....................	135,000	48,000	126,000	
Direct labor hours per unit:				
Machining department..............	0.8	0.5	0.2	
Assembly department...............	1.5	1.4	0.8	
Total direct labor hours:				
Machining department..............	108,000	24,000	25,200	157,200
Assembly department...............	202,500	67,200	100,800	370,500
Indirect labor hours:				
Machining department..............				31,500
Assembly department...............				18,600
Service departments...............				33,000
Total labor hours...................				610,800

exceeded estimates in the past. By the time the tentative sales budget came through, this process was well advanced and Mr. Wright was able to put together a production plan and production cost budget.

The first step was to convert the sales budget into a tentative product completion plan, as in the upper section of Exhibit 14–5. In this case, some increases in finished goods inventories were thought to be necessary to support the increased sales of the Drillmaster and Handyman models.

These completion schedules were then translated into labor requirements, product by product and department by department. The results of this operation are summarized in the lower portion of the exhibit. Because work-in-process inventories were not expected to change, labor requirements were based strictly on the number of units to be finished.

The production figures were then translated into materials purchases requirements. Major items were listed individually and the entire amount was stated at estimated purchase prices. These amounts are summarized in Exhibit 14–6. Once again, provision was made for modest increases in

Exhibit 14–6

CALDWELL COMPANY

Materials Purchases Budget

	Per Unit	Total
Materials required by production:		
Drillmaster....................	$8.85	$1,194,750
Superba......................	7.83	375,840
Handyman....................	6.16	776,160
Indirect materials and supplies.......		83,250
Total......................		$2,430,000
Increase in materials inventory.........		30,000
Total purchases....................		$2,460,000

inventories to accommodate the increased production rates.

Translation of the sales budget into production requirements was relatively easy in this case because the number of products was so small. With more products or custom production, Caldwell might have had to move directly from budgeted dollar sales to estimated production inputs, without an intervening list of product outputs. For example, the Danbury Company's tentative sales budget breaks sales down into three categories:

1. Major catalog products, budgeted in both physical units and sales dollars.
2. Minor catalog products, budgeted in dollars only.
3. Custom products, also budgeted in dollars.

The sales mix in the minor catalog products tends to remain relatively stable and historical mix ratios can be used to predict product output requirements. Custom products, on the other hand, are so diverse that common output units cannot be found. Instead, materials and labor requirements are based on average historical relationships between the sales value of production and labor and materials inputs.

Once the production input requirements have been estimated, management can put its production cost estimates into final form. The figures that Mr. Wright prepared for the Caldwell Company's factory are shown in condensed form in the upper part of the first table in 14–7. Actually, only the first four lines came from Mr. Wright. The allocations were pre-

Exhibit 14–7

CALDWELL COMPANY

Summary of Production Cost Budgets

	Machining Department	Assembly Department	Service Depart- ments	Factory Adminis- tration	Factory Total
Direct materials................	.....	.....	.....	.....	$2,430,000
Direct labor...................	$ 786,000	$1,111,500	.....	.....	1,897,500
Factory overhead:					
Indirect labor...............	$ 142,000	$ 59,000	$181,500	.....	$ 382,500
Other direct overhead........	464,500	209,900	152,500	$108,000	934,900
Allocations.................	236,000	206,000	(334,000)	(108,000)	.....
Total factory overhead......	$ 842,500	$ 474,900			$1,317,400
Total production cost..........	$1,628,500	$1,586,400			$5,644,900
Operating volume (direct labor hours).....................	157,200	370,500			
Variable overhead/hour.........	$ 1.50	$ 0.30			
Total fixed overhead...........	$ 606,700	$ 363,700			

Variable Product Cost per Unit	Drillmaster	Superba	Handyman
Direct materials.....................	$ 8.85	$ 7.83	$ 6.16
Direct labor:			
Machining department..............	4.00	2.50	1.00
Assembly department...............	4.50	4.20	2.40
Variable overhead:			
Machining department @ $1.50.......	1.20	0.75	0.30
Assembly department @ $0.30........	0.45	0.42	0.24
Total variable cost...................	$19.00	$15.70	$10.10

pared in the controller's office for the purpose of getting overhead rates for the direct production departments. Mr. Wright and Mr. Frank then worked together to estimate average cost variability in each department and came up with the rates shown in the lower part of the first table. Mr. Frank then applied these to the estimates of direct costs to get the revised product cost figures shown in the second table in the exhibit.

The revised product costs were slightly higher than those Mr. Frank had supplied earlier. Mr. Lloyd said that the increases were not great enough to cause him to revise his marketing plan, however, and Mr. Frank went ahead with assembling the profit plan.

The Production plan should be distinguished clearly from production *schedules*. Production schedules provide immediate instructions to first-line production personnel. They are seldom prepared more than a few months in advance, and are frequently revised from day to day as conditions change. The production plan, on the other hand, typically covers the entire year and is not revised. Its main purpose is to show how sales plans will be implemented, thereby giving production management a chance to evaluate alternative production methods and select the combination that seems to meet planned delivery requirements at minimum cost. In the process, it may identify the lack of adequate manpower, materials, or facilities to support the tentative sales plans. If production capacity cannot be increased rapidly enough at reasonable cost, then the sales plan will have to be cut back.

Informal contacts between sales and production personnel were very important in the development of Caldwell's production plan. Knowing at an early stage that sales of Drillmaster drills were likely to go up, Mr. Wright was able to include provision for an extra quality control inspector in his manpower and factory cost budgets. His recommendations for expenditures for new equipment and methods improvement were very much conditioned by the forecasts of increased volume, and early indications of this enabled him to do most of the spadework ahead of time.

The Profit Plan

The first place at which all of the foregoing components come together is in the annual profit plan, for the company in total and for each division or product line or both. Caldwell's tentative profit plan is shown in Exhibit 14–8. Most of the figures in this exhibit are from previous exhibits in this chapter. Inventories in this company are measured on a variable costing, first-in, first-out (Fifo) basis, so that the average cost of goods sold differs slightly from the unit costs given at the bottom of Exhibit 14–7, unit cost of the beginning inventory being lower than the amount budgeted for the year.

If the underlying components have been prepared carefully, with due attention to profit criteria and adequate exchange of information among functional executives, the profit plan ought to be in reasonable shape when it is put together. Profit is the principal basis on which overall corporate performance is judged, however, and management is likely to question parts of the plan if either they or the plan as a whole do not fit top management's expectations.

Divisional profit plans are likely to go through the same kind of scrutiny at divisional headquarters before being presented to corporate headquarters for further review and consolidation. A good division manager will be prepared to demonstrate that alternative courses of action have been considered and are likely to produce poorer results than the program being recommended.

Approval of the profit plan may be the most crucial single step in the control process. Approval is higher management's acceptance of the means selected and of the end to be achieved. When management receives a proposed profit plan, it can do any one of three things: (1) accept it, (2) send it back for revision, or (3) take steps to terminate the operation. In practice, some question is almost always raised about the adequacy of the plan, thus ruling out immediate acceptance. Termination, on the other hand, is unlikely to be ordered unless such a decision has

Exhibit 14–8

CALDWELL COMPANY

Annual Profit Plan
(in thousands)

	Drillmaster	Superba	Handyman	Total
Gross sales....................	$4,550	$1,200	$1,800	$7,550
Discounts and allowances.......	182	48	72	302
Net sales......................	$4,368	$1,152	$1,728	$7,248
Cost of goods sold............	2,455	748	1,211	4,414
Variable profit margin..........	$1,913	$ 404	$ 517	$2,834
Product-traceable fixed cost.....	89	22	38	149
Profit contribution..............	$1,824	$ 382	$ 479	$2,685
General expenses:				
Fixed factory overhead.........				$ 821
Marketing expenses...........				823
Administrative expenses........				198
Interest expense..............				80
Income taxes................				406
Total general expenses........				$2,328
Net income...................				$ 357

been considered before and deferred to give the division or product manager an opportunity to come up with a variable alternative.

The result is a response pattern like that schematized in Exhibit 14–9. Initial rejection ordinarily starts the process over again, as lower management seeks ways to improve the anticipated results. This is shown by the arrows looping back into the block at the upper left-hand corner of the exhibit.

No purpose would be served here by illustrating a reworking of the Caldwell budget. Revision is seldom very time-consuming, however. Most of the underlying figures can be used again and the direction of the necessary changes is usually fairly clear. In fact, the revisions are often hammered out on the spot, causing no delay at all. Another device that can be used to reduce the amount of last-minute revision is the same kind of informal cooperation that Mr. Lloyd and Mr. Wright found so productive as they were preparing their portions of the annual plan. If top management receives preliminary forecasts of the various components of the profit plan as the work progresses, it can offer comments and suggestions

Exhibit 14–9

SYSTEM RESPONSES TO PROPOSED PROFIT PLAN

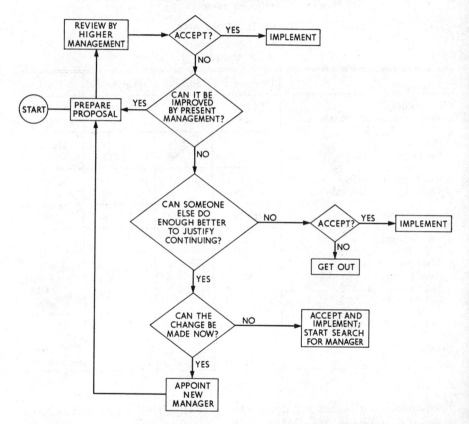

while the plan is still fluid. Ratification of the final profit plan under this system can be largely a formality in most years.

It should be emphasized here that acceptance of a plan implies a commitment to recognize this as satisfactory short-term performance. If Caldwell's top management is not convinced that $357,000 represents satisfactory performance in the circumstances, then it should send the plan back for another effort. Budget approval is an extremely important decision. It represents a commitment to the operation for the current period on the terms reflected in the budget. If current performance is unsatisfactory and top management feels that the fault is the manager's, it can seek a new manager. If the ailment is persistent, however, the same issue will arise in the next planning period, and the next, and the next, until management either is able to turn the operation around or gives up and gets out.

The Cash Budget

The operating plan that results from the process described above is not ready for presentation to top management until it passes one final feasibility test—does the firm have access to enough cash to finance the plan?

The usual procedure is to compute the cash receipts and disbursements implicit in the operating plan and merge this with the cash that would be

Exhibit 14–10

CALDWELL COMPANY
Preliminary Cash Forecast

Collections from customers...................		$6,939,000
Less: Payments to employees and vendors......	$6,414,000	
Interest............................	80,000	
Income taxes........................	355,000	6,849,000
Net cash receipts from operations.............		$ 90,000
Less: Equipment replacement................	$ 250,000	
Additional equipment.................	150,000	
Dividends...........................	160,000	560,000
Net cash outflow...........................		$ 470,000
Maximum cash available.....................		360,000
Minimum spending cutback required...........		$ 110,000

required by proposed expenditures on plant and equipment, long-range research and development, and other activities not immediately concerned with current operations. Exhibit 14–10, for example, shows a condensed summary of the preliminary cash forecast drawn up by Mr. Frank on the basis of the tentative operating plan and the proposals for discretionary spending. The operating receipts and expenditures in the exhibit differ from the amounts shown as revenues and expenses in earlier exhibits, partly because some expenses (e.g., depreciation) did not require current cash outlays, and partly because both accounts payable and accounts receivable balances were scheduled to rise during the year in line with the increase in company sales volume.

This exhibit shows that although the anticipated profit of $357,000 was acceptable, operations did not generate enough cash to finance both the increase in working capital required by the growth in sales and the proposals for dividends and expenditures on equipment. The equipment proposals had all met the company's normal profitability tests for this kind of expenditure, but the shortage of cash called for new and more stringent decision rules.

Discussion of these tests is partly premature and partly outside the scope of this text. It should be noted, however, that little success has been achieved to date in developing general decision rules that will permit direct comparison of proposals for dividends, capital expenditures, research and development, and educational development. Instead, the process is likely to be highly subjective, even extending back into the operating plan itself in an effort to find additional savings or sources of cash. For the Caldwell Company it was relatively easy. A small building used to store finished products was sold to a local insurance company for $120,000 and leased back on a 20-year lease at $10,000 a year. The planned dividend was cut back from $160,000 to $130,000, with the understanding that the cut would be restored if the cash situation in the fourth quarter proved more favorable than was anticipated. These two changes permitted the company to leave the operating plan intact and go ahead with the planned expenditures on equipment, still leaving a margin of liquidity to handle unexpected demands for cash.

LONG-RANGE PLANNING

Although the typical planning period is a year, it is not uncommon to find plans extending 2, 3, 5 or even 10 years into the future. These plans are frequently not as comprehensive as the company's annual budgets and may be limited to such major components as sales, capital expenditures, new product development, acquisition of capital funds, employment, or manager development. Even if a comprehensive long-range plan is drawn up, however, the estimates on which it is based reflect greater forecasting errors than estimates of the near future, and the only certainty is that the plan will have to be revised next year.

Justification for Long-Range Planning

Planning can be justified only by its ability to assist management in its current actions. Long-range planning permits management to view the probable chain of future actions that will follow as a logical consequence of the current decision, the first link in the chain. By this means, current alternatives can be evaluated in the light of how well they will fit into and affect the coordinated structure of future developments that are embodied in the plan.

Plans versus Targets

It should be emphasized that long-range plans reflect management's best current forecasts of the results to be achieved from the actions that management has tentatively decided to take. They should not represent the results of wishful thinking. A plan prepared without at least some realistic evaluation of implementation problems is more an expression of intent or desire than a road map to the future.

A fairly large government contractor some years ago decided to try to reduce its reliance on government business. The company's president told his planning director to draw up a timetable for increasing civilian business within five years from 20 to 50 percent of the total. Neither feasibility nor profitability was considered, and the resulting document was no more than a means of dramatizing a new company policy. During the next year, however, the division managers and the central headquarters acquisition staff worked to refine this timetable, with specific reference to the markets to be developed and the resources to be used. By the end of the year a real plan had evolved, very different from the original timetable but fully supported by the organization.

The original timetable in this case can be referred to as a target. Its purposes was to signal a change of direction and stimulate a search for means of implementing this change. It did not become a plan until ways and means were investigated and tested against the company's own standards of acceptability.

SUMMARY

Periodic planning, or budgeting, is not simply a matter of forecasting what the future has to offer. It is a highly creative process, in which executives at all levels are expected to evaluate and compare different possible courses of action, selecting those which seem more likely to meet company goals.

Budgeting, in other words, is a form of decision making. In many organizations the decisions made at budget time are the only really important ones. State and local governments are the most obvious examples, but this applies to the private sector as well.

In this chapter we have tried to convey a feeling for the complexity and dynamism of the budgeting process without getting bogged down in complex numerical examples. We have even omitted discussion of some parts of the budget altogether, such as research and development and administrative expense budgeting.

The picture presented here shows budget preparation starting at the top, with the formulation of broad statements of policy and the establishment of the basic framework. The next step is taken at the grass-roots level, as local managers work on their marketing plans, translate these into production plans, and back them up with proposals for capital investment. These plans are reviewed, revised, and consolidated as they move up the organizational ladder toward final top management approval. They all come together eventually in a series of profit plans and cash budgets that are both feasible and acceptable to top management.

As this would imply, budgeting is a responsibility of line management;

the controller or budget director administers the system and provides useful advice and assistance. When finally completed, the short-term plan, usually one year in length, becomes a managerial commitment and a bench mark against which future performance can be measured. The accompanying long-range plan, covering perhaps three or five years ahead, carries no such commitment, and is intended primarily as a device for avoiding current actions that would commit the organization to future actions that would conflict with the organization's basic objectives and policies.

EXERCISES AND PROBLEMS

1. Canyon, Inc. operates two stores that sell and install automobile seat covers and a few automotive supplies such as upholstery cleaner and auto washing compounds. The company's president has heard that budgetary planning is a good thing and has decided that a profit plan should be prepared for the coming year. The managers of the two stores have submitted the following tentative budgets:

	Downtown Store	Suburban Store
Sales revenue:		
Seat covers....................	$200,000	$360,000
Auto supplies.................	36,000	80,000
Total.......................	$236,000	$440,000
Store expenses:		
Supervisory & clerical salaries......	$ 23,600	$ 23,800
Installers' wages.................	20,400	40,000
Store clerks' wages..............	9,200	9,400
Rent...........................	19,200	17,600
Utilities.......................	3,000	4,200
Other..........................	1,400	2,600
Total.......................	$ 76,800	$ 97,600

During the coming year, the purchase cost of seat covers is expected to average 55 percent of selling prices, while the selling prices of auto supplies will be approximately double their purchase cost.

The president himself prepared a tentative head office budget for the coming year:

Executive salaries.........................	$ 50,000
Clerical salaries...........................	24,000
Advertising...............................	20,000
Rent.....................................	12,000
Office supplies............................	2,000
Utilities..................................	2,400
Legal and consultants' fees.................	3,400
Other....................................	1,000
Total...............................	$114,800

a)   Assemble these data into a tentative profit plan for the coming year.

b)   What problems do you think the president and the store managers encountered in preparing their tentative sales and expense plans? What were their principal sources of information?

c)   What criteria would you use in reviewing these proposals?

d)   Prepare a revised profit plan, using additional data that your instructor will provide.

2.* The Bowler Company manufactures three products from four purchased materials and parts. Materials must be ordered one month prior to desired delivery except for Part X, which requires a purchase order "lead time" of one and one-half months. It is the company's policy to place a new order for a material or a part whenever quantities on hand decline to less than a specified amount, known as the reorder point.

Materials for each job order are issued to production when that job order is started. Unit data relating to materials inventories are as follows:

Material or Part	Unit Price	Standard Purchase Lot	Reorder Point	Expected Inventory, Jan. 1	
				On Hand	On Order
W..................	$0.20	4,000	5,000	4,000	4,000
X..................	5.00	1,000	1,500	2,000	.....
Y..................	0.50	20,000	20,000	15,000	20,000
Z..................	2.00	5,000	4,000	7,000	.....

Standard materials specifications for the company's products, together with budgeted job order starts for the first three months of next year, are as follows:

Product	Materials or Parts per 100 Units				Budgeted Production Starts (Units)		
	W	X	Y	Z	January	February	March
A..............	210	...	340	105	1,000	1,200	1,300
B..............	140	210	400	...	300	200	400
C..............	...	...	360	120	1,500	1,400	1,400

For budgeting purposes it can be assumed that purchase orders are sent out at the middle of the month in which a reorder becomes necessary. Payment is made in the month of delivery, except for Part X, for which payment is made in the month following the month of delivery (1,000 units of Part X are expected to be delivered in December).

a)   Prepare budget schedules for orders, deliveries, and payments for materials and parts for the first three months of the year. Show calculations.

b)   Prepare budgeted inventory quantities for the end of each month.

3. The Erskine Sales Corporation serves as a manufacturers' representative for several manufacturers of automotive replacement parts. It has sales

---

* Solutions to problems marked with an asterisk can be found in Appendix B.

branches in each of the three major eastern cities. Sales and expense data for the current fiscal year are expected to show the following totals (in thousands):

	Boston	New York	Philadelphia	Head Office	Totals
Sales............................	$4,000	$10,000	$6,000	.....	$20,000
Cost of goods sold..............	2,700	6,750	4,050	.....	13,500
Gross profit.....................	$1,300	$ 3,250	$1,950	.....	$ 6,500
Expenses:					
Salaries and commissions.........	$ 900	$ 1,600	$1,200	$ 300	$ 4,000
Rent..........................	20	60	40	50	170
Travel expense.................	100	120	110	40	370
Advertising....................	10	20	20	30	80
Other expenses.................	5	15	10	20	50
Total expenses...............	$1,035	$ 1,815	$1,380	$ 440	$ 4,670
Net income before taxes...........	$ 265	$ 1,435	$ 570	$(440)	$ 1,830
Income taxes....................	xxx	xxx	xxx	xxx	950
Net Income.....................	xxx	xxx	xxx	xxx	$ 880

In planning for the coming year, the company's budget director obtained the following information:

(1) Expected automobile "population" in the region, classified by make and age of car, was obtained from the company's suppliers and was distributed to the branch managers.

(2) The company's suppliers announced their intention to raise list prices (charged by Erskine Sales to its customers) by 5 percent. Prices paid by Erskine Sales will be increased by 4 percent.

(3) Salaries and commissions per employee will be 3 percent higher next year.

(4) Sales forecasts received from the branches anticipate the following increases in physical sales volume: Boston, 6 percent; New York, 10 percent; and Philadelphia, 8 percent. The product mix, or relative proportions of total sales represented by each of the company's products, is expected to be the same next year as this year.

(5) To handle the increased sales volume, the following increases in personnel are anticipated: Boston, 2 percent; New York, 4 percent; Philadelphia, 3 percent; and head office, 2 percent. (These increases will occur in the indicated proportions at all salary levels.)

(6) Rent will be the same at all locations except New York, where a $30,-000 increase is expected on lease renewals.

(7) Travel expenses will be $10,000 greater in each of the branches and $5,000 greater in the head office.

(8) The New York office has asked for an increase in its advertising appropriation to $40,000. All other advertising appropriations are to remain at this year's level.

(9) Other expenses are expected to increase next year by 5 percent at all locations.

(10) Income taxes are budgeted at 30 percent for the first $25,000 of income and 50 percent for all income in excess of that figure.

a) Prepare a tentative operating budget for each branch office, for the head office, and for the company as a whole for the coming year.

b) Each of the three branches has indicated that it could expand sales by an additional 10 percent next year (that is, 10 percent of this year's physical sales volume) if it were permitted to hire additional salesmen and clerical employees. The added salaries and commissions, in excess of those already budgeted for next year, would be $120,000 at any branch for which such additional hiring is approved. Travel, advertising, and other expenses would be increased by $30,000 for any such branch. Head office expenses would be increased by $10,000 for each branch for which expansion approval is granted. Prepare calculations to indicate which branch or branches, if any, should be permitted to make the requested additions to their sales forces.

4.† DeMars College has asked your assistance in developing its budget for the coming academic year. You are supplied with the following data for the current year for the lower (freshman-sophomore) and upper (junior-senior) divisions:

	Lower	*Upper*
Average number of students per class...........	25	20
Average salary of faculty member.............	$15,000	$15,000
Average number of credit hours carried each year by each student......................	33	30
Enrollment (including scholarship students)......	2,500	1,700
Average faculty teaching load in credit hours a year (10 classes of 3 credit hours)	30	30

Lower division enrollment in the coming year is expected to increase by 10 percent, while the upper division's enrollment is expected to remain at the current year's level. Faculty salaries will be increased by a standard 5 percent, and additional merit increases to be awarded to individual faculty members will be $90,750 for the lower division and $85,000 for the upper division.

The current budget is $210,000 for operation and maintenance of plant and equipment; this includes $90,000 for salaries and wages. Experience of the past three months suggests that the current budget is realistic, but that expected increases for the coming year are 5 percent in salaries and wages and $9,000 in other expenditures for operation and maintenance of plant and equipment.

The budget for the remaining expenditures for the coming year contains the following:

Administrative and general.................	$440,000
Library.................................	160,000
Health and recreation.....................	75,000
Athletics...............................	320,000
Insurance and retirement..................	365,000
Interest................................	48,000
Capital outlay...........................	300,000

† Adapted from a uniform CPA examination.

The college expects to award 25 tuition-free scholarships to lower-division students and 15 to upper-division students. Tuition is $31 per credit hour and no other fees are charged.

The college has a small unrestricted endowment which has been invested in securities which now have a market value of approximately $2 million. In addition, commercial bank account balances total $50,000, but this amount is necessary to support the college's normal operations.

Budgeted revenues for the coming year from sources other than tuition are as follows:

From endowment......................... $114,000
From auxiliary services................... 235,000
From athletics.......................... 280,000

The college's only other source of funds is an annual support campaign held during the spring.

a) Prepare a schedule computing (1) the anticipated enrollment, (2) the total credit hours to be carried by students, and (3) the number of faculty members needed for each division.

b) Prepare a consolidated budget for the coming year, including revenue and expense figures on a divisional basis. How much must be raised during the annual support campaign to cover the budgeted expenditures?

c) In what ways should the structure of the available budget information be changed to facilitate periodic planning?

d) The college's president is concerned about the effect on the college's finances if enrollment falls below the budgeted levels. Prepare an alternative budget on the basis of a 6 percent reduction in enrollment in each division. The number of scholarships would not be reduced. In what ways would you use this additional information? What other analyses would you want to carry out?

5. Cycle World is a large retailer of bicycles, scooters, and motorcycles. Its showroom and parts department occupy the main floor of a modern building; a repair department is located in the basement.

Cycle World has never sold motor scooters, although it has serviced them in its repair department. The local representative of the Ivrea Scooter Company has been trying to induce Cycle World to act as its exclusive dealer in the area, so far without success. Ivrea's terms have become progressively more favorable in the hope of inducing Cycle World to accept, but it has now made what it says is its final offer. If Cycle World turns this down, Ivrea will set up its own sales branch.

Taking on the Ivrea line would require Cycle World to invest $20,000 in an inventory of scooters and repair parts. Adequate space is available to carry these added inventories. Ivrea would finance one half of this requirement, with no interest charge, but Cycle World would have to finance the remainder from other sources. Cycle World would also have to hire an additional mechanic, who would be trained at Irvea's expense before being transferred to the Cycle World payroll.

Judging from his experience in introducing a new line of light motorcycles a year ago, and using some figures provided by his bank, Cycle World's president has drawn up the following set of forecasts for the Ivrea line:

	First Year	Second Year
Revenues:		
Product sales..................	$50,000	$75,000
Repairs......................	3,000	5,000
Product warranty payments by		
Ivrea....................	1,500	2,000
Less: Bad debt losses..........	(1,000)	(1,500)
Net revenues...............	$53,500	$80,500
Expenses:		
Cost of goods sold.............	$33,000	$49,500
Mechanic's wages.............	6,500	6,800
Repair supplies................	1,000	2,100
Advertising...................	4,000	4,000
Other.......................	500	750
Total expenses..............	$45,000	$63,150
Incremental profit...............	$ 8,500	$17,350
Investment in receivables..........	$30,000	$20,000*

* The $20,000 is the *increase* in receivables investment *during* the second year. The total increase during the two-year period would be $50,000.

All of these figures represent increments to the figures arising from Cycle World's present business. The figures given for the second year seem likely to be representative of what later years would bring.

The owners of Cycle World have put their entire savings into the business and cannot sell shares to outsiders. The company is already substantially in debt, and the company's bankers would be willing to increase their loans to Cycle World by no more than $20,000, at an interest rate of 6 percent a year. If the company does not take on the Ivrea line, the bank will not increase the size of its loan.

Cycle World's present business is expected to generate a $15,000 excess of operating cash receipts over operating cash outlays in each of the next two years. The figures on operating cash outlays include interest on the present bank debt as well as the president's $14,000 salary. Reported net profit, before adjusting for the Ivrea addition, any additional borrowing, or any of the facts revealed below, would be approximately $14,000 a year.

Cash dividends to shareholders have been $12,000 a year, and the board of directors would encounter great opposition from several of the major shareholders (all close relatives of the president) if the dividend were to be reduced.

The head mechanic has put in a request for $2,000 to buy several pieces of shop equipment to replace equipment which no longer functions reliably. The annual depreciation charge would be about $100 greater if the replacements were made.

Finally, the Sussex Bicycle Company has notified Cycle World that it will no longer pay the full $5,000 cost of local advertising. Experience has shown that without this advertising, Cycle World's profits would be about $6,000 less than they are now. Sussex has offered to pay half of the cost of advertising, which it points out would still leave Cycle World with a $3,500 profit from sales of Sussex bicycles.

a) Prepare tentative profit estimates and cash forecasts from the above data for each of the next two years, assuming that the Ivrea line is taken on and that all the requested expenditures are made. By what amounts are the company's cash resources inadequate to finance all the requested expenditures? (Ignore income taxes.)

b) You do not have enough data to enable you to advise the president on a course of action. Identify some of the alternatives that he might consider and indicate what kinds of information you would like to have to help the president reach the decisions on which his final profit plan would be based.

6. The Airtight Company prepares its cash and profit budgets one quarter in advance. The following data are relevant to the budgets for the fourth quarter of the current year:

Sales are made on terms of net 30 days, and customer remittances are typically received 30 days after shipment. Accounts receivable on October 1 are expected to total $220,000. The company's product is sold at a price of $2.50 per unit.

Tentative sales and production budgets for the next four months are as follows (in units):

	Produced	Sold
October.	90,000	80,000
November.	100,000	90,000
December.	100,000	100,000
January.	110,000	110,000

Under a patent leasing arrangement with the Stopleak Company, Airtight pays Stopleak 5 cents for every unit it produces. Payments are made monthly on production during the preceding month. Production during September is expected to total 80,000 units.

Airtight's manufacturing costs, in addition to the royalty payment mentioned above, are as follows:

Materials.	$0.87 per unit
Payrolls.	$0.43 per unit + $20,000 per month
Other cash costs.	$0.12 per unit + $3,000 per month
Depreciation.	$5,000 per month
Taxes and insurance.	$2,000 per month

Materials are paid for in the month prior to the month in which production takes place. Factory payrolls are generally paid in the month to which they are applicable, subject to accrued but unpaid balances, as follows:

October 1.	$3,000
November 1.	$0.10 per unit produced in October
December 1.	None
December 31.	$0.10 per unit produced in December

Other cash manufacturing costs are paid 80 percent during the month of production and 20 percent in the following month. Taxes and insurance are paid at irregular intervals during the year. Payments for these items during the fourth quarter are expected to amount to $5,000 in November and $2,000 in December.

Manufacturing labor and overhead costs, including royalty charges, are absorbed into production by means of a predetermined burden rate based on the above data and a normal volume of 100,000 units a month. The under- or overabsorbed overhead is carried in a suspense account and closed out to the cost of goods sold in the final month of each quarter.

Cash dividends of $25,000 are to be paid to Airtight's stockholders in December. Budgeted expenditures on capital equipment amount to $15,000 in October and $10,000 in December. The effect of these capital expenditures on the monthly depreciation charge is to be ignored.

Selling and administrative expenses amount to $50,000 a month, all paid in cash. Income taxes are accrued at 52 percent of profit before taxes each month, but no income tax payments are to be made during the fourth quarter.

a) Prepare a tentative profit and loss budget for each of the next three months.

b) Prepare a tentative cash budget for each of the next three months.

CASE 14–1: VERLIES & WINST, N.V.†

During the first nine months of 1967, Verlies & Winst, N.V. operated its only factory two shifts a day plus a good deal of overtime work, and expected to continue at this production rate through the end of the year. At this rate, it was unable to meet the growing demand for its products, and inventories of finished products had been reduced during 1967 to amounts that the management felt were inadequate in view of the company's reputation for delivering its products promptly on the dates promised.

To correct this situation and to satisfy customer's demands, the company's executives in November 1967 decided to consider the desirability of moving to three-shift operations. To provide data useful for this decision, Mr. J. C. Verlies, the company's controller, was to prepare a profit plan and cash budget for 1968.

The Verlies & Winst product line consisted of two items of unusual design, both invented by the company's president, Mr. H. L. Winst. One product was a desk calendar holder of unusual design called "Dagmat"; the other was a desk-size device in which to list frequently called telephone numbers, sold under the name "Telemat."

In addition to Mr. Winst, the company's management consisted of Mr. Verlies and two product managers, one for each of the two products.

† Copyright 1967 by l'Institut pour l'Etude des Méthodes de Direction de l'Entreprise (IMEDE), Lausanne, Switzerland. Reprinted by permission. The monetary amounts have been restated as dollar amounts.

Because the company was small, Mr. Winst performed the duties of general sales manager and production manager, in addition to his functions as president.

Using an economic forecast supplied by the company's bank, together with reports of dealer sales and inventories gathered by the company's salesmen, the two product managers gave Mr. Verlies the tentative budgets for 1968 shown in Table 1.

Mr. Winst's estimates of maximum production capacity and "general factory costs" (all factory costs except materials, labor, and depreciation) were:

	Production Capacity (Machine-Hours)	General Factory Costs at Capacity Operating Rates
Two-shift operations............	91,450	$ 90,000
Three-shift operations...........	122,900	118,000

These estimates included allowances for labor overtime and also provided for a normal amount of time lost due to machine breakdowns and

Table 1

VERLIES & WINST, N.V.

Product Managers' Budget Proposals for the Year 1968

	Product	
	Dagmat	Telemat
1968 sales (in units).........................	400,000	300,000
Increase over 1967.........................	+ 100,000	+ 90,000
Price per unit (both years).....................	$ 1.00	$ 3.00
1968 production costs per unit:		
Material cost...............................	$ 0.25	$ 0.55
Labor cost.................................	$ 0.15	$ 0.45
Machine-hours required.....................	0.10	0.30
1968 product promotion expense................	$ 50,000	$ 60,000
Increase over 1967........................	+$ 12,500	+$ 18,000
Increase in finished goods inventories required with no increase in sales over 1967 (units)........	5,000	4,500
Additional increase in assets because of increased sales over 1967:		
Accounts receivable........................	+$ 20,000	+$ 54,000
Materials inventories.......................	+$ 2,500	+$ 4,950
Finished goods inventories (units).............	+ 5,000	+ 3,500
Work in process inventories...................	Negligible	Negligible
Increase in accounts payable accompanying increased sales..	+$ 2,500	+$ 4,950

other kinds of work interruptions. Factory personnel for the third shift could be obtained without difficulty, and new people required almost no training.

The increases in sales promotion expenditures in excess of 1967 levels would consist mostly of increases in local newspaper advertising and point-of-sale promotional displays. The projected increases in sales could not be obtained without these increased expenditures. No increase in the number of salesmen was anticipated.

Other estimates and budget proposals that were submitted to Mr. Verlies were:

General sales and administrative expenses (except depreciation)......	$210,000
Depreciation:	
Factory and factory equipment...............................	50,000
Office and sales facilities.....................................	25,000
Interest on long-term debt (maturing in 1975).....................	50,000
Dividends on common stock...................................	30,000
Research and development expenditures.........................	100,000
Equipment replacement expenditures...........................	90,000
Plant expansion expenditures (these additional facilities would not be completed in 1968)...	300,000
Interest to be paid in 1968 on short-term bank loans was at a rate of 5% on the balance of the bank loans outstanding at the end of 1967.	
Income taxes were computed at a rate of 47% of taxable income and were due in the first six months of the year following.	
Minimum cash balance..	140,000

Research and development expenditures are charged to expense as incurred. Depreciation for 1968 would not be affected by replacement expenditure decisions for 1968. Taxable income and reported income before taxes are identical in this company.

Mr. Verlies estimated that working capital balances would be as follows on January 1, 1968:

Cash...		$160,000
Accounts receivable.............................		186,000
Inventories....................................		33,350
Total....................................		$379,350
Less:		
Bank loan payable...........................	$30,000	
Accounts and interest payable...................	19,050	
Income taxes payable.........................	54,000	103,050
Working capital...............................		$276,300

Mr. Verlies was convinced that the company would be unable to obtain any new long-term capital during 1968. Cash had to be paid for all assets and services purchased except that trade credit (i.e., accounts payable) was available to finance increases in raw materials inventories. In addition, bank credit was available up to 50 percent of the sum of the face amount of accounts receivable and the total cost of all inventories. (Finished goods were costed at their materials and labor costs only, general factory costs being considered an expense). Bank credit was available in units of $10,000. For budgeting purposes, it was assumed that any amounts borrowed during the year would be borrowed on July 1, 1968. Interest on bank loans in force during 1968 would be paid in cash during January, 1969.

a) Did the company have adequate production capacity to service the tentative sales budget? What criteria would you use to allocate productive capacity between the two product lines whenever total capacity is inadequate to meet all demands?

b) Prepare a *factory cost* and *production volume* plan for 1968 that would have been technically feasible. Factory capacity should be assigned to the products in such a way as to maximize company profits, subject to the following restrictions: (1) the sales of each product are to be at least as large as they were the preceding year; and (2) inventories of finished goods must be built up to the minimum established for the level of sales anticipated in your *revised* sales plan for 1968.

c) Prepare a tentative cash budget for 1968, reflecting your factory cost and production volume plan and all the other estimates and budget proposals listed above. Is this budget feasible? In case of a shortage of cash, how should management decide which expenditures to cut back?

d) Prepare a profit plan for the year that is both technically and financially feasible, and which meets the restrictions listed under (b) above. Would this plan be accepted automatically, or would management be likely to subject it to further tests?

chapter **15**

Standard Costing for Control
of Labor and Materials Costs

Planning is only one side of the managerial control process described in Chapter 1. The other phase that concerns the accountant most closely is the use of feedback information in the implementation of management's plans. This is usually referred to as the control phase, although it can be described more accurately as measurement and reporting.

Feedback information can be used to help management control many aspects of performance in many different parts of the organization. For example, measures can be devised to monitor the company's performance on such matters as accident prevention, product quality, delivery time, cost control, or profit generation. In each case, the measurement and reporting technique must be adapted to the needs of management at each level and in each function.

A convenient place to begin our discussion of feedback systems is in the factory. The objective of this chapter is to explain how standard product costs can be used to help management control factory direct materials and direct labor costs. Factory overhead costs are more difficult to deal with, and will be discussed in later chapters.

THE STANDARD COSTING CONCEPT

In the absence of a standard costing system, cost control information typically takes the form of comparisons between current costs and those of a previous period or periods. This is seldom very satisfactory. Historical comparisons say whether costs are higher or lower than they were before, but they say nothing about whether they are too high or too low.

Standard costing systems take a different starting point. They consist of methods and procedures by which actual operating costs are compared with data from the standard product cost files so that the differences between these two sets of figures (the variances) can be analyzed and reported to management.

For factory direct labor or direct materials costs, the accountant usually divides the total variance into two types of components:

1. Quantity variances: the differences between actual and standard input quantities for the output actually achieved.
2. Price variances: the differences between actual and standard input prices.

Measuring Quantity Variances

The quantity variance is essentially an index of physical efficiency, an expression of the relationship between the quantities of resources used and the quantities of output derived from them. This means that it can always be measured in physical units if the right data are available. For example, suppose that combining 1.2 pounds of material A with 0.3 hours of labor is expected to yield one unit of product Y. This relationship can be expressed in a formula:

$$1.2 \text{ pounds } A + 0.3 \text{ labor hours} \rightarrow 1 \text{ unit } Y$$

Suppose further that on April 18, a batch of 10 units of Y was produced from 14 pounds of material A and required four labor hours. In schematic terms:

But 10 units of product Y can also be expressed in terms of their standard input content of 12 pounds of A (10 times 1.2) and three hours of labor (10 times 0.3). Substituting these equivalents and separating the materials from the labor, we have:

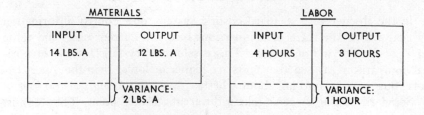

The differences between input quantities and output quantities (expressed as the equivalent number of standard input units), are the quantity variances, two pounds of A and one labor hour. In each case the actual input quantity exceeded the standard input quantity; such variances are referred to as unfavorable. If the actual input quantity had been less than the standard quantity, the variance would have been favorable.

These quantity variances can be expressed in monetary terms by multiplying the physical quantities by standard prices. If the standard price of A was $7 a pound and the standard wage rate was $5 an hour, the materials quantity variance would be reported as $14 (two pounds times $7) and the labor quantity variance would be $5 (one hour times $5).

Quantity variances are measured at standard prices rather than at actual prices, for two reasons. First, standard prices are clerically simpler to use, as we shall demonstrate shortly. Second, they facilitate interperiod comparisons of the quantity variance; that is, when the same set of standard prices is used month after month, a change in the size of the quantity variance can only mean that a change in the physical input-output relationship has taken place.

Measuring Price Variances

The final link between a product's standard cost and its actual cost is provided by the price variances—the differences between actual and standard input prices. For example, our batch of product Y was produced by a factory employee who was paid $5.25 an hour to do the work. The price variance for labor is called the labor rate variance, and amounted in this instance to 25 cents an hour for four hours, or $1 in total.

Schematically, the labor variances on this operation can be summarized as follows:[1]

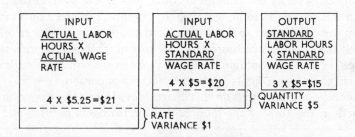

---

[1] The rate variance could be divided into two parts: the variance on the standard input quantity (in this case, three hours times $0.25, or $0.75) and the variance on the excess input quantity (one hour times $0.25, or $0.25). **The latter** component is

Reporting Quantity Variances

Variances should be reported to the executives who have the responsibility to control or respond to them. Quantity variances, for example, are ordinarily reported in the first instance to the first-line supervisors, who have primary responsibility for cost control. They may also be reported to the next management level or to methods engineering or other staff groups who have an interest in managing costs.

A department's quantity variances are also used by the department head's superior as a means of judging his effectiveness in cost control. Some systems require explanations of major variances each period, together with a statement of the manager's plans for dealing with them. Other systems call for explanations from the department head only if the variances persist.

The presence of a quantity variance does not necessarily mean that an operation is out of control, however. Some variation around standard performance is always anticipated, the result of random variations inherent in the operation itself. If a variance is due to random forces, it can be reduced only by changing the nature of the operation. Attempts to correct it without operational changes are bound to fail.

When quantity variances are too large to be accounted for by random forces, management should try to find out what caused them. If the causes are beyond the department head's control, then adaptive action or replanning may be appropriate; otherwise, corrective action is called for so that the variance will not arise again.

Statistical Control Limits

One device that can be used to identify nonrandom variances is the statistical control chart, illustrated in Exhibit 15–1. The dots on this chart represent the average variance recorded on a certain operation each day during a month. Working with historical data and readily available statistical tables, the company's cost accountants found that when the operation was under control they could expect the average daily variance on this operation to be less than 1.5 minutes per piece on more than 99 days out of 100. In other words, if the variance is greater than 1.5 minutes, the chances are more than 99 to one that a nonrandom force has been at work. Horizontal lines have been drawn at these levels to represent the control limits applicable to this operation.

Observations are plotted on this chart daily. When the upper limit was breached on the 10th of the month, the foreman was notified and asked

---

the joint product of price and quantity variation. The conventional procedure, however, is to measure the rate variance as a single quantity, as in the diagram: actual input quantity times the difference between actual and standard input prices. For a discussion of this point, see David Solomons, "Standard Costing Needs Better Variances," *N.A.A. Bulletin,* December 1961, pp. 29–39.

Exhibit 15–1

STATISTICAL CONTROL CHART

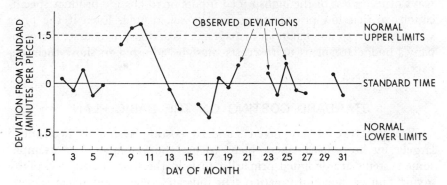

to investigate. He found the trouble, made the adjustment, and perform-ance was back within the normal range by the 12th of the month.

Strictly speaking, the control chart can be used only when an opera-tion (*a*) is well standardized, (*b*) is performed frequently, and (*c*) has generated a substantial amount of historical performance data. These conditions are seldom fully met, and formal control limits of this sort are seldom found in practice. The concept is applied directly or implicitly at all managerial levels, however, as managers decide what variances are large enough to investigate.[2]

Unfortunately, it is almost impossible to know whether the test ob-servations, fatigue allowances, and so forth represent normal or abnormal experience. Since judgment is required in any case, most companies prefer to set control limits for departmental variances by judgment rather than by formula. The control limit technique is used widely, however, in quality control work and to some extent in such tasks as identifying pieces of equipment that may require adjustment or overhaul.

Reporting Price Variances

Price variances are also reported to management, usually above the departmental level. If they are large, these too can be reviewed to see whether corrective action or replanning is needed.

In most cases, substantial price or rate variances are evidence that standard materials prices or wage rates are out of date. Purchasing and

---

[2] For some discussion on control limits in cost control, see Carl E. Noble, "Cal-culating Control Limits for Cost Control Data," *N.A.A. Bulletin,* June 1954, pp. 1309–17; and Edwin Mansfield and Harold H. Wein, "A Regression Control Chart for Costs," *Applied Statistics,* March 1958, pp. 48–57. Both of these articles are re-printed in David Solomons, *Studies in Cost Analysis* (2d ed.; Homewood, Ill.: Richard D. Irwin, 1969), pp. 444–62.

personnel departments ordinarily can influence them only within relatively narrow limits. The only really effective control response is to find ways of using less of the high-priced inputs or to change product specifications so that low-priced inputs can be substituted. Even if the price variances lead to no change in management's actions, of course, the company's budgetary plans or forecasts must be adjusted to show their impact.

STANDARD COSTING ON THE BASIC PLAN

The structure of any given standard costing system is determined largely by how management plans to use the variances. For example, some systems are designed primarily to help the first-line supervisor by giving him variance information that indicates where and when specific corrective actions are needed. This requires prompt, highly itemized reporting.

Other systems, in contrast, presume that the first-line supervisor can monitor his own operations by direct observation. Variance information in such systems is used mainly in performance review by the first-line supervisor to see whether his efforts have been successful, and by his superiors to identify persistent trouble spots. Variances for these purposes need to be reported less frequently and in considerably less detail than those used to pinpoint the need for specific corrective action.

In general, the more varied the work of the cost center, the more detailed and more frequent the reporting should be.

Quantity Variances under the Basic Plan

The simplest standard costing systems follow what we shall call the basic plan. Under the basic plan, no records are kept of the actual costs of performing individual operations or producing individual products. Instead, the labor and quantity variances for each cost center are determined only at the end of the reporting period, usually a month or a week, in the form of totals for the period.

Cost center quantity variances are identical in concept to the individual quantity variances described earlier in this chapter. That is, they measure the difference between the actual and standard input quantities required to achieve a given output. The only difference is that the cost center variance is the cumulative result of large numbers of individual variances. It is obtained by comparing total input with total output for the reporting period.

To see how quantity variances are generated under the basic plan, let us look at the system used by a small manufacturing firm, the Galahad Company. Its factory has two direct production departments—a large assembly department and a relatively small and simple forming department. The forming department manufactures only a few products, all of them component or replacement parts for products assembled in the assembly department. During July, the forming department used two kinds of materials, *A* and *B*, and one grade of direct labor to make two products, *P* and *Q*. Standard input requirements for these two products were:

$$1.2 \text{ pounds of } A + 0.8 \text{ hour of labor} \rightarrow 1 \text{ unit of } P$$
$$1.5 \text{ pounds of } A + 0.6 \text{ pound of } B + 1.3 \text{ hours of labor} \rightarrow 1 \text{ unit of } Q$$

Standard prices were $7 a pound for material *A*, $2 a pound for material *B*, and $5 an hour for direct labor. At these prices, the two products had the following standard costs:

	Materials	Labor
Product *P*	1.2 lbs. × $7 = $ 8.40	0.8 hrs. × $5 = $4.00
Product *Q*	1.5 lbs. × $7 = $10.50 0.6 lbs. × $2 = 1.20 $11.70	1.3 hrs. × $5 = $6.50

Input and output statistics for the month of July showed the following totals of physical units:

Inputs		Outputs	
Material *A*:	4,500 lbs.	Product *P*:	1,000 units
Material *B*:	1,100 hrs.	Product *Q*:	2,000 units
Direct labor:	3,500 hrs.		

Translating these at standard cost yielded the following totals:

Materials

Inputs	Outputs
4,500 × $7 = $31,500	1,000 × $ 8.40 = $ 8,400
1,100 × $2 = 2,200	2,000 × $11.70 = 23,400
$33,700	$31,800

Labor

Inputs	Outputs
3,500 × $5 = $17,500	1,000 × $ 4.00 = $ 4,000
	2,000 × $ 6.50 = 13,000
	$17,000

The aggregate standard cost of the month's output is sometimes referred to as the amount earned, reflecting the notion that each department "sells" its output at a "price" equal to its standard cost. The output in this case amounted to $31,800 for materials and $17,000 for labor.

The quantity variances for the month are derived by subtracting the inputs from the outputs, both measured at standard prices:

	Materials	Labor
Output.......................	$31,800	$17,000
Input........................	33,700	17,500
Variance.....................	$(1,900)	$ (500)

As the first column shows, the standard cost of the actual materials used exceeded the standard materials cost of the actual output by $1,900; this was the materials quantity variance for the month, and was unfavorable. Standard labor cost earned was $500 less than the standard cost of the actual amount of labor used, which means that the workers in the forming department turned out less production per hour than the standards anticipated. In other words, the labor quantity variance for the month amounted to $500 and was unfavorable.

The variance for material *A* in this instance could have been separated from the variance for material *B* simply by sorting the materials requisitions for the month. The basic plan system provides no basis for breaking the variances down by product or by worker, however, because materials requisitions and labor time tickets do not specify the job or provide data on standard quantities.

Measuring Departmental Outputs

As this illustration should indicate, departmental direct materials and direct labor inputs are relatively easy to measure. It is merely necessary to count the number of labor and materials units used during the period and multiply by the appropriate standard materials prices or wage rates.

The task of measuring a department's output, however, can be more complex than the illustration would seem to imply. To compute output, the number of product units completed during the period must be adjusted for any change in the amount of work in process between the beginning and end of the period, all priced at standard cost. Output, in other words, is a measure of the work done or progress made, and this need not be equal to the amount of product that was physically completed during the period.

For example, Galahad's forming department actually completed work on only 900 units of product *P* during the month of July. The remainder of its output of product *P* consisted of additions to the amount of work in process in the department. On July 1 the department had 200 units of product *P* in inventory. Part of the labor operations had already been performed on these units, with a standard labor cost of $1.60 per unit; all of the materials necessary to complete these units had already been applied. The standard cost of this beginning inventory therefore was as follows:

Materials: 200 units × $8.40 = $1,680
Labor: 200 units × $1.60 = $ 320

The inventory in process at the end of the month was up to 300 units. The standard labor cost of the work done on these units was $2.40, so that the standard cost of the ending inventory was:

Materials: 300 units × $8.40 = $2,520
Labor: 300 units × $2.40 = $ 720

The standard cost of the work actually done in the department during the month is computed in Exhibit 15–2. This shows that the forming

Exhibit 15–2

CALCULATION OF STANDARD COST EARNED

	Product	Number of Units	Standard Materials Cost	Standard Labor Cost
Completed....................	P	900	$ 7,560	$ 3,600
	Q	2,000	23,400	13,000
In process, July 31..............	P	300	2,520	720
			$33,480	$17,320
In process, July 1..............	P	200	1,680	320
Standard cost earned............			$31,800	$17,000

department actually did more work during the month than it would have had to do merely to process the units completed during this period. This excess appears as an increase in the standard cost of the work in process.

Notice that the standard cost of the work in process was not obtained by multiplying the number of units in process by the full standard cost of a completed unit. The reason is that these units were not in finished form on the inventory date and therefore were not equivalent to finished units. Instead, all in-process units are stated at the standard cost of the progress achieved to the date of the inventory. This requires both an inventory count and a determination of the number of operations which have been performed to date on the uncompleted units.

The Need for Dollar Variances

If production processes were all as simple as in this illustration, standard costing systems would be almost unnecessary. All variances could be stated in physical units, which often have a more direct meaning to the first-line supervisor. In the real world, however, each cost center is likely to use many different kinds of inputs, instead of just three, and to process many different products. The result is that statements of variances in physical terms become unwieldy; often only the dollar variances are reported.

This should not be thought of as a sacrifice of information, however. For one thing, the dollar totals are merely a convenient way of summarizing the underlying physical deviations from standard performance. Secondly, dollar variance information serves an important purpose in its own right, even when inputs and outputs are few in number. Expressing the variance in monetary terms gives management a measure of its relative importance, and a basis for deciding how much control effort is worthwhile.

Separating Materials Price Variances

Materials price variances in basic plan systems are measured when the materials are purchased. As a result of this practice, the amount of materials price variances recorded in the accounts depends on the quantity of materials purchased, whereas materials quantity variance totals relate to the quantity of materials used.

The main advantage of calculating price variances at the time of purchase is that this lets the accountant report them to management soon after they arise, not weeks or months later when the materials are finally used. It also permits substantial savings in the cost of materials bookkeeping, in that all materials inventories are measured at standard prices which remain unchanged for a year or longer. Detailed inventory records can be maintained in physical units only; when dollar totals are desired, these quantities can be multiplied by standard prices.

Aggregate price variances, even when reported separately for each broad class of materials, ordinarily provide little information for the purchasing agent. Purchasing decisions center on the item, not on the class of materials, and the purchasing agent can identify the variance when he places an order or at least when the order is confirmed by the vendor. Total price variance information is useful mainly in cash and profit planning, and has few other applications.

The Basic Plan in Perspective

Several things can be learned from this illustration. First, the use of standard product costs for control reporting presumes that costs ought to vary in direct proportion to variations in volume. Direct materials and direct labor costs in job order production are generally assumed to meet this requirement, with some exceptions that we shall discuss later. Similarly, standard product costs can be used as control standards in process production for all cost elements that tend to vary proportionately with volume.

Second, basic plan standard costing provides cost control comparisons in the form of cost center totals for each cost element. Actual costs are classified only by cost center and not by job. The argument is that since cost variances must be reported to the executives responsible for control, and since responsibility for cost control follows departmental lines, control reports should focus on the department rather than on products or job orders.

In this connection, it should be noted that the departmental variance totals provided by standard costing systems are most valuable when they are hardest to compute—that is, when the product line is broad, product mix is constantly changing, and production is on job orders. In process production, management can get some control information from comparisons between current departmental average costs and the average costs of prior periods. This is virtually impossible in job order production. To make departmental cost comparisons in the absence of standard costing, the accountant would have to identify the operations performed in the cost center during the period and then search through the files to find the records of prior performances of these same operations. To do this, he would need a much more elaborate data retrieval system than standard costing would require.

In other words, standard costing can improve the information basis for cost control either in job order or in process production; but the advantage is much greater in job order production, where the alternative is usually no control information at all.

Third, successful application of the basic plan hinges on management's ability to measure work-in-process inventories quickly and cheaply. Fortunately, in-process inventories in many processes can safely be assumed to be constant, so that output can be measured directly by the standard cost of the units completed during the period. In other cases, only a very few jobs are in process in any department at any time, and measurement is very simple. The simpler the solution to this measurement problem, the more frequently variance information can be reported. In some cases, daily reporting would be entirely feasible.

SINGLE PLAN STANDARD COSTING

The basic plan is adequate whenever management uses variance information primarily to provide a cumulative record of cost control performance or to signal the need for more detailed investigation. When management needs quantity variance information to identify specific

quantity variance
~ information

problems as they arise, however, a more complicated system is called for. In this kind of situation, variances need to be reported more frequently and in greater detail than is possible in basic plan systems. This typically requires identification of variances as they occur, operation by operation, rather than as end-of-period totals. Standard costing systems that do this can be called single plan systems.

Nature of the Single Plan

The principal feature of the single plan is that each charge for direct materials and direct labor is broken down into standard cost and variance components. In other words, both the actual and the standard input quantities are computed at the time the work is performed.

For example, if an operation calling for 5 standard labor hours is performed in 5.5 hours, two accounts will be charged, one for the standard hours and the other for the half-hour quantity variance. This requires a greater amount of data preparation time than basic plan standard costing because the input documents must show both standard and actual quantities.

Identifying Materials Quantity Variances

Identification of the materials quantity variance when it arises requires some means of identifying the actual materials consumption for each operation. The Faultless Company, a small metal-working company, accomplishes this by classifying materials requisitions into two categories: standard and supplemental. At the time a production order is prepared, a set of requisition cards is prepared for the standard quantities of materials shown on the standard cost sheet. The Faultless Company uses punched cards for this purpose, and a separate card is punched for each class of materials listed. When a cost center begins work on a job, the foreman presents to the stockroom the cards for the materials that he will require and obtains the standard quantity of materials specified.

Whenever additional materials are issued to cover excessive spoilage as the job progresses, a supplemental requisition card of a different color and with a distinctive code designation is prepared, showing the quantity and code number of each of the supplemental materials. Standard prices come from the standard cost file. Similarly, if a job is completed without consuming all of the materials issued, the excess materials are returned to the storeroom, where a returned materials card is filled out with the quantity of each material returned.

Identifying Labor Quantity Variances

The most common device used to identify the standard quantity of labor at the point of application is the prepunched or preprinted time ticket. If the job is of a standard lot size, these tickets may be prepared long before the job is scheduled, but in any event it is possible to prepare standard labor time tickets before the work begins. For the base plate job represented by Exhibits 12–1 through 12–3, for example, seven separate tickets probably would have been prepared, one for each of the operations called for on the standard cost sheet.

Identification of the labor quantity variance in a single plan system is ordinarily accomplished by entering actual labor time on the standard labor time ticket for each operation. This means that a labor variance can be reported for each operation performed. With suitable coding, variance totals can be obtained for each operation, each operator, each job, each product, or each machine.

Single Plan Reporting to Management

The structure and frequency of cost reports to management should be tailored continuously to the needs of current management. In many factories, for example, a tabulator run of the previous day's labor performance is placed on each foreman's desk at the start of each workday,

Exhibit 15–3

DAILY LABOR VARIANCE REPORT

DEPARTMENT Machining   DATE 3/6

SUPERVISOR P. B. Naum

Operator	Standard Hours Earned	Actual Direct Hours (Including Personal Time)	Variance	
			Hours	Percent of Standard
Brown, P...................	8.2	8.0	0.2	2.4
Conrad, T. T..............	8.6	8.0	0.6	7.0
Ennis, J...................	3.3	4.0	(0.7)	(21.2)
Gordon, L.................	8.4	9.5	(1.1)	(13.1)
King, M...................	7.9	8.0	(0.1)	(1.3)

with a separate line or lines for each operator. A truncated example of such a report is shown in Exhibit 15–3.

A daily labor report like this is not always necessary or desirable. There is such a thing as overcontrol, and too frequent reporting may actually defeat its own purpose by not making sufficient allowance for normal fluctuations in productive efficiency. Furthermore, the variance lists can become so long and unwieldy as to be virtually useless to management. It may be better to report less frequently, applying the exception principle to weekly or even monthly variances, and using the detailed variance data provided by single plan procedures solely as raw material for special analyses whenever aggregate quantity variances appear to be getting out of line.

AN APPRAISAL OF STANDARD COSTING

The use of standard costs for control reporting has much to recommend it. Management should weigh the advantages against the problems that must be solved to use standard costs for this purpose, however, and should try to select a standard costing plan that fits the company's specific situation.

Advantages of Standard Costs for Control

The advantages of using standard costs for control reporting fall under three broad headings:

1. Better control information.
2. Clerical economy.
3. Faster reporting.

Better Control Information.   Actual cost systems lack one important ingredient of good control information, a bench mark for comparison. This is provided by either of the standard costing plans described above. By comparing actual costs with standard costs, the accountant can identify the nature of the variance and the department or individual responsible for it.

Clerical Economy.   Although standard costing systems are often expensive to install, they do provide some clerical economies and these may even be greater than the initial installation cost. A full appreciation of these economies must await the discussion of methods of introducing standard costs into the accounts in the next chapter, but a few observations here may be suggestive.

One source of economy has already been mentioned. By pricing materials inventories at standard, Galahad is able to reduce the costs of materials accounting by eliminating actual costs from the stores ledger. In fact, the inventory ledgers can be maintained in physical quantities only; it is a simple matter to determine aggregate standard cost whenever this is required. This avoids the need for time-consuming and partly arbitrary allocations of discounts and surcharges among the various items covered by an invoice. It also eliminates recomputation of average unit cost after each purchase (moving average method) or the separate tracing of the costs of successive lots of inventory (Fifo method), thus reducing the clerical time required for cost recording and file maintenance.

The same benefit accrues from pricing other quantities at standard. Issues and returns of materials, interdepartmental transfers, and shipments and returns of finished goods can all be recorded faster, at lower cost, and with less chance of clerical error. Cost estimates also can be prepared faster and at far less cost if a standard cost file exists.

Another source of economy stems from the elimination of the historical job cost sheet. This eliminates a detailed posting operation, an operation that can be very costly. In a basic plan system, elimination of the job order cost sheet also permits the company to simplify its time-keeping and requisitioning procedures by eliminating the need to identify the time spent or the materials used on individual jobs.

Faster Reporting. Standard costing can make another kind of contribution by enabling the accounting department to issue reports to management more promptly after the end of a reporting period. For example, when a job is finished, this fact can be recorded immediately, without waiting for the complete posting of data from the requisitions and time tickets.

Furthermore, with fewer clerical operations to be performed, the accounts themselves can be brought up to date more rapidly. The means by which this can be done should become clear in the next chapter.

Problems with Standard Costing

The three main problems in standard costing systems are their cost, the difficulty of developing standards for all operations, and the danger of unfavorable employee reactions to the standards.

Cost. Installation of standard costing systems is often time-consuming and expensive, particularly if the company attempts to start out with detailed cost standards for all products and operations. For small companies, this installation cost may seem prohibitive, and the accountant should try to design simple systems that are both cheap to install and closely attuned to the simpler information needs of closely managed companies.

One possibility is to review the quantity data reported on job cost or departmental process costing records in the past. Preliminary standards derived from these can then be used to get the system going. The next step is to use these tentative standards to accumulate variances during a trial period.

In single plan systems the tentative standards can be compared directly with actual costs, and changes can be made wherever they seem appropriate. In basic plan systems the comparisons will relate to cost center totals. So long as a department's variances are small and no other evidence of consistent inefficiency is shown, it may be presumed that the usage allowances are satisfactory. If large variances arise and the department head cannot explain them, detailed data can be obtained by work study or by observation of a sample of the operations performed in the affected cost centers.

Nonstandard Products. Some portion of each month's output in job order production is typically of new products or product modifications for which no standards have been set. Most of these are merely new combinations of operations and materials already listed in the standard cost file, and standards can be derived fairly easily. When this is not the case, two solutions are possible. First, new standards might be developed for the new operations. If accuracy is attempted, the establishment of new standards is costly and could even delay production. Using rough approximations avoids these problems but may cloud the meaning of overall departmental variances.

The widely used alternative is to grant actual time allowances for unrated work. Actual costs can be accumulated on time tickets and totaled either for each job order or for each department in total. Job order totals can be compared with estimates, if desired, but the latter are not used as the basis for departmental reports. Departmental variances therefore pertain only to that portion of total production represented by input-rated operations.

Behavioral Problems. Most problems in employee relations under standard costing arise from poor execution or a basic misunderstanding of the system. The purpose of standard costing is to help management control costs, but management may try to use it as a means of inducing employees to reduce costs. Cost reduction is a laudable objective, and it may be achieved as a result of the development of standards, but it is not an automatic result. Cost reduction generally requires methods changes, and it cannot be assumed that employees will change their methods simply because someone tells them that they are not performing up to standard. We shall examine these problems more closely in Chapter 18.

Basic Plan versus Single Plan

Single plan standard costing requires a good deal of clerical preparation and standardization of operations. It has advantages when detailed analysis of variances by operation, machine, operator, or product is desired. Systems of this type require considerably more clerical time than basic plan systems, but they reduce the calculation and search time necessary to detail the variances. A single plan system is also likely to permit prompter preparation of monthly statements.

The actual cost data recorded under the single plan also provide a much broader data base for cost estimating. While one purpose of the standard cost files is to facilitate rapid cost estimation without the need for special cost studies, standards are not always up to date and they may even be wrong. Furthermore, some products or some operations may be subject to a wider variation in cost than others, and this may be an important factor in such questions as contract bidding. For all these reasons, the actual cost file may produce benefits.

Basic plan systems deliberately sacrifice this additional information in the interest of reducing clerical costs. Such plans are particularly well suited to operations in which in-process inventories either are negligible or do not change materially from period to period, but it is usually practicable to apply them to the variable inventory case. All that is required is an economical way of approximating the standard input costs of the work still in process at the end of the period.

Some chance always exists, of course, that the absence of significant variances covers up large compensating errors in the standards and that the department head is not perceptive enough to discover this. The probability that this kind of condition can long prevail is fortunately very small, particularly if the company has a continuing work study and methods improvement program in operation.

SUMMARY

Effective management control requires many kinds of feedback information. Standard costs are often used to provide information on the effectiveness of managerial control of factory direct labor and direct materials costs, and this chapter has described the kinds of information that standard costing systems can provide.

Standard costing systems are designed to assist management by identifying and reporting factory cost variances—differences between the actual and standard costs of the work done in any time period. Variances in costs that are expected to vary in proportion to variations in physical output—most often direct labor and direct materials—are usually broken down into two components, quantity variances and price variances. Attention in the factory itself is ordinarily focused on the quantity variances, and the accountant's task is to measure these and report them quickly and economically to the executives responsible for cost control.

Standard cost plans differ largely in terms of when and how variances are isolated. The simplest standard costing systems are known as basic plan systems, and the quantity variances produced under these plans are in the form of cost center totals—the differences between the actual quantities of the inputs consumed in the cost center and the standard input equivalents of the cost center's actual output in each time period. When these physical quantities are multiplied by standard input prices, the result is the dollar quantity variance that appears on the periodic performance reports.

The basic plan is relatively inexpensive. It identifies the cost centers in which quantity variances occur and provides management with a summary measure of cost control effectiveness in each cost center. Its weakness is that it fails to provide detailed information from which management can identify the products, operators, machines, or operations in

which the bulk of the variances occur. If management needs this information, a more expensive system may have to be used, either by modify-
ing the basic plan or by shifting to a more elaborate plan altogether.

The most elaborate standard costing systems, described as single plan
systems, attempt to determine all variances at the time the transactions are
recorded. This is accomplished by coding the production input documents for actual as well as standard input quantities for each direct
production operation.

The variances under this kind of plan ordinarily can be reported
more frequently than those in the basic plan system outlined in the
previous chapter. They can also be reported in more detail and classified
on several bases, if desired, but these detailed breakdowns and analyses
often can be dispensed with until large unexplained variances occur.

EXERCISES AND PROBLEMS

1.* The standard labor cost of a particular product is two labor hours per
unit at a standard wage rate of $3.80 an hour. A particular lot of 1,000 units
of this product required 1,900 labor hours at $3.85 an hour. Compute the
variances.

2.* Products A and B have standard direct labor requirements of two hours
and three hours a unit, respectively. The standard wage rate is $4 an hour.
During April, 1,500 units of product A and 4,000 units of product B were
manufactured. Direct labor for the period totaled 14,500 hours and cost
$59,000. Compute the labor variances.

3.* Standard direct labor cost of the product is $3 a unit. Operating data
for the month of July are:

Units in process, July 1 (one half processed)   500
Units finished during July 3,000
Units in process, July 31 (one fourth processed)   800

Compute the standard direct labor cost of the month's output.

4. Standard direct labor cost was $1 a unit for product A and $2 a unit for
product B. The standard labor cost of work in process was $2,000 on Septem-
ber 1 and $5,000 on September 30. The standard wage rate was $3 an hour,
and 7,500 direct labor hours were recorded during September. The direct
labor payroll for September totaled $23,000, and 4,000 units of product A and
7,000 units of product B were completed during the month.

a) Compute the standard direct labor cost of the month's output.
b) Compute the direct labor quantity variance, in dollars. How else could
      this same information be reported?
c) Compute the direct labor rate variance.

_____
  * Solutions to problems marked with an asterisk can be found in Appendix B.

5. Standard costs in the XYZ Company remain unchanged throughout the year. You have the following labor cost data for department 16:

	May	June
Actual direct labor hours............................	9,000	11,000
Actual direct labor wages...........................	$27,900	$36,300
Standard direct labor rate per hour.....................	$ 3.20	$ 3.20
Standard direct labor cost earned by production..........	$26,240	$33,600

Was the labor quantity variance better or worse in June than in May? How much better or worse? Show and explain your calculations.

6.* Material P is the sole ingredient in the two products manufactured in department X, products A and B. The following data are available:

Standard quantity of material P:	
Product A..	3 lbs. per unit
Product B..	4 lbs. per unit
Standard price of material P..........................	$6 per lb.
Material P purchased during October, 20,000 lbs.............	$110,000
Material P issued to department X in October...............	22,000 lbs.
Production during October:	
Product A..	5,000 units
Product B..	1,200 units

Compute the materials price and materials quantity variances for the month.

7. A department recorded the following data during three recent months:

	May	June	July
Actual direct labor cost.........................	$4,200	$4,675	$3,871
Actual direct labor hours........................	800	850	790
Standard wage rate.............................	$ 5	$ 5	$ 5
Standard labor cost of actual production...........	$4,500	$3,750	$3,400

a) Compute and analyze the labor cost variances for each month. The standard wage rate should be used to measure the size of the quantity variance each month.

b) Measure the labor quantity variance for each month using actual wage rates.

c) Measure any differences between your two sets of quantity variance figures. Give your reasons for preferring one to the other or for being indifferent to the choice.

8.† Follow the instructions given for each of the four exercises presented below:

---

† Copyright 1968 by l'Institut pour l'Etude des Méthodes de Direction de l'Entreprise (IMEDE), Lausanne, Switzerland. Adapted and reprinted by permission.

EXERCISE A

Luceri, Inc., reports factory materials and labor quantity variances to management monthly. It has two products, for which the following data are available:

	Materials Required per Unit	Labor Required per Unit	Units Produced during March
Product A...................	4 lbs.	1.5 hrs.	1,000
Product B...................	5	4.0	2,000

Usage of materials and labor during March was as follows: materials, 13,000 pounds; labor, 10,000 hours.

a) Compute materials and labor quantity variances for the month in terms of pounds of materials and labor hours. Indicate whether each variance is favorable or unfavorable.
b) The standard materials price is $4 a pound. The standard wage rate is $3 an hour. (1) Compute standard unit cost for each product in dollars. (2) Restate your quantity variances (from a) in monetary terms.

EXERCISE B

A. B. See, Inc., uses a standard cost system. It had no inventory of materials on December 1 and no work in process either on December 1 or on December 31. The following information was collected for the month of December:

(1) Materials:
        Standard price: $12 a pound.
        Purchased 10,000 pounds at a cost of $115,000.
        Used during December: 8,000 pounds.
(2) Labor:
        Standard wage rate: $2.50 an hour.
        Used during December: 2,700 hours at a cost of $7,000.
(3) Product output:
        Standard cost per unit of product:
            Materials: 3.9 pounds.
            Labor: 1.5 hours.
        Products manufactured during December: 1,900 units.

a) Compute labor and materials variances, in dollars, in whatever detail you think is appropriate.
b) Indicate to whom each of your variances should be reported.

EXERCISE C

Herren, Inc., uses a standard cost system. The following information was collected for one department for the month of December:

(1) Inventory of work in process, December 1 (at standard cost):
   Materials cost: $13,000.
   Labor cost: $8,000.
(2) Used during month:
   Materials (at standard prices): $30,000.
   Labor:
      At actual wage rates, $15,000.
      At standard wage rates, $16,000.
(3) Products finished and transferred out of the department during month
      (at standard cost):
   Materials cost: $31,200.
   Labor cost: $15,700.
(4) Inventory of work in process, December 31 (at standard cost):
   Materials cost: $9,000.
   Labor cost: $9,000.

Compute labor and materials variances in whatever detail you think is appropriate.

Exercise D

Smythe, Ltd. has a factory with four production departments. Department Baker receives partly processed products from department Able, adds component materials to them, and then transfers them to department Charlie for further work. A standard cost system is in use. The following data are available for department Baker for the month of February:

(1) Received from department Able during February:
   Product units received, 5,000.
   Unit cost in department Able:

	Standard	Actual
Materials..........................	$1.00	$1.10
Labor.............................	6.00	6.90

(2) Received component materials from stock room during month, at standard prices, $2,100; standard cost of these materials, 40 cents per product unit.
(3) Used 2,200 labor hours during February, $4,200 at standard wage rates; standard cost of department Baker labor was 90 cents per product unit.
(4) Transferred to department Charlie during February, 4,800 product units.
(5) Work in process inventories in department Baker were negligible both on February 1 and on February 28.
(6) Damaged 200 product units in processing operations; these units were not usable and had no salvage value. About half of the processing labor operations had been performed on these units before they were damaged. All of the component materials had been applied prior to the damage.

a) Compute labor and materials quantity variances for department Baker for the month of February.

b) Standard cost per product unit includes no allowances for losses of products during processing. How much of each of the variances computed in (*a*) was attributable to product losses? What do the remaining portions of the variances mean?

9. Product X is manufactured from material A in department 1. Material A has a standard price of $4 a gallon, delivered. The standard bill of materials for product X calls for 1.2 gallons of material A for every gallon of finished product. The following transactions took place during August:

(1) Purchased 10,000 gallons of material A at an invoice price of $3.80 a gallon, less a 2 percent discount for prompt payment.
(2) Paid freight charges on this shipment, $3,200.
(3) Issued 8,000 gallons of material A to department 1.
(4) Produced 7,000 gallons of product X.

Compute and analyze the materials cost variances for the month.

10. Materials price variances are identified at the time of purchase. Materials inventories are costed at standard purchase prices.

Material X is the raw material for product A. Product A is the only output of department 1. The standard materials quantity is 0.38 pounds of material X for a gallon of product A.

Material X has a standard purchase price of $8 a pound. The company purchased 3,000 pounds during January at a cost of $25,100. These materials were placed in warehouse W.

Department 1 used 4,000 pounds of material X during January. All of these came from warehouse H. They had been purchased six months earlier at a price of $7.50.

Department 1 produced 9,900 gallons of product A during the month of January.

Compute the materials price and materials quantity variances for the month.

11. Department A had six direct production workers on July 26, with the following hourly wage rates:

J. Cooley	$4.00
R. Donaldson	4.10
F. George	3.90
T. Sugarman	4.20
S. Taussig	4.00
L. Young	4.20

The standard wage rate for all workers in this department is $4 an hour. All have identical job descriptions; wage rates differ because of differences in seniority.

The time tickets for work in this department on July 26 showed the following details:

Name	Job No.	Indirect Acct. No.	Machine No.	Actual Hours	Standard Hours
Cooley..............	7762		X12	3.2	3.0
Cooley..............	7915		X12	1.4	0.9
Cooley..............		A14		0.6	...
Cooley..............	7915		X12	2.2	2.2
Cooley..............	7185		T44	0.8	0.6
Donaldson............	8044		T44	1.4	1.8
Donaldson............		A12		2.8	...
Donaldson............	7918		L95	4.8	4.3
George..............		A16		0.8	...
George..............		A14		0.4	...
George..............	7511		X16	2.0	1.2
George..............	7716		X16	1.1	0.5
George..............		A14		0.2	...
George..............		A17		3.5	...
Sugarman............	8345		X22	6.0	5.6
Sugarman............		A15		0.3	...
Sugarman............	7996		X16	2.2	2.3
Taussig.............	8212		L95	1.5	1.3
Taussig.............	7694		T44	2.3	2.5
Taussig.............		A14		0.6	...
Taussig.............	7694		T44	1.6	1.7
Taussig.............	7819		X22	3.0	2.8
Young...............		A12		1.0	...
Young...............	8076		X45	4.4	4.7
Young...............		A12		0.8	...
Young...............	8015		X45	1.1	1.3
Young...............	7995		X45	1.4	1.6

a) Assume that a single plan system is in use. Summarize these data and present a report of variances, in dollars, in any way that you think might be suitable. Be sure to distinguish variances that are likely to be controllable from those that are not.

b) Compute the variances showing only the amount of detail that would be available in a basic plan system. For this purpose you may assume that all the jobs referred to above were started and finished on July 26, leaving no work in process at the end of the day.

12.† Ross Shirts, Inc. manufactures short- and long-sleeved men's shirts for large stores. Ross produces a single quality shirt in lots to each customer's order and attaches the store's label to each. The standard direct costs for a dozen long-sleeved shirts are:

Direct materials, 24 yards @ $0.55............................	$13.20
Direct labor, 3 hours @ $2.45................................	7.35
Standard direct cost per dozen..............................	$20.55

During October 1969 Ross worked on three orders for long-sleeved shirts. Job cost records for the month disclose the following:

† Adapted from a uniform CPA examination.

Lot	Units in Lot	Material Used	Hours Worked
30...............	1,000 dozen	24,100 yards	2,980
31...............	1,700 dozen	40,440 yards	5,130
32...............	1,200 dozen	28,825 yards	2,890

The following information is also available:

Ross purchased 95,000 yards of material during the month at a cost of $53,200. The materials price variance is recorded when goods are purchased and all inventories are carried at standard cost.

Direct labor incurred amounted to $27,500 during October.

There was no work in process at October 1. During October, lots 30 and 31 were completed. All material was issued for lot 32 and it was 80 percent completed as to labor on October 31.

a) Compute the materials price variance for October and indicate whether it was favorable or unfavorable.

b) Compute the total amount of each of the following variances and indicate in each case whether the variance is favorable or unfavorable: (1) materials quantity variance in yards and dollars; (2) labor quantity variance in hours and dollars; (3) labor rate variance in dollars.

c) Identify, for each production lot, the variances that resulted directly from the production of that lot.

13. Hans Hasenpfeffer, a department foreman in Consolidated Industries' Rapperswil factory, receives a labor report each morning listing the previous day's performance of each worker in his department. This report contains one line for each task performed by each worker during the day. Below is an excerpt from the report for January 23 listing all tasks performed on that day by Anna Buri and Jorg Stubil, two workers in Mr. Hasenpfeffer's department:

Empl. No.	Employee Name	Rated Work				Other Actual Hours	
		Operation No.	Actual Hours	Standard Hours	Gain (Loss)	Nonrated Work	Nonpro- ductive
323	Buri, Anna	179–32	8.0	7.8	(0.2)		
886	Stubli, Jorg	176–40	2.2	1.4	(0.8)		
886	Stubli, Jorg						0.5
886	Stubli, Jorg					2.4	
886	Stubli, Jorg	179–32	2.9	2.0	(0.9)		

Nonrated work consists of all productive tasks for which no standards have been prepared. Nonproductive time is time spent waiting for materials, waiting for machine repair, etc. The twice-daily coffee breaks are not recorded as nonproductive time, however. Instead, standard labor hours include a provision for this factor.

Mr. Hasenpfeffer has 12 workers in his department, all of them paid on an hourly basis. The typical daily report consists of approximately 40 lines. All workers in this department are paid a fixed hourly wage, which varies considerably from worker to worker.

a) If you were Mr. Hasenpfeffer, what action, if any, would you probably take on the basis of the portion of the report dealing with Miss Buri and Mr. Stubli? Is Miss Buri a better worker than Mr. Stubli?

b) If you were Mr. Hasenpfeffer, would you want to see this report each morning? If so, how would you use it? Should a copy go to Mr. Hasenpfeffer's boss?

c) Describe the documents that are probably used to obtain the figures shown in each of the last five columns of this daily report.

d) This report is part of a much broader standard costing system that has been used in this factory for a number of years. Would you guess that this system is a basic plan system or a single plan system? Why do you think so?

chapter 16

Accounts for
Standard Costing

Although standard cost variances can be generated outside the ledger accounts, it is usually more economical or more convenient to tie them into the regular factory cost records. In this chapter we shall see how this can be done. We shall also examine the relationship between the inventory accounts under standard costing and the historical cost totals that are reported in the company's published financial statements.

ACCOUNTS FOR THE BASIC PLAN

Quantity variances in the basic plan are computed by comparing total production inputs with total production outputs for specified periods of time. Production input and output totals cannot be observed directly, however, but must be derived by summarizing a large number of individual transactions. To illustrate this process, let us see how the Galahad Company recorded its labor and materials costs during July.

Recording Materials Purchases

In Galahad's basic plan system, purchased materials enter the inventory accounts at standard prices; the materials price variances are recorded directly in a separate variance account. For example, Galahad purchased materials and parts from outside vendors during July for $75,000, less discounts of $1,500. The standard costs of these goods totaled $82,700, including provision for standard freight charges and discounts. In summary form, the entry to record the month's purchases was:

(1*a*)

Materials and Parts...................................... 82,700		
Materials Price Variance.............................		9,200
Accounts Payable......................................		73,500

In other words, the asset was recorded at standard prices, the liability for the goods was recorded at net actual prices (after deducting the discounts allowable) and the difference was placed in the variance account.

The purchase price variance was not actually this large, however. The standard prices for the materials and parts included a provision for freight charges, but the actual purchase prices did not always cover freight charges. Separate freight charges on Galahad's July purchases amounted to $8,500. This amount was charged to the variance account because the inventory account already contained a standard provision for these costs:

(1*b*)

Materials Price Variance.................................... 8,500		
Accounts Payable......................................		8,500

The standard cost of the goods in this case was $700 greater than the actual delivered cost ($75,000 minus $1,500 plus $8,500), and this amount appeared as the closing balance in the variance account:

Materials Price Variance

(1*b*)	8,500	(1*a*)	9,200
		Bal. 700	

This favorable variance may have resulted from lower quoted prices, smaller freight charges, or greater discounts than the company expected when it set the standards. Perhaps external conditions were better than anticipated, or the purchasing agent found a new supplier or a chance to get lower prices by buying some items in larger lots.

Using Accounts to Isolate Quantity Variances

The Galahad Company's basic plan system uses departmental work-in-process accounts to accumulate the data from which the quantity variances are calculated. To facilitate the calculation, separate accounts are maintained for labor and materials. The July 1 balances in the forming department's accounts were $1,680 for materials and $320 for labor. These were the standard costs of the work in process at the beginning of the month.

Recording the Inputs. Under the basic plan the actual direct labor and materials inputs are charged to the departmental work-in-process accounts at standard prices. For example, the quantities shown on the forming department's requisitions of direct materials during July were multiplied by the standard prices of those materials to get the standard costs of the materials issued. The resulting amounts, totaling $33,700 in all, were charged to the departmental materials-in-process account. The entries to record these transactions can be summarized as follows:

(2)

Materials in Process—Forming...............................	33,700	
Materials and Parts....................................		33,700

This entry identified the amounts for which the forming department was accountable and reduced the balance in the stockroom's inventory account.

Aside from updating the records of physical stocks in the storeroom each time goods are received, issued, or returned, Galahad makes no materials entries other than the summary entries illustrated above. A job cost sheet is prepared for each job at the time the job order is issued, but this job cost sheet is completely filled in at that time with the standard quantities and prices of labor and materials for the specific quantity of parts or products to be manufactured to fill the order. Actual quantities of labor and materials used on the job are never recorded on the job cost sheet.

Labor costs are charged to the departmental accounts in the same way—that is, these charges reflect the actual number of labor hours used, multiplied by standard wage rates. Forming department workers often work part of the time on indirect tasks, and during July their time was divided as follows:

	Actual Hours	Actual Hours × Standard Rate
Direct work on production orders............	3,500	$17,500
Indirect work.............................	340	1,700
Total.......................................	3,840	$19,200

The charges to the departmental accounts can be represented by the following entry:

(3)

Labor in Process—Forming.................................	17,500	
Indirect Labor—Forming..................................	1,700	
Payroll Cost Summary—Forming.......................		19,200

The indirect labor account is part of overhead and does not figure further in this illustration. Payroll Cost Summary—Forming is a temporary account known as a suspense account, serving as a temporary proxy for a wages payable account. Its full purpose will become clear in a moment.

Recording Completed Work. When a department finishes its work and transfers the goods to other locations, its accounts are relieved of the standard cost of the goods transferred. The forming department finished work during July on a number of job orders, including those that were in process at the beginning of the month. The output of one of these jobs was transferred to the company's finished goods warehouse, two small job lots went to the parts storeroom, and the other job lots were moved on to the assembly department for further work. The standard costs of these jobs were as follows:

	Units Completed		Standard Cost		
	Product P	Product Q	Materials	Labor	Total*
To finished goods...........	...	200	$ 2,340	$ 1,300	$ 3,640
To parts storeroom..........	200	100	2,850	1,450	4,300
To assembly department.....	700	1,700	25,770	13,850	39,620
Total.....................	xxx	xxx	$30,960	$16,600	$47,560

* In practice, standard product cost ordinarily includes a provision for factory overhead as well (see Chapter 20).

The entries to record these transfers had two effects: (*a*) to identify the amounts for which stockroom and assembly department managers were now accountable; and (*b*) to reduce the amount of costs for which the manager of the forming department remained accountable. These entries can be summarized as follows:

(4)

Finished Goods...	3,640	
Materials and Parts.....................................	4,300	
Materials in Process—Assembly..........................	39,620	
Materials in Process—Forming.......................		30,960
Labor in Process—Forming...........................		16,600

Notice that the standard labor costs of the forming operation became part of the materials costs of the assembly department. The assembly department manager receives processed material, not unprocessed materials and forming department labor. His labor cost account should show only the labor used in his own department.

Deriving the Variances. After all these transactions were recorded, the forming department's work-in-process accounts showed the following:

Materials in Process—Forming				Labor in Process—Forming			
Bal. 7/1	1,680	(4)	30,960	Bal. 7/1	320	(4)	16,600
(2)	33,700			(3)	17,500		
	35,380				17,820		
Bal. 4,420				Bal. 1,220			

These balances are very different from the standard costs of the work actually in process on July 31. Referring back to Exhibit 15–2, we find that the ending inventory had a standard materials cost of $2,520 and a standard labor cost of $720. In other words, the ending balance in the materials account was $1,900 too large and the balance in the labor account was $500 too large. These were the quantity variances for the month. They appeared in the work-in-process accounts because these accounts were charged with *actual* input quantities and were credited with the *standard* input quantities required by the jobs completed during the month. The ending account balances were therefore a mixture of the standard costs of the ending inventories and the variances for the month.

Once the standard cost of the ending inventory was determined, the work-in-process accounts were restored to their proper levels by transferring the variances to separate variance accounts. The materials variance in this case was unfavorable, requiring a debit to the variance account and a credit to the work-in-process account to bring the latter down to its correct balance:

Materials Quantity Variance—Forming....................... 1,900
    Materials in Process—Forming...........................   1,900

The Labor in Process—Forming account also had to be credited to bring it down to standard. The corresponding debit to the variance account indicates that the labor quantity variance was unfavorable:

Labor Quantity Variance—Forming............................. 500
    Labor in Process—Forming..................................   500

Using Accounts to Isolate the Labor Rate Variance

Galahad does not calculate the labor rate variance at the time labor is charged to work in process. Instead, it uses a payroll cost summary account to isolate this variance. As work is performed, the number of labor hours, multiplied by standard wage rates, is credited to this account, as in entry (3). The actual labor cost is debited to this account when the payrolls are prepared.

To see how this works, remember that Galahad credited $19,200 to the Payroll Cost Summary—Forming account during July, representing 3,840 hours at a standard wage rate of $5 an hour. The actual payroll for

July, covering the same 3,840 hours, amounted to $19,500. The entry to record this was:

(5)

Payroll Cost Summary—Forming	19,500	
Wages Payable		15,900
Taxes Withheld		3,600

The payroll summary account thus showed the following:

Payroll Cost Summary—Forming

(5) Actual labor hours × actual basic hourly wage rates...... 19,500	(3) Actual labor hours × standard hourly wage rates.......... 19,200	
Bal. 300		

Since the amounts on both sides of the account were based on the same number of labor hours (3,840), the $300 difference in the total could only be due to difference between actual and standard wage rates—that is, it was the labor rate variance. A credit balance would have shown up if actual wage rates had been lower than standard.

This rate variance measured differences between standard wage rates and actual straight-time pay rates. It did not include elements such as overtime premiums or shift differentials. These were segregated in payroll preparation and charged directly to overhead cost accounts.

Basic Plan Cost Flows

Exhibit 16–1 summarizes the mechanics of the basic plan by tracing the flow of materials costs through the Galahad Company's factory accounts. First, when materials are purchased, they are charged to the inventory account at standard prices, as shown in the upper left corner of the diagram. The differences between standard and actual prices are charged or credited at the time of purchase to a price variance account. (To eliminate unnecessary detail, only the net variance for the month is shown in this diagram.)

Next, the actual quantities of direct materials and parts issued to the production departments are charged to the departmental materials-in-process accounts at standard prices.

Third, the standard materials cost of work completed by each production department is credited to the departmental materials-in-process account. The accompanying debit, not shown in the diagram, is to an appropriate inventory account elsewhere—either Finished Goods, Materials and Parts, or Materials in Process—Assembly, depending on where the goods are taken.

The final requirement is to determine the standard materials content

Exhibit 16–1

MATERIALS COST FLOWS UNDER THE BASIC PLAN

Materials and Parts			Materials in Process–Forming		

Beginning Balance:
  Actual quantity X
  standard prices   130,000
	Actual quantity
	  issued X
	  standard prices:
	    To Forming 33,700
	    To Assembly 54,000
			Beginning Balance:
			  Actual quantity at
			  standard cost
			  (standard quantity
			  X standard price) 1,680
				Actual quantity of
				  goods finished at
				  standard cost
				  (standard materials
				  quantity X stand–
				  ard price) 30,960
					Completions

Actual quantity
  purchased X
  standard
  prices   82,700
		Issues	Actual quantity
			  received X
			  standard prices 33,700		

Ending Balance:
  Actual quantity
  X standard
  prices   125,000
				Excess of actual
				  quantity used
				  over standard
				  usage X standard
				  price 1,900	

Purchases			Ending Balance:
			  Actual quantity
			  at standard cost 2,520		

Materials Price Variance			Materials Quantity Variance–Forming		

Excess of actual over
  standard prices of
  materials purchased . . .
	Excess of
	  standard
	  over actual
	  prices of
	  materials
	  purchased 700
			Excess of actual
			  quantity used
			  over standard
			  usage X stand–
			  ard prices 1,900
				Excess of standard
				  quantity used over
				  actual usage X
				  standard prices . . .	

of the jobs still in process at the end of the period. The difference between this and the balance in the materials in process account is the departmental materials quantity variance for the period. This depends on the amount of materials used during the period, whereas the materials price variance relates to the quantity purchased during the period.

ACCOUNTS FOR THE SINGLE PLAN

The transactions documents in the single plan permit the accountant to record the quantity variances directly in variance accounts as they occur. The work-in-process accounts are used to record the standard cost of the work done. Barring errors, no variances should ever appear in the work-in-process accounts.

Materials Costs

Materials price variances in single plan systems are determined just as they are in basic plan systems. They are recorded at the time of purchase and the materials inventory accounts reflect standard prices only. This process needs no further illustration here.

Materials issued on standard requisitions are charged to the work-in-process account, but the standard costs of materials issued on supplemental requisitions are debited to variance accounts. For example, during September the machining department of the Faultless Company's factory requisitioned materials with a total standard cost of $34,150. Of this, $31,800 was on standard requisitions and $2,350 was on supplemental requisitions. The entries recording these transactions can be summarized as follows:

```
Materials in Process......................................  31,800
    Materials and Parts....................................          31,800

Materials Quantity Variance—Machining...................   2,350
    Materials and Parts....................................           2,350
```

The use of supplemental requisitions indicates excessive materials usage, and this is reflected in the debits to the quantity variance account. Conversely, returned materials cards are evidence of less than standard usage and lead to credits to the variance account. The standard cost of returned materials in this case was $450, summarized in the following entry:

```
Materials and Parts.........................................  450
    Materials Quantity Variance—Machining.....................         450
```

Because the amounts shown on the supplemental requisitions exceeded the total amounts shown on the returned materials cards, the materials quantity variance for the period was unfavorable. It is shown directly by the balance in the quantity variance account at the end of the period:

Materials Quantity Variance—Machining

Supplemental requisitions.... 2,350	Returned materials........... 450
Bal. 1,900	

The individual supplemental requisitions and returned materials cards then provide a basis for detailed analysis of the overall variance by job or product or type of materials.

Labor Costs

Labor rate variances can be isolated in single plan systems by the technique illustrated earlier for basic plan systems, using a payroll summary account. This procedure was described above and needs no further illustration here.

Recording the labor quantity variances is a different matter, however. Since time tickets are available for all work, the labor quantity variances can be recorded as they occur. The standard costs shown on the time tickets are debited to the work-in-process account, while the differences between these amounts and the actual time recorded on the tickets are either debited or credited to the variance accounts.

In this case, the standard labor cost of the work done during the month totaled $17,000, and this amount was debited to the Labor in Process account. An additional $930 in direct labor costs, again at the standard wage rate, was charged directly to the quantity variance account because actual times on some of the time tickets exceeded the standard times. This was partially offset by favorable variances on other jobs, however, and these totaled $430. These figures can all be summarized in a single entry:

Labor in Process..	17,000	
Labor Quantity Variance—Machining........................	930	
Labor Quantity Variance—Machining....................		430
Payroll Summary......................................		17,500

The Labor Quantity Variance—Machining account now has a debit balance of $500, reflecting labor performance slightly poorer than standard:

Labor Quantity Variance—Machining

(Actual hours — standard hours) × standard rates	930	(Standard hours — actual hours) × standard rates	430
Bal. 500			

Completed Work

The work-in-process accounts in single plan systems serve only to indicate the total standard cost of the work in process at any time. They are not used to isolate the quantity variances, and this usually means that the work-in-process account need not be departmentalized and that no entry is made when work is transferred from one department to another. Transfers are made from the work-in-process accounts only when all work has been completed and the products are transferred off the production floor.

The Fautless Company's factory output was the same as Galahad's—that is, the machining department completed production orders with standard materials costs of $30,960 and standard labor costs of $16,600, a total of $47,560. Of this, $3,640 represented finished goods, $4,300 was for fabricated parts, and the remaining $39,620 applied to goods transferred to the assembly department. Completion of finished goods and machined parts was recorded by entries with the following effect:

Finished Goods	**3,640**	
Materials and Parts	**4,300**	
Materials in Process..................................		5,190
Labor in Process.....................................		2,750

No entry was made to record the $39,620 standard cost of the work transferred to the assembly department because a single set of work-in-process accounts is used for all factory departments.

Comprehensive Inventory Accounts

Some systems go even farther than this illustration in reducing the number of work-in-process accounts, with the aim of reducing clerical cost and the chance of clerical error. Some use a single factorywide account for all in-process inventories, covering the standard labor, materials, and overhead costs of these inventories. Others keep inventory records by cost element rather than by stage of completion. For example, a single inventory account can be used to accumulate the standard cost of raw materials, the standard materials cost of the work in process, and the standard materials cost of finished goods. Under such a system, the materials inventory account is debited at standard prices when materials are purchased and credited only when finished products are sold or materials quantity variances are recognized. No entry of any kind is made to record the issuance of materials on standard requisitions.[1]

ADJUSTING STANDARD COSTS FOR PUBLIC REPORTING

Under most procedures, up-to-date inventory account balances represent the standard costs of the items on hand. When standard costs approximate average historical cost, these balances can be and generally are used to measure inventories for public financial reporting. Standard cost totals may differ from reported inventory balances, however, for three reasons:

1. Newly adopted standards measure anticipated costs and differ substantially from the previous standards which approximated historical cost.
2. Variances are so large that the firm's accountants insist that they be reflected in the reported inventory totals.
3. Standard costs represent current conditions but inventories are reported on a Lifo basis.

The balance of this chapter will be devoted to an examination of the ways in which an inventory adjustment account can be used to account for the discrepancy between standard cost and the balance sheet amounts in each of these cases.

The Inventory Adjustment Account

The balance in the inventory adjustment account on any balance sheet date is simply the difference between total standard cost of the inventory on hand and its average historical cost. It can be either a debit or a credit balance. To illustrate, assume that a company prices its inventories by the Fifo method, including an allowance for the appropriate portion of

---

[1] See Robert L. Beyer, *Profitability Accounting for Planning and Control* (New York: Ronald Press, 1963), pp. 77–80 and 128.

variances of all types. For convenience, this is referred to as the "actual" cost of the goods in inventory. Assume further that the labor cost assigned to the January 1, 1971, inventory was as follows:

	At Standard	At Actual	Difference
Labor in process................	$ 500,000	$ 530,000	$30,000
Labor in finished goods..........	800,000	848,000	48,000
Total.......................	$1,300,000	$1,378,000	$78,000

The method of estimating the "actual" cost will be discussed in a moment.

The difference between the actual and standard amounts could be carried as a debit balance in an inventory adjustment account:

Inventory Adjustment—Labor

Bal. 1/1	78,000	

A full balance sheet presentation would show:

Labor in inventories, at standard......................... $1,300,000
Plus allowance for actual costs in excess of standard.......... 78,000
Labor in inventories..................................... $1,378,000

Adjusting for Changes in Standards

On January 1, 1971, new standards were put into effect and the inventory account balances were adjusted upward to reflect the new standards. The labor in inventories at the new standards amounted to:

Labor in process............................... $ 550,000
Labor in finished goods......................... 880,000
Labor in inventories, at standard.................. $1,430,000

This was $130,000 more than the inventory accounts showed, and the adjustment was accomplished by the following entry:

Labor in Process... 50,000
Labor in Finished Goods.................................. 80,000
    Inventory Adjustment—Labor......................... 130,000

The adjustment account thus showed a $52,000 credit balance:

Inventory Adjustment—Labor

Bal. 1/1	78,000	Adjustment	130,000
		Adj. Bal. 1/1	52,000

This was purely an internal bookkeeping adjustment. The adjusted January 1, 1971 balance sheet still showed labor in inventories at $1,378,000:

Labor in inventories, at standard...................... $1,430,000
Less allowance to reduce inventories to actual cost......   52,000
Labor in inventories................................ $1,378,000

Adjusting for Large Variances

Although the available evidence is that most variances from standard cost are reported in full on the annual income statement, the wording of American Institute of Certified Public Accountants pronouncements supports the belief that large variances are likely to be divided between balance sheet and income statement.[2] Complete recosting of individual jobs or processes is not necessary, however. An adequate approximation can be obtained by the use of average cost-output ratios, using variance information already in the accounts.

During 1971, overhead costs were transferred into and out of the inventory accounts at standard, and no entries were made in the adjustment account. This produced the following year-end balances:

Labor in Process (Standard)	
Bal. 12/31 450,000	

Labor in Finished Goods (Standard)	
Bal. 12/31 1,100,000	

Inventory Adjustment—Labor

	Bal. 1/1	52,000

Thus, prior to adjustment, the total book value of the labor in inventories at year-end was $1,498,000 ($450,000 + $1,100,000 − $52,000).

The "actual" cost of the year-end inventories can be approximated in various ways, mainly the following:

---

[2] See Chapter 7 for a discussion of the options available to management for the disposition of cost variances and references to the available evidence on industry practice. Although the discussion in that chapter focused on overhead cost variances, it applies to labor and materials variances as well.

1. Multiply standard cost in inventories by the ratio of actual cost for the entire year to cost earned by production during the year.

2. Multiply standard cost in inventories by the ratio of actual cost for the final months of the year to costs earned by production during those months; the length of the period to be approximately that during which the ending inventory was manufactured (e.g., if standard cost in inventories totaled $1,550,000 and the standard cost earned by production in December, November, and October totaled $1,450,000, the cost ratios for the fourth quarter could be regarded as a close enough approximation).

The first of these is the easiest to apply, while the second is more fully consistent with the Fifo definition. Because the basic method is identical in each case and the differences in many cases will not be material in amount, an example using a simple annual average should serve to illustrate both.

Assume that factory labor cost for 1971 amounted to $5.4 million while the labor cost earned by production totaled $5 million. The ratio of actual to earned labor was thus 108 percent. Applying this ratio to the year-end inventory would yield the following:

	At Standard Cost	Conversion Ratio	At "Actual" Cost
Labor in process.............	$ 450,000	1.08	$ 486,000
Labor in finished goods.......	1,100,000	1.08	1,188,000
Total.....................	$1,550,000		$1,674,000

The "actual" cost total is $176,000 greater than the year-end book value, and the inventory adjustment account should have a debit balance of this amount at year-end. In other words, $176,000 of the $400,000 labor variance for the year would remain on the year-end balance sheet; the remaining $224,000 would go to the income statement. The entry to close the labor accounts for the year would be:

```
Inventory Adjustment—Labor.......................  176,000
Cost of Goods Sold................................  224,000
    Labor Variances....................................              400,000
```

After this entry was posted, the Inventory Adjustment—Labor account would have a debit balance of $124,000 (the $176,000 debit adjustment less the initial $52,000 credit balance). This is the amount by which average actual labor cost exceeded the standard labor cost of the inventories. The account balances could then be summarized on the balance sheet as follows:

Labor in inventories (at standard)...................... $1,550,000
Plus allowance for actual costs in excess of standard.......   124,000
Total... $1,674,000

This adjustment is admittedly an approximation, but it is probably sufficiently accurate for external financial reporting. Greater precision can be obtained by using separate adjustment factors for individual departments, but only at greater clerical cost.

Adjusting to a Lifo Basis

Lifo inventory pricing requires (1) the separate identification of the layer of inventory coming from each year's increment; (2) measurement of the physical inventory increment or decrement for the current year; and (3) estimation of the unit cost applicable to the increments and decrements.

This can be done item by item, but the use of standard cost in the inventory accounts is most readily applicable to composite inventory pools because it provides a ready means of measuring annual physical increments and decrements. For example, the physical inventories in the previous illustration, at 1971 standard costs, increased during the year:

End-of-year inventory................ $1,550,000
Beginning-of-year inventory........... 1,430,000
Increase in inventory................ $ 120,000

Beginning and ending inventory totals represent two sets of physical quantities multiplied by a single set of standard prices. Because both sets of quantity figures are multiplied by the same prices, the account change represents the combined effect of changes in the inventory mix and changes in the physical quantities of goods on hand. For application of the pooling method, the increment is interpreted to be entirely due to changes in physical quantities, on the ground that standard costs weight each item in proportion to its importance relative to the others. In other words, it is assumed that two $1 units are fully equivalent to one $2 unit. Without this assumption, the entire pooling concept must be abandoned.

To illustrate the method, suppose that the company adopted Lifo as of January 1, 1971. The book value of the labor costs in inventory at that time was $1,378,000, which was 96.36 percent of standard cost. At standard prices, the year-end inventory was $120,000 greater than the opening inventory, according to the calculations described in the last paragraph. The problem now is to estimate the "actual" costs of this increment.

The simplest solution would be to price the increment at current standard cost, $120,000:

Base quantity	$1,378,000
1971 layer	120,000
Total inventory at Lifo	$1,498,000

This would correspond to the sum of the labor balances in the inventory accounts and the inventory adjustment account, and no adjusting entry would be needed.

Although many companies take this simple approach, particularly if actual costs are not far from current standards, others include some or all of the current year's variances in the costing of the increment. For this purpose, the simplest approach is to use the ratio of actual to standard costs during the year.

In the example, this ratio was 108 percent for labor costs, and the 1971 layer would therefore be $1.08 \times \$120,000 = \$129,600$. The Lifo inventory at year-end thus would be $\$1,378,000 + \$129,600 = \$1,507,600$. The total standard cost was $1,550,000, and thus the inventory adjustment account would have to have a credit balance of $42,400 to bring the book value down to $1,507,600. The credit balance carried forward from the beginning of the year was $52,000, however, and this would require a $9,600 debit to this account in the year-end adjusting entries. In other words, the entry to write off the $400,000 labor variance for the year would be:

Cost of Goods Sold	390,400	
Inventory Adjustment—Labor	9,600	
Labor Variances		400,000

The calculations for an inventory liquidation are more complicated, but they are facilitated immensely by the availability of standard cost totals. For example, assume that in 1972 the labor in inventory at standard prices decreased by $150,000. Because both the current standard cost and the Lifo cost of each layer of the inventory are known, measurement of the decrement is simple and straightforward:

	At Standard Cost	Conversion Ratio	At Lifo "Actual" Cost
1971 layer	$120,000	108.00%	$129,600
Base quantity	30,000	96.36	28,908
Total decrement	$150,000		$158,508

This means that $8,508 would have to be credited to the inventory adjustment account at the end of 1972.

This procedure, of course, is also an approximation. The larger the inventory pool, the less homogeneous it is likely to be and the greater the error of approximation. The use of more than one pool, however, requires some means of dividing the variances among the various pools. Such a division increases the cost of bookkeeping. If the increase in accuracy is slight, this added cost will be hard to justify, particularly in that the adjustment has no managerial significance.

Disposition of Materials Price Variances

Materials variances are slightly different. The purchase price variance applies to raw materials and parts inventories as well as to the materials content of work in process, finished goods, and the goods that have been sold during the period. This difference requires some discussion.

Once again, full-year averages or partial-period averages could be used, but it is simpler to illustrate using the former. Suppose that the purchase price variance for the year was $600,000, and unfavorable, on a purchase volume of $10 million at standard prices. Ignoring the question of whether a 6 percent variance might be regarded as immaterial, the $600,000 could be spread in proportion to the standard materials cost distribution assumed in the following table:

	At Standard Cost	Conversion Ratio	At Actual Average Prices
Materials and parts inventory............	$ 3,000,000	1.06	$ 3,180,000
Materials in process inventory...........	500,000	1.06	530,000
Materials in finished goods..............	1,500,000	1.06	1,590,000
Materials in goods sold (less year-beginning inventory)................	5,000,000	1.06	5,300,000
Total...............................	$10,000,000		$10,600,000

This, of course, presumes that all inventories are carried on a Fifo basis; a Lifo adjustment would start with the materials content of the goods sold and would convert only increments in the inventory figures. With Fifo, however, the inventory adjustment account at year-end should include $300,000 for unfavorable materials price variances. The distribution of the materials quantity variances would of course not extend to the materials and parts inventory and could be based on calculations of the type illustrated for labor.

SUMMARY

Inventory account balances in standard costing systems reflect the actual quantities on hand, multiplied by their standard costs. Price variances are segregated in separate accounts as they occur.

Departmental quantity variances in basic plan systems are derived as end-of-period residuals in departmental cost summary or work-in-process accounts. These accounts are debited for the actual quantities of inputs used, at standard prices, and credited for the standard costs of the actual outputs. When adjusted for inventory changes, the balances in these accounts measure the quantity variances for the period.

In single plan systems, the quantity variances are identified first and then debited or credited directly to the variance accounts without passing through departmental work-in-process accounts on the way. Departmental work-in-process accounts can be eliminated.

Standard cost may be used for public financial reporting if it approximates actual historical cost. Differences between standard cost and average historical cost are represented by the balances in the current variance accounts. When these are material in amount, the accountant is supposed to divide them between the balance sheet and income statement in appropriate proportions. Inventories could be recosted for this purpose, but only at a high clerical cost. Generally satisfactory results can be obtained by pooling inventories and applying average variance ratios to each pool as a whole. Fairly simple methods of applying these averages are available, either for Lifo or for Fifo inventories.

EXERCISES AND PROBLEMS†

1. Using a basic plan of standard costing and carrying materials inventories at standard net delivered prices, record the following transactions in appropriate T accounts. You should include an account for each variance that you wish to identify separately.

Actual cost of materials purchased:	
Gross invoice price...............................	$50,000
Discounts received on purchases....................	800
Freight and delivery charges on materials purchased...	2,300
Standard cost of materials purchased.................	51,000
Materials issued (at standard prices).................	47,000
Direct labor:	
At actual wage rates............................	30,000
At standard wage rates..........................	28,000
Cost of goods finished (at standard):	
Materials......................................	40,000
Labor...	26,000
Cost of goods in process, end of month (at standard):	
Materials......................................	5,200
Labor...	5,100

There was no work in process at the beginning of the month.

---

† Additional problems on the topics covered by this chapter, incorporating overhead costs as well as direct labor and materials costs, can be found at the end of Chapter 20.

2.* The Durabilt Company, manufacturer of men's work clothes, uses a basic plan standard costing system. You are given the following information concerning the month of September:

Inventory, September 1:
Raw material.................................... $58,500
Material in process............................. 6,700
Labor in process................................ 2,400
Finished goods................................. 32,100
Purchases of materials:
Actual cost................................... 42,380
Standard cost................................. 44,620
Deliveries to finished goods:
Standard material cost......................... 40,350
Standard labor cost........................... 22,300
Direct labor at standard rates................... 23,600
Material put in process (at standard prices)........... 46,650
Standard labor and materials costs of products shipped
  to customers................................ 63,500
Direct labor payroll............................ 24,400
Inventory October 1:
Raw material.................................... ?
Material in process............................. 12,300
Labor in process................................ 4,700
Finished goods................................. ?

a) Enter the opening inventory balances in T accounts and record the above transactions.
b) Prepare a list of variances, and briefly state the meaning of each.

3.* Materials inventories are carried at standard cost, but for public financial reporting the year's variances are spread proportionately between the cost of goods sold and balance sheet accounts. You are given the following data:

(1) Inventories (at standard):

	January 1	December 31
Raw materials................................	$10,000	$15,000
Materials in process...........................	6,100	5,000
Materials in finished goods.....................	8,000	7,000
Materials quantity variance in inventory............	900 (cr.)	?

(2) Materials issued, at standard cost, $30,000.
(3) Materials quantity variance for the year (debit), $5,000.

a) Compute the Fifo cost of goods sold for the year.
b) Prepare an end-of-period entry to close out the Materials Quantity Variance account and adjust the Materials Quantity Variance in Inventory account to its appropriate year-end balance.

4. Department M performs two operations in the manufacture of product P. Operation 44 serves to combine material Z with the semifinished units received from a prior processing department. Operation 49 then completes department M's work on this product. This department's standard cost of a unit of product P is as follows:

* Solutions to problems marked with an asterisk can be found in Appendix B.

Materials:
    Semifinished product received from department K...... $ 4.50
    Material Z, 5 lbs. × $0.20......................... 1.00
Labor:
    Operation 44, 1.5 hours × $4..................... 6.00
    Operation 49, 2 hours × $5...................... 10.00
Total standard cost................................ $21.50

The following information relates to the month of July:

(1) 500 units of product P were in process in department M on July 1. Operation 44 had been performed on these units, but operation 49 had not been started.

(2) Department M received 2,000 units semifinished product from department K.

(3) Department M transferred 2,200 completed units of product P to department N.

(4) The July 31 work-in-process inventory consisted of 300 units on which no department M work had been performed.

(5) Department M received 9,500 pounds of material Z from the storeroom.

(6) Direct labor cost on operation 44, 3,000 hours, $11,500; on operation 49, 4,100 hours, $21,700.

(7) Departmental overhead costs were not included in standard product cost.

Prepare journal entries to record these transactions in such a way that the July 31 inventory account balances will show the standard costs of the work in process and each variance will appear in a separate account.

5.* The Irwin Seating Company manufactures a line of metal and wooden chairs for sale to large institutional buyers. Its standard cost system is similar to the single plan system described in this chapter. During September the following events took place in the wood chair department:

Materials purchased and placed in inventory:
    Standard prices............................... $123,000
    Actual prices................................. 131,000
Direct materials (at standard prices):
    Standard requisitions.......................... 140,000
    Supplemental requisitions........................ 12,000
    Returned to storeroom......................... 8,000
Direct labor:
    Standard hours at standard wage rates.............. 80,000
    Actual hours at standard wage rates................ 85,600
Direct labor payrolls:
    Accrued wages payable, September 1................ 8,200
    September payrolls, covering period of August 30–
        September 24, inclusive (paid entirely in cash)..... 79,500
    Accrued wages payable, September 30.............. 16,300
Chairs finished (at standard cost):
    Direct materials................................ 122,400
    Direct labor.................................. 76,500

Account for the above transactions, using T accounts, with a separate account for each cost variance that you are able to identify.

6. A company maintains three separate accounts for the materials, labor, and overhead content of inventories, plus accompanying accounts for the inventoried portion of cost variances. A standard costing system is in use, and inventories for public financial reporting are costed on a Fifo basis. Data for 19x1 are:

(1) Inventory balances, at standard cost:

	January 1	December 31
Labor in process..............................	$4,000	$ 7,000
Labor in finished goods........................	8,500	10,500
Labor variances in inventory (debit).............	500	?

(2) Direct labor, 8,050 hours (standard wage rate, $3 an hour; actual wages, $25,116).

(3) Labor quantity variance for the year at standard wage rates, $3,150 (unfavorable).

a) Compute the standard labor cost of goods sold.

b) Compute the labor cost of goods sold on a Fifo approximate average cost basis. (Suggestion: deal with quantity variances first.)

c) Prepare a journal entry to close out the year's variances and adjust the inventory accounts to their appropriate year-end balances.

d) Recompute the labor cost of goods sold for the year assuming a Lifo basis of inventory costing and inventorying only the appropriate portion of the labor rate variance.

7. Tufwun Products Company manufactures a limited line of machined products in its Albany factory. A basic plan of standard costing is in use at the factory, with materials inventories being carried at standard prices. The following information pertains to the operations of the milling department for the month of September:

(1) Direct labor in the department is divided into three basic pay grades at the following standard wage rates per hour:

Grade	Rate
101......................	$2.00
102......................	2.50
105......................	3.00

(2) Wages actually paid to employees will differ from these standard rates due to seniority provisions, etc. Actual hours worked and actual gross pay during the month were as follows:

Grade	Hours	Gross Pay
101.................	1,250	$ 2,520
102.................	1,500	3,900
105.................	1,520	4,200
Total..............	4,270	$10,620

(3) Production and product cost standards for the month:

| Product | Standard Materials Cost per Unit | Standard Milling Labor per Unit | | | | Units Com- pleted |
		101 Hours	102 Hours	105 Hours	Standard Labor Cost	
A..............	$2.00	0.5	1.0	..	$3.50	400
B..............	4.00	1.0	0.5	1.5	7.75	800
C..............	5.00	0.5	1.0	0.5	5.00	600

(4) Direct materials charged to the department were $7,600.

(5) There was no unfinished work in process in the department either at the beginning or at the end of the month.

(6) All units completed were transferred to the machining department.

Record the above information in appropriate T accounts. The account structure should facilitate the identification of the variances, and the ending balance in each account should have a clear meaning.

8. Eiseman, Inc. manufactures a line of children's sleds. It has a basic plan standard costing system in its factory. Materials price variances are separated at the time of purchase, and all materials inventories are costed at standard prices.

Factory overheads are regarded as wholly fixed and are charged to expense as incurred, without passing through the product inventory accounts. Factory overhead is expected to total $69,000 a month.

Standard costs and production and inventory data for the four models manufactured in the sled department during September were:

	Model 3	Model 5	Model 22	Model 30
Standard cost per unit:				
Materials................	$0.80	$1.20	$1.50	$ 2.00
Labor....................	2.00	4.00	6.00	10.00
Total.................	$2.80	$5.20	$7.50	$12.00
Units completed.............	5,000	10,000	4,000	2,000
Units in process, Sept. 1......	None	1,000	100	200
Units in process, Sept. 30.....	None	800	300	None

Units in process on any given date are assumed to be 100 percent complete as to materials and 50 percent complete as to labor.

The following transactions relate to the sled department during the month of September:

(1) Purchased materials on account (standard cost, $35,000), $35,400.

(2) Issued materials:
   Direct materials, at inventory cost, $24,500.
   Indirect materials, at inventory cost, $3,000.

(3) Accrued payrolls for the month (including indirect labor), $111,800.

(4) Direct labor hours (standard wage rate, $4 an hour), 23,800 hours.

(5) Indirect labor, $20,000.
(6) Other factory overhead, paid in cash, $50,000.

a) Prepare a schedule or schedules showing the standard costs of the inventories and goods completed. What were the standard materials and labor costs of the work done during the month?
b) Record the above information in appropriate T accounts. Be sure to enter the opening balances. Include entries that will bring the inventory accounts to their correct ending balances. A separate account should be provided for each variance that you wish to identify.

9. The company's factory has two departments and operates a single plan standard costing system. Separate accounts are maintained for (1) raw materials and parts, (2) work in process, and (3) finished goods inventories. The following data relate to the month of January:

(1) Direct materials issued and returned (at standard prices):

	Department A	Department B
Standard requisitions...........	$30,000	$45,000
Supplemental requisitions.......	4,800	2,700
Returns....................	2,500	3,100

(2) Direct labor distribution (at standard wage rates):

	Department A	Department B
Actual time....................	$21,000	$18,000
Standard time................	21,700	20,600

(3) Work completed:

	Department A		Department B	
	Standard Materials Cost	Standard Labor Cost	Standard Materials Cost	Standard Labor Cost
Transferred to department A....	.....	.....	$ 2,200	$ 1,000
Transferred to department B.....	$18,000	$12,000	.....	.....
Transferred to materials and parts inventory.............	4,200	3,000	9,300	5,000
Transferred to finished goods inventory..................	6,900	5,500	35,000	15,000

(4) Standard cost of goods sold: materials, $42,000; labor, $23,000.
(5) Direct labor payrolls, $42,000, including $750 overtime premiums in department A and $1,400 overtime premiums in department B.

a) Prepare a list of variances for the month in as much detail as the data permit.
b) Prepare journal entries to record the transactions.

c) Prepare the journal entries that would be appropriate if the company replaced its present inventory accounts with the following two accounts: Materials Costs in Inventories and Labor Costs in Inventories.

d) A run of the month's labor time tickets in department A showed that the following amounts, among others, were included in the labor quantity variance for the month (the department has a single standard wage rate of $3.50 an hour): (1) defective setup, 30 hours; (2) inferior materials, 50 hours; (3) standby machine used, 100 hours; (4) inexperienced operator, 80 hours; (5) one operator on two machines, 250 hours (favorable); (6) new machine, 120 hours (favorable). Prepare a revised list of labor variances for department A.

10. The Schouten Corportion employs a basic plan standard costing system. It uses a version of Fifo for public financial reporting. To simplify the bookkeeping, the Fifo cost of the year-end inventory is assumed to be equal to the standard cost of that inventory, measured at standard unit costs for the coming year.

The table below summarizes the data that were reflected in the factory accounts for labor and materials during 19x1:

	Trial Balance January 1, 19x1		Transactions during 19x1		Trial Balance December 31, 19x1	
Raw materials.......	43,000		(1) 120,000	(2) 114,000	49,000	
Materials in process...	12,000		(2) 114,000	(4) 110,000	16,000	
Labor in process......	3,000		(3) 25,500	(4) 25,000	3,500	
Finished goods.......	28,000		(4) 135,000	(5) 132,000	31,000	
Head office account...		86,000		(1) 133,000		246,700
				(3) 27,700		
Materials price variance............			(1) 13,000		13,000	
Labor rate variance...			(3) 2,200		2,200	
Cost of goods sold....			(5) 132,000		132,000	

A physical inventory was taken at the end of 19x1. The quantities on hand were multiplied first by 19x1 standard costs and then by the new 19x2 standards:

December 31, 19x1 Inventory at:

	19x1 Standards	*19x2 Standards*
Raw material......................	$49,500	$57,000
Material in process.................	17,000	19,000
Labor in process...................	6,000	7,000
Finished goods....................	29,000	32,450

The company was considering putting the materials content of its entire inventory on Lifo as of January 1, 19x1. For this purpose it computed the materials content of finished goods inventories as follows:

January 1, 19x1 inventory at 19x1 standards................ $19,000
December 31, 19x1 inventory at 19x1 standards............. 20,000
December 31, 19x1 inventory at 19x2 standards............. 23,000

a) Compute the Fifo cost of goods sold and prepare journal entries to adjust the inventories and close the variance accounts. Use any account titles that seem adequately descriptive.

b) Compute the cost of goods sold with materials on a Lifo basis and labor on a Fifo basis. Assuming that the entries called for in (*a*) have been made, prepare a single journal entry to provide for the conversion to the Lifo basis in materials.

11. The Prentice Company manufactures two products in its Denver plant. The plant uses a basic plan standard cost system for direct labor and direct materials costs. Factory overhead costs are not taken into product costs and are not introduced into this problem in any way.

The factory contains two production departments, X and Y. Production on both products is initiated in department X and completed in department Y. Materials inventories are carried at standard cost. Each department has two work-in-process accounts—Materials in Process and Labor in Process. The standard cost of materials received by a department from the storeroom is charged to the Materials in Process account of that department. The standard labor and materials costs of the operations performed in department X are charged to the Materials in Process account of department Y at the time the semifinished goods are transferred.

The standard costs for the two products are shown below. Note that operations and costs are listed in the order in which the work moves through the plant.

Product and Operation	Department	Labor Cost	Materials from Storeroom	Cumulative Cost
Product A:				
Op. 14.........	X	$2.00	$5.00	$ 7.00
Op. 12.........	X	1.50	0.10	8.60
Op. 20.........	X	1.00	0.50	10.10
Op. 18.........	Y	3.00	...	13.10
Op. 32.........	Y	1.00	0.90	15.00
Product B:				
Op. 11.........	X	0.10	0.30	0.40
Op. 16.........	X	0.25	...	0.65
Op. 27.........	X	0.20	0.05	0.90
Op. 32.........	Y	0.05	0.05	1.00

The following data describe the factory's operations during the month of July:

		Actual Prices	Standard Prices
(1)	Materials received from suppliers and placed in storeroom..............................	$31,402	$30,100
(2)	Materials issued from storeroom:		
	To department X...........................	xxx	20,530
	To department Y...........................	xxx	4,260
(3)	Actual direct labor:		
	Department X..............................	21,470	21,400
	Department Y..............................	15,351	14,620
(4)	Goods finished and transferred:		

Product	From Dept. X to Dept. Y	From Dept. Y to Finished Goods
A...............	3,100 units	3,000 units
B..............	14,000 units	15,000 units

(5) Work in process, July 1:
     Department X: 200 units of product A, complete through operation 12.
     Department Y: 1,000 units of product B, complete through operation 27.

(6) Work in process, July 31:
     Department X: none.
     Department Y: 50 units of product A, complete through operation 18.

a) Prepare journal entries to record the month's transactions, including interdepartmental transfers.

b) Prepare a list of variances, indicating for each whether it is favorable or unfavorable and the level of management at which control responsibility is likely to lie.

chapter **17**

Flexible Budgets and the
Control of Overhead Costs

Standard costing procedures constitute a highly effective means of generating information for use in the control of factory direct labor and direct materials costs. The purpose of this chapter is to see how similar kinds of control information can be generated for overhead costs. To reduce confusion, we shall limit our discussion almost exclusively to factory overheads, but the methods discussed here can be applied equally well to any overhead costs with similar characteristics.

OVERHEAD COST STANDARDS

Overhead cost control standards should represent what these costs ought to be. By analogy with labor and materials costs, standard overhead cost is an obvious candidate. How is this determined, and is it adequate to the cost control purpose?

Standard Factory Overhead Costs

Standard factory overhead costs are very similar to the overhead costs assigned to products by means of predetermined burden rates. The only difference is that standard overhead cost depends on some standard direct input quantity rather than the actual input quantity. For example, if the burden rate is $3 a direct labor hour and the product cost standard calls for 1.5 labor hours, then standard overhead cost is $4.50 a unit whether actual labor time averages 1 or 2 hours a unit.

In variable costing systems, standard overhead costs represent only the variable component of overhead costs. In most other systems the stan-

399

dard costs include some provision for fixed overhead costs, but all are based on the notion that the entire unit cost must be predetermined.

The volume base for standard overhead is quite clearly a normal volume rather than expected volume for the current year. Standard costs are predicated on normal operating conditions, and changes are seldom made unless factor prices or manufacturing techniques undergo structural changes. In the absence of such structural or permanent changes, a product manufactured in one year should be costed at the same amount as an identical product manufactured in the preceding year. This requires the use of the normal volume concept in setting standard overhead rates.

Inapplicability of Standard Overhead Costs to Cost Control

Two characteristics of overhead costs reduce the relevance of standard product costs to control reporting for overhead. First, overhead costs are common costs, not traceable to individual lots or units of product. For this reason, control standards must be derived from departmental figures rather than from data relating to specific products or operations.

Second, overhead costs include elements that do not vary in strict proportion to changes in production volume. If a significant proportion of total cost is fixed, standard overhead cost per unit will be too restrictive a control standard at low production volumes and too lenient at high volumes.

For example, suppose that overhead costs are expected to amount to $10,000 a month plus $1 for every unit of product manufactured, while standard overhead cost is $2 a unit. Production in November totaled 8,000 units. At this volume costs should have amounted to $18,000 ($10,-000 + 8,000 × $1 = $18,000), but total standard overhead cost was only $16,000 (8,000 units times $2). Comparison of actual costs with the $16,-000 figure would be useless for cost control purposes. In other words, overhead cost standards must be adjusted to levels appropriate to current volume.

The Flexible Budget

Taken together, these two characteristics of overhead costs require the development of departmental flexible budgets to serve as control bench marks. The flexible budget, also known as a semivariable expense budget, is actually a set of fixed budgets, one for each of a number of alternative production volumes.

Exhibit 17–1 shows the flexible budget for the drills department of a small metal products factory. The budget in this case is presented as a set of formulas so that the accountant can develop flexible budget allowances for any operating volume the department is likely to record. These

Exhibit 17–1

MONTHLY OVERHEAD COST BUDGET
Drills Department
(DLH—direct labor hour)

	Monthly Fixed Cost	Variable Cost per DLH	Budgeted Cost at Normal Volume (4,000 DLH)
Supervision:			
Less than 3,000 DLH..........	$2,000	...	
3,000–4,499 DLH.............	2,800	...	} $ 2,800
4,500 DLH..................	3,500	...	
Materials handling labor..........	....	$0.12	480
Idle or lost time.................	....	0.06	240
Other indirect labor..............	....	0.32	1,280
Overtime premium................	....	*	....
Supplies........................	....	0.14	560
Power..........................	....	0.20	800
Maintenance....................	600	0.10	1,000
Tools..........................	....	0.21	840
Floor space.....................	800	...	800
Equipment depreciation...........	600	...	600
General factory overhead.........	2,600	...	2,600
Total	$7,400†	$1.15†	$12,000

* Ten cents for each direct labor hour in excess of 4,500 hours a month.
† Totals apply only to normal operating range of from 3,000 to 4,499 direct labor hours.

formulas have been applied to the normal departmental volume of 4,000 direct labor hours to produce the budget allowances in the right-hand column; for any other volume a different calculation would have to be made.

Interpreting the Flexible Budget

Flexible budget allowances reflect the amount of cost that is reasonably necessary to achieve a given volume of activity, on the assumption that production is stabilized at that volume. As long as production activity in the drills department is relatively constant at a volume of 4,000 direct labor hours a month, departmental overhead cost should amount to about $12,000. If volume is stable at 3,500 hours, total overhead cost should be $7,400 + $1.15 × 3,500 = $11,425.

If volume changes from 4,000 hours to 3,500 hours, however, overhead cost in this department is unlikely to fall to this level. For one thing, adaptation to change takes time, and the change in cost is likely to lag behind the change in volume. Furthermore, if the reduction is expected to be temporary, management may even choose to reduce organizational stress by spending at the old level for a while. Under these conditions, the flexible budget allowances provide a distant rather than an immediate cost standard.

OVERHEAD COST REPORTING

The differences between actual cost center overheads and the flexible budget allowances for the period are reported to the first-line supervisor and, in condensed form, to his superiors. These differences are most commonly referred to as spending variances, although other terms such as budget variances and performance variances are also used.

A Monthly Report

A monthly report for the drills department is shown in Exhibit 17–2. Actual volume this month was 3,500 direct labor hours, and the total spending variance was $635, unfavorable.

Although the focus of this report is on the current month's results, shown at the left, the year-to-date columns at the right provide useful perspective on the current month's figures. The current variance in overtime premium, for example, was only slightly lower than the average for the previous four months, indicating a continuing situation that might need attention. The unfavorable variance in current maintenance costs,

Exhibit 17–2

DEPARTMENTAL OVERHEAD COST REPORT

DEPARTMENTAL OVERHEAD STATEMENT					
DEPARTMENT 10—Drills				PERIOD May, 19xx	
				VOLUME 3,500 hours	
Current Month				Year to Date	
Actual	Budget	(Over) Under		Actual	(Over) Under
$ 3,100	$ 2,800	$(300)	Supervision............	$14,600	$ (600)
410	420	10	Materials handling labor..	2,450	(218)
190	210	20	Idle or lost time........	1,754	(638)
1,125	1,120	(5)	Other indirect labor.....	5,340	612
280	...	(280)	Overtime premium......	1,545	(1,545)
530	490	(40)	Supplies..............	2,298	306
680	700	20	Power................	3,620	100
1,070	950	(120)	Maintenance...........	5,027	(167)
610	735	125	Tools................	3,815	91
785	800	15	Floor space...........	3,990	10
625	600	(25)	Equipment depreciation..	3,050	(50)
2,655	2,600	(55)	General factory overhead.	13,519	(519)
$12,060	$11,425	$(635)	Total................	$61,008	$(2,618)

on the other hand, accounted for most of the cumulative variance in that item. The department head would probably look into this, if he wasn't already aware of it; but his superior would probably be undisturbed by a single month's departure from the norm.

The Controllability Criterion

By printing so many figures on a single page, mixing the significant with the insignificant, the report shown in Exhibit 17–2 lacks visual impact. An easy remedy for this is to present key information in separate tables, attaching Exhibit 17–2 only for reference. These tables can also be supplemented or even replaced by charts and diagrams that have even greater immediacy.

More fundamental, however, is the need to distinguish between controllable and noncontrollable items. This has been done in Exhibit 17–3. The items "below the line" are completely beyond the department head's

Exhibit 17–3

DEPARTMENTAL OVERHEAD COST REPORT, EMPHASIZING CONTROLLABILITY

DEPARTMENTAL OVERHEAD STATEMENT			
DEPARTMENT 10—Drills		PERIOD May, 19xx	
		VOLUME 3,500 hours	
	Current Month		
	Actual	Budget	(Over) Under
Controllable:			
Materials handling labor................	$ 410	$ 420	$ 10
Idle or lost time......................	190	210	20
Other indirect labor....................	1,125	1,120	(5)
Supplies..............................	530	490	(40)
Power................................	680	700	20
Tools................................	610	735	125
Total controllable....................	$ 3,545	$ 3,675	$ 130
Partly controllable:			
Overtime premium......................	280	. . .	(280)
Maintenance..........................	1,070	950	(120)
Total responsibility..................	$ 4,895	$ 4,625	$(270)
Noncontrollable:			
Supervision..........................	$ 3,100	$ 2,800	$(300)
Floor space..........................	785	800	15
Equipment depreciation................	625	600	(25)
General factory overhead..............	2,655	2,600	(55)
Total departmental overhead............	$12,060	$11,425	$(635)

control; the items above the line he can influence to a significant degree. Thus although the total spending variance for the month is $635, $365 of this is below the line. These latter items may be controllable by someone else, but not by the foreman of the drills department.

The section on partly controllable costs emphasizes the shared aspect of cost control efforts. Maintenance costs, for example, depend not only on the department head's attention to careful handling of his equipment and his alertness to signs of maintenance problems, but also on the ability of the maintenance manager to see that maintenance work is promptly and satisfactorily done. Including this item in the drills foreman's total responsibility calls attention to his role in this process.

The practice of reporting noncontrollable costs below the line has a number of serious shortcomings, however. For one thing, reported variances are hard to ignore, no matter how clearly they are labeled uncontrollable. By the same token, large noncontrollable variances tend to obscure the department head's effectiveness in controlling costs. The bottom line catches the eye first and its apparent message is hard to ignore. Furthermore, when the noncontrollable variances grow large, they may make the controllable items look small by contrast, and the department head is likely to conclude that his control efforts are not very important.

The best remedy for these shortcomings is to eliminate noncontrollable elements from control reports altogether. If this suggestion is vetoed, the next best solution is to adjust the departmental charges for noncontrollable items to the budgeted amounts, thus keeping variances in these items out of the performance reports. These variances should be reported to the management levels at which control or decision responsibility lies. For example, if local property taxes are rising rapidly, the variances must be included in overall factory cost totals for headquarters review even though they have no place in the reports issued to first-line supervisors.

Cost Variability

Notice that the spending variance need not be separated into fixed and variable categories. Variability analysis is important in deriving the budget allowances, not in the interpretation of the variances. The only question is whether the variance is controllable or noncontrollable, and not whether is arises in fixed costs or in variable costs. This is fortunate because in many cases a completely satisfactory distinction between variances in variable costs and variances in fixed costs cannot be made. Many cost items do not fall precisely into either category, but must instead be placed in the intermediate class of semivariable costs. That is, it is impossible to decide, at the time of cost recording, whether a particular charge belongs in the fixed category or the variable.

Approved Departures from Budget

Because flexible budgets are highly static, higher management is very likely to authorize departures from flexible budget allowances for a variety of reasons: substitute equipment has to be used temporarily, workers are to be kept temporarily on standby rather than laid off when volume drops, and so forth.

One way to handle this is to wait until the variances are measured and then estimate how much was due to unexpected conditions. Another way is to anticipate the effects of changes and modify the budget allowances accordingly. The report shown in Exhibit 17–4 reflects this

Exhibit 17–4
BUDGET ALLOWANCE ADJUSTMENTS

DEPARTMENT 10—Drills				PERIOD May, 19xx	
				VOLUME 3,500 hours	
	Original Budget	Approved Variance	Adjusted Budget	Actual Cost	Unapproved Variance
Controllable:					
Materials handling labor...	$ 420	. . .	$ 420	$ 410	$ 10
Idle or lost time.........	210	. . .	210	190	20
Other indirect labor......	1,120	$ (60)	1,060	1,125	(65)
Supplies................	490	. . .	490	530	(40)
Power.................	700	. . .	700	680	20
Tools.................	735	(75)	660	610	50
Total controllable......	$3,675	$(135)	$3,540	$3,545	$ (5)
Partly controllable:					
Overtime premium.......	. . . .	200	200	280	(80)
Maintenance...........	950	. . .	950	1,070	(120)
Total responsibility........	$4,625	$ 65	$4,690	$4,895	$(205)

second approach. To reduce clutter, only the three rightmost columns should be reported to first-line management. The full report should be accessible, however, so that the department head can see for himself where the adjusted budget figures have come from.

Overhead Price Variances

The spending variance is likely to contain both price and quantity components. If the price component is significant, efforts should be made to isolate it, either by pricing overhead inputs routinely at standard prices or by end-of-period analysis of the overall variance.

For example, the materials handling labor variance in Exhibit 17–4 was $10, and favorable. Suppose, however, that the standard wage rate for materials handling labor was $3 an hour, while the actual rates averaged approximately $2.75. A $420 budget allowance is thus equivalent to a 140-hour allowance at standard rates, whereas the actual charge of $410 represents about 149 hours at the actual wage rate. Using the techniques that we developed in Chapter 15, we can subdivide the spending variance into two components, as follows:

Actual hours × actual rates		$410
Actual hours × standard rates (149 × $3)		447
Materials handling labor rate variance		$ 37
Budgeted hours × standard rates (140 × $3)	$420	
Materials handling labor quantity variance		(27)
Net spending variance		$ 10

If price variances are likely to be large, this same technique can be applied to each of the other departmental overhead items. Whether the price components of the spending variances belong in the monthly performance reports should depend on the location of responsibility for control over input prices.

DERIVING FLEXIBLE BUDGET ALLOWANCES

The development of flexible budget allowances is partly a technical question, usually requiring participation by trained staff personnel. Two questions usually arise in this connection:

1. What analytical method should be used?
2. What index or indexes of activity should be selected?

A third question is what data should be used, but this is usually moot. The ideal source would be controlled experiments to generate cost data at different volumes under current operating conditions. Unfortunately, experiments of this kind would take far too long and would disrupt the organization far too drastically to make this a practical alternative. Instead, the accountant must assemble data on costs and volumes from the records of previous periods.

The Analytical Method

The most sophisticated method of analysis in common use is statistical regression analysis, described in Chapter 3. Regression analysis has been made much more feasible in recent years by the development of standard computer programs, and its use is likely to increase. Even small companies without their own computer facilities can use these programs through time-sharing services. Even so, regression analysis is relatively expensive and time-consuming, and the available data are often too sparse to identify the underlying relationships very clearly.

The simplest and probably most widely used technique is the inspection of accounts, or judgment method. Under this approach, the foreman or staff analyst goes down the chart of accounts, classifying each account as wholly fixed, wholly variable, or a mixture of both. These decisions are based on personal knowledge and intuition, perhaps aided by rough scatter diagram plottings of historical data.

Having made this classification, the foreman or analyst estimates the monthly amount for each fixed cost element and the average unit cost for each proportionally variable element. The estimate of variable cost is often based on average historical cost per unit of activity adjusted for any changes in prices, wage rates, or other conditions that may have occurred or are expected to occur.

It may also be possible to budget step functions largely by the inspection of accounts method. For example, the number of foremen required in a responsibility unit is likely to vary only with fairly substantial changes in volume. Without going to the trouble of detailed cost analysis, the department head should be able to specify the volume level at which additional foremen will be required.

Inspection of accounts is an undeniably crude method. The question in each case must be whether regression analysis is likely to add enough to the accuracy of the relationship to justify the cost and effort. Simple scatter diagrams can often provide the necessary verification of judgmental estimates.

No matter what method is used, however, the results should be examined to see whether they seem to make sense. A regression line may fit the data very well, but still may not describe the current situation because the data are biased, atypical, or obsolete. Inspection of accounts also can produce nonsensical estimates if the estimator lacks experience or is unable to overcome his personal biases.

The Activity Index

The second major technical question is how to measure volume. An ideal volume index for the flexible budget is one that measures the factors that cause the costs. For example, if employees earn pension and vacation pay rights in proportion to their gross earnings, then labor dollars measure volume perfectly because they are the cause of pension and vacation overhead costs. Cause and effect are both clear and measurable.

Unfortunately, causes are seldom this easy to identify. Instead, we must try to find an index that correlates closely with changes in cost and therefore presumably correlates well with the underlying causal influences. Maintenance labor costs, for example, might be plotted against the number of units of product output, the number of pounds of materials processed, or the number of machine-hours used. In each case a regression line could be drawn through the observations. The closer the observations to the line, the higher the correlation between the actual cost at an output level and the cost predicted by the line. The best measure of volume is the one that gives the highest correlation.

Output Indexes.   According to this criterion, an output index can be used whenever a department's overhead costs vary more closely with variations in the total number of units of goods or services it produces than with variations in any other readily measurable quantity. This usually requires a fairly homogeneous output—for example, cement in a cement mill or premium notices in an insurance company; otherwise, changes in the product mix are likely to affect total overhead cost even when the total number of units remains unchanged.

A kind of synthetic output index can be derived from standard cost data. Each product can be represented by some element of its standard cost such as standard direct labor hours. Total output can then be measured by the total standard input content of all of the products or services produced in the department during the period. If standard input quantities correlate well with the factors that determine overhead cost, these indexes can be very useful.

Input Indexes.   Production is ordinarily so diverse that output indexes are too unreliable to use. When this is the case, input indexes are used, most commonly direct labor hours, machine-hours, or direct labor cost. In some cases the weight, bulk, or number of materials input units is the best index to use.

Once again the problem is to find an index that correlates closely with costs. For example, if direct labor hours is the base, it is assumed that overhead cost will vary with direct labor hours no matter what kind of operation is being performed in the cost center or which product is being produced. Alternatively, it might be said that the use of an input index assumes that neither variations in the operations mix nor variations in the output mix will influence the level of overhead cost. If mix variations influence cost materially, then a different volume index should be sought.

It can be argued that an input index is inherently inferior to an output index even if costs vary as a function of input rather than as a function of output. An input index permits relative efficiency or inefficiency in input usage to be reflected in the flexible budget allowances for the period, and the fear is that costs may be within the input-based allowances but still be too high from a competitive point of view. Unfavorable deviations from output-based standards eat into company profits even if costs are in line with input-based standards.

Unfortunately, to impose output-based standards when costs vary with input quantities is to attack the effect rather than the cause. The fault, if any, lies in the control of the direct inputs rather than in the control of overhead costs, and remedial action should be directed there.

Single versus Multiple Indexes.   In practice, most cost centers use a single index for all cost elements, the one index that best correlates with the sum of the cost center's costs. The use of two indexes rather than one would improve budget accuracy in most cost centers, because some cost elements tend to fluctuate with physical input quantities, while others, such as the cost of payroll benefits to employees, vary with dollar inputs.

Multiple indexes are subject to some dangers, however. For one thing, they increase the apparent complexity of the system and therefore may impair its usefulness by decreasing its chance of acceptance by operating foremen. Secondly, addition of a second index is costly, both in establishing the budget allowances and in periodic computation of the budget allowances. Finally, the techniques available for estimating cost relationships are far from perfect, and the use of multiple indexes may give an impression that the estimates are more accurate than they actually are.

In short, it may be preferable to continue with single cost center indexes except for staff analytical work. Whenever changes in input mix are big enough to affect cost variances materially, they can be removed in variance analysis. At other times the errors can be ignored in the interests of simplicity.

SUMMARY

Product unit standard costs are not relevant for control of factory overhead costs because factory overheads are neither wholly variable nor traceable to individual products. Instead, control standards are reflected in departmental flexible budgets, consisting of a series of budget allowance schedules for various volume levels within the normal operating range.

For this purpose, activity indexes must be selected which most closely correlate with short-run cost variations. These are mostly input indexes, such as direct labor hours, although output and synthetic output indexes can be used if they correlate well with overhead cost.

Methods used to estimate cost relationships depend on the nature of the operation and on the resources available for cost estimation. Of ultimate importance is the understanding and acceptance of the estimates by operating personnel, and this cannot be achieved by any doctrinaire adherence to a single formula.

Finally, it must be recognized that flexible budget techniques can never be expected to relieve management entirely of the difficult task of interpreting performance figures. It is impossible to design a reporting system such that the controllable variances reflect only the department head's performance and not the effects of causes and conditions outside his control. Causal analysis of variances is still necessary and may require the accumulation of supplementary statistics such as machine load factors, the length of production runs, and the mix of operations within each department. It also requires a considerable amount of informed judgment, and it is at this point that the real test of the cost accountant's experience and analytical skill begins.

EXERCISES AND PROBLEMS

1. The foreman of a certain factory department has control over three items of overhead cost:

Item A: This should amount to $300 per period plus 1 percent of the cost of materials used.

Item B: This should amount to $200 per period plus 5 percent of the cost of labor used.

Item C: This should amount to $400 per period plus 20 cents per hour of labor used.

These three indexes of volume vary from period to period, but not necessarily in the same proportions. In a typical period, the following activity takes place: materials used, $60,000; labor used (at an average wage rate of $3 a labor hour), $18,000.

It is considered impractical to use more than one index of activity as a basis for the flexible budget allowances in this department. You are asked to choose one of the three indexes mentioned above.

a) What criterion or criteria would you like to base this decision on?
b) Given only the data in the problem, which measure of activity would you select? Give your reasons.
c) What should the budget equation be?
d) Data for the first period under the plan are: materials used, $72,000; labor used (at an average wage of $3.20 per labor hour), $16,000; total controllable overhead, $3,500. Prepare a report (three lines) comparing actual overhead cost with the budget.
e) How much of the variance in (*d*) was due to the use of a single measure of volume instead of those? What problem is this likely to create?

2. The monthly flexible budget allowances for the assembly department of the Boyce Furniture Company for various numbers of direct labor hours are shown in the following table:

	10,000	10,500	11,000	11,500	12,000
Supervision.............	$ 1,800	$ 1,800	$ 1,800	$ 1,800	$ 1,800
Indirect labor.........	7,000	7,350	7,700	8,050	8,400
Supplies................	4,000	4,200	4,400	4,600	4,800
Power, fuel, and water..	1,000	1,050	1,100	1,150	1,200
Depreciation............	2,000	2,000	2,000	2,000	2,000
Space occupancy.........	3,000	3,000	3,000	3,000	3,000
General plant overhead..	2,800	2,800	2,800	2,800	2,800
Total...................	$21,600	$22,200	$22,800	$23,400	$24,000

Actual charges to the department for the month of March were as follows:

Supervision...................................... $ 1,900
Indirect labor...................................   7,700
Supplies..   4,020
Power, fuel, and water..........................   930
Depreciation....................................   1,950
Space occupancy.................................   3,000
General plant overhead..........................   3,000
Total.. $22,500

The actual volume of production during March totaled 10,500 direct labor hours.

a) Prepare a departmental overhead cost report for the month.
b) Comment on the possible causes of each of the variances shown on the report.

3.* The Riptide Company has a system of departmental flexible budgets for cost reporting. The fiscal year is divided into 13 "months" of four weeks each. The cost reports for one department for two successive months are summarized in the following table:

	Month 4			Month 5		
	Budget	Actual	Variance	Budget	Actual	Variance
Direct labor hours......	xxx	4,000	xxx	xxx	3,000	xxx
Nonproductive time, direct labor..........	$1,000	$ 800	$ 200	$ 750	$1,200	$(450)
Other indirect labor.....	4,000	3,700	300	3,500	3,600	(100)
Operating supplies......	600	650	(50)	450	430	20
Depreciation...........	2,000	2,100	(100)	2,000	2,150	(150)
Building service charges..	700	770	(70)	700	730	(30)
Total.................	$8,300	$8,020	$ 280	$7,400	$8,110	$(710)

a) Comment on the various items in these reports, indicating which items are likely to be of greatest significance in evaluating the cost control performance of the department supervisor.
b) Looking only at those items for which cost performance was poorer in month 5 than in month 4, what would be your reaction to the statement that the manager of this department had been lax in enforcing cost control during month 5? What remedial action would you suggest, if any?

4. Production volume in department X is measured by the number of standard direct labor hours earned by the department's output during any given period. Normal volume is 40,000 standard direct labor hours a month (each "month" consists of four consecutive weeks), and the flexible budget allowances for this volume of activity are:

---

* Solutions to problems marked with an asterisk can be found in Appendix B.

Supervision—fixed...............................	$ 2,000
Indirect labor—variable..........................	16,000
Supplies—variable................................	12,000
Maintenance—variable portion.....................	2,000
Maintenance—fixed portion........................	2,000
Depreciation—fixed...............................	10,000
Floor space charges—fixed........................	8,000

All variable cost elements are expected to vary in direct proportion to departmental output.

The department earned 45,000 standard direct labor hours during the "month" of March 2–March 29. The following costs were charged to the department during the month:

Supervision......................................	$ 2,100
Indirect labor...................................	19,000
Supplies..	13,200
Maintenance.....................................	3,900
Overtime premiums...............................	500
Depreciation....................................	10,000
Floor space charges.............................	8,500

a) Compute the month's flexible budget allowances and cost variances for each of these seven items. (Use the letters U and F to denote unfavorable and favorable variances.)

b) For each of the seven cost items listed above, indicate whether any variances are likely to be wholly or partly controllable by the department ment foreman. How might variances arise in the noncontrollable items?

5. The Broken Bend Manufacturing Company uses a standard costing system in its main factory. Direct labor and direct materials are charged to departmental work-in-process accounts which are credited for the standard cost of work completed. Factory overhead costs are also accumulated departmentally. Overhead budget allowances for department 23 are prepared on the following bases:

	Monthly Budget Allowance	
Account	Fixed	Variable per Standard DLH
Supervision..............................	$1,800	....
Inspection...............................	400	$0.160
Helpers..................................	600	0.500
Rework labor.............................	...	0.100
Labor downtime...........................	...	0.400
Other indirect labor.....................	...	0.040
Overtime premium........................	...	0.200
Supplies.................................	...	0.300
Power....................................	250	0.030
Vacation and holiday pay.................	204	0.300
Payroll taxes............................	168	0.312
Pensions.................................	140	0.260
Total....................................	$3,562	$2.602

During November, department 23 earned a total of 3,000 standard direct labor hours (DLH). The following transactions occurred during the month:

(1) Labor time tickets, extended at standard wage rates:

Direct labor	$11,620
Inspection	440
Helpers	1,960
Rework labor	540
Labor downtime	650
Other indirect labor	180

(2) Additional charges to department 23 from the factory payrolls for the month:

Supervision	$1,840
Overtime premiums	860

(3) Supplies issued, $310.
(4) Power consumed, $380.
(5) Additional payroll charges:
     Vacation and holiday pay: 8 percent of supervisory payrolls, 6 percent of all other departmental wages and salaries except overtime premium.
     Payroll taxes: 6 percent of departmental wages and salaries.
     Pensions: 5 percent of departmental wages and salaries.

a) Prepare a cost report for the month showing budget allowances, actual charges, and variances (to the nearest dollar).
b) Comment on any variances that are of particular interest.

CASE 17–1: SOCIETÀ RIGAZIO†

Società Rigazio manufactures a wide variety of metal products for industrial users in Italy and other European countries. Its head office is located in Milan and its mills in northern Italy provide about 80 percent of the company's production volume. The remaining 20 percent is produced in two factories—one in Lyon, France, and the other in Linz, Austria—both serving local markets exclusively through their own sales organizations.

Until 1964, the methods used by the Milan headquarters to review subsidiary operations were highly informal. The managing director of each subsidiary visited Milan twice a year, in October and in April, to review his subsidiary's performance and discuss his plans for the future. At other times the managing director would call or visit Milan to report on current developments or to request funds for specified purposes. These latter requests were usually submitted as a group, however, as part of the October meeting in Milan. By and large, if sales showed an increase over those of the previous year and if local profit margins did not decline, the

† Copyright 1965 by l'Institut pour l'Etude des Méthodes de Direction de l'Entreprise (IMEDE), Lausanne, Switzerland. Published by permission.

directors in Milan were satisfied and did nothing to interfere with the subsidiary manager's freedom to manage his business as he saw fit.

During 1963, Società Rigazio found itself for the first time in 12 years with falling sales volume, excess production capacity, rising costs, and a shortage of funds to finance new investments. In analyzing this situation, the Milan top management decided that one thing that was needed was a more detailed system of cost control in its mills, including flexible budgets for the overhead costs of each factory.

The Lyon mill was selected as a "pilot plant" for the development of the new system. Because the Lyon mill produced a wide variety of products in many production departments, it was not possible to prepare a single flexible budget for the entire mill. In fact, Mr. Spreafico, the company's controller, found that the work done in most of the production departments was so varied that useful cost-volume relationships could not even be developed on a departmental basis. He began, therefore, by dividing many of the departments into cost centers so that a valid single measure of work performed could be found for each one. Thus a department with both automatic and hand-fed cutting machines might be divided into two cost centers, each with a group of highly similar machines doing approximately the same kind of work.

The establishment of the cost centers did not change the responsibility pattern in the factory. Each department had a foreman who reported to one of two production supervisors; the latter were responsible directly to Mr. Forclas, the plant manager. Each foreman continued to be responsible for the operations of all the cost centers in his department. In some cases a cost center embraced an entire department, but most departments contained between two and five cost centers.

Once he had completed this task, Mr. Spreafico turned to the development of flexible budgets. For each cost center he selected the measure or measures of volume that seemed most closely related to cost (e.g., machine-hours) and decided what volume was normal for that cost center (e.g., 1,000 machine-hours per month). The budget allowance at the normal level of operations was to be used later as an element of standard product costs, but the budget allowance against which the foremen's performance was to be judged each month was to be the allowance for the volume actually achieved during that particular month.

Under the new system, a detailed report of overhead cost variances would be prepared in Lyon for the foreman in charge of a particular cost center and for his immediate superior, the production supervisor; a summary report, giving the total overhead variance for each cost center would be sent to the plant manager and to Mr. Duclos, the managing director of Rigazio France, S.A., Lyon. The Milan top management would not receive copies of any of these reports but would receive a monthly profit and loss summary, with comments explaining major deviations from the subsidiary's planned profit for the period.

The preparation of the budget formulas had progressed far enough by mid-1964 to persuade Mr. Spreafico to try them out on the September cost data. A top management meeting was then scheduled in Milan to discuss the new system on the basis of the September reports. Mr. Duclos and Mr. Forclas flew to Milan to attend this meeting, accompanied by the controller of Rigazio France and a production supervisor responsible for some 30 cost centers in the Lyon factory.

Mr. Enrico Montevani, Società Rigazio's managing director, opened the meeting by asking Mr. Spreafico to explain how the budget allowances were prepared. Mr. Spreafico began by saying that the new system was just in its trial stages and that many changes would undoubtedly be necessary before everyone was satisfied with it. "We started with the idea that the standard had to be adjusted each month to reflect the actual volume of production," he continued, "even though that might mean that we would tell the factory they were doing all right when in fact we had large amounts of underabsorbed overhead. In that case the problem would be that we had failed to provide enough volume to keep the plant busy, and you can't blame the foremen for that. When you have fixed costs, you just can't use a single standard cost per hour or per ton or per unit, because that would be too high when we're operating near capacity and too low when we're underutilized. Our problem, then, was to find out how overhead cost varies with volume so that we could get more accurate budget allowances for overhead costs at different production volumes.

"To get answers to this question, we first made some preliminary estimates at headquarters, based on historical data in the accounting records both here and in Lyon. We used data on wage rates and purchase prices from the personnel and purchasing departments to adjust our data to current conditions. Whenever we could, we used a mathematical formula known as a 'least squares' formula to get an accurate measure of cost variability in relation to changing volume, but sometimes we just had to use our judgment and decide whether to classify a cost as fixed or variable. I might add that in picking our formulas we tried various measures of volume and generally took the one that seemed to match up most closely with cost. In some cost centers we actually used two different measures of volume, such as direct labor hours and product tonnage, and based some of our budget allowances on one and some on the other. These estimates were then discussed with Mr. Forclas and his people at Lyon, and the revised budget formulas were punched into tabulating cards for use in monthly report preparation.

"Although you have a complete set of the cost center reports, perhaps we might focus on the one for cost center 2122 [Table 1]. You can see that we have used two measures of volume in this cost center, direct labor hours and product tonnage. During September we were operating at less than standard volume, which meant that we had to reduce the budget allowance to Fr. 12,617, which averaged out at Fr. 548.57 per ton. Our actual costs were almost exactly 10 percent higher than this, giving us an overall unfavorable performance variance of Fr. 1,265, or Fr. 55 per ton.

"I know that Mr. Duclos and Mr. Forclas will want to comment on this, but I'll be glad to answer any questions that any of you may have. Incidentally, I have brought along some extra copies of the formulas I used in figuring the September overhead allowances for cost center 2122, just in case you'd like to look them over." [See Table 2.]

Table 1

OVERHEAD COST SUMMARY—COST CENTER 2122
September 1964
(in francs)

	Standard Allowance at Normal Volume (500 Hours, 25 Tons)	Budgeted at Actual Volume (430 Hours, 23 Tons)	Actual, Month of September	(Over) Under Budget
Supervision.............	180	180	145	35
Indirect labor...........	1,500	1,360	1,610	(250)
Waiting time...........	105	90	177	(87)
Hourly wage guarantee....	70	60	30	30
Payroll taxes, etc.........	1,614	1,416	1,504	(88)
Materials and supplies.....	150	129	141	(12)
Tools..................	750	645	638	7
Maintenance...........	1,600	1,536	1,876	(340)
Scrap loss..............	2,110	1,941	2,456	(515)
Allocated costs..........	5,260	5,260	5,305	(45)
Total.................	13,339	12,617	13,882	(1,265)
Per ton................	533.56	548.57	603.57	(55.00)

a) Do you agree with Mr. Spreafico that 548.57 francs per ton (see Table 1) is a more meaningful standard for cost control than the "normal" cost of 533.56 francs?

b) Comment on the variances in Table 1. Which of these are likely to be controllable by the foreman? What do you think the production supervisor should have done on the basis of this report?

c) What changes, if any, would you make in the format of this report or in the basis on which the budget allowances are computed?

d) In developing the budget allowances, did Mr. Spreafico make any mistakes that you think he could have avoided? Does his system contain any features that you particularly like?

Table 2
FLEXIBLE BUDGET FORMULA—COST CENTER 2122
(in francs)

| | Allowance Factors | | |
	Fixed Amount per Month	Variable Rate	Remarks
Supervision............	180	....	Percent of foreman's time spent in cost center
Indirect labor...........	500	2.00/DLH	....
Waiting time...........	...	0.21/DLH	Wages of direct labor workers for time spent waiting for work
Hourly wage guarantee....	...	0.14/DLH	Supplement to wages of workers paid by the piece to give them guaranteed minimum hourly wage
Payroll taxes, etc........	204	2.82/DLH	Payroll taxes and allowances at 30% of total payroll, including direct labor payroll*
Materials and supplies.....	...	0.30/DLH	....
Tools..................	...	1.50/DLH	....
Maintenance............	800	32.00/ton	Actual maintenance hours used at predetermined rate per hour, plus maintenance materials used
Scrap loss..............	...	84.40/ton	Actual scrap multiplied by difference between materials cost and estimated scrap value per ton
Allocated costs..........	5,260	....	Actual cost per month, allocated on basis of floor space occupied

* Budgeted direct labor at standard volume, 500 hours at seven francs an hour; actual direct labor cost for September was 3,053 francs.

chapter **18**

Behavioral Factors
in Management Control

The planning and reporting systems outlined in the last four chapters constitute the essence of *responsibility accounting*. Their function is to cause people to behave in ways that help achieve the objectives of the organization. As a consequence, responsibility accounting systems must inevitably be based on certain assumptions about human behavior.

The main purpose of this chapter is to examine the validity of these assumptions and the effects that they have on the operation of the system. In the process we shall also look at some alternative assumptions that might be used in their place. The chapter will then close with a brief examination of some of the behavioral problems encountered in the administration of responsibility accounting systems.

THE ASSUMPTIONS OF RESPONSIBILITY ACCOUNTING

Despite variations from organization to organization, most of the following assumptions are implicit in responsibility accounting systems:

1. Organization personnel will strive to reach operational objectives embodied in the budget.
2. The budget should be set at a reasonably attainable level.
3. Managers should participate in the development of plans for their portions of the organization.
4. Managers should operate on the principle of management by exception.
5. Plans and reports should be prepared for all levels of management.
6. Managers should be charged or credited only for items within their control.

7. Dimensions of performance that cannot be measured conveniently in monetary terms are outside the accounting structure.

These assumptions in a sense are the behavioral properties prescribed by accounting writers. They may in fact describe quite poorly what actually takes place. Even so, discussion of these assumptions is likely to cover most of the major issues that arise in practice.[1]

Budgets as Operational Objectives

Responsibility accounting is built on the implicit assumption that management at all levels will strive to reach or surpass budgeted performance levels. In this view, the budget identifies the goals of the organization and establishes a standard of performance. For example, a sales budget might specify the emphasis to be placed on commercial and industrial sales and prescribe quotes for each sales sector. Once this has been done, the presumption is that people who have been delegated the responsibility for sales will attempt to achieve the budgeted objectives.

This assumption is so ingrained in the system that it was not even discussed in books and articles on budgetary control until very recently. The problem that went unrecognized for so long is that not everyone will be motivated automatically to achieve budgeted goals—that is, these goals may or may not be shared by the various individuals who make up the organization. An individual's goals are based on his needs, and achieving budgeted performance may make no contribution whatsoever to the satisfaction of these needs. If this is the case, then the budget will not motivate the individual. If an individual's goal and an organizational goal are identical, however, we say that *goal congruence* has been achieved.

For an individual to accept or *internalize* a budget or any other goal as his own, he must believe that achieving the goal will satisfy his needs better than not achieving it. A goal that an individual has internalized is known as his *aspiration level*, the performance level that he undertakes to reach.

Several factors influence the probability that an individual will internalize a budgeted goal as his level of aspiration. One of these is his past experience—success or failure in reaching budgeted goals. Another is the priority he assigns to the need for a sense of personal achievement. Still another is what he now expects to be able to achieve.[2] In short, the first implicit assumption of responsibility accounting is demonstrably

---

[1] A similar but not identical list can be found in G. H. Hofstede, *The Game of Budget Control* (Assen, The Netherlands: Koninklijke Van Gorcum & Comp., N.V., 1967), p. 62.

[2] For a discussion of these factors, see Timothy W. Costello and Sheldon S. Zalkind, *Psychology in Administration: A Research Orientation* (Englewood Cliffs, N.J.: Prentice-Hall, 1963), pp. 64–78.

wrong. The manager will not necessarily strive to achieve the budgeted performance level; his aspiration level can be quite different.

Reasonably Attainable Standards

A corollary of the first assumption concerns the performance level at which the budget is set. One way to assure efforts to attain budgeted performance levels is to set targets that are very easy to reach. Accounting writings have rejected this as suboptimal and have specified that the budgetary standards should represent performance levels that are described as "tight but attainable" or "reasonably attainable."

The assumption underlying this recommendation is that as long as standards or budgets do not exceed amounts that are reasonably attainable, the manager will internalize them. If budgets are set tighter than this, however, the manager and his subordinates will regard them as unrealistic and will cease to be motivated by them. In short, loose standards (in comparison with the reasonably attainable level) will lead to a slackening of effort; tight standards will be perceived as unrealistic and will fail to motivate anyone, except possibly in a negative direction.[3]

The process by which attainability is ascertained is not always specified. For direct production operations, the standard is assumed to emerge from analysis by experts. This was the basis for much of the standard cost data that we described in Chapter 12. Once these standards have been derived, it is assumed that the manager will accept them and try to meet them. Just how this is to be accomplished is a matter of managerial style, and not part of accounting.

We have already seen that the mere fact that a goal has been established by the organization does not assure that it will be shared by the individual making up the organization. This means that this assumption about the level at which budgeted performance is set assumes away the most crucial problem—how to get the manager to internalize such a standard.

Internalization of budgetary standards may not be the only way to motivate managers and workers to strive for higher performance levels. Stedry, for example, suggests that under certain conditions performance can be improved if higher management will impose unattainable standards on subordinates. Under laboratory conditions he found that his measurements of the subjects' aspiration levels were influenced by the level at which the imposed standards were set. He also found that performance that was significantly different from the aspiration level led to an adjustment of the aspiration level in the direction of the performance level that was actually achieved. As a result, he suggested that standards be changed

---

[3] For a concise expression of this point of view, see National Association of (Cost) Accountants, *How Standard Costs Are Used Currently* (New York, 1948), pp. 8–9.

from period to period so that they are met some of the time and slightly above the attainable level the rest of the time.[4] Hofstede also found that motivation is highest when standards are difficult to reach but are not regarded as impossible.[5]

Unfortunately, none of these studies indicates how to decide a priori what standard level will achieve an optimal motivation. Operating conditions are seldom identical in two successive periods and a standard that is motivational in one period may not work again. Furthermore, aspiration levels are individual, which means that budgetary standards would have to be different for each individual. Few managers, if any, will have either the time or the skill to carry this off.

Participation

Financial reporting on a responsibility basis is possible without the participation of subordinates in budget setting. This kind of participation, however, is usually regarded as the best way to get subordinate managers to internalize the standards embodied in the operating plans. That is, it is assumed to be an effective means of achieving goal congruence.[6] The argument is that the subordinate manager will be more likely to strive to achieve the planned results if he has developed the plan and has agreed with his superiors that it is feasible.

The Nature of Participation. Participation was an integral part of the periodic planning process described in Chapter 14. This description emphasized the subordinate's responsibility to originate proposals and the superior's responsibility to evaluate, question, and suggest changes.

These roles can also be reversed, at least in part. Superiors can propose, while their subordinates respond. If the system is to be participative, however, both parties must understand that proposals made by higher management provide a basis for discussion, not instructions. Participation means that decisions affecting a manager's operations are to some extent joint decisions of the manager and his superior. It is thus more than mere consultation, by which the superior informs himself of the manager's views but makes the decisions himself.

Participation does not mean that both the subordinate and his superior must be in full agreement on every decision. In some cases the superior will try to influence the decision but will not go as far as using his veto

---

[4] Andrew Stedry, *Budget Control and Cost Behavior* (Englewood Cliffs, N.J.: Prentice-Hall, 1960); and Andrew Stedry and E. Kay, *The Effects of Goal Difficulty on Performance: A Field Experiment* (Cambridge: Sloan School of Management, Massachusetts Institute of Technology, 1964).

[5] Hofstede, op. cit., pp. 152–56.

[6] This assumption is expressed or implied in many textbooks and in other writings on the subject. See, for example, Glenn A. Welsch, *Budgeting: Profit Planning and Control* (3d ed.; Englewood Cliffs, N.J.: Prentice-Hall, 1971), pp. 17, 22–23.

power, even though he feels that the subordinate is taking the wrong tack. More often, the superior's view will prevail and the subordinate will have to approve a plan that he feels is less than optimal. When this happens, something else must be present if goal congruence is not to be lost.

The Role of Group Dynamics. This is where group dynamics come into play. Every individual belongs to many groups—the family, the neighborhood, the work group, and so on. His aspiration level will depend in part on the levels prevailing in the groups that he belongs to.[7] The forces that operate within the group to achieve this result fall into the category of group dynamics.

Exhibit 18-1

POSITION OF THE BUDGETED MANAGER IN THE
SOCIAL NETWORK OF THE ORGANIZATION

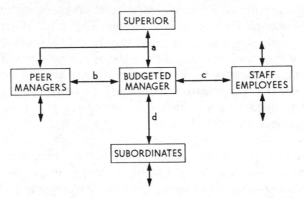

Group dynamics in work-related groups can have a significant effect on job-related aspiration levels. The manager, for example, belongs to at least four intersecting groups in connection with his work, as illustrated in Exhibit 18-1.[8] Here the organization is viewed as a network, with the manager at the center. He is seen sharing one group with his superior (labeled as group *a*), another with his subordinates (*d*), another with managers in similar positions elsewhere in the organization (*b*), and still another with the organization's staff (*c*). The dynamics of each of these groups will influence the manager's own goals, although not all to the same extent.

The amount of influence that group membership will have on the individual's aspiration levels depends on how strongly he is attracted to

---

[7] Kurt Lewin, "The Psychology of Success or Failure," in Harold J. Leavitt and Louis R. Pondy, *Readings in Managerial Psychology* (Chicago: University of Chicago Press, 1964), pp. 25-31.

[8] This diagram is from Hofstede, op. cit., p. 57. Two groups are said to intersect if some but not all members belong to both groups.

that group. The strength of the attraction determines the *cohesiveness* of the group, the degree to which individual members value their group membership.

The individual joins or remains in a group mainly because he believes that it will help him attain his own individual goals.[9] The greater the value placed on membershp, the greater will be the likelihood that different members will have similar goals. This is the individual's way of insuring his continued membership in the group. ("Membership" here means social acceptance rather than nominal affiliation in a formally constituted group). Valuing his own membership and anxious to keep it, the individual will tend to reject goals that he believes conflict with the goals prevailing in the group. He will tend to accept goals that seem to be consistent with those of others in the group. The more strongly the available information seems to indicate acceptance by others in a cohesive group, the greater the likelihood that the individual will adopt the goal as his own.

Other Influences. The patterns and effects of group dynamics are not the same at all times and in all situations. Different managers, for example, find that different managerial styles are suited to their different personalities. Similarly, different styles may be appropriate for different kinds of tasks or in different cultural environments. A democratic style may be completely inappropriate, at least in the short run, if the subordinate has never experienced it in situations that he regards as comparable.[10]

For example, the introduction of participative budgeting in a large electrical equipment factory some years ago was received very coldly by most of the first-level supervisors, despite enthusiastic support from their superiors and the presence of a highly sensitive, multifunctional installation team in the factory for a period of many months. The reason seemed to be that the foremen were reluctant to accept the risk of censure for failure to achieve targets that they had set themselves. Without participation, blame could always be assigned elsewhere, at least in the foremen's minds. It took many months to rid most of the foremen of this fear.

Interviews with the top managers of a number of Europe-based multinational companies revealed similar tendencies. They reported that their managers in some countries, even at fairly high levels, were reluctant to participate in budgetary planning. Those in other countries, given the same top management environment, were both ready and eager for greater autonomy.

The Role of Participation. Several conclusions about the role of participation should emerge from this discussion. First, participation does

---

[9] Edwin H. Caplan, "Behavioral Assumptions of Management Accounting," *Accounting Review*, July 1966, pp. 496–509; also in William J. Bruns, Jr., and Don T. DeCoster, *Accounting and Its Behavioral Implications* (New York: McGraw-Hill Book Co., 1969), pp. 113–30.

[10] This was one of the findings from Hofstede's study (op. cit., pp. 188–89).

not automatically produce goal congruence. The gap between the individual's goals and those of the organization may be too great to be bridged. Second, conditions may be such that a more authoritarian managerial style will be more effective in raising the aspiration levels of subordinates. In other words, participation may not be the only means of validating the first assumption of responsibility accounting, the willingness of managers to internalize budgeted performance standards.

The strength of participation comes from two sources. First, it can be used to strengthen the bonds among the members of the group—that is, increase cohesiveness by providing more effective communication. Second, it can increase the visibility of the progress that each member of the group is making toward internalization of a goal. The first of these increases the desire of the individual to share the goals of others in the group; the second increases his ability to do this.[11]

Management by Exception

The emphasis on variances in accounting reports reflects the assumption that all is well if standards are being met. If this view is correct, management should devote its attention only to those areas in which significant variances are observed. This is the essence of the method of allocating executive time known as management by exception.

The danger in this is that the system will be perceived as emphasizing failure, with only an unusual degree of success coming to the attention of management at higher levels. Although meeting the budgetary standard represents successful performance, it receives no attention at all. Furthermore, the recognition given to favorable variances often seems to be weaker than the response to unfavorable variances.

Seeing these evidences of apparent bias, subordinates are led to view the system as punitive rather than informative. A common result is that people become defensive. They may question the fairness of the standard or use various devices to cover up variances as they arise and prevent them from being reported.

The focus on failures can also place a premium on cautious behavior. This may be consistent with the organization's goals, but not necessarily. For example, a food manufacturer cannot allow a foreman to try to re-

---

[11] For a more complete discussion of the role of participation in the budgeting process, see Selwyn Becker and David Green, Jr., "Budgeting and Employee Behavior," *Journal of Business*, October 1962, pp. 392–402; Andrew W. Stedry, "Budgeting and Employee Behavior: A Reply," *Journal of Business*, April 1964, pp. 195–202; and Selwyn Becker and David Green, Jr., "Budgeting and Employee Behavior: A Rejoinder to a 'Reply'," *Journal of Business*, April 1964, pp. 203–5. These three papers are also in Bruns and DeCoster, op. cit., pp. 327–56. Additional discussion can be found in George J. Benston, "The Role of the Firm's Accounting System for Motivation," *Accounting Review*, April 1963, pp. 347–54 (also in Bruns and DeCoster, pp. 161–72).

duce cost by departing from the standard procedures used to kill bacteria, no matter how big the potential cost saving. The penalty to the company for failure of this experiment could be catastrophic, and any such experiement must take place in a formal research context.

In a research organization, in contrast, management may want to encourage the research staff to try new approaches that raise immediate costs but offer the possibility of completing projects successfully well ahead of time. Since these approaches may not work, however, the result may be unfavorable cost variances. If these are emphasized unduly, the research staff is likely to play it safe. This may have serious effects on the company's competitive position.[12]

This suggests that care should be taken to minimize the punitive role of the reporting system and emphasize its usefulness to the subordinate himself. Furthermore, major efforts should be made to emphasize positive as well as negative aspects of performance, to provide "positive reinforcement."[13] Still another desirable action would be to make sure that the organization's objectives have been identified and that measurements of progress toward objectives that are difficult to state in financial terms are made and communicated to the executives concerned.

Multilevel Plans and Reports

The performance of the organization as a whole is the sum total or product of performance in the various responsibility centers. Managers at lower levels, no less than their superiors, need to plan and monitor the activities within their jurisdictions. The responsibility accounting structure therefore is extended to the lowest level of management.

If a manager's performance is poor and his efforts to improve fail, frequent reminders of his continuing failures are more likely to reduce his aspiration levels than to raise them. Furthermore, if these same reports go to his superior, the latter will have more occasions to review and criticize his performance. This will create friction between the manager and his superior and make achieving goal congruence more difficult.

A lesser danger is that the system may lead the first-line supervisor to try to manage more by responding to the reports and less by direct contact with the operations under his control. Reports and formal plans are designed to supplement on-the-spot observation, not supplant it, and this must be made clear.

---

[12] In their study of large research organizations, Sayles and Chandler found a good deal of evidence of these tendencies. Leonard R. Sayles and Margaret K. Chandler, *Managing Large Systems: Organizations for the Future* (New York: Harper & Row, 1971), p. 299.

[13] Jacob G. Birnberg and Raghu Nath, "Implications of Behavioral Science for Managerial Accounting," *Accounting Review*, July 1967, p. 478; also in Bruns and DeCoster, op. cit., p. 21.

Neither of these is inherent in the accounting system itself. Both can arise only if the system is misconstrued by management. The accountant may be able to do something about both of them, however, by emphasizing the objectives of the reports; by working with managers at all levels to make the reports seem less mechanistic, less impersonal; and by helping managers to identify the origins of variances that have arisen. To accomplish this, the accountant should play the role of a facilitator rather than that of an appraiser of the manager's performance.

The Controllability Criterion

Responsibility accounting systems attempt to exclude noncontrollable variances from periodic performance reports. This may have two undesirable effects. First, it may provide incentives to try to shift responsibility. If the manager can get an unfavorable variance classified as outside his jurisdiction, he can improve his own performance record. Second, overemphasis on controllability may lead to a greater compartmentalization of the organization. Nowhere does the responsibility accounting structure recognize organizational interdependence. It may even increase interdepartmental conflicts, as each manager seeks to improve his own record or protect himself from blame, without regard for what happens elsewhere.

For example, sales and production ordinarily take place in different departments in a manufacturing firm. One department gets the orders; the other fills them. The sales force wants to be able to offer its customers the widest possible choice of products and features, all for prompt delivery. The task of the production manager, on the other hand, is a lot easier with long production runs and a steady delivery schedule. This requires fewer products, long lead times, and few or no special modifications to meet individual customer's needs. The production manager complains that the sales manager accepts orders that are very expensive to fill; the sales manager objects to the production manager's inflexibility and insensitivity to marketing problems. Both are right; the problem is how to get both men to consider both points of view.

Cooperation is also important within a single functional area such as marketing or production or research. Sayles and Chandler, for example, found that an emphasis on departmental responsibility in a large research organization seemed to be incompatible with the need for cooperation.[14]

Many companies have attempted to obtain the necessary coordination among production, sales, and other functions by appointing product managers, one for each product. The product manager sees the interrelationships and attempts to reconsile the needs of the various parties. The project manager in a research organization has the same job, although usually with more authority than most product managers have.

---

[14] Sayles and Chandler, op. cit., pp. 299–304.

Accountants have not tried to attack this problem to any significant extent. One possibility is to issue reports on a project, product or program basis rather than for individual departments. Thus a factory manager might get several reports, one for each product he manufactures. Each of these reports would include sales figures as well as engineering and production costs. The implication would be that responsibility is shared rather than divided. Similarly, each department foreman might get a report or reports showing total performance in a group of departments as well as a separate report for his own department.

The impact of the controllability criterion is not primarily an accounting problem. The partial solution suggested in the last paragraph is really an organizational solution; the accountant cannot make this change unless line management has decided to enlarge the boundary of the responsibility center itself and introduce group responsibility.

It may even be that the positive benefits of interdepartmental conflict make it undesirable to try to eliminate it entirely, even if that were possible. Interdepartmental conflict may be better than intradepartmental conflict, for example, and may be a relatively harmless way of letting the manager let off steam. It may also be a way of getting problems out in the open where they can at least be attacked, and maybe even solved.

Management's problem is to decide how much conflict is desirable. the accountant's problem is to design the reporting system so that it doesn't produce more conflict than management wants. Strong interdepartmental arguments centering on accounting reports should at least lead to a reappraisal of the reporting structure.

Monetary Measurements

The accounting structure typically ignores dimensions of performance that cannot be measured conveniently in monetary terms. Consequently, only financial performance is measured periodically, routinely, and throughout the organization. It is not that other dimensions are unimportant or even that the accountant thinks them unimportant; it is merely that they are difficult to measure.

The danger here is that managers will be motivated to emphasize those things that are measured to the neglect of things that are not. For example, the manager of a staff department may be led to concentrate exclusively on minimizing the current cost of performing his current functions. By ignoring the development of personnel in his department, however, he may be depleting his human capital. This may not show up in the accounting reports for several years.[15]

One possibility is to develop a set of nonfinancial measures to supple-

---

[15] For a discussion of the problems of accounting for human capital, see R. Lee Brummet, Eric G. Flamholtz, and William C. Pyle, "Human Resource Measurement—A Challenge for Accountants," *Accounting Review*, April 1968, pp. 217–24.

ment the financial measures. If such measures could be derived, the periodic reports could give them equal prominence, reducing the danger of so-called "dysfunctional" consequences.[16]

Assuming that the difficult problems of measurement can be solved, the major difficulty with multivariate reporting is that it does not identify priorities. For example, the manager needs guidance when faced with a proposal that will reduce cost but increase product delivery time. Operations research models typically try to provide this guidance by converting product delivery time (and other nonfinancial measures) into monetary terms, but this is not always possible.

To resolve this issue, the company might try to develop a composite measure of performance, with each dimension assigned a weight in proportion to management's perceived priorities. The outlook for this solution is bleak, however. Managerial weighting systems are implicit rather than explicit, and extremely difficult to translate into numerical form. Even more fundamentally, the implicit weights refuse to stay constant. Market share may be the watchword today, but a share-oriented composite measure of performance will be obsolete when cost-cutting becomes the order of the day.[17]

In short, no final solution to this problem has yet been found. A useful first step is to identify the major dimensions of performance, whether measurable or not. If this has been done, each of these can be incorporated into the performance review process. The accountant can contribute by seeking ways of measuring the nonfinancial aspects; higher management can help by trying to make the managerial reward structure more visible. In the final analysis, however, the process has to remain fluid, somewhat subjective, and the individual manager can never wholly escape the task of estimating the weights implicit in the structure.

BEHAVIORAL PROBLEMS IN SYSTEM ADMINISTRATION

Undesired behavioral responses to budgetary control systems sometimes arise from the methods of implementation rather than from any inherent defects. Two possible sources of such responses are:

1. Insensitivity on the part of the budgeting staff.
2. The use of budgets as pressure devices.

---

[16] The General Electric Company made an ambitious attempt to do this. See Robert W. Lewis, "Measuring, Reporting and Appraising Results of Operations with Reference to Goals, Plans and Budgets," in *Planning, Managing and Measuring the Business*, Series II, Business Planning and Control, Report No. 3 (New York: Controllership Foundation, 1955), pp. 29–41. See also Stanley E. Seashore and Ephraim Yuchtman, "Factorial Analysis of Organizational Performance," *Administrative Science Quarterly*, December 1967, pp. 377–95.

[17] V. F. Ridgeway, "Dysfunctional Consequences of Performance Measurement," *Administrative Sciences Quarterly*, September 1956, pp. 240–47.

Insensitivity of the Budgeting Staff

A frequent complaint is that the accountant or budget department staffer is insensitive to operating problems and to the needs of the operating man. In many of his contacts with the operating manager, the budget man appears to play an adversary's role. His job is to criticize budget proposals, to investigate variances, to enforce compliance with prescribed procedures. In short, he is paid to find fault with the operating manager, and the more faults he finds the more successful he is likely to be.

Furthermore, the budget man is likely to report his findings in the first instance to his boss or to higher levels of operating management rather than to the first-line supervisor himself. Otherwise, he has no proof of his own productivity. The supervisor is likely to resent this and take out his resentment in a refusal to cooperate with the staff man.

As a consequence, the accountant creates defensiveness, hostility, and conflict. The accountant who is aware of these problems can avoid them or at least minimize their impact. One way is by changing his attitude toward his job and toward the operating executive. Unfortunately, some accountants do take great pleasure in finding and reporting others' mistakes. A better way to handle it is with the man who made the error, so that he can do something about it.

A closely related possibility is to change most accountants' formal role to that of facilitators. In this way, most of the accounting people would spend their time providing feedback and working with the line manager on his problems and decisions. For example, the accountant can try to make sure that the operating manager has adequate technical help before budgetary plans are submitted, thereby reducing the number of defects that will be uncovered during the review process. Similarily, if he is engaged in post-mortem investigations, he can incorporate in his reports the steps that the manager is taking to respond to variances that have arisen.

Staff-line problems cannot be completely avoided by devices such as these. Plans do have to be reviewed and performance does have to be monitored. The effect should be to eliminate conflict where it is unnecessary and where it serves no purpose. This should keep the unintended responses within manageable limits.[18]

Budgets as Pressure Devices

In a landmark study two decades ago, Argyris found that first-line production supervisors regarded the budget as an effort by higher man-

---

[18] For a very perceptive set of observations about the relationships between accountants and operating personnel, see Herbert A. Simon, George Kozmetsky, Harold Guetzkow, and Gordon Tyndall, *Centralization vs. Decentralization in*

agement to maintain pressure on the organization.[19] With the budget set at a level that was difficult to reach, the supervisors felt the strain of efforts to translate this pressure into improved performance. Pressure took the form of higher management's demands for constant improvement of performance. The budget was the vehicle through which these demands were made; periodic comparisons with budgeted performance were used to enforce them.

One effect of this kind of pressure was to increase output or reduce cost. Another was to increase the amount of pressure *against* improvement. As performance improved, the counterpressure increased until the two forces were equally strong and further improvement became impossible. Tensions tend to mount under these circumstances, as management has to work harder to keep the gains that have already been made. Grievances mount and the relationships between the supervisor and his subordinates deteriorate.

Argyris and others have found that supervisors react to pressure in various but predictable ways. One response is to internalize the pressure by working harder, checking on subordinates more often, in effect trying to transmit the pressure to the next level. This tends to produce the results described in the preceding paragraph.

The supervisor's capacity for internalization is limited, particularly when it ceases to lead to improved results. At this point, and even before, the supervisor is likely to seek ways of relieving the pressure. One way is to unite with his subordinates against "the boss." That is, pressure may lead him to identify more with the manager-subordinate group (group *d* in Exhibit 18–1) and less with the manager-superior group. By doing this, he can create problems for the superior and thereby transmit the pressure back up the line where it came from.

In his efforts to relieve pressure, the manager is also likely to try to transmit it laterally to his fellow supervisors and to staff personnel. In other words, he will identify less with the manager-peer and manager-staff groups that appear in Exhibit 18–1. This is likely to be reflected in increased interdepartmental warfare and in worsened relationships with the staff. Instead of seeking cooperative solutions to problems, the manager is likely to try to avoid the risk of failure and to try to shift to others the blame for any failures that do occur. The staff gave poor advice, other departments didn't do their job properly, the staff interfered and therefore is responsible for what went wrong—in short, failure is attributed anywhere as long as it is outside the supervisor's own department.

Organizing the Controller's Department (New York: Controllership Foundation, 1954).

[19] Chris Argyris, *The Impact of Budgets on People* (New York: Controllership Foundation, 1952); and "Human Problems with Budgets," *Harvard Business Review,* January–February 1953, pp. 97–110.

Another way of relieving pressure is to seek ways of beating the system. Methods improvements will not be disclosed to staff or higher management to avoid a subsequent tightening of standards. Materials will be hoarded for use when variances are unfavorable. Records will be falsified by misclassifying costs or misrepresenting output.[20]

It should be recognized that the pressure that the supervisor transmits to his subordinates may not come from higher up. Argyris found that some supervisors use the budget as an excuse for an authoritarian leadership style. By blaming the budget, which can't answer back, the supervisor hopes to prod his workers to do better. By making the budget department the villain of the piece, the supervisor hopes to avoid unpleasant conflicts with his subordinates. It is an easy way out, but it may lead to the same kinds of tensions and counterpressures that we cited earlier as likely responses by the supervisor when pressure is exerted on him.

Argyris's basic solution to the problems raised by pressure was to find ways to reduce the pressure. One avenue was to train budget staff people in human relations, to make them more aware of problems that might arise so that they would not unwittingly contribute to the belief that the budget was there to place the supervisor under pressure.

The main problem, however, stems from management's use of the budget as a pressure device or—what amounts to the same thing—from the supervisor's belief that management is using it in this way. The solution to this must focus on the line manager rather than on the budgeting staff.

SUMMARY

The responsibility accounting structure is based on a number of implicit assumptions about the behavior of individuals and groups making up the organization. The most fundamental of these is that individuals will strive to achieve the performance levels represented in the current operating budget. The mechanism that is relied upon to accomplish this is participation in managerial decision making by managers at all operating levels. Participation is designed to get the managers to internalize the budgetary standards, thereby converting them into personal aspiration levels.

This process is more effective if members of the organization are highly cohesive. If the budgetary standards are accepted by the group, each member of the group is more likely to accept them for himself.

The accounting structure also contains potentially destructive elements. Management by exception and the concept of controllability, for example, can lead to excessive departmentalization of effort and counterproductive efforts to shift blame or the chance of being blamed. Furthermore, the very nature of the accountant's job creates opportunities for

[20] Melville Dalton, *Men Who Manage* (New York: John Wiley & Sons, 1959).

conflict with operating personnel. If senior management tries to use the budget as a pressure device, these opportunities multiply.

Solutions to most of the behavioral problems that arise in connection with the budgetary control system lie outside the accounting area. The accountant can contribute to these solutions, however: first, by being more sensitive to the needs and attitudes of operating personnel; and second, by devising methods of measurement and reporting that will further the control objectives of operating management.

EXERCISES AND PROBLEMS

1. Campo Motor Parts, Inc. manufactures a wide variety of automotive parts and supplies. A basic plan standard costing system is in use in each of its factories.

One of the company's lines is a line of windshield wipers for trucks and passenger vehicles. The windshield wiper consists of four principal mechanical parts: the blade, the blade holder, the wiper arm, and a mounting bracket. The blade holders and wiper arms are made in the metal shop, the mounting brackets are made in the casting department, and the blades are purchased from a rubber manufacturer.

Holders, arms, brackets and blades are assembled in the assembly department. The blades, blade holders, and arms are brought together in a subassembly. This is then fitted on a mounting bracket. If the subassembly fits, the assembled mechanism is placed in a box and readied for transfer to the shipping room, where it is mated with an electrical actuating mechanism that is produced elsewhere in the factory.

Each batch of parts is inspected before delivery to the assembly department. Slight flaws are difficult to detect, however, and often show up only as the units are being assembled. A particularly common problem is a poor fit between the arm and blade assembly and the mounting bracket. This can be corrected by the assembler, but the correction takes from 10 to 60 seconds.

The standard assembly time includes provision for a normal percentage of defective parts and subassemblies. Whenever a sizable unfavorable labor quantity variance arises, however, the chief of assembly is inclined to claim that defective parts were the cause. The head of the castings department says that process control in his shop is so tight that the mounting brackets cannot be at fault. The metal shop foreman, for his part, believes that the chief of assembly is merely trying to pass the buck. If excessive defects do occur, however, he says that they must come from the casting process.

The plant manager has learned to live with this kind of bickering, but lately the problem has become much worse. Several months ago the company introduced a new type of wiper, requiring much tighter-fitting parts. Engineered standard times were established for the new model on the basis of time studies. Labor variances in the castings department and the metal shop have been negligible; in the assembly department they have been large and unfavorable. The product manager insists that if these cost problems cannot be licked he will subcontract the work to an outside firm. The plant manager doesn't want this to happen and has asked your advice.

a) Is it likely that the standard costing system is partly responsible for the high costs of the new model? Give reasons to support your point of view.

b) What changes, if any, would you make in the measurement and reporting system to alleviate the problems that have arisen? Give reasons for the position you have taken.

2.† Ray Carlson, president of Scientific Equipment Manufacturing Company, wants to introduce standard costing into his company's factory. As a result of his participation in a two-week management development course at a nearby university, Mr. Carlson is convinced that some kind of standard costing system is just what he needs to strengthen his control over factory cost. The factory now has a simple job order costing system, and no one has ever attempted to establish standard costs.

Scientific Equipment makes and sells a line of highly technical equipment for industrial users. The company is located in a small midwestern city with a population of 80,000 people. Quality, or the supplier's ability to meet exacting technical specifications, is a major consideration for most of the company's customers when deciding where to place an order.

Production is organized on a job order basis, and orders are typically manufactured to customer specifications. Most of the orders can be filled by producing items of standard design and specifications, or items which require only minor modifications of the standard designs. Jobs requiring major redesign and the use of nonstandardized production techniques amount to 30 percent of the total. The cost estimates that Mr. Carlson uses in developing price bids for this kind of nonstandardized business have been close to the actual costs of filling the orders in most cases, or at least close enough to satisfy Mr. Carlson.

Scientific Equipment is a small company, with about 75 employees. The two largest segments of the work force are 30 machine operators and 20 assemblers. The machine operators are all men. Their jobs require a considerable degree of skill and experience. The assemblers, on the other hand, are all women. Their jobs are relatively routine but require a good deal of concentration to avoid costly assembly defects. The employees generally lunch together in a nearby cafeteria. Many of the men socialize off the job, and so do several of the women.

Mr. Carlson is considering engaging a consulting firm to develop and install a standard costing system. A letter from the managing partner of the consulting firm contained the following key paragraphs:

"In order to motivate people to their maximum productivity, standards must be based upon the company's best workers and what they can achieve. If the standard were lower, the high performers could meet it too easily and it wouldn't offer sufficient motivation for the low performers. I'd set the standard at the level of performance of the top 10 to 15 percent of your employees. This would establish a high aspiration level for your people and, therefore, motivate their best efforts.

"I also suggest that superior performance be well rewarded. This means

---

† From a problem by Eric Flamholtz.

that employees who exceed standard should receive a substantial bonus, while those who do not exceed standard should receive no bonus."

Since Mr. Carlson does not feel qualified to evaluate this kind of statement, he has contacted the faculty member who conducted the sessions on standard costing at the local university (you), asking what you think of the philosophy underlying the proposed system.

a) Prepare a reply to Mr. Carlson. Should he engage the consultant?
b) If you agree with the consultant's basic approach, outline how you would implement it at Scientific Equipment Manufacturing Company. If you disagree with the consultant, state the basic principles underlying an alternative system and outline how you would go about developing a standard costing system for this company.

CASE 18–1: FABRIQUES DE TABACS LUXEMBOURGEOISES, S.A.†

Fabriques de Tabacs Luxembourgeoises, S.A. was one of the first to adopt the new uniform standard costing and reporting plan designed at parent company headquarters in New York. "I was very enthusiastic," Sam Burton, the Belgian company's controller, said later. "I could see why the head office needed to standardize, and I thought we could get a good deal out of it here, too. I still think so, but most of our local people still prefer their old ways and don't really use the reports we prepare. I'm beginning to wonder whether we couldn't cut back a little and save some money."

Fabriques de Tabacs Luxembourgeoises is a wholly owned subsidiary of Union Tobacco Company, Inc., a United States corporation. It has about 450 employees and an annual sales turnover of about Fr. 100 million, divided among about 15 different brands of cigarettes.‡ The company manufactures all of its own cigarettes from imported tobacco leaf.

The Reporting System

"Most of our reports are prepared for New York headquarters," Mr. Burton said. "All of the Union Tobacco subsidiaries use the same forms for these reports, for reasons that should be obvious. Our main report in this group is the monthly profit and loss statement. The form itself has too many technical terms for you, but I have prepared a simplified version that you might find useful [Table 1].

---

† This case has been extracted from a longer and more comprehensive case on this same company. Copyright 1969 by l'Institut pour l'Etude des Méthodes de Direction de l'Entreprise (IMEDE), Lausanne, Switzerland. Field research for the case was carried out primarily by Mr. Peter Mollet of the management services staff of Price Waterhouse & Co., Paris. The company's name and other superficial details have been disguised. Reproduced by permission.

‡ At the time this case was written, the Belgian franc was worth about $0.02.

Table 1

FABRIQUES DE TABACS LUXEMBOURGEOISES, S.A.
Monthly Profit and Loss Statement†
(monetary totals in thousands of francs)

	Budget		Actual		Variance
Sales of cigarettes (in thousands)	304,035		303,826		* 209
	Value	Average	Value	Average	Value
Turnover.....................	319,649	1,051	313,400	1,031	*6,249
Turnover and excise taxes..........	244,795	805	240,448	791	4,347
Net turnover...................	74,854	246	72,952	240	*1,902
Total variable cost.................	34,384	113	34,592	114	* 208
Leaf & casing.................	20,440	67	21,050	69	* 610
Duty........................	5,314	17	5,452	18	* 138
Filter & wrapping..............	7,540	25	7,520	25	20
Royalty......................	570	2	570	2	...
Volume/mix variance...........	520	2	....	...	520
Contribution	40,470	133	38,360	126	*2,110
Other operating exp.	21,770	72	24,210	79	*2,440
Prod. sal. & wages.............	7,590	25	7,530	25	60
Other production	3,270	11	3,540	11	* 270
Marketing	5,790	19	6,490	21	* 700
Advertising	2,320	8	3,720	12	*1,400
Administration................	2,800	9	2,930	10	* 130
Operating profit..................	18,700	61	14,150	47	*4,550
Other income and expense (net)......	1,050		680		* 370
Profit before tax.................	19,750		14,830		*4,920
Taxation.......................	7,940		5,410		2,530
Net profit......................	11,810		9,420		*2,390

† The actual form has an identical set of columns for year-to-date figures, plus a pair of columns for the actual results of the comparable period (year-to-date) in the previous year. These columns have been omitted here to facilitate study of the line-to-line relationships within the report. "Turnover" is the local term for sales revenues.
* Unfavorable.

"You can see that we place great emphasis on the variances. Each month I attach to the report a detailed commentary on the variances, running about two pages. Our accounting system is designed to collect some of the information on which this commentary is based, but we also have to ask the production and sales people for information that we can't get otherwise. We can do a lot more now than we used to be able to, though, thanks to our new standard costing system. I can give you a copy of our standard costing manual, if you think that would be helpful."

The Standard Cost System

Union Tobacco's standard costing manual states that the main purpose of standard costing is to permit the calculation of variances, "thus providing Management with detailed control information." The manual continues:

Although normally Standard Costing relates only to expenditure, it is proposed that the system shall be applied in the Group to Turnover, Excise and all Variable Expenses which are taken into account in arriving at Contribution.

The Production Standards—e.g., quantity of cigarettes produced from a kilo of Leaf, processing Gains/Losses, etc.—must be realistic and capable of achievement. . . . Once the Production Standards are agreed, it is the Accountant's responsibility to establish Standard Cost averages for each stage of processing and for each element of Variable Expense for each Brand and Packing.

At each stage of processing, Standard Production Performance is compared to actual Production Performance, both valued at Standard averages. The differences, or variances, after allowing for Standard Gains/Losses, etc., are therefore obtained.

It is these variances concerned with processing performance which are of interest to Factory Management, for they represent the deviation of Actual Performance from the Standard Performance they have set themselves. It is Factory Management initially who will give the reasons and the action which has been taken or is to be taken where necessary. Such action may, in the first instance, be confined to improving the Actual Performance in future months. On the other hand, as Standard Costing gives a continuous record of Variances, experience and time may indicate that a re-examination of the Production Standard is necessary.

It is important that the Variances arising at the various stages are examined in total as well as individually. It may be that after the Master Budget is prepared a decision is taken to introduce a cheaper packing material. This would produce a favorable Price Variance but because of a much higher wastage in processing, the value of an unfavorable Usage Variance may be considerably greater than the favorable Price Variance. Equally there could be a waste of Labor arising from constant machine stoppages.

The number of Variances which are reported must obviously be influenced by Management's need to measure effectively Actual Performance and a comprehensive list of the types of Variances is given below. Not all of these Variances would arise in any one month and some of them would only arise infrequently.

Variable Production Cost Summary Sheet

Variances from standard variable production cost (i.e., materials costs) are calculated and analyzed for each brand each month. These variances are then summarized and reported on a variable production cost summary sheet like the one illustrated in Table 2. This report is not forwarded to

Table 2

FABRIQUES DE TABACS LUXEMBOURGEOISES, S.A.

Variable Production Cost Summary Sheet for August
(in Luxembourg francs)

	Leaf and Casing	Duty	Wrapping	Filter	Royalty	Total
In-process, start.................	5,978,005.30	1,494,719.90	12,026.80	42,039.00		7,526,791.50
Issues............................	20,459,417.20	5,115,228.50	4,232,628.80	2,854,365.20	565,260.20	33,226,899.90
Total.............................	26,437,423.00	6,609,948.40	4,244,655.60	2,896,404.20	565,260.20	40,753,691.40
In-process, end...................	5,728,711.10	1,432,443.30	24,799.10	65,570.50		7,251,524.00
"Actual" value of material used...	20,708,711.90	5,177,505.10	4,219,856.50	2,830,833.70	565,260.20	33,502,167.40
Variances:						
Opening stock...........			*0.50			*0.50
Price...................	*152,100.30	*38,001.80	59,673.10	19,703.70		*110,725.30
Reweighed...............	*133,635.50	*33,287.60	:::::	:::::		*166,923.10
Formula.................	*12,848.00	*3,216.50	:::::	:::::		*16,064.50
Substitution............	*116,553.50	*30,017.20	:::::	:::::		*146,570.70
Transfers...............	16,133.70	4,038.60				20,172.30
Processing & usage......	18,414.50	4,698.10	*3,941.40	*54,584.60		*35,413.40
Yield...................	*239,295.90	*60,558.20				*299,854.10
Fractional..............	*154.90	39.60	*27.70	25.60		*117.40
	*620,039.90	*156,305.00	55,703.50	*34,855.30		*755,496.70
Standard value of material used...	20,088,672.00	5,021,200.10	4,275,560.00	2,795,978.40	565,260.20	32,746,670.70

* Unfavorable.

company headquarters in New York and need not be prepared unless local management finds it useful.

The importance of this report is stressed in the standard costing manual:

The Summary is a most important part of the Standard Costing procedure for it enables Management to see at a glance the Variances between Actual Performance valued at Actual and Standard for each element of Cost and in total. From the working papers significant Variances can be broken down by Blends, Brands or type of Wrapping Material to enable Management to take corrective action where necessary.

While the Variable Production Cost Summary Sheet gives to Factory and Other Management the overall Variances from Standard by types for each element of material, etc. used in Production it will be necessary to demonstrate these in greater detail for Management.

The complete detail is shown on the Working Sheets which have been designed so that Management can see clearly from them the individual variances; for example, the Standard Wrapping Cost Sheet shows for each type of material used the variances both in Units and Value. This obviates the need to list Variances separately on a further Schedule. It should therefore be sufficient to pass these working papers to Factory Management who will, on returning them to the Accountant, attach a note with their comments and action where necessary.

Comments on the System

"As I told you before," Mr. Burton said recently, "the local reporting structure is a matter for each local company to decide. Two years ago, a team from New York headquarters visited each subsidiary to explain the newly developed standard costing and budgetary control system and to ask each of us to adopt it for our own internal operations.

"Many of our sister companies said no, but we put it into effect here in Luxembourg in record time. We felt then, and still feel, that the new system was the only way to get an adequate explanation of the differences between actual results and the budgeted figures. We also thought it would have other local benefits in improving cost control in the factory and in pointing out opportunities for cost reduction.

"It is still too early to tell whether we're going to get the full benefit from this system, but I am hopeful. I just wish that more of our people would take an interest in the reports. M. de la Salle, our managing director, does ask me to investigate particularly large variances from time to time, but he's the only one. So far, we have always found that the necessary remedial action has already been taken or that the variance itself was the product of unrealistic standards or what my people like to call 'hiccups' in the system."

Jack Williams, the deputy managing director with primary responsibility for marketing, makes no use of the monthly variance reports. "I'm no production man, and I leave that end of things to Bob Waterman. Manufacturing costs are very important in this business, but I'm satisfied that he is doing a good job. I see no reason to poke my nose in there."

Waterman has been production manager in Luxembourg for the past 15 years. He is outspokenly skeptical of the value of the new standard costing and reporting system in general, and of the variable production cost summary sheet in particular. "You can't run a factory from behind a desk," he says. "Even if you could, you can't do anything with data that reach you weeks later. When something is going wrong, you have to correct it on the spot, not when the accounting department gets around to telling you about it.

"The secret of success in this business is to make the right cigarette for the market, using as little tobacco as you can—none at all, if you can get away with it. What I mean, of course, is that we have to control our tobacco losses very closely. We can't eliminate them completely, but our job is to keep them at a minimum. The difference between a 4 percent and a 5 percent loss factor can be as much as half a million francs a month.

"The only way that I can control my tobacco losses is on a mix-by-mix basis. My girls weigh each batch before and after each operation. They also collect and weigh the sweepings and rejects. If we're out of line with previous runs on the same brand, we look into it right away.

"With many brands and several kinds of packaging, all this work on standard costs is not worthwhile. In theory, the standards are based on scientific observation, but you know as well as I do that they are based on past results—these things always are. The problem is that this process is difficult to standardize. I get some really big variances on many of my runs, and I'm just glad that I don't have to report on variances on a brand-by-brand basis. Fortunately, favorable variances on some brands are enough to offset unfavorable variances on others, so that they cancel each other to a large extent.

"On wrapping material, all I need to know is how much winds up in the wastepaper basket. These waste reports that I get from the accounting department are very hard to understand. I have to go behind the figures to find out whether the wastage is big enough to worry about. It never is. I used to have a very simple report showing the amount of material used, the wastage percentage, and the approximate value of the waste. This was much better. I could go into the factory floor and show the foreman something that he could understand."

Suggestions of the Cost Accountant

Jean Michelet, Burton's cost accountant and head of the 22-man costing department, is enthusiastic about the new system of standard costing for materials: "You can't imagine how much we've been able to find out with this new system. Several times we've gone out to the factory floor to check on a big variance, and have found boxes of spoiled materials hidden behind machines so that the foreman wouldn't spot them.

"The system is far from perfect, but most of our problems stem from the hostility of the factory people. We need their help to get data for better standards and for our analysis of variances, but they're not very cooperative. Even so, the new system has saved us a lot of work here, and we can get our reports out in a fraction of the time it used to take before we went to standards.

"We're new at this, of course, but I hope in time to see us do as well with this system as our Dutch sister company. They had had no figures on wastage at all, and when they went on standard costs their costs went down fantastically. Naturally, the Dutch management were very pleased.

"To bring our system up to the Dutch level, we should get regular reports from the clerks and foremen on the factory floor. These should deal with things that have gone wrong, such as wrong mixtures, stock losses, and machine stoppages. If I had this kind of information, I could explain the variances more fully and prepare summaries of the recurring sources of trouble. This shouldn't cost us anything, because the clerks and foremen have odd bits of free time that they could use for this work. The only possible extra cost that I see is an hour or two of my own time each month to collate and report on the data."

a) What behavioral problems, if any, were created by the installation of the new uniform standard costing and reporting system? Could they have been anticipated? How could they have been avoided?

b) What should Mr. Burton do about the Variable Production Cost Summary Sheet?

CASE 18–2: SUSSEX PRODUCTS, LTD.†

Sussex Products, Ltd. is a manufacturer of a diversified line of industrial cleaning compounds, disinfectants, and pesticides located in Lower Grinling, Sussex, England. Its production division consists of six manufacturing plants and a small divisional headquarters staff.

The exchange of letters given below relates to an internal audit carried out at the company's Leatherslade plant early in 1964. A partial organization chart, showing the formal organizational relationships among the persons mentioned in this case is as follows:

† Copyright 1965 by l'Institut pour l'Etude des Méthodes de Direction de l'Entreprise (IMEDE), Lausanne, Switzerland. Reproduced by permission.

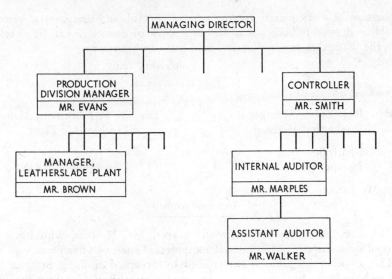

Questions

a) Whose side would you take in this dispute?
b) What, if anything, could Messrs. Evans, Smith, and Marples have done to avoid the difficulties which arose?

Exchange of Letters

FROM: P. J. Evans, Manager
Production Division

To: T. P. E. Brown, Manager
Leatherslade Plant

cc: Controller
Internal Audit Dept.

3rd September, 1963

Dear Mr. Brown:

Internal Control

We draw your attention to the following section of our regulations for internal control (ACC/17—12/6/59):

"The allocation of duties and responsibilities within a plant shall be designed in such a way that there will be a system of checks and balances whereby the work of one employee shall always be checked by the work of another employee, working independently."

We are, of course, of the opinion that plant managers should do their utmost to avoid loss to the company from fraud by employees. On the other hand, we are also particularly anxious to keep paperwork in our productive units to a strict minimum. We therefore point out that there should be no duplication of work merely for the sake of control, and that control systems should be devised in such a way that the work of one clerk can be checked with the work that another clerk would have done anyway.

Yours very truly,

FROM: P. J. Evans, Manager   To: T. P. E. Brown, Manager
       Production Division   Leatherslade Plant

cc: Controller
       Internal Audit Dept.   13th January 1964

Dear Mr. Brown:

Internal Audit

This letter serves to introduce the bearer, Mr. Marples, who has been charged by management to undertake an internal audit of your plant.

The scope of his audit is determined by accepted auditing practice and will include in particular an examination of control procedures in the light of the company's regulations for internal control (ACC/17—12/6/59).

Mr. Marples is to have access to all the books of account and records necessary to complete his audit and we are sure we can rely on you to see that he is provided with all the explanations of which he stands in need.

He will discuss with you the findings of his audit before he leaves your plant.

Yours very truly,

FROM: T. P. E. Brown, Manager   To: P. J. Evans, Manager
       Leatherslade Plant   Production Division

CONFIDENTIAL   22nd January 1964

Dear Mr. Evans:

Internal Audit

This is to confirm my phone call to you today during which I informed you of the unfortunate happenings of last week.

As I explained, I find it difficult to hold myself responsible for the reactions of my people to the internal auditors' attitude to their task. Quite apart from the auditors' inability to observe the common forms of politeness and business etiquette with supervisory staff and their attempts to browbeat employees with many years' service with the company, matters were brought to a head this week when Mr. Marples' assistant was discovered after the normal closing hours hiding behind the stocks in the finished goods warehouse. I can only assume that the purpose of this subterfuge was to spy on warehouse staff who were having to work overtime as a result of the delay occasioned in their work by the lengthy checking and rechecking of finished goods stocks insisted on by the auditors.

As you know, our union is becoming particularly militant in preparation for our negotiations with them which are due this spring. I therefore requested that the audit at present be discontinued and resumed later in the year.

You, however, stated that for head office reasons the audit must go on.

Yours very truly,

FROM: F. G. Marples   To: B. W. Smith
      Internal Auditor   Controller

CONFIDENTIAL   22nd January 1964

Dear Mr. Smith:

Leatherslade Plant Audit 1964

This is to confirm my telephone call of yesterday evening, during which I reported on the first week of our audit here.

As this is a first audit, one naturally expects some difficulties to arise, but I very much regret to report that in this instance there seems to be some definite ill will in the reaction of plant management.

I had the usual discussion with the plant manager on the second day we were here and explained to him the purpose and scope of our audit, but unfortunately was unable to elicit any positive reaction from him. In the following days the atmosphere rapidly degenerated to the point where both Mr. Walker and I were followed whenever we left the office to check anything in the plant.

The day before yesterday Mr. Walker returned to the finished goods warehouse to recover some notes which he had inadvertently left there, whereupon he was grasped by both arms by one of the factory foremen who had followed him there and taken by force to the manager's office.

I would not normally bother you with the details of such rather childish behavior were it not for veiled threats subsequently issued by Mr. Brown that this incident, which I consider to have been rigged, was to be used for political purposes at head office.

Yours very truly,

17th February 1964

REPORT ON INTERNAL AUDIT

Leatherslade Plant
13/ 1/60—3/2/60

Period of Audit

13th January, 1964 to 3rd February 1964.

Conclusions

We found that most of the clerical routines in the plant were performed conscientiously, accurately, and on time, although certain recording functions could, we felt, be improved. We also found, however, that the internal control system in the areas of labor payroll, raw materials, and finished goods was defective and have made recommendations that the allocation of tasks amongst employees should be changed.

. . . .

Cash and Stamps

At the time of our cash check the cash book had not been written up for four days. There was some evidence of subsequent alterations to entries in the cash book and some entries were not easily legible.

We recommend that the cash book be kept up to date at all times and that faulty entries be corrected in the orthodox manner.

. . . .

Accounts Payable

We found the recording of creditors accounts up to date and correct insofar as our verifications could determine. We noted, however, that the creditors' accounts clerk orders certain technical materials, checks them on arrival, and signs for them having been received. From the point of view of internal control, the person keeping creditors' accounts records should not participate either in the ordering or reception of supplies and in any event supplies should not be ordered and vouched for upon receipt by the same person.

. . . .

Manufacturing Account

Weekly manufacturing losses for raw materials showed the following variations during November and December:

Week 1............ 2.0%	Week 4............ 2.1%	Week 7............ 2.0%
Week 2............ 1.9	Week 5............ 1.8	Week 8............ 5.2
Week 3............ 4.8	Week 6............ 1.9	Week 9............ 1.8
	Average: 1962–63:............ 2.0%	

No satisfactory explanation was given for the extraordinarily high losses of week 3 and week 8.

The final check on quantities produced is afforded by the quantities shown as entering to the finished goods warehouse. The quantities produced are recorded under the supervision of the manufacturing foreman; the quantities entering the warehouse are recorded by the warehouseman. The manufacturing foreman and the warehouseman are, however, related by marriage. We feel that to ensure adequate control, the recording of goods produced should be made entirely independently of the recording of goods entering the warehouse.

. . . .

Labor Payroll

Our check of the labor payroll for the first week of December revealed two errors in the calculation of overtime pay. These errors were rectified during our audit.

We noted that the employee who calculates the labor payroll also pays out wages to the employees. Although the payroll calculations are checked by another person, we nevertheless recommend that the payout of wages be made by someone in no way connected with the calculation of the payroll—preferably the cashier.

. . . .

We wish to extend our thanks to Mr. Brown and his staff for the assistance rendered to us during our audit.

FROM: T. P. E. Brown, Manager   To: P. J. Evans, Manager
        Leatherslade Plant   Production Division

cc: Controller
        Internal Audit Dept.   2nd March 1964

Dear Mr. Evans:

Internal Audit

I have for comment the report on January's audit.

Although the tone of the report would seem to be unfavorable, the substance of it seems to me to be a commendation, particularly of our office staff. The only mistakes the auditors could find were a few corrections in the cash book (the cash balance agreed with cash on hand), 7d. missing in the stamps (which even the auditors did not think worth mentioning), and two minor errors in our large payroll (which even the workers concerned had not noticed).

Failing to find anything seriously wrong with our accounting, they therefore had to comment on theoretical weaknesses and on matters outside the scope of their audit.

No comment was made to the auditors on the manufacturing losses they mention, as these had already been discussed with you in correspondence and as such manufacturing matters are clearly not the concern of auditors.

Nor can I admit that auditors should attempt to reassign jobs amongst plant employees. The payroll clerk orders and checks certain technical supplies as he previously worked in the fitter's shop and is the only office employee qualified to do so.

I fail to see how our warehouseman's marriage last summer to the manufacturing foreman's younger sister has anything whatsoever to do with his trustworthiness.

The remarks concerning Mr. Thompson, who is in charge of the payroll, seem particularly misplaced. He has worked for us now for 27 years and is known and respected by all our employees. To entrust the payout to Miss Allen, our cashier, who has been with us only 18 months and who is now only 22 years of age, just does not seem to me to be a feasible proposition.

I fully realize that our auditors are young, zealous, and without a great deal of experience of business, and I hope that the coming years will temper their theories with reality.

Yours very truly,

chapter 19

Factory Overhead
Cost Allocations for
Performance Reporting

Interdepartmental cost allocations of the sort described in Chapter 10 are often carried beyond the development of departmental burden rates for product costing into the routine cost reporting structure. That is, all or part of the costs of service departments are charged each month to other service departments and to production departments.

These after-the-fact allocations serve a managerial purpose if they reflect in one department's periodic performance reports that department's consumption of another department's services. For one thing, the department head may be able to control service department costs indirectly by controlling his consumption of services. For example, the manager of a machining department has no jurisdiction over the amount of fuel consumed in producing electric power in the company's power plant, but he may be able to exercise considerable control over the amount of power consumed in his department.

Allocations may also serve an attention-directing and decision-making purpose even if service consumption is not controllable. The maintenance manager, for example, often has the sole responsibility for maintenance costs, which are nevertheless classified by department and even by individual pieces of equipment. These data can serve to identify trouble spots and also can be used by higher management in equipment replacement and similar decisions. They should be reported to the operating department heads, however, only if the latter are expected to share cost control responsibility.

After-the-fact allocations may also be made for purposes of product or project costing. Certain kinds of cost-plus contracts, for example, call for average historical costs rather than predetermined burden rates.

The purpose of this chapter is to see how ex-post allocation methods should be reflected in periodic performance reports. Barring contract provisions or legal requirements to the contrary, ex-post allocations for product or project costing should be based on the principles discussed in Chapter 10 and need no further discussion here.

ALTERNATIVE ALLOCATION METHODS

Data for control reporting should reflect differences between actual input quantities consumed and the input quantities budgeted under current conditions. The inputs here are the number of units of service department services consumed by a specific department. Any cost allocation, therefore, should reflect the department's use of service department services. The question is how the measures of usage should be costed.

Postdetermined Transfer Prices

Allocations based on indexes of service consumption require the use of transfer prices, defined in Chapter 10 as charging rates per unit of service consumed. The most common variant of the transfer price method, reflecting a bias against leaving any undistributed or overdistributed balances in service department accounts, is to compute the average actual service department cost per unit of service consumed. This average cost is an after-the-fact or postdetermined transfer price, and it changes every period.

For example, suppose that during October the maintenance department's costs totaled $24,000 on a work load of 4,000 service hours, an average of $6 an hour. Department M used 500 maintenance labor hours. Using the after-the-fact transfer price, the amount charged department M for maintenance labor for October would be $500 \times \$6 = \$3,000$.

The advantage of this method is that it does reflect service consumption, which is presumably the only variable subject to even partial control by the managers of service-consuming departments. It does this only imperfectly, however. For example, suppose that department M's flexible budget allows 100 maintenance department labor hours a month plus one maintenance labor hour for every 20 direct labor hours. The normal work load for the maintenance department is 5,000 maintenance labor hours a month, and at this level it has an operating cost budget of $25,000 a month, an average of $5 a maintenance labor hour. (This does not include repair parts, which are ordinarily charged separately.)

On this basis, department M's monthly maintenance labor allowance is computed from the formula:

$$\text{Budget} = \$500 + \frac{\$5 \times \text{Direct labor hours}}{20}$$

If department M recorded 10,000 direct labor hours during October, its maintenance labor budget allowance would be:

$$\text{Budget} = \$500 + \frac{\$5 \times 10,000}{20} = \$3,000$$

This is just equal to the amount charged to the department, and thus the monthly cost report would show a zero maintenance labor variance. If the budget allowance were expressed in hours, however, a favorable variance of 100 maintenance hours would appear.

The problem is probably obvious. Unless physical flexible budget allowances are recomputed on a $6 basis, the departmental variance will reflect both a price effect (variation in cost per hour) and a quantity effect (variation in hours used). In other words, the amount charged against one department depends not only on the amount of service consumed but also on the total amount of service provided to all departments and on the efficiency with which the service department is managed. Thus a variance can appear in the periodic cost report even though service consumption by the department has been kept under control.

Predetermined Transfer Prices

The main defect in the actual cost transfer price method can be eliminated by fixing the transfer price in advance. For example, if maintenance hours are to be charged to other departments at a fixed rate of, say, $5 an hour, the charge for maintenance will depend solely on this rate and on the number of maintenance hours spent in each department. The figures are:

Charged to department M (500 hours × $5)................	$2,500
Budgeted (as above).......................................	3,000
Spending variance (100 hours × $5).......................	$ 500

In other words, the use of predetermined transfer prices keeps price effects from creeping into the overhead spending variances calculated for service-consuming departments. The alternatives to this are to segregate the price effect in variance analysis or to adjust the budget allowances each period to the new average cost figures. Both of these procedures are cumbersome and thus inferior to the predetermined transfer price.

A maintenance department illustration was used here for simplicity and because maintenance costs are usually allocated by transfer prices. It is not always clear, however, just how much responsibility production department managers have for the amount of maintenance work performed. Directly they may have none, with responsibility for both preventive maintenance and repairs lodged in the maintenance manager or managers. Even so, there is often much the operating manager can do to affect the amount of maintenance required, and this is therefore often regarded as an item to be controlled jointly by the maintenance and operating managers.

Activity Charges

If measures of service consumption are unavailable, the periodic charge for service cannot measure the effect of the department head's efforts to control his service demands. Even so, management often insists on allocations as a means of keeping department heads aware of costs being incurred for their benefit elsewhere in the company. Although some authorities feel that allocations of this sort are self-defeating in that they merely distract the manager's attention from the items he can control, empirical evidence on this point is lacking and demands for those allocations are so widespread that the accountant must be prepared to devise schemes that will afford the least possible danger of misinterpretation.

One possibility is to use an activity charge, such as a rate per factory labor hour. This is appropriate if service center costs vary with the volume of activity in other departments. If activity charges are used, they should be predetermined, to keep service department variances out of the periodic performance reports of other departments. For example, suppose that factory office costs normally amount to $3,000 at a normal factory operating level of 30,000 labor hours a month, an average of 10 cents an hour. Normal volume in department M is 6,000 labor hours a month and the department therefore would budget 6,000 × $0.10 = $600 a month as its share of factory office costs. If total factory volume drops to 25,000 hours, however, all other figures remaining the same, average office cost will increase to $0.12 and the charge to department M will go up to 6,000 × $0.12 = $720. The extra $120 would appear as an unfavorable variance on the monthly performance report. Variations in the cost of operating the service department would have a similar effect on the amount charged to department M and on the reported variance.

Variances of this kind are not connected to managerial performance in department M, and should not appear on the periodic cost reports. The best way to accomplish this is to use predetermined rates. The rate for factory office costs, for example, could be fixed at 10 cents a labor hour both in the flexible budget and in the actual monthly charges. This would keep factory office cost variances completely out of department M's performance reports, where they do not belong.

Charges for Facilities Provided

When the costs of the service department are fixed, it makes little sense to vary the charge each month on the basis of current levels of factory activity. Such costs are incurred to provide service department

Exhibit 19-1

THE STANDOFF COMPANY
Costs and Operating Statistics
(Month of October)

	Total	Service Departments				Production Departments		
		Electric Power	Buildings	Factory Administration	Equipment Maintenance	Machining	Welding and Plating	Assembly
Costs incurred:								
Supervision and clerical help	$14,600	...	$1,000	$8,200	$1,000	$1,600	$ 900	$ 1,900
Indirect labor	31,900	...	2,100	...	8,300	9,500	5,000	7,000
Operating supplies	3,050	...	300	1,200	250	650	350	300
Equipment depreciation	2,253	...	100	200	300	1,053	400	200
Miscellaneous	2,950	...	300	1,130	870	205	195	250
Electric power	1,686	$1,686	...	...	...	...	...	...
Building depreciation, taxes, insurance	2,070		2,070	...	...	...	...	...
Total cost	$58,509	$1,686	$ 5,870	$10,730	$10,720	$13,008	$ 6,845	$ 9,650
Operating statistics:								
Direct labor hours	20,110	...	...	...	1,960	6,400	1,750	10,000
Total labor hours	31,510	...	900	...	1,960	10,300	3,850	14,500
Power consumed (kwh.)	84,300	...	11,000	...	4,900	51,000	11,900	5,500
Maintenance hours	1,960	...	...	...	...	1,800	100	60
Machine-hours	xxx	...	...	...	...	8,400	...	...

capacity, and the allocations should reflect occupancy of that capacity. To accomplish this, each cost center should be charged a fixed amount per month, determined in advance on the basis of the proportion of the service center's capacity that has been provided for each of the beneficiary cost centers—in other words, a *capacity charge*, based on an index of the amounts of service facilities provided to each.

For example, assume that factory office costs are fixed and that factory office capacity is closely related to the total labor hours budgeted for the factory. The factory office is staffed to meet the following normal service load per month:

Department	Labor Hours
M	1,500
P	7,000
X	6,000
Y	8,000
Z	5,000
AA	2,500
Total	30,000

Under the fixed charge or lump-sum method, department M would be assigned 1,500/30,000 of the $3,000 budgeted monthly factory office cost, or $150. Department P would be assigned 7/30 of the total ($700), and so on. These charges would not be changed, no matter what the total labor hours or service costs were in any month.

Once again, the advantage of this method is that the amount charged for noncontrollable fixed costs can be budgeted in advance and no variance in this charge will appear in the monthly cost statements. Thus the monthly report for department P would show budgeted costs of $700, "actual" costs of $700, and no variance.

AN ALLOCATION ILLUSTRATION

To illustrate the application of these methods in a systematic way, let us continue the Standoff Company illustration that we began in Chapter 10. Actual costs and operating statistics for the month of October are shown in Exhibit 19–1.

The Allocation Method

The Standoff Company's system is to use predetermined transfer prices whenever reliable usage measurements are available, and predetermined activity charges or capacity charges when they are not. These rates are derived from the annual budget figures and remain unchanged throughout the year. Therefore, the October allocations were based on the rates developed in Chapter 10:

Unassigned overhead:

Electric power............................ $0.02 per kwh.

Service department costs:

Buildings (including building depreciation,
taxes, and insurance).................. 0.12 per sq. ft. of budgeted floor space

Factory administration.................. 0.10 per direct labor hour
+0.30 per budgeted labor hour

Equipment maintenance.................. 5.80 per maintenance labor hour

Electric Power. Meters in the three production departments and in the equipment maintenance department record the amount of electricity consumed for motive power in those departments. The remaining power is used for lighting the factory and factory office and for operating a few simple pieces of office equipment. Separate metering of office power consumption has been deemed uneconomical, and all such power passes through the buildings department meter, along with power for lighting.

Electric power, in other words, is partly traceable to specific departments, but the company finds it more convenient to record power costs initially in a single factorywide account and then distribute them among the five departments in which meters are installed.

Using the operating statistics at the bottom of Exhibit 19–1, the allocation of power costs for October was:

	Consumption (kwh.)	Cost Allocation
Buildings.........................	11,000	$ 220
Equipment maintenance..........	4,900	98
Machining......................	51,000	1,020
Welding and plating............	11,900	238
Assembly......................	5,500	110
Total.....................	84,300	$1,686

Buildings. Buildings department and building ownership costs are both fixed and noncontrollable by the other department heads. The allocation, therefore, was by a series of capacity charges, equal to the amounts budgeted at the beginning of the year, averaging $0.12 a square foot. The allocations were:

	Occupancy (sq. ft.)	Cost Allocation
Factory administration..........	5,000	$ 600
Equipment maintenance..........	3,000	360
Machining......................	20,000	2,400
Welding and plating............	7,000	840
Assembly......................	15,000	1,800
Total.....................	50,000	$6,000

Factory Administration. The costs of the factory administration department are partly fixed and partly variable. Capacity charges, amounting to $0.30 per budgeted labor hour, are used to allocate the budgeted fixed costs, while an activity charge of $0.10 for each actual direct labor hour is used for the variable costs. (For this purpose, maintenance hours are classified as direct labor hours.) The allocations for October were:

	(1) Actual Direct Labor Hours	(2) Activity Charge (1) × $0.10	(3) Capacity Charge (from Budget)	(4) Total Charge (2) + (3)
Equipment maintenance..........	1,960	$ 196	$ 600	$ 796
Machining.....................	6,400	640	3,000	3,640
Welding and plating.............	1,750	175	1,200	1,375
Assembly......................	10,000	1,000	4,800	5,800
Total....................	20,110	$2,011	$9,600	$11,611

Equipment Maintenance. A clear measure of service consumption is available for equipment maintenance service, and a transfer price can be used. Using the predetermined rate of $5.80 per maintenance labor hour, the allocation for October was:

	Maintenance Labor Hours	Cost Allocation
Machining.......................	1,800	$10,440
Welding and plating...............	100	580
Assembly........................	60	348
Total........................	1,960	$11,368

The maintenance charging rate was broken into fixed and variable components in Chapter 10 for product costing purposes. The Standoff Company's accountants gave some thought to applying this breakdown to the monthly allocations, but decided against it on the ground that the fixed component was relatively small, just 20 percent of the total.

Service Department Variances

The cost distribution sheet for the month is shown in Exhibit 19–2. Since predetermined rates were used, all three service departments show over- or underdistributed balances. These do not necessarily indicate favorable or unfavorable performance efficiency on the part of the department managers. Seasonal patterns in cost recognition, volume fluctuations, and external price changes, to mention only a few of the possible causes, may account in large part for under- or overdistribution of service department costs. In other words, further analysis is necessary to identify the effects of individual factors influencing costs.

Exhibit 19–2

THE STANDOFF COMPANY
Cost Distribution Sheet
(Month of October)

	Total	Service Departments				Production Departments		
		Electric Power	Buildings	Factory Administration	Equipment Maintenance	Machining	Welding and Plating	Assembly
Costs incurred:								
Supervision and clerical help	$14,600	...	$1,000	$ 8,200	$ 1,000	$ 1,600	$ 900	$ 1,900
Indirect labor	31,900	...	2,100	...	8,300	9,500	5,000	7,000
Operating supplies	3,050	...	300	1,200	250	650	350	300
Equipment depreciation	2,253	...	100	200	300	1,053	400	200
Miscellaneous	2,950	...	300	1,130	870	205	195	250
Electric power	1,686	$1,686	...	...	...	...	...	...
Building depreciation, taxes, insurance	2,070	...	2,070	...	...	...	...	...
Total cost	$58,509	$1,686	$5,870	$10,730	$10,720	$13,008	$6,845	$ 9,650
Allocations:								
Electric power	...	(1,686)	220	...	98	1,020	238	110
Building services	...	...	(6,000)	600	360	2,400	840	1,800
Factory administration	...	...	...	(11,611)	796	3,640	1,375	5,800
Equipment maintenance	...	...	...	...	(11,368)	10,440	580	348
Total	$58,509	...	$ 90*	$ (281)†	$ 606*	$30,508	$9,878	$17,708

* Unfavorable variance.
† Favorable variance.

Monthly Performance Reports

Each of the six factory departments has a set of flexible budget schedules for the current year. These are used in preparing monthly cost reports along the lines described in Chapter 17. Exhibit 19–3 shows the October report for the machining department. The budget allowances appropriate to a monthly volume of 8,400 machine hours in the machin-

Exhibit 19–3

THE STANDOFF COMPANY
Monthly Departmental Cost Report
Machining Department, October

	Actual	Budget	(Over) Under Budget
Controllable and partially controllable:			
Indirect labor..................	$ 9,500	$ 9,660	$ 160
Operating supplies.............	650	630	(20)
Electric power.................	1,020	945	(75)
Equipment maintenance.........	10,440	9,048	(1,392)
Factory administration..........	3,640	3,630	(10)
Miscellaneous.................	205	420	215
Total controllable.............	$25,455	$24,333	$(1,122)
Noncontrollable:			
Salaries......................	1,600	1,600	....
Equipment depreciation.........	1,053	1,000	(53)
Building services..............	2,400	2,400	....
Total overhead costs..........	$30,508	$29,333	$(1,175)

ing department are shown in the second column, while the "actual" costs for the month, taken from Exhibit 19–2, are shown at the left.

Because predetermined transfer prices were used, the variances in electric power and equipment maintenance charges can be identified immediately as variances due to the quantities of service used during the month. The charges do not reflect variations in power rates, changes in the efficiency of the maintenance department, or fluctuations in the total maintenance department load. In this case, because all maintenance was charged at a single rate of $5.80 an hour, it is apparent that the department used 240 maintenance hours more than its flexible budget allowed for the production volume achieved in October ($1,392 ÷ $5.80 = 240).

No variance in building service costs appears on this report because predetermined capacity charges were used to allocate these costs. The small variance in the charge for factory administration costs reflects the deviation between the actual number of man-hours and the number of man-hours actually used during October, at 10 cents an hour. Since this is partly controllable, the variance is shown "above the line," in the upper portion of the report.

Modifications to the System

The Standoff Company's system might be criticized on three grounds. First, it includes allocations of noncontrollable fixed costs, and these serve no managerial purpose. If managerial allegiance to full cost can be broken, these allocations could be eliminated without any information loss. If the allocation has to be made, however, the predetermined capacity charges are the best vehicle for making it.

Second, the system does not report the variable and fixed components of cost separately. Separate charges are computed for factory administration costs, but the amounts are reported as a single total. For maintenance, a single rate covers both the fixed and the variable components. Switching to a system of dual rates would indeed be more consistent with the basis on which the burden rates were computed in Chapter 10, but the quality of the control information would be improved only marginally. For example, a variable cost rate would reinforce the manager's awareness of the short-run effects of his decisions to use maintenance services, but the full cost rate is simpler to compute and is likely to lead to the same control response.

In fact, if the rate used is a reasonable approximation to attributable cost, charges on this basis may even be preferable. Decisions to use services often have impacts on the amount of capacity provided, and variable cost charges may stimulate service use unduly. Computer services are likely to fall in this category.

The third criticism is that this system ignores interservice-department service consumption. The equipment maintenance department, for example, might very well provide services to the other two service departments as well as to the production departments, and a more refined system would provide charging rates for these services. This refinement was omitted from the illustration in this chapter in the interest of simplicity. To introduce it in practice, charging rates should be computed by the simultaneous allocation procedure described in Chapter 10, using fairly simple computer programs for this purpose. If this is not practical, however, the rates obtained by the simpler sequential allocation procedure illustrated here can be used without serious error.

SUMMARY

Reassignment or allocation of overhead costs from one cost center or department to another is an important feature of most cost accounting systems. Many such allocations are carried out with little understanding of the purposes they are intended to serve.

Allocations before the fact serve an inventory costing purpose by placing service department costs into the production department budgets used for burden rate determination. Before-the-fact allocations can also serve a planning purpose by indicating long-run or short-run cost variability in response to changes in production volumes or capacities. Finally, allocations after the fact serve a control purpose if they reflect service consumption by other departments.

Because after-the-fact allocations serve only a control objective, the design of the allocation system should reflect the desired characteristics of control information. An allocation scheme that meets this specification consists of:

1. Predetermined transfer prices for services with measurable consumption units (consumption charges).
2. Predetermined fixed charges for the fixed component of the costs of service centers without readily traceable outputs (capacity charges).
3. Predetermined activity charges for the variable component of the costs of service centers without readily traceable outputs (activity charges).

The predetermined rates and amounts should be developed as part of periodic financial planning; for planning purposes the fixed and variable components of departmental transfer prices should also be identified. After-the-fact allocations of the second and third classes can be omitted unless management feels that they serve to keep department heads aware of the costs of ancillary activities, thus possibly stimulating suggestions for methods improvement and cost reduction.

EXERCISES AND PROBLEMS

1. General factory overhead and factory service department costs may be allocated or recirculated to production departments in many ways. All costs may be allocated, or just the variable costs. If all costs are allocated, separate treatment may be given the fixed and variable components. They may be allocated on the basis of a rate per unit of activity in the production departments, or on the basis of a rate per unit of service performed. The rates may be determined in advance, or after actual general and service department costs are accumulated.

Discuss the relative merits of the three following methods of allocation:

a) After-the-fact allocations of full service department costs on the basis of a single rate per unit of activity in the production departments.
b) Predetermined allocations of full service department costs on the basis of a single rate per unit of activity in the production departments.
c) Predetermined allocations of variable service department costs on the basis of a single rate per unit of service performed by the service departments.

2. The costs of a service department, such as maintenance, are frequently distributed to the departments which utilize its services by multiplying a "charging rate" by the number of man-hours of service provided to each other department. The charging rate is computed so as to provide for a complete distribution of service department costs, using the following formula:

$$\frac{\text{Actual direct service dept. costs} + \text{actual costs allocated to service dept.}}{\text{Total man-hours of service provided to all other departments}}$$

During the month of July, the milling department of the Grope Company called for very little maintenance service, but the maintenance department's charge for services performed for the milling department during July was in excess of the milling department's budget allowance for the month.

a)   What conclusions would you draw from this unfavorable variance?
b)   Can you suggest any improvements in the company's accounting treatment of maintenance department costs?

3.† The budgeted costs of the power service department amount to $9,520 a month; of this amount $2,500 is considered to be a fixed cost. Costs during April amounted to $9,300.

Power consumption in this factory is measured by the number of horsepower-hours. The monthly power requirements of the factory's four other departments, in horsepower hours, are as follows:

	Producing Departments		Service Departments	
	A	B	X	Y
Needed at capacity production......	10,000	20,000	12,000	8,000
Budgeted........................	8,000	15,000	8,000	5,000
Used during April................	8,000	13,000	7,000	6,000

What dollar amounts of power service department costs should be allocated to each of these four departments for the month of April?

4.* The Warren Manufacturing Company has four producing departments —milling, machining, assembly, and painting—and three service departments— factory office, plant operation, and storeroom. The company's records contain the following information for the month of July:

Department	Actual Direct Overhead Costs	Square Feet Floor Space	No. of Employees	Average % of Requisitions
Milling...................	$40,000	18,000	28	26%
Machining................	35,000	12,000	14	10
Painting..................	42,000	15,000	11	24
Assembly.................	30,000	9,000	9	40
Factory office.............	19,490	3,000	7	
Plant operation............	22,110	5,000	3	
Storeroom................	24,460	10,000	2	

† Adapted from a uniform CPA examination.

* Solutions to problems marked with an asterisk can be found in Appendix B.

The actual costs of the service departments for the month are to be re-distributed, using a sequential allocation procedure. The departments are to be dealt with in the following sequence, using the indicated bases for cost allocation:

> Plant operation—square feet of floor space.
> Factory office—number of employees.
> Storeroom—average percentage of requisitions.

Prepare an overhead cost distribution sheet for the month.

5. The following information has been taken from the overhead cost budget for a direct production department and from the accounting records of this department for the month of December:

	Budgeted		Actual Cost
	At Normal Volume	At Actual Volume	
Cleanup labor...................	$ 400	$ 400	$ 550
Indirect labor...................	3,000	3,600	3,400
Overtime premium...............	300	500	750
Steam.........................	1,500	1,800	1,700
Heat, light, depreciation, and			
insurance....................	2,000	2,000	2,400
Factory administration...........	800	800	800

All budgeted figures are at standard prices and standard wage rates. Indirect labor and cleanup labor are charged to the department at standard wage rates. Steam is purchased from a local utility at a price which varies with the price of soft coal; steam costs are charged to the departments on the basis of the average steam price for the month multiplied by consumption determined on the basis of meter readings. Heat, light, depreciation, and insurance costs are charged to the departments on the basis of the percentage of the factory's floor space occupied at the beginning of the year.

Indicate what figures you would report to the department head, how you would arrange these figures on the department head's report, and what further data you would like to obtain to make the report more useful to the department head and his superiors. Give your reasons.

6. Service department S provides services to other departments of the company's manufacturing division. The amount of service provided depends on the needs of the other manufacturing departments, as determined by their respective managers.

The normal operating volume for department S is 10,000 service hours a month. Budgeted cost is $20,000 plus $2.50 per service hour. Actual department S cost for February was $42,000, at a volume of 8,000 service hours, including 1,100 service hours performed in production department M.

The normal operating volume for department M is 15,000 direct labor hours a month. At this volume, department M's budget allows for the consumption of 1,000 department S hours. During February, department M operated at a volume of 12,500 direct labor hours, and at this volume it had a budget allowance of 900 department S hours.

a) How much should department M be charged for department S services for the month of February? State your reasons.

b) Compute the variance in the charge for department S services that would appear on department M's cost performance report for the month, using the allocation method you developed in (a). Give a one-sentence explanation of the meaning of this variance.

c) Compute the variance in departmental costs that would appear on department S's cost control reports for the month.

7.* The Tensile Steel Company is reviewing its semivariable overhead budget system in the interest of securing better control over service departments and of charging the cost of these departments to producing departments in the most effective manner possible. Below are budget data for the maintenance and the finance (accounting, payroll, clerical, etc.) departments and operating and cost data for the month of September.

Maintenance Department Budget:

(1) Normal level of output: 12,000 maintenance labor hours a month.
(2) Average hourly rate for maintenance workers, $3.50.
(3) Other maintenance department costs:

Item	Fixed per Month	Variable per Maintenance Labor Hour
Supervision and indirect labor.......	$ 5,000	$0.30
Supplies and tools................	2,500	0.60
Miscellaneous....................	3,300	0.10
Total........................	$10,800	$1.00

Finance Department Budget:

(1) When the factory is operating at a normal level of activity, the factory as a whole employs 1,000 people.
(2) The budget of the finance department is $18,000 a month plus $1 for each factory employee.

September Data:

(1) Maintenance labor hours worked, 13,300.
(2) Maintenance department costs, $72,900.
(3) Factory employment, 1,200 employees.
(4) Finance department costs, $20,000.

a) Specify rules for allocating the costs of the two departments, state their rationale, and illustrate them with the September data.

b) What are the most likely explanations of the differences between the actual costs of these two departments and the amounts allocated to other departments by your methods?

8. The management of Blake-Emmich wants to have departmental cost statements that will be all-inclusive so that the department head will be cognizant of his share of the total costs of operating the factory, but which will be used primarily for control purposes. The monthly budget of the machining department includes the following categories of costs:

(1) Fixed costs which are distributed among the factory's departments on a "fair and equitable" basis: the machining department's share of these costs is $12,000 a month.

(2) Fixed costs which are direct to the department, the amount of the cost being determined by the factory superintendent: $2,000 a month.

(3) Fixed costs which are direct to the department, the amount of the cost being determined by the department head: $600 a month.

(4) Variable direct costs for which the department head determines the amount of inputs used but not input prices: $4 a standard direct labor hour.

(5) Variable costs of service departments for which the machining department head determines the amount of service used: five units of service per standard direct labor hour, at an average variable service department cost of $0.20 a unit.

(6) Variable costs of service departments for which the service department head or the factory superintendent determines the amount of service used: four units of service per standard direct labor hour at $0.30 a unit.

The machining department's output for July was the equivalent of 2,000 standard direct labor hours.

a) Compute a machining department flexible budget allowance for July for each of the six cost categories listed above.

b) Comparisons between these flexible budget allowances and the "actual costs" charged to the department for July will be embodied in a monthly departmental cost report. Indicate for each category how "actual cost" should be measured and reported. Remember that the report is to be used for control purposes.

9. Service department 101 provides services to a number of production departments. The cost budget for the department at a normal volume of 5,000 service hours per month, together with actual departmental charges for the month of March, is as follows (4,000 hours of service were provided to production departments during March):

	Budget at Normal Volume		March Actual
	Amount	Fixed or Variable	
Servicemen labor............	$15,000	V	$14,000
Supervision................	2,000	F	2,000
Indirect labor..............	4,000	V	3,000
Supplies...................	1,000	V	1,100
Depreciation...............	5,500	F	5,600
Rent......................	2,500	F	2,900
Total.................	$30,000		$28,600

Depreciation charged each month is 1 percent of the original cost of equipment installed in the service department. The rental charge is based on the department's pro rata share, based on floor space occupied, of the costs charged to the building service department's accounts during the month.

Production department 76 uses department 101 services, and the foreman in charge of department 76 is expected to control his use of these services. Normal production volume in department 76 is 10,000 machine-hours. Department 76's use of department 101 services is budgeted at one service hour for every 10 machine-hours. A full cost charging rate is used.

Service hours are charged to production departments on the basis of average actual service department cost for the month multiplied by the number of service hours used during the month. During March department 76 operated a total of 11,000 machine-hours and used 900 hours of department 101 service.

a) Compare department 76's budget allowance for department 101 service: (1) at normal volume, (2) at 11,000 machine-hours.
b) Compute the service charge to department 76 for March.
c) Analyze department 76's March budget variance in department 101 charges, showing a breakdown between the variance due to factors over which department 76 had some control and the variance due to other causes.

10. The Zeta Company operates a factory with six production departments, three service departments, and a plant office. Any cost which can be traced to one of these departments is charged to that department at the time it is incurred. All other costs are charged to the plant manager.

Costs charged to the plant manager are of two kinds: (1) those relating to building occupancy, such as building depreciation, insurance, and taxes; and (2) general administration costs, such as the plant manager's salary. Actual occupancy costs for the month are allocated to all departments on the basis of floor space, prior to the distribution of service department costs. General administration costs, together with plant office costs, are not distributed.

The costs of the service departments are charged to the production departments on the following bases:

Department	Amount Distributed Monthly	Basis of Distribution
A..........	Total budgeted cost	Fixed amount to each production department, determined in advance
B..........	Total actual cost	Average service cost per service hour times service hours used by each production department
C..........	?	Fixed amount per service department hour, determined in advance, times actual service hours used by each production department

The factory uses a flexible budget and issues reports to each of the 10 departments. These reports show variances between actual costs and the flexible budget standard for the volume of activity in each department during the month. The flexible budget for service department A is the same amount each month (i.e., no variable costs).

a) What variances from flexible budget allowances, if any, would you expect to find in production department M in connection with the amounts charged to it by each of the service departments and by the plant manager for occupancy costs? What meaning can be attached to each of these variances?

b) What undistributed balances, if any, would you expect to find in the summary account for each of the service departments and for building occupancy? What meaning can be attached to each of these balances?

11. Each year, as part of the process of developing burden rates for the direct production departments in its factory, the Premier Company allocates the budgeted costs of its four factory service departments to the budgets of the four direct production departments. A sequential allocation system is used. The allocation sequence and the rates that were derived from it in 19x1 are as follows:

Buildings department.......... $0.17 per square foot
Office..................... $140 per employee
Maintenance department....... $4.80 per maintenance labor hour
Shipping room.............. $0.12 per machine-hour

These rates reflect the following average monthly statistics from the 19x1 budget:

	Floor Space (Square Feet)	Total Employees	Maintenance Labor Hours	Machine-Hours
Department 101...........	18,000	50	560	8,000
Department 102...........	16,000	40	610	12,000
Department 103...........	33,000	100	930	16,000
Department 104...........	20,000	60	500	10,000
Office..................	10,000	34	....	.....
Buildings...............	1,000	11	....	.....
Maintenance.............	1,000	17	....	.....
Shipping room...........	2,000	6	....	.....
Total...............	101,000	318	2,600	46,000

Monthly cost reports are issued to the managers of each of the company's four producing departments and four service departments. Although these reports are to reflect the full cost concept, they are to be used primarily in reviewing the effectiveness of cost control in each department. Production department managers are presumed to share responsibility with the maintenance department manager for the number of maintenance labor hours used.

The following operating and overhead cost data were recorded for the month of November:

	Direct Departmental Overhead	Total Employees	Maintenance Labor Hours	Machine-Hours
Department 101..........	$ 12,100	54	600	8,200
Department 102..........	21,200	42	650	13,000
Department 103..........	18,400	96	900	15,800
Department 104..........	15,600	50	550	8,000
Office..................	35,300	33	...	.....
Buildings...............	19,200	11	...	.....
Maintenance.............	10,500	18	...	.....
Shipping room...........	4,700	6	...	.....
Total..............	$137,000	310	2,700	45,000

Buildings department costs are entirely fixed and indivisible. Office costs are fixed but highly divisible. Maintenance costs are mostly variable with the volume of maintenance work done. Shipping room costs are fixed but divisible.

Prepare a service department cost distribution sheet for the month of November, using any method of cost distribution that you deem appropriate. Defend your choices.

12. "I get overcharged by the computer center every month, and I'm getting pretty tired of it," Patrick Denning said. Mr. Denning was the manager of his company's research department, a heavy user of the computer.

"I know we use a lot of computer time," he continued, "but the amount they charge me has gone up a lot faster than my usage. Besides, I know that most of the costs down there are fixed costs. It seems to me that incremental cost would be a better basis for the charge."

Donald MacKenzie, the controller, admitted that Mr. Denning's charges had gone up, but cited figures to show that the increases were justified. "We have worked out an hourly rate for the central processor," he said, "and everyone is treated alike. The hourly cost has gone up every year as we have expanded the system and gotten more sophisticated software. We don't raise the rate within the year, though. The rate is based on the budget for the year and each department has a budgeted allocation. If they don't use more time, they don't get charged more.

"The annual rate covers all of the costs that have been budgeted for operating the computer center during the year. We divide this by the number of hours that we expect to devote to productive work, and this gives us the rate. We don't attach any of the costs to idle time or to the time we use for training purposes within the center. These are necessary and we feel that everyone should bear his fair share of the total.

"Actually, Pat Denning has kept pretty well within his budget limits over the years. I don't know what he's complaining about. Besides, his department uses more of the expensive software than anyone else. If anything, we should charge him more than we do now."

a) Why is Mr. Denning upset? Does he have reason to worry?
b) What, if anything, should Mr. MacKenzie do in response to Mr. Denning's complaints?

chapter 20

Standard Cost
Variance Analysis

Standard cost variances don't always mean exactly what they seem to say. What seems to be a labor quantity variance may actually turn out to be the result of variations in materials yields, or vice versa. Similarly, the variances that arise when standard costing is applied to joint products may mean nothing more than that the product mix differs from standard. Finally, the incorporation of standard overhead costs into the system introduces an element that may obscure the spending variances. The purpose of this chapter is to discuss some of the methods the accountant can use to deal with these three kinds of problems.

ANALYSIS OF QUANTITY VARIANCES

Although the first-line supervisor can often provide an explanation of the major sources of quantity variances, more formal techniques are also available, either to *identify* the causes or to indicate their relative *magnitudes*. Two approaches are possible: (1) identification of the causes of variances as they occur; or (2) after-the-fact analytical separation of the variances stemming from various sources.

Classification by Causes

One means of identifying the amount of the variance arising from particular causes is to classify them when they occur. For example, the time spent by direct production workers on activities not directly connected with specific jobs can be recorded as indirect labor. Separate accounts can be established for such categories as machine maintenance time, time spent waiting for production materials, and idle time resulting from machine breakdowns, with separate time tickets being prepared when one of these occurs. An equivalent alternative is to leave the entire variance in the labor variance account, but code some or all parts of it with numbers identifying the causes of the variance.

To see what this means, let us look first at the information required to identify two kinds of variances and then at a more ambitious scheme to identify all labor variances at the source.

Effect of Product Rejections. Some variances arise from defects in materials or workmanship that cause quality control inspectors to reject individual product units or even whole production lots. In a basic plan system, such variances remain part of the residual quantity variance unless provision is made for transferring costs to separate accounts during the period. Single plan systems require immediate separation of the variances from the work-in-process accounts, but may either leave them as part of the overall quantity variance or transfer them to separate overhead accounts.

If the production losses are recouped by issuing and processing new materials to bring the production lot up to the specified quantity, then the costs of these extra materials and operations can be charged directly to the departmental variance accounts as they are incurred. Similarly, the costs of rework labor and other costs of reprocessing defective goods to bring them up to specifications should also be charged to variance or overhead accounts. The temporary error in the work-in-process account balance thus disappears as soon as the deficiency is made good, and no adjustment of the work in process account is necessary. If the lost units are not replaced, however, the work-in-process account must be relieved of the cumulated standard costs of all operations prior to the point of rejection.

Effect of Equipment Substitution. Product cost standards are generally based on the use of a particular type of machine to do each operation, but scheduling difficulties may cause department foremen or the scheduling department to use substitute equipment in order to meet delivery schedules when the preferred equipment is fully utilized by other work. Use of standard operation time cards for the charge to work in process will leave an amount in the labor quantity variance account representing the effect of the use of nonstandard equipment.

This problem may be serious enough to justify considerable attention. If use of nonstandard equipment is frequent enough, separate cost standards may be prepared for each type of equipment used for performing each operation. When nonstandard equipment is used, the departmental accounts are credited with the standard cost of the operation on the machine actually used. Inventory accounts, however, are debited only for standard product cost, based on the use of standard equipment. The difference is debited to an overhead account, attributed to the scheduling function.

For example, assume that a drilling operation on a piece part is normally assigned to a new drill press with a standard time of 21 hours for a standard lot. It can also be performed on a slower machine in 23 hours. The standard wage rate on both machines is $5 an hour. The standard cost of the operation when performed on the slower machine is thus 23 hours at $5 an hour, or $115 instead of $105. A charge of $10 could therefore be made to an overhead account bearing a title such as Use of Nonstandard Equipment—Machining.

Complete Classification by Causes. Identification of all of the causes of labor or materials quantity variances requires much more elaborate procedures than those needed to measure the effects of one or two fairly well-defined causes. One such scheme is illustrated in Exhibit 20–1. This form provides a virtually complete classification of labor quantity variances by cause. It presumes a single plan system and requires the foreman to assign a reason for each variance in excess of 10 percent. These classified variances are then tabulated and reported monthly to the foreman and to plant management.

This kind of system is difficult to police, and most companies are content to limit routine variance separation to a few main items, leaving more detailed investigation of residual variances to special analysis if and when required.

Analytical Separation of Variances

Analytical measurement of the variances from various sources is feasible only if relationships between cost and factors other than product output are known or can be approximated. To illustrate the method, we shall examine the analytical approach applicable to three possible sources of labor variances:

1. Variations in materials yields.
2. Labor substitution.
3. Variations in labor mix.

The accountant's task in each case is to estimate the amount of the total variance resulting from this particular cause. When this is removed, the residual indicates the amount to be attributed to other causes.

Effect of Variations in Materials Yields on Labor Variances. In materials-paced operations, such as much of process production, the amount of labor required is a function of the materials used rather than a function of output. For this reason, an unfavorable materials quantity variance would normally be accompanied by an unfavorable labor quantity variance.

To illustrate, assume that one pound of materials is expected to yield five units of product. One hour of processing labor is required for each

Exhibit 20–1

DEPARTMENTAL DIRECT LABOR VARIANCE REPORT

Code	Reason for Variance	Control-ability	Month of			Year to Date		
			Actual Hours	Variance Hours	Cost	Actual Hours	Variance Hours	Cost
0	No reason. Variances less than 10 percent.	C						
1	Estimated running time too high. Reported to standards department.	N						
2	Estimated setup time too high. Reported to standards department.	N						
3	Men's effort and/or ability above average.	C						
5	New machine, standard has not been changed.	N						
6	Change in methods, standard has not been changed.	N						
7	New or improved tools, standard has not been changed.	N						
8	Used setup from previous jobs.	C						
9	Time set for man operating one machine. Ran two.	C						
10	Time clock registers to 0.1 hour only.	N						
11	Work done under special supervision.	C						
	TOTAL GAINS							
0	No reason. Variances less than 10 percent.	C						
51	Standard too low. Reported to standards department.	N						
52	First time job was made.	C						
53	Slow or obsolete machine used.	N						
54	Planning not correct. Was changed. Standards department notified.	N						
55	Could not follow operation as planned, delivery requirements.	N						
56	Operations in previous departments not performed as planned.	C						
57	Time set for man operating two machines. One available.	N						
58	Quantity too small.	N						
59	Extra setup result of machine break down.	N						
60	Extra work.	N						
61	Two men had to be assigned to job due to nature of job.	N						
62	Learner, apprentice, or student.	N						
63	Man inexperienced. Undergoing instructions.	N						
64	Different operators used due to difficulty of job.	C						
65	Assisting inexperienced operator on another machine.	N						
66	Man's effort and/or ability below average.	C						
67	Operation not performed correctly. Additional time required.	C						
68	Parts spoiled. Had to make additional parts.	C						
69	Tools not available at time job was started.	N						
70	Trying out new tools.	N						
71	Tools not correct when job was started. Had to be corrected.	N						
72	Broke tool. Time lost redressing and sharpening.	C						
73	Oversized material used.	N						
74	Castings warped, but are within foundry tolerances.	N						
75	Casting not to dimensions. Time lost waiting for instructions.	N						
76	Material too hard. Frequent sharpening of tools required.	N						
77	Improper supervision.	C						
79	Illegible blue prints.	N						
80	Blowholes and porous casting.	N						
81	Sheet stock—secondary material or scrap ends used.	N						
99	Full quantity or operations not complete.	N						
	TOTAL LOSSES							
	GRAND TOTAL							
Efficiency % Controllable by Foreman		C						
Efficiency % Noncontrollable		N						
Efficiency % Overall								

Reproduced by permission from "The Analysis of Manufacturing Cost Variances, Research Series No. 22," *N.A.(C.)A. Bulletin*, August 1952, pp. 1545–84.

10 pounds of materials processed, and the standard wage rate is $5 an hour. The standard labor cost of a unit of product is thus:

$$(0.1 \times \$5) \div 5 = \$0.10 \text{ a unit}$$

Suppose now that 10,000 pounds of materials are processed, using 1,000 labor hours and yielding 45,000 units of product. The labor quantity variance will be:

```
Standard cost of output: 45,000 × $0.10........................  $4,500
Actual labor hours at standard wage rate.......................   5,000
Labor quantity variance (unfavorable).........................  $ (500)
```

In this case, however, the entire labor quantity variance is a reflection of the materials quantity variance, because actual labor hours are exactly one tenth of the number of pounds of materials processed, which is the precise relationship assumed in the product cost standard. Thus the two quantity variances might reasonably be combined in a single quantity variance for management reporting.

In other words, whenever labor costs are governed by materials input flows rather than by output quantities, three components of the direct labor cost variance might be identified:

(1)   Actual hours × actual wage rates
(2)   Actual hours × standard wage rates
          Labor rate variance: (1) − (2)
(3)   Required hours × standard wage rates
          Labor performance variance: (2) − (3)
(4)   Earned hours × standard wage rates
          Effect of materials variance on labor cost: (3) − (4)

(The term *required hours* has been coined to refer to the standard hours required by the given quantity of materials inputs; *earned hours* refers to the standard hours reflected in product standard cost.)

The term labor performance variance is used here to distinguish the residual component from the materials-related portion of the labor quantity variance. Whether the variance is subdivided in this way should depend on the materiality of the materials-related component.

Effect of Labor Substitution. Labor variances sometimes arise not because workers are paid at a higher or lower rate than the standard rate for their particular pay grade but because work which is supposed to be performed by a worker in one pay grade is actually performed by a worker in another grade. Variances of this kind are known as labor substitution variances.

To illustrate, suppose that the machining department is required to perform four different operations on a particular production order, for a total of 47 standard labor hours. The workers in this department fall into two pay grades, each with its own standard rate. The standard machining labor cost of this production order is $241, derived from the following figures:

Operation	Hours	Rate	Cost
Cutting....................	5.5	$6	$ 33
Drilling...................	21.0	6	126
Beveling..................	6.0	4	24
Polishing.................	14.5	4	58
Total....................	47.0	xxx	$241

Suppose now that the operators normally assigned to polishing are fully scheduled and that to meet delivery schedules on this order one of the drill press operators is assigned to perform the polishing operation. The operator's time will be charged to the department at the standard wage rate for his own pay grade ($6). The $2 an hour difference between this and the standard rate for the operation is due to a nonstandard labor assignment.

To summarize, if the worker's actual rate is $6.50 and he spends 16 hours on the polishing operation, the following variances can be distinguished:

(1) Actual hours × actual rate......................... 16 × $6.50 = $104
(2) Actual hours × standard rate for actual pay grade.... 16 × $6.00 =   96
      Labor rate variance: (1) − (2)................. $ 8
(3) Actual hours × standard rate for specified pay grade.. 16 × $4.00 =   64
      Labor substitution variance: (2) − (3)..........   32
(4) Standard hours × standard rate for specified pay
      grade..................................... 14.5 × $4.00 =   58
      Labor performance variance: (3) − (4)..........   6
      Total variance: (1) − (4)...................... $46

Effect of Variations in Labor Mix. A single wage rate is sometimes used to cost the labor of a number of pay grades. If the actual pay grade mix differs from the mix on which the standard rate was based, a labor mix variance will result.

For example, suppose that a $5 standard wage rate was used in the machining department, based on an assumed 50-50 mix of the workers in the two pay grades. The department worked 3,500 hours during September, including 1,900 hours in the $6 grade and 1,600 hours in the $4 grade. Total hours at grade standard wage rates were as follows:

1,900 × $6.......................... $11,400
1,600 × $4..........................   6,400
Total............................... $17,800

The difference between this sum and the actual gross wages for the period is the adjusted labor rate variance. The difference between $17,800 and the amount charged to the department (3,500 hours × $5 = $17,500) is the labor mix variance, $300 in this case. Whether the mix variance should be reported to the department head depends on whether he has significant control over the labor mix.

STANDARD COST VARIANCES FOR JOINT PRODUCTS

Standard costs for joint products also provide a basis for variance analysis. Standard joint cost can be established for a batch of products, produced in standard proportions. This can then be divided among the joint products by some method that satisfies income measurement criteria.

For example, suppose that the standard inputs for 100 pounds of finished product include 100 pounds of materials at a standard price of $4 a pound and 20 hours of labor at $5 an hour. Ignoring other processing costs for simplicity, the total standard cost for a 100-pound batch is thus $500. The process yields products in three grades and standard cost has been computed by the relative market value method, as shown in Exhibit 20–2.

Exhibit 20–2

ESTABLISHING STANDARD UNIT COSTS FOR JOINT PRODUCTS

Grade	(1) Standard Pounds of Output per 100 Pounds of Materials	(2) Estimated Market Price per Pound of Output	(3) Market Value per 100 Pounds (1) × (2)	(4) Percent of Total Market Value	(5) Total Cost Allocated (4) × $500	(6) Standard Cost per Pound (5) ÷ (1)
Firsts.......	60	$13.20	$ 792	72%	$360	$6
Seconds.....	30	8.80	264	24	120	4
Culls........	10	4.40	44	4	20	2
Total...	100	xxx	$1,100	100%	$500	xxx

Actual labor and materials costs of the joint products can differ from the standard for a number of reasons, mainly the following:

(1) Materials prices and labor wage rates may differ from standard (price and rate variances).
(2) The process may use more or fewer labor hours or materials quantities than the standard amounts required by the total physical output actually produced (yield variances).
(3) The output may consist of a nonstandard percentage composition of the various joint products (mix variances).
(4) The required or budgeted labor or materials quantities may not be proportional to the volume of output (volume variances).
(5) The inputs used may have been of nonstandard quality (input quality variances).

Input price and rate variances pose no new problems and can be ignored here. Volume variances can be skipped because they will be dealt with in the next section. This still leaves three items in the list: yield variances, mix variances, and input quality variances.

Mix and Yield Variances

The mix and yield variances ordinarily are unsegregated components of the labor and materials quantity variances. They must be segregated analytically. Continuing the example, we find that the following labor and materials inputs were recorded during November:

	Input Quantity	Input Cost at Standard Prices
Materials...................	10,000 lbs.	$40,000
Labor.......................	2,240 hrs.	11,200
Total.....................	xxx	$51,200

Actual yields for the month were:

	Quantity (Pounds)	Standard Cost per Pound	Standard Cost Earned
Firsts...................	6,200	$6	$37,200
Seconds.................	2,800	4	11,200
Culls...................	500	2	1,000
Total.................	9,500	xxx	$49,400

The total quantity variance was thus $51,200 minus $49,400, or $1,800 and unfavorable.

To break the quantity variance into mix and yield components, we must first adopt a physical measure of total output. In this case, the output of each product can be measured conveniently in pounds. The standard cost of a standard output mix is $5 a pound ($500 for 100 pounds of finished products). If the actual output (9,500 pounds) had been distributed among the three products in the standard proportions of 60–30–10, it would have had a standard cost of 9,500 × $5 = $47,500.

The standard cost earned by the actual yield was greater than this, $49,400. The $1,900 difference between these two figures was the *mix variance*, reflecting a higher percentage yield of firsts than in the standard mix.

The difference between the standard cost of the actual input quantities used and the standard cost of a standard mix is the *yield variance*. In this case the yield variances amounted to $3,700 and were unfavorable, computed as follows:

	(1) Standard Input Cost per 100 Pounds Output	(2) Standard Input Cost per 9,500 Pounds Output	(3) Actual Inputs at Standard Prices	(4) Yield Variance (3) − (2)
Materials............	$400	$38,000	$40,000	$(2,000)
Labor...............	100	9,500	11,200	(1,700)
Total.............	$500	$47,500	$51,200	$(3,700)

The variance analysis so far can be summarized as follows:

(1) Actual cost (at standard prices)................... $51,200
(2) Standard cost for standard mix.................... 47,500
     Yield variance: (1) — (2)...................... $(3,700)
(3) Costs earned (actual mix)........................ 49,400
     Mix variance: (2) — (3)....................... 1,900
     Total quantity variance: (1) — (3)............... $(1,800)

The mix variance can be further subdivided by product, if desired:

	Standard Cost of Actual Yield, Actual Mix	Standard Cost of Actual Yield, Standard Mix	Product Mix Variance
Firsts................	$37,200	$34,200	$3,000
Seconds..............	11,200	11,400	(200)
Culls................	1,000	1,900	(900)
Total...........	$49,400	$47,500	$1,900

The same kind of information could be shown in a tabulation of percentage yields, but the conversion into dollar equivalents has the advantage of showing the relative desirability of physical yield variances in the various grades. Furthermore, it permits tying the physical comparisons in with the accounting records so that the entire variance can be analyzed.

Input Quality Variances

Variations in yield or mix are sometimes related systematically to variations in such factors as materials quality or crew size. To illustrate the kinds of analysis that can be performed if information on these relationships is available, let us assume that the materials used during the month were of a quality higher than standard. Information available to the company indicates that materials of this quality should have yielded the three products in 70–25–5 proportions, total output weight remaining the same. This means that 100 pounds of output in these proportions would earn standard costs of $530, or $30 more than for materials of standard quality:

	Product Yield (Pounds)	Standard Cost per Pound	Standard Cost Earned
Firsts......................	70	$6	$420
Seconds....................	25	4	100
Culls......................	5	2	10
Total.................	100	xxx	$530

In other words, a favorable mix variance would be expected to arise from the higher quality of the materials used.

The analysis of the quantity variance so far can be summarized as follows:

(1) Actual cost (at standard prices)................... $51,200
(2) Standard cost for standard mix, standard quality
       (95 × $500).............................. 47,500
       Yield variance: (1) − (2)..................... $(3,700)
(3) Standard cost for standard mix, actual input quality
       (95 × $530).............................. 50,350
       Input quality variance: (2) − (3)..............   2,850
(4) Costs earned (actual mix)...................... 49,400
       Operating mix variance: (3) − (4)..............   (950)
       Total variance: (1) − (4)...................... $(1,800)

This shows that the total mix variance should have been $950 more favorable than it was, given the quality of the materials used, and operating performance was actually unfavorable. The yield variance was not affected by the variation in materials quality.

The analysis is not yet finished, however. A richer product mix ordinarily entails higher input costs, in the form of higher materials prices, higher wages rates, or increased input quantities. Oil refineries, for example, often increase gasoline yields in peak driving months by subjecting intermediates to more intensive processing. Similarly, the yield of low-sulphur fuel oil, which has a higher market value, can be increased by purchasing more expensive grades of crude oil.

Suppose that the improved mix in the example above was obtained by purchasing a higher grade of raw materials with a standard price of $4.25 a pound, or a premium of $25 for each 100 pounds of output. The net input quality variance is thus only 5 cents a pound, or $475 for the month:

	Per 100 Pounds	November (9,500 Lbs.)
Improved product mix.....................	$30	$2,850
Increased materials cost....................	25	2,375
Net input quality variance.................	$ 5	$ 475

The $2,375 in increased materials cost in this case would have to be extracted from the purchase price variance if the process was charged at standard prices for standard materials. It would have to be removed from the yield variance if the process was charged for the standard price of the actual materials used.

VARIANCES FROM STANDARD OVERHEAD COST

Variances from standard overhead cost differ from direct labor and direct materials variances in two ways: (1) they can be analyzed only for the cost center as a whole, not by individual products or individual production workers; and (2) they are seldom meaningful for periods shorter than a month. In both cases, the reason is that standard overhead costs do not measure direct relationships between specific inputs and product outputs.

Two-Variance Analysis

Whenever costs are expected to vary in response to changes in standard labor hours (or standard machine-hours, standard materials input, etc.) rather than actual hours, variances from standard overhead cost earned can be analyzed by a two-variance method similar to that developed in Chapter 7 for overhead variances in historical job order costing systems.

To illustrate, let us return to the simple numerical example that we used in earlier chapters. Actual overhead during May was $12,060 and the standard labor content of the work performed during the month amounted to 3,400 hours. The burden rate was $3 an hour, and the standard overhead cost for the month was 3,400 × $3 = $10,200. This was the amount of overhead "earned" by the factory, and was $1,860 less than the actual overhead cost for the month.

Suppose further that actual overhead costs are expected to vary more closely with standard direct labor hours (DLH) than with actual direct labor hours and that the flexible budget allowances can be summarized in the following formula:

Budgeted overhead cost per month = $7,400 + ($1.15 × standard DLH)

The flexible budget allowance for a volume of 3,400 standard or earned labor hours is thus $11,310:

$$\text{Budget} = \$7,400 + (\$1.15 \times 3,400) = \$11,310$$

The variance analysis can now be summarized in the format developed in Chapter 7:

(1)	Actual costs charged...........................	$12,060	
(2)	Budgeted costs for earned hours..................	11,310	
	Spending variance: (1) − (2)...................		$ (750)
(3)	Costs absorbed by earned hours..................	10,200	
	Volume variance: (2) − (3)...................		(1,110)
	Total variance: (1) − (3).....................		$(1,860)

This same analysis is diagrammed in Exhibit 20–3. The amounts of overhead earned at different volumes are shown by the height of the straight line rising from the lower left-hand corner of the chart. The amounts budgeted are shown by the height of the other line. The amounts earned and budgeted for this month's volume of 3,400 standard direct labor hours are shown as large dots on these lines. The actual amount spent is shown by another dot. The total variance is the vertical distance be-

Exhibit 20-3

TWO-VARIANCE ANALYSIS ILLUSTRATED

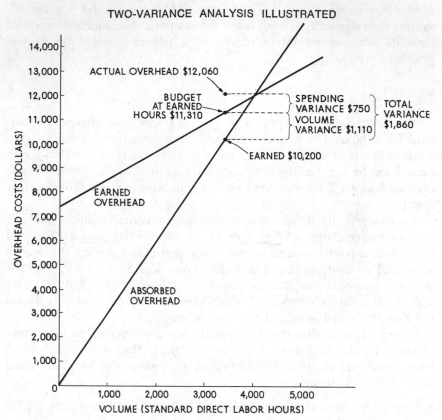

tween the actual cost and the amount absorbed at this volume. This total is divided into two parts, the distance between the actual and budgeted amounts representing the spending variance and the distance between the amount budgeted and the amount absorbed representing the volume variance.

Notice that the *actual* number of direct labor hours was not reflected in this analysis in any way. The budget formula indicates that overhead costs will rise or fall with changes in standard labor hours but will be entirely unaffected by variations in the amount of labor actually used to produce a given output. If this assumption is not valid, then the two-variance method should not be used.

Three-Variance Analysis

Whenever overhead costs tend to vary with the amount of some input rather than with physical output, a three-variance analysis is called for, dividing the total variance into three components:

1. Spending variance: the difference between actual overhead and the flexible budget allowance for the actual quantity of input used.
2. Input efficiency variance: the difference between the flexible budget allowance for the actual quantity of inputs used and the allowances for the standard input quantity for the work done during the period.
3. Volume variance: the difference between the amount of overhead earned and the amount budgeted for the work done during the period.

In this case the calculations can be summarized in the following table:

(1)	Actual costs....................................	$12,060	
(2)	Budget at actual hours..........................	11,425	
	Spending variance: (1) − (2)....................		$ (635)
(3)	Budget at earned hours.........................	11,310	
	Labor efficiency variance: (2) − (3)............		(115)
(4)	Earned at earned hours.........................	10,200	
	Volume variance: (3) − (4)..................		(1,110)
	Total variance: (1) − (4)......................		$(1,860)

The calculation of the volume variance is the same as in the two-variance method and needs no further discussion. The big change is the introduction of the budget allowance for the actual amount of input used. Since overhead costs are now presumed to vary with actual labor hours, the flexible budget allowances for use in control reporting should be based on actual labor hours rather than on standard hours. The input quantity this month was 3,500 direct labor hours, and the overhead budget at this volume is:

$$\text{Budget} = \$7,400 + (\$1.15 \times 3,500) = \$11,425$$

Since actual overhead costs for the month totaled $12,060, the spending variance was $12,060 − $11,425 = $635.

The spending variance calculated in this way differs by $115 from the $750 spending variance calculated by the two-variance method. This difference measures the effect on overhead cost of the difference between actual hours and earned hours. Since actual labor hours exceeded earned hours by 100 hours, the budget allowance for variable overhead costs was increased by $115 (100 hours at $1.15 an hour). This is the input efficiency variance, in this case known as the labor efficiency variance. (If overhead costs varied with the number of machine-hours used, this would be called a machine efficiency variance.)

Whether the spending variance is $635 or $750 depends on the underlying pattern of cost variation. If overhead costs vary with labor inputs, then $635 is correct. If overhead depends on the rate of output, however, the answer is $750. In other words, the size of the spending variance depends on the determinants of overhead cost and not on the method of analysis; in any given situation, only one method is appropriate.

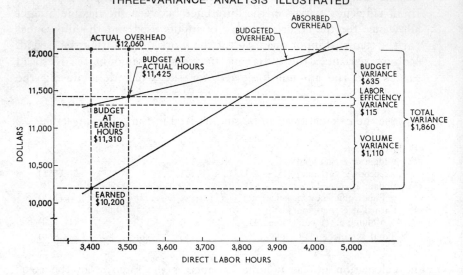

Exhibit 20-4

THREE-VARIANCE ANALYSIS ILLUSTRATED

The full progression from the amount earned to the actual amount spent is illustrated in Exhibit 20–4. The amount earned is identified by the point on the Earned line at the 3,400-hour mark. The vertical distance between this point and the point on the Budgeted line above is the volume variance. The labor efficiency variance is shown by the vertical distance traveled by a movement along the budgeted line from 3,400 to 3,500 hours. Finally, the spending variance is shown by the distance between the budget allowance for 3,500 hours and actual overhead cost for the month.

Four-Variance Analysis of Overhead Variances

The volume variance ordinarily represents the over- or underabsorption of fixed costs. To the extent that it has any meaning at all, the fixed cost component of the burden rate measures the average cost of providing departmental capacity to do business. An unfavorable volume variance, therefore, indicates the amount of capacity underutilized. (A favorable volume variance is harder to explain, but it can be said to represent the capacity costs that are doing double duty.)

Assuming that factory capacity is measured in labor hours, it is apparent that the more output achieved in each direct labor hour, the greater the total production capacity of the plant. Thus it might be argued that the effect of direct labor performance on fixed cost absorption should be measured to show how much of the factory's capacity has been consumed or released by off-standard labor performance.

To illustrate, the effect of the 100-hour unfavorable direct labor performance in the example is to make this much of the factory's capacity unavailable for other uses. In other terms, one sixth of the volume variance in this case is due to unfavorable labor performance. The fixed cost component of the burden rate is $1.85 an hour ($7,400 in fixed costs divided by the normal volume of 4,000 hours), and at this rate a lost capacity variance of $185 could be separated from the rest of the volume variance, thus bringing the total to four variances in all.

This fourth variance can be calculated in other ways, but it deserves little attention. It makes sense only if the department is operating at capacity and thus can increase production only if capacity utilization can be improved. In the absence of serious problems of capacity limitation, the two-variance or three-variance method should be completely adequate.

Seasonal Variances

For interim reporting it is sometimes desirable to estimate the effects of seasonal variations in cost and in volume. Seasonal variations in cost are simple to deal with once the seasonal pattern has been identified. For example, May may be a month of high fixed costs in the machining department because heavy maintenance expenditures are normally scheduled for that month. By adjusting the budgeted fixed costs for May to, say, $8,400, the spending and volume variances can be recalculated:

(1)	Actual costs...................................	$12,060		
(2)	Budget at actual hours, month of May..............	12,425		
	Spending variance: (1) − (2)....................		$	365
(3)	Budget at earned hours, month of May............	12,310		
	Labor efficiency variance: (2) − (3)............			(115)
(4)	Earned at earned hours.........................	10,200		
	Volume variance: (3) − (4)...................			(2,110)
	Total variance: (1) − (4).....................			$(1,860)

The adjustment of the budget leads to a shift of $1,000 from the spending variance to the volume variance; the labor efficiency variance remains unchanged because the variable cost rate remains the same.

Seasonal variations in volume require a different form of analysis. If volume is seasonal, the volume variance is really made up of two elements, one reflecting the seasonal influence and the other the departure of actual volume from the volume budgeted for the month. Continuing the example, suppose that the volume normally budgeted for May is 3,800 earned hours instead of the 3,400 earned hours actually achieved. The amount of overhead absorbed at this volume would be 3,800 × $3 = $11,400. The amount budgeted, including the $1,000 in extra fixed maintenance costs, would be:

$$\text{Budget} = \$8,400 + (\$1.15 \times 3,800) = \$12,770$$

The budgeted volume variance therefore would be $1,370:

Absorbed at 3,800 earned hours	$11,400
Budgeted at 3,800 earned hours	12,770
Budgeted volume variance	$(1,370)

The actual volume variance during May was $2,110, or $740 greater than the normal volume variance for the month. This $740 is the adjusted volume variance for the month, indicating the departure of volume from its anticipated level. The seasonal variance should cancel itself out during the course of the year.[1]

Recording Standard Overhead Costs

No matter what kind of standard costing system is in use, the overhead-in-process accounts do not serve as a vehicle for deriving departmental cost variances. This is the function of the overhead summary and overhead earned accounts.

For example, suppose the the opening balance in the overhead-in-process account was $2,600, representing the standard overhead cost of the work already done on the units in process at the beginning of the month. Suppose further that products with standard overhead costs totaling $11,000 were completed and transferred to the finished goods stockroom during the month. After recording these transfers, the overhead-in-process account appeared as follows:

Overhead in Process—Machining

Beg. bal.	2,600	Completions	11,000

At the end of the month, the inventory count indicated that the work in process had a standard overhead cost of $1,800. The amount of overhead earned is the amount that must be debited to the overhead-in-process account to produce this balance. In this case, the amount was $10,200 and was recorded by the following entry:

Overhead in Process—Machining	10,200	
Overhead Earned—Machining		10,200

At the end of the month the accounts showed the following:

---

[1] This discussion presumes that seasonal adjustments have been made to the budgeted data and that separate flexible budget formulas are therefore available for each interim reporting period or season. The possibility of applying statistical techniques to isolate the seasonal influence after the fact is discussed by Werner Frank, "Seasonal Adjustment of Accounting Data," *Management Services*, November–December 1965, pp. 51–55.

Overhead Summary—Machining		Overhead Earned—Machining	
Actual Cost 12,060			Earned by production 10,200

Overhead in Process—Machining

Beg. bal.	2,600	Completions	11,000
Earned	10,200		
	12,800		
End bal. 1,800			

The total overhead variance is now represented by the difference between the balances in the overhead summary and overhead earned accounts and can be analyzed by the methods described earlier.

SUMMARY

Most standard costing systems, whether single plan, basic plan, or something else, provide for identifying certain kinds of variances at the source and recording them in special variance accounts classified as part of factory overhead. Examples include overtime premiums and shift differentials, separated from the labor rate variance; and setup time, rework labor, and equipment substitution variances, separated from the labor quantity variance. Classifications such as these not only reduce the size of the residual unexplained variance but also eliminate from direct materials and direct labor most of the influences that cause them to vary disproportionately with volume.

Standard costs can also be used in joint production to provide indexes of the shifts in relative product yields. The calculations in this chapter are suggestive of what can be done in this connection.

Extension of standard costing to factory overhead requires still another kind of variance analysis. Variances from standard overhead cost include not only the spending variances described in Chapter 17 but volume variances, and sometimes input efficiency variances, as well. These latter components do not measure the effectiveness of overhead cost control and must be extracted from the total overhead variance.

EXERCISES AND PROBLEMS

1.* The standard unit costs per pound and standard yield rates of three joint products are as follows:

---

* Solutions to problems marked with an asterisk can be found in Appendix B.

Product	Yield Ratio	Cost
A......................	30%	$2
B......................	45	3
C......................	25	5

The total weight of product output is expected, under normal conditions, to equal the weight of the materials processed. Processing costs vary as a function of the weight of the materials processed.

During August, 5,000 pounds of materials were processed. At standard prices and wage rates, materials and labor cost $17,300. Output for the month totaled 1,600 pounds of A, 2,400 pounds of B, and 950 pounds of C. Fifty pounds of materials were lost in processing.

a) What is the standard cost of processing 100 pounds of materials?
b) Calculate the total quantity variance for August and break it down into mix and yield components.

2.* A department's employees are grouped into three pay grades, with standard hourly wage rates as follows:

Grade	Rate
1...........................	$2.50
2...........................	3.00
3...........................	4.00

A single department-wide standard wage rate of $3.50 an hour is used for product costing. Data for October are: (1) actual department wages, $30,000; (2) standard labor cost of the month's output, $32,000; (3) actual labor hours: grade 1—2,000; grade 2—4,000; grade 3—3,000.

Analyze the department labor variances for the month.

3. Actual wages total $15,000. The standard wage rate used for product costing is $4 an hour. Actual labor time totals 4,000 hours: 2,500 hours of grade A labor, with a standard wage rate of $5 an hour, and 1,500 hours of grade B labor, with a standard wage rate of $3.50 an hour. The month's output has a standard labor cost of $15,800.

a) What are the standard proportions of grade A and grade B labor implicit in the $4 standard wage rate used for product costing?
b) Compute and analyze the variances.
c) How much labor cost would be charged to the Work in Process account to reflect the month's operations if the company were on a single plan standard costing system? A basic plan system?

4. Given the following data, compute and analyze the overhead cost variance:

Actual factory overhead....................	$29,000
Standard overhead cost of goods finished......	27,000
Standard overhead cost of goods in process:	
Beginning of month.....................	5,000
End of month.........................	7,700
Standard overhead cost....................	$3 per direct labor hour
Flexible budget...........................	$15,000 + $1.50 per direct labor hour
Actual direct labor hours..................	9,500

5.* Standard costs and budget allowances in a machining department are as follows:

Flexible budget:

Machine-Hours	Manufacturing Overhead Costs
8,000	$20,000
10,000	22,000
12,000	24,000
14,000	26,000

Standard burden rate = $2 per machine-hour.

Standard manufacturing overhead cost:

Product A............. 1 machine-hour per unit = $2 per unit.
Product B............. 1.5 machine-hours per unit = $3 per unit.

During April the department produced 4,000 units of product A and 4,000 units of product B. A total of 9,500 machine-hours was recorded during April, and actual manufacturing overhead costs totaled $21,750.

Compute and analyze the factory overhead cost variances for the month.

6. A process yields three joint products, X, Y, and Z. A batch of 100 pounds of materials has a standard yield of 100 pounds of products: 50 pounds of X, 30 pounds of Y, and 20 pounds of Z.

Standard materials cost for a 100-pound batch amounts to $300. Standard labor cost is $100 for a batch. The products sell at prices of $2.20, $11, and $22 a pound, respectively.

During February 80 batches were processed. The materials used cost $25,000, at standard purchase prices. Labor costs, at standard wage rates, amounted to $8,800. The month's output totaled 7,500 pounds, as follows:

Product X................ 4,000 pounds
Product Y................ 2,400 pounds
Product Z................ 1,100 pounds

a) Compute standard labor and materials costs for a unit of each product.
b) Compute and analyze the variances for the month.

7. The Dade Corporation operates a single plant, manufacturing molded plastic products. It uses a basic plan standard costing system in which all price variances are removed at the time of purchase or payroll preparation. Production in the molding department is performed by crews of men in three separate wage rate classifications. A "standard crew hour" consists of 10 man-hours, distributed among the three pay grades as follows:

Pay Grade	Hours	Standard Rate	Standard Cost
FA–1......	2	$3.50	$ 7.00
FA–2......	3	2.80	8.40
FA–3......	5	2.40	12.00
Total......	10	xxx	$27.40

Standard output is 1,000 pounds of finished product per standard crew hour, and on this basis standard labor cost per 1,000 pounds of product is $27.40.

During February charges to the molding department included 650 hours of FA–1 labor, 1,000 hours of FA–2 labor, and 1,600 hours of FA–3 labor. Output of the molding department totaled 330,000 pounds of finished product. There were no in-process inventories either at the beginning or at the end of the month. The department operated 160 hours during February, using two production crews throughout the period. All of this was classified as productive time except for five hours of idle time recorded by one crew while machinery was being repaired. The departmental payroll for the month totaled $9,000.

a) Compute any variances that you can identify.

b) Trace the labor costs of the molding department through T accounts. Indicate for each T account what the ending balance represents. If possible, design your accounts so that only one variance remains in each.

8. A department's overhead cost budget is $48,000 a month plus $2 for each actual direct labor hour. Actual direct labor cost during September was $69,000 (15,000 hours at $4.60 an hour). Actual overhead was $77,500. The department's output for the month had a standard cost of:

Labor, 15,500 hours at $4.50	$ 69,750
Overhead, 15,500 hours at $5	77,500
Total	$147,250

Materials cost variances for the month were negligible.

Departmental variances are classified as controllable or noncontrollable, favorable or unfavorable. The controllable variances are then totaled, and if the total of the favorable controllable variances exceeds the total of the unfavorable controllable variances the foreman is paid a bonus amounting to 5 percent of the difference (the "net favorable controllable variance"). If the net controllable variance is zero or unfavorable, the foreman receives no bonus. The foreman has no control over wage rates or volume, but all of the overhead costs are controllable.

Prepare a list of the variances you can compute from the above data; indicate for each whether it is controllable or noncontrollable, favorable or unfavorable; and compute the amount of the foreman's bonus, if any.

9. The Rushby Chemical Company manufactures a certain product by mixing three kinds of materials in large batches. The blendmaster is charged with the responsibility of maintaining the quality of the product, and this often requires him to alter the proportions of the various ingredients. Standard costs are used to provide materials control information. The standard materials inputs per batch are:

	Quantity (Pounds)	Price (per Pound)	Standard Cost of Materials
Bulk material	420	$0.06	$25.20
Coloring material	70	0.12	8.40
Setting material	10	0.25	2.50
Total batch	500	xxx	$36.10

The finished product is packed in 50-pound boxes; the standard materials cost of each box is therefore $3.61.

During January, the following materials were put in process:

Bulk material.................	181,000 lbs.
Coloring material.............	33,000
Setting material..............	6,000
Total......................	220,000 lbs.

Inventories in process totaled 5,000 pounds at the beginning of the month and 8,000 pounds at the end of the month. It is assumed that these inventories consist of materials in their standard proportions. Finished output during January amounted to 4,100 boxes.

a) Compute the total materials quantity variance for the month and break it down into mix and yield components.

b) Who, if anyone, in the management of the company would be interested in seeing this breakdown of the quantity variance?

10. The overhead costs in one department are budgeted on the basis of the following formula:

$$\text{Overhead costs} = \$100,000 + \$3 \times \text{actual direct labor hours}$$

Other data are: (1) normal volume is 50,000 direct labor hours; (2) actual overhead cost, $225,000; (3) actual direct labor hours used, 40,000; and (4) standard direct labor hours in actual output, 39,000.

a) Calculate and analyze the overhead variance. What managerial use, if any, would be made of each of the variances you have calculated (i.e., who is being evaluated and in what connection)?

b) Calculate the overhead variances that would be appropriate if the overhead budget equation were as follows:

$$\text{Overhead costs} = \$100,000 + \$3 \times \text{standard direct labor hours}$$

11. Factory overhead is budgeted on the basis of the following formula:

$$\text{Overhead} = \$500,000 + \$2 \text{ per labor hour used} + 20\% \text{ of actual labor cost}$$

Standard product costs are based on a standard labor rate of $5 an hour and a standard overhead cost of $7 a labor hour.

Actual overhead cost in June was $845,000. The total standard cost of the June output was $1,920,000, made up of the following:

Materials..................	$ 600,000
Labor.....................	550,000
Overhead..................	770,000
Total.....................	$1,920,000

Materials variances were negligible in June, but there was an unfavorable labor quantity variance of $20,000 and an unfavorable labor rate variance of $57,000, the latter caused by a 10 percent wage increase due to a new labor union contract.

Foremen are held responsible for labor quantity variances. Responsibility for overhead costs is in the hands of the plant manager, and he would like your assistance in explaining the $75,000 unfavorable variance in overhead costs. What would you tell him?

12. A department has two kinds of machines which are interchangeable but not equally efficient. Standard labor hours per unit of product on each type of machine are:

Product	Model X	Model Y
A................	1.0	1.2
B................	2.0	2.6
C................	3.0	2.8
D................	4.0	5.0

Standard product cost is based, in each case, on the more efficient machine model for that product—that is, C's standard cost is based on model Y machine time, while standard cost for the other three products presumes the use of model X machines. The data for March are:

(1) Actual labor hours, including items (4) and (5) below, 2,200.
(2) Standard wage rate, $3.50 an hour.
(3) Actual wages, $8,000.
(4) Labor hours waiting for machine repair, 40 hours.
(5) Labor hours correcting defects in products rejected in inspection: product B, 50 hours; product C, 30 hours.
(6) Production (units of product) on each type of machine:

Product	Model X	Model Y
A................	500	...
B................	200	100
C................	...	150
D................	140	50

a) Compute and analyze the labor variance for the month in as much detail as the data permit. Explain the meaning of each variance component that you identify.

b) Assuming that a maximum of 1,460 hours on model X machines and 1,200 hours on model Y machines was available for production during the month, after subtracting waiting and rework time and allowing an adequate margin for variations in efficiency, did the department achieve the most efficient scheduling of its equipment? How is any scheduling inefficiency reflected in the labor variance? Explain and quantify if possible.

13. The Schuyler Corporation uses a standard costing system in its factory. Statistical studies have shown that variation in overhead costs in department X is more closely correlated with direct labor input than with product output. The departmental burden rate is $2 per direct labor hour, and 15,000 direct labor hours were recorded during November. Additional data are:

	Budget		Actual, November
	Fixed per Month	Variable per Direct Labor Hour	
Supervision..................	$ 5,600	...	$ 5,900
Indirect labor..............	500	$0.60	10,200 =
Supplies....................	...	0.25	3,400
Department S service.........	...	0.10	1,750 ← ?
Building service.............	6,500	...	7,600
Total.....................	$12,600	$0.95	$28,850

The standard overhead cost content of work in process was $8,000 on November 1 and $10,000 on November 30. The standard overhead cost content of the work completed and transferred out of the department during the month was $29,500. Production departments are charged for department S service at a rate of $5 per service hour. Production department managers have responsibility for controlling the amount of department S service used. Building service costs are allocated to production departments on the basis of floor space occupied. The actual costs of department S for November averaged $5.20 per service hour.

a) What is the normal volume of activity in department X?
b) What was the total of direct labor hours earned by department X during November?
c) What was the effect on total departmental overhead cost of the variation from standard direct labor efficiency during November?
d) What was the overall departmental variance for November?
e) What is the meaning of the variance in building service costs for department X?
f) Prepare a brief summary of actual overhead costs and budget allowances for the month reflecting only those variances attributable in whole or in part to *overhead* cost control in department X (i.e., exclude those variances due to variations from standard direct labor efficiency).

14.† Joe is concerned about the large unfavorable labor quantity variance that arose in his department last month. He has had a small favorable variance for several months, and he thinks that his crew worked just as effectively last month as in previous months. This makes him believe that something must be wrong with the calculations, but he admits that he doesn't understand them. The variance was reported as follows:

Standard labor cost of output (120,000 pounds at 6.45¢)....... $7,740
Actual labor hours at standard wage rate.................. 8,585
Labor quantity variance................................ $ (845)

The product is made in batches which start with 1,200 pounds of material. The standard calls for the following labor quantities for each batch:

† From a problem prepared by Carl L. Nelson.

Labor Class	Standard Wage Rate	Standard Labor Hours	Standard Labor Cost
Class 6........	$4.50	3	$13.50
Class 5........	4.00	6	24.00
Class 3........	3.00	9	27.00
Total.........		18	$64.50

The raw material is of uneven quality, and the product yield from a batch varies with the quality of the raw materials used. The standard output is 1,000 pounds, resulting in a standard labor cost of 6.45 cents a pound.

Joe's work force is a crew of 12 men. The standard crew consists of two class 6 men, four class 5 men, and six class 3 men. Lower rated employees cannot do the work of the higher rated employees, but the reverse is possible with some slight loss in efficiency and a resulting increase in labor hours.

The standard work day is nine hours. Last month had 23 working days, for a total of 207 standard working hours. Premiums for overtime hours are charged to overhead accounts and do not enter this problem.

Last month, 165,000 pounds of material were used to produce 120,000 pounds of product. The actual amounts of labor used were as follows:

Labor Class	Labor Hours	Labor Rate	Labor Cost
Class 6........	390	$4.50	$1,755
Class 5........	980	4.00	3,920
Class 3........	970	3.00	2,910
Total.........	2,340		$8,585

Joe's work force last month, assigned to him by the personnel department, consisted of two class 6 men, five class 5 men, and five class 3 men.

What would you tell Joe? Can you get him "off the hook" with the plant manager?

15. In the Travis Paper Company, the principal costs are centered about the paper machines. The company, therefore, attaches great importance to the calculations of machine rates by which manufacturing overhead is assigned to products. Furthermore, the operating executives give considerable attention to the analysis and interpretation of cost figures and in particular to overhead cost variances. In periods of abnormally high or low production, the variances are analyzed to separate controllable from noncontrollable gains or losses.

By running three eight-hour shifts each 24 hours, one of the Travis Paper Company's machines has a normal annual volume of 6,000 hours. An hourly machine rate that will adequately distribute budgeted machine overhead to products at this volume is as follows:

Fixed charges, $61,800/6,000............. $10.30
Variable charges, $98,400/6,000.......... 16.40
Total................................. $26.70

During the first three months of 19x1, the machine actually ran 1,490 hours; the first quarter ordinarily provides 30 percent of the total year's production. The overhead account for this machine at the end of the quarter showed the following data:

Machine No. 2 Overhead

Fixed charges	14,485	Fixed charges (1,490 × $10.30)	15,347
Variable charges	23,304	Variable charges (1,490 × $16.40)	24,436
	37,789		39,783
		Overabsorbed balance 1,994	

The costs chargeable to machine no. 2 were:

	Normal Annual Charges	Actual 1st Quarter 19x1
Fixed charges:		
Watchman and fire brigade...........	$ 1,800	$ 450
Taxes.............................	7,560	1,890
Insurance.........................	4,980	1,245
Depreciation.......................	33,000	8,250
Building repairs....................	10,460	1,625
Supervision........................	2,400	600
Accounting and office...............	1,000	250
Laboratory........................	600	175
	$61,800	$14,485
Variable charges:		
Indirect labor.....................	$ 5,400	$ 1,318
Supplies...........................	12,260	3,154
Water.............................	1,620	364
Teaming and yard expense...........	6,720	1,520
Stock handling.....................	1,980	430
Repairs to machinery...............	8,160	1,880
Power and light....................	54,220	12,408
Heat.............................	8,040	2,230
	$98,400	$23,304

Determine, insofar as possible, the sources of the $1,994 variance and measure how much of this variance comes from each source. On the basis of your analysis, prepare a brief statement for submission to the general manager.

Review Problems

16.* The Abel Company manufactures three products in two factory departments. It uses a full cost, basic plan factory standard costing system. You have the following data for department I (DLH is direct labor hours):

	Product A	Product B	Product C
Standard unit cost:			
Department I materials....................	$ 3	$ 6	$ 9
Department I labor (at $4 an hour).........	8	12	10
Department I overhead (at $6 per DLH)....	12	18	15
Inventory and production (units):			
Department I work in process, March 1.....	. . .	100	200
Completed and transferred to department II, March.............................	300	500	400
Department I work in process, March 31....	200	100	. . .

Work in process at both beginning and end of the month was complete as to materials and half-processed. Other data for the month were:

Materials inventories, March 1 (at standard prices)........	$11,400
Materials purchased ($5,400 at standard prices)............	5,850
Materials issued to department I (at standard prices)........	6,000
Actual direct labor payroll, department I (3,500 DLH)......	14,200
Actual overhead, department I...........................	25,500

At normal operating volume and with actual DLH equal to standard DLH, variable overhead totals $8,000 and fixed overhead amounts to $16,000. It is assumed that variable overhead varies in direct proportion to variations in the number of direct labor hours used.

a) Enter these data in appropriate T accounts. Try to set up accounts that will help you identify the variances.

b) Prepare a list of variances for department I for the month of March. Be sure to label each variance clearly.

17. The Blue Ribbon Corporation uses single plan standard full costing in accounting for manufacturing costs in one of its plants. The following information applies to the month of January 19x1:

(1) Inventories at standard, January 1, 19x1:

Materials..	$20,000
Materials in process.............................	5,000
Labor in process.................................	2,000
Manufacturing overhead in process.................	3,000

(2) January materials purchases, $14,500 (total standard cost of items purchased, $14,800).

(3) Materials requisitioned for production (at standard prices):

On standard quantity requisitions...................	$12,000
On supplemental requisitions.......................	1,000

(4) Freight bill on January materials purchases, $800.

(5) January direct labor payroll, $9,200 (5,000 actual hours, 5,200 standard hours; the standard labor rate is $1.80 an hour).

(6) Factory overhead costs incurred or accrued during January, $14,000 (the standard burden rate is $1.50 a direct labor dollar).

(7) Work finished during January:

Standard material cost.............................	$11,000
Standard labor cost...............................	9,540
Standard factory overhead cost.....................	14,310
Total standard cost of work finished................	$34,850

Overhead costs in this factory are expected to total $10,000 a month plus 90 cents for every standard direct labor hour.

a) Enter the opening balances in T accounts and record the month's transactions.

b) For the month of January 19x1 compute, as accurately as you can, two materials variances, two labor variances, and as many overhead variances as you believe relevant.

18. A company has two products, with the following standard costs and the following production for the month of March:

	Product A	Product B
Standard cost per unit:		
Materials..................................	$ 1	$ 2
Labor......................................	4	3
Overhead..................................	8	6
Total.....................................	$13	$11
Units in process (all materials applied, but only one half of labor operations performed and one half of overhead earned):		
Beginning of month........................	1,000	3,000
End of month.............................	2,000	3,000
Units completed during month..............	4,000	5,000

Factory overhead costs for the month were budgeted from the following formula:

Overhead = $60,000 + 0.5 (actual direct labor hours × standard wage rates)

The following costs were recorded during the month:

(1) Materials purchased: standard cost, $20,000; actual cost, $21,200.
(2) Direct materials issued (at standard prices): $17,000.
(3) Direct labor payrolls, actual hours worked: at standard wage rates, $31,600; at actual wage rates, $34,000.
(4) Miscellaneous overhead costs: $75,000.

a) Prepare a list of variances for the month. Indicate for each whether it was favorable or unfavorable. Show your calculations.
b) Compute the standard cost of work in process at the end of the month.

19. Inventory balances at the Mooseheart Company factory, all priced at standard cost, were as follows on March 1:

Materials............................. $1,500
Materials in process.................... 600
Labor in process....................... 200
Overhead in process.................... 180

The following transactions occurred during March:

(1) Materials received from vendors: actual price, $1,290; standard price, $1,200.
(2) Materials issued (at standard prices): direct materials, $1,150; indirect materials, $100.
(3) Summary of labor time tickets for the month (at standard wage rates): direct labor, $2,020; indirect labor, $340.
(4) Actual payroll for the month, $2,450—includes overtime premium, $60, and apprentice pay, $15, to be charged to overhead; these two amounts are not included in the figures given in item (3).

(5) Other overhead charges for the month, $1,300.

(6) Goods completed during March, and standard product costs:

Product	Units Completed	Standard Cost per Unit			
		Materials	Labor	Overhead	Total
X..........	100	$1.00	$2.00	$1.80	$4.80
Y..........	200	1.50	4.00	3.50	9.00
Z..........	300	3.00	2.50	2.00	7.50

(7) The month's flexible budget allowances for factory overhead can be calculated from the following formula:

$$\text{Overhead costs} = \$1{,}000 + 0.4 \times \text{standard direct labor cost}$$

(8) Standard costs of work in process on March 31:

> Materials in process................. $500
> Labor in process.................... 400
> Overhead in process................. 350

a) Enter the opening inventory balances and record the transactions described in items (1) through (6) in appropriately titled T accounts.

b) Compute aggregate variances for materials, labor, and overhead, and subdivide these in any way you deem appropriate. Indicate for each variance whether it is favorable or unfavorable.

20. The Poquette Corporation uses standard costing systems in all its plants. Departmental flexible budget allowances are computed monthly, based on standard direct labor hours earned in each department. Each department has three work-in-process accounts, one each for materials, labor, and overhead. Materials and labor are charged to their respective work-in-process accounts at standard prices and wage rates. Marketable or reusable scrap is credited to departmental materials-in-process accounts at standard prices. Factory overhead costs are accumulated in departmental overhead summary accounts, and at the end of the month a charge is made to overhead in process on the basis of standard direct labor hours earned for the month. Completed production is credited to the departmental work-in-process accounts as finished work is transferred out of the department.

The refining department of the Poquette Corporation's Minneapolis plant processes a certain raw material for use in a number of the company's products. The standard cost of a ton of the refined material is:

> Raw materials:
> 3,400 pounds of concentrate at $0.05...................... $170
> 500 pounds of processing chemical at $0.15.................. 75
>   Less: 1,800 pounds of recoverable residue at $0.02.......... (36) $209
> Labor, 3 crew hours at $25 per crew hour..................... 75
> Overhead, 3 crew hours at $65 per crew hour................. 195
> Total standard cost per ton................................. $479

The following data summarize the refining department's operations for the month of October:

Materials received in department:

Concentrate.....................................	665 tons
Processing chemical............................	94 tons
Recoverable residue.............................	370 tons
Actual crew labor at standard wage rates............	$29,200
Actual crew hours..............................	1,180 crew hours
Actual overhead cost............................	$79,200
Refined materials completed......................	380 tons

Actual crew hours include 10 crew hours of unproductive time. Standard product cost includes no provision for this kind of unproductive time. The amount of work in process was unchanged during the month.

The number of labor crew hours varies with the number of tons of concentrate used, in the proportions reflected in the standard cost sheet. Overhead varies with the number of actual crew hours, and the flexible budget for the department can be computed from the following formula:

$$\text{Budget} = \$30,000 + \$33.75 \text{ per actual crew hour}$$

Analyze all variances for the month in as much detail as you can. Use any method of analyzing and classifying the labor and overhead variances that seems appropriate.

21. The King Supply Company's factory is organized in four production departments and three service departments. A full cost, basic plan standard costing system is in use.

Budgeted overhead costs for the current year, at normal volume, together with other pertinent data, are as follows (DLH is direct labor hours):

Department	Floor Space	No. of Employees	Dept. 23 Man-Hours Used	Normal Volume per Month	Budgeted Direct Dept. Overhead
Production 11.....	20%	80	600	10,000 DLH	$30,000
Production 12.....	25	120	900	15,000 DLH	50,000
Production 13.....	35	60	1,200	20,000 machine-hours	59,300
Production 14.....	9	50	300	5,000 DLH	20,000
Service 21........	..	6	...	....	10,000
Service 22........	8	24	...	....	19,000
Service 23........	3	20	...	3,000 man-hours	22,500

For the purpose of developing departmental predetermined burden rates, budgeted service department costs are distributed in sequence as follows:

Department	Basis
Service 21...........................	Floor space
Service 22...........................	Number of employees
Service 23...........................	Service 23 man-hours

The following data relating to factory overhead costs were recorded during April:

Department	No. of Employees	Dept. 23 Man-Hours Used	Production Volume	Direct Dept. Overhead Cost
11.........	75	500	9,000 DLH	$29,000
12.........	125	500	16,000 DLH	55,000
13.........	58	1,200	21,000 machine-hours	61,000
14.........	60	300	6,500 DLH	23,000
21.........	6	...	....	8,800
22.........	22	...	....	19,200
23.........	16	...	2,500 man-hours	19,000

Service department costs are distributed monthly on the following bases:

Service 21: To all departments on basis of budgeted monthly cost of floor space occupied.

Service 22: To all departments except service 21 on basis of budgeted rate per employee.

Service 23: To production departments on basis of budgeted rate per department 23 man-hour.

The flexible budget for one of these departments, department 14, is available to you in the following form:

	3,500 DLH	6,500 DLH
Direct departmental overhead.............	$17,000	$23,000
Number of employees....................	38	62
Department 23 man-hours used............	250	350

Direct departmental overhead, number of employees, and department 23 man-hours used are expected to vary as the number of direct hours varies within this range. The variations are expected to be in proportion to the variations in the number of direct labor hours, except that the number of employees must be a whole number. If a fraction of an employee is needed, a whole employee will be provided in the department.

You also have the following additional information pertaining to department 14 for the month of April:

(1) Direct materials issued (at standard prices): $4,200.

(2) Standard cost of work received from other departments: $214,800.

(3) Direct labor payrolls ($39,000 at standard wage rates): $40,300.

(4) Work in process April 1 (at standard cost): materials in process, $106,-900; labor in process, $12,000; overhead in process (2,000 standard direct labor hours), ____?

(5) Work in process April 30 (at standard cost); materials in process, $87,200; labor in process, $4,800; overhead in process (800 standard direct labor hours), ____?

(6) Standard cost of goods finished: materials, $230,000; labor, $44,400; overhead (7,400 standard direct labor hours), ____?

a) Distribute budgeted service department costs and compute predetermined burden rates for each of the four production departments for the current year.

b) Prepare an overhead cost distribution sheet for the month of April.

c) Compute the total overhead cost variance for the month for each of the four production departments and the total amount over- or underdistributed for each of the three service departments.

d) Prepare a complete variance summary for department 14.

chapter 21

Control Reporting for
Nonmanufacturing Activities

Planning budgets are probably the most widely used control bench marks for nonmanufacturing activities. Measures of deviations from plan are useful, but other kinds of control information should not be overlooked. The purpose of this chapter is to see how accounting can help management control the costs of various types of nonmanufacturing activities.

COST CONTROL IN REPETITIVE SERVICE ACTIVITIES

Three types of nonmanufacturing activities were recognized in Chapter 13: (1) repetitive service activities; (2) diversified service activities; and (3) independent programs. Repetitive service activities are a good place to start because they are most similar to direct production operations.

Developing Cost Standards

Control standards for nonsupervisory labor and other divisible costs in repetitive service centers can be based on functional unit costs, determined by the methods outlined in Chapter 13 above. Basically, this is a three-step method:

1. Select a work unit or governing factor by which to measure the volume of functional activity.
2. Estimate the amount of divisible costs reasonably necessary to support a standard or normal volume of activity.
3. Divide estimated cost by standard volume to get standard unit cost.

Standards developed in this way are based on the concept of attributable cost. They make no distinction between those that are fixed and those that are variable in the short run. Since most repetitive service costs are fixed, attributable cost standards are more relevant to functional planning than they are to the evaluation of current managerial performance. Comparisons with attributable cost standards identify short-run departures from linearity. If work loads are running light, average cost will be high, and comparisons with unit cost standards will give management a

Exhibit 21–1

SERVICE DEPARTMENT FLEXIBLE BUDGET

FLEXIBLE BUDGET ALLOWANCES			
DEPT. Warehouse			YEAR 19xx
Item	Budget Allowances		Normal Budget (10,000 Units per Week)
	Fixed (per Week)	Variable (per Unit)	
Supervision	$122	. . . . .	$ 122
Labor	246	$0.180	2,046
Clerical	55	0.003	85
Overtime	. .	0.011	110
Warehouse supplies	. .	0.086	860
Office supplies	32	0.002	52
Maintenance	87	0.010	187
Employee benefits	43	0.020	243
Other	52	0.001	62
Total	$637	$0.313	$3,767

chance to review its staffing requirements. Unit cost standards can also serve as a basis for advance planning when substantial changes in volume are contemplated.

It should be emphasized that these standard unit costs should be restricted to cost elements that are directly related to the number of work units. Inclusion of an arbitrary allocation of common costs or a unitization of indivisible fixed costs weakens the standard as an indicator of expected or desired cost performance. In other words, aggregate budget allowances rather than standard unit costs should be used for the indirect costs of repetitive service activities. And for short-term managerial performance review, the flexible budget technique should be used. In fact, two sets of flexible budgets may be called for, one based on short-term variability and another in which divisible fixed costs are unitized.

An illustrative flexible budget of the second kind is shown in Exhibit 21–1. The department is a warehouse, and a single work unit has been selected for all of the department's activities: the total number of pallet loads received in and shipped by the warehouse during a period. Budgeted fixed costs per week and average variable costs per load have been derived from a study of the relationships between the various cost elements and the number of loads handled (the warehouse units).

Recording Actual Costs

The next step is to prepare a chart of accounts for each department or cost center. To permit the isolation of variances for each activity, the chart of accounts would have to provide for separate accumulation of actual cost data for each activity performed within the cost center. The warehouse referred to in Exhibit 21–1 presents no such problems because the department engages in only one activity, but this is not always the case. For example, the same man may perform both the delivery and the unloading functions, and it is extremely difficult to obtain reliable information on how he splits his time between these two activities.

Fortunately, classification of actual cost data by function is not essential. The departmental budget allowance is a composite allowance, reflecting the total volume of departmental activity. When more than one activity is performed, this total represents the actual number of work units performed for each activity. Thus if total costs can be accumulated departmentally, they can be compared with departmental standards. To illustrate, if the cost rates are 25 cents a mile and $1 per delivery and the bulk trucks logged 8,000 miles and made 4,000 deliveries during the month, the budget allowance is:

Bulk delivery labor, 8,000 × $0.25	$2,000
Bulk unloading labor, 4,000 × $1	4,000
Total budget allowance	$6,000

Reporting Cost Variances

Control reports for repetitive service activities are much the same as for manufacturing activities. Budget allowances for each reporting period are derived from the predetermined flexible budgets and standard unit costs on the basis of the recorded number of work units. Comparison of actual functional costs with these allowances serves to locate the source of major variances and indicate where further investigation of underlying causes is desirable. When two or more functions are combined in one administrative unit, these comparisons may well be in summary form for the department as a whole, particularly if separate identification of the actual costs of each task or function is impractical. An example of a report of this kind is shown in Exhibit 21–2.

Some companies provide variance information in much greater detail. One system, for example, reports efficiency percentages weekly for each

Exhibit 21–2

SERVICE DEPARTMENT COST REPORT

DEPARTMENTAL COST SUMMARY

DEPT. Warehouse   MONTH AND YEAR March, 1967

OPERATING VOLUME 36,000 Units   NO. WEEKS 4

	This Month			Year to Date	
Item	Budget	Actual	(Over) Under	Actual	(Over) Under
Supervision	$ 488	$ 488	. . .	$ 1,680	$(94)
Labor	7,464	7,602	$(138)	26,704	(808)
Clerical	328	310	18	1,115	(22)
Overtime	396	256	140	1,250	136
Warehouse supplies	3,096	2,745	351	9,525	1,311
Office supplies	200	243	(43)	702	(34)
Maintenance	708	815	(107)	2,167	(176)
Employee benefits	892	880	12	3,045	34
Other	244	212	32	840	(38)
Total	$13,816	$13,551	$ 265	$47,428	$ 309

member of the clerical staff engaged in repetitive service operations.[1] To do this, the company keeps records of output (earned standard hours) for each employee. This is unlikely to be an expensive operation, but it could produce misleading signals if assigned work loads are uneven.

Since most costs are fixed, the main use of these reports should be to measure functional efficiency, not to evaluate managerial performance. For example, the functional managers cannot be blamed if low output per man-hour results from low system demand. Major variances should lead to a review of staffing requirements. Current control comparisons can be made only for those costs that are expected to vary with volume in the short run.

Control Through Competitive Comparisons

One alternative to cost standards derived from analysis of the operation itself is the cost of performing similar functions at other locations within the company. Nonmanufacturing service operations at different locations are often quite comparable. Once differences in service volume and in locational factors have been allowed for, this kind of competitive standard can help management distinguish good performance from bad.

A second possibility is to use market standards derived from data generated outside the firm. Most companies perform some services that

[1] Thomas G. Eshelman, "How Hanes Hosiery Uses Clerical Work Measurement," *Management Services*, March–April 1966, pp. 37–43.

could easily be purchased from outsiders. Typical examples include company print shops, photo services, cafeterias, and power plants, although the last of these is more typically regarded as a manufacturing activity. These activities are characterized by readily identifiable service units for which market prices can be estimated with a high degree of reliability. For this reason, the cost of equivalent services performed by outsiders may be useful as an overall bench mark for evaluating the desirability of providing the service internally.

For example, the company may own the building in which its offices are located. The rental value of comparable floor space in the same locality is $3.50 per square foot. Multiplying this figure by the number of rentable square feet provides an aggregate standard against which to compare the costs of owning, maintaining, and operating the building, including provisions for interest on invested capital. Standards of this type do not provide a basis for the control of specific items of cost, but they do indicate overall objectives and measures of effectiveness.

CONTROL OF DIVERSIFIED SERVICE COSTS

Unit cost standards are less useful for diversified service activities, for two reasons. First, because service activity is highly heterogeneous, a reliable index of volume is difficult to find. Second, even if an index can be found, the costs are often divisible only in large volume increments, so that a wide unit cost variation can take place without indicating inappropriate staffing levels.

Fixed budget allowances provide little additional control information. Variances from fixed budget allowances are unlikely to be significant—except perhaps in such items as travel expense and telephone charges—so that the major instrument of cost control is the preparation of the budget allowances rather than the enforcement of these allowances.

The major effort here should be to find ways to reduce costs. Administrative payrolls, if unchecked, have a tendency to grow. Cost reduction requires the definition of the function or task performed and an examination to see whether this task can be either eliminated or accomplished at lower cost. Because the major element of diversified service cost is the cost of personnel, these efforts are customarily concentrated on job evaluation. Comparisons with previous years are more useful in budgeting this kind of cost than in any other portion of the budget, although even here the consequences of corporate growth tend to reduce the significance of interperiod comparisons.

CONTROL OF PROJECT RESEARCH AND DEVELOPMENT COSTS

Independent program activities are perhaps best exemplified by research and development activties. These are of three types: project research, general research, and development. Development work is ordinarily the closest to commercial exploitation, the most specific, and the least subject to uncertainty about its results. General research, at the other extreme, often has no specific anticipated commercial applications, is not well specified as to expected inputs and outputs, and is characterized by extreme uncertainty as to its benefits.

Control procedures for general research are ordinarily very simple and reflect a company's faith in its research scientists. Time may even be made available for general research as a kind of fringe benefit, a means of attracting research workers and keeping them content. Activities of this kind will be given little attention in this chapter, which will focus instead on project research and development.

Control Criteria

Once the decision is made to undertake a research or development project, the laboratory generally gears itself to spend the money. Differences between budgeted and actual amounts in any given time period are usually very small. For this reason, cost control must be exercised primarily through control over appropriations rather than over expenditures.

Many possible criteria have been suggested to guide management in establishing budgets for independent program activities. Most of them are based on some rule of thumb, such as x percent of sales or y dollars per year, but there is only one real test of the advisability of an appropriation—will it produce profits at a rate sufficient to justify the cost?

The main trouble with this test is the difficulty of quantifying it. Forecasts of the benefits to be derived from specific programs or projects are subject to considerable error ranges, and the same is often true of forecasts of project costs. Confronted with this uncertainty, management is often tempted to abandon the profitability approach and select some method that seems to offer security by tying the appropriation to some norm indicative of what others are doing or what has been done in the past. This places an even greater responsibility on the company's analytical staffs to attach profit estimates, even of the roughest sort, to appropriation requests. Errors of estimation are always present in managerial decision making, but it is better to have some indication of expected profitability, no matter how rough, than no guidance at all.

Project Approval

Control procedures for project research and development are essentially of three types: (1) initial approval, (2) progress review, and (3) reapproval.

In a typical case, projects are submitted for approval as part of the annual budget review. Budget results are usually stated in two ways:

first by projects, and second by descriptive category of cost, in total for all projects. If the research effort is sufficiently great, separate departmental budgets will also be presented.

Exhibit 21–3 illustrates one kind of project estimate form, in this case covering a small project for the development of a new product. If the research division is departmentalized, this will usually be expanded by a further classification of project costs by department. In this exhibit, project labor costs are subdivided by task and the tasks are grouped into phases, each phase ending at some readily recognizable point in the development process. The estimated time to complete each phase is shown at the bottom of the sheet, and project totals, including a rough estimate of profit potential, are shown in the summary section at the top of the

Exhibit 21–3
RESEARCH PROJECT ESTIMATE

RESEARCH DIVISION
PROJECT ESTIMATE SHEET

PROJECT NO. 16321   DATE 10/15/x0
PROJECT TITLE Sandfly Attachment   TYPE New Product
PROJECT SUPERVISOR G. Hill

Completion Estimate 9 Months   Cost Estimate:

Estimated Annual Profit $30,000   Labor $ 8,000
                                              Materials   7,200
                                              Equipment   4,800
                                              Total $20,000

Task	Phase 1, Specifications		Phase 2, Drawings		Phase 3, Prototype	
	Hours	Cost	Hours	Cost	Hours	Cost
Synthesis and analysis	300	$2,400				
Design specifications	50	400				
Breadboarding	100	700				
Layout	50	350				
Parts list			80	$ 400		
Schematics			150	750		
Test specifications			50	400		
Fabrication					300	$1,200
Assembly					100	300
Wiring					50	300
Test					100	800
Total Labor	500	$3,850	280	$1,550	550	$2,600
Materials and purchased parts	$2,000		$ 500		$4,700	
Equipment	$3,000		. . .		$1,800	
Completion time	4 months		2 months		3 months	

form. Additional supporting sheets, not shown here, present further detail on the nature of the project and on the derivation of the estimates.

Networking

Other projects pose more difficulties. The various part of the projects are not entirely sequential but require close coordination and careful scheduling. For complex projects, the most useful scheduling tool is the activity network.

Networking is a subject in itself, but the basic concept can be spelled out fairly quickly. Exhibit 21–4 is a typical, although very simple, net-

Exhibit 21–4

PROJECT NETWORK

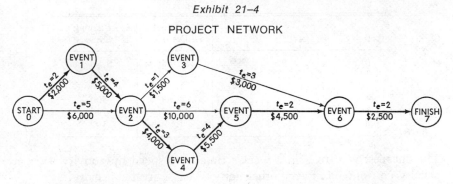

work. The circles represent *events* that occur at specific moments during the course of the project; the connecting lines stand for *activities*, the means of getting from one event to another. The direction of progress toward completion of the project is indicated by arrowheads on the activity lines. The numbers labeled t_e on the activity lines indicate the expected number of weeks required to complete each activity. Thus the network in Exhibit 21–4 indicates that it will take two weeks to get from the start of the project to event No. 1. The expected cost of this activity is $2,000.

Notice that activities are both concurrent and sequential. For example, two separate sets of activities must be completed independently in order to reach event No. 2—these are concurrent sets of activities. The activities linking events 4 and 5 and events 5 and 6, on the other hand, are sequential—the second one cannot be started until the first one is completed.

Networks are used to make the interdependencies visible, to facilitate resource scheduling, and to identify those activities that are likely to be most critical to the timely completion of the project. The activities shown as heavy lines in Exhibit 21–4 constitute the *critical path*—the sequence of activities requiring the longest total elapsed time from start to finish. If the critical path is too long to meet a desired completion date, it may be possible to devote more resources to one or more of the activities on the critical path and thus shorten the total time requirement. Shortening the time required for an activity on one of the slack paths, on the other hand, would not advance the completion date at all.

To assist management in these decisions, networking procedures often require estimates of *cost slopes* for all or most activities—that is, the added costs that would be necessary to reduce the amount of estimated time by specified amounts, or the amounts that would be saved by slowing the activity down.

For example, suppose that the time required by the critical path in Exhibit 21–4 is one week too long. The one-week cost slopes for increasing or decreasing estimated time for all activities on the critical path are:

Activity	Cost Penalty to Decrease	Cost Saving If Increased
01	$2,000	$ 0
12	1,000	200
24	1,500	900
45	500	500
56	800	700
67	1,500	100

The cheapest way to gain a week's time is to speed up activity 45 at a penalty cost of $500. Every other activity has a greater penalty.

An additional possibility is also available in this case. The company could save $900 by slowing the pace on activity 24. To offset the delay this would cause, activity 56 could be speeded up by one week at a penalty of $800, leaving a net saving of $100. In fact, if the cost slope on activity 45 were linear, so that the penalty cost of a second time reduction would cost no more than the first, then this would be the obvious solution and the net saving would be even greater. At some point, however, the cost slope is likely to become nonlinear and it is best to require specific forecasts for each possible time increment or decrement.

The most widely known networking technique is PERT (program evaluation and review technique).[2] Most PERT networks or programs are very large and require high-capacity electronic computers. The networking technique can be applied to simpler tasks without the use of computers, however, both inside and outside the research division.

Summary Budgets

Although projects should be justified individually, the entire research and development budget is likely to be reviewed by top management as

---

[2] For a simple introduction, see Harry F. Evarts, *Introduction to PERT* (Boston: Allyn & Bacon, 1964).

Exhibit 21–5

RESEARCH BUDGET REQUEST FORM

RESEARCH DIVISION
PROJECT BUDGET SUMMARY

YEAR 19x1

Project No.	Project Supervisor	Costs to Date	Costs This Year				Future Costs	Total Costs	Annual Profit Expected
			Labor	Materials	Equipment	Total			
16214	P. Jones	$13,500	$21,200	$1,800	$ 600	$23,600	$ 10,000	$ 47,100	$20,000
16285	F. Tons	84,050	15,600	3,400	1,000	20,000	. . . . . .	104,050	70,000
16312	L. Peters	27,140	5,000	200	. . . .	5,200	. . . . . .	32,340	10,000
16318	A. Stern	. . . . .	30,000	6,500	2,500	39,000	50,000	80,000	40,000
16320	N. Rossi	. . . . .	10,000	2,000	4,000	16,000	100,000	116,000	60,000
16321	G. Hill	. . . . .	8,000	7,200	4,800	20,000	. . . . . .	20,000	30,000

a unit. Exhibit 21–5 is a form used by one company to summarize the direct costs of all the projects underway or proposed for the coming year. Each project is listed separately. Separate columns are provided for past costs of continuing projects; estimated costs for the current year; estimated costs for future years, if any; expected completion date; and estimated annual profits on completion. This is normally accompanied by a second budget schedule, such as that shown in Exhibit 21–6, which summarizes the individual project requests for the current year, together with the overhead costs of the research organization. This is broken down into months for cash budgeting purposes.

Progress Reporting

Comparisons between budget allowances and total costs for the period are of little value in the control of project research and development costs. Most costs are either salaries or are closely related to salaries. Total expenditures for these inputs are controlled by decisions to hire personnel, and these, in turn, are the outcome of project approvals. In other words, aggregate expenditure rates are controlled by budget approval, and follow-up budget comparisons of this sort serve only to indicate overall departures from anticipated rates of expenditure.

A second defect in departmental comparisons is that research activity typically focuses on the project rather than on the department. An alternative, therefore, is to compare expenditures with budget allowances periodically on a project basis. For example, a monthly report might take the form illustrated in Exhibit 21–7.

This kind of reporting does serve to identify projects on which rates of expenditure are out of line with preestablished schedules, but it ignores one vital element—progress. Project costs have no meaning except in comparison with the progress achieved toward project objectives. Thus Exhibit 21–7 would seem to indicate that project 16321 is running far in excess of its budget, but it may be that resources were available much sooner than had been anticipated and that more progress had been made than originally scheduled.

Exhibit 21–6

CURRENT RESEARCH BUDGET SUMMARY

RESEARCH DIVISION BUDGET SUMMARY	
	YEAR 19x1
	DATE 12/2/x0
Description	**Annual Total**
Project costs:	
Labor	$150,000
Materials	33,000
Equipment	39,000
Total project costs	$222,000
Executive salaries	$ 30,000
Clerical	12,000
Overtime premium	8,000
Payroll charges	26,000
Professional services	20,000
Travel	5,000
Telephone	1,500
Insurance	1,800
Maintenance	4,000
Shop supplies	6,000
Office supplies	2,200
Depreciation	5,000
Space charges	10,000
Unclassified	4,500
Total	$358,000

The existence of networks permits a two-way kind of research performance reporting: (1) actual progress versus planned progress, and (2) actual cost versus planned cost for the progress actually achieved. Comparisons of the first kind tell management whether a project is on schedule, whether one or more slack path activities have been delayed or have run so far over the time estimates that they are now on the critical path, etc. Comparisons of the second kind indicate whether schedules have been maintained within the anticipated cost limits. They may also help in project reevaluation.

Exhibit 21–8 is a pictorial version of a progress report of this sort. This focuses attention on three aspects of project performance: (1) total spending to date against budgeted spending to date (the "expenditure lag"); (2) total spending against budgeted spending for the work performed ("cost overrun"); and (3) progress to date in comparison with the original plan (indicated by the expected completion delay or "schedule slippage").

Notice that this chart focuses on the future rather than the past. Both costs and completion dates are reestimated and compared with original estimates. These comparisons are then used in deciding whether to continue the projects, modify the objectives, alter the expenditure rates, and so forth.

Exhibit 21–7

PROJECT COST COMPARISON REPORT

RESEARCH DIVISION
MONTHLY PROJECT COST REPORT

PROJECT NO. 16321   MONTH April
PROJECT TITLE Sandfly Attachment   SUPERVISOR G. Hill

START DATE 3/6/x1
SCHEDULED COMPLETION 11/30/x1

| | This Month | | To Date | | |
	Actual	Budget	Actual	Budget	Variance
Salaries, professional	$ 800	$ 550	$1,550	$1,000	$ (550)
Salaries, technical	300	220	900	450	(450)
Laboratory services	15	. . .	15	. . .	(15)
Drafting supplies	25	30	95	100	5
Outside services	. . .	. . .	20	. . .	(20)
Purchased parts	350	. . .	350	. . .	(350)
Equipment	1,350	500	3,100	3,000	(100)
Total	$2,840	$1,300	$6,030	$4,550	$(1,480)

Charts like the one in Exhibit 21–8 could be constructed for project segments as well as for the project as a whole, as long as the chart of accounts is subdivided to permit recording of actual costs by segments. In the typical case, the clerical cost of recording project costs by individual activities is prohibitive, and so larger groups of activities known as *work packages* are treated as costing units for this purpose.[3]

---

[3] See U.S. Department of Defense and National Aeronautics and Space Administration, *DOD and NASA Guide, PERT/COST* (Washington D.C.: U.S. Government Printing Office, 1962), for a description of this and related techniques.

Exhibit 21–8

INTEGRATED PROJECT PROGRESS CHART

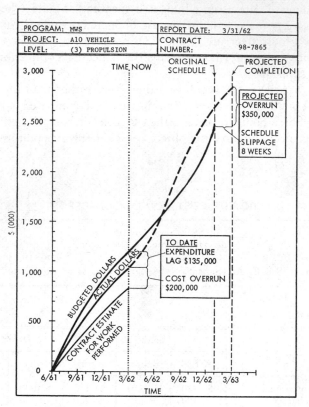

Project Reapproval

The periodic progress reports not only serve to alert management to departures from plans so that appropriate adjustments can be made but also provide an occasion for reappraisal of project desirability. Projects are typically reviewed annually for this purpose, even if the initial time and expenditure schedules are being met. They may also be reviewed whenever either time or cost overruns become serious enough to call for such a review.

Some projects even include one or more profitability investigation activities in project sequences or networks, and probably more should do so. One reason is that external conditions are constantly changing; a product that would have excited the market when research was started may be completed out of fashion or favor now. Additional expenditures should be made only if they will pay off.

A second reason has a similar impact. As research progresses, the nature and cost of the ultimate product may become much clearer, and this may not fit the anticipated market conditions as well as the original design and cost expectations.

Finally, progress may be so much slower or so much costlier than originally planned that the revised estimates of future time and costs can no longer be justified by the expected benefits. Once again, the project should be terminated and the resources devoted elsewhere.

Departmental Performance Review

Each project is typically the direct responsibility of a project manager who may or may not have other duties as well. Some companies supplement project cost accumulations with departmental accumulations of direct, as well as indirect, project costs. Each project is identified with a specific department, usually the department to which the project manager is normally assigned. The cost of any work on a particular project that is performed by personnel of other departments in the research division is charged to the project and to the project manager's department as well. The department supplying the service is credited for a corresponding amount. An alternative is to provide for a departmental classification of work performed, by project, so that hours or costs accumulated on all projects in each department can be compared with the hours or costs budgeted for the tasks actually performed on those projects in that department.

The administration of research divisions is an exceedingly complex subject, and one that has only recently been studied by analytical methods. Cost control techniques are only one phase of the greater problem of research administration, albeit an important phase. The discussion in the preceding paragraphs has merely scratched the surface, because every company is to a certain extent unique in its research activities. The cardinal point, however, is that no system of control in this field can be successful unless it recognizes that the justification of research is future profit and not merely adherence to arbitrarily established expense budgets.

CONTROL OF MARKETING COSTS

The costs of generating firm orders for delivery of the company's products generally consume a larger portion of the sales dollar than any other nonmanufacturing expense. These are the company's marketing costs or, to use a term often used by accountants, order-getting costs.

Order-getting activities are independent program activities, as that term has been used here, and some of them bear striking similarities to research and development activities. Market research is perhaps the most obvious example; media advertising is another. Others differ from research and development, however, in that they are continuous rather than discrete. This second group is exemplified by direct selling costs consisting mainly of sales salaries and commissions, travel, entertainment, samples, and dealer aids and other forms of direct assistance to customers.

The Control Problem

The fundamental difficulty in establishing viable control standards for order-getting costs was stated succinctly in a research report of the National Association of Accountants (then National Association of Cost Accountants):

Order-getting costs cannot be budgeted by establishing a simple and direct relationship between sales orders and costs. The principal reason for this is that order-getting activities are a cause rather than a result of sales and the volume of orders obtained depends to some extent upon the amount spent for advertising, sales promotion and selling. This contrasts with the manufacturing cost budget where production costs can be budgeted after the volume of goods to be produced has been determined because the volume of production does not depend upon the amount of money spent for materials, labor, and factory overhead. . . . The lowest unit cost or total cost is not always the preferred objective in controlling order-getting costs because such a cost may fail to yield the most profitable volume which can be attained.[4]

Any effort to establish standard costs per unit of sales is bound to founder on the problem of circular reasoning. The number of calls made or the number or dollar value of orders received may be useful indices of effort or results, but they do not constitute units of output to which a standard cost can be attached. For example, the salesman can reduce cost per call merely by lengthening his stay in a particular city and shortening the duration of each call, but the company's sales may suffer as a result. Sales and the cost of obtaining sales are inescapably interdependent.

Budget Preparation

As with research and development activities, the most crucial stage in the control of marketing costs is the development of the marketing plan. Once the plan is approved, expenditures are likely to follow rather closely.

The budgeting process was discussed in Chapter 14, but one point needs reemphasis here. Sales and selling expenses are interdependent, and budgets for these items must be developed simultaneously. Starting with sales forecasts for existing levels of selling effort, the branch or product

---

[4] National Association of Accountants, "Cost Control for Marketing Operations —General Considerations, Research Series No. 25," *N.A.C.A. Bulletin*, Vol. 35, No. 8 (April 1954), pp. 1085–86.

managers should consider the desirability of various changes; e.g., increasing or decreasing the number of salesmen, changing the degree of specialization in the sales force, or altering the amount of attention to be given to different groups of customers or different products.

Marketing Response Functions. The most useful tool the marketing manager could have is a set of marketing response functions. For example, suppose that sales volume is determined by the number of sales calls made and the number of samples distributed. The relationship between sales volume and one of these determinants is a response function. If these functions were known, they could be expressed in mathematical terms and marketing planning would become very simple. The manager would merely increase the size of his marketing budget until the incremental response no longer generated a large enough margin to pay for additional effort.

Unfortunately, marketing response functions are ordinarily so complex that existing techniques are inadequate to identify them. The effect of spending on samples depends not only on the total number of samples provided but also on the accompanying program for advertising the product and calling on customers. Furthermore, the functions are almost certainly nonlinear. Whereas the first $1,000 spent on samples may generate $10,000 in gross profits, the second may bring in only $7,000, the third $3,000, and the fourth only $100. The analyst is likely to be happy to get a usable estimate of the effects of small changes in existing or proposed programs.

The basic analytical technique for this purpose is regression analysis, usually applied to routinely collected historical data. Occasionally data can be obtained from controlled experiments, but good experimental opportunities are rare, and widespread application of this idea must await the development of better methods of data collection.[5]

Expense Rates. In budgeting such expenses as travel, entertainment, dealer aids, and samples—that is, expenses that supplement or implement personal selling effort—the manager ordinarily uses historical averages. These are usually broken down by territory and perhaps also by type of customer or channel of distribution. Past averages are only suggestive, but without them forecasting is likely to be far wider of the mark.

Analysis of Results

The results of marketing effort are communicated to the marketing manager through the medium of routine periodic profit contribution re-

---

[5] An early discussion of this idea can be found in Joel Dean, "How Much to Spend on Advertising," *Harvard Business Review,* January 1951, pp. 65–74. The usefulness of this kind of data to marketing management is ably described by David B. Montgomery and Glen L. Urban, *Management Science in Marketing* (Englewood Cliffs, N.J.: Prentice-Hall, 1969).

ports of the kinds discussed in the next chapter. This kind of routine profit reporting is often supplemented by separate analyses of sales and of expenses.

Sales Analysis. Sales analysis uses only the sales figures themselves, without reference to costs of any kind. Individual sales transactions (or orders received) are classified on a number of bases—e.g., industry, territory, size of order, and channel of distribution. By analyzing sales mix patterns period after period, the marketing manager can see who is buying his products and who isn't, which distribution channels are on the way up and which on the way down, and so on. He can then change his marketing plan or work with his subordinates to correct trends that he regards as unfavorable.[6]

Expense Rate Analysis. Another approach is to examine relationships between marketing inputs and outputs for different segments of the sales force. For example, the following ratios might be calculated for each salesman:[7]

Calls per day.
Sales per call.
Travel expense per day.
Selling expense per call.
Miles traveled per day.

The multidimensionality of selling effort and the lack of precise comparability among markets or territories make it difficult to develop a science of ratio analysis. The ratios are valuable insofar as they aid the analyst in identifying important patterns, and for this it is the overall picture that is important rather than the absolute size of any one ratio. For example, one salesman may have a high cost per call and few calls per day but a much larger sales volume and a higher profit contribution than his fellows. If the sales territories are comparable, this may indicate the greater effectiveness of a policy of selective selling. Another salesman may have many calls per day and greater-than-average sales per call but a low gross margin, indicating a tendency to sell what is easiest to sell or to cut selling prices and then move on quickly to the next customer.

SUMMARY

Cost control techniques in nonmanufacturing activities are typically much more primitive than those used in the factory. Industrial standards

---

[6] See National Industrial Conference Board, *Sales Analysis, Studies in Business Policy No. 113* (New York, 1965).

[7] For an exhaustive survey of these ratios, see Spencer A. Tucker, *Successful Managerial Control by Ratio-Analysis* (New York: McGraw-Hill Book Co., 1961), chaps. 6–9.

were born in the factory and so was cost accounting, and movement into other areas has been slow.

This may be due to a number of factors, such as the desire of white-collar workers to keep a separate identification from blue-collar workers, the diversity and nonstandardized nature of the output of most non-manufacturing activities, the commonness of a large proportion of non-manufacturing cost, and in some cases the reverse causal relationship between output and cost.

This chapter has discussed the cost control problems of three separate categories of nonmanufacturing activities—repetitive service, diversified service, and independent program activities. The first two of these are closely similar to manufacturing activities in that the costs are incurred as a functional response to an externally imposed service demand. Unit cost standards, flexible budgets, and departmental cost reporting techniques can be useful for these activities.

Independent program activities are those that are undertaken to achieve a discretionary objective—that is, their output is not provided to service either customer orders or current production requirements. They can be undertaken or not, depending on whether the anticipated results satisfy a company decision rule.

Two kinds of independent programs may be distinguished: discrete and continuing. The former is exemplified by research and development activities; the latter by sales promotion and direct selling. For both classes, traditional input-output standards are inapplicable because the input costs are more volume-determining than volume-determined. The most valuable technique for controlling these costs is to test budget proposals by the criterion of expected profits. Once budget allowances for these activities are approved, it is unlikely that actual costs will be materially less than the amounts budgeted.

This before-the-fact control can, however, be supplemented by various other techniques. Any program that can be broken down into a number of sequential phases can be monitored by periodic cost and progress reports. For continuing programs, input-output or cost-input ratios may have some usefulness in interunit or intertemporal comparisons. The crucial stage in both cases, however, is the decision to spend, and it is on this stage that control efforts are ordinarily centered.

EXERCISES AND PROBLEMS

1. The travel expense budget for the New Orleans branch of the Winchell Company amounts to $8,500 for the current fiscal year. It is now the last month of the fiscal year, and $8,473 has already been charged to New Orleans branch travel expense. Travel expense vouchers received from the New Orleans branch manager in this morning's mail amount to $286.

a) As controller of the company, would you refuse to honor the vouchers, notify the president, ask the branch manager for an explanation, charge the amount in excess of budget to another account that has an unexpended balance, or would you take some other action?

b) If the New Orleans branch manager had consulted you at the beginning of the month, before the travel expenses had been incurred, what action would you have taken?

2.* Draw a network to fit the following data and trace the critical path. (Each activity is identified by a two-digit number, the first digit denoting the preceding event and the second digit indicating the event that signals the end of the activity.)

Activity	Estimated Time (Weeks)
01	1
02	3
03	5
14	2
25	4
35	3
46	6
56	2
57	1
69	4
78	2
89	2

3. The Montgomery Company sells its products in three territories. Management has established the following standard administration expenses to be used in preparing profit and loss statements for each territory:

Credit	$ 5.00 per new account
Collection	10.00 per overdue account
Bookkeeping	0.35 per transaction
Stenographic	0.60 per letter
Other clerical	1.00 per customer account
Executive salaries	0.03 per sales dollar
Other administrative expense	0.02 per sales dollar

The following data were recorded for the month of October:

	Territory A	Territory B	Territory C
New accounts	80	140	100
Overdue accounts	50	60	60
Transactions	10,000	18,000	16,000
Letters	400	500	600
Customer accounts	500	1,000	800
Sales	$200,000	$300,000	$250,000

a) Compute the amount of head office administration cost per dollar of sales in each territory for the month of October.

---

* Solutions to problems marked with an asterisk can be found in Appendix B.

b) Comment on the usefulness of the comparison of these costs among territories.

4. A company charges the managers of its three product divisions for head office services, using the following charging rates:

Department	Rate
Credit department................... $	0.30 per order
Billing department...................	0.95 per order
Payroll department...................	2.50 per employee
Accounts receivable department.........	0.40 per order
General accounting department..........	0.30 per entry
Treasurer............................	0.35 per customer remittance
General sales manager................	2,000.00 per month to each product division
Legal department....................	3,000.00 per month to each product division
Executive management................	10,000.00 per month to each product division

Statistics for the month of February were as follows:

No. of orders received...................	3,900
No. of employees.......................	860
No. of entries...........................	9,300
No. of customer remittances.............	4,600

Head office expenses and flexible budget allowances for February were:

Department	Actual	Budget
Credit.........................	$ 1,350	$ 1,400
Billing.........................	4,150	4,000
Payroll.........................	2,400	2,200
Accounts receivable..............	1,730	1,800
General accounting...............	2,910	2,850
Treasurer......................	1,680	1,700
General sales manager............	5,630	6,000
Legal.........................	6,200	9,000
Executive management............	30,400	30,000

a) Compute and analyze the month's variances for each head office department.

b) How would you expect management to respond to large volume variances in the head office departments? How, if at all, do they differ from factory overhead volume variances?

5. The Villard Company recently initiated a new product development project estimated to cost $31,500. The list of activities constituting this project, together with estimates of the number of weeks each activity would take and the cost to carry it out, is shown in the table below. In this table each activity is identified by a two-digit number, the first digit denoting the preceding event and the second digit indicating the event that signals the end of the activity:

Activity	Estimated Time (Weeks)	Estimated Cost
01.........	2	$ 1,100
12.........	1	500
23.........	3	2,500
24.........	7	3,500
25.........	2	2,200
34.........	3	3,300
35.........	1	400
45.........	5	4,000
49.........	3	1,600
56.........	2	900
67.........	1	1,200
68.........	6	4,200
78.........	2	700
79.........	4	4,100
89.........	3	1,300
Total........		$31,500

Eight weeks after this project was initiated, activities 01, 12, 24, and 25 had been completed and activity 23 was approximately half finished. It was estimated that an additional two weeks and $1,500 would be necessary to finish activity 23. No other estimates had to be revised. As originally approved, the schedule called for completion of activities 01, 12, 23, and 25 in the first eight weeks, with activity 24 to be five-sevenths finished and activity 34 to be two-thirds finished. Costs incurred during the first eight weeks were:

Activity	Amount
01................	$1,150
12................	250
23................	2,400
24................	3,000
25................	2,500
Total.............	$9,300

a) Draw a network to represent this project.
b) List the events through which the critical path passes and indicate the number of weeks which the project was originally expected to take.
c) Prepare a report summarizing costs and performance on this project during the first eight weeks. Has the critical path changed in any way?

6. Sherman Products, Inc. manufactures and sells laundry detergents, floor wax, tooth paste, and a wide variety of related products throughout the United States and Canada. To facilitate sales management, the market is divided into 12 major sales regions, each with its own regional manager. Each region is subdivided into territories, each territory being the exclusive province of a single salesman.

The company's controller and his staff have developed a highly detailed reporting system that most regional managers have adopted for their own use. This system focuses on monthly measurements of each salesman's performance in four key areas: orders received, calls made, initial orders received, and net profit. Orders received are classified by size, measured in dollars. Calls are classified by customer group, as follows:

Group A: regular customers, annual sales volume at least $10,000.
Group B: prospects, no purchases during previous fiscal year.
Group C: regular customers, annual sales less than $10,000.

"Initial orders" are the first orders of the year from group B customers.

One of these monthly reports, for salesman Jones, is shown below:

		Last Month			This Territory, Same Month Last Year
	Jones Actual		Jones, Planned	Average, All Salesmen	
	No.	Amount			
Orders received:					
$ 0– 250	45	$ 3,000	.....	$ 3,100	.....
251– 500	20	7,000	.....	8,100	.....
501–1,000	8	6,000	.....	11,200	.....
1,001–2,000	4	5,000	.....	7,800	.....
2,001–5,000	2	8,000	.....	6,300	.....
More than $5,000	1	6,000	.....	3,500	.....
Total	80	$35,000	$32,000	$40,000	$33,000
Cost of goods sold (at standard)		$26,000	$22,500	$28,000	$23,000
Direct expenses		2,200	2,250	2,300	2,100
Marketing overhead (5% of sales)		1,750	1,600	2,000	1,650
Administrative overhead (8% of sales)		2,800	2,560	3,200	2,640
Net profit		$ 2,250	$ 3,090	$ 4,500	$ 3,610
Initial orders received	5	$ 1,000	$ 1,500	$ 2,500	$ 1,200
Calls made:					
Group A customers	30		40		25
Group B customers	20		20		26
Group C customers	50		30		45
Total Calls	100		90	100	96

Jones's report goes to the regional manager, who uses it to identify ways in which Jones can improve his performance. He does the same for each salesman. In addition, these reports help him to differentiate the better salesmen from the poorer ones.

Marketing and administrative overheads are almost entirely fixed costs.

a) Compute the following: (1) sales and expense variances for the month; (2) Mr. Jones's contribution to company profits for the month; (3) cost per call—actual and planned for Mr. Jones, all-salesmen average, and same territory last year; (4) sales per call, as in (3); (5) profit to sales ratios, as in (3).

b) Using the figures from (a), whenever pertinent, and any others that you deem appropriate, analyze Mr. Jones's performance for the month.

7.† Cheerful Calorie Contributors, Inc., operate a chain of ice cream stores. The company has expanded steadily for several years, opening a new store every month, on the average. As a result of this experience, management has been able to develop a fairly precise standard operating procedure for opening a new store. The chief operating officer has drawn up the following description of this procedure:

The first step in opening a store is finding a desirable location in the general area we wish to enter. This generally takes about four days. As soon as we find our location, our engineering department begins drawing plans for the store, including layouts for furniture and for built-in freezers. Plan preparation takes six days.

During this time our real estate department is negotiating rental terms. Since we pay premium rates and obtain virtually every location that we choose, we do not delay the drawing up of the plans for the two days that these negotiations consume.

After terms are negotiated, the lease must be drawn up by our legal department and approved by outside counsel. This process takes six days. We do not actually start installing furniture or freezers until the lease is approved.

When the engineering department completes its plans, they are submitted to the city for approval. This takes seven days. Neither the furniture nor the freezers can be installed before plans are approved by the city.

Furniture can be ordered as soon as plans are completed, since if the city rejects the location, the furniture can be used elsewhere. It takes eight days for furniture to be ordered and delivered. (The ordering process takes one day and delivery is made seven days later.) Installation in the store requires four days.

No ordering time is involved in the case of freezers, since CCC keeps a supply on hand, but building them in and installing and testing the necessary electrical and plumbing facilities takes nine days.

Once the plans have been drawn, the personnel department can identify a manager and hire a staff, a process requiring five days. Then the manager and staff must be trained for six days at CCC's large modern training facility. Once trained, they can begin planning the operation of the store and order the necessary inventory of ice cream and supplies, a process that requires four days. (The inventory arrives at the end of this four-day period, but of course cannot be received or stored until the day after the freezers and furniture have been installed.)

After inventory, freezers, and furniture are all in place, a final preopening cleanup is required. This takes two days.

a) Construct a network describing this process and identify the critical path.
b) How long does the entire process take?
c) The company has found that by devoting additional resources to some of these activities, the time it takes to complete them can be reduced. The following actions are the only possibilities:

---

† From a problem prepared by John C. Burton.

Additions	*Time Saving*
$200...........................	One day in installing freezers
$100 (in addition to the $200 above).	A second day in installing freezers
$150...........................	One day in hiring staff
$ 50...........................	One day in installing furniture
$120...........................	One day in training staff
$175...........................	One day in drawing plans
$210 (in addition to the $175 above).	A second day in drawing plans
$300...........................	One day in preopening cleanup

Which of these options would you recommend if the company wants to reduce total project time by one day? By two days? By three days? Show your calculations.

Management is in a great hurry to open its next store. What is the shortest possible time in which the project can be completed? What is the incremental cost of shortening the time table in this way?

CASE 21–1: SPACE CONSTRUCTORS, INC. (B)†

After restudying other elements of the overall construction program, Mr. Alison and Mr. Phillips decided that a 10-week schedule for the construction of the remote control building would be acceptable. They were able to draw the critical path diagram shown in Figure 1.

Mr. Alison was field construction supervisor for Space Constructors, Inc. Mr. Phillips was project engineer in charge of the job of constructing a remote control building. This project was an integral part of the work covered by a large construction contract that had been awarded to Space Constructors some months earlier.

Using this information, Mr. Alison and Mr. Phillips agreed on the cost and production schedule summarized in Table 1. "I think that we can meet

Figure 1

SPACE CONSTRUCTORS, INC.
Revised Critical Path Diagram for Remote Control Building Project

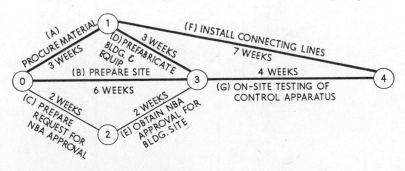

Note: Doubled lines indicate critical paths.

---

† This case was prepared as a follow-up to "Space Constructors, Inc.," Case No. EA-P380 (copyright 1965 by the President and Fellows of Harvard College). Copyright 1969 by l'Institut pour l'Étude des Méthodes de Direction de l'Entreprise (IMEDE), Lausanne, Switzerland. Reproduced by permission.

Table 1

SPACE CONSTRUCTORS, INC.

Construction Schedule for Remote Control Building Project

Activity	Cost to be Incurred During Week										Total
	1	2	3	4	5	6	7	8	9	10	
A	$1,667	$1,667	$1,666	.....	.....	.....	.....	.....	.....	.....	$ 5,000
B	2,333	2,333	2,334	$ 2,334	$ 2,333	$2,333	.....	.....	.....	.....	14,000
C	1,250	1,250	.....	.....	.....	.....	.....	.....	.....	.....	2,500
D*	.....	.....	.....	6,000	6,000	6,000	.....	.....	.....	.....	18,000
E	.....	.....	.....	4,000	4,000	.....	.....	.....	.....	.....	8,000
F	.....	.....	.....	1,643	1,643	1,643	$1,643	$1,643	$1,643	$1,642	11,500
G	.....	.....	.....	.....	.....	.....	2,500	2,500	2,500	2,500	10,000
Total	$5,250	$5,250	$4,000	$13,977	$13,976	$9,976	$4,143	$4,143	$4,143	$4,142	$69,000

* Crash schedule, providing for maximum permissible amount of overtime work.

the 10-week deadline with this schedule," Mr. Phillips said, "but we'll have to watch our progress very closely as we go along. We'll take our first reading at the end of three weeks and see where we stand. If we have to make adjustments, we can make them then."

"I guess that's soon enough," Mr. Alison replied, "but we can't lose sight of the costs on this project. We've gone way over our estimates on those underground installations, and we have to be particularly careful to keep our costs under control on the remaining parts of the contract."

On Monday, October 1, work began on activities A, B, and C. All personnel were scheduled to work a regular five-day week during each of the first three weeks, with no overtime.

At the end of the third week, Mr. Phillips asked each of his project supervisors to report the amount of progress they had made on the activities under their supervision. The following information reached Mr. Phillips's desk late Monday afternoon, October 22:

Activity	Date Started	Completed as of Oct. 19	Weeks Needed to Complete
A.................	10–1	100%	...
B.................	10–1	33	4
C.................	10–1	100	
D.................	10–18	10	3

Activity starts and completions were reported routinely to Mr. Phillips, so he already knew that activity A had been completed three days ahead of schedule and that as a result the project supervisor had been able to start activity D two days ahead of schedule. Because of this head start, the amount of overtime work scheduled for activity D had been reduced. No overtime work was performed on any activity during the first three weeks.

Activity F, on the other hand, had not been started early. The necessary personnel had been fully assigned to other projects and the project supervisor had not been able to get them rescheduled. They had reported for work on the remote control building site on Monday, October 22, however, and Mr. Phillips saw no reason why activity F should not be completed on time.

Mr. Phillips also received two reports from his cost accountant. The first of these was the regular weekly cost report for the project, shown in Table 2. The second was a revised set of cost estimates, prepared during the early afternoon by the cost accountant in cooperation with the project supervisors. Expected future costs per week for each activity were:

B..............	$2,500
D..............	5,500
E..............	unchanged
F..............	unchanged
G..............	unchanged

Table 2

SPACE CONSTRUCTORS, INC.
Weekly Cost Report for Remote Control Building Project
(week of October 15–19)

Activity	This Week			Cumulative		
	Budgeted Costs*	Actual Costs	(Over) Under	Budgeted Costs*	Actual Costs	(Over) Under
A..........	$1,666	$ 500	$ 1,166	$ 5,000	$ 4,900	$ 100
B..........	2,334	2,300	34	7,000	6,800	200
C..........	....	350	(350)	2,500	2,350	150
D..........	....	1,500	(1,500)	....	1,500	(1,500)
Total.......	$4,000	$4,650	$ (650)	$14,500	$15,550	$(1,050)

* From Table 1.

a)   A program of the kind illustrated in Figure 1 cannot be implemented unless enough resources of the required kinds can be made available at the dates indicated. How would you use the data summarized in Table 1 to test the feasibility of the proposed construction schedule?

b)   Why did Mr. Phillips want a performance report at the end of three weeks? What kinds of decisions did he have to make at that time?

c)   In the light of your answer to question (*b*), what was wrong with the weekly cost report (Table 2)?

d)   Prepare a report or reports that would have told Mr. Phillips what he needed to know about his performance during the first three weeks of the remote control building project.

e)   What should Mr. Phillips have done on the basis of the information provided by your report?

chapter **22**

Routine Reporting
of Activity Profitabilty

Periodic reports on the profitability of company divisions, subsidiaries, or product lines are intended to serve some or all of the following purposes:

1. To help division managers and their superiors appraise the financially measurable aspects of managerial performance in the division.
2. To provide top management with a measure of the profitability of the resources invested in the division.
3. To guide division managers toward decisions that will increase company profit.

This chapter will concentrate on the second of these, the measurement of the profitability of the resources used in a particular activity. For convenience, this discussion can be divided into two parts: (1) top management's interest in the reports; and (2) the interest of the division, subsidiary, or product-line manager.

REPORTING TO TOP MANAGEMENT

Routine reports to top management on activity profitability typically measure the rate of return on the funds that have been invested in the activity, referred to as the *return on investment* (ROI) or *return on capital employed:*

$$\text{Return on investment} = \frac{\text{Profit}}{\text{Investment}}$$

Another ratio that is often referred to in activity evaluation is the *margin on sales:*

$$\text{Margin on sales} = \frac{\text{Profit}}{\text{Sales}}$$

While margin-on-sales ratios are often highly revealing in trend analysis, they do not indicate resource profitability because they ignore the amount of resources committed to the division, and this is the major scarce resource that management is expected to administer.

For example, two divisions of a company might show the following profit record:

	Division A	Division B
Sales.................................	$10,000,000	$5,000,000
Profit................................	2,000,000	500,000
Investment............................	10,000,000	2,000,000
Percentage margin on sales.............	20%	10%
Percentage return on investment........	20%	25%

Division B ranks lower than division A on the basis of sales, profit, and margin on sales, but it yields a return on investment considerably greater than that of division A.

The return-on-investment ratios are used in activity analysis in two ways:

1. To determine whether the activity is profitable enough to support the amounts of resources devoted to it.
2. To identify activities that need top management attention, either to deal with emerging problems or to capitalize on opportunities that have arisen.

Our task in this section is to study how return on investment ratios are calculated for individual activities and to see how well they relate to management's information needs. For convenience, we shall start with a divisional organization in which each division has its own product lines, its own sales force, and its own manufacturing facilities. Other kinds of situations will be examined later.

Measuring Divisional Profit

Return-on-investment computations typically require some form of net profit calculation. Starting with the revenues recorded in division accounts, the following expense deductions are ordinarily made:

1. Cost of goods sold.
2. Division-traceable nonmanufacturing expense.
3. Other nonmanufacturing expense.

The main difficulty, of course, lies in measuring the fixed component of the third of these categories. Enough has been said about this problem in previous chapters to indicate that any figure purporting to represent the amount of net profit emanating from the division is bound to be inaccurate. Fixed costs that bear no apparent relationship to divisional activity represent a general charge against company revenues as a whole. They provide general management capacity and have no relevance to the evaluation of individual divisions or product lines. Costs for which no index of attributability can be found are often allocated, however, on some arbitrary basis (such as in proportion to gross sales). To the extent that these allocations are arbitrary, the net profit figure will be arbitrary, too.

Exhibit 22–1

PACKAGING DIVISION INCOME STATEMENT
(for the month of March)

	Amount	Percent
Net sales..................................	$3,495,000	100.0
Standard variable cost of sales................	$1,908,000	54.6
Factory fixed costs..........................	274,000	7.8
Factory cost variances, net..................	13,000*	0.4*
Divisional overhead:		
Marketing.............................	538,000	15.4
Administration.........................	73,000	2.1
Total expense......................	$2,780,000	79.5
Profit contribution.........................	$ 715,000	20.5
Head office charges........................	360,000	10.3
Net income before taxes....................	$ 355,000	10.2

* Favorable (subtracted from subtotal).

Exhibit 22–1, for example, is a monthly income statement for the packaging division of Conglomerate, Inc. This shows very little detail because top management is interested primarily in the overall result, not in its component parts. Supporting schedules like those presented later in this chapter are available if top management wishes to look more closely at this division's performance. The net income figure means something only if the head office charges reflect the attributable cost concept, and this seldom happens.

The accountant also faces difficulties in measuring the revenues to be reported for an activity. For example, the packaging division may be able to sell some of its products only because the customer buys the products of another division of Conglomerate, Inc. This means that the revenues recorded in the other division's accounts understate the amount of revenue attributable to its activity. Or, the sales of a division selling plastic containers may cut into the sales of the company's glass and paper products division. The plastics division's recorded sales revenues therefore overstate the amount of revenues attributable to its activities.

The difficulty of reflecting these complementary and substitute relationships is so great that accountants never attempt it except in special ad hoc analyses. The revenues for routine profit measures are those immediately traceable to the activity in question.

Measuring Divisional Investment

Turning to the divisional or product-line investment figures, two subjects need examination:

1. The definition of invested capital.
2. The assignment of assets to divisions.

Definition of Invested Capital. Divisional investment may be defined in many ways, the most important being (1) the division's share of corporate stockholders' equity, (2) total assets, (3) net investment, and (4) traceable assets. Stockholders' equity is the book value of the owners' investment in the assets of the firm. Total assets represent all assets of the division, including a share of corporate cash and other assets that are administered centrally. Net investment is the division's share of total assets less noninterest-bearing current liabilities—in other words, the division's share of the total investment of stockholders and lender creditors. Traceable assets include all assets that can be identified specifically with the division, regardless of their physical location.

Stockholders' equity is clearly inapplicable as a measure of divisional investment. The funds provided to a division cannot be identified specifically as debt funds or equity funds. The financing mix is a characteristic of the corporation and is the same for all divisions. Division management is entrusted with a portion of the company's total capital which consists of both debt and equity, and any distinction at the division level is unavoidably arbitrary. Certain subsidiaries, it is true, engage in their own financing, and for these an argument can be made for using the parent company's equity as the investment base, on the ground that this equity was provided from parent company funds, both debt and equity.

Net investment and total assets are substantially identical in concept, although not in absolute amount. Both require allocations of centrally administered assets. Of the two, net investment is more closely comparable to the cost-of-capital figures underlying minimum investment standards, because it includes only those funds that are provided to the firm specifically for an interest-like return—i.e., owners' equity, long-term debt, and short-term interest-bearing debt.

Defining divisional investment as traceable assets avoids the allocation of centrally administered assets to individual divisions, but it makes comparisons among company divisions vulnerable to intracompany variations in asset administration. For example, one division may handle all its own inventories and receivables, whereas another may utilize central billing and warehousing and thereby bury some of its investment in the common pool. For this reason, most companies prefer to use some variant of total assets or net investment.

Assignment of Assets to Divisions. Many of the assets that relate to the activities of a specific division can be traced to that division from the organizational account classification. In addition to these, every company has some assets that are administered centrally, either because they are necessary to perform central office or service functions or because central administration represents a more efficient use of resources.

At this juncture we should distinguish between assets that are truly common to more than one division and those that presumably could be traced to specific divisions by a finer subdivision of the account codes. Cash, for example, can never be traced satisfactorily to the operations of individual divisions, whereas it is often possible to identify receivables by division even though billing and accounts receivable operations are performed centrally.

Centrally administered assets of this latter type may be subcoded in the accounts to permit divisional identification. If this step is regarded as excessively costly, at least two solutions are available. First, the percentage distribution might be approximated by sampling techniques; for example, a sample of open customer accounts might be taken to approximate the true distribution of all receivables among divisions. Second, studies might be undertaken to determine the statistical relationship between asset balances and divisional activity. For example, receivables might be found to bear a fixed relationship to sales volume, the exact ratio differing for each division because of differences in terms, collection policies, or industry customs. This second method is likely to be inferior to sampling because statistical relationships frequently get out of date.

Assets that are truly common to more than one division presents a more difficult problem. The relevant investment base for activity evaluation is the amount that is uniquely devoted to the support of the division's operations. For common assets, the allocation criterion that satisfies this definition is the criterion of avoidable investment—that is, what portion of the common investment would be unnecessary if this division were not present?

Implementation of this concept is extremely difficult, and few companies even try to apply it. Some make no allocations at all; others use arbitrary but plausible formulas. Exhibit 22–2, for example, shows the investment attributed to the packaging division. Traceable current lia-

Exhibit 22–2

PACKAGING DIVISION NET INVESTMENT
(as of March 31)

Direct investments:

Accounts receivable	$ 4,192,000
Inventories:	
Finished goods	3,307,000
Work in process	1,488,000
Raw materials, parts and supplies	953,000
Prepayments	59,000
Property, plant and equipment, net	10,528,000
Total direct investment	$20,527,000
Direct current liabilities:	
Accounts payable	$ 1,287,000
Accruals	174,000
Total direct current liabilities	$ 1,461,000
Net direct investment	$19,066,000
Centrally administered assets:	
Cash	2,500,000
Other	1,954,000
Net investment	$23,520,000

bilities amounting to $1,461,000 are deducted from traceable assets to leave a net direct investment of $19,066,000. Allocated investments bring the total net investment up to $23,520,000.

The allocation of centrally administered assets permits the calculation of a return-on-investment figure that has the appearance of comparability to companywide profitability rates and standards. Assuming that March is an average month, the return on investment can be calculated by multiplying the month's earnings by 12 and dividing by net investment:

$$\frac{12 \times \$355,000}{\$23,520,000} = 18.1\%$$

Interpreting the Return on Investment

The basic return-on-investment standard for use in activity evaluation is the rate of return that the company's management regards as the minimum which new investments in comparable activities must meet, as discussed in Chapter 26 below. For newly established or rapidly growing activities, this may be replaced by the ratios budgeted for the current period, but this substitution is only temporary.

The reason for using an investment decision criterion is that the main objective of activity analysis is to monitor the wisdom of management's investment decisions. The main interpretation placed on a below-standard return-on-investment figure is that the activity is an unprofitable one that must be either rescued or abandoned.

While this interpretation may be reasonable, three things should be borne in mind. First, routine periodic measures of return on investment are ex-post measures of resource productivity—they show what the company has achieved by its past decisions to engage in this activity, not what it would lose if the activity were discontinued now. Decisions must be based on estimates of the latter—that is, the relevant figure is an ex-ante measure of investment performance, relating estimates of the annual cash receipts that would be lost if the activity were discontinued to the cash that could be realized and released for use elsewhere by liquidating the assets now supporting it. The amounts invested in the past to support the activity are sunk costs, irrelevant to current decisions.[1]

Second, as we mentioned earlier, routine ex-post measures do not reflect any complementarity or substitutability that may exist between the sales reported for this activity and those reported for others. Some companies have been able to withdraw from certain activities at a sacrifice of as little as 10 percent of the revenues previously ascribed to those activities, while eliminating most of the costs.

Third, the arbitrary nature of most allocations of centrally administered costs and assets makes the return-on-investment percentages inapplicable for decision making. Only if all allocations reflected the attributability concept would the ratios be comparable to the company's minimum profitability standards.

Despite these shortcomings, return-on-investment ratios continue to be used quite widely as measures of activity profitability. Part of the explanation may be that the impact of allocations and unrecorded interdependencies among divisions is immaterial. Whatever the reason, however, the ratios should be used only as crude signals, a means of directing attention to activities that need investigation.[2]

Effects of Price Level Fluctuations

The property, plant and equipment figure in Exhibit 22–2 reflected original historical cost less accumulated depreciation. After a period of inflation, however, long-life property is a mixture of assets acquired at many different price levels. Divisions with an older asset mix will have a lower historical cost investment base and lower depreciation charges than younger divisions and therefore will tend to report a higher return on investment. This may serve to cover up a deteriorating profit situation until price levels stabilize and investment replacement at higher prices begins to make itself felt in lower return-on-investment figures.

This problem differs in no fundamental way from the price level prob-

[1] For a review of abandonment analysis, see Gordon Shillinglaw, "Profit Analysis for Abandonment Decisions," *Journal of Business*, Janurary 1957, pp. 17–29.

[2] For a lucid discussion of some of the problems encountered in interpreting return-on-investment figures, see John Dearden, "The Case Against ROI Control," *Harvard Business Review*, May–June 1969, pp. 124–35.

lem in external financial reporting and seems no nearer to solution. If there is any difference at all, it is that few division managers have major responsibility for so-called holding gains and losses on their asset port-folios; but this is relevant to the use of divisional profit figures in man-agerial evaluation rather than in activity evaluation, which is the concern of this chapter.

Costing inventories at current standard cost and long-lived assets at some approximation to current replacement cost, by the use of explicit index numbers or otherwise, might be a good solution to the problem of interdivisional comparability, but the expense of making the replacement cost calculations is unlikely to be justifiable except as part of a company-wide adjustment for public reporting purposes. (Some of the large Dutch companies do in fact make such adjustments both for internal and for external reporting.)

REPORTING TO DIVISION MANAGEMENT

When company divisions comprise a number of distinct activities, the same kind of return-on-investment breakdown used by top management for activity evaluation may be useful to division management. If the divi-sion manager suspects that the company's position could be improved by discontinuing one of the division's activities, he should apply the same kind of incremental analysis that top management would use in evaluating the division's activities as a whole.

Adoption of the division's operating plan for the period is an implicit rejection of the abandonment alternative, however. Once the plan has been adopted, the division manager's primary interest in the profit gener-ated by his own operations focuses on the question of whether it equals or exceeds the profit planned for the period. The deviations between planned and actual results can then be studied for the purpose of helping management initiate corrective or adaptive action. The absolute level of the return on investment is of no significance unless the unfavorable profit variances get so large that the abandonment alternative is brought back to life.

Alternative Profit Concepts

The profit contributed by any one segment can be measured on at least four different bases:

1. *Variable profit:* revenues less the variable costs attributable to these revenues.
2. *Profit contribution:* variable profit less traceable fixed costs.
3. *Attributable profit:* profit contribution less the nontraceable fixed costs that could be eliminated if the segment were to be abandoned.

4. *Net profit:* attributable profit less a pro rata share of all other non-traceable fixed costs.

If the division manager has initial responsibility for abandonment decisions, the attributable profit concept should be applied. Even when this is done, however, the variable profit and profit contribution figures should be clearly identified, because these reflect the only variables that are subject to current operating control.

Exhibit 22–3, for example, makes no attempt to allocate nontraceable costs to individual product lines within the division. The columns relating to the division's three product lines—White Shield, Red Label, and Commercial—are carried down only to the product profit contribution level, the amount available to cover the nontraceable fixed overheads and provide a margin for the profit of the division and the company as a whole. Divisional net income is the sum of the segment profit contributions, less the total of the fixed costs not traceable to individual segments. For the reasons set forth in Chapter 13, allocations of sales salaries and travel

Exhibit 22–3

PACKAGING DIVISION
Product Profit Contribution Statement
(for the month of March)

	Total	White Shield	Red Label	Commercial
Net sales.....................	$3,495,000	$1,619,000	$1,031,000	$845,000
Variable cost of sales........	1,908,000	793,000	577,000	538,000
Variable profit margin.........	$1,587,000	$ 826,000	$ 454,000	$307,000
Product fixed costs:				
Factory....................	$ 68,000	$ 25,000	$ 19,000	$ 24,000
Marketing.................	98,000	60,000	30,000	8,000
Total product fixed cost............	$ 166,000	$ 85,000	$ 49,000	$ 32,000
Product profit contribution.....	$1,421,000	$ 741,000	$ 405,000	$275,000
Divisional fixed costs:				
Manufacturing..............	$ 193,000			
Marketing.................	440,000			
Administration.............	73,000			
Total divisional fixed cost............	$ 706,000			
Division profit contribution.....	$ 715,000			
Head office charges...........	360,000			
Net Income before Taxes......	$ 355,000			

expense are unlikely to improve the information content of the product-line profitability statements and should be omitted.

Comparison Reports

The profit report shown in Exhibit 22–3 is of limited usefulness because it provides no comparison bench mark, but the profit contribution concept can be applied in comparative statements as well. Exhibit 22–4,

Exhibit 22–4

PACKAGING DIVISION
District Profit Performance Report

DISTRICT SALES AND EXPENSE SUMMARY				
DISTRICT Boston			MONTH	March
	Budget	Actual	Deviation	Actual % of Sales
Net sales billed...............	$500,000	$514,000	$14,000	100.0
Cost of sales.................	280,000	286,000	(6,000)	55.6
Gross margin.................	$220,000	$228,000	$ 8,000	44.4
District office costs:				
Branch salaries..............	$ 2,800	$ 2,800	...	0.5
Sales salaries...............	25,200	25,900	(700)	5.0
Travel.....................	7,900	6,800	1,100	1.3
Entertainment..............	800	1,300	(500)	0.2
Local advertising...........	1,000	1,000	...	0.1
Storage and delivery........	6,500	6,800	(300)	1.4
Branch office expense.......	700	1,100	(400)	0.2
Other.....................	100	300	(200)	0.1
Total district cost.........	$ 45,000	$ 46,000	$(1,000)	8.9
District profit contribution......	$175,000	$182,000	$ 7,000	35.4

for instance, shows a report that might be issued to a district sales manager as an overall summary of his district's profit contribution.

A glance at this report will tell the district manager that his actual sales volume was $514,000, that this gave him a gross margin $8,000 larger than his profit plan called for, and that his district profit contribution for the month was $7,000 greater than his profit objective.

While this kind of report is useful as an overall summary, it does not provide the district manager with any explanation of the *sources* of the main deviations. Another report that he might receive is shown in Exhibit 22–5; it would permit him to monitor the performance of his individual salesmen. Although many companies limit such summaries to sales volume alone, the interjection of product costs and traceable fixed expenses can add a significant dimension to the sales figures. Salesman Kelly, for example, sold $4,000 more than Williams during the month but showed an $800 smaller profit contribution. Williams, on the other hand, failed to meet his profit objective for the period, as did three of the other salesmen.

Some companies prefer to show figures for the comparable period of the previous year in addition to the deviations from the profit plan. No

Exhibit 22–5

PACKAGING DIVISION
District Salesman Report

	SALESMAN PERFORMANCE SUMMARY					
DISTRICT Boston					MONTH March	
				Profit Contribution		
Salesman	Net Sales Billed	Variable Cost of Sales	Salary and Expenses	Amount	Budget Deviation	% of Sales
Brown...............	$ 40,000	$ 21,900	$ 2,500	$ 15,600	$ (800)	39.0
Cannon..............	31,000	18,300	3,200	9,500	(1,900)	30.6
Evars................	63,000	32,000	4,300	26,700	3,700	42.4
Johnson..............	30,000	18,100	2,900	9,000	(2,400)	30.0
Kelly................	54,000	30,600	4,200	19,200	400	35.6
Lusso................	47,000	25,800	3,100	18,100	2,800	38.5
McGregor............	76,000	42,200	3,800	30,000	4,000	39.5
Nelson...............	55,000	31,400	3,400	20,200	1,500	36.7
Stern................	68,000	38,700	3,600	25,700	2,200	37.8
Williams.............	50,000	27,000	3,000	20,000	(1,600)	40.0
Total...............	$514,000	$286,000	$34,000	$194,000	$ 7,900	37.7
Branch expenses.........				12,000	(900)	2.3
District profit contribution.......				$182,000	$ 7,000	35.4

serious objection can be raised to this practice as long as it does not lead to de facto displacement of the current year's profit plan as the relevant bench mark. Graphic presentations of year-to-date performance against planned performance are also useful supplements to the tabulated figures in most cases.

The district manager might receive another report, summarizing the same data but arranged as in Exhibit 22–6, if he is expected to influence product mix. Notice that in this exhibit a much smaller percentage of expenses is assigned to individual segments of the district's business than in the salesman report. Salesmen's salaries and expenses are traceable to individual salesmen, but not to individual product lines. The only product-

Exhibit 22–6

PACKAGING DIVISION
District Product Sales Report

	PRODUCT CONTRIBUTION REPORT					
DISTRICT Boston					MONTH	March
Product Line	Net Sales Billed		Variable Cost of Sales	Other Product Expenses	Profit Contribution	
	Actual	Variance			Actual	Variance
White Shield............	$204,000	$26,000	$102,000	$1,000	$101,000	$14,000
Red Label...............	133,000	(50,000)	77,000	...	56,000	(11,000)
Commercial.............	177,000	38,000	107,000	...	70,000	5,000
Total.................	$514,000	$14,000	$286,000	$1,000	$227,000	$ 8,000
Other branch expenses.....					45,000	(1,000)
District profit contribution..					$182,000	$ 7,000

traceable district costs, in contrast, were the costs of local advertising for
the White Shield line, amounting only to $1,000.

It should be noted that no effort has been made in this illustration to
assign repetitive service costs to individual products, individual salesmen,
or individual districts. As we pointed out in Chapter 13, distribution
cost analysis is decision-oriented, and after-the-fact allocations are unlikely to be useful in decision making. If the amounts are large, however,
predetermined charging rates might be used to make the profit contribution figures more accurate.

Reporting to Marketing Management

Profit reports for higher levels of marketing management are similar
in structure to those just illustrated, but the level of aggregation is higher.
For line management, the basic segmentation is typically along organizational lines, as in Exhibit 22–7. A product manager would receive a similar
type of report showing the profit contribution of his own product line.

Notice that none of these marketing performance reports has shown
any factory cost variances. Manufacturing performance measures become an integral part of routine profit reports only at the level at which
manufacturing and marketing responsibility are joined, in this case at the
divisional level. They should be shown on the product performance reports only if they arise at least partly as a result of characteristics of the
product or of methods of distributing it. Excessive unfavorable factory
cost variances, for example, may signify an ultraliberal product modification policy or fundamental technical difficulties that product management
should recognize when formulating the marketing plan.

Exhibit 22–7

PACKAGING DIVISION
Marketing Department Performance Report

DISTRICT SALES PERFORMANCE SUMMARY (000 omitted)						
					MONTH	March
District	Net Sales Billed	Variable Cost of Sales	District Selling Expense	District Profit Contribution	Budget Deviation	Contribution % of Sales
Boston......................	$ 514	$ 286	$ 46	$ 182	$ 7	35.4
New York....................	946	453	84	409	25	43.2
Baltimore...................	472	285	53	134	(33)	28.4
Atlanta.....................	348	197	42	109	15	31.3
Pittsburgh..................	588	328	63	197	3	33.5
Cleveland...................	627	359	58	210	(2)	33.5
Total..................	$3,495	$1,908	$346	$1,241	$16	35.5
Central marketing expense:						
Administration..............				$ 40	$ 1	
Market research.............				26	(1)	
Advertising.................				103	10	
Other......................				23	(3)	
Total..................				$ 192	$ 7	5.5
Department profit contribution...				$1,049	$23	12.6

One final problem deserves brief recognition at this point. Promotional effort is often made and its cost dimension recorded in the accounts before the resultant sales revenues are recorded. Somtimes this is due to a time lag between effort and results; sometimes it is due to a time lag between results (sales orders) and accounting recognition of these results (revenues).

Most accounting systems are content to overlook these time lags, trusting in the good judgment of marketing executives and top management to make due mental allowances when reviewing reported results. Another possibility is to recognize revenues for internal reporting purposes on the basis of orders received, no matter what basis is used for external reporting. This would not solve the problem raised by the first kind of time lag, but it would adjust for the second, assuming that the bookkeeping details could be worked out economically.

Report Format

The format of the reports in this chapter has been designed to illustrate an important set of concepts. In practice, the objective is different and the format should be designed accordingly. The main purpose of periodic reports is to direct the manager's attention to key figures, to draw him along without losing him in a mass of inconsequential detail. Details should be relegated to supporting schedules or left in the accounts until the manager calls for them. Furthermore, terminology should be shaped in the company's own image. Every industry has its own jargon, and nothing is to be gained by a pedantic insistence on standard accounting terminology.[3]

SUMMARY

Periodic reports on the profit performance of individual divisions, product lines, or other company activities, emphasizing the rate of return on investment in each activity, can give top management a rough idea of the wisdom of past internal investment decisions. By contrasting the return on investment with the standard rate used in capital expenditure decisions within the company, these reports may help management identify activities that should be expanded and those that should be reduced in size or discontinued.

The relevance of historical return-on-investment figures to these decisions is highly limited, however. They are always affected to some extent by more or less arbitrary allocations of centrally administered operating costs and investments, and they ignore the interdependencies that often exist between activities that the company regards as independent enough to justify separate measurement. Most important, they relate to the past, whereas decisions of this sort should be based on forecasts of the incremental cash flows that would be affected.

The activity manager's interest in these reports is quite different. He uses them to identify or quantify problems and opportunities as they arise within his area of responsibility. His performance standard for this purpose is the operating plan or budget, perhaps supplemented by information on the performance of similar activities both inside and outside the company. For this he needs more detail than top management and is less concerned with overall profit-investment relationships for the activity as a whole.

Multiple classification of costs and revenues permits the development of profit performance reports on several bases simultaneously—by product line, by district, and perhaps by distribution channel or customer grouping as well. With profit contribution figures for each activity, local management can gain a good deal of insight into the structure of its own operations.

---

[3] For some interesting suggestions on report construction, see Clarence C. Benedict, "An Integrated System of Variance Analysis for Operating Control Reports," in American Management Association, *Special Report No. 25: Reporting Financial Data to Top Management* (New York, 1957), pp. 127–59.

EXERCISES AND PROBLEMS

1. The asset and liability records of the Deutsch Instruments Company show the following account balances (in thousands of dollars):

	Un-distributed	Division A	Division B	Division C
Cash............................	$360	$ 10	$ 20	$ 15
Receivables......................	400	...	....	....
Inventories.......................	...	300	450	400
Plant and equipment...............	100	500	1,500	1,000
Allowance for depreciation.........	(40)	(200)	(700)	(300)
Total Assets...................	$820	$ 610	$1,270	$1,115
Accounts payable.................	$ 30	$ 80	$ 140	$ 100
Accrued liabilities.................	30	20	30	25
Bonds payable....................	200	...	....	....
Total Liabilities................	$260	$ 100	$ 170	$ 125

No further divisional identification of undistributed asset balances is possible, but the president of the company has insisted that divisional net profits be expressed as a percentage of divisional investment, including a share of undistributed investment. Further information on company activities for the most recent year follows (in thousands of dollars):

	Division A	Division B	Division C
Net sales.........................	$1,500	$2,400	$2,100
Division payroll.....................	400	600	500
Materials received..................	500	800	800
Head office expense distributed........	80	120	100
Division net profit..................	150	300	380

Compute net investment for each division and justify the methods that you have used in your computations.

2. The Ray Manufacturing Company is decentralized in several divisions, including the textile products division. The following statistical information relates to the company as a whole and the textile products division for the month of June. All budget data have been taken from the planning budget for the month.

	Entire Company		Textile Products	
	Budget	Actual	Budget	Actual
Number of employees.............	5,000	4,600	800	780
Total payrolls....................	$ 3,500,000	$3,175,000	$ 480,000	$ 485,000
Factory payrolls..................	$ 2,400,000	$2,200,000	$ 375,000	$ 365,000
Net sales........................	$10,000,000	$9,000,000	$1,500,000	$1,600,000

Actual head office selling and administrative expenses are fully distributed among the divisions each month. All head office expenses are assumed to be fixed with respect to volume. Budgeted and actual head office expenses, together with the relevant allocation bases, were as follows during the month of June:

	Basis	Budget	Actual
Accounting department...............	Employees	$120,000	$115,000
Manufacturing department	Factory payrolls	60,000	62,000
Marketing department................	Net sales	50,000	51,000
Advertising.........................	Net sales	200,000	280,000
Executive offices....................	Total payrolls	70,000	68,000

a) Prepare a head office expense budget for the textile products division, based on budget data only, and compute the amount of head office expenses to be charged to the division for the month.

b) Compute the variances in the charges for these five items that will appear in the textile products division profit report for the month. What effect do they have on divisional return on investment? What relevance do they have to activity evaluation?

3. The XYZ Company manufactures all of its products in a single factory and sells them through two channels of distribution: through dealers and directly to the ultimate consumer. In addition, it bills its customers for work performed for those customers by the XYZ customer engineering department. Revenues from these three business segments last month were as follows:

Dealer sales..................................	$28,000
Direct sales..................................	36,000
Customer engineering..........................	15,000
Total...	$79,000

Sam Fletcher, an experienced accountant, has just been hired to replace Bob Danvers, who retired two months ago after 25 years as the company's controller. The first day on the job, Sam learned that profit figures for individual revenue segments had never been collected, although sales revenues had been reported regularly and promptly to top management every month. Fearing that the lack of information might be very costly to the company, he has managed to collect the following information on last month's operations:

(1) Standard cost of goods sold:
   Dealer sales: variable costs, $11,000; fixed costs, $4,000.
   Direct sales: variable costs, $13,000; fixed costs, $5,000.
(2) Total factory costs:
   Direct materials: standard, $10,000; actual, $10,500.
   Direct labor: standard, $12,000; actual, $13,200.
   Factory overhead: standard, $17,000; actual, $20,400.
(3) Factory overhead volume variances included in (2) above: $3,000 (unfavorable).
(4) Cost variances in opening inventory, none.
(5) Commissions on direct sales, $2,700.
(6) Dealer discounts, $10,500.

(7) Other direct expenses (fixed):
  Dealer sales department, $1,000.
  Direct sales department, $4,500.
  Customer engineering department, $15,800.
(8) Product advertising (budgeted at 3 percent of direct and dealer sales), $2,500.
(9) Time spent by customer engineers on work not billable to customers:
  For dealer sales customers, $600.
  For direct sales customers, $150.
(10) General sales division overheads, $1,500.
(11) Administrative expenses, $4,900.

a) Prepare a summary profit report for each business segment and for the company as a whole. Use whatever format you feel is appropriate, but be prepared to defend your choice. (Ignore income taxes.)
b) How would your report be used? What conclusions, if any, might Sam Fletcher draw from it?

4. A company has two products, X and Y. The following data are available for a recent month:

	Product X	Product Y
Selling price.	$5.00	$2.00
Standard manufacturing cost:		
Materials.	$0.50	$0.45
Labor.	1.00	0.50
Overhead.	1.50	0.75
Total.	$3.00	$1.70
Units produced and sold.	50,000	200,000
Sales discounts & allowances.	$ 12,500	$ 4,000
Advertising and other direct selling costs.	$ 20,000	$ 20,000
Salesmen's commission per unit.	$0.25	$0.05

Both products use the same manufacturing facilities and all present facilities would still be required if only one of these two products were manufactured.

Variable overhead costs constitute 80 percent of standard manufacturing overhead.

Manufacturing cost variances are apportioned between the two products on the basis of relative total standard direct labor cost per month. The manufacturing cost variances reflected in the net income (loss) for the month were:

Overhead volume.	$ 3,000 unfavorable
Overhead spending.	1,375 favorable
Materials and labor price.	19,875 unfavorable
Materials and labor quantity.	26,500 unfavorable
Total.	$48,000 unfavorable

None of these variances is traceable to a specific product.

Costs of sales promotion, general company administration, etc. not otherwise specified above are regarded as fixed and are not traceable to either product. They amount to $52,000 a month and are allocated between the two products on the basis of relative gross sales dollars. Elimination of either product would permit a reduction in these costs of $10,000 a month.

These data are typical under current conditions, and no significant changes are anticipated in the near future.

a) From these data prepare a profit contribution statement in good form, including an "allocated charges" section at the bottom to bring each product down to a fully allocated net income figure.

b) If the company were to discontinue the manufacture of product X, it could reduce working capital by $10 million. Discontinuation of product Y would release $2 million in working capital for other purposes. This company requires a 20 percent return on investment before taxes. Would you recommend discontinuation of either product? State your reasoning. (Do not evaluate the desirability of discontinuing both products and going out of business entirely—not enough data are provided.)

c) Indicate how you think the vice president of marketing should use the statement prepared in (a).

5. The Top Equipment Company is organized into several divisions. The value division sells all of its output to outside customers and buys all of its materials and parts from outside suppliers. The asset and liability sections of the division's last two balance sheets are as follows (in thousands):

	January 1, 19xx		December 31,19xx	
Cash................................		$ 380		$ 400
Accounts receivable....................		450		520
Inventory............................		780		850
Land, buildings, and equipment...........	$2,280		$2,300	
Less: Allowance for depreciation........	1,110	1,170	1,200	1,100
Total Assets.......................		$2,780		$2,870
Wages, accounts, and taxes payable........		$ 300		$ 350
Mortgage loan payable.................		550		500
Total Divisional Liabilities...........		$ 850		$ 850

The income statement for 19xx is considered indicative of the division's profit potential for the future (in thousands):

Sales..		$4,250
Less: Cost of goods sold...................................	$3,410	
Selling and administrative expense.....................	470	3,880
Division profit contribution...............................		$ 370
Less: Allocated headquarters expense......................		120
Division Net Income before Taxes........................		$ 250

The cost of goods sold figure includes $110,000 in annual depreciation charges.

Wages, accounts, and taxes payable are all traceable to the valve division.

The mortgage loan payable calls for interest at a rate of 5 percent and is a long-term obligation of the Top Equipment Company, secured by a mortgage on the land, buildings, and equipment of the valve division. This loan would be paid off if the division were to be liquidated. Interest on this loan is not charged to the valve division.

Liquidation expenses, including such items as terminal pay of employees and losses from liquidation of inventory and receivables, would total $320,000. The disposal value of the land, buildings, and equipment is approximately $820,000.

Replacement cost of the fixed assets is considerably in excess of their book value. The replacement of the existing facilities with equivalent brand-new facilities would cost approximately $3,700,000.

Annual outlays on plant and equipment necessary to maintain the division's competitive position would amount to $160,000 if the division were to continue in operation.

Headquarters expenses are allocated among the company's divisions as a uniform percentage of divisional sales.

Compute divisional rate of return (*a*) on a going-concern basis, and (*b*) on a liquidation basis. Comment on the differences between the two figures and indicate how you think they would be used.

6. The Andrews Company is organized in divisions, each one with its own products, its own factories, and its own sales force. A balance sheet and an income statement are prepared every month for each division, and a return-on-investment figure is computed.

The Hastings Pump division is one of the Andrews Company's smaller divisions. Unlike some other divisions, it sells all of its output to customers outside the company and none to sister divisions within the company. It also buys all of its materials and parts from outside suppliers, so that no transfers between divisions take place.

The balance sheet for the Hastings Pump division as of the end of last month showed the following amounts (in thousands):

Assets

Cash...		$ 400
Accounts receivable.............................		520
Inventories.......................................		850
Land, buildings, and equipment.....................	$2,300	
Less: Accumulated depreciation.....................	1,200	1,100
Total Assets.....................................		$2,870

Liabilities

Accounts, taxes, and wages payable..................	$ 340	
Mortgage payable..................................	500	
Total Liabilities.................................		840
Net Headquarters Equity in Divisional Assets..........		$2,030

Last month's income statement was as follows:

Sales...		$350,000
Less:		
Cost of materials and supplies used.................	$ 89,300	
Labor and labor-related costs......................	177,600	
Cost of outside services used......................	56,100	
Depreciation on divisional plant and equipment.......	9,000	
Headquarters charges.............................	17,500	
Mortgage interest expense........................	2,500	343,000
Net Income......................................	~~353,000~~	$ 7,000

The return on investment for the month was found to be 2.9 percent, computed as follows:

$$\frac{12 \times \$7,000}{\$2,870,000} = 2.9\%$$

(The net income for the month figure was converted to an annual equivalent by multiplying by 12.)

Receivables, inventories, and fixed assets are all wholly traceable to the division. The figure shown for cash, however, is obtained by dividing the company's cash balance among the divisions in proportion to each division's share of total company sales.

Accounts, taxes, and wages payable are all traceable to the division.

The balances in the accounts for inventories, receivables, and payables were approximately the same at the end of the month as at the beginning.

Inventories are measured at standard cost, which is approximately equal to current replacement cost.

The mortgage loan payable calls for interest at a rate of 6 percent and is a long-term obligation of the Andrews Company, secured by a mortgage on the land, buildings, and equipment of the Hastings Pump division.

The disposal value of the land, buildings, and equipment is approximately $820,000. Replacement of these assets with equivalent brand-new facilities would cost approximately $3,680,000.

Plant and equipment expenditures during the month amounted to $5,000. These were capitalized in their entirety. Normally, the company spends about $13,000 a month for new equipment and plant renovation to keep the division's facilities in efficient operating condition.

Headquarters expenses are allocated among the company's divisions as a uniform percentage of divisional sales.

If the division were to be liquidated, the company would be able to recover 100 percent of the book value of the division's receivables and inventories. The company's total cash requirements would decrease by $100,000 if liquidation took place. Liquidation costs, including such items as terminal pay of employees, would total $320,000.

The Andrews Company estimates that its cost of long-term investment capital is approximately 12 percent.

a) Prepare a revised balance sheet and a revised income statement, making whatever changes are necessary to make the statements as useful as possible for activity evaluation. Describe and justify the changes you have made. You should assume that income taxes are zero.

b) Prepare a second set of statements, using only the information that you would normally expect the Hastings Pump division to have available on a regular basis. The purpose of these statements would be to assist the Andrews Company's top management in activity evaluation. If these statements differ from the statements you prepared in (a) above, indicate the reasons for the differences.

CASE 22–1: THE FEDERAL COMPANY

The Federal Company was a medium-sized manufacturer of consumer soft goods. The headquarters marketing staff in Cleveland was responsible for overall planning and direction of all marketing activities, while responsibility for field selling activities was assigned to the managers of the company's six regional branch offices.

David Halsey, Federal's marketing vice president, was experimenting with a new financial reporting format that he hoped would help him make better promotional expenditure decisions. "Our move to profit contribution reporting several years ago was a step in the right direction," he said, "but it didn't go far enough. For one thing, sales are still reported several months after the promotional activity takes place. This makes for some pretty funny profit contribution figures sometimes.

"For another, they still don't tell me whether I'm spending the right amount in each market area. For example, I was pretty sure that we were spending too much in the Atlanta branch, but I couldn't prove it. I couldn't put the squeeze on the branch manager, either, because he was turning in a larger profit contribution than any of the other branches. I want the system to help me answer this kind of question."

The new reporting system had been worked out by Jack McClendon, Federal's controller. "We made a special study," he said, "trying to find out how long it takes before promotional effort pays off. Frankly, the results aren't very clear, but they have given us something to think about. For instance, we found that calling on a customer more frequently seemed to increase the average order size as well as the total sales volume. I don't know how far we can carry that, but we're certainly going to follow up on it.

"We did find that the orders received in a month correlate pretty well with the current month's field selling and local advertising expenses. I've talked this over with Dave (Halsey) and we've agreed to report sales and cost of goods sold internally on the basis of orders received. That will mean a little more bookkeeping—the company's financial statements will still show revenues from shipments—but I think the benefits are worth it."

Mr. Halsey explained his experimental report structure to the case writer. "The main feature of these reports is that they focus on month-to-month changes rather than on departures from the budget. We still get monthly reports of variances from the profit plan for control purposes, but they don't help us much in decision making.

"Let me show you what I mean. Here is last month's report for the Atlanta branch [Table 1]. The figures in the right-hand column show

Table 1

THE FEDERAL COMPANY
Profit Performance Report, Atlanta Branch
(dollar figures in thousands)

	This Month	Change from Same Month Last Year
Sales (net orders received)......................	$5,000	+$450
Standard variable manufacturing cost.............	2,010	+ 181
Standard variable distribution cost................	253	+ 22
Gross margin................................	$2,737	+$247
Field selling expenses.........................	669	+$ 71
Local advertising.............................	523	+ 65
Administration...............................	128	+ 4
Total branch expenses........................	$1,320	+$140
Branch Profit................................	$1,417	+$107
Effectiveness Ratios:		
Gross margin to sales........................	0.55	...
Field selling and advertising to sales.............	0.24	...
Branch profit to sales........................	0.28	...
Branch profit to field selling and advertising......	1.19	0.79

the changes from the same month a year ago. I'm not sure that that's the right way to go, but we felt that it would be better than a comparison of two successive months.

"Our real emphasis is on the ratios at the bottom of the report. The ratios in the left-hand column are conventional percentage figures. Every company uses these. Our big interest is in the ratio to the right, and I don't know of anyone else who calculates this one. It shows the relationship of the *change* in profit or the *change* in sales to the change that has taken place in marketing costs. We call this our 'response function.' At Atlanta, for example, we got 79 cents for every extra dollar that we spent on field selling and advertising. This is the $107,000 change in branch profit divided by the $136,000 change in field selling and advertising costs."

"That means that you didn't get your money back, doesn't it?"

"No, it's a net figure. We've already deducted the $136,000 from the profit figure, so that we're okay as long as the ratio is positive."

"I'm not sure how much good that ratio will do you," said the case writer. "A lot of other things could have happened, and you can't assume that the increase in sales was all due to the added marketing costs."

"I can't argue with you on that, but we don't take the ratios one by one. What we really want to do is compare the branches, as we do here [in Table 2]. This shows that we were wrong about Atlanta. With a profit ratio of 0.79, it is now giving us more for our added promotional dollar than we get in any other branch. In fact, we're considering spending more money in Atlanta rather than less. Seattle and Denver are at the other extreme. Both of them have negative ratios, and we may decide to cut back on our efforts there."

"I don't understand what the negative ratios mean. Why should they lead you to reduce your promotional outlays in those branches?"

"Well, look at Seattle, for instance. We put an extra $70,000 in there, but our branch profit went down by $7,000. That's a negative response to our effort. The extra $70,000 wasn't a very good investment, in my opinion."

"I can understand the minus figures for Seattle, but what about Denver? There your profit actually went up."

Table 2

THE FEDERAL COMPANY
Branch Profit Comparison
(dollar figures in thousands)

	Atlanta	Cleveland	Houston	Boston	Denver	Seattle
Results						
Sales:						
This year	$5,000	$4,560	$3,076	$3,249	$1,865	$2,722
Change from last year	+ 450	+ 333	+ 243	+ 390	− 67	+ 132
Promotional expense:						
This year	1,192	684	369	520	375	599
Change from last year	+ 136	+ 107	+ 90	+ 135	− 44	+ 70
Branch profit:						
This year	1,417	1,280	831	1,007	634	517
Change from last year	+ 107	+ 76	+ 40	+ 72	+ 5	− 7
Effectiveness Ratios						
Current period:						
Gross margin to sales	0.55	0.52	0.42	0.49	0.58	0.46
Promotional expenses to sales	0.24	0.18	0.12	0.16	0.20	0.22
Branch profit to sales	0.28	0.28	0.27	0.31	0.34	0.19
Response function (change in branch profit to change in promotional expenses)	+ 0.79	+ 0.71	+ 0.44	+ 0.54	− 0.11	− 0.10

"That's right. We spent less than last year, and we lost some business as a result—sales were down by $67,000. Fortunately, the gross margin on the lost sales was less than the amount we saved in marketing expense. That's what a nega... ...tio means. Whenever I see a minus sign, it tells me that I can make money by spending less on marketing. With a plus sign, I figure that the market isn't saturated yet, so I should put in a little more money. It doesn't tell me how much more or less to spend, but it gives me the direction."

"How do you allow for changes in general economic conditions? It seems to me that these could have such huge effects on the changes that your ratios would lose all their validity."

"We haven't figured out how to grapple with that one yet. One way is to deal with quarterly data instead of monthly data and compare each quarter with the one before instead of the one a year earlier. The drawback there is that seasonal influences are important in our business, and I don't think the figures would be very useful. Another possibility is to adjust the figures in some way for changes in the gross national product or some other index of the volume of business generally. Even without these changes, though, I think we can use the ratios productively. Don't forget that a change in business conditions is likely to affect all of our markets. Other things being equal, a change of this kind would produce either minus signs in all branches or plus signs in all branches. We're looking for differences, knowing that the ratios aren't precise and that all they can do is suggest directions we might want to move."

a)   Do you agree that Federal should spend more money in Atlanta and less in Denver and Seattle?

b)   Do you think that the new reporting system will provide Mr. Halsey with better information for decision making? What changes, if any, would you make in the system to make it more useful?

chapter 23

Measuring Managerial
Profit Performance

A company is divisionalized whenever certain related activities are grouped together for administrative direction and control by high-level executives. Whenever this is accompanied by the delegation of the responsibility for a segment of the company's profits, the company is said to be *decentralized*. The purpose of this chapter is to examine how routine profit performance reports can be used by top management to exert control over the operations of decentralized units.

THE DECENTRALIZATION CONCEPT

Decentralization has sometimes been referred to as a state of mind rather than as a description of a specific organization structure. Before looking at the profit measurement problems of a decentralized unit, therefore, it may be appropriate to ask what decentralization is expected to accomplish and what kinds of units can appropriately be referred to as decentralized.

Objectives of Decentralization

Decentralization is intended to increase overall corporate profitability in three ways:

1. By transferring decision-making responsibility to executives who can devote all of their efforts to individual markets or product lines.
2. By bringing subordinate executives into more direct contact with the ultimate profit objectives of the firm, thereby motivating them to work toward these profit objectives.

547

3. By providing an integrated training ground for the top managers of the future.

Sharing the Work Load. Perhaps the most important objective is to cope with the sheer weight of the decision-making responsibility in a large corporation. Even with versatile electronic computers at its disposal, a centralized management cannot give enough time to each area of its operations. Furthermore, division executives have a closer, more detailed familiarity with their own products or markets and presumably can react faster to changing conditions. In other words, decentralization aims to recreate in the large organization the conditions that give life and flexibility to the small company without sacrificing such advantages of size as diversification of risk, centralized financing, and specialization in the planning and advisory functions of management.

Spreading Profit Motivation. The profit objectives of the large corporation often have little meaning to the functional executive. A manufacturing executive sees all problems with a cost overlay, while marketing executives are likely to focus their attention on sales volume and distribution cost. Decentralization places subordinate executives in charge of operations that are relatively self-contained, thereby permitting them to identify directly with profit figures. It is hoped that this will motivate them to work for greater corporate profit.

Training Future Managers. Closely related to this is a third objective of decentralization, namely, to provide a more comprehensive training ground for the top managers of the future. The ranks of top executives are continually being thinned by death and retirement, and there is a need for replacements who have been schooled in various aspects of business management and are thereby better prepared to face the major problems that can be resolved only at the top management level. This kind of experience is best obtained at lower levels, where the inevitable mistakes are likely to be smaller.

Profit Centers

The profit-oriented divisions in a decentralized company are generally known as profit centers. The manager of the profit center is responsible for using the division's assets to generate profit for the company as a whole. To this end, he is given authority to decide what kinds of inputs to use, how much of each, and where to get them, in much the same degree as the manager of an independent firm.

In return for this authority, the profit center manager is expected to use profit criteria in decision making, and his performance is measured in part by the amount of profit he is able to generate.

Although profit centers are never quite as autonomous as independent companies, the division which has its own manufacturing and distribution facilities, with few dealings with sister divisions within the company, is ideally suited for designation as a profit center. The profit reported for such a division is largely independent of operating performance elsewhere in the company, thus facilitating the interpretation of reported profit.

In most cases, profit centers deal with individual product lines or geographic regions. Product divisions are most common when manufacturing facilities tend to be specialized by product line or when product distribution calls for separate sales forces for individual product lines. Geographic divisions are generally indicated if marketing problems differ

Exhibit 23–1

PRODUCT-LINE ORGANIZATION STRUCTURE

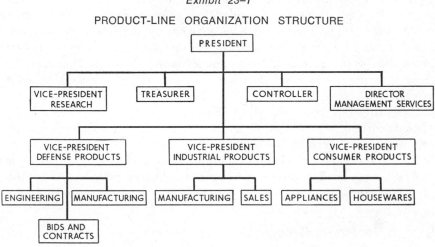

more among regions than among products and if the economics of manufacturing produce regional manufacturing facilities instead of specialized factories for each product line serving the entire nation.

Exhibit 23–1 illustrates a division structure based on separate product lines. Seven executives report directly to the president: treasurer, controller, vice president–research, director–management services, and three operating vice presidents. Company operations are centered around three separate product lines, each under a vice president who has overall responsibility for sales and production in his division.

Two of these divisions, the defense products division and the industrial products division, are organized internally along functional lines. The structure of these functional organizations differs between the two divisions because of differences between them in the nature of their products and of the markets that they serve, but the nature of the responsibility of each of the functional heads is similar to that of his corporate counterparts in centrally administered companies. The consumer products division, on the other hand, is subdivided further around two distinct groups of consumer products that are marketed through separate sales forces and manufactured in separate production facilities.

Divisions of this sort can be referred to as profit centers as long as the division manager is able to control enough of the major determinants of profit. How much is enough is difficult to say, but one proviso is that the division must sell most of its output to outside customers. On this count, manufacturing divisions cannot be treated as profit centers. The sales volume achieved by a manufacturing division is entirely dependent on the number of orders obtained by the marketing division or divisions, and thus is not subject to the manufacturing manager's control.

A second proviso is that the manager must be free to choose his sources of supply. This means that most marketing divisions are not true profit centers. The marketing division manager does face the market, however, and he can influence most of the determinants of divisional profit except the unit cost of the merchandise he sells. This may be enough to warrant treating the marketing division as if it were a profit center.

No matter how it is defined, decentralization never represents a complete delegation of authority. Even in the most decentralized companies, top management retains some vestige of authority, particularly over financing and capital expenditures. In any case, divisional autonomy is limited by the need to conform to overall company policies and by the need for coordination.

Service Centers in Decentralized Companies

Both at the corporate level and within each profit center there are units that are not organized on a profit responsibility basis. These are called *service centers* or *budget centers* to distinguish them from profit centers. The managers of these departments are also responsible for costs, but they generally have no direct profit responsibilities.

Corporate service departments are typically classified as service centers, but exceptions are sometimes made. For example, one company has a photo and reproduction shop which performs a wide variety of blueprinting, photostating, and printing of reports, forms, and so forth on demand for other parts of the company. In this operation it competes with outside organizations to which its customers within the company have free access. It is expected to justify its existence by providing services of a quality and at prices which compare favorably with those offered by outside competition.

This shop cannot be a profit center as long as the shop manager is not free to solicit business from outside customers, but treating it as one may help to achieve some of the objectives listed earlier. The division manager is expected to compete with outside suppliers by offering better or faster service at the same market price. In adding or dropping personnel, he is expected to use a profit criterion rather than a cost or volume criterion. In short, the use of this device may serve to create a favorable climate in which the manager feels motivated to work toward company profit goals.

PROFIT REPORTING FOR MANAGERIAL EVALUATION

When a company is decentralized, top management's primary means of control is provided by its participation in divisional planning. This form of control is reinforced and supplemented by a variety of other controls, including supervision by corporate staff of the work of divisional staff, periodic inspection visits by top management, and executive conferences and training courses. One of the most important of these controls is the system of periodic profit performance reports.

Purposes of Periodic Profit Reports

One purpose of periodic profit reports is to provide top management with a measure of the profitability of the resources invested in the division. This purpose was discussed in the previous chapter.

A second objective is to provide top management with a measure of the financial performance of division management. Managerial performance has many dimensions, of which current profit performance is only one, but reporting on this dimension is absolutely essential. The managers of any business unit are always accountable to the suppliers of capital for the ways in which this capital has been used to meet the stated objectives. For the profit center, top management is the supplier of capital. If its objective for the use of that capital is to produce income, the accountability of the profit center manager must be regarded primarily as accountability for the amount of income produced.

A third objective of periodic profit reporting is to guide division managers toward decisions that will increase company profits. Knowing that divisional profits will be reported, the division manager is presumably motivated to forecast the impact of his decisions on the reported profit of his own division and to choose those solutions that will increase this figure. If reports to top management were not made, this motivation might very well be reduced.

Requirements of Managerial Evaluation Standards

Standards to be used in evaluating the profit performance of division managers need to meet two major requirements: (1) current attainability by competent division managers, and (2) consistency with the degree of divisional profit controllability. Their essential characteristic is that they provide a basis for evaluating how well management has utilized the resources at its command in the environment in which it has operated.

Attainability. The first requirement of a sound profit standard—attainability by competent division management—is somewhat difficult to define in unambiguous terms. Each division is to a certain extent unique with respect to the conditions that affect its performance. Profit differences can be created by variations in the age or condition of production facilities; by differences in local wage structures, transportation costs, and raw material prices; by differences in the types of products handled or customers served; or by differences in the degree of competition faced in the marketplace. Each manager's performance should be evaluated in the light of the situation facing him. This means that the standard must be different from division to division and must be changed from period to period as conditions change. A standard that is not in tune with current operating realities may serve adequately as a target or long-range objective, but it is not a standard of satisfactory managerial performance.

Controllability. The second criterion, the need for consistency with the extent of divisional profit controllability, applies with equal force to the standard and to the measure of divisional profit. Both the measure of profit and the standard with which it is to be compared should be defined to exclude any variances that are not to some significant extent within the control of the division managers.

This criterion must be interpreted with a dash of common sense. No variable is ever completely and absolutely controllable; controllability always means the ability to influence an item of cost or revenue within limits, and these limits may be either very broad or extremely narrow. No measure of profit, no matter how carefully defined can hope to be a precise reflection of a manager's effectiveness in profit control. The danger lies in trying to avoid the problem by adopting a profit definition that eliminates so many of the possible sources of variances that the manager is relieved of most of his profit control responsibilities.

For example, changes in local property taxes are clearly outside the scope of divisional controllability, as is the amount of most central administrative expense allocated to the divisions. Variations in divisional sales, however, are an important aspect of managerial performance even though they may result in large part from changes in general business conditions. To define controllability so narrowly as to exclude this latter kind of variation would be to reduce profit comparisons to mere statements of cost variances. Changes in the business environment can and should be considered in evaluating profit deviations, but not in computing those deviations. The difference is significant. The division manager can do little to influence local property assessments, but he is expected to react to market changes so as to take advantage of favorable opportunities or reduce the impact of unfavorable developments.

Selecting the Performance Standard

For activity evaluation, the relevant profit standard is the rate of return that management is willing to accept for new capital expenditures. This is the same for all divisions or at least for all divisions in the same risk category.

This kind of uniform standard is inapplicable in managerial evaluation, however, because it violates the criterion of attainability. For example, one of the divisions of Conglomerate, Inc. is a local transit company. Its after-tax rate of return on investment is 3 percent, calculated by the methods described in Chapter 22. This is far below the 12 percent rate of return on investment that Conglomerate, Inc. insists upon in its negotiations for the acquisition of new subsidiaries, but top management is highly pleased with the division manager's performance. He has increased the operating cash flow, has developed bus charter business to increase his average load factor, and has far exceeded top management's expectations for this division.

The educational services division, in contrast, is earning 16 percent, but its growth is far slower than management had hoped for and slower than other companies in the field have actually achieved. Turnover of personnel is very high, despite high salaries, and most of the cash flow comes from operations that were well established before the present division manager was appointed two years ago.

The inescapable conclusion is that *budgeted profit* provides a better profit standard for managerial performance evaluation than any uniform ratio applied across the board. A carefully conceived profit budget is by definition attainable with good management under expected operating conditions. The budget may be as high or as low as these conditions seem to warrant.

This approach permits the manager himself to influence the criteria by which he will be judged. In a sense, it is like letting a student write his own examination questions. To reduce the likelihood that the manager will use this opportunity to set unrealistically low budgets, top management must judge his performance at least as much by the quality of his budget proposals as by his success in carrying them out, and both parties must understand this clearly in advance. In addition, top management must carry out a rigorous, critical review of all budget proposals, usually with strong central staff participation. The conflicts between staff and division management that arise inevitably in this situation must be accepted as part of the cost of decentralization, and it is top management's responsibility to see that they are contained within reasonable limits.

The use of desired performance ratios as profit standards stems from a confusion of long-run desirability with short-run attainability, or a confusion of managerial evaluation with activity evaluation. The mere fact that management desires a certain return on investment does not make this a valid standard for use in evaluating current managerial performance, although it may have some relevance in examining the profitability of the activities that make up the division. The continuing emphasis on these ratios leads to time-consuming and fruitless efforts to allocate centrally administered investments, despite the fact that the periodic performance report is not intended to be, and in fact cannot be, a faithful indicator of the profitability of investment in the division.

The Residual Income Approach

Advocates of the return-on-investment approach to divisional profit reporting for managerial evaluation rely heavily on the argument that the use of divisional profit budgets established without reference to the amount of invested capital reduces the accountability of the division manager for the prudent use of capital funds. Clearly, some mechanism must be provided to regulate internal capital investment. Capital is invested to produce profits. If profit expectations are inadequate, the investment should not be made. Investment control, however, is not achieved primarily through routine historical comparisons:

1. Most of the division's plant and equipment investment remains substantially unchanged for long periods and is thus not currently controllable.
2. Control over current capital expenditures is achieved by project review and justification procedures that emphasize future expectations rather than past performance; most of these decisions are made at the top management level rather than by the division managers.

Control over the division manager's exercise of his limited authority over capital expenditures is best accomplished by incorporating provisions for planned cost reductions and profit improvement in the operating profit budget. This should be accompanied by procedures that will require division managers to justify new capital expenditures on the basis of anticipated profitability and to limit severely expenditures on projects that cannot meet such tests.

One portion of divisional investment, however, is subject to a substantial degree of current control at the division manager level, and this is the investment in working capital, particularly investments in inventories and receivables. The division manager may be able to control receivables by selecting his customers and by regulating his efforts to collect overdue accounts. He can influence inventory levels by changing reorder levels and by adjusting production schedules. Variations in controllable investment, however, do not customarily enter the profit budgets, because the normal accounting procedure is to make no charge for implicit interest on capital investment.

One solution to this problem that has been adopted by a number of companies is to include a provision for a normal return on controllable investment in the divisional profit budgets and to charge the divisions

Exhibit 23–2

PACKAGING DIVISION
Profit Performance Report
(for the month of March)

	Actual	Budget	Favorable (Unfavorable) Deviation
Net sales...........................	$3,495,000	$3,600,000	$(105,000)
Standard variable cost of sales............	$1,908,000	$1,930,000	$ 22,000
Factory fixed costs....................	274,000	270,000	(4,000)
Other factory cost variances, net.........	13,000*	5,000	18,000
Divisional overhead:			
Marketing........................	538,000	535,000	(3,000)
Administration....................	73,000	75,000	2,000
Carrying charge on controllable investment........................	64,000	59,000	(5,000)
Total expense..................	$2,844,000	$2,874,000	$ 30,000
Residual income......................	$ 651,000	$ 726,000	$ (75,000)

* Favorable (subtracted from the subtotal).

for the actual controllable investment balances. The profit contribution figure that remains after this deduction is known as *residual income*.[1]

For example, a monthly profit report for the packaging division of Conglomerate, Inc. is shown in Exhibit 23–2. In this case a capital usage charge is made at a rate of three fourths of 1 percent a month on the total of the division's receivables and inventories, less accounts payable and accruals. For convenience, end-of-month balances are used for this purpose on the ground that fluctuations in these amounts during the month are unlikely to be large. The charge for March, therefore, was:

[1] For an extended discussion of this concept, see David Solomons, *Divisional Performance: Measurement and Control* (New York: Financial Executives Research Foundation, 1965), Chaps. 3 and 5.

$$0.0075 \times \$8,479,000 = \$64,000 \text{ (to the nearest thousand)}$$

The \$8,479,000 figure was derived from the month-end balances in Exhibit 22–2.

The \$22,000 favorable deviation in the standard variable cost of sales results at least in part from the unfavorable variance in sales. In fact, none of the variances shown in this exhibit are very meaningful as they stand, because the underlying causes remain concealed. The analytical techniques described in Chapter 24 have been designed to throw light on these questions.

The capital charge in this case is known as *imputed interest*—"imputed" because it does not arise from a contractual borrowing arrangement with an outside lender. It serves to emphasize to the division managers the importance of controlling the size of the working capital balances. It also ties in very nicely with the inventory control formulas used by many companies to achieve a balance between the costs of carrying inventories and the economies of long production runs and stable production levels.

The use of imputed interest could be extended even further, to cover the company's investments in assets that are not controllable by division management. The purpose would be to integrate the managerial performance report with the company's activity evaluation criteria. If this idea is applied, a division with a positive residual income would be one that generated enough income to justify the historical investment in that division. The schizophrenic use of a dollar figure to appraise management and a ratio to evaluate the activity would thus be avoided.

Residual income has another advantage over a ratio calculation. Decisions that will increase total company profit and provide an incremental return in excess of the minimum profit standard can actually decrease the division's average return on investment. If the division has been earning, say, 25 percent and the proposed action would reduce this to 23 percent, division management may hesitate before going ahead. Even if performance is being judged on the basis of comparisons with profit plans, the absolute level of this key ratio is difficult to ignore and may affect the attitudes of top management and division management as well. The exclusive use of residual income figures can remove this danger.

Profit Controllability

The use of the profit plan as a bench mark for performance evaluation imposes one final constraint on the design of divisional profit reports: each division's profit should be independent of variations in performance efficiency elsewhere in the company. If one service or profit center's unit costs exceed or are less than the budgeted amounts, this has no bearing on the managerial performance of the managers of the profit centers using these goods or services. Such deviations must be excluded from the evaluation reports.

The solutions here are the same as those suggested in the chapter on interdepartmental allocations of factory overhead costs. Charges should be predetermined lump sums if the division manager cannot control his consumption of the services in question. If consumption is controllable, predetermined rates should be used.

For example, in Exhibit 23–2 a three fourths of 1 percent rate was used to calculate both the amount budgeted and the actual investment carrying charge for the month. Usually the budgeted rate will serve for the entire year, but if conditions change rapidly enough to warrant a change in the rate, the budgeted charge should be adjusted accordingly. In short, profit deviations should never result from changes in the basis on which allocations are made.

The Danger of Suboptimization

The most serious criticism that has been leveled at the concept of profit decentralization is that it can lead to suboptimization—that is, decisions that increase current division profit but hurt the company as a whole.

One source of suboptimization is a poorly designed set of divisional boundaries, so that various company divisions compete with each other rather than with outside firms. Some degree of internal competition may promote the company's long-term interests, by leading to better service to the company's customers; but if divisional overlaps are substantial, management may wish to reorganize along somewhat different lines.

Suboptimization can also arise if management cuts back unwisely on discretionary expenditures in order to show more profit in the current period. Preventive maintenance expenditures, for example, often can be deferred for months on end before the costs of breakdowns, product defects, and repairs rise enough to offset the apparent savings.

This problem has not been completely solved. Some central administration of such items as maintenance is probably required, but the degree of central interference in divisional affairs is an extremely ticklish problem. Perhaps the best weapon that top management has is its authority to review and modify divisional budgets.

Still another possible source of suboptimization is the existence of complementary relationships among profit centers. One division may be able to supply another division at a lower cost than that for which the same goods or services can be obtained from outside sources. If the charges for these goods or services are uneconomically high, however, the buying division may choose to go outside. These interdivisional charges are known as transfer prices; the transfer pricing problem is covered in Chapter 25.

SUMMARY

Many companies have found it desirable to decentralize decision-making responsibility to a number of semiautonomous divisions or profit centers. The profit center manager is expected to base his decisions on profit criteria, and his performance is judged in part on the amount of profit he is able to generate.

The operating cost and investment allocations necessary to derive return-on-investment figures have little bearing on managerial evaluation. Divisional circumstances vary so widely that managerial performance has to be judged against tailor-made division profit plans rather than against a uniform companywide return-on-investment standard.

For managerial evaluation purposes, the return-on-investment ratio need not be computed even if the division manager can control divisional working capital or other assets. Instead, imputed interest on controllable investment can be deducted from the division's profit contribution to yield a figure known as residual income. Variances between planned and actual levels of residual income can then be analyzed by the methods described in Chapter 24.

The measurement system should be designed to eliminate noncontrollable variances from the periodic reports. It should also attempt to minimize the likelihood of suboptimization, the problem that we shall deal with in Chapter 25.

EXERCISES AND PROBLEMS

1. The profit plan of the Dorsey Corporation's Industrial Products Division was summarized as follows (in thousands):

Sales.....................................		$2,000
Less:		
Standard cost of goods sold..................	$1,400	
Factory cost variances......................	80	
Selling expense............................	300	
Administrative expense......................	150	
Income taxes at 40%.......................	28	1,958
Net Income................................		$ 42

To carry out this profit plan, the division budgeted the following balance sheet totals (in thousands):

Current assets.......................................	$ 600
Fixed assets...	800
Total Assets......................................	$1,400
Current liabilities....................................	400
Net Investment......................................	$1,000

Actual sales volume for the year amounted to $2.2 million. The standard cost of goods sold was $1.5 million. Divisional selling expenses totaled $290,000 and divisional administrative expenses (excluding allocations of headquarters costs) amounted to $73,000. Factory cost variances amounted to $110,000, unfavorable. Accounts receivable, inventories, and other current assets traceable to the Industrial Products Division totaled $500,000; current liabilities were $380,000. Fixed assets traceable to the division amounted to $780,000.

All goods sold by this division are manufactured in the division's own factory. Selling expenses are all traceable to the division. They do not vary significantly with variations in actual sales.

Budgeted administrative expenses included a charge for the costs of the Dorsey Corporation's central administrative offices. This charge was computed at 4 percent of sales. Central administration costs do not vary in response to changes in sales volume within the year. As the company expands, however, these costs tend to rise and the 4 percent average has been relatively constant for many years.

The budgeted factory cost variances were entirely overhead volume variances.

The budgeted net investment in current assets included $150,000 in cash. Cash balances are administered by the corporate treasurer's office and are allocated among the divisions on the basis of divisional sales.

Budgeted fixed assets included $50,000 as the Industrial Products Division's share of the company's investments in its headquarters offices. All remaining items in the net investment were traceable to the division and administered locally.

Production and sales volumes for the year were identical. The company's target minimum rate of return on investment is 10 percent for all divisions.

a) Prepare a profit report for use in appraising managerial performance in the Industrial Products Division during the year. Use the residual income approach.
b) Prepare a brief description of the principle or principles you followed in (a), referring to items in the report to show how these principles were applied.
c) What additional information would you want to have before evaluating division management's performance for the year?

2. The sales manager of the Valli Products Company is preparing a tentative sales budget for the coming year. The bulk of the company's organization is concentrated in two divisions, a sales division and a manufacturing division. The manufacturing division consists of a small head office staff and two factories, one for each of the company's two product lines, known as the Valor line and the Valmaid line. The sales division consists of the sales manager and his central staff, two product managers and their staffs, and a field sales organization.

The field sales force is organized by branch territories, with each salesman responsible for covering all present and potential customers in his portion of the territory assigned to his branch. The salesmen report to a branch manager. Branch managers report directly to the sales manager, but they also receive sales promotion advice and assistance from two product managers, each of whom is responsible for one of the product lines.

Sales, standard cost of sales, and branch expenses are reported monthly for each branch. Sales, cost of sales, and salesmen's commissions are also classified by product line; most other branch expenses are not allocated between product lines. Each product manager has a small staff responsible for providing technical assistance to purchasers of products in his product line. He also controls expenditures against annual budgets for advertising and product development and improvement.

This divided responsibility for sales promotion at times places a strain on the sales organization, as each product manager attempts to induce the field sales force to devote more time to his product line. Each salesman receives an annual bonus computed on the basis of his branch's reported profit, and the product managers vie with each other in pointing out the profitability of their respective lines.

The tentative budget for the sales division for the coming year, as prepared by the sales division controller from budget estimates submitted by responsible executives within the division, is as follows (all figures are in thousands of dollars):

	Valor	Valmaid	Undistributed	Total
Sales..........................	$35,000	$20,000	....	$55,000
Cost of sales..................	21,000	14,000	....	35,000
Gross margin...................	$14,000	$ 6,000	....	$20,000
Commissions..................	$ 1,400	$ 800	....	$ 2,200
Other branch expenses..........	100	50	$ 2,800	2,950
Product manager expenses.......	300	200	....	500
Other divisional expenses.......	.....	.....	2,680	2,680
Total expenses.............	$ 1,800	$ 1,050	$5,480	$ 8,330
Divisional profit..................	$12,200	$ 4,950	$(5,480)	$11,670
Percentage of sales...............	34.8%	24.7%	....	21.2%

The Valmaid product manager was immediately concerned over the effect of these figures on branch managers' and salesmen's willingness to push Valmaid sales. He asked the division controller to find out what had happened to his profit margin, which had never been less than 30 percent and had often been higher in the past. The controller discovered that the cost of sales for each line had been prepared by the manufacturing vice president on the basis of sales forecasts compiled from the branch managers' tentative budgets. These forecasts had indicated that whereas the Valor line plant would be operating at virtually full capacity for the next year, the Valmaid plant would be seriously underutilized. The tentative factory cost budgets for the coming year showed the following (all figures in thousands of dollars):

	Valor	Valmaid
Standard costs:		
Direct labor..............................	$ 5,000	$ 4,000
Direct materials...........................	8,000	3,000
Factory overhead..........................	9,000	6,000
Total standard cost......................	$22,000	$13,000
Volume variance...........................	(1,000)	1,000
Net cost of goods manufactured................	$21,000	$14,000

Factory overhead costs are approximately 70 percent fixed at standard volume in the Valmaid plant and 50 percent fixed at standard volume in the Valor plant. Sales commissions are proportionate to dollar sales. All other division expenses are substantially fixed.

a) Given the existing profit measurement system, prepare a statement that will indicate to salesmen the relative profitability of the two lines insofar as this relates to the bonus calculation.

b) Compute the effect on total company profit of increases in sales volume in each of the two lines.

c) A salesman believes that by giving more attention to the Valmaid line he can increase its sales by 20 percent, but that if he does so, he will lose $1.10 in Valor sales for every dollar of additional Valmaid sales. Assuming that the annual bonus is 10 percent of net branch profit before taxes, how would you advise the salesman to act? Is this action in the best interests of the company?

d) Discuss the company's treatment of manufacturing volume variances. Should these be charged to the sales division? To the product managers? To the sales branches?

e) From what you know of this company's operations, are there any changes in organization structure that might be considered? Discuss these changes. Are there any other changes in the profit reporting structure that you might suggest?

3. The following financial report was prepared for the Hepplewhite division of the Duncan Company for the first two months of the 19x1–x2 fiscal year which began on March 1, 19x1 (all figures are in thousands of dollars):

	Comparative Results of Business			
	Actual, April, 19x1	Two months to April 30		
		Forecast 19x1	Actual	
			19x1	19x0
Sales:				
Product A..........................	$190	$ 500	$ 453	$484
Product B..........................	223	700	522	377
Product C..........................	65	100	132	91
Product D..........................	12	50	28	39
Total sales......................	$490	$1,350	$1,135	$991
Cost of sales:				
Product A..........................	$112	$ 300	$ 266	$312
Product B..........................	107	336	251	183
Product C..........................	38	58	76	44
Product D..........................	6	25	14	22
Total cost of sales..............	$263	$ 719	$ 607	$561
Gross profit on sales................	$227	$ 631	$ 528	$430
Expenses:				
Home office commissions..........	$ 28	$ 66	$ 66	$ 66
Selling...........................	58	128	121	79
Administrative....................	27	52	61	63
Development......................	27	77	63	106
Total expenses..................	$140	$ 323	$ 311	$314
Net profit before taxes..............	$ 87	$ 308	$ 217	$116
Taxes at 50%..................	44	154	109	58
Net Profit..........................	$ 43	$ 154	$ 108	$ 58

	Comparative Financial Condition		
	2–28–x1	4–30–x1	Change
Assets:			
Cash..........................	$ 16	$ 20	$ 4
Receivables....................	277	101	(176)
Inventories.....................	2,451	2,324	(127)
Fixed assets—net...............	1,295	1,291	(4)
Deferred charges—net...........	19	(67)	(86)
Total assets....................	$4,058	$3,669	$(389)
Accounts payable..............	189	94	(95)
Net investment...................	$3,869	$3,575	$(294)
Return on investment..............	10.8%	17.5%	+6.7%

Home office commissions reflect predetermined payments for central administrative services rendered.

Development expenses consist of current research division charges to projects which have been requested and approved by the Hepplewhite division.

Cash balances represent imprest funds only. All payrolls and most payments to vendors are made by the home office.

Accounts receivable and accounts payable consist of billings and invoices in transit between Hepplewhite and the home office.

All materials, work-in-process, and finished product inventories of the Hepplewhite division, together with plant and equipment listed in the corporate property records as belonging to Hepplewhite, are shown on the Hepplewhite statements. There is no allocation of centrally administered assets.

The company uses 10 percent after taxes as its cost of capital in capital expenditure decisions.

Factory flexible budget allowances for March and April amounted to $282,-000. Overhead absorbed totaled $308,000, and actual overhead totaled $273,000. Overabsorbed overhead as of April 30 accounts for part of the credit balance in deferred charges.

The standard before-tax P/V ratio is 50 percent for product A, 60 percent for product B, 55 percent for product C, and 50 percent for product D. All expenses other than the cost of goods sold are assumed to be fixed with respect to volume.

a) How well does the return-on-investment figure, as calculated above, measure the profitability of this division's activities?

b) How well does it measure managerial performance?

c) Prepare a revised report for the two-month period, incorporating any improvements that you deem desirable and feasible, given only the information above.

4.† The Burton Beneficial Company is a manufacturing firm with three divisions and a home office in New York. The company is decentralized, with each division manager responsible for the profits of his division. The company's consolidating income statement for an entire year is shown in Table 1. (In this table, both "managed" and "committed" costs are regarded as wholly fixed; there are no variable overhead costs.)

The company's inventories are carried on the books at their variable cost, calculated on a last-in, first-out basis. If current costs had been used during the period instead of Lifo cost, the cost of goods sold for the various divisions would have been as follows:

> Division A......... $25,000 (no change)
> Division B.........   9,000
> Division C......... 15,000

---

† From a problem prepared by Professor John C. Burton.

Table 1

THE BURTON BENEFICIAL COMPANY
Consolidating Income Statement

	Consolidated	Consolidating Adjustments	Home Office	Division A	Division B	Division C
Sales—outside	$100,000			$60,000	$25,000	$15,000
Interdivisional sales		$(20,000)		.....	5,000	15,000
Total sales	$100,000	$(20,000)		$60,000	$30,000	$30,000
Manufacturing costs:						
Product costs—outside sales:						
Direct labor	$ 7,000			$ 2,000	$ 3,000	$ 2,000
Raw materials	7,000			3,000	2,000	2,000
Raw materials—intercompany purchases	.....	$(20,000)		20,000		
Product costs—intercompany sales:						
Direct labor	6,000				1,000	5,000
Raw materials	5,000				2,000	3,000
Total cost of goods sold	$ 25,000	$(20,000)		$25,000	$ 8,000	$12,000
Committed costs:						
Depreciation	12,000			9,000	2,000	1,000
Rents and royalties	1,000			500	300	200
Insurance	1,000			300	400	300
Other fixed overhead	5,000			3,200	800	1,000
Managed costs—manufacturing:						
Operating costs	9,000			5,000	3,000	1,000
Policy costs	6,000			3,000	2,000	1,000
Total manufacturing costs	$ 59,000	$(20,000)		$46,000	$16,500	$16,500
General and administrative costs:						
Managed costs:						
Research and development	$ 5,000		$ 3,000			$ 2,000
Other	8,000		7,000			1,000
Committed costs:						
Administrative salaries	6,000		6,000			
Rent	1,000		1,000			
Depreciation	1,000		1,000			
Home office allocation	.....		(18,000)	$ 9,000	$ 4,500	4,500
Total general and administrative costs	$ 21,000		$	$ 9,000	$ 4,500	$ 7,500
Selling costs:						
Managed costs:						
Advertising	$ 4,000			$ 2,000	$ 1,500	$ 500
Sales department costs	3,000		1,000	1,000	800	200
Committed costs:						
Fixed sales overhead	3,000		1,000	1,500	500	.....
Total selling cost	$ 10,000		$ 2,000	$ 4,500	$ 2,800	$ 700
Income before income tax	$ 10,000		$ (2,000)	$ 500	$ 6,200	$ 5,300
Provision for income tax	5,000		5,000			
Net Income	$ 5,000		$ (7,000)	$ 500	$ 6,200	$ 5,300

Depreciation is, of course, recorded on a historical cost basis. If depreciation had been charged on the basis of replacement costs during the period, the depreciation for the various divisions would have been as follows:

Division A............ $10,000
Division B............ 4,000
Division C............ 5,000

The home office carries an investment account for each division, reflecting the net investment in that division on a historical cost basis. The investment accounts did not vary substantially during the year in question and at year-end had the following balances:

	Original Cost	*Replacement Cost*
Division A...........	$100,000	$120,000
Division B..........	60,000	80,000
Division C..........	40,000	100,000

The figures in the second column reflect an estimate of the current replacement cost of the net assets of each division.

The division managers constantly argue over who is doing the better job. The manager of division A, for example, says that the net income figure for his division is a poor indication of his performance. In the first place, he points out that his division purchases goods from the other two divisions on which they make a profit. In addition, he notes that his division's cash flow is the highest, and this is highly significant. He is also suspicious of the accounting practices of the other divisions, claiming that their accounting departments make more profits than their operations. Finally, he complains about the method of allocating home office general and administrative expense. The other division managers also have a variety of complaints.

a) Analyze the performance of the three divisions, and prepare a brief report in which the divisions are ranked according to their profitability to the company.
b) Comment on any aspect or aspects of the company's reporting system that you found particularly desirable or undesirable. What do you think is the difference between "managed" and "committed" costs?

CASE 23-1: DUNDEE PRODUCTS, INC.

George Dickson would like to take on a new customer, but is worried about his rate of return on investment (ROI). Mr. Dickson is in charge of the Cleveland branch of the Esco division of Dundee Products, Inc., a large conglomerate. Esco is a national distributor of industrial supplies, purchased from a number of manufacturers and sold through a network of 17 regional branches. Most of Dundee's other divisions deal in consumer goods; none of them sells any of its products through the Esco division.

Like the managers of the other branches, Mr. Dickson reports to Frank Corbett, Esco's executive vice president. Each branch is treated as a small profit center and each branch manager has virtually complete discretion over the methods of sales promotion to be used, the products to stock, and the customers to be served within his own geographical area. All products are selected from a list supplied by Esco's central purchasing office.

Selling prices are set at Esco's headquarters, but each branch manager can alter the terms of sale to reflect differences in risk and profitability of doing business with different customers. Each branch does its own billing and collection work. The profit performance of the branches and their managers is judged each year on the basis of the rate of return achieved on the investment in the branch, mainly the investment in storage space, the inventories on hand, and the receivables outstanding.

The Profit Plan

Each September, every branch manager submits a tentative profit plan to Mr. Corbett. This plan is a complete summary of the manager's marketing plans, including estimates of the amounts he proposes to spend for field selling, the sales level he expects to reach, the costs of warehousing, and the levels of his investments in inventories and receivables. The anticipated first-year effects of proposed investments in physical facilities and equipment are also reflected in this tentative plan.

The proposed profit plans are reviewed critically by Mr. Corbett and his staff, who question the assumptions on which the projections have been based, make sure that alternative plans have been studied carefully, see whether the proposals are within the company's capacity, offer suggestions for improvement, and provide technical help in revising the proposals.

Once Mr. Corbett and the branch managers have come to an agreement, the plans are consolidated into an overall profit plan for the Esco division as a whole. Last-minute adjustments are sometimes made at this stage, but most of the inconsistencies ordinarily have been removed during the staff review.

The profit plans from all of the Dundee divisions are reviewed by corporate staff. Divisional plans are discussed informally as they are being formulated, and as a result relatively few changes are made in the plans after formal submission. The main reason for change at this point is a refusal by top management to fund facilities and equipment proposals at the levels anticipated by the division managers. This requires a reworking of the budgetary proposals in the light of the revised guidelines.

The current profit plan for the Cleveland branch is summarized in the first column of Table 1. Cleveland has been one of the division's most profitable outlets in the past, with rates of return ranging from 17 to 21 percent, but a major expenditure of funds on a new warehouse building and new materials handling equipment has brought the budgeted rate of return down to the 13.6 percent figure shown in Table 1. Even

Table 1

DUNDEE PRODUCTS, INC.
Esco Division, Cleveland Branch
Pro Forma Profit Plan
(dollar figures in thousands)

	Current Plan	Adjusted for Cut-Rate Line*
Net sales............................	$2,728	$3,740
Cost of goods sold†.................	1,982	2,792
Gross margin........................	$ 746	$ 948
Branch expenses‡...................	264	334
Income before tax....................	$ 482	$ 614
Income tax..........................	265	338
Net income..........................	$ 217	$ 276
Current assets:		
Cash◊..............................	$ 35	$ 50
Accounts receivable.................	253	398
Inventories.........................	702	1,132
Total current assets.................	$ 990	$1,580
Less accounts payable◊.............	346	431
Net working capital..................	$ 644	$1,149
Land...............................	91	91
Buildings (net of depreciation)..........	704	704
Equipment (net of depreciation)........	185	215
Net investment, end of year............	$1,624	$2,159
Average net investment:		
End of year........................	$1,624	$2,159
Beginning of year..................	1,572	2,111
Average net investment..............	$1,598	$2,135
Rate of return (ROI).................	13.6%	12.9%

* Based on 12 months' operations for comparative purposes.
† Purchase price plus estimated headquarters purchasing department cost.
‡ Including charges for head office services.
◊ Based on head office estimates of amounts attributable to this branch.

so, this is substantially greater than the 9 percent after-tax figure adopted by Dundee's top management as a minimum profit standard for investments in warehouses and sales offices.

Measurement Methods

For internal reporting, Dundee measures investments in physical facilities at original cost less straight-line depreciation. Inventories in the Esco division are costed on a first-in, first-out (Fifo) basis. Receivables are shown at full face value, less an allowance for uncollectible amounts that is adjusted once a year on the basis of a headquarters staff review of the outstanding account balances.

All payrolls and payments to vendors are processed at Esco's divisional headquarters; the branch managers control only small petty cash accounts and have no direct liabilities of their own. The branch profit plans include a provision for cash and accounts payable, however, based on head office staff estimates of the amounts attributable to each branch's operations. These provisions are calculated from standard formulas, which are also used to compute the amounts shown in the monthly performance reports for each branch.

Investments in facilities and working capital at divisional and corporate headquarters are very small, and none of this investment is allocated to the individual branches.

Each branch is charged at predetermined unit prices for head office services such as payroll preparation and vendor payment. In addition, a flat charge of 2 percent of sales is made to cover the average cost of head office administration. Division headquarters charges each branch with the net invoice price of all goods consigned to the branch, plus 1 percent of this amount to cover the cost of the divisional purchasing department, which does all the purchasing for the branches.

The New Opportunity

The operations at the Cleveland branch are proceeding more or less according to plan, and Mr. Dickson expects that when all the results are in at the end of the year he'll be very close to the planned levels of revenue and expense.

His new warehouse was built to meet the company's anticipated growth in the Cleveland area in the next 10 years, however, and a good deal of space is currently unused. Reasoning that his method of operation would enable him to offer better warehousing service to local companies with large inventories of nonperishable merchandise than local storage warehouses could provide, Mr. Dickson has spent a considerable amount of time during the past few months looking for one or two such customers.

Preliminary contacts with Cut-Rate Drugs, Inc., a St. Louis-based supplier of cosmetics, proprietary medicines, and other articles typically sold in drug stores, have progressed to such a point that Mr. Dickson has to make up his mind whether to expand into this line of business. Under the proposed arrangement, Cut-Rate would ship its products to the Cleveland warehouse, billing the Esco division on terms of net 30 days. This merchandise would be stored in a separate section of the warehouse.

In accordance with the Cut-Rate method of operation, all store deliveries would be in full case lots. Delivery would be made by four driver-salesmen who would be transferred from the Cut-Rate payroll. Cut-Rate would also lease its local fleet of four delivery vehicles to Mr. Dickson for the duration of the agreement. Mr. Dickson would become responsible for billing the drug stores and collecting the amounts due from them for the merchandise.

"This looks like a natural for us," Mr. Dickson said last week. "Only the sales force would be separate. Otherwise, the operation would be just like what we're doing now with our regular lines. We carry stock, sell, deliver, and collect, and we're pretty good at our job. I see no reason why we shouldn't do just as well with the Cut-Rate line. They're doing the same sort of thing in Denver and Atlanta, and seem to be making a go of it.

"The figures seem to bear me out, too. We'd get an extra $59,000 in profit on a $535,000 increase in investment, a rate of return of about 11 percent. The return to the company would be even greater, because our figures reflect the 2 percent surcharge that headquarters skims off the top of all our operations. I can't see how headquarters costs would go up by a penny as a result of this operation.

"The only problem is that our overall rate of return would go down from 13.6 percent to about 12.9 percent on an annual basis. You can see this in the right-hand column of the pro forma budget I gave you this morning [Table 1]. We've already come down from 17 percent as a result of the new warehouse and I don't think I'm going to look very good if I ring in with an even lower rate this year. I think I have a crack at the division manager's job when Frank Corbett retires in a couple of years and I don't want to do anything to rock the boat now. Frank tells me that he'll okay the increase in my inventories and receivables if I want to go ahead, but I'm afraid of that drop in the ROI."

"What kind of commitment would you have to make with Cut-Rate?" the case writer asked. "Could you get out of this easily if it didn't work out the way you expected?"

"Oh, we'd have no problem there. The deal is that either party could cancel the arrangement on six months' notice, and it would take us six months to clean things up anyway. They'd buy back the unsold inventory at book value. The salesmen would go back to Cut-Rate, too, unless they wanted to stay with us and we had room for them."

"What's in it for Cut-Rate? What's wrong with the way they've been operating? I've been taught to be suspicious of people who want to give up part of their business."

"Well, anything's possible, of course, but I think this is on the level. They've been supervising the local sales force from St. Louis, using a local storage warehouse as a transshipment depot. The salesmen are okay, but they've had a lot of trouble with the warehouse. Those people are good at dead storage, but they don't know the first thing about field warehousing. That's our business, and the people at Cut-Rate are pretty sure that we can increase their volume and cut their costs, too. Besides, they have a lot of money tied up in inventories and receivables. We figure that with our controls we can handle the higher volume with a smaller investment. It's unprofitable for them and very profitable for us, and you can't find a better basis for a deal than that."

a) Should Mr. Dickson go ahead with the Cut-Rate venture? Prepare a summary of the calculations and arguments on both sides of these questions.

b) How would you decide whether the Cleveland branch's reported profit or return on investment is satisfactory or unsatisfactory? What profit standards would you adopt in this connection, and where would you get them?

c) Do you think that Mr. Dickson's worries about his branch's declining return-on-investment figures are justified? Suggest changes in the content and structure of Table 1 that would help relieve him of worries that do not serve the corporation's objectives.

chapter **24**

Profit Analysis

Deviations from profit plans measure the effects of changes in conditions, poor forecasting, or variations in managerial effectiveness. Since the reasons for these deviations are not always clear, further analysis and explanation are usually necessary.

The main purpose of this chapter is to outline a method that the accountant can use to break the total profit variance into a set of interrelated components. This will be followed by a brief discussion of an alternative approach, focusing on ratios and trends, and an even briefer reference to efforts to measure incremental profit relationships directly.

PROFIT VARIANCE ANALYSIS

An ideal variance analysis would identify the ultimate or primary cause of each element of the overall profit variance. So much would be attributed to orders lost due to price competition, so much to higher materials prices resulting from an increase in rail freight tariffs, and so on.

Because this ordinarily can be done only for a small part of the total variance, the variance analysis has to focus on intermediate causes or symptoms rather than on the primary causes. Examples of categories into which profit variances ordinarily can be split are:

1. Deviations from budgeted selling prices (sales price variances).
2. Deviations from budgeted physical sales volume (sales volume variances).
3. Deviations from budgeted product sales mix (sales mix variances).
4. Deviations from budgeted input prices (input price variances).
5. Deviations from standard costs and flexible budget allowances (input quantity and spending variances).
6. Deviations due to product costing procedures, accounting adjustments, etc.

Basic Mechanics

At its simplest, profit variance analysis merely adds two variances—a selling price variance and a sales volume variance—to those already described in previous chapters. To illustrate, let us assume that the ABC Company manufactures and sells a single product. The company uses absorption costing, and all short-term cost relationships are linear. Budgeted factory costs amount to $120,000 a month plus $3 for each unit produced, and the product sells at a price of $5 a unit. To simplify the presentation, we have assumed that the company has no selling and administrative expenses.

The profit budget appropriate to a normal production and sales volume of 100,000 units a month is as follows:

	Total Amount	Average per Unit
Units sold	100,000	xxx
Units produced	100,000	xxx
Sales revenues	$500,000	$5.00
Standard cost of goods sold	420,000	4.20
Gross margin	$ 80,000	$0.80
Factory cost variances	. . . . . .	. . .
Net income before taxes	$ 80,000	$0.80

Sales Volume Variance. The month of May was expected to be normal in all respects. Therefore, the budget for the month was the same as the budget for a normal month. Actual results for May and the resulting profit variance were as follows:

	Actual	Budget	Variance
Units sold	90,000	100,000	(10,000)
Units produced	100,000	100,000	. . . . .
Sales revenues	$450,000	$500,000	$(50,000)
Standard cost of goods sold	378,000	420,000	42,000
Gross margin	$ 72,000	$ 80,000	$ (8,000)
Factory cost variances	. . . . . .	. . . . . .	. . . . .
Net income before taxes	$ 72,000	$ 80,000	$ (8,000)

The entire profit variance this month was a sales volume variance. It can be computed by multiplying the physical variance in sales volume (10,000 units) by the standard gross margin per unit:

Sales volume variance = 10,000 units × $0.80 = $8,000

Production Volume Variance. The situation in June was different. The budgeted profit was again at its normal level, and actual sales equaled the budgeted amount, but production fell 10,000 units below the budget for the month. The results were as follows:

	Actual	Budget	Variance
Units sold..................	100,000	100,000	.....
Units produced..............	90,000	100,000	(10,000)
Sales revenues...............	$500,000	$500,000	.....
Standard cost of goods sold..	420,000	420,000	.....
Gross margin................	$ 80,000	$ 80,000	.....
Factory cost variances........	(12,000)	......	$(12,000)
Net income before taxes......	$ 68,000	$ 80,000	$(12,000)

The factory cost variance in this case was due entirely to the deviation of production volume from the amount budgeted—that is, it was a production volume variance. We can demonstrate this by comparing the amount of cost budgeted at actual volume with the amount absorbed at this volume:

$$\text{Absorbed: } 90,000 \times \$4.20 \dots \dots \dots \$378,000$$
$$\text{Budgeted: } \$120,000 + (90,000 \times \$3) \dots \dots \ 390,000$$
$$\text{Production volume variance} \dots \dots \dots \underline{\$(12,000)}$$

Since this is equal to the reported variance, all other factory cost variances either were zero or canceled each other. (Note that since we have assumed the cost function to be linear, the production volume variance was due entirely to a variance in fixed cost absorption. It is the overhead volume variance that we encountered in earlier chapters.)

Sales and Production Volume Variances Combined. Production, sales, and net income were again budgeted at normal levels in July, but the results were as follows:

	Actual	Budgeted	Variance
Units sold..................	95,000	100,000	(5,000)
Units produced..............	90,000	100,000	(10,000)
Sales revenues...............	$475,000	$500,000	$(25,000)
Standard cost of goods sold...	399,000	420,000	21,000
Gross margin................	$ 76,000	$ 80,000	$ (4,000)
Factory cost variances........	(12,000)	......	(12,000)
Net income before taxes.......	$ 64,000	$ 80,000	$(16,000)

The production volume variance was identical to that recorded in June because production volumes were identical in the two months. The sales volume variance can be computed once again by multiplying the deviation in physical sales volume (5,000 units) by the standard gross margin per unit ($0.80)—that is, it was $4,000 in July. The total variance therefore can be analyzed into two parts:

Sales volume variance	$ (4,000)
Production volume variance	(12,000)
Total profit variance	$(16,000)

Sales Price Variance. The ABC Company's management once again budgeted a normal profit for the month of August. The results were only slightly better than in July:

	Actual	Budgeted	Variance
Units sold	95,000	100,000	(5,000)
Units produced	90,000	100,000	(10,000)
Sales revenues	$478,000	$500,000	$(22,000)
Standard cost of goods sold	399,000	420,000	21,000
Gross margin	$ 79,000	$ 80,000	$ (1,000)
Factory cost variances	(14,000)	......	(14,000)
Net income before taxes	$ 65,000	$ 80,000	$(15,000)

Sales and production volumes were identical to those recorded in July; therefore, the sales volume and production volume variances were the same as those computed for July. The difference was that for the first time the company experienced a sales price variance. If the actual sales of 95,000 units had been made at the budgeted (standard) price, sales revenues would have been 95,000 × $5 = $475,000. Since actual sales revenues actually amounted to $478,000, the $3,000 difference must have arisen because actual prices averaged slightly more than $5.

Factory Spending Variance. Factory cost variances in June would have totaled $12,000 if the production variance had been due entirely to production volume. Since the actual variance amounted to $14,000, the remaining $2,000 can only be attributed to other factors—either input prices or input consumption. With the additional information usually available in the factory records, these could be identified by department and classified as materials, labor, or overhead spending variances by the methods described in earlier chapters. For convenience, in this chapter we shall refer to the entire amount as a factory spending variance.

Variance Summary. The variances for August are summarized in Exhibit 24–1. The total variance is the difference between the net income figures in the first and last columns. This is broken down in stages—each

Exhibit 24–1

BASIC VARIANCE CALCULATION

	Standard Prices and Costs			Actual Prices, Standard Costs, Actual Sales, Actual Production	Actual Net Income
	Planned Sales, Planned Production	Actual Sales, Planned Production	Actual Sales, Actual Production		
Sales revenues............	$500,000	$475,000	$475,000	$478,000	$478,000
Standard cost of goods sold.	420,000	399,000	399,000	399,000	399,000
Gross margin..............	$ 80,000	$ 76,000	$ 76,000	$ 79,000	$ 79,000
Factory cost variances......	...	...	(12,000)	(12,000)	(14,000)
Net income before taxes.....	$ 80,000	$ 76,000	$ 64,000	$ 67,000	$ 65,000

Sales Volume Variance $(4,000)   Production Volume Variance $(12,000)   Sales Price Variance $3,000   Factory Spending Variance $(2,000)

column is identical to its neighbor except in one element, such as price or volume.

In one sense, this is an arbitrary procedure. The sales volume variance could just as easily be calculated at $5.03, the average actual price (actual revenues of $478,000 divided by actual sales volume of 95,000 units). The sales volume variance then would be 5,000 units × ($5.03 − $4) = $4,150. This might even be a better measure of the effect of the volume deviation on company profit in a given period.

Standard prices are usually used, however, to permit direct comparisons of the volume variances of different time periods. If volume is always measured at the same prices, then any change in the volume variance is the result of a change in volume, not a mixture of price and volume effects. The issue here and the possible solutions are the same as in the calculation of price and quantity variances in factory costs described in Chapter 15.

Sales Mix Variances

In a multiproduct firm or activity, profit may vary because high-margin products have increased or decreased their relative share of total volume. The effect of this variation is known as the sales mix variance.

From the analyst's point of view, the sales mix variance is a component of the total of the sales volume variances of all of the products in the line. For example, suppose that the ABC Company has two products instead of one. Budgeted and actual data for the month of September

Exhibit 24–2

PRODUCT PROFIT DATA FOR SEPTEMBER

	Product A		Product B		Total Amount
	Per Unit	Total	Per Unit	Total	
Budget:					
Units sold...................		80,000		20,000	
Units produced.............		80,000		20,000	
Sales revenues..............	$3.75	$300,000	$10.00	$200,000	$500,000
Standard cost of goods sold......	2.85	228,000	9.60	192,000	420,000
Gross margin...............	$0.90	$ 72,000	$ 0.40	$ 8,000	$ 80,000
Actual:					
Units sold...................		76,000		21,500	
Units produced.............		80,000		20,000	
Sales revenues..............	$3.75	$285,000	$10.00	$215,000	$500,000
Standard cost of goods sold......	2.85	216,600	9.60	206,400	423,000
Gross margin...............	$0.90	$ 68,400	$ 0.40	$ 8,600	$ 77,000
Variances:					
Units sold...................		(4,000)		1,500	
Units produced.............		. . .		. . .	
Sales revenues..............		$(15,000)		$ 15,000	. . .
Standard cost of goods sold......		11,400		14,400	$ (3,000)
Gross margin...............		$ (3,600)		$ 600	$ (3,000)

are shown in Exhibit 24–2. This shows that the gross margin for the month, $77,000, was $3,000 less than the amount budgeted.

We can calculate the individual product sales volume variances quite easily, using the variance in units sold and margin per unit from the exhibit:

	Units Sold	Margin	Variance
Product A............	(4,000)	$0.90	$(3,600)
Product B............	1,500	0.40	600
Total..............			$(3,000)

Although both of these components were volume variances, the $(3,000) total in the right-hand column could not have been a volume variance because total volume was exactly equal to the budgeted amount, $500,000. This means that the overall sales volume variance had to be zero. Instead, the $3,000 decline in profit resulted from a deterioration in the sales mix due to the substitution of $15,000 in sales of product B for an equal volume of sales of product A. Since product B had a lower profit margin than A, net income fell.

To demonstrate the method more adequately, let us look at a situation in which both mix and aggregate volume changed. Sales volume, mix, and profit rate in October were once again budgeted at normal levels— that is, budgeted net income was $80,000. The actual volume and mix, however, were as follows:

	Product A	Product B	Total
Units sold..........................	68,000	22,000	90,000
Sales revenues......................	$255,000	$220,000	$475,000
Standard cost of goods sold.........	193,800	211,200	405,000
Gross margin......................	$ 61,200	$ 8,800	$ 70,000

(handwritten in margin: 255,000)

(handwritten in margin: 285)

(handwritten in margin: 9.6)

(handwritten in margin: 193,800)

(handwritten in margin: 211,200)

(handwritten in margin: 405)

Production volume, sales price, and factory spending variances were all zero, and the total profit variance for the month was $80,000 − $70,000 = $10,000, unfavorable.

The volume variance for each product is easy to calculate. The standard profit margin for product A, for example, was $0.90 a unit. Since volume was 12,000 units less than the amount budgeted for this product, the sales volume variance was 12,000 × $0.90 = $10,800, unfavorable. The standard profit margin for product B was only $0.40, but volume exceeded the budgeted amount by 2,000 units. The sales volume variance for this product therefore was 2,000 × $0.40 = $800, favorable. The total of these two variances was $10,000, accounting for the entire profit variance for the month.

To break the total of the product sales volume variances down into aggregate mix and volume components, the analyst needs two figures: (*a*) a figure representing the variation in overall physical volume: and (*b*) a measure of the average profitability of one unit of overall volume. In this case, sales revenue was selected to measure volume. Since the sales price variance was zero, the difference between budgeted and actual sales ($500,000 − $475,000 = $25,000) is a measure of the change in physical volume in which each product is weighted in proportion to its standard selling price.

Using this measure of volume, the standard unit profit was 16 percent of sales (from Exhibit 24–2). The sales volume variance for October was:

$$\text{Sales volume variance} = \$25,000 \times 16\% = \$(4,000)$$

This says that if sales of the two products had stayed in their budgeted proportions, a $25,000 change in volume would have reduced the gross margin by $4,000. In fact, the effect was much greater than that, $10,000. The $6,000 difference was the sales mix variance.

Exhibit 24–3

CALCULATION OF SALES MIX VARIANCE

	Standard Prices		
	Planned Volume, Standard Mix	Actual Volume, Standard Mix	Actual Volume, Actual Mix
Sales revenues........................	$500,000	$475,000	$475,000
Standard cost of goods sold...........	420,000	399,000	405,000
Gross margin........................	$ 80,000	$ 76,000	$ 70,000
		Sales Volume Variance $(4,000)	Sales Mix Variance $(6,000)

The same figures can be derived more systematically by a line-by-line analysis of the income statement, as in Exhibit 24–3. Once again, each column differs from its neighbor in only one respect, and this difference provides an explanation for the variance figure shown between the two columns at the bottom of the exhibit.

Analysis without Physical Unit Data

This analysis of mix and volume variances was conducted without the use of unit cost and unit price data. It is fortunate that this is possible, because in multiproduct companies the variances ordinarily will be calculated for groups of products rather than for each product individually. The products in a given product group ordinarily are related to each other in some way, but they are usually different enough to prevent any meaningful physical measure of total volume. Without a unit of physical volume, there can be no unit price or unit cost.

In these cases, an artificial "unit" must be used for each product line. This is obtained by weighting the different products in the group. In the last illustration, actual and standard selling prices were the same. More often, however, actual selling prices depart from their budgeted levels, and either standard costs or standard selling prices are better weights.

For example, suppose that product group X consists of several hundred different products. The aggregate physical volume in this group is to be measured by what the company calls standard sales dollars, obtained by multiplying the unit sales of each product by its standard selling price. Budgeted standard sales dollars for November totaled $300,000.

The next step is to compute aggregate budgeted deductions from standard sales dollars. This can be done product by product if the data are available, but the usual approach is to use predetermined ratios for the group as a whole. Suppose that the standard ratios for product group A are 5 percent for discounts and other forms of price adjustments, 76 percent for the standard cost of goods sold, and 3.8 percent for salesmen's commissions. (Sales commissions are paid at the rate of 4 percent of net sales.)

Based on these ratios, the budget for November showed the following totals:

	Amount	Percent
Standard sales dollars (at standard prices).........	$300,000	100.0
Price adjustments............................	15,000	5.0
Net sales (at budgeted prices)...................	$285,000	95.0
Standard cost of goods sold....................	228,000	76.0
Gross margin................................	$ 57,000	19.0
Sales commissions...........................	11,400	3.8
Product margin..............................	$ 45,600	15.2

Actual sales of product group X in November totaled $320,000, again at standard selling prices. The income statement for the month showed the following, based on actual ledger account balances:

Standard sales dollars (at standard prices).............	$320,000
Price adjustments.............................	25,000
Net sales (at actual prices).......................	$295,000
Standard cost of goods sold......................	250,000
Gross margin.................................	$ 45,000
Sales commissions (4% × $295,000)..............	11,800
Product margin...............................	$ 33,200

This product margin was $12,400 less than the amount budgeted, and this is the variance that we need to analyze.

Sales Volume Variance. The first step is to multiply the standard sales dollars figure by the standard percentages listed above. This will show the amounts that would have been reported if volume had changed but everything else had remained the same. The figures are:

	Percent	Amount
Standard sales dollars (at standard prices).........	100.0	$320,000
Standard price adjustments for this volume.......	5.0	16,000
Standard net sales at this volume.................	95.0	$304,000
Standard cost of goods sold for this volume.......	76.0	243,200
Standard gross margin for this volume............	19.0	$ 60,800
Standard sales commissions....................	3.8	12,160
Standard product margin for this volume..........	15.2	$ 48,640

The effect of sales volume changes alone was the difference between $48,640 and the product margin originally budgeted, $45,600, a favorable variance of $3,040. (The same result can be obtained by multiplying the $20,000 variance in standard sales dollars by the standard product margin of 15.2 percent.)

Sales Mix Variance. If the products in the group had been sold in their budgeted proportions, the standard cost of goods sold would have been $243,200 (76 percent of $320,000). Actually, it was $250,000, indicating that high-cost, low-margin products accounted for more than their share of actual sales during November. The difference between these two figures, $6,800, was the sales mix variance for the month.

Sales Price Variance. If actual sales volume had been made at budgeted prices, actual net sales would have amounted to $304,000, as shown in the last table above. Net sales actually totaled only $295,000, indicating that an unfavorable and unbudgeted price variance of $9,000 took place.

The measure of the price variance does not end here, however. Sales commissions were based on net sales, not standard sales dollars. The price reduction therefore led to a slight reduction in sales commissions, from the $12,160 appropriate to net sales of $304,000 to the $11,800 actually paid on actual net sales. The net sales price variance therefore was as follows:

Price adjustments in excess of standard . . . . $ (9,000)
Effect of price adjustments on sales
    commissions (4%)   360
Sales price variance . . . . $ (8,640)

Variance Summary. The variance calculations are summarized in Exhibit 24–4. Again, each variance is measured by the difference between the figures on the bottom line in two adjacent columns. Taken together, these three components account for the $12,400 variance between the

Exhibit 24–4

VARIANCE ANALYSIS SUMMARY PRODUCT GROUP X

	Standard Prices			Actual Prices, Actual Volume, Actual Mix
	Planned Volume, Standard Mix	Actual Volume, Standard Mix	Actual Volume, Actual Mix	
Standard sales dollars	$300,000	$320,000	$320,000	$320,000
Price adjustments	15,000	16,000	16,000	25,000
Net sales	$285,000	$304,000	$304,000	$295,000
Standard cost of goods sold	228,000	243,200	250,000	250,000
Gross margin	$ 57,000	$ 60,800	$ 54,000	$ 45,000
Sales commissions	11,400	12,160	12,160	11,800
Product margin	$ 45,600	$ 48,640	$ 41,840	$ 33,200

Sales Volume Variance $3,040   Sales Mix Variance $(6,800)   Sales Price Variance $(8,640)

amount budgeted and the product margin actually realized during the month.

Other Indexes of Volume. The same kind of analysis can be applied if standard selling price data are not available. For example, physical volume totals can be used if the various products in the line do not differ widely in such physical characteristics as weight or cubic volume—that is, if management is accustomed to thinking of aggregate output in physical terms.

Another possibility is using the standard cost of goods sold as the unit of volume. This has the advantage of being generally available, but the arithmetic is more complicated and the calculations are more difficult to explain.

Profit Variance Analysis under Variable Costing

Profit variance analysis is slightly simpler when variable costing is in use. If factory overhead costs are linear, the production volume variance disappears. The orders of magnitude will also be different. Because only variable costs are used in computing the product profit margins, the sales volume variances for the individual products will be larger than under absorption costing. Because different products absorb fixed costs at different rates, however, the aggregate sales volume variance or the aggregate sales mix variance can be either larger or smaller and might even have a different algebraic sign.

Limitations of the Analysis

Useful though it is, this analytical technique suffers from three defects. One of these has already been mentioned. The relative sizes of the various variances depend on the sequence in which they are computed. That is, the size of the volume variance will depend on whether it reflects actual or standard prices, and so on. Confusion can be minimized by adopting a standardized sequence, but the resulting variances give only orders of magnitude and cannot be interpreted literally.

Second, the profit plan does not necessarily represent what the manager should have been able to accomplish during the period, given the conditions that actually prevailed. In an attempt to deal with this, Demski has provided a model by which the total variance can be divided into two parts, one representing the difference between the original plan and the correct plan in the prevailing circumstances, and the other measuring the difference between the adjusted plan and the actual results.[1] This

---

[1] For descriptions of this model, see Joel Demski, "An Accounting System Structured on a Linear Programming Model," *Accounting Review*, October 1967, pp. 701–12, and "Predictive Ability of Alternative Performance Measurement Models," *Journal of Accounting Research*, Spring 1969, pp. 96–115.

latter component can then be subjected to the kind of analysis described in this chapter. Although application of this model requires more data than are generally available, the approach represents an improvement over existing practice and deserves efforts to implement it.

The third defect is even more fundamental. Even if the first two defects could be overcome, this analysis does not indicate *why* the price variance is as large or as small as it is or why volume failed to meet the budgeted amounts. In fact, the variances may even be interdependent. Volume may be down because price is too high, the mix may be good because the more profitable product is underpriced, and so on.

All that technical variance analysis can do is provide a convenient summary of symptoms. Identification of the underlying causes then becomes a matter for managerial detective work. The technical breakdown can be very useful, however, in pointing the finger at areas that should be investigated. If the analysis shows that the main problem seems to be the sales mix, management is likely to be much closer to finding a solution than if this information were not available.

PROFIT RATIO AND TREND ANALYSIS

A second approach to profit performance reporting is through ratio and trend analysis. At its simplest, this takes the form of a single chart showing the progress of earnings or return on investment from period to to period. This kind of chart can have a strong visual impact, and is widely used. It throws little light on the forces that affect reported performance, however. Recognizing this, some companies supplement the return-on-investment chart with a series of back-up charts, each one dealing with some dimension of performance.

One such chart system is diagrammed in Exhibit 24–5. Each block in this exhibit represents a separate chart or table. The words appearing in the spaces between vertically adjacent blocks describe the relationship between these blocks and the block they are joined to at the left. The basic return-on-investment (ROI) ratio, for example, can be broken into two component ratios:

$$\text{ROI} = \frac{\text{Profit}}{\text{Investment}} = \frac{\text{Profit}}{\text{Sales}} \times \frac{\text{Sales}}{\text{Investment}}$$

A drop in the return-on-investment ratio that is accompanied by a decline in the earnings percentage has a different meaning from a drop that is accompanied by a reduction in turnover.

A low turnover ratio, for example, may have arisen because total investment increased more rapidly than sales. The increment in investment, in turn, may have been located entirely in the finished goods inventories.

Exhibit 24–5

RELATIONSHIP OF FACTORS AFFECTING RETURN ON INVESTMENT

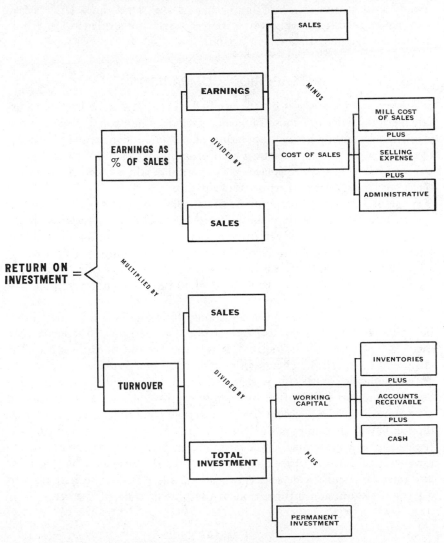

Source: E. I. duPont de Nemours & Co., *Executive Committee Control Charts: A Description of the duPont Chart System for Appraising Operating Performance* (Wilmington, Del., 1959).

Management knows, therefore, that the explanation for the decline in turnover must be sought in the reason for the inventory build-up. By moving farther and farther to the right on this diagram, management can get deeper and deeper into the details of the company's operations. In the process, the major causes of the problem may come to light.

The ratios and other figures used in this system are used by top management to identify favorable and unfavorable trends. While a declining sales margin percentage means nothing in itself, it may be a very bad sign if asset turnover is not increasing at the same time. Unexpected movements revealed in this way initiate a search for explanations, which in turn can trigger management action.

INTERPERIOD COMPARISONS

Profit variance analysis can be applied to the difference between current period results and those of earlier periods. The proper place for this is in the preparation of new operating plans, when management is trying to decide what prices to set or which promotional methods to use. Once the plan has been set, it displaces prior-period results as the proper bench mark for managerial performance evaluation.

Straight historical interperiod comparisons do not give the manager the information he really would like to have. He needs *response functions*, the incremental effect of variations in his operating plan. If he knew that additional salesmen would pay off handsomely in two of his sales territories, while taking salesmen away from two 'other territories would sacrifice nothing, he probably would try to arrange for the transfers.

Routine measurement of these response functions is still in the future, but one possibility is to use interperiod comparisons to approximate them. A response ratio calculated in this way would be the ratio of the change in results to the change in cost or price or effort.[2]

One difficulty with this is that the results of promotional effort lag behind the effort itself, often by many months and unevenly distributed over time. Another problem is that external conditions change, so that the increment in results is due only in part to the increment in effort. If management recognizes these possibilities, however, it may be able to use these incremental ratios to good effect. In the absence of a good environment for small-scale experimentation, this may be the best way to get response function information in the present state of the art.

SUMMARY

Comparisons of actual results with the amounts budgeted provide only the crudest of signals to management. The techniques described in this chapter have been developed to provide signals that are more finely tuned.

The most significant of these techniques is profit variance analysis, by which the overall profit variance for a given product line or division is

---

[2] For an interesting proposal along these lines, see Richard A. Feder, "How to Measure Marketing Performance," *Harvard Business Review*, May–June 1965, pp. 132–42. Case 22–1, The Federal Company, dealt with a similar proposal.

subdivided into portions identified as stemming from factors such as selling price variations, fluctuations in sales and mix, inventory movements, and so on.

Another technique is interperiod ratio comparison. Although these comparisons ordinarily ignore planned ratios, and although the various ratios are not independent of each other, this kind of analysis does identify trends that seem to be developing and may help management decide to take action before the need for action otherwise would have become apparent.

Instead of interperiod ratio comparisons, the analyst may decide to work with interperiod differences, hoping to approximate marketing response functions. This is the only one of the three techniques described here to attempt to identify causes as opposed to symptoms. Although its use is fraught with difficulties, it can provide information in a highly useful form.

EXERCISES AND PROBLEMS

1.*￣ From the information below, compute the amount of the profit variance due to variations in (a) selling prices, (b) sales volume, and (c) other factors, in as much detail as you deem appropriate.

	Budget	Actual
Sales...............................	$60,000	$60,500
Cost of goods sold:		
Direct material.....................	$10,000	$11,200
Direct labor........................	13,000	14,700
Factory overhead....................	13,000	14,100
Total cost of goods sold............	$36,000	$40,000
Gross margin........................	$24,000	$20,500
Selling and administrative expenses......	18,000	18,500
Net profit...........................	$ 6,000	$ 2,000
Units sold...........................	10,000	11,000

Additional information: (1) Materials prices and wages were at budgeted levels. (2) Production volume and sales volume were identical. (3) Factory overhead is budgeted at $7,800 plus 40 percent of direct labor cost. (4) Selling and administrative expenses are assumed to be wholly fixed.

---

* Solutions to problems marked with an asterisk can be found in Appendix B.

2. The ABC Sales Company operates a wholesale outlet. It buys merchandise from two or three manufacturers and sells these goods to retailers. Its planned and actual results for a recent period were as follows:

	Planned	Actual
Selling price per unit	$10	$9.50
Sales volume, units....................	50,000	52,000
Cost of goods sold....................	$300,000	$318,000
Selling and administrative cost..........	$100,000	$115,000
	+$0.20 a unit	

a) Calculate planned net income for the period.
b) Calculate actual net income for the period.
c) Analyze the difference between (*a*) and (*b*) to measure the effects on net income of deviations in sales volume, selling price, and merchandise purchase prices, and the effect of departures from budgeted selling and administrative expense. Ignore income taxes.

3. A firm has made the following estimates of the percentage of expenses to sales revenue, based on a normal sales volume of $10 million:

Variable manufacturing....................	30%
Fixed manufacturing......................	40
Variable selling and administrative..........	15
Fixed selling and administrative.............	5
Total expense...........................	90%

Inventory is measured at full absorption cost, based on normal volume. Anticipated sales volume for the current period is $8 million. All production cost variances are taken directly to the income statement as they arise.

a) What would be the effect on net income of increasing sales by $1 million without an increase in production?
b) What would be the effect on net income of increasing production by a quantity of goods that has a sales value of $1 million without an increase in sales?

4. Woodbridge, Inc., after several years of profitable operation, showed a loss of $2 million in 19x3, accompanied by a severe cash shortage. Woodbridge seethed with activity as a result: new financial controls were installed, and a new sales manager was hired. By the end of 19x4, the new organization was fully operating and Mr. James Woodbridge, the company's president, was optimistic about the future despite the 19x4 loss of $1.3 million on sales of $5 million.

Looking ahead, Mr. Woodbridge was convinced that the firm could attain a volume of $10 million in a few years, with the following profit results (in thousands):

Sales.............................		$10,000
Variable production costs...........	$5,000	
Fixed production costs.............	2,000	
Variable selling costs..............	1,000	
Fixed selling costs.................	1,000	9,000
Net income before taxes............		$ 1,000

Variable costs were expected to vary in proportion to changes in physical volume. Standard product costs in the factory were established on the basis of the physical volume required for an annual sales volume of $10 million. All production cost variances were to be taken directly to the income statement for the period in which they arose.

The initial profit budget for 19x5 called for sales of $6.5 million (at standard prices) and a net loss (before taxes) of $400,000. Actual volume for 19x5 was $7 million, also at standard prices. At this volume a loss of $200,000 was budgeted, but the company's cash position had improved so much by the end of 19x5 that Mr. Woodbridge thought the company might have broken even. Therefore, he was aghast when he received the following income statement (in thousands):

Sales (at actual prices).................		$6,860
Standard cost of goods sold.............	$4,900	
Selling expenses.......................	1,720	
Factory overhead volume variance........	900	
Other factory cost variances............	30	7,550
Net loss.............................		$ (690)

"What happened?" he gasped. Tell him, in as much detail as possible.

5. The return on investment in the Able Division fell from 20 percent in the first quarter to 14.7 percent in the second quarter. You are given the following data (in thousands):

	First Quarter	Second Quarter
Sales................................	$100	$105
Cost of goods sold...................	$ 60	$ 66
Operating expenses...................	20	24
Income taxes.........................	8	6
Total expenses...................	$ 88	$ 96
Net income..........................	$ 12	$ 9
Traceable investment:		
Receivables......................	$ 50	$ 54
Inventories......................	60	62
Plant and equipment..............	120	122
Total traceable assets...............	$230	$238
Accounts payable.................	20	25
Net traceable investment.............	$210	$213
Centrally administered assets.........	30	32
Net investment......................	$240	$245

a) Verify the computation of the return-on-investment ratios given above.
b) Break the return-on-investment ratios down into component ratios. Try to explain what has happened, using ratios only.

6.* A company sells three products. Sales and cost of sales last month were as follows:

	Units Sold	Revenue	Unit Cost
Budget:			
Product X..............	10,000	$20,000	$1.20
Product Y..............	5,000	30,000	4.20
Product Z..............	4,000	20,000	4.00
Total...............		$70,000	
Actual:			
Product X..............	12,500	$26,200	$1.20
Product Y..............	4,000	23,600	4.20
Product Z..............	5,000	24,500	4.00
Total...............		$74,300	

Compute and analyze the profit variance for the month, product by product and in total.

7. Van Dyk Corporation distributes cigars, cigarettes, and pipe tobacco to retail outlets. Cigars have the biggest percentage of profit markups, and cigarettes have the smallest. The markups also vary to some extent from brand to brand within each product class, but these variations are relatively small.

Johann van Dyk, the company's president and chief stockholder, is worried. The warehouse seems as busy as ever, the delivery trucks seem to be as heavily loaded, but profits have been close to zero for several months.

Last month was very much like earlier months. Budgeted and actual data for the month were as follows:

	Budget		Actual	
	Cases	Amount	Cases	Amount
Sales:				
Cigars.................	500	$ 60,000	300	$ 35,000
Cigarettes.............	2,125	204,000	2,300	220,000
Pipe tobacco...........	800	24,000	700	22,000
Total...............		$288,000		$277,000
Cost of goods sold:				
Cigars.................		$ 36,000		$ 22,000
Cigarettes.............		163,200		180,000
Pipe tobacco...........		16,800		15,000
Total...............		$216,000		$217,000

Operating expenses are almost entirely fixed within the customary operating range and have been running very close to budget.

Mr. van Dyk thinks that he may have to press the manufacturers for an increase in the spread between the prices he pays and the prices charged the retail dealers. Before doing this, however, he has decided to ask you to analyze last month's figures. Analyze the profit variance for the month and prepare a table summarizing the results of that analysis. What advice would you give to Mr. van Dyk?

8. The annual profit plan of the Moontide Company's Crescent Division included a budgeted net income of $10,000 for the month of June. Actual net income for the month amounted to $12,800. Detailed information on products A and B was as follows:

(1) Budgeted profit:

	A	B	Total
Units sold..........................	30,000	10,000	
Net sales..........................	$150,000	$100,000	$250,000
Standard cost of goods sold..........	120,000	70,000	190,000
Gross margin.......................	$ 30,000	$ 30,000	$ 60,000
Selling and administrative expense....			$ 32,000
Factory cost variances (unfavorable)..			18,000
Total deductions.................			$ 50,000
Net income before taxes.............			$ 10,000

(2) Standard product cost (full cost basis):

	A	B
Direct materials..........	$1	$1
Direct labor..............	1	2
Factory overhead.........	2	4
Total..................	$4	$7

(3) Budgeted factory overhead cost: $90,000 + (0.5 × standard direct labor cost). A zero overhead spending variance was budgeted for June.
(4) Budgeted production volume: product A, 30,000 units; product B, 10,000 units.
(5) Budgeted selling and administrative expense: $27,000 + 2 percent of net sales.
(6) Actual profit reported for the month of June:

	A	B	Total
Units sold..........................	36,000	9,000	
Net sales..........................	$181,000	$84,000	$265,000
Standard cost of goods sold..........	144,000	63,000	207,000
Gross margin.......................	$ 37,000	$21,000	$ 58,000
Selling and administrative expense......			$ 33,000
Factory cost variances (unfavorable)...			12,200
Total deductions.................			$ 45,200
Net income before taxes.............			$ 12,800

(7) Actual production volume during June; product A, 34,000 units; product B, 9,200 units.
(8) Actual factory overhead cost during June: $114,800.

a) Prepare an analysis of the month's operations, indicating insofar as possible the sources of the $2,800 departure from budgeted net income.

b) Without actually making any calculations, explain how the results of your analysis would differ if a variable costing system were in use. Would the total variance be the same or different? Which of the component variances would change in amount?

CASE 24–1: TREFLAZ, S.A.[†]

Treflaz, S.A. was a large distributor of a wide range of consumer and industrial products in Switzerland. Products were sold to wholesalers, retailers, and directly to large institutional consumers (such as hospitals and laboratories). The organization was divided into 11 product sales departments, each responsible for the sale of a particular group of products, and 12 service and administrative departments.

Sales department X reported the following sales, cost of goods sold, and operating expenses for the month of September 1959 (in thousands of francs):

$$
\begin{array}{lr}
\text{Net sales}\dots\dots\dots\dots\dots\dots\dots\dots\dots\dots & 340.4 \\
\text{Cost of goods sold}\dots\dots\dots\dots\dots\dots\dots & 191.0 \\
\text{Operating expenses}\dots\dots\dots\dots\dots\dots\dots & 95.4
\end{array}
$$

Each sales department prepared a budget at the beginning of each year. Because of seasonal factors, department X's September budget differed slightly from one twelfth of the annual budget for the fiscal year 1959–60. The figures were (in thousands of francs):

$$
\begin{array}{lr}
\text{Budgeted net sales, entire year}\dots\dots\dots & 3,900.0 \\
\text{Budgeted net sales, September}\dots\dots\dots & 318.0
\end{array}
$$

Cost of goods sold was budgeted on an annual basis by multiplying budgeted annual physical unit sales of each product by standard cost or purchase price per unit. This was then expressed as a percentage of budgeted net sales for the department. The resulting ratio was multiplied by budgeted monthly sales to compute budgeted cost of goods sold for each month. For department X in 1959–60 the figures were:

$$
\begin{array}{lr}
\text{Budgeted cost of goods sold, entire year, percent of} \\
\quad\text{budgeted net sales}\dots\dots\dots\dots\dots\dots\dots\dots\dots & 54.4\% \\
\text{Budgeted cost of goods sold, September (54.4\% }\times \\
\quad\text{budgeted net sales)}\dots\dots\dots\dots\dots\dots\dots\dots\text{Fr. } 173,000
\end{array}
$$

Operating expenses were divided into four categories: (1) direct—traceable to specific sales departments; (2) allocated—allocated to sales departments by formula; (3) freight—traceable to specific sales departments; (4) reserves and interest—provisions for costs that will not be known with certainty until some future period, plus imputed interest on working capital.

---

† Copyright 1965 by l'Institut pour l'Etude des Méthodes de Direction de l'Entreprise (IMEDE), Lausanne, Switzerland. Reproduced by permission.

Table 1

DEPARTMENT X
Budgeted Operating Expenses for Fiscal Year 1959–60
and Actual Expenses for September 1959
(francs in thousands)

	Budgeted			
	Fixed Amount per Year	Variable Percentage of Sales	Basis for Charging Department	Actual Expenses September
Direct cost of department X:				
Salaries and premiums........	Fr. 84.0	. . .	Traceable	Fr. 6.9
Commission of representatives.	. . . .	3.0	"	10.2
Fringe benefits..............	16.8	. . .	"	0.3
Office supplies..............	12.0	. . .	"	1.9
Depreciation on equipment and furniture.................	9.2	. . .	"	0.8
Price lists, brochures.........	3.6	. . .	"	1.3
Travel and entertaining.......	24.0	. . .	"	1.9
Postage, telephone, and telegraph...................	24.0	. . .	"	2.3
Demonstrations and samples...	2.4	. . .	"	. . .
Quality control and research...	54.0	. . .	"	4.5
General selling expense.......	18.0	. . .	"	2.6
Subtotal................	Fr. 248.0	3.0	....	Fr. 32.7
Cost allocated to department X:				
Buildings (depreciation, maintenance, etc.).............	Fr. 67.2	. . .	Fixed sum	Fr. 5.6
Management..............	. . . .	2.0	Fixed %	6.8
Data processing............	. . . .	2.8	"	9.5
Inventory handling..........	. . . .	4.4	"	15.0
Subtotal................	Fr. 67.2	9.2	....	Fr. 36.9
Freight.....................	. . . .	1.8	Traceable	Fr. 3.3
Reserves, interest:				
Provision for advertising.....	. . . .	4.2	Fixed %	Fr. 14.4
Provision for bad debts.......	. . . .	0.5	"	1.7
Provision for unsalable inventories...................	. . . .	0.2	"	0.7
Provision for free replacement of goods sold.............	. . . .	0.5	"	1.7
Interest on inventories........	Fr. 27.3	. . .	*	2.9
Interest on accounts receivable...............	19.5	. . .	*	1.1
Subtotal................	Fr. 46.8	5.4		Fr. 22.5
Total................	Fr. 362.0	19.4		Fr. 95.4

* Charge based on fixed precentage of departmental inventories and receivables; all other "fixed per centage" charges are based on actual net sales.

Flexible budgets were prepared for expenses in each of these four categories, on the bases described in Table 1. These budgets for 1959–60 can be summarized in the formula:

Budgeted operating expense = Fr. 30,200/month + 19.4% × net sales

The budget allowances for 1959–60 were (thousands of francs):

> Entire year (budgeted net sales of Fr. 3,900,000) 1,118,600
> September (budgeted net sales of Fr. 318,000)   91,900

Actual operating expenses charged against department X's revenues for September totaled Fr. 95,400, as detailed in the right-hand column of Table 1.

Budgeted net sales were stated on the basis of standard list prices† in force at the beginning of the fiscal year. Actual net sales were recorded on the basis of the amounts actually billed customers, but a supplementary record was kept of the standard list prices of all goods sold. For September, actual net sales at standard list prices amounted to Fr. 355,500.

a) Prepare a summary report analyzing department X's profit variance for the month of September, in as clear and as concise a form as possible. This report should show, among other things, the total variance from budgeted profit, the effect of deviations from budgeted physical sales volume, the effect of deviations from budgeted or standard list prices, and the amounts due to ineffective cost control and other causes, to the extent that these effects can be identified. (Note: You need not accept the company's classifications into direct, allocated, etc., if you feel that some other classification would be more meaningful.)

b) Do you agree with the company's methods of charging expenses to department X? Give your reasons.

c) Which variances should be reported to the department managers?

---

† The company actually kept a record of actual sales at gross or dealer prices and computed standard net prices by multiplying these by a predetermined average discount percentage. The result is approximately the same as that described here.

chapter **25**

Intracompany
Transfer Pricing

From a profit measurement viewpoint, the ideal profit center is one that buys all its raw materials and parts from outside companies and sells its entire output on the market, with no intracompany purchases or sales. Unfortunately, convenience in profit measurement cannot be the dominant criterion in establishing profit centers, and interdivisional transfers do take place. The prices at which these transfers are recorded are known as transfer prices. The purpose of this chapter is to see why transfer pricing is important, what alternative pricing methods are available, and how management might choose among them.

ISSUES IN TRANSFER PRICING

The prices used to record transfers of goods between divisions serve two main purposes:

1. Before the fact, to guide division managers toward decisions that will lead to an economic allocation of resources.
2. After the fact, as one determinant of the profit attributed to each profit center.

Resource Allocation

Goods transferred from one division or subsidiary to another are *intermediate products*. The objective of such a transfer is to subject the product to further processing, use it in the manufacture of another product, or offer it for sale in another market. Management needs some mechanism for deciding whether to allocate the product to these uses and, if so, in what quantities. In a centralized company, the central decision-making authority can examine the incremental cost of further processing and compare it with the probable increment in sales value of the final product over that of the intermediate product. In a decentralized company, however, the manager of the final product division treats the price at which the intermediate product is transferred to him as an incremental cost.

The transfer price, in other words, establishes the cost of the buying division's raw materials. When combined with the estimated costs of processing the materials and marketing the output, this cost can be compared with estimated end-product market values to determine the estimated profitability of various possible courses of action. The transfer price also guides the management of the supplying division by establishing the sales value of one of its outputs to one of its customers. This value can be compared with the net value of other uses of the supplying division's capacity to determine their relative profitability.

Another type of resource allocation decision is the make-or-buy decision. The company has the option of manufacturing a certain part, subassembly, or intermediate product or of buying it from an outside supplier. Given the available facilities, the question is one of comparing outside purchase prices with incremental internal manufacturing costs. When the company is decentralized, however, the intermediate product may be made by one division and the final product by another. The manager of the final product division, given authority to decide such matters, will compare outside purchase prices with internal transfer prices and base his decision largely on this comparison.

Suboptimization and the Opportunity Cost Criterion

The transfer price will serve its decision-making objectives satisfactorily only if it will lead division management to make the same decisions that headquarters management would make if it had the time to study the problem and apply all the data available to the managers of both divisions. If the transfer price leads to departures from this ideal, it is said to cause suboptimization.

As an example of suboptimization, suppose that a supplying division can sell a product (product X) to an outside customer for $1,000 less incremental selling costs of $180. Alternatively, the supplying division can transfer product X internally to another of the company's divisions which will use it as a raw material in the manufacture of product Z. The buying division can sell product Z to an outside customer for $1,800, against which it must charge the cost of "materials" (product X) and also $850 in further processing and marketing costs. For some reason, a transfer price of $1,100 has been established for product X.

If he based his decision on the transfer price, the manager of the buying division would choose not to buy product X and process it into product Z, basing his decision on the following calculation:

Potential revenues..............................		$1,800
Incremental costs:		
Materials (product X)........................	$1,100	
Processing and selling........................	850	1,950
Estimated processing loss........................		$ 150

Given all of the above information, however, a manager responsible for both divisions would decide that the interdivisional transfer would be in the company's interests:

Estimated revenues, processed product Z..............		$1,800
Less: Estimated revenues, unprocessed product X....		1,000
Incremental processing revenue......................		$ 800
Estimated processing and selling costs, processed product Z....................................	$850	
Less: Estimated selling costs, unprocessed product X...............................	180	
Incremental processing and selling costs.........		670
Estimated incremental processing profit..............		$ 130

The reader by now will recognize this as simply another application of the concept of opportunity cost. If the supplying division had priced its output to the buying division at $820 (product X's outside sale value less incremental selling costs), the manager of the buying division would have arrived at the profit-maximizing solution:

Estimated revenues..............................		$1,800
Estimated costs:		
Materials (product X)..........................	$820	
Processing and selling..........................	850	1,670
Estimated incremental processing profit..............		$ 130

Suppose now that the selling price of product Z was only $1,500. At a transfer price of $820, the buying division would not buy product X:

Estimated revenues..............................		$1,500
Estimated costs:		
Materials (at net market price)..................	$820	
Processing and selling..........................	850	1,670
Estimated incremental processing profit (loss).........		$ (170)

This would be the correct decision if only one unit of product X were available. Suppose, however, that the supplying division had the capacity to serve both the outside customer and the internal buyer at an incremental processing cost of $500 for each. The correct decision in this situation would be to use product X to make product Z:

Estimated revenues...............................		$1,500
Estimated costs:		
Materials (at incremental cost)....................	$500	
Processing and selling...........................	850	1,350
Estimated incremental processing profit..............		$ 150

At a transfer price of $820, the buying division manager would see only the $170 processing loss, with no incentive for him to buy.

The problem is that although $820 is the market price, this is not a good measure of the sacrifice the supplying division would have to make to provide a unit of product X to the buying division. The supplying division's sacrifice in this case would be the $500 in incremental processing cost; no sale to outside customers would be lost. Thus $500, not $820, is the appropriate measure of opportunity cost in this situation.

In other words, an economical resource allocation solution could be reached in either of these situations by division managers acting independently, but only if the transfer price was equal or close to opportunity cost. This is the general rule: an appropriate transfer price for managerial guidance in decision making is one that approximates opportunity cost.

Performance Measurement

Transfer prices have a second impact, this time on the image of the division and of its management that will be transmitted to top management. When transfers of goods are made, a portion of the revenue of one profit center becomes a portion of the cost of another. This means that the price at which transfers are made can influence the earnings reported by each profit center.

For example, suppose that a division has budgeted residual income of $210,000 but reports only $116,000, as shown in the following table:

	Actual	Budget	Variance
Sales.........................	$1,600,000	$1,650,000	$(50,000)
Cost of goods sold..............	$1,150,000	$1,100,000	$(50,000)
Divisional overhead.............	235,000	240,000	5,000
Investment carrying charge.......	99,000	100,000	1,000
Total charges...............	$1,484,000	$1,440,000	$(44,000)
Residual income................	$ 116,000	$ 210,000	$(94,000)

If internal transfers are important, the big profit variance could be due mainly to low transfer prices on the products the division sells to sister divisions or high transfer prices on the products it buys internally.

The danger is that top management will allow the transfer price to influence its appraisal of the division manager's performance or, which amounts to the same thing, that the division manager will think the transfer price is affecting his performance rating unfairly. This can lead to dissension and can even defeat the main purpose of profit decentralization by impairing the manager's motivation to produce profits. The transfer pricing system should be designed to prevent this kind of dysfunctional effect.

BASES FOR TRANSFER PRICING

Many different bases for transfer pricing have been tried or proposed. The principal alternatives are:

1. Full cost (or full cost plus).
2. Marginal or variable cost.
3. Market price.
4. Market-based negotiated price.
5. Market price minus commission.
6. Variable cost plus subsidy.
7. Programmed prices.

Whichever of these is used, it should be set before the transfer is made rather than afterward. This permits a division manager to know in advance what price he will receive or what price he will pay for transferred goods, thus eliminating one source of uncertainty and permitting a division manager to predict more accurately the effects of his decisions on his reported profit.

Full Cost

The major defect of full cost as a basis for transfer pricing is that it fails to provide a sound guide to decision making. For example, suppose that a division manager is faced with the problem of choosing between an outside vendor and an internal supplying division for all or part of his requirements of a certain intermediate product. The full cost transfer price is $12, but the product can be obtained from an outside vendor at a delivered price of $10 a unit. Given these conditions, the division manager has a $2 incentive to buy the product outside, other things such as reliability and quality being equal.

But now suppose that the internal supplying division is operating at 60 percent of capacity and that the incremental costs in this division amount to $9 a unit. If the product is purchased outside, the supplying division will lose a $3 contribution toward its fixed costs and the loss in total company profit will be $1 a unit. Top management can prevent suboptimization only by lowering the transfer price or by ordering the buying division to purchase the product internally. In either case, one of the managers will see his authority reduced and his profit responsibility diluted.

Full cost may have a further distorting effect on executive decisions. As long as a division manager is operating below practical capacity— that is, on the relatively flat portion of his average variable cost curve —he will be willing to produce to satisfy both internal and external demands for his goods. But if he is pressing the limits of his capacity, he will be likely to favor the outlet for his goods that offers him the highest current revenue. Under these circumstances, market prices for the inter- mediate product are most likely to be higher than full cost; and unless a higher authority intervenes, sales to the outside market are likely to take precedence over internal transfers. The usual result is that the full cost transfer price system breaks down at this point as top management steps in to insure the flow of goods to other divisions.

The fact is that full cost transfer prices are incompatible with the resource allocation objectives of a decentralized company. They do not provide a sound basis on which top management can delegate decision- making authority to division managers—authority over sources of supply and outlets for each division's products. For this reason full cost transfer prices should be restricted to situations in which this authority is not granted, in fact, to companies or divisions that are not really decen- tralized.

Marginal Cost

A marginal cost transfer pricing system works in the following man- ner.[1] Each division manager is provided with a schedule representing the marginal cost of each of his supplying divisions at various volumes of operations. This provides him with a basis for calculating the prices he must pay for additional quantities of the intermediate products. To these he adds his own marginal cost figures to determine a composite mar- ginal cost schedule for the final products. He then adjusts his volume to the level at which the additional or marginal revenue from the sale of an additional unit of the final product is just adequate to cover total mar- ginal cost.

In more formal terms, this means that the division manager will accept additional orders for the final product as long as the price received ex- ceeds combined marginal cost, assuming that additional orders do not require price reductions on the business already obtainable at higher prices. When there is an outside market for the intermediate product, the respective amounts to be sold in the final and intermediate markets can be determined by finding that point at which the marginal cost of

---

[1] For a full exposition of the marginal cost method, see Jack Hirshleifer, "On the Economics of Transfer Pricing," *Journal of Business*, Vol. 29, No. 3 (July 1956), pp. 172–84.

manufacturing the intermediate product is just equal to the marginal revenue from sale of the intermediate product and is also equal to the net marginal revenue (marginal revenue less marginal processing cost) from sale of the final product.

To illustrate this process, let us assume that division S manufactures product X for sale to outside customers. Division B manufactures and sells product Y to outside customers, using one unit of product X in the manufacture of each unit of product Y. The marginal cost schedules are as follows:

Units per Month	Marginal Cost per Unit	
	Division S	Division B*
13,000 and less..................	$1.50	$1.00
14,000.........................	1.55	1.00
15,000.........................	1.60	1.05
16,000.........................	1.65	1.10
17,000.........................	1.70	1.15
18,000.........................	1.75	1.20
19,000.........................	1.80	1.25
20,000.........................	1.85	1.30

* Excluding cost of product X.

The resource allocation decision in this company is to be made by the manager of division S, and he receives the following schedules of marginal revenues:

Units per Month	Marginal Revenue per Unit		Net Marginal Revenue per Unit Product Y*
	Product X	Product Y	
6,000 and less...........	$2.00	$4.00	$3.00
7,000.................	1.90	4.00	3.00
8,000.................	1.80	4.00	3.00
9,000.................	1.70	4.00	3.00
10,000.................	1.60	3.75	2.75
11,000.................	1.50	3.50	2.50
12,000.................	1.40	3.20	2.20
13,000.................	1.30	2.85	1.85
14,000.................	1.20	2.55	1.55
15,000.................	1.10	2.00	0.95

* Marginal revenue less marginal cost in division B.

Looking only at his outside market, the manager of division S would produce 11,000 units. At any lower volume marginal revenue would be greater than the $1.50 marginal cost of product X; at higher volumes marginal revenue would be too low to cover the marginal cost. Alternatively, if division S were to supply only division B and ignore the outside market for product X, the division could produce up to 14,000 units of X; because up to that volume, the net marginal revenue from product Y would exceed the marginal cost of the intermediate product, product X.

Patently, division S cannot do both of these, and some means must be found for deciding how much of product X is to go in each direction. This is done by giving priority to the use with the higher net marginal revenue, moving down the ladder until marginal revenue no longer exceeds marginal cost. In this case, a total of 12,000 units of X should be transferred to division B before any units are produced for sale to outsiders, because up to that point net marginal revenue from product Y is greater than $2, the net marginal revenue of the first sales of product X on the outside market.

Now it becomes profitable to produce for outside customers. By increasing production to 13,000 units of X, the manager of division S can meet the requirements for product Y and also sell 1,000 units of X at a marginal revenue of $2 and a marginal cost of $1.50. In ·fact, he can increase production to 19,000 units, supplying 12,000 units of X to division B and selling 7,000 units of X on the market, before the marginal revenue from sales of X falls below the $1.85 net marginal revenue to be derived ·from the sale of additional product Y. Sale of the 7,000th unit of X produces a marginal revenue of $1.90 and a marginal cost of $1.80, so this is profitable.

Increasing production of Y to 13,000 units adds net marginal revenue of $1.85 and also brings production of X up to the 20,000-unit level, at which marginal cost equals $1.85. It is unprofitable to expand production of either product beyond this point because additional revenue will be less than additional cost. Therefore, the optimum output of X is 20,000 units a month and the optimum output of Y is 13,000 units a month.

The difficulties of developing marginal cost and marginal revenue schedules that change with volume in this way are substantial. Few companies have cost structures that are delineated clearly enough to justify anything but a constant marginal cost assumption, and marginal revenue is even more of a mystery. Within some volume limits, however, marginal cost may indeed be constant, and within these limits marginal cost may be a reasonable measure of opportunity cost.

A second defect is even more fundamental, in that in some situations a marginal cost transfer pricing system cannot be administered without abrogating the decision-making autonomy of the various profit centers. For example, if marginal cost increases with volume, it will depend on the total demands of the buying division and the supplying division's external customers. Thus neither division can make its output decisions independently. A division is thus essentially a cost center rather than a profit center to the extent that it obtains or supplies products internally.

Capacity operations place additional strains on a marginal cost transfer pricing system. When the supplying division is operating at capacity, the net revenue available from outside customers often appears to be greater than marginal cost. In theory, this could not happen, because the firm would increase its rate of output until marginal cost equaled marginal revenue. In fact, the firm's knowledge of its marginal costs is almost never good enough to extend the cost schedule to this point; or else the firm is unwilling or unable to engage in subcontracting or other high-cost devices to expand its short-run capacity to deliver products.[2] As a result, when the supplying division is operating at capacity, top management may have to permit the division manager to depart from the previously calculated marginal cost or else may have to direct him to divert his production to internal customers at a sacrifice in his reported profit. Under the former solution, the marginal cost basis for transfer pricing is acknowledged to be inadequate; under the latter, divisional authority is abrogated.

The third defect of a straight marginal cost transfer pricing system is that it ignores the performance measurement aspects of internal profit reporting. As long as marginal cost is lower than average full cost, under marginal cost transfer pricing all divisions will show a loss except those divisions that make sales to the outside market. If these divisions also supply intermediate products to other units within the corporation, then their profit reports will reflect a mixture of "profits" on outside sales and "losses" on internal sales.

Reported losses need have no ill effects at all on the use of divisional profit statements in the evaluation of managerial performance, provided that evaluation is based on achievement of predetermined goals which have been established in a critical, creative manner. Unfortunately, no matter how intellectually it is committed to this point of view, management often finds it emotionally difficult to accept a low profit figure as evidence of good or satisfactory performance. Furthermore, executive promotion often seems to come faster, the monetary rewards to be greater, and people easier to recruit in divisions with good profit records, and a transfer pricing system that a division manager feels is unfairly depriving him of these advantages is likely to breed resentment.

The activity evaluation aspect may be even more important, particularly during periods of idle capacity. Here all the profits on internally transferred goods will be lodged in the internal buying divisions, and the supplying divisions may find it correspondingly more difficult to justify capital expenditure proposals.

---

[2] Economic capacity can be defined as the volume at which marginal cost becomes high enough to exceed average cost. Joel Dean, *Managerial Economics* (Englewood Cliffs, N.J.: Prentice-Hall, 1951), p. 305. Common definitions of practical capacity assume implicitly that expansion of operations to this point is not feasible.

Market Price

If the profit centers were, in fact, independent businesses, any transfer of intermediate products would require a market transaction for which a market price could be recorded. The independent firm is judged on its ability to buy and sell at market and make a profit. If a purchase price is too high, the independent firm will not buy; if its selling prices are too high, it will not sell.

By analogy, if a profit center cannot afford to pay market prices, it should not be permitted to buy internally at less than market. If it can sell outside at market, it should not be required to sell internally for less.

The implicit assumption in this argument is that market prices truly represent the opportunity cost of the intermediate product. In the strictest sense, market price is truly representative of opportunity cost only if intermediate markets are perfectly competitive—that is, if the company's activity in the market, either in buying or in selling, has no influence on the market price. If the company's sales of the intermediate product act to depress market prices, the marginal revenue from these sales will be less than market price; if the company's purchases force market prices upward, marginal cost will be greater than market price.

Perfectly competitive conditions exist only in the rarest of circumstances; so in a strict sense, market price is almost never a fully adequate basis for transfer pricing. Management must always deal with an imperfect world, however, and the main question is not whether a transfer pricing system is perfect but rather whether it is sufficiently reliable to be workable. In general, a market price transfer system may be regarded as workable whenever the intermediate product is one which is traded actively and in substantial quantities at prices that approximate those available in published quotations.

The number of instances in which published market prices can be used as transfer prices without adjustment is very small. Markets for many intermediate products are established only through promotional effort and negotiation with prospective purchasers. For others, published prices are available, but they represent such a small quantity of transactions that they cannot be regarded as reasonable approximations to opportunity cost. Finally, product differentiation may make it difficult to find market quotations that are strictly relevant to any one company's transfer price problem. In these circumstances, some solution other than quoted market price must be sought.

Market-Based Negotiated Price

Most transactions between independent firms are not made at publicly quoted prices but at prices in which there is an element of negotiation. At a minimum this consists of obtaining bids from two or more potential suppliers and placing orders with the firm that seems to offer the most favorable package. This suggests that an analogous procedure might be adopted for internal transfer pricing, leaving the respective division managers free to negotiate with each other to determine the appropriate price. Only if the division managers are unable to come to an agreement on price will top management be called upon to intervene in what is called "umpiring."

Four conditions are necessary to make a negotiated transfer price system workable:

1. There must be some form of outside market for the intermediate product.
2. Any available market information should be communicated to both parties to the negotiation.
3. Both parties must have freedom to deal outside.
4. Top management must indicate its support of the principle of negotiation.

In a sense, these conditions are also part of the definition of a profit center. Delegation of profit responsibility is possible only insofar as it is accompanied by the delegation of authority to make decisions that determine profitability, including the selection of sources of supply and the pricing of the division's products, within the framework of general company policies. This authority may be restricted in various ways, but it cannot be completely withheld if the various divisions are to operate as profit centers. When both input and output prices are determined at higher levels, as they are for many sales divisions or subdivisions, the resulting profit figures may still be useful as a means of summarizing the promotional and cost control activities of the unit managers, but they provide little useful guidance to managerial decision making.

The existence of an outside market for the intermediate product is important in negotiation because it provides both parties with an alternative. Dissemination of information relating to this outside market should reduce the bargaining range and permit negotiation to take place in an atmosphere conducive to producing transfer prices that are fair approximations to opportunity cost. In the absence of an outside market, the bargaining range is likely to be considerably wider because the buying and selling divisions are in the position known to economists as bilateral monopoly—that is, the market for the intermediate product consists of two firms, one buying and one selling, and neither has an outside alternative. The buyer may buy or not buy or, at the extreme, he may equip his division to manufacture the intermediate product. The seller may sell or not sell or, at the extreme, he may equip his division to manufacture the final product. Under these conditions the market price is likely to be indeterminate within a fairly wide range, and relative profit of the two divisions will depend on the bargaining ability of the respective division managers.

It should be reemphasized that the mere existence of an outside market for the intermediate product is insufficient to secure the success of a negotiated transfer price system. Even if the market is there, the lack of real freedom to buy or sell outside tends to weaken the effectiveness of negotiation as a means of promoting sound resource allocation. In the circumstances that make published market prices unacceptable and that therefore require negotiation, opportunity cost cannot be determined with sufficient reliability unless there is some way to test the market. Freedom to enter the market provides the necessary mechanism. If a buying division manager can purchase outside for a certain price, freedom to go outside will permit him to negotiate a price internally that will reflect this opportunity. He may even be willing to pay a price in excess of market in order to obtain the advantages of an assured supply, better quality control, and reduced purchasing costs, but this merely expands the effective bargaining range.

Freedom to buy outside is particularly important when substanital capacity for the manufacture of the intermediate product exists internally, capacity that would be made idle if the products were to be acquired outside. Paradoxical as this may seem, it is under conditions such as these that it is most important to have internal transfer prices that best reflect the company's opportunity costs. Without buying freedom, transfer prices are less likely to feel the pressure of competitive forces and will remain higher than they should be to guide the manager of the buying division in his pricing and output decisions. With his costs kept at artifically high levels, he will be unable to accept orders that would prove profitable to the company as a whole.

It should be remembered that freedom to deal outside does not necessarily mean that a substantial volume of purchases will actually be made from outside suppliers when idle internal capacity exists. Freedom must be accompanied by an obligation to negotiate internally. The buying division manager will normally prefer to buy from another unit of his company if he can obtain intermediate products at competitive prices. On the other side, the supplying division that is faced with idle capacity should be willing to reduce transfer prices to retain the business as long as some margin remains over the incremental costs of serving the internal customer. Admittedly, the manager of the supplying division is in a poorer bargaining position at this point. Although he has the option of seeking additional business outside to utilize his capacity, if idle capacity is widespread in the markets for the intermediate products this may not be a very effective weapon in negotiation. What the division manager should consider is whether he would make a larger profit or a smaller loss by accepting an internal order at a reduced price instead of rejecting it. Given this, there is no reason why freedom to deal outside will result in underutilization of capacity unless it is more profitable to the company.

The fourth requirement for a successful negotiated transfer price system—strong top-management support—is essential to reduce the amount of umpiring that top management is called upon to do. A system of negotiation can be undermined quickly if top management is ready to step in and arbitrate disputes whenever they arise. Appealing to the umpire is a form of dodging responsibility. Unless top management makes it clear that appeals for arbitration will reflect unfavorably on the executive ability of the negotiators, umpiring is likely to become frequent and the resulting transfer prices will serve as unreliable guides to resource allocation decisions.

Market Price Minus Commission

Effective negotiation is not always possible because one or more of the requisite conditions cannot be met. The absence of outside markets is the most serious drawback to negotiation because, as we have seen, buyer and seller have no alternative sources of supply or markets. One transfer pricing basis that has been used frequently when the buying division is largely a marketing organization and the selling division manufactures products for sale through the buying division is the market price minus a sales commission.

The absence of a market for the intermediate products means that these divisions are not profit centers but rather pseudo profit centers in which decision-making authority is restricted within fairly narrow limits. Nevertheless, as we have pointed out, the advantages of creating an awareness of profit and of providing a summary measure of financial performance in profit terms may justify separate profit reporting of these two units. If the company were to market its products through independent distribution companies, the price paid for marketing services would be represented by the spread between the final market price of the product and the net proceeds to the manufacturer. This suggests that something similar might be adopted when the marketing organization is not independent but is an internal operating unit. After deducting from revenues the marketing division's commision on sales, the residual is credited to the manufacturing division.

Under this system the basic resource allocation decisions are made by top management, not by the managers of the affected divisions. List prices and standard markups are established by top management. The sales division manager may or may not be given authority to grant price concessions; but if he is given this authority, any price concessions that he may make are not reflected in the transfer price. The reason for this is that sales management is evaluated on its ability to perform the marketing function. Changing the transfer price eliminates the fixed point of reference dividing the manufacturing from the selling function. Just as manufacturing cost standards are not changed monthly to conform to the latest cost experience, transfer prices should not be changed to reflect factors that are subject to the control of only one of the parties to the transaction. Allowing actual prices to influence the transfer price has the effect of guaranteeing a profit to the sales division, with the manufacturing division absorbing most of the losses from depressed market conditions.

Variable Cost plus Subsidy

Market or market-based negotiated prices are the only prices that are fully consistent with the concept of decentralization and profit center autonomy. Unfortunately, the availability and accessibility of intermediate markets which make systems of this sort workable are frequently absent. Nevertheless, management may still wish to report profit on a divisional basis in order to get divisional executives thinking in terms of profit rather than cost or sales volume.

Under these circumstances, in which internal buying and selling divisions are inextricably interdependent, some companies have turned to a modification of the marginal cost approach. This approach substitutes standard variable cost per unit for marginal cost and adds a monthly lump-sum subsidy to cover the fixed costs of the internal supplier of the intermediate product. This subsidy normally also includes a provision for profit, so that as long as the supplying division adheres to budgeted performance it will report a profit.[3]

A system of this kind can be made quite workable as long as it is clearly understood that the supplying divisions are essentially budget centers rather than profit centers. The main difficulty arises when the supplying division markets a portion of its output directly to outside markets. The lump-sum subsidy under these circumstances amounts to a reservation of a portion of the supplying division's capacity by the final product division, and the question of how much to reserve is extremely difficult.

For example, suppose that a division has been selling half of its output internally and half to outside customers, and that the subsidy has been established on the basis that this allocation will continue. During the year the final product division finds that its sales are running ahead of budget, and the manager requests additional quantities of the intermediate product. If the supplying division has idle capacity, this additional demand can or should be met at standard variable cost and no

---

[3] For an outline of one such proposal, see Myron J. Gordon, "The Use of Administered Price Systems to Control Large Organizations," in Charles P. Bonini, Robert K. Jaedicke, and Harvey M. Wagner (eds.), *Management Controls: New Directions in Basic Research* (New York: McGraw-Hill Book Co., 1964), chap. 1.

distortion of the supplying division's profit should result. But if the supplying division is operating at or near capacity, the additional volume for the final product division can be obtained only by diverting capacity from outside sales of other products of the supplying division or by incurring costs in excess of standard variable cost, perhaps by increased subcontracting, increased use of overtime, or use of less productive stand-by equipment. In this hybrid situation, who makes the decisions and how are these decisions reflected in the transfer prices?

There are no clear-cut answers to these questions. Because much of the output of the supplying division is sold to outside customers, it may be regarded as a modified profit center with a considerable degree of authority to make decisions as to production and sales. Perhaps the best solution is to provide for direct negotiation between the supplying division and the final product division. Because he wishes to make as favorable a profit showing as possible, the supplying division manager will be unwilling to accept any price that will not cover his opportunity costs of increasing deliveries to the final product division. If the increased output can be obtained only by curtailing production of other products now being sold outside the company, he will demand the same dollar markup over variable cost from his internal customer that he would lose by restricting sales to his outside customers. If he can expand his total output, he must demand a price that is at least adequate to cover the incremental cost of production by the more costly methods. The final product division manager will be willing to pay these higher prices for additional quantities of product only if their sales value is adequate to cover the transfer price plus any additional costs that he may incur in further processing and distribution.

Thus when a division is operating at capacity, supplying both inside and outside markets, there is a market price mechanism for resource allocation even when there is no independent market for a specific intermediate product. But when the supplying division is operating at less than full capacity, market forces are inoperative in determining the transfer price, and the standard variable cost plus subsidy may be the only practicable approach.

Mathematically Programmed Prices

The main conceptual barrier to the use of a marginal cost transfer price is that it does not measure opportunity cost when the supplying division is operating at capacity. This defect can be remedied if the operations can be programmed mathematically.

For example, an oil company controls the output of one of its large refineries with the help of a linear programming model. Part of the output of one of the refinery's products is transferred to a nearby petrochemical plant. The linear programming model is solved every quarter for various transfer volumes, and the petrochemical division manager is given a schedule listing the transfer prices for various quantities. He can then decide how much he wants to buy.

When the refinery is operating below capacity, the transfer prices represent the marginal cost of serving the petrochemical plant. At full capacity, however, the transfer price is the sale value of the transferred output. Since this is considerably higher than marginal cost, the petrochemical manager will often find it profitable to buy substitute materials from outside sources.

This is not a perfect solution. These transfer prices are predicated on estimates of production and sales of all of the refinery's products for three months in advance. As conditions change, the optimal refinery mix also changes, and with it the opportunity cost of goods transferred to the petrochemical division. The transfer price remains unchanged, however, and this can lead to some suboptimization. It can also lead to complaints from one manager or the other that he is being deprived of profits that are rightfully his. The refinery manager's freedom of action is particularly circumscribed by this system.

Another problem is that this method is difficult to apply if intermediate products are transferred to more than one buying division. The output decisions of the various divisions are interdependent, and a full programming solution would require fully centralized decision making. To maintain the appearance of decentralized decision making without suboptimization, several writers have advocated an iterative procedure rather than a firm set of predetermined transfer prices.[4] Under this plan each division manager would supply a central analytical staff with preliminary estimates of their output plan and input needs. The central staff would enter these plans into a large-scale linear program and transmit the resulting quantities and transfer prices to the division managers.

Upon receipt of the results of this first run, the division managers would review their initial plans and submit revised estimates to headquarters. The linear program would be run again with these data and the results would once again be sent to the division managers. By the end of the third or fourth iteration, the divisional plans would approximate the optimal solution and further iteration would become unnecessary.

Whether this procedure would preserve the decentralization pattern or undermine it is a behavioral question for which no data are available.

---

[4] William J. Baumol and Tibor Fabian, "Decomposition, Pricing for Decentralization and External Economies," *Management Science,* September 1964, pp. 1–32; Andrew Whinston, "Price Guides in Decentralized Organization," in W. W. Cooper, H. J. Leavitt, and M. W. Shelly II (eds.), *New Perspectives in Organization Research* (New York: John Wiley & Sons, 1964), pp. 405–48; Nicholas Dopuch and David F. Drake, "Accounting Implications of a Mathematical Programming Approach to the Transfer Price Problem," *Journal of Accounting Research,* Spring 1964, pp. 10–24.

The method would seem to have a positive benefit if the quality of the data considered by the division manager in later iterations were higher than the quality of the data he supplied initially to a central decision staff. The method may also be applicable whenever divisional autonomy is clearly limited, as in the case of many distant subsidiaries of multinational companies.

The method itself is based on a belief that divisional managers, if left to themselves, will inevitably suboptimize to an intolerable extent. If this is really true, decentralization probably is inappropriate, and no amount of window dressing will be effective.

SUMMARY

Transfer prices on goods or services transferred to or from a profit center should guide the profit center manager toward decisions that will lead to an economic allocation of resources. They should also be perceived as fair by the profit center manager, so as not to weaken his motivation.

A transfer price that meets the first of these criteria is one that approximates opportunity cost to the supplying division. If each party to the transfer has adequate access to outside markets, a system of negotiated market-based transfer prices can meet this test and also retain the appearance of fairness.

The use of any nonnegotiated transfer price is an abrogation of the profit center manager's authority. Negotiation is not always feasible, however, because outside markets are thin or nonexistent. If management wishes to retain a profit center structure, substitutes for negotiation must be found.

The best practical alternative will ordinarily be to transfer at estimated average variable cost, marginal cost information not being generally available. To preserve the appearance of fairness, this should be accompanied by a system of lump-sum subsidies by which the buying divisions reserve portions of the selling division's capacity. If control by a linear programming model is feasible, this may be used instead.

Whenever a nonnegotiated solution is adopted, care should be taken to insure that variances between budgeted and actual transfer prices do not appear on the periodic profit reports. Since these are outside the manager's control, his performance rating should not be affected by them.

EXERCISES AND PROBLEMS

1. The Apex Machinery Company manufactures and distributes a line of textile machinery and supplies and a line of machinery for nontextile industrial trades. The company's operations are organized as shown in the following chart:

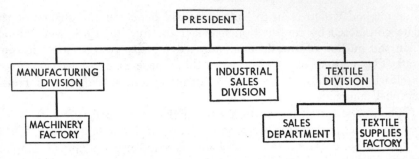

All machinery, including both textile and industrial trades machinery, is manufactured in the machinery factory of the manufacturing division. The textile division manufactures its own supplies in its supplies factory but purchases all its requirements of machinery from the manufacturing division. The machinery is highly technical and cannot be obtained from independent manufacturers.

The management of the Apex Machinery Company wishes to prepare profit reports for each of the company's three divisions, and you have been asked to recommend a transfer pricing system. The manufacturing vice president has suggested that machinery be transferred at standard manufacturing cost plus 10 percent. The industrial sales division has suggested list price less 25 percent, an arrangement that is common among manufacturers' agents in this market. You need not recommend either of these proposals if you feel that some other arrangement would be superior.

2.* The Hull division of the Ballou Company manufactures and distributes a broad range of industrial chemicals. One of these, product X, is also sold to another Ballou Company division, the Hingham division, which uses it as a raw material in the manufacture of several products.

The Hull division's income statement is classified by product line, and the section relating to product X is as follows (in thousands):

Sales—outside (100,000 lbs. @ $2)...............		$200
Sales—Hingham (50,000 lbs. @ $1.80)............		90
Total sales.................................		$290
Product-traceable costs:		
Variable manufacturing costs ($0.90/lb.)........	$135	
Sales commissions—outside sales...............	10	
Depreciation...............................	20	
Other traceable fixed costs....................	40	205
Product profit contribution.....................		$ 85
Share of divisional fixed costs....................		60
Net Profit before Taxes.........................		$ 25

Common fixed costs, including such items as executive salaries and sales branch operating expenses, are allocated among the division's product lines at a flat $0.40 a pound.

An outside supplier has offered to supply the Hingham division with a product similar to and a perfectly satisfactory substitute for product X, at a

* Solutions to problems marked with an asterisk can be found in Appendix B.

firm contract price of $1.60 a pound, delivered at the Hingham factory. The Hingham division manager has proposed that the interdivisional transfer price of product X be reduced to $1.60 to meet the competing offer. Otherwise, he threatens to purchase the substitute product from the outside vendor.

The manager of the Hull division has refused to meet this price on the grounds that this is less than his cost. You are a staff assistant to the manager of the Hingham division, and he has asked you to draft a short memorandum to the Hull division manager in support of the proposed $1.60 price.

3.† The Alma Products Company is decentralized into a number of operating divisions. In the words of the company's controller, under this arrangement "practically absolute authority is granted to the division to carry on its everyday operations." The controller described the company's interdivisional transfer pricing system in the memorandum quoted in the following paragraphs.

"Our plan is to use market price as the intercompany pricing base where the material is a prime one that can be purchased from an independent source in the same form and quality as obtained from the affiliated unit. The controller's organization doesn't set the price in this case. Representatives of the buying and selling units sit down and develop prices with just as evident interest on either side as would be shown if they were dealing with someone outside of the family.

"On all other items we have used cost as the basis of transfer value between divisions. This transfer value is established for a quarterly period and is the sum of current manufacturing cost and a percentage thereof to cover other allocable items not ordinarily included in the manufacturing cost of the product. This latter arrangement has the effect of putting all of the gross profit into the company that does the selling and which must stand the selling and merchandising expense. Just so there won't be any question about it, the buying divisions' representatives look just as caustically at the costs involved as they would if they were doing the job of manufacturing from the very beginning. It is in this type of transaction that the controller's responsibility enters, as in our organization he has the job of creating the cost base upon which the price is established."

a) Discuss the soundness of this system in view of the company's announced practice of delegating to divisional executives "practically absolute authority" for decision making.

b) What purpose is served by having buying division representatives look "caustically" at transfer prices that are established by the controller's organization? What problems do you foresee under this arrangement and how do you think they can be solved?

4. Professor E. G. Heide recently received the following letter from a former student:

"Dear Professor Heide:

"I found your paper on Divisional Profit Standards very much to the

---

† Based on an article by L. R. Feakes in *The Controller*.

point. We are working on our divisional reporting structure now, and much that you say seems to fit our situation.

"In my limited experience so far, the most difficult aspect of this problem has always been the matter of transfer pricing. I wonder if you could comment on the merit of the following approach which I believe takes into account the effect of below-capacity operation of the supplying division in a market where price and to a large extent market share are constant. This, you will admit, is the case in many industries today, especially where oligopolies exist.

"Consider division A, whose operations can be described as shown on the diagram labeled Table 1.

Table 1

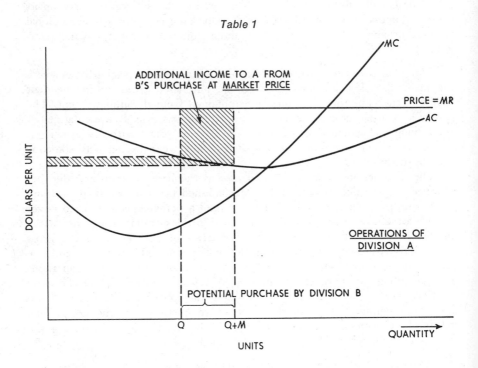

"Division B wishes to purchase a quantity M of material produced by division A, whose cost curves are shown and whose output, not counting the contemplated interdivisional transfer, is limited to Q, its 'share of market.' A forced purchase of the material at market price by division B would be, in effect, a 'windfall profit' for division A; while purchase at marginal cost would cause division A to lose money. I would suggest that the additional income to A that could result from B's purchase of the material at market cost be divided evenly between A and B, resulting in a transfer price above A's average cost—i.e., a profit to A—and below the market cost, i.e., a saving for B.

"If the purchase price were set at average cost, A's manager would have no incentive to make the transfer of material, while if the price were set at market cost, B might prefer to go 'outside' for marginal reasons like 'service,' and if so, would adversely affect corporate earnings. The 50–50 split could become a matter of company policy, and thus avoid negotiations each time a transfer cost has to be established.

"I look forward to hearing from you."

Draft a reply for Professor Heide's signature.

5. The Barnaby Corporation was formed two years ago as a merger of two previously independent companies, Dover and Elmsford. These two companies, now Barnaby divisions, have been operated since the merger just as they were before the merger, as if they were still independent businesses. Each has its own sales force and its own production facilities. Interdivisional transactions are rare and the company has never established a transfer pricing policy.

The Dover division now buys 10,000 metal handles a month from the Fowler Company for use on one of its products, a canister-type vacuum cleaner. The Elmsford division recently offered to supply these handles to Dover at a price of 90 cents apiece. The Dover division manager was interested, but not at a 90-cent price. His current price was 82 cents and the Fowler Company offered him a firm contract for his next year's requirements at this price.

The Elmsford division has a modern, well-equipped factory. Although its equipment is not ideally suited to the production of small items like the Dover handles, labor and materials costs on such items are only a few cents higher than in more suitably equipped plants.

Because of his high costs, Dick Baker, the manager of the Elmsford division, doesn't see how he can cut the price much below 90 cents. According to his own calculations, cost would be 85 cents, as follows:

Materials	$0.55
Labor	0.10
Factory overhead	0.20
Total	$0.85

Because this would be an internal sale, no selling expense would be incurred.

Mr. Baker knows that many of his factory overhead costs are fixed and that he has more than enough idle capacity to take on this business without difficulty. Only about 30 percent of the factory overhead cost of making the handles represents incremental cost. Furthermore, he would have no difficulty in expanding his work force by the small amounts necessary to take on the production of these handles. Mr. Baker feels, however, that any business that does not cover at least its share of fixed factory overhead offers no long-term promise and is better left alone. It reduces the average rate of profitability and ties down part of the division's productive capacity.

The Dover division manager has just decided to continue buying the handles from the Fowler Company at the 82-cent price.

a) On the basis of the data available to you, do you believe that the Dover division should buy its handles from the Elmsford division?

b) If you had the power to set the transfer price in this situation, what price would you set?

c) Assuming that the calculations in (a) indicated that Elmsford should supply the handles, should the top management of the Barnaby Corporation step in and order the Dover division to buy them from Elmsford at the transfer price you selected in (b)?

6. Division A manufactures and sells product X both to outside customers and to division B. Both division A and division B are regarded as profit centers, and each manager is expected to try to maximize divisional profit.

Division A has no marketing organization of its own, but instead sells its products to outside customers through a network of manufacturer's agents. The manufacturer's agents maintain no inventories, but are responsible for investigating customers' credit ratings, billing, and collections.

Product X is priced to customers at 95 cents a pound. The agents' commission on sales of this product is 25 cents a pound, leaving 70 cents a pound for division A. Experiments conducted several months ago indicated that reducing customer prices by 10 cents a pound (to 85 cents) and agents' prices by 15 cents a pound (to 55 cents) had no noticeable effect on the number of pounds sold to outside customers. The agents have also said that sales to their customers would fall considerably if the price were to be raised, but no attempt has been made to verify this.

Division A's sales to division B are billed at 70 cents a pound. The transfer price is set by the manager of division A and is not subject to negotiation. All sales are in batches of 1,000 units each.

Division B uses one pound of X in the manufacture of each unit of its product, product Y. The demand function for product Y is as follows:

Price	Units Sold per Week
$2.00	1,000
1.60	2,000
1.40	3,000
1.25	4,000
1.10	5,000
0.95	6,000
0.80	7,000

Division A is now selling 10,000 pounds of X each week to its outside customers. The following cost estimates have been prepared for the two division managers. Each division manager has access to his own cost data only—he does not see the cost estimates for the other division.

Division A		Division B	
Pounds Produced per Week	Total Production Cost	Units Produced per Week	Total Production Cost*
10,000	$6,000	0	$1,000
11,000	6,400	1,000	1,500
12,000	6,800	2,000	1,850
13,000	7,200	3,000	2,200
14,000	7,600	4,000	2,550
15,000	8,000	5,000	2,900
16,000	8,400	6,000	3,250
17,000	9,000	7,000	3,700

* Exclusive of the cost of product X.

a) How many pounds of product X would division B be likely to buy each week at a price of 70 cents a pound?

b) Assuming that the division managers were instructed to negotiate the transfer price, what transfer price do you think might result? How many pounds of product X would division B buy at this price? Would it make any difference if each negotiator had access to the information available to the other? (The price to outside customers would not be affected by these negotiations.)

c) How many units of product Y would be manufactured if a single division manager were responsible for the activities of both of these divisions? Compare this figure with the one derived in (*b*) and comment on the similarity or difference.

CASE 25–1: THE WOLSEY CORPORATION

The Wolsey Corporation established an industrial products division about 15 years ago. Its purpose was to find applications in industrial markets for products and technology that other company divisions had developed successfully for the company's commercial and consumer markets.

In its first 14 years, the industrial products division was required to buy from other company divisions any component part or product that it required and that was manufactured by those divisions for sale to outside customers. For special parts not manufactured by other divisions for sale to outside customers, the industrial products division was required to use internal sources if other divisions had adequate capacity and facilities. As a result, approximately 85 percent of the materials cost in industrial products plants represented parts and processed materials transferred from other divisions. These transfers were made at standard product cost.

Early last year the president of the Wolsey Corporation issued the following directive:

MEMORANDUM TO: Division Managers
SUBJECT: Interdivisional Transfers

1. To place all divisions on a more competitive footing, each division manager is hereby authorized to negotiate with outside vendors for the purchase of all processed materials, component parts, and products now purchased from other divisions of the company, except (*a*) products sold directly under the company's brand name without further processing, and (*b*) components and processed material on Schedule T-146, for which specifications and drawings are classified company confidential.

2. Before any order is placed with an outside vendor for an item currently being supplied from another division, that division must be given a chance to meet the outside price and promised delivery schedule. No such procedure need be followed on orders in amounts of less than $500.

3. Before any order is placed with an outside vendor for a new item, all divisions should be notified and given a chance to bid on the item. This procedure need not be followed for orders amounting to less than $500.

4. Transfers between divisions will continue to be made at standard cost for all items that have not been covered by the negotiations referred to in paragraphs 2 and 3 above. These standard costs are to be approved in all cases by the corporate methods department. Negotiated prices that are less than standard cost will be reported to the accounting depart-department on Form PR-12-60, and do not require review by the corporate staff.

5. The cooperation of all personnel is requested to make this system effective. Each division will keep a record of outside purchases and the savings accomplished thereby.

Shortly after this memorandum was circulated, the president called a meeting of division managers to explain the new procedure and to answer questions that had arisen. The manager of the small machinery division was skeptical. He said, "Does this mean that if I have idle capacity I can be forced to transfer at less than standard cost? It seems to me that that is just the time when I need transfers at standard cost more than ever to help me absorb my overhead." Most of the other division managers were more sympathetic to the new system, although they were not certain exactly how it would work.

Upon his return from this meeting, the manager of the industrial products division instructed the divisional controller to obtain outside quotations on a metal housing used in one of the division's products. This housing was then being cast in the small machinery division's foundry at a standard cost of $22.17 per casting. The castings were then machined to required tolerances in the industrial products division, and the standard cost of this operation was $6.18. Inquiries at local foundries produced a bid from the Gray Foundry Company of $23.75 per casting, plus $175 for the cost of an aluminum pattern. These castings would be produced by a more modern process and would not require any machining in the industrial products division. Annual requirements were expected to average 500 castings.

The manager of industrial products then prepared the following cost estimate and submitted it to the small machinery manager, noting that unless the indicated price could be met, the order would be placed with Gray Foundry:

```
Cost of outside purchase:
   Pattern...............................  $    175
   Castings—500 at $23.75................     11,875
Total purchase cost.....................    $12,050
   Less: Cost of machining, 500 at $6.18....      3,090
Maximum transfer price..................    $  8,960  = $17.92 per casting
```

The manager of the small machinery division exploded when he received this estimate. "This is just what I was afraid of. You don't even know whether these people can live up to their promises and you want me to accept an order at less than cost. How do you expect me to cover my overhead? They are only quoting you this price to get your business, and once you are on the hook, they will raise their prices. As long as I have idle capacity, it is foolish to go outside—the whole company will suffer if you do very much of this. Against my better judgment, however, I'll quote you a price of $19.62. This doesn't cover depreciation on foundry equipment, and it's as low as I can go."

The industrial products manager rejected this offer and placed an initial order for 200 castings with the Gray Foundry Company, whereupon the small machinery manager appealed to the president, claiming that the new system was unworkable and unreasonable.

The president had hoped to avoid participation in disputes of this kind, but since this was the first case he felt that it warranted his attention. A staff assistant was assigned to study the problem and he made the following breakdown of standard costs:

	Variable Cost	Fixed Cost	Total Standard Cost
Casting...........	$17.95	$4.22	$22.17
Machining........	4.15	2.03	6.18

He also found that materials price variances in the foundry were likely to be unfavorable, amounting to $0.12 per casting.

a) Prepare an analysis that will indicate whether future castings should be acquired from the Gray Foundry Company or from the small machinery division.

b) Discuss the transfer pricing policy outlined in the president's memorandum, commenting on any features that you feel should be changed.

c) Would you expect the new policy to require any substantial amount of top management mediation to settle disputes of the kind arising in this problem? Explain.

CASE 25–2: HOPPIT CHEMICAL COMPANY

The Moorhouse division of the Hoppit Chemical Company has 14 chemical plants located in various parts of the United States. Its profit contribution after deducting all divisional overheads runs about $50 million a year, and in exceptionally good years may even reach $75 million.

The company's Allworth division is much smaller, with only two plants and an annual profit contribution of about $2.5 million. Four years ago, the Allworth division constructed a new plant on a site adjacent to one of the main plants of the Moorhouse division. The idea was to take advantage of a plentiful supply of a chemical known as amalite, a product of the Moorhouse plant. Amalite was made in the Moorhouse plant from the waste residue thrown off by the plant's primary production process.

Before the Allworth plant was built, amalite had been manufactured only intermittently, whenever its market price was high enough to justify the conversion expenditures. The market for amalite had been weak for some time, however, and the Hoppit market research department forecasted that this condition would continue to prevail for many years to come as amalite was gradually displaced by petroleum derivatives in one of its main uses. Under these circumstances, it seemed a good move to build the new plant to convert amalite into another chemical product with a considerably higher market value.

A transfer price system was devised and accepted by the managers of both divisions when the new plant went into production. Under this system, Allworth's management initiated the process each quarter by telling Moorhouse how much amalite it expected to need during the next quarter. The Moorhouse division then quoted a set of prices for different quantities of amalite to be delivered during that quarter. These prices were based primarily on the estimated incremental costs of processing different quantities of Moorhouse waste into amalite. For example, during the first two years the plant was in operation, a typical transfer price schedule was as follows:

Transfers (pounds)	Total Transfer Price
1,000,000 or less.........	$0.40 per lb. (minimum 500,000 lbs.)
1,000,000–2,500,000......	$400,000 + $0.30 per lb. in excess of 1,000,000
More than 2,500,000......	$850,000 + $0.40 per lb. in excess of 2,500,000

With this schedule in hand, Allworth's management could then decide how much amalite to order from Moorhouse during the next quarter.

The transfer pricing system also provided that transfers would be made at anticipated net market price whenever the Moorhouse plant's capacity for producing amalite was expected to be inadequate to serve all of its outside customers and Allworth too.

The Allworth plant was not completely dependent on Moorhouse amalite for raw materials. It could also use a commercially available product known as flemite. The purchase cost of flemite was considerably higher than the transfer prices prevailing during the first two years of the new plant's operations, however, and flemite was not used. Outside purchases of amalite were impractical for the same reason. Although the market price of Moorhouse's amalite was lower than its incremental cost during these two years, high transportation costs prevented Allworth from buying amalite from outside suppliers.

Each year each division manager in the Hoppit Chemical Company is required to prepare a profit plan. In drawing up their plans, the Allworth and Moorhouse managers get together and agree on a forecast of the transfer prices expected to prevail during the coming year. This price schedule is then built into the divisional profit plans for the year.

Shortly after the beginning of the current year, the market price of amalite took a sudden jump to 50 cents a pound, and Moorhouse could sell all it could produce at this price. Moorhouse therefore set 50 cents as the transfer price for the second quarter. Because flemite was available at a price of 45 cents, however, Moorhouse sold most of its amalite on the market and bought flemite to meet its supply commitment to the Allworth plant. Both division managers agreed that this was in the best interest of the Hoppit Chemical Company.

At the same time, however, Mr. C. P. Jones, the Allworth division manager, refused to approve the transfer charge at 45 cents on the ground that this would create a substantial profit variance, amounting to approximately $250,000 a quarter, through no fault of anyone in the Allworth division. As Mr. Jones pointed out, when the plant was constructed he could have signed a long-term contract with outside suppliers of amalite at a price of 40 cents a pound, but he was not allowed by Hoppit's top management to do so. Mr. Jones felt that Moorhouse was under an obligation to continue to supply amalite or a substitute at a price within the range that was forecasted when the plant was built.

Mr. John England, Moorhouse's chief cost analyst and the man responsible for the transfer price calculations, did not agree. "Even if they had signed a contract like that," he said, "we would still have to make our decisions on the basis of current market conditions. If Allworth can't make an incremental profit on the basis of current market prices, then the plant should be shut down until materials prices go back down or selling prices of the Allworth products go up. If we let them have this stuff at 40 cents, the company could be losing as much as 5 cents on every pound they use."

a) Do you feel that Mr. Jones is justified in asking for a long-term price commitment from Moorhouse, or is Mr. England right in saying that the transfer price should always reflect current market conditions?

b) Should the transfer pricing system be changed, and if so in what way? Can you identify any other defects in the system? Explain your reasoning.

Part IV

Cost Accounting
for
Decision Models

chapter **26**

Capital Expenditure Analysis

Management decision models ordinarily use data from the company's accounting system. The three chapters in Part IV will examine the relevance of accounting data to three different kinds of decision models. The purpose of this chapter is to study the data requirements of models for capital expenditure decisions.

THE INVESTMENT PROBLEM

An investment outlay may be defined as an expenditure of cash or its equivalent in one time period or periods to obtain a net inflow of cash or its equivalent in some other time period or periods.

For example, suppose that a company has an opportunity to rearrange the layout of one of its factories at an outlay of $50,000. This will permit the company to save $20,000 a year in the manufacture of a product which it expects to produce for the next three years. The cash flows in this example can be arranged in a timetable like the following:

Years from Now	Cash Inflow (+) or Outflow (−)
0	−$50,000
0 to 1	+ 20,000
1 to 2	+ 20,000
2 to 3	+ 20,000
Total	+$10,000

This is a typical investment problem—a cash outflow is made immediately to get cash inflows in each of the next three periods. The decision cannot be based on the anticipated cash flows for the first period alone.

623

Types of Investment Problems

This definition of an investment problem embraces a wide variety of situations. For example, a decision to buy raw materials in larger lots is an investment decision because it will require larger inventories. The profitability of the outlays made to increase the inventories depends on the size of the future cash savings to be realized through large-scale buying.

Plant abandonment is also an investment problem. Continued operation of the plant requires the company to forgo the cash that it could release by shutting down, selling plant and equipment, and releasing working capital for other uses. The amount of this released cash appears in the timetable as an inflow (+). Against this must be weighed the cash outflows represented by the cash flow that would be generated by product sales that would be lost by abandonment.

For example, suppose that a company could realize $500,000 if it were to close and sell one of its plants which otherwise could be operated to yield positive cash flows totaling $750,000, spread over the next five years. The comparison could be set up this way:

Years from Now	Abandon	Keep	Difference
0	+$500,000	0	+$500,000
0 to 1	0	+$250,000	− 250,000
1 to 2	0	+ 200,000	− 200,000
2 to 3	0	+ 150,000	− 150,000
3 to 4	0	+ 100,000	− 100,000
4 to 5	0	+ 50,000	− 50,000
Total	+$500,000	+$750,000	−$250,000

Thus the total cash flow from continued operations is $250,000 greater than the alternative under consideration, but it comes later. This makes it an investment problem or, more precisely, a disinvestment problem.

This could be regarded as an investment of the current disposal value of the facilities to obtain the cash flows from future product sales. It is merely necessary to reverse the algebraic signs in the table above and the comparison becomes identical to the one considered earlier.

Few investment problems are as simple as the one illustrated above, although it is often permissible to assume that they are. A more typical case is exemplified by the plant acquisition proposal portrayed in Exhibit 26–1. An initial outlay of $1 million for plant, equipment, and working capital is shown as a shaded block below the zero line at the left of the diagram. The expected annual cash inflows from operating the plant amount to $50,000 in the first year, $150,000 in the second, and $200,000 a year in the 3rd through 13th years. The inflows are expected to decline to $150,000 in the 14th year and to $100,000 in the

Exhibit 26–1

TIME PROFILE OF AN INVESTMENT PROBLEM

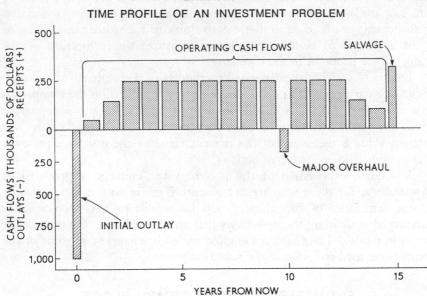

15th. All of these inflows or receipts are represented by shaded blocks above the zero line.

Management expects the plant to be useful for 15 years, after which it will either be sold or rebuilt. The cash value of the plant, equipment, and working capital at that time is expected to be $300,000. This is treated as a cash receipt and is shown as the rightmost shaded block above the line.

Finally, a major overhaul of facilities, costing $150,000, is expected to be necessary at the end of the 10th year. Without this, the company could not obtain the cash inflows of the final five years. This outlay is shown in Exhibit 26–1 as the second shaded block extending below the zero line.

The Decision Model

Probably the most important category of investment problems in most firms comprises proposals for the expenditure of funds to build, acquire, replace, or expand long-life productive assets—i.e., *capital* expenditures. In the aggregate, these proposals typically exceed the amount of cash available for investment. For this reason, management needs methods and procedures for deciding which proposals should be accepted.

Management would find it very difficult to evaluate a capital expenditure proposal that was supported only by a number of cash flow estimates. For example, it may be accurate to describe a proposal by listing one cash outlay and six future cash receipts, but before making a decision management needs to relate these cash flows to each other. Some means must be found to combine the estimates into a single measure of the value of the proposal to the company.

The most widely recommended method is to discount all of the cash flows to their present value at a discount rate representing the company's cost of capital. The decision rule implicit in this model is to accept only those proposals that seem to promise a positive net present value. Net present value is the excess of the present value of the cash receipts over the present value of the cost outlays.

A detailed explanation of the present value concept is provided in Appendix A for those who are not already familiar with it. Our concern in the remainder of this chapter will be to discuss the problems encountered in defining the cash flows that are called for by the investment decision model.[1] The chapter will close with a brief survey of some of the procedures used to facilitate the selection process.

ESTIMATES OF PROJECT CASH FLOWS

It is conceptually unnecessary in capital expenditure analysis to distinguish different types of cash flows. The timetable requires a distinction only between inflows and outflows. For analytical convenience, however, six separate parameters can be recognized:

1. The impact of income taxes.
2. The amount and timing of the initial investment outlay.
3. The amounts and timing of subsequent investment outlays.
4. The amounts and timing of operating cash flows.
5. Economic life.
6. End-of-life salvage values.

Before examining these, however, we need to look briefly at the question of how to date cash flows that take place within the year rather than at the beginning or the end.

Dating the Cash Flows

Outlays and receipts of cash are likely to be spread more or less continuously over the life of the investment. A year's operating cash receipts,

---

[1] For a discussion of the model and of the cost of capital, see James Porterfield, *Investment Decisions and Capital Costs* (Englewood Cliffs, N.J.: Prentice-Hall, 1965); Myron J. Gordon, *The Investment, Financing, and Valuation of the Corporation* (Homewood, Ill.: Richard D. Irwin, 1962); and Ezra Solomon, *The Theory of Financial Management* (New York: Columbia University Press, 1963).

for example, are likely to come in throughout the year, not all at one time.

Ideally, cash flows should be dated as accurately as possible and the compounding interval should be adjusted to the frequency with which the cash is typically reinvested.[2] If cash flows can be reinvested monthly, monthly compounding should be used. This will assign a smaller present value to a cash flow that takes place late in the year than it assigns to one that occurs earlier.

In practice, cash flows are assumed to come in or go out only once a year, and present value is calculated on the basis of annual compounding. Present values computed on this basis will be slightly inaccurate, but the error is small relative to the errors inherent in the estimates of future cash flows. We shall adopt this convention for the illustrations and problems in this chapter. Operating cash flows will be assumed to take place at year-end. Investment outlays will be dated at the year-end nearest to the date of the anticipated cash outlay.

The Impact of Income Taxes

The present value of a proposal depends on both the amounts and the timing of the cash flows that would follow acceptance of the proposal. Since income taxes affect the cash flows, proposals should be analyzed on the basis of after-tax cash flows.

Many countries attempt to stimulate certain kinds of investment expenditures by granting them favorable tax treatment. One kind of tax inducement is the investment credit, by which a taxpayer is permitted to deduct from his current tax payments an amount equal to a specified percentage of his total expenditures on certain types of property. This increases the present value of an expenditure proposal by decreasing the total amount of taxes to be paid during the life of the facilities acquired.

Other tax inducements are more subtle in that they merely postpone tax payments. This reduces the present value of the payments and increases the net present value of the after-tax cash flows, presumably making the investment more attractive. For example, suppose that certain facilities costing $100,000 normally have a four-year amortization period for tax purposes, but that a special provision permits the entire amount to be written off during the first year. If the income tax rate is 40 percent[3] and the discount rate is 10 percent, the present value of the normal tax deductions is $31,690, computed as follows:

---

[2] See Appendix A for a discussion of the compounding interval.

[3] The effective tax rate varies slightly from state to state and is subject to change. For simplicity, a rate of 40 percent will be used throughout this section. Although actual rates are ordinarily in the neighborhood of 50 percent, for illustrative purposes it is clearer to use the 40 percent rate, which produces different figures for income tax and after-tax net income.

Years from Now	Annual Deduction	Income Tax Effect	Present Value @ 10%	
			Multiplier	Amount
1..................	$ 25,000	$10,000	0.909	$ 9,090
2..................	25,000	10,000	0.826	8,260
3..................	25,000	10,000	0.751	7,510
4..................	25,000	10,000	0.683	6,830
Total..............	$100,000	$40,000		$31,690

The present value of the privilege of writing the entire amount off during the first year would be 0.909 × $40,000 = $36,360. The $4,670 difference between $36,360 and $31,690 is what the faster write-off is worth to the company.

Initial Investment Outlay

The initial outlay is defined as the net expenditure of cash or its equivalent required by the proposal. This includes all expenditures necessary to carry out the proposal, whether for plant and equipment or for working capital, whether capitalized on the balance sheet or written off immediately as expense for external financial reporting or tax purposes.

In a narrow sense, no outlays are made for some elements of working capital. For example, the fact that cash balances are required by the proposal means that the cash will still be in the company's possession. It will be immobilized, however, unavailable for other uses. This makes it a cash "flow."

The increment in accounts receivable balances, on the other hand, is included because the estimates of operating cash flows usually reflect sales revenues rather than collections from customers. If sales exceed collections by, say, $4,000, the operating cash flows will be overstated by this amount. This is corrected by inserting the $4,000 into the timetable as an investment outlay, preferably at the same point in time as the operating cash flows.

Current asset requirements can be financed in part by short-term, noninterest-bearing credit, mainly trade payables. To this extent cash is not immobilized. Increases in trade payables and accruals therefore should be deducted from the increases in current assets required by the proposal.

To get a better picture of the initial investment outlay, let us suppose that a company is considering a proposal to modernize one of its plants. The following expenditures would be made prior to the start of operations.

Equipment	$ 80,000
Installation	10,000
Working capital	5,000
Training and test runs	7,000
Total expenditures	$102,000

In practice, these outlays would be spread over many weeks or months, but it is conventional to assume that they are all incurred at the same time, usually when the facilities are placed in full operation. For convenience, this can be designated as the zero date. If the expenditures are spread over a year or more, of course, the zero date should be earlier and part of the outlay should be shown as occurring one or more years later, depending on the circumstances.

This proposal also calls for the use of a machine already owned by the company but now idle. This is one of the resources that would be tied up if this proposal were accepted, and its opportunity cost should be included as part of the investment outlay. The best alternative to the proposed use of this equipment is to sell it for $12,000, and this is regarded as part of the outlay because the company is depriving itself of this amount of cash if it accepts the proposal. A cash receipt forgone is always equivalent to a cash outlay made.

Finally, if the proposal is accepted, a machine now serving a standby purpose can be disposed of. This machine represents resources now unavailable for general use but which will be made available by acceptance of this proposal. Opportunity cost is once again the measure of the resources released, in this case equal to the scrap value of the machine, which is $6,000. The displaced resources, in other words, can finance $6,000 of the gross before-tax outlays required by the proposal.

The initial outlay before taxes can now be computed from the above figures:

Equipment	$ 80,000
Installation	10,000
Working capital	5,000
Training and test runs	7,000
Presently owned surplus equipment to be used (resale value)	12,000
Gross outlay	$114,000
Less: Presently owned operating equipment to be replaced if proposal is accepted (resale value)	6,000
Net investment outlay before income taxes	$108,000

Let us assume that the first two of these items—equipment and installation costs—are subject to a 7 percent tax credit (a tax reduction), so that the cash flows are:

Gross outlay	$90,000
Less: Tax reduction at 7 percent	6,300
After-tax outlay	$83,700

The working capital outlays have no special tax treatment in this case, so that after-tax and before-tax outlays are identical. The training and test-run costs are fully deductible from current revenues, however, and thus the after-tax cash flow is only 60 percent of the before-tax outlay:[4]

Gross outlay..	$7,000
Less: Tax reduction at 40 percent...................	2,800
After-tax outlay....................................	$4,200

The fifth item on the list, the standby equipment, has a before-tax opportunity cost of $12,000, its current resale value. The records show that its book value for tax purposes (in technical language, its adjusted basis) is $20,000. If the proposal is rejected, the equipment will be sold, an $8,000 loss will be reported on the income tax return, and the company's taxes will be reduced by $3,200. If the proposal is accepted, on the other hand, the equipment cannot be sold and the company's taxes will be $3,200 more than they would have been had the equipment been sold and the loss declared for tax purposes. This $3,200 increase in taxes is an outlay attributable to the modernization proposal. The after-tax outlay required to retain this surplus equipment therefore is:

(1)	Before-tax cash flow.................................	$12,000
(2)	Book value for tax purposes..........................	20,000
(3)	Taxable gain or (loss): (1) − (2).....................	$(8,000)
(4)	Tax or (credit): (3) × 40%...........................	(3,200)
(5)	After-tax cash flow: (1) − (4).......................	$15,200

The tax effect of the disposal of the replaced facilities is similar. Assuming a book value for tax purposes of $1,000, the calculations are:

(1)	Before-tax cash flow.................................	$6,000
(2)	Book value for tax purposes..........................	1,000
(3)	Taxable gain or (loss): (1) − (2).....................	$5,000
(4)	Tax or (credit): (3) × 40%...........................	2,000
(5)	After-tax cash flow: (1) − (4).......................	$4,000

These adjustments are all summarized in Exhibit 26–2. In this case the net difference between the before-tax and the after-tax amounts is relatively small, less than 4 percent; in other cases it will be much higher.

The assumption that tax payments or receipts take place simultaneously with the before-tax cash flows is a simplification. The time lag before tax payments are due is relatively short, however, and a difference in timing probably should be recognized in the timetable only if the deferral is longer than six months. Recognition of lags shorter than this would require similar adjustments to other kinds of cash flows and the use of a shorter compounding interval.

---

[4] Although different parts of the cash flow are likely to be subject to different tax treatments, a uniform 40 percent rate will illustrate the method without extraneous complications.

Exhibit 26–2

CALCULATION OF AFTER-TAX INVESTMENT OUTLAY

Item	Outlay before Tax	Tax Effect	Outlay after Tax
Equipment, installed.................	$ 90,000	$(6,300)	$ 83,700
Working capital....................	5,000	0	5,000
Training and test runs..............	7,000	(2,800)	4,200
Surplus equipment used.............	12,000	3,200	15,200
Equipment replaced.................	(6,000)	2,000	(4,000)
Total...........................	$108,000	$(3,900)	$104,100

Subsequent Investment Outlays

It is often possible to anticipate, at the time a proposal is made, special outlays in later time periods that are more like investment outlays than operating expenditures. These, too, may be for equipment or working capital, treated as expense or capitalized, and should be adjusted for their tax effects.

In the example, replacement expenditures amounting to $20,000 would have to be made at the end of the fifth year and must be entered in the timetable at that point.

Economic Life and Discounting Period

The economic life of any particular asset may be defined as the time interval that is expected to elapse between the time of acquisition and the time at which the combined forces of obsolescence and deterioration will justify retirement of the asset.

As in human life expectancy calculations, this is a probabilistic notion. Of any group of similar wasting assets, death will come to some soon after birth; others may have lives of 50 years or even longer. Exhibit 26–3 shows one company's experience with the mortality of one type of industrial equipment. In this case the median historical life expectancy was approximately 13 years, meaning that half of the machines lived longer and half were retired before the end of 13 years.

Project Life. Historical data of this sort may be useful in estimating the economic lives of the facilities provided for specific investment proposals, particularly when the proposals are for the replacement of existing equipment. The economic life of an investment project, however, may be very different from the life of any one of the assets required by the project. It may include buildings with a life of 50 years, production equipment with a life of 15 years, test equipment with a 3-year life, and working capital with an infinite life. The estimated life of such a project is determined not so much by the lives of the physical facilities as by the expected duration of the earnings stream generated by the project. This may encompass two or more life cycles of particular kinds of physical assets, or it may be shorter than a single cycle.

Life is usually estimated as the interval before major facilities replacement or renovation will probably be required or before market obsolescence is expected, whichever is shorter. To the extent that life is terminated by a progressive evaporation of the source of earnings, it may

Exhibit 26–3

ILLUSTRATIVE SURVIVAL CURVE FOR INDUSTRIAL EQUIPMENT

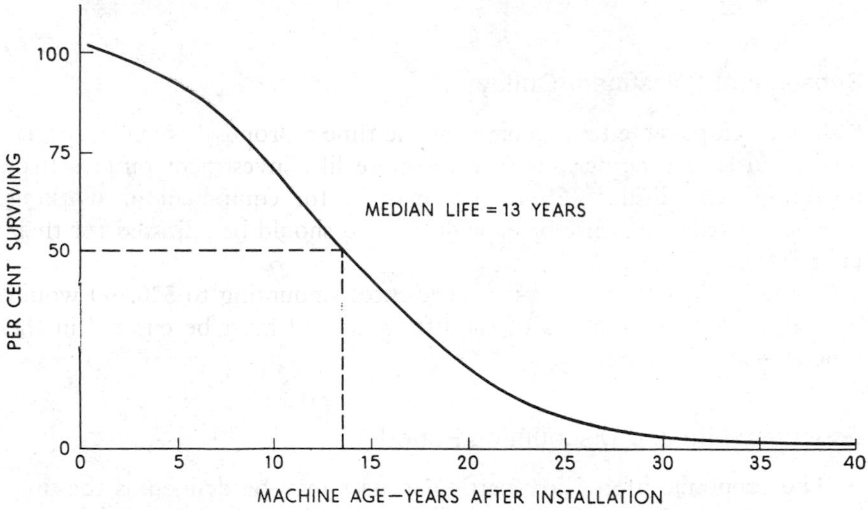

be possible to estimate life on the basis of the time pattern of the expected earnings stream. For example, if operating and maintenance costs are expected to rise as facilities age, the stream of anticipated cash flows may decline as time goes by. Life in this case may be estimated by finding the point at which the present value of expected future cash flows is less than the estimated disposal value of the assets.

Alternatively, as newer and better equipment becomes available in the future, the spread between the annual costs of operating and maintaining a machine purchased now and the comparable costs of the best machine available for purchase will increase. At some point this cost spread will be great enough to justify replacement even if operating and maintenance costs of the equipment purchased now have not risen substantially.

Unequal Lives. Another problem arises when the alternatives being compared differ in estimated life. For example, a meat-packer may be faced with the problem of acquiring transportation equipment to move its products from central packing plants to regional distribution points. It can purchase either railroad cars or tractor-trailer combinations. Railroad cars are expected to last 20 years, the tractor-trailers only 6.

One way of attacking this problem is to repeat the investment cycle for the shorter-lived facilities as many times as necessary to cover the expected life cycle of the longer-lived alternative. Thus the meat-packer would need to use 3⅓ tractor-trailer cycles to provide comparability with the 20-year railroad car life. An estimate of the salvage value of the fourth tractor-trailer investment would have to be inserted into the timetable at the end of 20 years to make the time periods comparable.

The alternative to this procedure is to define the discounting period in terms of the life of the shorter-lived alternative. Unfortunately, this requires an estimate of the recoverable value of the longer-lived facilities at this intermediate point, and intermediate resale values may not be an adequate reflection of the service value of the equipment at this point in time. If used equipment markets were perfect, the estimated resale value at any point in time would be an accurate reflection of the present value of the future services of the equipment, but markets are not perfect. Resale values tend to drop sharply in the early years of ownership and then decline more gradually as the equipment ages. For this reason, the use of intermediate salvage value for long-lived equipment is likely to penalize the longer-lived alternative.

Fortunately, errors in these forecasts are seldom as serious as it might seem. At the discounting rates that are used in capital expenditure analysis, cash flows that take place more than 15 years ahead have relatively little effect on the total present value of the project. The present value of $100,000 15 years hence, discounted at 10 percent, is only $23,900. This dampens the effects of errors in the salvage value estimates.

For the modernization proposal, management estimates that the plant could remain in operation for about 10 years before another major renovation would be required, and all calculations will be based on a 10-year life.

Operating Cash Flows

The modernization expenditures are expected to reduce operating costs and permit the company to accept certain orders that it is not now equipped to handle. Although the cash costs of operating the plant would undoubtedly rise as the facilities grew older, the difference between the before-tax cash flows associated with the company's current facilities and those incurred in operating the renovated facilities would be relatively constant at $30,000 a year.

Allocations. Increments in interdepartmental allocations of service department costs and other internal charges and credits often correspond poorly to the changes in cash flows. One company, for instance, applies factory overhead to products by means of a predetermined burden rate of $2 a direct labor dollar. It is very unlikely, however, that the company will save $2 in overhead for every dollar of direct labor it saves. In fact, most labor-saving investments actually increase total company overhead rather than the other way around.

Interdepartmental cost allocations can be misleading in a very similar way. In both cases, the effects on indirect costs should be estimated explicitly, not by applying a figure representing average full cost. The incremental principle should be kept clearly in mind: How will the choice of one alternative instead of another affect total cash flows for the company as a whole?

In the example, renovation of the facilities would decrease the amount of floor space required and would reduce the internal space charge for the modernized operation. The opportunity cost of the space saved is zero, however, and the cash flow estimate therefore has ignored this apparent difference in costs.

Income Taxes. Although depreciation represents a cost allocation rather than a current cash flow, it does affect the amount of taxes paid by the company as a whole. The depreciation figures used to estimate this amount are the figures allowed for tax purposes, of course, rather than those used for internal or external reporting.

The renovation proposal, it will be recalled, calls for before-tax incremental outlays totaling $108,000. Of this amount, $7,000 would be immediately deductible from taxable income, and $5,000 represents working capital which is not depreciable. This leaves three parts of the initial outlay to affect taxes on the incremental operating cash flows:

	Before-Tax Cash Flow	Tax Basis	Depreciation Rate for Tax Purposes
New equipment................	−$ 90,000	$ 90,000	20% of declining balance
Surplus equipment incorporated in the project..................	− 12,000	20,000	
Total equipment required........	−$102,000	$110,000	
Equipment replaced by the project.	+ 6,000	1,000	$500 a year
Net equipment required.........	−$ 96,000	$109,000	

Depreciation on the surplus equipment should be deducted because it will be included on the annual tax returns in this way only if the proposal is accepted. It therefore affects the incremental tax.

Taken together, the new and surplus equipment has a depreciable total (tax basis) of $110,000. The first year's tax depreciation is 20 percent of this, or $22,000. This reduces the tax basis to $88,000, and the tax depreciation for the second year is 20 percent of $88,000, or $17,600.

The depreciation calculations for the entire 10-year period are summarized in Exhibit 26–4. For simplicity, declining-balance depreciation has been used for the full 10 years; in practice, a slightly more complicated schedule is likely to be necessary. We have also assumed that retirements will be zero and that the additional expenditures at the end of five years are added in full to the tax base. Finally, we have assumed that tax depreciation will be based on the estimated life of the project rather than some other amount. These assumptions are seldom wholly valid. They make the illustration easier to follow, but they should not be used in a practical application without verification.

Exhibit 26–4
DEPRECIATION ON NEW AND RETAINED FACILITIES

Year	(1) Tax Basis, Start of Year	(2) Additions	(3) Tax Depreciation 20% × [(1) + (2)]	(4) Tax Basis, End of Year (1) + (2) − (3)
1	$110,000	...	$22,000	$88,000
2	88,000	...	17,600	70,400
3	70,400	...	14,080	56,320
4	56,320	...	11,264	45,056
5	45,056	...	9,012	36,044
6	36,044	$20,000	11,209	44,835
7	44,835	...	8,967	35,868
8	35,868	...	7,174	28,694
9	28,694	...	5,739	22,955
10	22,955	...	4,591	18,364

The tax depreciation figures in Exhibit 26–4 do not represent incremental tax depreciation. If the proposal is rejected, the standby equipment will be kept. Tax depreciation of $500 a year will be recorded for the first two years, until the equipment is fully depreciated. This means that incremental tax depreciation for each of the first two years is $500 less than the figures shown in Exhibit 26–4.

The deduction of depreciation on the replaced equipment may be more easily understood if it is recognized as a simple time shift. If the proposal is accepted, the equipment will be replaced and $1,000 will be deducted immediately from taxable income. If the proposal is rejected, on the other hand, the equipment will be retained and the $1,000 will be deducted from taxable income during the next two years.

After-Tax Cash Flows. One way to compute the after-tax cash flow is to compute after-tax net income and add back depreciation and other incremental tax deductions that do not represent current cash outlays. Another is to compute the present value of the so-called *tax shield,* the effect of depreciation and similar charges on future income taxes.

Exhibit 26–5

CALCULATION OF AFTER-TAX OPERATING CASH FLOWS

Year	(1) Cash Flow before Taxes	(2) Tax Depreciation*	(3) Taxable Income (1) − (2)	(4) Income Tax 40% × (3)	(5) Cash Flow after Taxes (1) − (4)
1..............	$ 25,000	$ 21,500	$ 3,500	$ 1,400	$ 23,600
2:.............	25,000	17,100	7,900	3,160	21,840
3..............	25,000	14,080	10,920	4,368	20,632
4..............	25,000	11,264	13,736	5,494	19,506
5..............	25,000	9,012	15,988	6,395	18,605
6..............	25,000	11,209	13,791	5,516	19,484
7..............	25,000	8,967	16,033	6,413	18,587
8..............	25,000	7,174	17,826	7,130	17,870
9..............	25,000	5,739	19,261	7,704	17,296
10.............	25,000	4,591	20,409	8,164	16,836
Total..........	$250,000	$110,636	$139,364	$55,744	$194,256

* The figure for each of the first two years differs from that shown in Exhibit 26–4 by $500, placing it on an incremental basis, as explained in the text.

Probably the clearest format is the one illustrated in Exhibit 26–5. With the before-tax figures in the left-hand column, the three middle columns are used to compute the income tax effect. The after-tax cash flow is then found by deducting the tax from the before-tax cash flow.

Notice how the declining-charge depreciation has changed the constant annual before-tax cash flow into a stream of gradually declining amounts. This makes this proposal more valuable than if only the straight-line method were available.

End-of-Life Salvage Value

End-of-life salvage value consists of the after-tax amount realizable from liquidation of the working capital and sale of the facilities. Alternatively, it is equal to the internal value of the assets to the company at the end of the project's life, if this is greater than liquidation value.

Suppose that the estimated liquidation value of the working capital 10 years from now is equal to its book value for tax purposes ($5,000), and that the liquidation value of the equipment would be $20,000. From the bottom line of Exhibit 26–4 we find that the book value of the equipment would be $18,364, leaving a taxable gain of $1,636. At a tax rate of 40 percent, the tax would be $654 and the after-tax cash flow would be $5,000 + $20,000 − $654 = $24,346.

This is not the incremental amount, however. The after-tax figures should represent differences between the cash flows available if the proposal is accepted and those available if it is rejected. If the project is turned down, the company will retain its rights to the standby equipment that will be sold if the proposal is accepted. Suppose that the liquidation value of this equipment 10 years from now would be $1,500. This amount would be fully taxable, since the equipment would be fully depreciated after only two years. The tax would be $600 and the after-tax amount would be $900. The incremental end-of-life salvage value, therefore, would be $24,346 − $900 = $23,446.

Calculation of Present Value

All of the cash flows for the modernization proposal are summarized in Exhibit 26–6. If the company requires an after-tax return on investment

Exhibit 26–6

CALCULATION OF PRESENT VALUE

Years from Now	Investment Cash Flow after Taxes	Operating Cash Flow after Taxes	Total Cash Flow after Taxes	Present Value @ 10%	
				Multiplier*	Amount
0..............	−$104,100	. . .	−$104,100	1.000	−$104,100
1..............	. . .	+$23,600	+ 23,600	0.909	+ 21,452
2..............	. . .	+ 21,840	+ 21,840	0.826	+ 18,040
3..............	. . .	+ 20,632	+ 20,632	0.751	+ 15,495
4..............	. . .	+ 19,506	+ 19,506	0.683	+ 13,323
5..............	− 20,000	+ 18,605	− 1,395	0.621	− 866
6..............	. . .	+ 19,484	+ 19,484	0.564	+ 10,989
7..............	. . .	+ 18,587	+ 18,587	0.513	+ 9,535
8..............	. . .	+ 17,870	+ 17,870	0.467	+ 8,345
9..............	. . .	+ 17,296	+ 17,296	0.424	+ 7,334
10..............	+ 23,446	+ 16,863	+ 40,309	0.386	+ 15,559
Total..........					+$ 15,106

* From Table 1, Appendix A.

of at least 10 percent, the present value of this proposal is $15,106, as shown in the bottom line of the exhibit. This means that, if the estimates are correct, the future operating cash receipts will be large enough to pay back the amounts invested ($104,100 and $20,000) and pay interest on these amounts at an annual rate of 10 percent, with enough left over to increase the company's value by $15,106. Other things being equal, this proposal should be accepted.

Selecting the Right Bench Mark

In most cases, the above calculations would be correct. Sometimes, however, the implied alternative of continuing operations as they are now is not the relevant bench mark. Perhaps the product can be manufactured elsewhere in the company, using equipment that is already available. Or, the present facility may no longer meet local safety standards and cannot be operated without renovation.

In the present case, the problem is slightly different. The plant could operate for another 10 years, but the operation would be too unprofitable to justify keeping it going on that basis. Suppose that the company could liquidate the present plant, equipment, and working capital now for $500,000 after taxes. If the plant were kept open, its annual operating cash flow after taxes would be about $60,000, but routine replacement expenditures would run about $40,000 a year. At the end of 10 years the plant, equipment, and working capital would bring in about $400,000, again after taxes.

Exhibit 26–7

PRESENT VALUE OF CONTINUING PRESENT OPERATION

Years from Now	Cash Flow after Taxes			Present Value @ 10%	
	If Sell Now	If Keep	Difference	Multiplier	Amount
0....................	+$500,000	...	−$500,000	1.000	−$500,000
1 to 10.............	...	+$ 20,000 a year	+ 20,000 a year	6.145	+ 122,900
10.................	...	+ 400,000	+ 400,000	0.386	+ 154,400
Total..............					−$222,700

These figures are summarized in Exhibit 26–7. It is clear that unless something drastic can be done to improve the cash flows, the plant should be closed.

This being the case, continued operation is no longer the relevant bench mark. The question now is whether the proposed modernization is good enough to restore this operation to health. If not, the additional expenditure would be wasted. The comparison, in other words, should be between the proposal and the best available alternative, in this case to close down. The calculation is:

Present value if operated in present condition.................... −$222,700
Present value of contribution from renovation................... + 15,106
Net present value.. −$207,594

The renovation proposal is not good enough. Instead of pouring good money after bad, the company should close the plant and reinvest the proceeds elsewhere.

Uncertainty Adjustments

None of these calculations has reflected the uncertainties inherent in the estimates. Two aspects of uncertainty must be considered:

1. Uncertainty as to future value of an important independent variable (such as aggregate disposable personal income).
2. Uncertainty as to the parameter, or the relationship, between a given value of an independent variable (disposable personal income) and the value of a dependent variable (e.g., product sales).

For example, suppose that aggregate disposable personal income in a given market area is an important factor in determining the level of sales of a new product. Personal income is the net result of many forces operating within this market area, and the exact level of personal income cannot be forecast with certainty. The best that the forecaster can hope to do is to estimate the probabilities associated with each possible level of personal income. He can make statements as to the expected value (the average of all possible values weighted by the percentage probability of each) and the dispersion around this value. From this he can make statements as to probabilities, such as that there is a 95 percent probability that personal income will be between x and y next year.

As to the second aspect of uncertainty: even if it were possible to predict personal income with complete certainty, the relationship between personal income and sales of the product could be forecast only in terms of probabilities. Again the analyst is faced with the problem of forecasting the frequency distribution of possible outcomes for a given level of personal income.

The most elaborate way of dealing with these twin uncertainties is to multiply the two probability distributions for each of the cash flows to obtain a combined distribution of the possible values of that cash flow. Unfortunately, the complexity of this method places severe limits on its usefulness.

Another possibility, still very sophisticated but often feasible, is to construct a decision tree, a series of "if . . . , then . . ." statements, in which a probability figure is attached to each major possible outcome. This gives management a visual image of the range of ultimate possibilities and the relative likelihood of each. It also provides an analytical structure that management can use to organize its thinking.[5]

A cruder approach is to bracket the anticipated cash flows with pessimistic and optimistic estimates. Pessimistic figures, for example, might indicate a negative present value of, say, $20,000 for the renovation proposal, whereas optimistic figures might yield a positive present value of $80,000. This is crude in that it ignores the probabilities associated with the various outcomes, but it does give management some feel for the risks associated with estimating errors.

---

[5] For an extended discussion, see David B. Hertz, "Risk Analysis in Capital Investment," *Harvard Business Review*, January–February 1964, pp. 95–106, and "Investment Policies that Pay Off," *Harvard Business Review*, January–February 1968, pp. 96–108; also John F. Magee, "Decision Trees for Decision Making," *Harvard Business Review*, July–August 1964, pp. 126–38, and "How to Use Decision Trees in Capital Investment," *Harvard Business Review*, September–October 1964, pp. 79–96.

The Sunk Cost Fallacy

Despite general understanding of the incremental principle, capital expenditure decisions are sometimes influenced by the amounts spent in the past to provide equipment or to develop new products. Suppose, for example, that an automobile company has spent $200 million to design, test, tool, and market a new model. Sales have been disappointing and management is considering discontinuing the model. The first year's operating loss, as shown on the company's internal profit report, was (in millions):

Sales..		$400
Less: Out-of-pocket operating costs...........................	$380	
Amortization of past tooling and development costs........	80	460
Net operating loss...		$(60)

One mistake would be to conclude that the company must continue the model because it has not yet recovered its initial investment. The $120 million of the original $200 million development cost that has not yet been charged to expense is irrelevant to the decision. The question is not whether all past costs have been recovered or charged to expense, but rather whether future receipts from sale of the product are likely to cover future outlays with enough left over to justify continued expenditure of management time and continued investment of liquid resources.

A second and perhaps more common mistake is to decide that the new model should not be continued unless its future revenues will cover not only future costs but depreciation of past outlays as well. For example, assume that the company is considering the following profit plan for the next year (in millions):

Sales..		$450
Less: Out-of-pocket operating costs...........................	$400	
Amortization of past tooling and development costs........	60	460
Estimated net operating loss.................................		$(10)

A recommendation based on net profit rather than incremental profit would be to discontinue the model rather than incur a $10 million loss, despite the forecast of a $50 million incremental cash profit.

These are two illustrations of the sunk cost fallacy, the notion that costs not yet recovered are somehow relevant for decision making. The relevant concept in both cases is opportunity cost: What is the present salvage value of the investment, and by how much will that salvage value decline if the investment is not liquidated now?

Treatment of Interest

Interest on long-term debt is a component of the cost of capital. The discounting process allows for this component, and neither interest nor debt amortization should be deducted explicitly from project cash flows even when the project is financed specifically by a particular issue of long-term debt.

Nonseasonal short-term interest-bearing debt should be classified as long-term debt for this purpose, because it provides part of the long-term capital to finance the project. Interest on seasonal short-term debt, on the other hand, is an explicit cash outlay that is not provided for by the discounting process. It should be deducted in computing annual cash flows. Similarly, interest on any seasonal investments of project funds can be regarded as a cash inflow for the project.

INTERNAL RATE OF RETURN

Management is used to return-on-investment figures as measures of investment yield. This suggests that the profitability of investment proposals might usefully be expressed as a return-on-investment ratio instead of as net present value.

Unfortunately, a simple ratio of average annual earnings to the average book value of the investment during the project's life is inaccurate because it overlooks the vital element of timing.[6] Instead, many companies use the internal rate of return, defined as that rate of discount at which the sum of the positive present values is equal to the sum of the negative present values. In other words, the internal rate of return is the rate at which the net present value of the cash flows is zero.

Calculating the Rate

The equations for the internal rate of return cannot be solved explicitly. Instead, a cumbersome trial-and-error procedure must be used. Although computer programs are available to take the burden out of this, it may be useful to do it once manually, using a simpler set of cash flows than in the previous illustration.

Suppose that a $48,000 outlay will produce cash flows of $10,000 a year for 10 years, with no end-of-life salvage. The first step in computing the rate of return for this project is to discount all of the cash flows at some rate that seems likely to be close to the true rate. Suppose that we choose 15 percent as this first trial rate. Using the multiplier for 15 percent on the 10-year line in Table 2 of Appendix A (5.019), we find that the present value of the cash inflows exceeds the present value of the initial outlay by $2,190:

```
Outlay: $48,000 × 1.000.........................     −$48,000
Receipts: $10,000 × 5.019.......................     + 50,190
Net present value...............................     +$ 2,190
```

[6] An even simpler measure in the *payback period*, the number of years that will elapse before cumulative net cash receipts are just equal to the initial outlay. This measure ignores economic life and reflects the timing of the cash flows only crudely and incompletely.

This indicates that the project earns more than 15 percent on the investment, but it doesn't show how much more. The next step is to try another rate, higher than the first. Discounting at 20 percent, the present value of the cash receipts is $41,920, and this is $6,080 less than the present value of the outlay. This means that the project earns less than 20 percent. The true before-tax rate of return is somewhere in between, approximately one quarter of the distance between 15 percent and 20 percent:

$$\text{Approximate rate} = 15\% + \frac{\$2,190}{\$2,190 + \$6,080} \times (20\% - 15\%) = 16.3\%$$

The Incremental Rate of Return

The internal rate of return is very easy to misuse. Suppose that the company's minimum acceptable rate of return is 12 percent, and that an alternative proposal to the one described above has been made: to buy a different kind of equipment at a price of $64,000. The annual cash cost saving with this machine would be $13,000 instead of $10,000. Once again we could compute the internal rate of return by trial and error:

	Present Value at 15%		Present Value at 20%	
	Factor	Amount	Factor	Amount
Outlay..........................	1.000	−$64,000	1.000	−$64,000
Inflow ($13,000 a year).............	5.019	+ 65,247	4.192	+ 54,496
Net present value.................		+$ 1,247		−$ 9,504

The overall rate of return here is approximately 15.6 percent. Although this is slightly less than the 16.3 percent calculated for the original proposal, this second proposal is actually the better of the two. What is relevant is not the return on the full $64,000 but rather the return on the added $16,000 investment that would be required if this more expensive equipment were to be purchased instead of the equipment represented by the $48,000 outlay. If this added investment produces a rate of return in excess of the company's minimum requirements, then the additional expenditure should be made.

In this case the incremental cash savings available to justify the additional investment outlay are $3,000 a year ($13,000 less the $10,000 obtainable with the lesser expenditure). This works out to a rate of return of approximately 13.4 percent:

	Present Value at 13%		Present Value at 14%	
	Factor	Amount	Factor	Amount
Outlay..........................	1.000	−$16,000	1.000	−$16,000
Inflow ($3,000 a year)..............	5.426	+ 16,278	5.216	+ 15,648
Net present value.................		+$ 278		−$ 352

This means that the incremental cash flows are more than adequate to meet the company's 12 percent standard, and the proposal to buy the more expensive equipment should be accepted.

The net present value method reaches this same conclusion by a simpler route. The cash flow stream for each proposal is discounted at 12 percent, the preferred alternative being the one that offers the greater present value at this rate. The results of this computation are summarized in Exhibit 26–8. The present value of the receipts from proposal B exceeds the outlay by $9,450. The comparable figure for proposal A is only $8,500, indicating that proposal B should be selected. No differential calculations are necessary, although a difference column is introduced for

Exhibit 26–8

PRESENT VALUE OF MUTUALLY EXCLUSIVE PROPOSALS

		Proposal A	Proposal B	Difference (B − A)
(1)	Initial outlay......................	−$48,000	−$64,000	−$16,000
	Cash receipts:			
(2)	Annual amount...................	+$10,000	+$13,000	+$ 3,000
(3)	Discount factor (Table 2).........	5.650	5.650	5.650
(4)	Present value at 12%, (2) × (3)....	+$56,500	+$73,450	+$16,950
	Net present value, (1) + (4).........	+$ 8,500	+$ 9,450	+$ 950

added emphasis; nor is it necessary to perform trial-and-error calculations to find the internal rate of return for each proposal and for the increment between them.

In this simple example, either method would lead to the correct solution, but there are circumstances, by no means rare, in which it is not clear in what order to take the various alternatives so as to provide information on incremental rate of return. For example, suppose that there are three alternatives: one requiring no immediate outlay, another calling for an outlay of $60,000 now and $60,000 two years from now, and the third requiring a lump-sum outlay of $100,000 now. The second alternative obviously requires the greatest total investment, but part of this investment can be deferred for two years. The greatest immediate outlay is called for by the third alternative. In this case, it is far simpler to apply the present value test to the alternatives than to compute differential rates of return.[7]

---

[7] For a discussion of situations in which the internal rate of return and net present value will point to different decisions, see James Porterfield, *Investment Decisions and Capital Costs* (Englewood Cliffs, N.J.: Prentice-Hall, 1965).

ADMINISTERING THE CAPITAL EXPENDITURE PROGRAM

The methods used to administer a capital expenditure program may be almost as important as the evaluative techniques, and therefore deserve a brief description.[8]

Preparing the Capital Budget

At the time of annual budget preparation, each division manager or department head is asked to submit a tentative list of the proposals that he plans to make during the coming year, together with a brief justification of each. These lists are combined with schedules of planned expenditures on projects that will already be approved and under way at the beginning of the year.

The consolidated expenditure schedule is then presented to the top management budget committee. If the estimated supply of funds falls short of the demand, the committee will have to ration the funds to the more profitable projects or explore alternative ways of raising additional funds. If the supply of funds exceeds the demand, management may raise the dividend or use the excess funds to improve its financial position. It may also inaugurate a vigorous program of seeking out new investment opportunities, taking the company into new products, increasing expenditures on research and development, or acquiring other companies.

Appropriation Requests

Budget approval seldom serves as the final authorization to undertake a capital expenditure project. Most systems require the submission of a written appropriation request for each proposal at the time the sponsor is ready to begin committing funds to it. The main purpose is to give the sponsor more time to plan as well as an opportunity to consider events that have occurred since the budget was prepared. It also gives the firm more flexibility in that all of its resources are not fully committed at the start of the year. If an emergency or an extraordinarily profitable opportunity arises during the year, it can be initiated at once without upsetting the overall budget figure. It is only necessary to delay or cancel other projects if additional investment funds cannot be obtained on short notice from other sources.

Each appropriation request must show the reasons why the sponsor believes it should be undertaken. For many projects, this is a detailed estimate of future cash flows, either from reduced costs or expansion of capacity. For others the justification is more qualitative, with the sponsor's assertion that the benefits will be substantial even though presently

---

[8] For a description of representative practice, see National Industrial Conference Board, *Managing Capital Expenditures* (New York, 1963).

unmeasurable. One part of good capital budget administration is to encourage efforts to estimate benefits as well as costs.

Approval Authority

While proposals may originate anywhere in the organization, the manager who will be responsible for the results of a project is usually expected to sponsor the request. Typically, each proposal must be approved by each person in the sponsor's chain of command, up to the level at which final approval authority is lodged.

In larger firms, final approval authority is usually delegated to managers at lower levels. Department heads may approve individual projects smaller than, say, $10,000; division managers may have authority to approve projects up to some higher amount, such as $100,000; and the president may be able to approve projects up to amounts as large as $500,000 or even $1 million, the limit depending on the size of the company and its past history. Final decisions on major projects are almost always made or ratified by the board of directors.

Delegated approval authority is almost always limited and subject to audit. Lower level managers are still expected to apply company profitability standards to proposals within their authority limits, and they are usually subject to limits on the total amounts that they can approve.

Project Coordination and Review

Once an appropriation request is approved, someone must be assigned the responsibility for implementing the project. For small projects, this is usually the task of the manager who will be responsible for managing the new facilities. For major expenditures, it may be a full-time assignment lasting many months.

After the full project expenditure has been made, the actual and budgeted outlays are reported to the capital budget committee or controller's department. If the actual expenditure has exceeded the budget by a significant amount, the person in charge of the project will have to submit an explanation, usually in writing.

Some firms have experimented with post-completion audits of capital expenditures. A year after the project has been placed in operation, or longer if necessary, a study is made to ascertain whether the project realized the anticipated benefits. Unfortunately, these audits have seldom been very successful. Typically, the assumptions under which the proposal was made no longer hold, and the opportunity costs are not recorded in the accounts. Furthermore, except for very large projects, the portion of the company's profit stemming from a specific capital investment is very difficult to isolate.

The best control devices in any case are careful scrutiny of individual proposals and incorporation of the estimated results into departmental operating budgets. Although the results of individual projects cannot be isolated, their combined effects can be examined as part of the conventional periodic performance review.

SUMMARY

The company's future depends heavily on the wisdom of its current capital expenditure decisions. Development of expenditure proposals requires imagination and foresight, accompanied by a clear understanding of how project profitability should be measured.

The desirability of individual proposals should be measured, insofar as possible, by forecasts of the cash flows that they would generate. These forecasts should be combined in such a way that the profitability of the proposal can be compared with a companywide standard of minimum acceptable profitability, usually based on the company's cost of investment capital.

A good way to bring these figures together is to discount the anticipated cash flows at the minimum acceptable rate of return to find their net present value. If the present value of the cash inflows exceeds the present value of the cash outflows, the proposal ordinarily should be accepted.

The most difficult problem for the accountant is to prepare or review estimates of the anticipated cash flows. Because taxation affects different kinds of cash flows differently, all estimates should be placed on an after-tax basis, and opportunity costs should be clearly recognized. Investment outlays, operating cash flows, and end-of-life salvage values all enter into the analyses, and the bulk of this chapter has been devoted to a discussion of the problems of measuring these three kinds of cash flows.

EXERCISES AND PROBLEMS

1.* Using the tables in Appendix A, compute net present value at 10 percent and the internal rate of return for each of the following series of cash flows. All figures are stated on an after-tax basis.

a) Initial outlay...................................... $10,000
    Annual cash receipts............................... $ 1,750
    Estimated life..................................... 10 years
    Salvage.. None
b) Initial outlay...................................... $10,000
    Annual cash receipts:
        First five years............................... $ 2,000
        Second five years.............................. $ 1,500
    Estimated life..................................... 10 years
    Salvage.. None

---

* Solutions to problems marked with an asterisk can be found in Appendix B.

c) Initial outlay.. $10,000
   Annual cash receipts:
     First five years.................................. $ 1,500
     Second five years................................ $ 2,000
   Estimated life.................................... 10 years
   Salvage.. None

d) Initial outlay.. $10,000
   Annual cash receipts............................... $ 1,350
   Estimated life.................................... 10 years
   Salvage.. $ 4,000

e) Initial outlay.. $10,000
   Annual cash receipts............................... $ 1,750
   Estimated life.................................... 15 years
   Salvage.. None

2. A capital expenditure proposal is expected to produce the following cash flows:

Outlays:
   Two years before operations commence.................. $10,000
   One year before operations commence................... 30,000
   One day before operations commence.................... 20,000
   At the end of 10 years of operations.................. 20,000
Receipts:
   Each year for the first three years of operations........... 5,000
   Each year for the next 10 years....................... 10,000
   Each year for the next five years..................... 8,000
   At the end of 18 years of operations.................. 12,000

a) Compute the net present value of this proposal at a discount rate of 15 percent.

b) Calculate the internal rate of return.

3. The ABC Company is considering a proposal to buy materials handling equipment to achieve economies in its warehousing operation. The total cost of the equipment, together with auxiliary investments in pallets and supplies, is $30,000. The equipment is expected to be useful for seven years before replacement becomes economical. Scrap value is expected to be negligible. Annual cash savings are expected to be $5,000 the first year, $7,000 the second year, and $8,000 in each subsequent year as the warehouse reaches full-capacity operation. The ABC Company requires a minimum return on investment of 20 percent a year before taxes. Assuming that the decision is to be based on before-tax cash flows, should this proposal be accepted?

4. Peter Brown has an opportunity to buy a certain business, paying $50,000 immediately and $20,000 at the end of each of the next five years. It is anticipated that the net cash receipts from the operation of this business will amount to $25,000 a year for the next 15 years and $15,000 a year for the 5 years after that. Mr. Brown wishes to retire 20 years from now and believes that he can sell the business at that time for $30,000. If he buys the business, he expects to spend $2,000 a year on capital replacements and improvements during the first five years, $3,000 a year during the next five years, $4,000 a year during the third five years, and nothing thereafter.

The above figures do not provide for any compensation for Mr. Brown's services. If he buys the business, he must leave his present job, in which he is earning $8,000 a year. Furthermore, if he buys the new business, he must liquidate certain investments of comparable risk that now yield a return on investment of 10 percent before taxes.

Would you advise Mr. Brown to make the purchase? Show your calculations.

5. Frank Destry has been offered the opportunity to submit a bid for the right to provide catering services in a private club. The contract would run for eight years, and Mr. Destry estimates that his net cash receipts from the catering business would amount to approximately $12,000 a year. If he accepts the contract, he will have to make an initial investment of $2,000 in equipment. What is the maximum price that Mr. Destry can afford to bid for the catering privilege, assuming that he requires a 14 percent return on his investment?

6.* A proposal is made to purchase and install a new machine to replace an existing machine. The existing machine has a book value of $20,000, current salvage value of $8,000, and annual depreciation of $3,000. Annual out-of-pocket operating cost is now $10,000.

The replacement machine would cost $50,000 delivered. It would cost $10,000 to train employees to operate the machine, and this amount can be written off immediately for tax purposes. An immediate tax credit of 7 percent of the capitalizable outlay is available as an investment credit to reduce current taxes. Annual out-of-pocket operating cost of the new machine would be $3,200.

The first year's tax depreciation on the new machine would be 30 percent of the amount capitalized. The income tax rate is 40 percent.

a) Compute the net incremental after-tax investment outlay required by this proposal.
b) Compute the after-tax net cash operating savings for the first year of operation of the replacement machine.

7. Company X is considering a proposal to increase the degree of automation in one of its manufacturing departments. The following estimates have been made:

(1) Initial outlay, $100,000, of which $20,000 would be expensed immediately for tax purposes. No investment credit would be applicable.
(2) The capitalized portion of the initial outlay would be depreciated for tax purposes at a straight-line rate of 10 percent per year.
(3) The net annual before-tax cash savings would be $22,000, starting immediately after installation.
(4) The facilities would be obsolete at the end of six years of operation, at which time they would be dismantled at a cash cost of $5,000 and sold for scrap. Scrap recovery at that time would be $1,000.
(5) The company's effective income tax rate is expected to be 50 percent.

Compute the following:

a) After-tax initial outlay.
b) Expected after-tax annual cash inflow for the second year.

c) Anticipated effect of this proposal on the company's reported after-tax net income for the third year.

d) After-tax cash flow at the end of six years, when the facilities are dismantled.

8. The Artling Corporation manufactures four products in four identical processing operations. The only differences among the four products are in the raw materials used. The facilities are completely interchangeable, although they differ slightly, with newer machines having higher depreciation and generally lower operating costs than older machines. Processing costs (that is, all costs other than material costs) are determined by the machines used, not by the product being manufactured.

The company is now considering a proposal to acquire a fifth set of processing facilities to manufacture a new, higher grade of product, using a more expensive raw material that has just come on the market. All machines, new as well as old, would still be completely interchangeable, but the new machine would probably be used to make the new product.

The following table shows all of the costs per pound that would be incurred in the factory to operate the machines:

Product	Machine Used	Selling Price	Materials Cost	Depreciation Cost	Other Costs	Profit Margin
A........	1	$0.60	$0.15	$0.12	$0.31	$0.02
B........	2	0.66	0.20	0.12	0.30	0.04
C........	3	0.73	0.25	0.13	0.28	0.07
D........	4	0.81	0.30	0.13	0.29	0.09
E*........	5*	0.90	0.35	0.14	0.29	0.12

* Proposed.

Depreciation cost per pound is based on estimated annual production of 200,000 pounds of each product and an estimated life of 10 years. Estimated salvage value of the production equipment is zero; in fact, once the facilities are installed, their only market value is their scrap value.

In support of the proposal to add the fifth product and corresponding facilities, the sales manager of the Artling Company has pointed out that this would increase the company's gross profit margin by $24,000 on an added sales volume of 200,000 pounds annually. Variable selling and administrative costs amount to 5 percent of sales.

Compute the incremental annual cash flow that you would use in deciding whether the proposed investment is adequately profitable. State your reasoning. (Note that you are not asked to indicate whether the proposed investment in new facilities would be adequately profitable to justify the required outlays. This is solely an exercise in estimating the annual earnings data that would enter into the evaluation of this problem. You may ignore income taxes.)

9. Many companies evaluate at least some of their capital expenditure proposals on a before-tax basis. That is, before-tax cash flows are tested against a

standard representing the before-tax cost of capital. The main reason for doing this is to simplify the calculations.

You have the following figures in connection with a proposal to purchase and install new factory equipment:

The company's cost of capital is 10 percent after taxes; this is assumed to be equivalent to 20 percent before taxes.

Initial investment outlays amount to $80,000, of which $30,000 can be expensed immediately for tax purposes.

The capitalized portion of the initial outlay is subject to special amortization treatment. Fifty percent of the capitalized cost can be written off in equal annual installments during the first five years. The remainder is subject to depreciation at the normal straight-line rate of 6 percent per year, including the first five years.

The investment is expected to produce net cash receipts (before taxes) of $16,500 a year for the first five years, $11,500 a year for the next five years, and $6,500 a year for the third five years.

It is expected that the facilities will be retired at the end of 15 years and that salvage value will be $5,000.

All taxes are to be computed on the basis of a 50 percent tax rate.

Analyze this proposal on both a before-tax and an after-tax basis. How, if at all, would your recommendation to management be different if you used the before-tax basis instead of the after-tax basis?

10.* The expected life of a facility proposal is 10 years, the installed cost will be $50,000, and the expected end-of-life salvage value is zero. The equipment will replace facilities now in use that have a book value of $30,000 and a market value of $10,000. The remaining tax life of the old facilities is eight years.

Double-rate, declining-balance depreciation will be used on the new facilities, but the 7 percent investment credit is not available for tax purposes. The present facilities are being depreciated by the straight-line method down to an end-of-life salvage value of zero.

Estimated before-tax, before-depreciation cash savings amount to $20,000 per year. The tax rate is 50 percent, and all savings are assumed to take place at the end of each year.

a) Compute the incremental after-tax present value of this proposal at 10 percent.
b) Compute the incremental after-tax internal rate of return on this proposal.

11. A company is thinking of discontinuing manufacture and sale of product A. You are given the following information:

(1) The projected monthly income statement for product A is as follows:

Sales......................................		$80,000
Less:		
Cost of goods sold (standard)...............	$64,000	
Selling and administrative expenses..........	25,000	89,000
Net Income (Loss).........................		$(9,000)

(2) Product A is manufactured in two departments, and its standard unit   .
cost is as follows:

	Dept. X	Dept. Y	Total
Materials............	$1.00	$0.50	$1.50
Labor...............	1.50	0.75	2.25
Overhead............	3.00	1.25	4.25
Total...............	$5.50	$2.50	$8.00

(3) The budgeted overhead cost structure in the two departments is as
follows ("D.L.$" stands for "direct labor dollars"). Before using these
figures, see items (4) and (5) below.

	Dept. X	Dept. Y
Traceable fixed overhead.......	$40,000 per mo.	$20,000 per mo.
Traceable variable overhead....	$0.80 per D.L.$	$0.60 per D.L.$
Allocated costs..............	{ $20,000 per mo. +$0.20 per D.L.$	{ $ 6,000 per mo. +$0.20 per D.L.$
Standard monthly volume......	60,000 D.L.$	30,000 D.L.$

(4) A study reveals that traceable fixed costs in department Y include a
$2,000 step function for each 6,000 direct labor dollars—that is, fixed
costs increase by $2,000 a month any time that monthly departmental
production volume increases by a full 6,000 direct labor dollars. (If
volume increases by 11,000 direct labor dollars a month, the fixed cost
increase is still $2,000; but if the increase is 12,000 direct labor dollars,
the fixed cost goes up by $4,000 a month.) Traceable fixed costs in de-
partment X have no step function.

(5) Of the allocated costs, the only items likely to be eliminated by the
discontinuation of product A amount to $500 a month in department X
and 6 cents a direct labor dollar in department Y.

(6) Selling and administrative costs charged to product A include (a)
$5,000 a month for product advertising, free samples, product display
material, etc.; (b) 10 cents per sales dollar for salesmen's commissions
and patent royalty payments; (c) 4 cents per sales dollar as an allocation
of field selling expenses, market research, etc.; and (d) 11 cents per
sales dollar for the product's share of head office expenses. Total company costs in these latter two categories would be unaffected by the discontinuation of product A.

(7) The sales force estimates that sales of substitute products in the company's line could be increased by $10,000 a month if product A were
abandoned. The average ratio of variable profit to selling price for
these products is 40 percent, and the increased volume in these lines
would not affect fixed costs in any way.

(8) It is estimated that the only investment that would be released by withdrawal of product A from the market would be working capital with a
book value of $300,000. This figure includes inventories at their book

value of $150,000; before-tax proceeds from liquidation of these inventories would total about $110,000.

(9)   The income tax rate is 50 percent and the required minimum rate of return on capital expenditure proposals is 8 percent after taxes.

(10)   Remember that all figures except those given in items (8) and (9) are *monthly* figures.

Should product A be withdrawn from the market? Show and label your calculations, explaining your reasoning if necessary.

12. The Barnstable Company manufactures and distributes through retail outlets a line of electrical products and appliances. Distribution of the company's products is accomplished through 12 regional branch offices, each of which has responsibility for maintaining adequate inventories, granting customer credit, and for collecting accounts receivable. List prices are established in the head office of the Barnstable Company, but each branch manager has authority to set his own policy on discounts, returns, and allowances to meet competitive conditions in his region.

For a number of years the company has followed the practice of preparing income statements for each branch. The San Francisco branch profit has declined from approximately $50,000 a year five years ago to a loss of $38,000 last year. Last year's income statements for this branch and a somewhat larger branch at Los Angeles were as follows (in thousands):

	San Francisco	Los Angeles
Gross sales (at list prices).....................	$488	$675
Discounts, freight, returns, and allowances......	72	58
Net sales....................................	$416	$617
Manufacturing cost of goods sold (at standard)...	293	367
Gross margin...............................	$123	$250
Branch expenses:		
Salaries and commissions.....................	$ 73	$104
Travel and entertainment.....................	15	16
Office expense..............................	12	13
Bad debt losses.............................	5	3
Miscellaneous..............................	6	5
Total branch expenses......................	$111	$141
Branch margin..............................	$ 12	$109
Home office charges.........................	50	74
Branch Net Profit (Loss).....................	$(38)	$ 35

Capital invested at the branch consists of $90,000 in receivables (after deducting a provision for uncollectible accounts) and $50,000 in inventories. Because the branch has no depreciable assets, no depreciation charges are included in the branch expenses.

The controller of the Barnstable Company has undertaken an analysis to determine whether it would be profitable to close the San Francisco branch and serve the region from Los Angeles. Analysis of costs and expenses has produced the following estimates:

If the San Francisco branch remains in operation, branch margins at both the San Francisco and Los Angeles branches are likely to remain at last year's levels for the foreseeable future.

If the San Francisco branch were closed, approximately $400,000 in gross sales could be retained by salesmen working out of Los Angeles. Discounts, freight, returns, and allowances on these sales would total $60,000 a year. The product mix in the San Francisco area would be the same at this lower volume as at the current sales volume.

An analysis of the company's factory costs indicate that manufacturing costs are approximately 70 percent variable and 30 percent fixed at standard volumes.

Salesmen are paid a salary plus commission. Sales commissions are computed at 12 percent of net sales. In addition, each salesman receives a salary. If the San Francisco office were closed, two of its salesmen would be added to the Los Angeles sales force. All other San Francisco sales personnel, each with an annual salary of $2,000, would be transferred to other positions in the company, as replacements for other employees who are retiring or leaving the company.

Closing of the San Francisco office would eliminate completely all other San Francisco branch expenses, but it is estimated that expenses of the Los Angeles office would be increased by $36,000 per year in addition to the specific items mentioned above.

Home office administrative expense is distributed to the branches at 12 percent of net sales. Past experience has indicated, however, that the variable portion of these expenses is only 4 percent of net sales.

The Los Angeles investment in inventory and receivables would increase by $20,000 and $80,000, respectively, if the San Francisco branch were closed and the San Francisco area were served from Los Angeles.

After taxes at 50 percent, the company's minimum acceptable return on investment is 8 percent.

a) If you had to choose between operating the San Francisco branch and abandoning the territory entirely, what would you do? Show your calculations.

b) Given the added choice of serving the territory from Los Angeles, which of the three alternatives would you recommend? Show your calculations.

13.† Ace Publishing Company is in the business of publishing and printing guidebooks and directories. An outside printer has offered to do all of Ace Publishing's printing and shipping work for the next five years. If the proposal is accepted, Ace will close its print shop and shipping department.

Under the terms of the proposed contract, the volume of work done last year would be printed at a cost of $550,000 a year. From the information below, prepare an analysis of this proposal that will indicate whether it should be accepted.

—————
† Adapted from a uniform CPA examination.

(1) The company's cost accounts for the preceding fiscal year showed the following balances:

	Departments		
	Publishing	Printing	Shipping
Salaries and wages..............	$275,000	$154,000	$25,000
Materials and supplies............	50,000	250,000	10,000
Building occupancy..............	75,000	80,000	10,000
Equipment depreciation...........	5,000	40,000	5,000
Telephone and telegraph..........	12,000	3,700	300
General and administrative........	40,000	30,000	4,000
Total........................	$457,000	$557,700	$54,300

(2) A review of personnel required reveals the following:
  (a) All printing department personnel could be released except one clerk at $5,000, two layout men at $7,000 each, and one proof-reader at $6,000.
  (b) All shipping department personnel could be released except one mailing clerk, $4,000.
  (c) One cost clerk whose salary of $6,000 is now included in general and administrative cost could be released.
(3) Termination pay equal to three months' pay would be paid for all released personnel. This pay would be expensed immediately for tax purposes.
(4) The cost of envelopes and stamps for mailing material to an outside printer would be $5,000 a year.
(5) Printing and shipping room machinery having a net book value of $300,000 can be sold for $200,000. This disposal value is unlikely to change materially over the next five years.
(6) If printing is discontinued, the company will retain its present building, but will sublet a portion of the space at an annual rental of $50,000. Taxes, heat, light, and other occupancy costs will remain at current levels.
(7) Long-distance telephone and telegraph charges are identified and distributed to the responsible departments. The remainder of the telephone bill, representing basic service at a cost of $4,000, is now allocated in the ratio of 10 to publishing, 5 to printing, and 1 to shipping. The discontinuance of printing is expected to reduce the basic service cost by $500 a year.
(8) General and administrative expenses include the cost of payroll taxes, retirement and insurance premiums, and the like, amounting to approximately 10 percent of salaries and wages. This portion is charged to departments on the basis of total departmental payroll. Payroll taxes, etc., on termination pay (item [3] above) would amount to 8 percent, not 10 percent. All other general and administrative costs would be unaffected by discontinuation of printing.

(9) A $100,000 reduction in required working capital would be made possible by discontinuation of printing.

(10) Volume, prices, and wage rates are expected to remain approximately constant at last year's level for the next five years.

(11) If the company's printing and shipping facilities are retained, annual expenditures for equipment in these two departments will average $30,000 a year (capitalized for tax purposes), and annual equipment depreciation charges for tax purposes will remain approximately constant at their present levels for the next five years. (Assume that all property retired is fully depreciated; ignore any scrap values.)

(12) The effective income tax rate is 50 percent, both on operating income and on capital gains and losses. Taxable income from other sources permits the company to take full and immediate advantage of the tax credits arising out of losses or tax write-offs.

(13) The company's minimum rate of return on investment proposals is 10 percent after taxes.

CASE 26–1: SOVAD, S.A.[†]

Mr. Walter Weber, general manager of Sovad, S.A., looked across his desk at Mr. Karl Huber, the company's sales manager. Mr. Huber had just suggested that Sovad increase its capacity to manufacture automatic timing devices.

"All right," said Mr. Weber, "let's see if the profits from the increased sales will give us a big enough return on investment. As soon as you're ready, give Mr. Berner (the company's controller) your estimates of sales and what you'll need for advertising and sales promotion. He can work with purchasing and manufacturing to get the rest of the data he needs. I'll ask him to give me a recommendation on your proposal sometime next week."

Sovad, S.A. was a manufacturer of industrial controls and precision instruments, with headquarters and manufacturing facilities in Winterthur, Switzerland. Its manufacturing operations in 1967 were conducted entirely in Winterthur, but more than half of its 1967 sales were made in other countries.

First introduced in 1964, the company's automatic timers had been well received by Sovad's customers both at home and abroad. By 1967 Sovad was selling all that it could manufacture. Mr. Huber was convinced that he could expand his sales in Switzerland by large amounts if adequate factory capacity could be provided.

Before coming to Mr. Weber with his suggestion, Mr. Huber had discussed the idea of expansion with Mr. Gluck, the company's director of manufacturing. "Our Winterthur factory is already crowded," Mr.

---

† Copyright 1968 by l'Institut pour l'Etude des Méthodes de Direction de l'Entreprise (IMEDE), Lausanne, Switzerland. Reprinted by permission.

Gluck told him. "The authorities won't give us a building permit to expand it, but I know of some vacant space that we can rent in Zurich for Fr. 50,000 a year. We could put all the timer operations in there." Zurich is only 20 kilometers from Winterthur and Mr. Gluck was confident that he could supervise manufacturing operations in both places without difficulty.

Working with Mr. Gluck, Mr. Huber prepared the preliminary estimates shown in Table 1. As he gave this exhibit to Mr. Berner, Mr.

Table 1

ZURICH TIMER FACTORY

Preliminary Profitability Estimate

Sales (30,000 units at Fr. 50)		Fr. 1,500,000
Out of pocket expenses:		
Factory labor and materials (30,000 units at Fr. 28.40)	Fr. 852,000	
Rent	50,000	
Other factory costs (not including depreciation)	70,000	
Marketing expenses	160,000	
Total expenses		1,132,000
Profit contribution		Fr. 368,000
Equipment required:		
New equipment to be purchased	Fr. 250,000	
Old equipment, to be moved from Winterthur	0	
Cost of moving old equipment from Winterthur and installing it at Zurich	5,000	
Total		Fr. 255,000

$$\text{Payback period} = \frac{\text{Fr. } 255,000}{\text{Fr. } 368,000} = 0.69 \text{ years} = 8.3 \text{ months.}$$

Huber remarked that an eight-month payback period was hard to beat. He hoped that Mr. Berner wouldn't take too long to pass the proposal on to Mr. Weber for approval.

In the course of his examination of these figures, Mr. Berner discovered two things. First, the sales and expense figures given in Table 1 were not expected to be achieved until the third year of the new factory's operation. Second, they represented the *total* sales and expenses of the timers. Since the company was already selling 10,000 timers a year, Mr. Berner did not believe that the profit on these units should be used to justify the opening of the new factory. As he put it, "The data that we need are differential or incremental figures, the differences between having the new factory and not having it." Mr. Huber estimated that he would be able to sell 30,000 timers a year after a two-year introductory period. His detailed estimates of annual sales and marketing expenses are summarized in Table 2.

Mr. Berner knew that these volumes of sales would require sizable investments in working capital which Mr. Huber had omitted from

Table 2

ZURICH TIMER FACTORY

Estimated Annual Timer Sales
and Marketing Expenses

	Annual Sales		Annual Marketing Costs
	Units	Value	
If all timers are manufactured in Zurich:			
Year 1............................	20,000	Fr. 1,000,000	Fr. 260,000
Year 2............................	25,000	1,250,000	260,000
Year 3 and after..................	30,000	1,500,000	160,000
If timers are not manufactured in Zurich...	10,000	Fr. 500,000	Fr. 60,000

Table 1. On the basis of the company's past experience, he estimated that the cumulative balance of working capital required at the beginning of each year would be as follows:

If timers are manufactured in Zurich:
Year 1.................................... Fr. 700,000
Year 2.................................... 750,000
Year 3.................................... 800,000
If timers are not manufactured in Zurich............ Fr. 300,000

When questioned about the manufacturing cost estimates in Table 1, Mr. Gluck gave Mr. Berner the figures shown in Table 3. Mr. Gluck explained that if the Zurich factory were opened, all automatic timer production would be shifted to Zurich. If the expansion proposal were to be rejected, however, the cost of producing 10,000 timers a year at Winterthur would be Fr. 31 per unit plus Fr. 20,000 a year. All of these costs could be eliminated if operations were transferred to Zurich.

Mr. Berner also questioned Mr. Gluck about the equipment that would be moved from Winterthur to Zurich. "That is the old test equipment that we are now replacing here in Winterthur," he replied. "It's perfectly adequate for the timers, and it saves us from buying new equipment for

Table 3

ZURICH TIMER FACTORY

Estimated Factory Costs

	Variable Costs per Unit	Fixed Costs per Year		
		Rental	Depreciation	Other
Year 1.................	Fr. 29.60	Fr. 50,000	Fr. 25,000	Fr. 70,000
Year 2.................	28.80	50,000	25,000	70,000
Year 3 and after.........	28.40	50,000	25,000	70,000

the new location. It's fully depreciated on our books, but it's in perfect condition and I see no reason why it wouldn't last for years.

"If we don't open up in Zurich, we'll sell this old equipment locally for about Fr. 10,000. If we keep it, our only cost will be about Fr. 5,000 to get it from Winterthur to Zurich. We can subtract this Fr. 5,000 from the taxable income from our other operations right away, even before we start operating at Zurich."

For purposes of analysis, Mr. Berner and Mr. Huber agreed that the new Zurich plant should be able to operate for at least 10 years and that the company's investment in working capital would be a reasonable measure of the value of the Zurich assets at the end of that time.

In evaluating capital expenditure proposals, Mr. Berner used an income tax rate of 30 percent of ordinary taxable income. Gains on the sale of equipment were also taxed at a 30 percent rate. Depreciation for tax purposes on the new equipment to be purchased for the Zurich plant would be Fr. 50,000 a year for five years.

a) Prepare a time table of the before-tax cash flows that are relevant to the evaluation of this expansion proposal. Do you agree with Mr. Berner that these should be differential figures?

b) If Sovad required at least a 20 percent return on investment before income taxes, should Sovad have opened the Zurich factory?

c) How would your analysis differ if you were to use after-tax cash flows and a minimum acceptable rate of return of 14 percent?

CASE 26–2: PORTIA MILLING COMPANY

The Portia Milling Company operated several flour mills in the Midwest. The president of the company had assembled what he felt was an exceptionally competent management team capable of encompassing a much larger operating volume than the company's existing facilities could supply. Accordingly, when he heard that the owner-managers of the Grindell Flour Company were contemplating retirement from the business, he hurried to open negotiations for the purchase of their business.

The Grindell company had annual sales of approximately $25 million and profits after taxes of about $350,000 a year. Sales and profits had been roughly constant for the last five years, and the Grindell mills had been operating close to their maximum capacity. Grindell's top executives are all members of the same family. Their compensation for the most recent year was:

J. C Grindell, president	$85,000
J. P. Grindell, treasurer	75,000
L. M. Marcus, sales manager	50,000
F. N. Noble, division manager	23,000
R. B. Grindell, division manager	23,000

The president and treasurer would retire if the company were to be sold. Mr. Noble, who also serves as the president of a local bank, would undoubtedly leave the company if he were asked to fill a position at the Portia headquarters. Mr. Marcus and R. B. Grindell would be expected to remain with the business if it were acquired by Portia. Mr. Marcus would stay on in the merged company at his current salary and in his current position. R. B. Grindell would take on a newly created job in the Portia head office, also at his current salary.

The Grindell division managers had responsibility for local sales as well as for mill operations. Portia, on the other hand, was organized functionally, with an integrated sales force and mill managers who were responsible for manufacturing only. Portia's mill managers received salaries and bonuses amounting to about $15,000 a year each, and this pattern would be imposed on the two Grindell mills if they were acquired. Two new mill managers would have to be hired to take over the management of the mills from Mr. Noble and R. B. Grindell. No other executives would have to be hired if the Grindell facilities were to be acquired.

Portia's president anticipated that certain other economies could be made if Grindell were acquired. For one thing, consolidation of bookkeeping operations was expected to reduce clerical costs by $40,000 a year.

Second, the company would be able to take more complete advantage of the cost advantage of "milling in transit" privileges. Flour can be shipped by rail at the lower rates applicable to grain shipments provided that it has been milled from grain shipped by rail and that the outbound shipment of flour continues to move in the same geographic direction as the grain shipment. Portia's president had made calculations indicating that realigning the areas served by each mill would produce $50,000 a year in freight savings.

Third, acquisition of Grindell's grain elevators, with some idle capacity, would permit Portia to save $20,000 a year in elevator rentals.

Finally, the ability of the company to serve chain bakeries with plants in both territories was expected to increase the sales of the combined companies by $1 million a year and the profits before taxes by $25,000, in addition to the other sources of increased profits discussed above.

Portia's management proposed to make an offer for the inventories, prepaid expenses, facilities, trademarks, and goodwill of the Grindell Flour Company. Grindell's cash, receivables, and certain other assets would not be acquired, nor would Portia assume any obligation for Grindell's liabilities. The price to be paid would be an agreed-upon sum plus the book value of inventories and prepaid expenses at the date of the acquisition. Grindell's inventories and prepaid expenses amounted to $1.2 million at the seasonal low.

In addition to the purchase price, Portia would have to invest $1.8 million at the seasonal low to finance the increase in the company's balances of cash and receivables that would accompany this major expansion of its operations.

Funds for all of these items would have to come from the Portia Milling Company's long-term financial resources. The purchase price would be paid with $2.5 million in 6 percent debentures and the remainder in cash. Capital required for the cash payment would be obtained from the Portia Milling Company's present funds and from the proceeds from the sale of additional shares of stock to the present stockholders. If the acquisition were consummated at a time at which the Grindell inventories and pre-paid expenses were greater than their seasonal low, funds to pay for the excess would be obtained by drawing on Portia's line of bank credit. The line of credit was also adequate to finance extra seasonal requirements of cash and receivables.

The Grindell Flour Company's income statement reflected $50,000 in annual interest charges on its funded debt and $100,000 in interest on short-term borrowing to meet peak seasonal needs. Seasonal borrowing requirements were expected to remain approximately the same under Portia management as under Grindell management.

If the Grindell facilities were acquired, Portia would have to spend about $100,000 a year on new equipment to keep the facilities in first-rate condition. These expenditures would be capitalized for tax purposes and depreciated on a regular basis. This would serve to keep the annual de-preciation charge at $100,000. Depreciation on the company's financial statements was the same as that shown on the company's tax returns.

Portia's minimum return on investment was based on an estimate of the company's cost of capital. Its policy was to regard favorably any pro-posal that was expected to yield a return of 8 percent after taxes on long-term permanent investment. Peak seasonal investment requirements were not treated as investment, but the cost of seasonal borrowing was charged as one of the elements of the cash flows attributed to a proposal.

Although Portia expected the Grindell business to become a permanent integral part of the Portia operations if it were acquired, there was always the possibility that the loss of the close relationship of the business to the Grindell family would lead to some loss in sales. For this reason Portia's president decided to use 10 years as an estimate of economic life, with a resale value of $2 million plus the value of working capital at the end of that time. A tax rate of 50 percent was in force at the time of these negotiations and was not expected to change.

Prepare a statement showing the maximum price that Portia could af-ford to pay for the physical facilities, trademarks, and goodwill of the Grindell Flour Company. Also show how much money Portia would have to obtain from its working capital and from sales of its common stock to finance the acquisition.

chapter **27**

Costs for Product Pricing

A company's long-term survival depends on its ability to obtain prices for its products that will cover all costs and leave a satisfactory margin of profit, adequate to compensate investors for the use of their funds. While this is true in the aggregate, the cost of any one product may be a poor basis for pricing that product, partly because cost itself can be calculated in a number of ways and partly because cost calculations completely ignore the effect of price on the number of units sold.

The purpose of this chapter is to see what kinds of information, particularly cost information, are likely to be relevant in representative pricing situations.

OUTLINES OF THE PRICING PROBLEM

A useful classification of pricing problems is in terms of the kind of event that creates the need for a decision, such as the following:

1. A new product has been developed for addition to the line.
2. Historical profit reports indicate that some products, or all products in the aggregate, have been yielding lower profits than management deems necessary for long-run survival.
3. The sales force reports substantial losses in sales volume due to customer resistance to existing prices.
4. An opportunity arises to bid for a special order for a custom product to be manufactured to the buyer's specifications or engineered to meet his specific requirements.
5. An offer is made by a prospective buyer to purchase a product at a specified price.
6. A mass market exists but cannot be penetrated at existing prices.

This list by no means exhausts all the possible circumstances under which pricing decisions must be made. Other problems include the de-

termination of the discount structure for different categories of customers, the relationships between the prices of substitute or complementary
products or between the prices of different sizes or qualities of products
of a particular type, on-season and off-season differentials, and geographic
structures of product prices. Most of the fundamental questions in pricing are met in examining the six kinds of pricing situations listed above,
however, and it is on these that we shall concentrate our attention.

Economic Theory in Product Pricing

The general approach to product pricing that is implicit in most
microeconomic theory (theory of the individual firm and its relation to

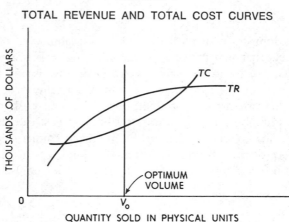

Exhibit 27–1

TOTAL REVENUE AND TOTAL COST CURVES

other firms) is that analysis for pricing is merely a special kind of incremental analysis. The optimum price is the price that will yield the maximum excess of total revenues over total cost.

To illustrate this concept, the economist uses a diagram similar to that
shown in Exhibit 27–1. If an unlimited number of units of the product
could be sold at the same price, the total revenue line (TR) would be a
straight line rising from the zero point in the lower left-hand corner of
this diagram. In most market situations, however, it is assumed that additional products can be sold only by reducing prices or increasing promotional effort per unit sold. This means that although total sales revenue
will increase as more and more units are sold, the increase in total revenue
will decline gradually as sales expand.

For example, if 10 units can be sold at a price of $2, 11 units can be
sold at a price of $1.90, and 12 units can be sold at a price of $1.80, we
have:

Price	Quantity Sold	Total Revenue	Addition to Total Revenue
$2.00......................	10	$20.00	xxx
1.90......................	11	20.90	$0.90
1.80......................	12	21.60	0.70

Lowering the price from $2 to $1.90 increases total revenue by 90 cents; a further price reduction to $1.80 increases total revenue by only 70 cents. In Exhibit 27–1 this falling off in the rate of increase in total revenue is represented by a gradual reduction in the steepness of the total revenue line as further price reductions become less and less effective in stimulating sales.

The total cost line (TC) in Exhibit 27–1 is the same one discussed in Chapter 3, gradually becoming steeper as volume increases due to the increasing difficulty of expanding output with a given set of productive facilities. As long as total revenue is climbing more rapidly than total cost, total profit will increase with increases in volume. At some point, however, the two rates of climb will become equal, which means that the increase in total cost due to the addition of one more unit of volume is just equal to the increase in total revenue, or a zero increase in total profit. The volume at which this occurs is indicated in Exhibit 27–1 as volume V_0, at which the slopes of the two curves are equal and the curves are parallel. To the right of this point, total cost is increasing more rapidly than total revenue, which means that any attempt to increase volume beyond V_0 will reduce total profit. V_0, therefore, is the optimum volume, and the price at which this volume can be obtained is the optimum price.

These relationships can also be expressed in terms of marginal revenue and marginal cost. Marginal cost was defined in Chapter 3 as the increment in total cost as the result of increasing volume by one unit. Marginal revenue is the increase in total revenue that results from the sale of one additional unit of product. Marginal revenue (MR) and marginal cost (MC) at any volume are determined by measuring the rates of climb or slopes of the total revenue and total cost curves at that volume. Because the curves in Exhibit 27–1 reflect the assumptions that the slope of the total revenue curve will decrease and that the slope of the total cost curve will increase as volume expands, a line representing marginal revenue will slope downward to the right as volume expands and the marginal cost line will slope upward to the right.

These curves are shown in Exhibit 27–2. Marginal revenue is less than price because a price reduction lowers the revenue from all units that would be sold at higher prices. For example, if 10 units can be sold at a price of $2 per unit and 11 units can be sold if the price is $1.90, the mar-

Exhibit 27–2

MARGINAL REVENUE AND MARGINAL COST CURVES

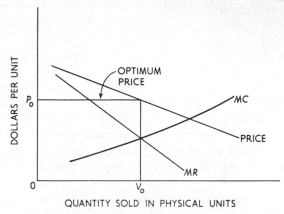

QUANTITY SOLD IN PHYSICAL UNITS

ginal revenue at a volume of 11 units is $20.90 (11 × $1.90) minus $20 (10 × $2), or $0.90.

The optimum price is determined by the intersection of the marginal revenue and marginal cost curves. Lowering the price below this level would increase revenues by less than it would increase costs. Raising the price above the optimum would decrease revenues by more than it would decrease costs.

Limitations of the Model

Although this model illustrates the general nature of the incremental profit approach to product pricing, it is very much oversimplified. First, the available data are seldom good enough to give management more than a rough idea of the shape of the revenue curve. Second, revenues depend on many factors other than the company's own price. For example, a company can seldom assume that management's decisions as to price will not induce retaliatory pricing decisions by competing manufacturers. The circumstances under which this assumption is largely valid are those of *monopoly* (no directly competing product in the market) or *monopolistic competition* (many sellers of similar but not necessarily identical products, with no single seller having a large enough share of the market to permit his competitors to identify the effects of his pricing decisions on their sales).

In the intermediate situation, known as *oligopoly* (a market in which a few large sellers occupy a large share of the market), the marginal revenue curve of the individual seller depends on the reactions of his competitors to changes in his selling prices. If the oligopolistic seller finds that his competitors will raise their prices when he raises his and lower their prices when he lowers his, then his revenue curve (demand curve) takes the same general shape as the demand curve for the market as a whole, except insofar as product differentiation affects the price sensitivity of his sales. If, on the other hand, he finds that his competitors will match his price reductions but will not follow his price increases, than a different situation arises. If one seller tries to raise his prices, his sales will fall off sharply as customers shift their purchases to other firms whose prices have not risen. If he lowers his prices, on the other hand, his competitors will follow suit and the only source of increased revenue will be this seller's share of any general expansion of total industry sales.

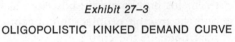

Exhibit 27–3

OLIGOPOLISTIC KINKED DEMAND CURVE

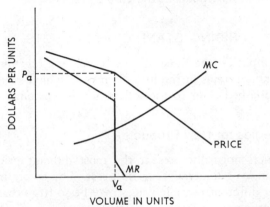

This effect is shown in Exhibit 27–3, in which both the price curve or demand curve and the marginal revenue curve are interrupted or "kinked" at the sales volume (V_a) expected at the existing price (P_a). Although marginal revenue at this volume may be greater than marginal cost (as in Exhibit 27–3), any attempt to expand volume by price reductions will produce a substantial drop in marginal revenue. In this illustration the reduced marginal revenue is less than marginal cost, and thus the price reduction would be unprofitable.

A kink of this sort is likely to appear immediately only if most other firms in the industry are not operating at the limits of practical capacity. If capacity is fully utilized, competitors might find it profitable to meet any price rises, which would eliminate the kink. If they do not raise their prices but cannot absorb any additional volume immediately, the kink effect will not be felt by the high-priced seller until outside capacity has grown sufficiently to permit competitors to take advantage of all the orders that are forthcoming at existing prices. If most sellers suspect the existence of a kink of the kind illustrated here, and if they also assume that total industry sales are inelastic (relatively insensitive to price reductions), this is enough to explain why prices in many oligopolistic industries do not decline significantly during periods of idle capacity.

A third defect in the marginal model is that price is only one element in the marketing mix. The amount and kind of selling effort, the package design, and the distribution outlets chosen all have a heavy influence on the amount of product that will be sold at any given price. This adds a third dimension to the analysis, ruling out any simplistic application of the two-dimensional model.

These limitations prevent the direct use of the marginal model in most pricing situations. It remains highly useful, however, as a point of departure, a means of stating the pricing problem in conceptual terms, and this can be the most crucial point in the entire process.

PRICING STANDARD PRODUCTS

In most companies, the bulk of the company's revenues arises from the sale of standard items in the line—items for which specifications and design are established prior to the solicitation of customer orders.

Pricing Strategies for New Products

New products normally present the most difficult pricing problem, because the range of uncertainty is so great. The errors in estimates of sales volume at different possible prices may be so large that the resulting incremental profit comparisons are virtually useless for decision making.

Two basic strategies are available to the developer of a new product. *Skimming pricing* is a policy of high prices during the early period of a new product's life, followed by a progressive lowering of prices as the market matures. *Penetration pricing,* on the other hand, calls for low initial prices to permit rapid acceptance in large segments of the market.[1]

The ideal skimming price is one that maximizes short-run profit, and it should be derived by the direct application of the economic model described above. A penetration price, in contrast, requires a short-run profit sacrifice to reap long-run gains. Which of these to choose depends on the characteristics of the product and its market.

For example, high initial prices may be a profitable way to utilize the novelty appeal of a new product when the responsiveness of sales to lower prices is slight, but this possibility carries the danger of inroads by price-cutting competitors as the product catches on and the sensitivity of sales volume to price (price elasticity of demand) increases. Automobiles,

---

[1] Joel Dean, *Managerial Economics* (Englewood Cliffs, N.J.: Prentice-Hall, 1951), pp. 419–24.

radios, television sets, nylon, and many pharmaceutical products have all gone through a skimming pricing stage before lower prices provided a basis for penetration of mass markets.

Skimming pricing may also provide a form of insurance against unexpected costs of manufacturing or distribution. It is easier to lower prices than it is to raise them, and manufacturing or engineering difficulties may raise product cost substantially above the estimates during the early shakedown period. The apparent security offered by a skimming price disappears, however, whenever the competing products are relatively close substitutes for the new product or whenever competitive entry into the market is easy. This explains, for example, why manufacturers of household detergents probably could not use skimming pricing successfully even if they wanted to.

Pricing Experiments

Some companies have used experimental techniques with a great deal of success to produce more reliable estimates of the effect of price on sales. For example, one company recently prepared a new product for national distribution, but before the national market was approached the product was introduced in three representative regional markets. Every attempt was made to ensure the comparability of the three regions and to standardize the methods of sales promotion. Three prices were selected for testing, one in each market. Analysis of the sales response in the three markets indicated that although profit per unit was highest at the highest of the three prices, product demand was such as to yield a greater total profit at the intermediate of the three prices. The estimated sales and costs are shown in Exhibit 27–4. At a retail price of $2.45, the product was expected to return $54,000 less in sales than at a $1.95 retail price, but the

Exhibit 27–4

ESTIMATED PROFIT–PRICE RELATIONSHIP

	At $1.95	At $2.45	At $2.95
Estimated unit sales................	800,000	600,000	300,000
Price to dealers....................	$1.17	$1.47	$1.77
Estimated revenues.................	$936,000	$882,000	$531,000
Variable costs:			
Variable manufacturing costs.......	$504,000	$378,000	$189,000
Variable selling costs..............	80,160	70,920	40,860
Traceable fixed costs...............	135,000	135,000	120,000
Total costs....................	$719,160	$583,920	$349,860
Net cash flow......................	$216,840	$298,080	$181,140

contribution toward fixed costs and profits was expected to be the greatest at the $2.45 price.

Product Value Analysis

Another approach is to estimate the value of the product to various potential users and set a price that is less than the product's value to the bulk of the market.

For example, a machinery manufacturer has a file of detailed estimates of the costs of operations in its customers' factories. When a new product is developed, experienced engineers estimate the potential cost savings for large and small customers. A rough estimate of the demand schedule is prepared from these data—sales of 100 machines if the price is $20,000, sales of 250 machines if the price is $15,000, and so on. Matching this against cost estimates points toward the optimum price.

Product value analysis ordinarily enters into pricing implicitly rather than explicitly. Although few companies have the kinds of value estimates described above, they are seldom completely in the dark. An experienced executive may be able to tailor prices to customer values without even realizing that he is doing anything so systematic. One British company went so far as to try to develop a pricing formula based on the customer values implicit in the pattern of prices set by the company's chief executive.[2] This may not be feasible in the general case, but the question of customer value should not be ignored.

Cost-Based Pricing Formulas

Few prices are based on explicit estimates of cost-price-volume relationships. In most companies, the pricing process begins with an estimate of unit cost and price is arrived at by adding a markup to this.[3] For the retailer, cost ordinarily means the purchase price of the merchandise to be sold; for the manufacturer it means factory cost, derived by the methods outlined in Chapters 4–12 above. For personal service organizations, cost estimates are usually limited to labor time and materials.

The most crucial element in the cost-based formula is the percentage markup. One approach is to estimate the amount of investment attributable to the new product and set the price to achieve a specified return on investment at a given volume. For example, suppose that cost is $10 a unit at an assumed annual volume of 100,000 units. If $1 million in investment is required and the target rate of return is 20 percent, the target markup would be:

---

[2] Wilfred Brown and Elliot Jaques, *Product Analysis Pricing* (London: Heinemann Educational Books, 1964).

[3] For a survey of industry practice, see A. D. H. Kaplan, Joel B. Dirlam, and Robert F. Lanzillotti, *Pricing in Big Business: A Case Approach* (Washington, D.C.: Brookings Institution, 1958).

$$\frac{20\% \times \$1,000,000}{100,000} = \$2 \text{ a unit}$$

In other cases, specific product investment is negligible and the markup is set on the basis of estimated companywide or divisionwide profit objectives.

The main objection to this approach is that it ignores the relationship between price and volume. The competitive situation varies from product to product, and a $2 markup may be so high for this product that volume will only reach 50,000 units. Alternatively, it may be far lower than customers are willing to pay and the company may be unable to meet the demand at a $12 price.

The answer is twofold. First, the target markup is often varied from product line to product line to correspond to well-established differences in custom or competitive position. Department stores, for example, typically vary the markup from department to department. Cosmetics might carry an 80 percent markup on cost, whereas the markup on major appliances might be only 30 percent.

Second, actual prices are likely to differ from target prices. The alert pricing executive will shade the markup on some products and increase it on others because he senses the presence of real differences in competitive position. By the same token, conditions change, and the markups that have been normal for the past 20 years may suddenly turn out to be unobtainable. The neighborhood grocer found this out in the thirties, when the supermarket established a new pattern in food retailing; and the same fate befell the full-service department store with the growth of discount retailing in the fifties.

A legitimate question at this point is why cost should be used at all if the executive is going to vary the margin so freely. A quick answer often is that cost serves as a pricing "floor," shielding the seller from the risk of loss. Unfortunately, the protection it offers is illusory. It is entirely possible for the company to lose money even though every product is priced higher than cost. The reason is that many costs are fixed, so that unit cost depends on volume. A high price can drive customers away, reducing sales volume so far below the estimated volume that average cost is greater than price.

Another possible answer is that the decision maker must make his decisions in the face of a host of uncertainties. He cannot possibly cope with all of these uncertainties, and to keep his sanity he has to find some way of ignoring some of them or of getting others to accept responsibility for dealing with them. He may for this reason accept a pricing formula that seems reasonable on the surface purely as a means of avoiding the need to deal with this one source of uncertainty.

This form of *uncertainty absorption* would not last long if it seemed to produce consistently unacceptable results. There must be other reasons to explain the durability of a pricing method that appears to ignore demand factors entirely.

Perhaps the best explanation is that a cost estimate may help the decision maker to predict either his competitor's costs or a competitive price. For example, if he has been operating for some time in a market in which markups over cost average 50 percent, he may be able to assume that the same relationship will hold on new products as he calculates their costs.

This kind of thinking is particularly valid in oligopolistic industries. Recognizing that price competition is likely to be self-defeating, the pricer may set a price that he feels will not attract competitors unduly and then focus his competitive efforts on other factors such as delivery, credit terms, and so forth. If every company uses its full cost as a basis for pricing standard products, a substantial measure of price stability can be achieved even under conditions of idle capacity.

A closely related reason for formula pricing is that many firms have so many products that they cannot afford to analyze the price-volume relationships for them all. Once again, by using a pricing rule that seems to work reasonably well, management can devote more time to other dimensions of the marketing mix.

Full Cost versus Variable Cost Pricing Formulas

Most cost-based pricing formulas are so-called full cost formulas. The unit cost entered in such a formula is an estimated or standard full manufacturing cost, including provision for fixed costs of both production and factory service departments.

As previous chapters have pointed out, a unit cost defined in this way is subject to two influences that tend to cloud its meaning. First, many interdepartmental factory service department and general factory overhead costs cannot be attributed clearly to particular production departments. They are nevertheless allocated, but on arbitrary bases. Second, unitization of fixed costs requires a selection of normal volume levels in individual departments. This selection is inevitably subjective.

To avoid these two forms of subjectivity, many accountants have turned to variable cost formulas based on the variable costing principle described in Chapter 9. They argue further that restriction of unit cost to the variable costs makes it not only clearer but more relevant to pricing decisions.

Most of the arguments against this solution are misdirected. It is claimed, for example, that prices based on partial costs will inevitably be lower than prices based on full cost. This ignores the fact that "full" cost ordinarily includes only factory costs and is just as much a partial cost as variable cost. Standard markups over full cost include provision for average selling and administrative expenses; there is no reason why standard markups over variable cost cannot include provision for average fixed costs.

The most telling argument against variable cost pricing formulas for pricing standard new products is that they ignore very real differences in input requirements. It must be remembered that the purpose of the cost element in the pricing formula is to supply guidance as to what a competitive price is likely to be. If a variable cost base accomplishes this, well and good; if not, something else should be tried. Empirical evidence on this point is almost completely lacking, but it might be presumed that long-run normal prices will bear some relation to what we have been calling attributable cost. If a company is unlikely to cover the costs attributable to a product, then it ordinarily will not introduce it.

Notice that this is not the same as full product cost. Factory service department costs for which a clear index of attributability is unavailable should not be allocated to production departments. Similarly, the indivisible portion of production department fixed costs should be excluded from product-costing burden rates used for pricing. On the other hand, provision should be made in unit cost for any significant product-related selling and administrative costs for which an attributability index can be found.

If this position is accepted, one final problem still remains—to select an appropriate volume level for unit cost determination. The irrationality of using expected current volume has already been pointed out, but this does not settle the question of how to measure normal volume. As with everything else in this area, the real test is pragmatic—if it works, it's right. A good starting point, however, is what might be called "designed capacity." For factory costs, this is the average operating level assumed by the designers when they were deciding how big a plant to build. It will typically be less than maximum physical capacity and will depend to some extent on industry practice as to number of shifts worked in a normal week.

Use of Unit Cost Targets in Product Design

The preceding discussion has presumed that a price is to be set on a product that has been developed and is ready for commercialization. In many cases, however, selling price is known and the question is what kind of a product can be offered at this price.

For example, automobile manufacturers often start with a tentative price at which they want a particular model to sell. Each proposed design is costed, element by element, to test its feasibility at this target price. Features are then added or subtracted, components are redesigned, or new price quotations are sought from parts suppliers, until target cost levels are achieved. Clothing manufacturers typically follow a very similar procedure.

The cost estimates used in these calculations are of the same order as those described above, although here the presumption in favor of attributable costing is ordinarily much stronger.

Reviewing Prices of Established Products

Part of the basic rationale for cost-based formula prices disappears once the product is placed on the market. Some of the uncertainty surrounding the initial pricing decision is dissipated by the flow of field sales data. These data seldom provide a very precise indication of price-

Exhibit 27–5

PRODUCT PROFITABILITY CHART

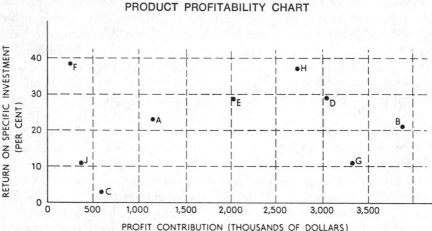

PROFIT CONTRIBUTION (THOUSANDS OF DOLLARS)

volume relationships, but they often can point to prices that seem to be out of line, either too high or too low.

Many companies continue to use cost-based formula prices as bench marks against which to compare actual prices. Existing products often differ widely in relative profitability, and routine pricing review can be highly important.

The review of existing prices may take either of two forms: a study of the present and past profit patterns or a projection of the probable effects of price changes. Studies of the first type are frequently made on a routine basis; forward projections are seldom made unless past profits are lower than the desired normal or someone makes a proposal to reduce price as a means of taking advantage of a sales opportunity. One company uses a chart similar to that illustrated in Exhibit 27–5 to identify products with relatively weak earnings positions. It singles out for intensive review any products that fall in the lower left-hand segment of this chart.

This procedure may be objected to on the grounds that products that fall in the upper right-hand segment may present the company with a greater degree of pricing latitude and a greater potential for increased profit. Furthermore, the return-on-investment figure may include so many arbitrary allocations of cost or investment that little significance can be attached to vertical distances above the base line. Nevertheless, charts of this type or trends of period-to-period movements in product profitability are useful in pointing out possible weaknesses, and this is all that can be asked of any purely historical review. Decisions as to what to do about these weaknesses require estimates of the future, and therefore must depart from the record of the past.

Pricing review is seldom entirely separable from the review of the other determinants of product-line profitability, and comparison of actual prices with target prices or profitability rankings will not necessarily answer the immediate questions of whether to raise or lower prices or discontinue certain products. Market data are essential to these decisions, and the decision maker will ordinarily need more cost data than single estimates can supply. Ideally, both variable cost and attributable cost should be available: variable cost for short-horizon decisions and attributable cost for long-horizon problems.

PRICING CUSTOM PRODUCTS

An eastern manufacturer of specialized parts for automotive and industrial equipment manufactures more than 2,000 distinct products. Approximately half of these products are manufactured to order on the customer's specifications or to meet a specific customer requirement, and this custom business contributes more than half of the company's total sales volume for the year. Except for the standard catalogue items, pricing in this company is largely a matter of bidding or negotiating with individual customers for specific orders or for a planned sequence of deliveries of a custom-designed product. This kind of pricing is typical of a wide variety of products, primarily products to be used by other manufacturers, ranging from ocean-going tankers to salesmen's calling cards.

The Role of Cost

Pricing this kind of business ordinarily starts with cost estimates prepared expressly for the particular order or contract. A bill of materials and list of operations is prepared by the methods engineering staff or similar group on the basis of the product specifications. A cost estimator then has the task of assigning prices to the estimated physical input requirements. Most custom products represent specialized combinations of fairly standard operations, and standard operating times can be extracted from the current cost files if these are kept reasonably current. Otherwise, detailed estimates of operating times need to be prepared by the engineering or manufacturing staff. Estimated input quantities are then converted into estimated dollar costs with the aid of price lists, wage rate schedules, and, in some cases, inquiries of materials vendors.

At this point we come head on once again with the question of the definition of unit cost. The time horizon for pricing decisions on custom products is ordinarily much shorter than the adjustment period under-

Exhibit 27–6

PRODUCT COST ESTIMATE SHEET

PRODUCT NO. 172–41-B	COST ESTIMATE SUMMARY			PREPARED BY _____
QUANTITY 1,000				DATE _____

Materials:		Direct Labor and Machine Time:			
Tooling	$ 507.00				
Fixtures, etc.	. . . . . .	*Dept.*	*Setup*	*Operating*	*Machine-Hours*
Process	728.00	12	$ 6.25	$ 450.00	200
Total	$1,235.00	14	1.25	175.00	110
		17	2.50	130.00	150
		22	3.00	650.00	300
		24	1.25	85.00	20
		Total	$14.25	$1,490.00	780

Direct materials and direct labor	$2,739.25
Variable manufacturing overhead	548.00
Variable administrative costs	54.80
Total specific cost	$3,342.05
Fixed manufacturing overhead at $1.20 per machine-hour	936.00
Fixed selling and administrative at 15% of manufacturing cost	641.71
Normal profit at 12% of cost	590.37
Target price	$5,510.13

lying the attributable cost figures, and this argues for the availability of variable cost data. It can be argued, however, that such estimates should be accompanied by estimates of attributable cost. If variable cost data provide a basis for specifying the floor beneath which prices will seldom if ever be reduced, attributable cost data can still perform their major function of providing some indication of what a normal price might be expected to be.

A cost estimate summary in this form is shown in Exhibit 27–6. In this example, the normal fixed manufacturing cost is $1.20 per machine-hour, fixed selling and administrative cost is applied at a rate of 15 percent of total manufacturing cost, and the profit necessary to produce a target return on investment of 20 percent before taxes is applied at 12 percent of total product cost.

Adjusting to the Market

The pricing executive now has the responsibility of deciding whether the market situation will support a price in excess of this "normal" price or whether the normal price must be shaded to permit a successful bid. He will be guided in this by his recent experience in bidding for jobs and by the extent of expected utilization of factory capacity.

For example, if the company is operating at high levels of capacity utilization, the pricer will not do much price shading below the normal level except possibly on orders that appear likely to lead to repeat business when greater available capacity exists. If recent bids at normal levels have found ready acceptance, he will feel justified in increasing the provision for profit on bids for new work. If substantial idle capacity exists, however, and full cost bidding has been failing to secure orders, the pricing executive faced with the choice of losing the order or quoting a price that is lower than the normal level is likely to accept the latter course and bid at some point intermediate between the estimated specific cost of the order and the normal price.

This description should provide ample support for the statement that pricing is an art rather than a science. The pricing executive must be alert to general market conditions and to differences among customers in their willingness to pay higher prices. Even when substantial idle capacity exists, it is not uncommon to find many orders priced at or above normal levels because all sections of the company's markets are not subject to the same competitive conditions.

PRICE DISCRIMINATION

Business executives face many other kinds of pricing situations, but we have space to consider only one more question—price discrimination. Price discrimination consists of charging different prices to different customers, and the term is intended to have no ethical overtones. Some discrimination can be defended on social grounds; some cannot.

For example, a uniform price charged both to customers across the continent and to those next door is nondiscriminatory according to the definition in the preceding paragraph, but it can be regarded as socially undesirable because it deprives the next-door customer of his locational advantage. For this reason, discrimination is often defined as differences in the net proceeds from sales to different customers after deducting freight and delivery costs.

The private benefit from price discrimination is probably obvious. Suppose that a customer will buy one television set if the price is $200 but will buy two sets only if he can get the second set for $110. The cost attributable to the manufacture and sale of a television set is $80. In this situation, the company can make $30 more if it can sell the two sets at the buyer's maximum price than if it has to adhere to a one-price policy:

First Set	Second Set	Revenue	Cost	Profit
$200	. . .	$200	$ 80	$120
200	$110	310	160	150
110	110	220	160	60

Successful price discrimination always requires an ability to segment the market and to prevent shifts of customers from one segment to another. Petroleum marketers generally find it difficult to confine gasoline price wars to narrow areas because price cuts at one station lead station operators in adjacent areas to cut their prices, too.

The safest way to prevent erosion of the price structure through individual price concessions is through product differentiation. Price concessions on standard products are difficult secrets to keep; but when product differences are present, it is much more difficult for individual customers to find out whether price concessions are being granted. The product differentiation must appear to be important, of course, so that other buyers do not regard the cheaper product as a satisfactory substitute for the standard item.

The seller also needs to consider the likelihood that a price concession now will spoil the market for future sales. Fortunately, this danger is often more imagined than real. If excess capacity exists in the future, the company will probably be happy to grant the same kind of price concessions it finds profitable now. If, on the other hand, the excess capacity disappears in the future, the company will not be willing to grant price concessions in order to obtain added sales, and therefore the possibility of spoiling future markets may not be a serious objection.

Price discrimination can be either systematic, in the form of standard discounts or price concessions to certain classes of customers, or sporadic, as the seller responds with special price concessions to meet specific competitive conditions. Both forms of discrimination are restricted in the United States by the provisions of the Robinson-Patman Act. This act provides that price discrimination between customers is unlawful if it is likely to lessen competition substantially unless the price differential can be justified by a cost differential or unless the lower price is made in good faith to meet a price quoted by a competitor.

As we noted in Chapter 13, few companies have been able to justify their price differentials by evidence on cost differentials. The best defense is to differentiate the product sufficiently so that the product sold at a lower price is not a perfect substitute for the standard product. There is nothing in the law to require that markups be uniform for all products. One authority on antitrust law has stated: "If in fact there is an actual and substantial difference in grade and quality of two commodities, they may be sold at different prices, and the difference in price apparently need not be measured by the difference in cost, consumer acceptance, value or any other standard."[4]

Companies whose share of specific product markets is relatively small are less vulnerable to Robinson-Patman charges than companies with large market shares, because it is more difficult to substantiate a charge of probable lessening of competition on the basis of a small market share.

SUMMARY

Application of the profit maximization decision rule to pricing decisions requires data on price-volume and cost-volume relationships. In the absence of the former, most companies fall back on pricing formulas, most of them based on estimates of product unit cost.

These pricing formulas seem illogical, and often are, but their main purpose is to assist management in determining what a "normal" price might be. For pricing new products to be added as standard items in the regular product line, management may wish to follow a skimming pricing policy by setting a price in excess of the normal price, or a penetration pricing policy by setting price at or near the normal level.

Cost estimates for this purpose are perhaps most logically based on the attributable cost concept, although the real question is which formula provides the best indication of the normal price. If attributable cost or its conceptually weaker cousin, full cost, is used, it should be supplemented by data on variable cost for use in decisions with shorter time horizons. The pricer must then use his own judgment as to what markup to seek. Judgment is the essential ingredient in product pricing; cost data are merely aids to the exercise of this judgment.

EXERCISES AND PROBLEMS

1. The Weiss Company manufactures a highly machined precision part that is used in the manufacture of certain kinds of industrial equipment. The selling price is $350. Standard cost is as follows:

Material, 30 pounds at $2	$ 60
Direct labor, 15 hours at $5	75
Variable overhead	30
Fixed overhead	40
Total standard cost per unit	$205

The company was recently offered an order by a Canadian concern for 200 units at a price of $250 each. Freight charges and Canadian import duty, to be paid by the seller, would total $15,000. There was no danger that units

---

[4] Mathias F. Correa, "Discrimination in Prices," in *How to Comply with the Anti-trust Laws*, edited by Jerrold G. Van Cise and Charles Wesley Dunn (New York: Commerce Clearing House, 1954), p. 159.

shipped to Canada would be reshipped to Weiss's domestic customers because of high U.S. tariffs on imports of this product.

The Canadian company had never done business with the Weiss Company, and the sales manager pressed strongly for the sale on the ground that this was an opportunity to expand into a new market. The controller was out of town when this offer came in and was not consulted. The president turned down the sales manager's recommendation and instructed him to reject the offer.

Due to a number of factors, unabsorbed overhead variances amounting to $5 a unit have been budgeted for the coming year. Labor and materials quantity variances have been negligible, but the standards do not reflect recent increases in materials purchases prices and wage rates. Materials prices have increased 3 percent above standard, and wage rates have increased 5 percent. Wage and price changes affecting overhead costs account for $1 of the budgeted underabsorption of fixed overhead.

a)   Do you agree with the president's decision? Support your position with
     arguments based on data provided above.
b)   Are there any considerations that might justify a course of action other
     than that which you have supported?

2. The sales manager of the Franglais Company has been asked to submit a price quotation for 100,000 units of a product used by one of the Franglais customers.

The out-of-pocket cost of filling the order, if it can be obtained, is $90,000. Three possible prices are being considered, $1, $1.25, and $1.50. The sales manager is not certain how busy competitors' factories are, but in the light of their bids on recent jobs he thinks that the chance of their operating at a rate as high as 80 percent of capacity or higher is only 20 percent. Similarly, he believes that the probability that competitors are operating at 60 percent of capacity or less is 30 percent.

He estimates that if competitors' operating rates are 80 percent or higher, he can secure the order at any bid up to and including $1.50. If competitors are operating between 61 and 79 percent of capacity, a price of $1.25 or less will secure the bid, but if competitors' operating rates are 60 percent or less it will take a bid of $1 to land the order.

a)   Prepare a payoff table to reflect these data.
b)   Assuming that the decision rule is to maximize the expected value of the
     monetary return, which bid should be submitted?

3.* The Magellan Company has been selling its product at a price of $0.80 and has decided to investigate the profitability of increasing the price to compensate the company for recent increases in operating cost. The controller of the company has analyzed the company's costs, and although he recognizes that his analysis is imperfect, he has derived the following cost estimates:

---

* Solutions to problems marked with an asterisk can be found in Appendix B.

Monthly Output (Units)	Operating Costs	
	Fixed Cost	Marginal Cost per Unit
50,000 and less.............	$10,000	$0.60
50,001–60,000.............	10,000	0.61
60,001–70,000.............	10,000	0.62
70,001–80,000.............	11,000	0.64
80,001–90,000.............	11,000	0.67
90,001–100,000............	11,000	0.71
100,001–110,000............	12,000	0.75
110,001–120,000............	12,000	0.79
120,001–130,000............	13,000	0.85

The market research department has recently studied prices and performance of competitive products and has derived an estimate of the effect of price on sales volume. The manager of market research has presented the following figures to the controller hesitantly, saying that he doesn't know how reliable they are but that they are the best he can do. He adds that in good years sales would exceed these figures, but on the average he thinks his estimate would be borne out.

Price per Unit	Monthly Unit Sales
$0.75......................	100,000
0.80......................	90,000
0.85......................	80,000
0.90......................	70,000
0.95......................	60,000
1.00......................	50,000

Prepare a statement that will indicate the most profitable price at which the product might be sold.

4.* The Hammer Company manufactures a product that it distributes through its own sales branches in the midwestern United States. The company's president, Mr. Martin, was recently approached by a West Coast distributor who was interested in obtaining a franchise for distribution of the product in seven western states not now served by the company. The distributor proposed that he purchase the product from Hammer at a price of $32.50 f.o.b. the Hammer factory and offer it for sale to retailers at a price of $42.50. He would pay freight charges to the West Coast, averaging $3.50 a unit. No sales commissions would have to be paid on these sales. Mr. Martin promised that he would consider the offer.

The product is now sold to retailers in Hammer's present market area at a price of $44 delivered. Sales commissions are computed at 5 percent of sales. Freight averages $1.50 a unit. Other selling and administrative costs are regarded as fixed and amount to $4.50 a unit. Manufacturing cost amounts to $29.50 a unit, as follows:

Materials...........................	$18.70
Labor..............................	3.00
Variable overhead..................	3.30
Fixed overhead....................	4.50
Total.............................	$29.50

Manufacturing capacity is adequate to handle the increased volume, which Mr. Martin estimates would amount to 1,000 units a month, but fixed factory overhead would probably increase by $1,500 a month.

a) Would you advise Mr. Martin to accept the arrangement suggested by the West Coast distributor?

b) What factors other than those mentioned above should be considered in making this decision?

5. Daniel Seder Associates is a market research firm, specializing in testing consumer reactions to new products. Its methods are slightly different from its competitors, and it has built a good reputation.

Prices in this industry are ordinarily quoted on the basis of a flat fee, the amount depending on the size of the job. In preparing his bids, Mr. Seder has been using a flat price of $20 an hour, and has gotten all the work he could handle at that price.

Mr. Seder decided a few months ago to experiment with different bidding formulas to see whether he could increase his earnings by putting in higher bids on new work. The results were interesting; at various prices per hour, the percentage of bids accepted was:

$30.00..............	32%
27.50..............	42
25.00..............	50
22.50..............	56
20.00..............	60

The total volume of work available for bidding calls for about 5,000 professional hours in an average month. Mr. Seder figures that he can handle up to 2,800 hours of work a month, which would give him about half of the local market. In fact, this is the level at which he has been operating for many months.

The costs of the professional staff are approximately constant from month to month. The bulk of the field work is done by a regular staff of part-time employees, but a few smaller firms are available to fill in (at higher prices) when the Seder load gets too heavy. Based on his past experience, Mr. Seder estimates that his monthly costs will be as follows:

Volume (Hours)	Total Cost
1,500..............	$33,500
1,700..............	34,900
1,900..............	36,300
2,100..............	38,700
2,300..............	40,300
2,500..............	41,900
2,700..............	43,900
2,800..............	44,100

What hourly price should Mr. Seder use in bidding? Present an analysis to back up your recommendations.

6. The Aybec Foundry Company is feeling the effects of a general over-capacity of the foundry industry in the Boston area. Its monthly production cost budget for the next six months is based on an output of only 500 tons of castings a month, which is less than half of practical capacity. The prices of castings vary with the composition of the metal and the shape of the mold, but they average $175 a ton. The condensed monthly production cost budget at the 500-ton level is as follows:

	Core Making	Melting and Pouring	Molding	Cleaning and Grinding
Labor........................	$10,000	$16,000	$6,000	$4,500
Variable overhead............	3,000	1,000	1,000	1,000
Fixed overhead..............	5,000	9,000	2,000	1,000
Total labor and overhead.....	$18,000	$26,000	$9,000	$6,500
Labor and overhead per direct labor hour................	$9.00	$6.50	$6.00	$5.20

Operation at this level has brought the company very close to the break-even point. The lack of work also means that some of the most highly skilled workers will probably have to be laid off, and the production manager is worried that he might find it difficult to get them back when volume picks up later on. Accordingly, when he learned that a customer was soliciting bids for a large casting order, he called in the plant accountant and instructed him to prepare a bid "at cost." He reasoned that if he could keep his work force together, that would be enough profit for the contract.

The order is for 90,000 castings, each weighing about 40 pounds, to be delivered on a regular schedule during the next six months. Materials required would cost $1 per casting after deducting scrap credits. The direct labor hours per casting required for each department would be:

Core making......................... 0.09
Melting and pouring.................. 0.15
Molding............................. 0.06
Cleaning and grinding................ 0.06

Variable overhead would bear a normal relationship to labor cost in the melting and pouring department and in the molding department. In core making and cleaning and grinding, however, the extra labor requirements would not be accompanied by proportionate increases in variable overhead. Variable overhead would increase by $1.20 for every additional labor hour in core making and by 30 cents for every additional labor hour in cleaning and grinding. Standard wage rates are in effect in each department, and no labor variances are anticipated.

To handle an order as large as this, certain increases in fixed factory overhead would be necessary, amounting to $1,000 a month for all departments combined. No increases in selling and administrative expense are anticipated, but the company uses a standard selling and administrative expense rate of

$12 per ton of castings in its pricing work. Production for this order would be spread evenly over the six-month period.

a) Prepare a revised monthly factory cost budget, reflecting the addition of this order.

b) What is the lowest price that the plant manager could quote without selling at a loss? Show your calculations.

7. Aberdeen Appliances, Inc., is bringing out its 19x1 line of household appliances. Sales during 19x0 were at record levels and an equally good year is forecast for 19x1. Disposable consumer income is expected to be at all-time record levels, and the entire appliance industry is booming.

The appliance business has always been highly competitive, and Aberdeen feels that at least part of its success has lain in its ability to keep its costs at competitive levels. The contract that has just been negotiated with the labor union representing the company's factory employees has raised wage rates by 10 percent for next year, however, and management is worried about the effects on the profit margin.

The 19x0 model was sold to dealers at $25. In view of the higher costs of the new model, management is considering setting the price on the 19x1 model at $27. This would keep the percentage markup over standard cost at 35 percent, the level prevailing for the 19x0 model.

The old and new standard costs for Aberdeen's electric buffet grill–deep fryer combination are shown in the following table. The new standard costs reflect the new wage rates, changes in model design, and changes in manufacturing methods.

	19x0	19x1
Materials and parts....	$ 8.50	$ 9.10
Labor....	4.00	4.30
Factory overhead....	6.00	6.50
Total....	$18.50	$19.90

Standard overhead costs are based on estimated costs at normal volume. Factory cost variances on this product in 19x0 amounted to about 10 cents, mostly unfavorable materials price variances. The introduction of new production equipment has created difficulties with the local labor union, however, and Aberdeen Appliances is now budgeting an unfavorable labor quantity variance of 50 cents a unit on the grill-fryer combination. Other variances are expected to be minimal.

No estimates of the sensitivity of sales volume to changes in price have been made, and none can be made before management must reach a decision on the price for the new model.

To the extent that you can judge from the data given, should the price on the new model be set at $27, lower than this, or higher than this? Give reasons for your answer.

8. Dave Seeberger, president of Olympic Instruments, Ltd., feels that the time has come for a price increase on the company's most important product. "Our costs on this line have gone up 32 percent since our last price increase," he said, "and I think that justifies a price hike now. We're almost down to the break-even level and for the first time in 20 years we can't pay a dividend to

the stockholders. It's a good thing that we have a higher margin on most of our other products. Without those we'd really be in the soup!"

The product is sold directly to industrial users at a price of $160. The factory cost estimates at the time of the last price increase and at present are shown in the following table:

	Then	Now
Materials...............	$ 17.50	$ 20.40
Labor..................	32.50	40.00
Factory overhead.........	65.00	91.60
Total factory cost........	$115.00	$152.00

The product specifications have not been changed since the previous price increase. Wage rates have gone up by 30 percent, but some labor has been saved as a result of methods changes that have been effected during this period.

Factory overhead is assigned to products on the basis of a plantwide burden rate, reflecting estimated costs at current volume. The rate is brought up to date once a year. The overhead cost files at the time of the increase and at present show the following:

	Then	Now
Burden rate (per direct labor dollar)....	$2.00	$2.29
Estimated monthly volume (direct labor dollars)..................	$120,000	$110,000
Variable overhead cost..............	$ 36,000	$ 31,900

All of the company's salesmen are on salary and all selling and administrative costs are regarded as fixed. Even so, they have gone up in total from $70,000 a month to $75,000 a month. Sales have dropped from about $700,000 a month to $550,000, despite price increases on some other products.

Brad Pierce, Olympic's sales manager, is against any price increase. "We have a tough enough time now," he said. "Our competitors' list prices are about the same as ours, but my guess is that they're doing a little unofficial price cutting. Everybody in the industry has cut back, but we've been hit harder than most. Our market share on this product has fallen from about 50 percent to maybe 40 percent. If anything, we should be offering a few deals of our own, not raising prices."

a) Prepare an analysis of costs that Mr. Seeberger can use as he studies this situation.

b) Should the price be increased at this time? If not, what should Mr. Seeberger do?

9. The Oppenheim Company is just completing the construction of a new facility to manufacture a new product. This product is intended for sale to manufacturers of a wide variety of products in which it would be used as a component part, ordinarily hidden from the view of the ultimate consumer.

Competing products sell at prices ranging from $3.80 to $4.80, but differences in product specifications and design make direct comparisons difficult. Furthermore, the company believes that there is some price shading for large volume customers, but has thus far been unable to determine its extent.

Sales in this market are quite difficult to forecast, at least in part because individual orders tend to be fairly large and the loss of one order can make the difference between a good forecast and a highly inaccurate one.

In making the decision to enter this market, the Oppenheim management believed that it would be able to sell 150,000 units a month within three years after commencing operations if its prices were competitive. Market conditions have changed materially since the initial decision was made, and even with heavy promotional outlays at the outset, the company is not confident that it can meet the original sales target.

The company's reputation for product quality and delivery performance is such, however, that the sales manager has suggested setting a premium price of $5 a unit. He is quite confident that he can sell 80,000 units a month in the first year at that price. In fact, he thinks it unlikely that he could sell more than 80,000 units a month in the first year no matter how low a price was set. Buyers in this market try out new components in their less popular lines, often waiting two or three years before incorporating components of improved design into their major products, and this latter portion of the market tends to be highly price-sensitive.

It is estimated that materials will cost 80 cents a unit at monthly volumes of 100,000 units or less and 70 cents a unit if monthly volume is in excess of that figure. Labor costs will amount to $1.40 a unit. Factory overhead is to be budgeted at $90,000 per month plus 42 cents a unit. By-products from the process are expected to yield 24 cents for each unit of the main product manufactured. The plant's output can be increased to 250,000 units a month, but for all output in excess of 200,000 units a month labor cost will increase to $1.70 a unit and variable overhead will rise to 65 cents a unit.

An intensive sales promotion campaign is now being prepared to launch the new product. Advertising and special promotion activities costing $750,000 will be spread over the first year of the new product, in addition to salesmen's commissions of 5 percent of sales. Thereafter it is expected that selling costs attributable to the new product will be $20,000 a month plus commissions. No change in administrative or other nonmanufacturing expenses is expected to accompany the introduction of the new product.

The company's selling and administrative expenses (including advertising and salesmen's commissions), together with its reported net income before taxes, have in the past averaged about 40 percent of manufacturing cost. This comes very close to a pricing formula that the company has used on many occasions: budgeted manufacturing cost at normal volume plus 45 percent.

a) Compute unit cost on whatever basis you feel would be most helpful to management in setting an initial price on this product. Prepare a summary report to present this figure and any others that you would want management to see, including any charts or diagrams that you would find useful in getting your analysis across.

b) Approximately what price would you like to see the management of the Oppenheim Company set on this product? What reasons underlie your recommendation?

10. "We price to achieve a target return on investment," Al Doherty said. "First, we estimate the amount of facilities and working capital necessary to support each product. Eighteen percent is our target return on investment, before taxes, and this gives us the amount of profit we have to achieve. Then we figure out what it will cost us to operate at normal volume. Adding this to the target return gives us the price to set."

"Don't you consider the effect of price on volume?"

"Not directly. We figure that if we can't reach normal volume at a price that gives us our target return, then we don't want the product."

Mr. Doherty is the marketing vice president of Usher Enterprises, Inc., a medium-sized manufacturer of adhesives, abrasives, and industrial chemicals. He is responsible for the entire marketing program, including the establishment of product selling prices. For major pricing decisions he has a price advisory committee made up of the controller, the production manager, the industrial engineer, and himself, but the final decision is his because his performance is judged on the basis of return on investment.

At the moment Mr. Doherty is wrestling with the problem of setting a price on a new product for use in the paper processing industries. Usher's major competitor, Hinden Products, Inc., has a product with characteristics that have given it an enormous competitive advantage in paper processing industries. It sells for $3, and at this price has forced all competing products out of this market.

The only problem with the Hinden product is that it is costly to use. Users have to spend between $0.50 and $2 for auxiliary materials for every pound of the Hinden product they use. Mr. Doherty estimates that the cost penalties for using Hinden's product are as follows:

Cost Penalty	Pounds Sold (Monthly)
$0.50	40,000
1.00	80,000
1.50	120,000
2.00	160,000
Total	400,000

Usher's new product would eliminate these cost penalties.

Paper industries' consumption of the Hinden product has been growing at a rate of about 100,000 pounds a year, or 8,300 pounds a month. Hinden sells the same product to other industries in which it does not have a cost penalty, but Usher's sales organization is inadequate to cover these other industries. The decision on Usher's new product will be based solely on its performance in the paper processing industries.

Introduction of the new product would be fairly easy. Investment in plant and equipment and working capital would amount to $5 million plus $10 for each pound of product sold in an average month. Introductory promotional costs would be negligible because Usher's salesmen are already in regular contact with customers in the paper processing industries, and no large initial burst of media advertising would be required.

All cost estimates have been prepared on the basis of a normal volume of 200,000 pounds a month. Factory costs for the new product would amount to $200,000 a month plus $2 a pound, up to a volume ceiling of about 250,000 pounds a month. Beyond that, cost penalties would begin to increase rather rapidly and would quickly become prohibitive. Rather than go above 250,000 pounds a month, management would either limit sales or begin the construction of additional facilities.

Selling and product management costs for the new product would average $60,000 a month. These costs would be classified as fixed.

The company's central administration costs average 6 percent of factory cost at normal volume. These are fixed costs and would not change immediately if the new product were introduced. They would probably creep up gradually, however, for an eventual increase of about $20,000 a month.

Engineering and research and development costs to date have totaled $600,000. This amount has been capitalized and will be charged against operations on a straight-line basis over the next 60 months. (If Usher decides not to introduce the product, the entire amount will be expensed immediately.)

a) What price would be set if the company's pricing formula were used? Show your calculations.

b) Do the data indicate that the price should be set at the target level? Make calculations that you think would help management decide what price to set and indicate how they might be used.

11. The president of the Gregson Products Company makes all the product pricing decisions. He is now trying to decide on a price to be placed on a new type of floor wax, called "Flow-On," that has just been perfected by the company's research department. Although a number of competing brands of liquid floor wax are now on the market, the company has not previously marketed any kind of floor wax. The company's products are distributed in a seven-state regional market, rather than nationally.

Labor, materials, and manufacturing overhead costs per gallon at different volumes (gallons per week) are expected to average as follows:

	10,000	15,000	20,000	25,000	30,000
Materials..............	$1.00	$1.00	$0.95	$0.95	$0.95
Labor.................	0.50	0.45	0.40	0.40	0.43
Factory overhead.......	1.55	1.05	0.80	0.69	0.68
Total.................	$3.05	$2.50	$2.15	$2.04	$2.06

These costs are also typical of those facing the company's major competitors.

The manufacturing process is such that it requires 24-hour, three-shift operation of the production facilities. Changes in the rate of output are achieved by increasing or decreasing the number of processing units in service. In designing the facilities, the company's engineers were asked to design for efficiency at a "normal" operating level of 25,000 gallons a week, or 80 percent of maximum physical capacity. The company's efficient competitors are able to achieve about an 80 percent utilization, on the average.

The company's salesmen are paid on a flat salary basis. Introduction of this new product, however, would require the permanent addition of two new salesmen at an average salary of $180 per week each. All other selling and administrative costs would be unchanged by the introduction of this new product. On a companywide basis, the selling and administrative cost averages about 30 percent of manufacturing cost. If the company's profitability targets were met, company net income would be approximately 20 percent of manufacturing cost, but in the past few years the reported net income has averaged about 15 percent of factory cost.

The company's research people are convinced that "Flow-On" is superior to any existing liquid floor wax. The leading competing product sells at a retail price of $5 per gallon. At the prevailing trade discount of 40 percent off list, the manufacturer's realization at this price is $3 a gallon. The other five brands in the company's market area are less popular and sell at retail prices ranging from $3.95 to $5.35. No quality product is marketed at a price of less than $4.75, and sales of the $5.35 product have been rather small, although it is marketed by a well-established manufacturer of branded household products.

The sales manager is planning an extensive promotional campaign to launch the new product. He is convinced that he can sell 25,000 gallons of "Flow-On" per week once the product is established, as long as the price is no higher than that of the leading competitor. This would represent a market share of about 15 percent, but the impact on competitors would be lessened considerably by expansion of total sales of floor waxes in this area as a result of the extra promotion of the new brand.

The president is less optimistic than the sales manager. He, too, hopes for a sales volume of 25,000 gallons per week, but does not expect to reach this level of operations until normal growth of the market expands industry sales sufficiently several years hence. He thinks that 20,000 gallons a week is more likely as long as prices are competitive, and that sales might even be as low as 15,000 gallons per week.

a) As controller of the Gregson Products Company, you have been asked to supply the president with a figure representing the cost per gallon of "Flow-On." Prepare a short report, providing the figure(s) that you think is (are) most likely to be relevant in this situation and explaining to the president what your figures mean and why you selected them.

b) There is no time for experiments that would test the price elasticity of demand. No one in the company can give you any information other than that supplied above. What price would you establish and why?

12. The Lundstrom Company's factory consists of three production departments and two service departments, with the following normal monthly overhead costs:

	Production Departments			Service Departments	
	A	B	C	M	N
Direct overhead:					
Variable...............	$ 5,200	$16,000	$10,500	$ 7,500	.....
Fixed—divisible........	6,000	4,500	2,000	.....	.....
Fixed—indivisible.......	800	1,500	3,000	2,000	$10,000
Allocated (full cost basis):					
General factory........	2,000	2,000	2,000	.....	.....
Department M.........	1,000	4,000	5,000	.....	.....
Department N.........	5,000	2,000	2,500	500	.....
Total...............	$20,000	$30,000	$25,000	$10,000	$10,000
Normal volume...........	20,000 dir. lab. hours	10,000 dir. lab. hours	12,500 machine-hours	2,000 service-hours	100,000 sq. ft.

Consumption of service department M's services is regarded as a divisible fixed cost in department A and as proportionately variable with volume in departments B and C. General factory overheads are entirely fixed and largely indivisible.

Product X has just been developed by the Lundstrom Company and is now ready for commercialization. It will be listed in the company's next product catalog, and orders will be taken for immediate or deferred delivery at list price.

Product X will compete with more than 100 products offered by 36 competing companies in the Lundstrom market area. Its biggest competition will come from the Deane Company's product P, which now sells 5,000 units a month, about 35 percent of the potential market for product X, at a unit price of $59. Lundstrom's market share in other product lines in its own region ranges from 5 to 35 percent, with most products between 10 and 15 percent. Prices in this market have been relatively stable for several years.

Product X has a number of significant advantages over product P and other competing products already on the market, and competitors will not be able to match these distinctive features for at least a year. The Lundstrom sales department is enthusiastic about the new product and feels that at a competitive price product X could achieve a good share of the market, perhaps as much as 15 percent, during the first year. Whether it could keep or increase its market share in subsequent years would depend in part on customers' experience with the product and in part on competitors' responses to product X.

The company's development engineers estimate that after an initial six-month learning period, production inputs for a unit of product X will be: direct materials, $5; direct labor, $25; department A, three direct labor hours; department B, 1½ direct labor hours; and department C, two machine-hours. Errors in the engineers' estimates at this stage of product development have generally been within 10 percent of actual costs in the past, and underestimates have been just as frequent as overestimates.

Markups over factory cost on the company's other regular products average about 40 percent of full factory cost and generally range between 25 and 45 percent.

Most selling and administrative expenses will be the same no matter what price is set on product X. Selling costs attributable to this product are expected to amount to about $5,000 a month, not counting any special price deals that might be made to stimulate sales during the introductory period.

a) Prepare a unit cost estimate or estimates that you feel would help management arrive at a price for product X. Discuss your reasoning.

b) Recommend a selling price for product X. Support your recommendation, using figures from the problem to whatever extent you deem appropriate.

c) How, if at all, would your answer to (a) differ if the decision were whether to accept a single order for 100 units of product X to be shipped to a customer outside Lundstrom's ordinary sales area at a time when factory capacity in each department is only 75 percent utilized?

d) Assuming that product X is now in the line, selling 500 units a month, and that factory production capacity is not fully utilized, what unit cost figure would you use in a rough test of the desirability of discontinuing production and sale of product X? Explain.

CASE 27-1: CLOVIS, S.A.†

Clovis, S.A. manufactures a line of roller skates which it sells in France and other European countries. The company has just received a proposal from Empire Importing Company of New York to introduce Clovis skates into the U.S. market, but at lower net prices than the company now receives on its European sales.

Clovis has no foreign subsidiaries, all foreign sales being made through independent wholesale distributors in the various countries. The company sells three models of detachable skates (detachable skates are attached to the wearer's regular street shoes by means of straps or clamps) and four models of shoe skates (skates fastened at the factory to special skating shoes). The company's requirements of all of these models are manufactured in the company's plant at Lyon, France.

Annual sales volume is now approximately three million pairs of detachable skates and 500,000 pairs of shoe skates. Shoe skate sales have remained approximately constant for the past several years, but unit sales of detached skates have declined approximately 25 percent from the level of a few years ago, despite successive price reductions in most European markets, as competitors have increased their shares of the market at Clovis's expense. The overall European market is about the same size as it was a few years ago.

Empire Importing is convinced that it can market the Clovis detached skates in the United States as high-quality items. Typical cost and price data for one of these, Model TM-5, are shown in Table 1. The other two detachable models have similar cost-price relationships in the three countries listed in the table. Markups over manufacturing cost in other European countries are less than in Switzerland but greater than in Italy. Cost-price relationships for the shoe skates are somewhat different, but Empire Importing does not believe that they could be marketed effectively in the United States, at least at this time, and thus data on these models need not be considered in evaluating this proposal.

The proposal is to offer the products for sale through department stores and discount houses in the eastern part of the United States. Empire Importing would sell Model TM-5 to retailers at a price of $3.50 a pair (approximately Fr. 17.15), plus freight from New York. Empire would pay Clovis Fr. 9.20 a pair, plus all shipping charges and U.S. import duties, estimated at Fr. 4.50 a pair for the TM-5. It would be responsible for all

---

† Copyright 1965 by l'Institut pour l'Etude des Méthodes de Direction de l'Entreprise (IMEDE), Lausanne, Switzerland. Reproduced by permission.

advertising and sales promotion in the United States, would bear all U.S. credit risks, and would have exclusive rights to market Clovis skates east of the Mississippi River for a period of five years.

Mr. J. R. Martell, Clovis's sales manager, is strongly attracted by this proposal. Empire executives are convinced that they can sell 100,000 pairs of skates this year and that within three years they will be able to increase their U.S. volume to 300,000 pairs a year. Manufacturing overhead is now underabsorbed, and capacity exists in the Lyon factory to manufacture

Table 1

SELECTED PRICE AND COST DATA

(all figures in French francs per pair)

	France	Switzerland	Italy
Price data			
Retail price....................	24.00	30.08	24.30
Wholesale price.................	18.00	22.00	18.10
Factory price...................	13.80	15.12	10.35
Cost data:			
Manufacturing cost:			
Variable cost................	6.70	6.70	6.70
Fixed cost...................	2.10	2.10	2.10
Selling and administrative expense			
—fixed...................	1.50	1.50	1.50
Average shipping costs*..........	1.50	1.80	2.10
Import tariff*..................	. . .	1.51	1.65
Approximate retail price range:			
Competing products.............	20.50–34.00	22.13–42.56	9.41–23.52
All Clovis models...............	20.50–30.50	26.67–36.89	18.82–24.30†

* Paid by wholesale distributor; factory prices do not cover shipping costs or import duties.
† Model TM-6, Clovis's most expensive model, is not marketed in Italy.

more than the 300,000 pairs per year required to supply Empire Importing. The overhead rates from which the unit cost figures in Table 1 were derived were based on an annual volume of about 3,600,000 pairs of detachable skates and 500,000 pairs of shoe skates. Most fixed overheads are not traceable to any one product, but represent capacity costs for the combined production of detached and shoe skates and skate parts.

The present level of fixed costs could probably be maintained if sales were to increase by 100,000 pairs a year, but additional supervisory and clerical personnel would be required to handle a larger increase. Clovis's accounting department has assembled estimates that the accompanying increases in total fixed costs would average approximately Fr. 180,000 a year from the second year onward. Variable manufacturing cost per pair would be approximately as shown in Table 1.

Mr. Pepincourt, Clovis's president, is not entirely convinced of the wisdom of entering the U.S. market on this basis. The company's policy has been to market no product at less than full cost, although in some countries such as Italy the profit margin above full cost has been very thin. Furthermore, expansion into the U.S. market would mean that Clovis would have to spend approximately Fr. 150,000 three or four years from now to replace certain items of factory equipment now in use. If the company does not accept the Empire Importing proposal or find other ways to increase volume, production lines can be reorganized at negligible cost, thereby making it possible to dispose of this equipment now. Thus the Empire proposal would commit Clovis to an investment which Mr. Pepincourt is reluctant to make. On the other hand, the working capital necessary to support the company's entry into the United States would be negligible.

The equipment referred to in the previous paragraph has no salvage value at the present time, but depreciation on it is included in factory fixed costs at Fr. 15,000 a year. Other fixed costs associated with this equipment amount to approximately Fr. 60,000 a year.

Shipping charges and European tariffs are high enough so that re-exportation of Clovis skates from New York to Europe would not be feasible, but Mr. Pepincourt is worried nevertheless that if he agrees to this proposal his sales manager will begin to propose major price concessions in other markets as well.

Should Clovis skates be introduced in the United States at the price proposed by Empire Importing Company? Be sure to consider the arguments advanced both by Mr. Martell and by Mr. Pepincourt.

chapter 28

Short-Run Optimization
Models

Management now has access to a wide variety of decision models for problems with relatively short time horizons. Some of these models recognize more than one time period, but most of them are single-period models. The purpose of this chapter is to examine the problems of using accounting data to provide the estimates required by two models that are usually regarded as short-term models:

1. Rationing of existing capacity.
2. Establishing order quantities and reorder points.

This is not a fully representative selection. Neither of these models deals with uncertainty except in a very modest way; each employs relatively simple mathematics. The problems of converting accounting data into decision-oriented estimates are no different for the more complex models, however, and our objective can be served most efficiently by an examination of simple models only.

CAPACITY RATIONING: SINGLE CONSTRAINT MODELS

Scarcity of any kind poses a problem of rationing. In wartime the scarcity of productive resources requires some means of assigning relative priorities so as to insure the flow of resources into their most essential applications. Similarly, when a business finds that its capacity to perform certain functions is fully utilized, it must find some way of rationing the available capacity among alternative uses. This requires a decision criterion and measures of the relative desirability of the various possible uses of the capacity.

All-or-Nothing Model

If the cost function is linear and capacity can be measured in terms of a single limiting factor, the rationing problem would seem simple. Suppose that two products can be produced in a given set of facilities. One product has a P/V ratio of 40 percent; the other's ratio is 60 percent. The demand for the 60 percent product is so great that the company could not fill all of the orders it expects to receive for this product, even if production of the other product were discontinued entirely.

On the surface, it would appear that the best solution would be to fill orders for the 60 percent product only. Four objections to this solution are worth noting, however.

Four objections to this solution can be advanced. First, other short-term alternatives could be considered, such as finding some means of obtaining additional capacity quickly or raising prices on either or both products. Many companies alter the amount of subcontracting of parts and subassemblies as a means of adjusting capacity to product demand, and some even subcontract the entire fabrication process on a portion of their output. Parts or products with the smallest relative margin between purchase price and manufacturing cost are subcontracted first, then followed by others with larger and larger cost-price spreads.

Few companies are either willing or able to take the second course and raise product prices to adjust for short-run capacity limitations. Instead, they extend promised delivery times, become more selective in the orders they accept, or adjust their promotional activities to emphasize the most profitable products or channels of distribution. All these are means of administrative rationing, which is always an alternative to rationing through the pricing mechanism.

The second objection is that the P/V ratios may not reflect all the dimensions of profitability. Many customers buy several of the company's products, and any attempt to limit sales to high-margin items may induce these customers to seek alternative sources of supply. In other words, the demand for an individual product may bear either a complementary or substitution relationship to the demand for another product or products.

Closely related to this is the question of intertemporal independence of demand. By withdrawing from the market for one product now, future sales of that product may be lost. This is an investment problem in concept, but in many and probably most cases the costs of reentering a market are so great that explicit investment evaluation is unnecessary.

The final objection is that the linearity assumption does not apply to a shift as large as this. Beyond a relatively narrow limit, increased sales of one product are obtainable only at the cost of additional promotional expenditure. These cut into the profitability of the high-profit items, and beyond some point further expenditures will not be productive.

Trade-Off Model

Some simple capacity rationing models recognize the diminishing productivity of promotional expenditures. One such model is illustrated in Exhibit 28–1. The vertical distance between the marginal profit line for product A and the base of the chart represents the added profit that could be derived by devoting a small additional amount of capacity to this product. It is assumed that marginal profit declines as more and more capacity is devoted to this product, reflecting increasing marketing costs for each additional unit sold. In other words, the line is fairly high at the left of the diagram, where very little effort is being devoted to product A. As more and more of the plant's capacity is devoted to this product, however, the marginal profit falls, reaching a low point at the right-hand margin, where product A is taking up all of the plant's capacity.

Exhibit 28–1

SINGLE-CONSTRAINT RATIONING MODEL

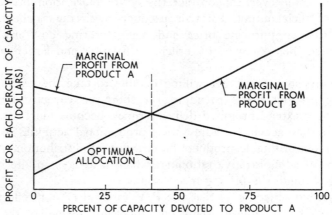

The line for product B has the same meaning, except that its percentage of plant capacity must be read from right to left. (In a two-product facility, giving 75 percent to product A means giving 25 percent to product B, and so on.) Thus the height of the marginal profit line for product B indicates the profit that would be lost by diverting an additional unit of capacity to product A. As long as the two marginal profit figures differ, the company can gain by substituting the product with the greater marginal profit for the other. The optimum solution is indicated by the point of intersection of the two curves.

Practical Application

This model gives management a useful approach to capacity rationing decisions, but the data are seldom adequate to a full implementation. Instead, its direct application probably has to be limited to the identification of the direction of desirable changes in capacity allocation, leaving the extent of such changes to managerial judgment.

An example drawn from practice may illustrate this point. A flour mill has three classes of customers: high-volume chain bakeries, independent commercial bakers, and wholesale distributors of packaged family flour. The mill has been operating with three shifts, seven days a week, for several months, and a number of orders have been lost due to the inability to meet required delivery schedules. Although some salesmen have a higher percentage of family flour and chain bakery business than others, all salesmen contact customers in all three categories.

Product specifications are different for each group of customers, and for this reason mill hours per hundredweight are also different. Because mill hours are the capacity-limiting factor, relative profitability cannot be indicated adequately by variable profit per hundredweight. The real question is which class of business provides the greatest profit per mill hour. Data relevant to this question are shown in the following table:

	Chain Bakeries	Independent Bakeries	Family Flour
Variable profit per cwt.............	\$ 0.0734	\$ 0.0896	\$ 0.0942
Cwt. per mill hour................	280	260	245
Variable profit per mill hour........	\$20.552	\$23.296	\$23.079

This comparison reveals two important facts. First, the chain bakery business is far less profitable than either of the other two categories. This is no surprise to management, because competitive bidding for the trade of the bulk buyers has consistently led to lower prices on this portion of the business. Management is quite satisfied to see that the profit contribution per mill hour on the sales to chain bakeries is as high as it is, because the mill could not operate without the substantial volume afforded by this segment of the business.

The second fact revealed by the table is that family flour, with a higher variable profit per hundredweight than independent bakery sales, represents a less profitable utilization of capacity. On the basis of this comparison, the company's salesmen might be instructed to continue contacting their more regular customers in each category but to place more promotional effort in the independent bakeries. They might also be authorized to offer firmer delivery promises to the independent bakers than to the wholesale distributors of family flour. The family flour business would not be given up entirely, however, because this would leave idle capacity that could not be filled profitably by expansion of sales in other lines.

MULTIPLE-CONSTRAINT RATIONING MODELS: LINEAR PROGRAMMING

Capacity is seldom unidimensional. Typically, it represents a composite of the separate capacities of various departments or functions of the firm. Whenever a product or other segment of the business utilizes two or more services which have limited service capacity, a more complex form of analysis is required.

Two-by-Two Optimization Model

In the simplest case, two products, customers, or projects compete for the use of two scarce resources. For example, suppose that a company has two products, each of which is processed in the same two production departments. The available data are:

Product	Variable Profit per Unit	Machine-Hours Required per Unit		Order Backlog (Units)
		Dept. X	Dept. Y	
A....................	$10	4	2	1,000
B....................	6	1	‑ 3	2,500

Capacity   *4500*   *7500*

Capacity is 4,500 hours in department X and 7,500 hours in department Y.

Product A is the more profitable of the two, and one solution would be to produce the 1,000 units of product A, filling in with product B until one department's capacity was reached. Department X's capacity would be critical in this case, and the solution would be:

Product	Output	Capacity Utilized		Variable Profit
		Dept. X	Dept. Y	
A....................	1,000	4,000	2,000	$10,000
B....................	500	500	1,500	3,000
Total................		4,500	3,500	$13,000
Capacity available.......		4,500	7,500	
Idle capacity..........		0	4,000	

The existence of idle capacity in department Y suggests that it might be profitable to shift some production from A to B, which uses department Y more intensively. If one unit of A were to be dropped, this would permit production of four units of B, because it would release four hours of department X capacity. Four units of B contribute $24 of profit instead of $10, for a net gain of $14 for every unit of A that is dropped.

A second possible solution, therefore, would be to produce as much product B as department Y could handle. Since one unit of product B requires three hours in department Y, this department's capacity would be completely absorbed by 2,500 units of product B. These units would contribute $15,000 in profit. This is better than the first solution, but this time some of department X's capacity would be idle:

| Product | Output | Capacity Utilized | | Variable Profit |
		Dept. X	Dept. Y	
A....................	0	0	0	0
B....................	2,500	2,500	7,500	$15,000
Total.................		2,500	7,500	$15,000
Capacity available.......		4,500	7,500	
Idle capacity..........		2,000	0	

Once again the opportunity cost analysis is revealing. If a unit of product B were to be withdrawn, this would release capacity in department Y to make one and a half units of product A. The gain would be $15 (1½ × $10); the loss would be $6. Thus a net gain of $9 would result from this shift.

The optimum solution obviously lies somewhere between these extremes. When department X is underutilized, it pays to substitute product A for product B. When department Y is underutilized, it pays to substitute product B for product A. This suggests that the optimum solution will be reached when both departments are fully utilized.

One way to reach this solution is to use the substitution ratio in department Y. By cutting back one unit of product B, capacity is released for one and a half units of product A. This substitution will keep department Y fully occupied and will use five hours of department X's idle capacity:

Added production of A: 1½ × 4..................... 6 hours
Less: Reduced production of B: 1 × 1................. 1 hour
Net increase in use of department X................... 5 hours

Because department X had an idle capacity of 2,000 hours, both departments will be fully utilized if 400 units of B are subtracted from the preliminary solution. This will release enough capacity to produce 600 units of A. The profit under this solution is:

$$600 \times \$10 + 2{,}100 \times \$6 = \$18{,}600$$

This is $3,600 greater than the better of the two previous solutions. The amount of the improvement could have been predicted, because the benefit from substituting one and a half units of A for one unit of B was found to be $9 and we made 400 of these substitutions.

The feasibility of the solution can be checked by deriving the input requirements:

Product	Units Produced	Hours Required	
		Dept. X	Dept. Y
A......................	600	2,400	1,200
B......................	2,100	2,100	6,300
Total....................		4,500	7,500

Linear Programming

The knowledgeable reader will long since have recognized this as a special case of a widely used technique known as linear programming. Linear programming consists of a set of mathematical procedures by which management finds the capacity-occupancy pattern that will maximize or minimize a performance measure that management has selected. In the illustration above, the performance measure was incremental profit, capacity was measured in the number of hours available, and the occupancy pattern was described by the number of units of each of two products to be manufactured.

Any extensive consideration of the techniques of linear programming is beyond the scope of this text. Some discussion of the basic elements of a linear program is necessary, however, to indicate the kinds of accounting data that the method requires.

Constructing the Program. The first step in constructing a linear program is to identify the *decision variables* that management can influence. In the illustration, two such variables were identified:

1. A = number of units of product A to be manufactured.
2. B = number of units of product B to be manufactured.

The next step is to identify the relationship between these variables and the measure to be maximized or minimized. This relationship is known as the *objective function,* because it shows the relationship (function, in mathematical terms) between the decision variables and the measuring units in which management expresses its objective. In this case the objective was profit maximization and the objective function was:

$$\text{Profit} = \$10 \times A + \$6 \times B$$

The next step is to identify the conditions that an acceptable solution must meet. These are referred to as the *constraints.* The constraints in the illustration were:

1. The capacity of department X is 4,500 hours.
2. The capacity of department Y is 7,500 hours.
3. Output of product A cannot be negative.
4. Output of product B cannot be negative.

The first constraint can be expressed mathematically as an inequality— that is, production of the two products must use no more than 4,500 hours in total. Mathematically:

$$\text{Hours used for } A + \text{hours used for } B \leq 4{,}500$$

(The symbol $\leq$ means "is less than or equal to.") Since we know that each unit of product A requires four hours of department X time and each unit of product B requires one hour, we can restate the inequality as follows:

$$4A + 1B \leq 4{,}500 \qquad \text{(Department X capacity constraint)}$$

A similar translation of the capacity constraint for department Y yields the following inequality:

$$2A + 3B \leq 7{,}500 \qquad \text{(Department Y capacity constraint)}$$

The third and fourth constraints would seem superfluous, but they must be introduced to rule out nonsensical solutions that might otherwise emerge from a mechanistic application of the mathematical problem-solving technique. The mathematical expression of the constraints is as follows:

$$A \geq 0$$
$$B \geq 0$$

(The symbol $\geq$ means "is greater than or equal to.")

Graphic Soultion. This problem can be solved by a number of different linear programming techniques. We shall illustrate only one, the graphic method, as the clearest way to show the logic underlying them all.

Exhibit 28–2

GRAPH SHOWING FIRST CONSTRAINT

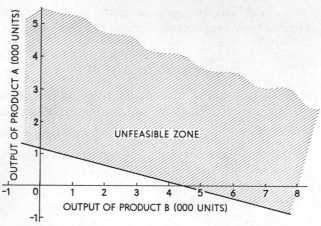

The first step is to prepare a sheet of graph paper and draw in the constraints. Exhibit 28–2 shows a graph with a line representing the first constraint drawn in. The position of this line is determined by computing the values of B corresponding to any two values of A. (Since the relationship between the two is linear, identification of any two points is enough to locate the position of the line.)

For example, when output of product A is zero, the constraint becomes:

$$4 \times 0 + B \leq 4{,}500$$

That is, when output of A is zero, output of B cannot exceed 4,500 units.

The second value of A can also be selected arbitrarily, say at 1,000 units. The inequality becomes:

$$4 \times 1{,}000 + B \leq 4{,}500$$

Solving this, we find that the output of product B cannot exceed 500 units when 1,000 units of product A are manufactured.

The straight line drawn through these two pairs of values in Exhibit 28–2 marks the dividing line between an acceptable solution and one that is not feasible. All points above this line—that is, those falling in the shaded area in the diagram—are ruled out by the inability of department X's resources to handle the load.

This process can be repeated for each of the constraints, with the results shown in Exhibit 28–3. The line representing the department Y constraint was constructed by exactly the same procedure as the one used for department X. The third and fourth constraints are represented

Exhibit 28–3
GRAPH SHOWING ALL CONSTRAINTS

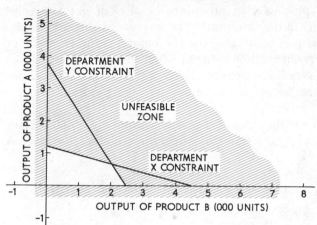

by the shadings that rule out all of the negative values of A and B. All feasible solutions therefore lie in the unshaded area in the diagram.

Although a large number of solutions are feasible, they are not all equally desirable. To choose among them, we must find some way of superimposing the objective function on the diagram. This is the most difficult step to visualize, but the procedure is basically very simple. We start by picking any output combination and computing the anticipated profit from that combination. Because it will be easy to plot on the diagram, suppose that we pick the combination of no units of A and 2,000 units of B. The profit would be:

$$\text{Profit} = 0 + \$6 \times 2,000 = \$12,000$$

The next step is to find another output combination that provides this same \$12,000 profit. Again, the easiest solution is to let B equal zero, so that the output of A is:

$$\$12,000 = \$10 \times A + 0$$

The output of A would be 1,200 units.

These two points have been plotted in Exhibit 28–4 and a straight line has been drawn between them. Because the profit relationship is assumed to be linear, every point on this line represents an output combination that will produce a \$12,000 profit contribution. We call this an "isoprofit" line. Even more important, all points to the "northeast" of this line represent an output combination that would yield more than \$12,000. Since many feasible combinations lie in this zone, it stands to reason that the company can increase its profit by selecting a combination farther to the northeast.

The graphic solution procedure consists of drawing other isoprofit lines parallel to the first, moving progressively outward. Each line stands for a higher profit total than the one before, as shown in the exhibit. The maximum profit solution is found when an isoprofit line crosses the outer edge of the feasible output zone. Any other output is on a lower isoprofit line, and the output combinations on higher isoprofit lines are all unfeasible.

In this case, the maximum possible profit is $18,600, obtainable when the output of A is 600 units and the output of B is 2,100 units. At no other

Exhibit 28–4

LINEAR PROGRAMMING: GRAPHIC SOLUTION

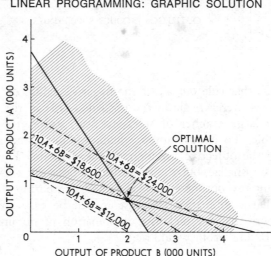

combination can the company make as much as $18,600, and all other output combinations producing $18,600 fall in the unfeasible zone.

Notice that this solution is at the point of an angle at the edge of the feasible zone. This will always be the case unless the maximum isoprofit line coincides with one of the constraint boundaries. In that limiting case, a number of combinations will be equally desirable.

In summary, the capacity constraints define the feasible region. The best combination of outputs is found by moving the isoprofit line out until it reaches the farthest limit of the feasible region. This combination normally will be at the intersection of two of the constraint lines or at the intersection of one constraint line and either the vertical or horizontal axis.

Other Solution Methods. Most linear programs are too complex for graphic solution and must be solved by other means. The method most commonly used is the simplex method, described in any standard operations research textbook.[1] Computer programs for the simplex method are widely available, and most linear programs are solved on the computer in a minute fraction of the time a manual solution would require.

Shadow Prices. The constraints in linear programs are ordinarily less rigid than the mathematical formulation would imply. If the payoff is great enough, management often can find a way to alter the constraint. The linear program can be used to identify the constraints that are most worth changing.

For example, suppose that department X's capacity could be increased by one hour, to 4,501 hours. Suppose also that fractional outputs are feasible. We saw earlier that we could substitute one and a half units of product A profitably for one unit of product B if we had five hours of idle time in department X. Total use of department Y would be unaffected by this substitution. This means that one additional hour of time in department X would permit the following adjustment:

$$\text{Product A:} \quad +\tfrac{1}{5} \times 1\tfrac{1}{2} = +0.3 \text{ unit}$$

$$\text{Product B:} \quad -\tfrac{1}{5} \times 1 \quad\ = -0.2 \text{ unit}$$

The profit contribution of a unit of product A is \$10; that of product B is \$6. The extra hour of capacity therefore would increase total company profit by $0.3 \times \$10 - 0.2 \times \$6 = \$1.80$. In other words, an hour of department X capacity is worth \$1.80. This is referred to as department X's shadow price.

A similar calculation can be made for department Y. Additional capacity in department Y, unaccompanied by an increase in the capacity of department X, could be used only by substituting some units of product B for product A. Since a unit of A requires four hours in department X and a unit of B takes only one hour, the substitution would be in a four-to-one ratio. Adding four units of B would increase usage of department Y by 12 hours, less the 2 hours saved by the cutback in production of A there, a net increase of 10 hours. Since we are only adding one hour of capacity, we can handle only one tenth of this substitution, permitting the following adjustment:

$$\text{Product A:} \quad -\tfrac{1}{10} \times 1 = -0.1 \text{ unit}$$

$$\text{Product B:} \quad +\tfrac{1}{10} \times 4 = +0.4 \text{ unit}$$

The addition of an hour of department Y capacity therefore would be worth $0.4 \times \$6 - 0.1 \times \$10 = \$1.40$. This means that the capacity constraint in department Y is \$0.40 an hour less costly than the one in de-

---

[1] For an elementary but very clear exposition, see Richard I. Levin and C. A. Kirkpatrick, *Quantitative Approaches to Management* (New York: McGraw-Hill Book Co., 1965), chaps. 8 and 9. Saul I. Gass, *Linear Programming: Methods and Applications* (3d ed.; New York: McGraw-Hill Book Co., 1969) provides a more complete explanation.

partment X. Management should be willing to pay up to $0.40 more for extra department X hours than for department Y hours.

Accounting Data Required

Familiarity with linear programming can help the accountant in three ways. First, the simple act of formulating the constraints may permit him to show the operating executive how past and present decisions are narrowing the number of feasible solutions. This may lead to a desirable review of these decisions.

Second, he may be able to use linear programming to prepare recommended utilization schedules and to identify profitable ways of altering the existing constraints. In other words, he can use linear programming in performing his role as advisor and analyst for line management.

Third, knowledge of the method is essential if the accountant is called upon to provide data for others to insert in their linear programs. The main criterion that must be met in providing cost data for this purpose is that the cost be variable with product output, roughly in proportion to the change in the volume of output. Put another way, this means that the only costs that need to be considered are those that will be affected by the way capacity is utilized. Since linear programming can deal only with linear relationships, increments or steps in fixed costs must be either excluded or averaged. If the steps are relatively close together, they should be averaged into the variable costing figure. Otherwise they should be excluded.

Another question is how to deal with increments in rates of variability. For example, capacity operations may require the use of high-cost suppliers for, say, 10 percent of total materials. The full penalty price presumably should be used to cost the materials used, on the ground that this approximates marginal cost. This will give products with low materials requirements a larger share of the optimal product mix. If their share becomes big enough, the need for high-cost purchases may disappear and the cost penalties will become inapplicable. If the adjustment is this large, more complex models must be used.

A more difficult question is how to deal with costs that vary with the degree of utilization of capacity but are not affected by the product mix. For example, suppose that capacity in department X is measured in labor hours. Restrictions on the size of the labor force usually also preclude variations in the composition of the labor force at capacity operation. This means that total labor cost will be the same no matter which products are manufactured, as long as all of the capacity is used.

Department X's labor costs should not be left out of the objective function in this situation, however, because linear programming does not preclude solutions that do not use all of the available capacity. For example, suppose that department X labor cost at $5 an hour had not been

b : $5/hr

deducted in computing the objective function above. Since product A uses four hours and product B uses one hour of department X labor, deducting this cost would lead to the following objective function:

3 × B   20 ÷ A

$$\text{Profit} = \$1 \times B - \$10 \times A$$

Since production of even one unit of product A would be unprofitable, it is clear that the best decision in this case would be to produce no product A at all. Department Y's capacity would limit output of product B to 2,500 units and these would use only 2,500 hours of department X time, leaving 2,000 hours of idle capacity. The labor cost of these 2,000 hours is a variable cost and is incremental to any decision between full utilization and less than full utilization. Only those costs that will be the same whether capacity is used or not should be excluded from the objective function.

Sensitivity Analysis

The development of shadow prices is an example of a simple form of a technique known as sensitivity analysis. This has been defined as a method of determining the responsiveness of the conclusions of an analysis to changes or errors in parameter values used in the analysis.[2] The conclusions referred to in this definition can be either the action recommendation or the estimated value of the objective function. Of these, the sensitivity of the action recommendation is the more important and deserves to be the focus of our attention.

The analyst's main task is to identify the range of values of one of the parameters for which a given action recommendation would be valid. Changing the constraints by tiny amounts, for example, would require immediate changes in the production schedule, as we saw in the preceding section on shadow prices. Changes in the relative profit contributions of the two products would have no effect at all unless the change was extremely large.

To illustrate this latter point, let us return to Exhibit 28–4. The optimal production decision is indicated by the intersection of the $18,600 isoprofit line and the two departmental capacity constraint lines. The isoprofit lines in this diagram reflect an assumption that a unit of B is 60 percent as profitable as a unit of A. If the relative profit changes, the slope of the isoprofit lines will change. As the value of A increases, the isoprofit lines become flatter. The intersecting point will not change, however, unless product A becomes more than four times as profitable as product B. In that case the highest isoprofit line would be reached by producing only product A and no product B. This is illustrated in Exhibit

---

[2] Alfred Rappaport, "Sensitivity Analysis in Decision Making," *Accounting Review*, July 1967, p. 441

Exhibit 28–5
EFFECT OF CHANGE IN RELATIVE PROFIT RATIO

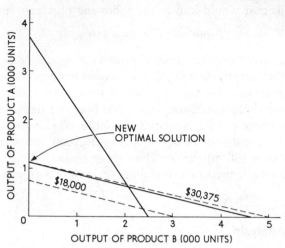

OUTPUT OF PRODUCT B (000 UNITS)

28–5. Here the profit contributed by a unit of A is assumed to be $27, while B continues to contribute $6 a unit. The highest isoprofit line the company can reach is the $30,375 line reached by producing 1,125 units of A and no B at all:

$$\text{Profit} = 1{,}125 \times \$27 + 0 = \$30{,}375$$

This line cannot be reached at any other output combination.

The recommendation at the other end of the scale would not be affected unless a unit of product B was more than one and a half times as profitable as a unit of product A. Beyond this point, the slope of the isoprofit line would be greater than the slope of the department Y constraint, so that the highest feasible isoprofit line would be reached at an output of 2,500 units of B and no production of A.

In other words, the action recommendation would be the same within a very wide range of relative profit values:

$$\left(\frac{P_A}{P_B} = \frac{4}{1}\right) \geqq \text{Actual ratio} \geqq \left(\frac{P_A}{P_B} = \frac{2}{3}\right)$$

The estimated ratio is $10/$6, far from either end of the range.

The reason for this application of sensitivity analysis is uncertainty. Management probably does not know the profit contribution figures with certainty, and this analysis indicates how serious this lack of knowledge is likely to be. Sensitivity analysis is also useful even in the absence of uncertainty, however, in the evaluation of constraints that we mentioned earlier. This consists of examining the effects of altering, adding, or eliminating individual constraints. The key question in each of these applications is how the change will affect the value of the objective function.

INVENTORY DECISION MODELS

One of the most frequent routine actions is the placing of a purchase order. Management must decide what to buy, from whom, when, and in what quantity.

Given the number of these decisions, it is perhaps not surprising that a large number of models have been developed to permit management to routinize at least some of these decisions—primarily how much to buy at any one time and when to place the order. In the next few pages we shall attempt to explain one of the simplest of these models and look briefly at the kinds of data that it requires.

The Basic Variables

Most inventory models represent a systematic, programmed method of making purchase or production order decisions. The key relationship in most if not all of these models is between the size of the order and the average amount of inventory on hand. At a given usage rate, the average inventory quantity will vary directly with the size of the order.

For example, suppose that a company needs 10 units of a certain item each week. It now buys a week's requirements at a time—that is, each order is for 10 units. The inventory on hand varies from 10 units (just after the receipt of the latest order quantity) to zero (just before the receipt of the next order quantity). If the consumption rate is steady during the week, the average inventory will be halfway between 10 and zero, or 5 units.

This behavior pattern is illustrated in the left-hand panel of Exhibit 28–6. Inventory quantity starts at 10, falls gradually to zero, and then

Exhibit 28–6

EFFECT OF ORDER QUANTITY ON AVERAGE INVENTORY

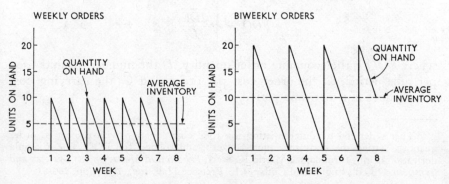

bounces back to 10 when the new shipment is received. The inventory level in the right-hand panel shows the same pattern, but the purchase quantity is doubled, to 20 units. This means that orders have to be placed only every other week, but the average inventory goes up to 10 units.

This relationship is significant because costs are ordinarily affected by the number of orders placed in a given time period and by the average inventory quantity. Weekly purchases, for example, require 50 times as many orders as annual purchases, and therefore approximately 50 times as much clerical time, 50 times as many forms, and 50 times as much postage. The average inventory is only one 50th as large, however, which means that less storage space will have to be provided, less insurance will be carried, less capital will be tied up, and fewer units will deteriorate or become obsolete.

The other major variable that is common to all inventory models is the rate at which the item is used, usually referred to as the *demand rate* or *demand*. Other things being equal, both order size and average inventory will be large if the demand is great and small if it is small.

The Basic Model

The simplest inventory decision models stop here, using only the variables described above. Their objective is to minimize total inventory cost, given a stable level of demand that is known with absolute certainty. The objective function is:

Annual Cost = Number of orders per year × cost per order + average inventory quantity × carrying cost per unit

Since inventory carrying costs at a given demand level vary directly with order size and purchase costs vary inversely, cost minimization is a matter of increasing the order quantity until the marginal carrying cost of further increases in inventory would exceed the marginal reduction in ordering cost. The simplest formula used to calculate this point is:[3]

$$EOQ = \sqrt{\frac{2DC_o}{C_c}}$$

where *EOQ* is the economic order quantity, *D* the number of units used per time period, C_o the order cost per order, and C_c the carrying cost per product unit per time period.

---

[3] This is derived by differentiating the total cost equation with respect to order quantity, setting the derivative equal to zero, and solving for EOQ. For a simple derivation of this formula, see Martin K. Starr, *Production Management: Systems and Synthesis* (2d ed.; Englewood Cliffs, N.J.: Prentice-Hall, Inc., 1972), pp. 280–81.

Safety Stocks and Reorder Points

Orders typically must be given to suppliers many days or weeks before delivery is desired. This interval is known as the *lead time*, and an essential element of any inventory decision model is the *reorder point*, identified by the model as the signal to place a new purchase order.

Lead time would pose no problem if the assumptions underlying the basic model always held true—that is, an order would be placed when the quantity on hand was just equal to the quantity that would be used during the lead time. This would insure that the new shipment would arrive just as the existing stock was exhausted.

The real world is not this simple. Both the rate of use and the length of the lead time are uncertain. This means that *stock-outs* can occur—that is, the inventory on hand is inadequate to fill a customer's order on the desired delivery date. In the case of factory materials and parts, a stock-out represents a failure to fill a requisition when a particular item is needed in production.

Stock-outs can be costly. If the result is the loss of a customer order, at least part of the cost is the opportunity cost of the lost order. If the result is an outside purchase to fill the customer's order, the cost is the penalty that must be paid for prompt delivery. If the result is deferred delivery to the customer, the cost will include the present value of repeat orders that now will be lost. In all three cases, the stock-out may increase the amount of idle time and disrupt production flows, thereby increasing factory costs for the volume of work done.

Management can reduce the number of stock-outs by providing a *safety stock*—the amount expected to be on hand at the time an inventory replenishment shipment is received. Safety stocks are not costless, however. By increasing the average inventory quantity, they increase inventory carrying costs. The problem is to adjust the size of the safety stock so that the carrying cost of the last unit in the inventory is equal to the stock-out cost avoided by having that unit in stock.

To illustrate, let us suppose that the economic order quantity for a part used in the factory is 200 units, with an average usage of 20 units a week. The lead time is four weeks. Assuming that both the lead time and the demand are known with certainty, the company will always reorder when 80 units are on hand. Unfortunately, both the lead time and the demand are uncertain quantities This means that if the company carries no safety stocks, it will be out of stock some of the time (whenever more than 80 units are demanded between the time of reorder and the time the goods are received).

To illustrate the general approach without overcomplicating the arithmetic, let us assume that lead time is certain but that demand varies between 10 and 30 units a week, with the various demands occurring at the following frequencies:

Weekly Demand (units)	*Percentage Probability*
10	5
15	10
20	70
25	10
30	5

In other words, demand is expected to exceed the 80-unit reorder date inventory during 15 percent of the reorder intervals, when weekly demand is more than 20 units.

Management has several options here. One is to carry a zero safety stock and accept the likelihood of being out of stock 15 percent of the time. Another is to reduce the stock-out frequency to 5 percent by carry-

Exhibit 28-7

CALCULATION OF OUT-OF-STOCK COSTS

(1) Safety Stock (units)	(2) Units Short per Order Period	(3) Order Periods per Year	(4) Prob- ability	(5) Expected Units Short per Year (2) × (3) × (4)	(6) Expected Annual Stock-Out Cost (5) × $18
0	20	5	0.10	10	
	40	5	0.05	10	
				20	$360
20	20	5	0.05	5	90
40	0	5	0.00	0	0

ing a 20-unit safety stock—that is, by placing the order while five weeks' supply is on hand instead of four. Finally, the stock-out probability can be reduced to zero by increasing the safety stock to 40 units, a two-week normal supply, reordering when 120 units are in inventory.

To choose among these alternatives, management needs two sets of estimates: (1) how the stock-out costs are associated with each safety stock level, and (2) the inventory level corresponding to each safety stock level.

Stock-Out Costs. The calculation of the first of these is summarized in Exhibit 28–7. Starting on the first line, we see that with a zero safety stock the company will be 20 units short 10 percent of the time. Since orders are placed every 10 weeks, on the average, and the factory operates 50 weeks a year, five orders will be placed in an average year. This means that 10 units will be out of stock on an annual basis (20 × 10% × 5 times a year).

The next line in the exhibit shows that the zero safety stock will lead to a few 40-unit stock-outs as well as the 20-unit stock-outs covered on the first line. This will happen 5 percent of the time, or 10 units a year. If stock-out costs amount to $18 a unit, annual stock-out costs of a zero safety stock will be $360. Similar calculations for two other safety stock levels are summarized on the final two lines.

Average Inventory Level. Introduction of a safety stock increases the average inventory level. The number of units in the safety stock can be used as a rough measure of the increase, but if management wants a more precise figure, the probability figures will have to be introduced.

Exhibit 28–8

INVENTORY LEVELS WITH NO SAFETY STOCK, 80-UNIT REORDER
LEVEL, 200-UNIT ORDER QUANTITY, AND 10-UNIT WEEKLY DEMAND

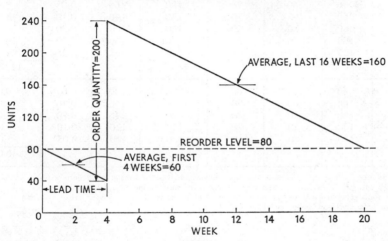

For instance, the figures in the illustration show that with a zero safety stock a reorder should be placed when the inventory reaches 80 units. If weekly demand is only 10 units, then 40 units will still be on hand when the new shipment arrives. This is shown in Exhibit 28–8. The inventory level gradually declines from 80 to 40, as shown by the short sloping line in the left-hand portion of the exhibit.

Immediately after the goods are received, the inventory level goes up to 240 units (40 units on hand plus the standard order quantity of 200 units). After this peak, it falls gradually to 80 units, at which point another order is placed and the cycle is completed. Since demand is at a rate of 10 units a week, this decline takes 16 weeks, as shown in the right-hand portion of the exhibit.

Assuming a steady rate of demand, the average inventory for this safety stock level and this demand level will be 60 units during the first 4 weeks (halfway between 80 and 40) and 160 units during the last 16

Exhibit 28–9

CALCULATION OF INVENTORY COSTS OF SAFETY STOCKS
(in units)

(1) Safety Stock	(2) Used during Lead Time	(3) On Hand at Order Arrival 80 − (2)	(4) Reorder Interval	(5) Remainder of Cycle	(6) Entire Cycle	(7) Probability	(8) Expected Average Inventory (6) × (7)
			Average Inventory during:				
0	40	40	60	160	140	0.05	7.0
	60	20	50	150	120	0.10	12.0
	80	0	40	140	100	0.70	70.0
	100	0	32*	140	91	0.10	9.1
	120	0	26.7*	140	83	0.05	4.1
							102.2
20	40	60	80	180	160	0.05	8.0
	60	40	70	170	140	0.10	14.0
	80	20	60	160	120	0.70	84.0
	100	0	50	150	100	0.10	10.0
	120	0	41.7*	150	91	0.05	4.5
							120.5
40	40	80	100	200	180	0.05	9.0
	60	60	90	190	160	0.10	16.0
	80	40	80	180	140	0.70	98.0
	100	20	70	170	120	0.10	12.0
	120	0	60	160	100	0.05	5.0
							140.0

* Inventory will reach zero before the new shipment arrives. If demand is 25 units a week, an 80-unit inventory will last 3⅕ weeks. The average inventory is 40 units during this period and zero during the next ⅘ of a week. The weighted average for the entire four weeks is 32 units. Similar calculations can be made for other order-level–order-point combinations.

weeks (halfway between 240 and 80). The average for the entire 20 weeks between reorder points will be:

$$\frac{4 \times 60 + 16 \times 160}{4 + 16} = 140 \text{ units}$$

Similar calculations can be made for every possible combination of safety stock and demand level. These have been summarized in the first six columns of Exhibit 28–9.[3]

The expected average inventory level can now be calculated by multiplying each possible inventory level by itse probability. The results of these calculations are shown in the right-hand column of the exhibit.

Calculating the Optimal Safety Stock. With these figures we can calculate the optimal safety stock. If annual carrying costs amount to $6 a unit, then the analysis will show the following:

[3] Calculations can also be made for negative safety stocks. In this case they are clearly suboptimal, because the probability of stock-outs with a small negative safety stock of 20 units would increase to 85 percent.

Safety Stock	Carrying Cost	Stock-Out Cost	Total Cost
0..............	$613.20	$360	$973.20
20..............	723.00	90	813.00
40..............	840.00	0	840.00

In other words, the company can minimize the cost of its safety stock by providing a safety stock of 20 units and a reorder level of 100 units (the safety stock plus the normal consumption during the four-week lead time).

Data Requirements

Many other inventory desision models have been developed, most of them more complex than the one described above. Most of them require the same kinds of data, however, and discussion of the data requirements of one will serve them all.

Order quantity models call for three kinds of physical unit data: demand, out-of-stock, and inventory quantities. Although many companies fail to record out-of-stock data, measurement of these quantities poses no conceptual problems. The main task is to make sure that information is available in usable form.

Cost data are more difficult to prescribe. Three cost factors must be estimated:

1. Order cost.
2. Carrying cost.
3. Stock-out cost.

Order Costs. Historical order-cost data can be accumulated in the ledger accounts. The order cost used in inventory models should be a cost that varies in some sense with the number of orders placed. Most order costs are completely fixed in the short run, but some of them must be changed as the total load on the purchasing or order department is increased and can be reduced as the load falls. In other words, the attributable cost concept is applicable here. If the fixed costs are relatively divisible, they should be unitized and included in the order cost factor. Otherwise they should be excluded.

The reason for this approach is that aggregate order cost depends on the joint outcome of thousands of order quantity decisions. Although a single extra order will cost little more than a few cents for paper and postage, a 10 percent increase is likely to require an additional order clerk and a 20 percent increase may call for another purchasing officer.

Just what constitutes "reasonable" divisibility is difficult to say, but one approach is to see how sensitive the order quantity is to variations in order costs. If it is highly sensitive, the number of orders will be affected considerably. The accountant can then check to see whether the change in cost appropriate to the change in the number of orders corresponds to the figures used in the calculation.

Carrying Costs. Carrying costs are of two different kinds: those that vary with the cost or value of the average inventory, and those that vary with the physical quantity of the average inventory. Insurance, financing, and spoilage costs are in the former category; the cost of warehouse space may vary with the latter.

Once again, and for the same reason as for order costs, carrying costs should be based on the attributable cost concept. Few personnel costs fit this definition, however. One reason is that most labor costs associated with inventory storage are related to stacking and unstacking, and these are unrelated to the length of time the goods are in inventory. Only if larger inventories require additional storage locations is the labor cost increment likely to be material in amount.

Financing costs are ordinarily determined outside the ledger accounts. Implicit interest for simple models should be based on the cost of capital figures that are used for capital expenditure decisions. These are seldom, if ever, equal to the explicit interest rates on borrowed funds. The reason is that the economic order quantity decision affects the amount of long-term capital that must be raised. Only complex models that recognize seasonal demand patterns call for the introduction of short-term borrowing rates on seasonal inventories.

Stock-Out Costs. Stock-out costs are the most difficult to measure and estimate. As we noted earlier, the cost depends on the consequences of the stock-out—loss of current sales, premium payments for rush delivery, loss of future sales, extra factory costs, or some combination of these.

If the results of the stock-out is lost sales, the cost ordinarily can be measured by the product's P/V ratio. In most cases standard variable manufacturing cost will be a reasonable approximation of the marginal cost of production. Variable sales commissions and other short-run variable selling and administrative costs should also be entered at average variable cost. Step-function increments in fixed costs should be excluded, because the aggregate volume of stock-outs is likely to be insufficient to permit significant reductions in divisional fixed costs.

If stock-outs lead to rush orders and subcontracting rather than lost sales, the stock-out cost is the difference between the internal variable cost of manufacture and the costs of dealing outside. The latter should include such hidden penalties as the costs of extra telephone calls, the costs of preparing specifications and choosing among suppliers, and the costs of expediting delivery.

The costs of idle labor time, including allowances for fringe benefits and other related costs, must also be included in the stock-out cost. This refers to idleness of wage-rated employees, not salaried personnel; again on the grounds that the volume differential seldom will be large enough and last long enough to permit any significant adjustment of salary costs to lower aggregate volume. For this reason, idle time costs are likely to be considerably smaller in connection with models governing reorder points of purchased merchandise than for goods purchased for processing or internal consumption.

Penalty costs are unlikely to be available routinely in historical accounting records, and in most cases the usefulness of these data will be too small to warrant collecting them on a regular basis. Rough estimates, perhaps based on a sampling of past order records, are probably as much as can be hoped for.

SUMMARY

Management now has an almost bewildering number of quantitative decision models to choose among. Each of these has its own data requirements. This chapter has attempted to throw some light on these requirements by discussing two different kinds of optimization models.

The first section of the chapter dealt with a group of capacity rationing models, by which management can decide which of two or more competing uses of capacity should be favored. Both single-constraint and multiple-constraint models were examined, the latter in a simple linear programming format. For the linear program, incremental costs must fit a linear formula—that is, a single unit cost figure must be used for each product or other potential use of capacity. This usually means average short-run variable costs.

One short section was also devoted to an introduction to sensitivity analysis. Although linear programming lends itself very easily to sensitivity analysis, any decision model can be examined for sensitivity, both to examine the impact of uncertainty on the quality of the decision and to explore the desirability of altering, adding, or eliminating constraints.

The final section introduced a simple inventory decision model, by which economic order quantities and reorder points can be determined if management is willing to make certain simplifying assumptions about the behavior of product demand. For these models the appropriate cost concept is attributable cost, because the aggregate effect of the decisions to be based on the model is likely to introduce changes in fixed costs.

These same ideas can be applied to other decision models as well, including those that recognize uncertainty. The main problem is to determine the scope of the choices to be made. The wider the scope, the larger the cost increment. Determination of the scope therefore serves to specify the cost definition that should be used.

We have not attempted to delve very deeply into the models themselves, nor have we discussed the practical limitations of simple models like the ones described. Our objective was merely to go far enough to identify the data requirements of the models and indicate the criteria by which data choices can be made.

EXERCISES AND PROBLEMS

1.* Product A has a unit profit contribution of $5, while product B's profit contribution is $8 a unit. The company could sell as many as 2,000 units of each product without reducing the unit profit contribution.

A unit of product A requires two hours in department X and two hours in department Y. A unit of product B requires one hour in department X and four hours in department Y.

Department X has 3,000 hours available for these two products, while department Y has 6,000 hours available.

a) Construct the objective function and formulate the constraints.
b) What is the optimal production schedule? What is the anticipated profit contribution at this level of production?
c) How sensitive is the scheduling decision to variations in the profit contribution of product A?

2. The attributable cost of processing a purchase order is $36. Attributable carrying costs average 20 percent of average inventory cost. The company expects to buy 10,000 units of material X during the next year at a purchase price of $2.50.

Stock-out costs for this material are measured by the cost of idle labor time plus penalty costs for emergency deliveries. Management estimates that these amount to $1 for each unit that is not on hand when it is needed.

The average lead time is three weeks. (For convenience, the year is assumed to consist of 50 weeks.) The consumption of this material during the reorder period is expected to correspond to the following pattern of probable usage:

Usage During 3-Week Period	Probability of this Usage
300	0.02
400	0.05
500	0.19
600	0.45
700	0.23
800	0.06

a) Determine the economic order quantity, using the formula supplied in this chapter.

---

* Solutions to problems marked with an asterisk can be found in Appendix B.

b) What safety stock should be carried? Show your calculations. What is the reorder point? Show your calculations. (The desired safety stock should be some multiple of 100 units.)

3. Department 17 is fully utilized, producing several products. It is now operating two shifts, with 4,000 labor hours a month on the first shift and 3,000 labor hours a month on the second shift. Third-shift and overtime operations are not feasible.

Labor costs of the second shift are recorded separately from those of the first shift. Output statistics are also recorded separately. Materials, supplies, utilities, and all other nonlabor costs are not assignable to individual shifts.

Output in department 17 is measured by the number of standard direct labor hours (standard hours) for the work done. Costs and output in a normal month are as follows:

	First Shift	Second Shift	Total
Output (standard hours)...........	4,200	2,800	7,000
Actual direct labor hours..........	4,000	3,000	7,000
Direct labor.....................	$20,000	$15,000	$35,000
Indirect labor...................	4,000	3,000	7,000
Supervision.....................	4,500	3,200	7,700
Shift differential (on direct and indirect labor.................	...	1,800	1,800
Labor benefits and payroll taxes....	5,700	4,600	10,300
Supplies........................			3,500
Power...........................			4,200
Other costs.....................			14,000

Direct labor performance is poorer on the second shift than on the first shift because the best workers are assigned to the first shift and because the employees work less efficiently during evening hours than during the daytime.

Analysis of historical data indicates that cost variability in this department is as follows:

Item	Variability Pattern
Direct labor.............	100% variable with direct labor hours
Indirect labor...........	70% variable with direct labor hours
Supervision.............	100% fixed and indivisible for each shift
Shift differential........	Proportional to second-shift direct and indirect labor
Labor benefits and payroll taxes.................	Proportional to total gross wages and salaries
Supplies................	100% variable with weight of materials used
Power..................	100% variable with weight of materials used
Other costs.............	10% variable with direct labor hours

On the average, products processed in department 17 require one standard direct labor hour for every four pounds of materials.

How much of department 17's costs should be inserted in the objective function as part of the unit cost of a product requiring four pounds of materials and two standard direct labor hours in this department?

4. A single large machine is the only equipment used in one of the Beaman Company's factory departments. Quite a few different products are processed on the machine, and management is interested in finding the most economical lot size in which each product should be manufactured.

One cost that must be considered in determining the most economical lot size is the cost of changing the machine over from one product to another—the setup cost. The following information has been obtained for use in computing the setup cost for product A:

Two men from the maintenance department have to spend four hours each to set up the equipment, which is located in department P.

Maintenance department employees have a basic wage rate of $7 an hour. It is the company's policy to provide its maintenance force with a 40-hour week, adjusting the size of the maintenance staff only if changes in the size of the work load are substantial and likely to persist.

Department P's machine is operated by a crew of six men whose basic wage rate is $6 an hour. While the machine is being set up, these men perform minor finishing operations and carry out other productive tasks to the extent that such work is available. Experience indicates that they are idle approximately 60 percent of the time required for machine setup.

Department P's costs other than direct materials, the wage of the operating crew, and setup labor are expected to average the following monthly amounts:

Depreciation	$ 760
Power	280
Space	160
Payroll taxes and insurance	592
Maintenance labor	440
Foremen	1,200
Operating supplies	300

All payroll taxes and insurance costs on both direct and indirect labor are classified as overhead. They average approximately 8 percent of the gross payroll. Payroll taxes and insurance on setup and maintenance labor are not charged to department P but remain in maintenance department overhead accounts.

Operating supplies and maintenance labor costs charged to department P (as in the table above) are expected to be roughly proportioned to the number of productive hours of the operating crew.

Department P's depreciation, power, space, and foremen costs are regarded as fixed costs.

Maintenance department costs other than labor and payroll taxes and insurance are completely fixed.

A typical month has 20 producing days of eight hours each.

Establish the cost of setting up the machines and explain how you derived your figures.

5. A company manufactures three products, A, B, and C. These three products have been well received in the market, and at current selling prices the company can sell all that it can produce. Data for these three products are as follows:

	A	B	C
Selling price........................	$15	$19	$24
Materials cost......................	5	10	13
Other variable costs (paid when incurred).........................	6	4	7
Portion of selling price collected in month of sale.....................	⅓	0	0

Each product requires one unit of its own special raw material. These materials are not interchangeable—that is, A's material may not be used for B or C, B's may not be used for A or C, and so on. The raw materials inventories will be as follows on January 1:

$$
\begin{aligned}
&200 \text{ units of material for A @ } \$5\ldots\ldots\ldots\ldots\ldots \$1,000 \\
&120 \text{ units of material for B @ } \$10\ldots\ldots\ldots\ldots\ldots 1,200 \\
&\ \ 50 \text{ units of material for C @ } \$13\ldots\ldots\ldots\ldots 650
\end{aligned}
$$

Additional quantities of these materials can be acquired from nearby suppliers on a few hours' notice. Materials are always paid for in cash when they are received.

The products pass through two departments. The maximum machine time available during January is 400 hours in department 1 and 800 hours in department 2. Machine time for processing a unit in each department is:

	Hours Required by a Unit of		
	A	B	C
Department 1...............	½	1	¼
Department 2...............	1	1	4½

Departmental fixed costs (for both departments) will be $900 in January. This includes $200 in depreciation charges; the balance will be paid when incurred.

The January 1 cash balance is expected to be $6,660. The ending cash balance cannot be less than $3,000. Due to a seasonal shutdown, the company will have no outstanding accounts receivable on January 1.

Formulate an objective function to maximize profits and specify the constraints this function is subject to.

6. The management of Danielson, Inc. is preparing its production schedule for the next three months. The company sells two products, A and B, which it manufactures in two departments, X and Y. Department X has a total capacity of 2,700 labor hours a month, while department Y has a monthly capacity of 3,000 machine-hours.

Danielson is now entering its busy season. Orders are flowing in at a record rate, and management knows that it will not be able to fill all of them. Fortunately, the two products are bought by different customers, so that refusal of orders for one product will not lead to cancellation of orders for the other.

The company's accountants have gathered the following information on unit costs, prices, and input requirements for the two products:

	A	B
Materials used (lbs.).....................	2	1
Labor hours, department X...............	1	3
Machine-hours, department Y.............	2	3
Selling price.............................	$47	$53
Salesmen's commissions..................	2	1
Direct labor cost:		
Department X.........................	5	15
Department Y.........................	6	12

The Danielson company has 1,800 pounds of materials in inventory. More materials are on order, but will not be delivered in time for use during the next quarter. The materials now on hand cost $7 a pound; the units on order will cost $8 a pound when delivered.

Overhead costs in department X vary with the number of direct labor hours used, at a rate of $1 per direct labor hour. Variable overhead costs in department Y amount to one third of departmental direct labor cost.

a) Develop the objective function and express the constraints in a form suitable for the use of linear programming.

b) Prepare a recommended monthly production schedule for the next three months.

c) How, if at all, would your recommendation change if you found that two former company employees, now in retirement, would be willing to return to work in department X for a few months on a part-time basis at regular wage rates? These men would be willing to put in a total of 200 hours a month during the next three months.

d) Danielson, Inc. could increase the price of product A by $7 a unit without losing a significant number of orders. How, if at all, would such a change affect your recommendation?

7. The Acme Belt Company has decided to determine purchase order quantities on the basis of the following simple formula:

$$EOQ = \sqrt{\frac{2C_pD}{pC_s}}$$

in which EOQ is the optimal number of units per purchase order, p the purchase price per unit, C_p the cost of purchasing (per order), C_s the annual cost of storage (per dollar of investment in inventory), and D the total number of units needed a year. The three cost parameters—p, C_p, and C_s—are to reflect the following elements:

Purchase price: p
Invoice price
Freight and carting

Purchase order cost: C_p
Forms and supplies
Order preparation
Processing payments
Receiving and inspection

Storage cost: C_s
Insurance
Taxes
Interest
Breakage and spoilage
Space rental
Warehouse operation

You have the following information:

The invoice price of product X is $10 a unit, with a 5 percent discount on purchase orders in excess of 1,000 units. Annual consumption of product X averages 10,000 units.

Freight charges on product X amount to $2.50 a unit.

The purchasing department is responsible for preparing all purchase orders. It processes approximately 2,000 purchase orders a month. Its costs consist of the salaries of the purchasing agent and his assistant ($2,500 a month, including fringe benefits); salaries of six order clerks ($4,000 a month, including fringe benefits); and the costs of forms, supplies, and other variable inputs ($200 a month).

Payments are processed in the accounting department. Work sampling studies indicate that the labor cost of processing an order, including fringe benefits, averages $4 an order. The rental cost of the data processing equipment for the time used to process an average order amounts to $1. Electricity and other variable costs of data processing amount to 20 cents an order.

All purchased items are inspected in the shipping and receiving department. Wages in this department amount to $6,000 a month, plus $1,200 for the foreman. Approximately one third of the workers' time is devoted to receiving and inspecting incoming goods, with the remainder being devoted to shipping finished products. The foreman's time is not included in this percentage. No estimates of how he spends his time are available.

Annual insurance and personal property taxes amount to 7 percent of the cost of the average amount of inventory on hand.

The company has a small amount of short-term, seasonal bank debt at an interest rate of 6 percent a year. Capital expenditure proposals are expected to produce a return on investment of at least 20 percent before taxes.

Breakage and spoilage each month amount to one 12th of 1 percent of the items in storage.

The company rents one warehouse on a 20-year lease at an average annual cost of $2 a square foot. Comparable warehouse space in the area now rents for $3 a square foot. The company's warehouse can be sublet only in its entirety. A unit of product X requires one fifth of a square foot of space, but space must be available for twice the anticipated average inventory quantity. One fifth of the total floor space must be reserved for aisles, etc.

All warehouse labor costs are incurred to move goods into and out of the warehouse. They average 10 percent of the average inventory cost in an average year.

a) Compute the three cost parameters. Explain your treatment of each item.
b) To what extent would historical records help you provide the data from which these cost parameters could be derived? What information sources would you use to supplement or replace historical records for this purpose? What analytical methods would you apply to your basic data?

8.† In November 19x4 the Springfield Manufacturing Company was in the process of preparing its budget for 19x5. As the first step it prepared the following pro forma income statement for 19x4 based on the first 10 months' operations and revised plans for the last two months.

Sales.....................................		$3,000,000
Materials...............................	$1,105,000	
Labor....................................	310,000	
Factory overhead........................	775,000	
Selling and administrative................	450,000	2,640,000
Net Income before Income Taxes..........		$ 360,000

These results were better than had been expected and operations were close to capacity, but Springfield's management was not convinced that demand would remain at present levels and hence had not planned any increase in plant capacity. Its equipment was specialized and made to its order; a lead time in excess of one year was necessary on all plant additions.

Springfield produced three products with the following annual sales volumes:

100,000 units of product A @ $20.....................		$2,000,000
40,000 units of product B @ $10.....................		400,000
20,000 units of product C @ $30.....................		600,000
Total sales.......................................		$3,000,000

Management had ordered a profit analysis for each product and had the following information:

	A	B	C
Material........................	$ 6	$ 4.00	$17.25
Labor...........................	2	1.00	3.50
Factory overhead................	5	2.50	8.75
Selling and administrative...........	3	1.50	4.50
Total costs......................	$16	$ 9.00	$34.00
Selling price....................	20	10.00	30.00
Profit..........................	$ 4	$ 1.00	$(4.00)

Factory overhead was applied on the basis of direct labor cost at a rate of 250 percent; approximately 20 percent of the overhead was variable and did vary with labor costs. Selling and administrative costs were allocated on the

† Prepared by Professor Carl L. Nelson.

basis of sales at the rate of 15 percent; approximately one half of this was variable and did vary with sales in dollars.

As the next step in the planning process, the sales department was asked to make estimates of what it could sell. These estimates were reviewed and accepted by the firm's consulting economist and by top management. They were as follows:

Product A .... 130,000 units
Product B 50,000
Product C 50,000

Production of these quantities was immediately recognized as being impossible. Practical capacity was 66,000 machine-hours in department 1 and 63,000 machine-hours in department 2. The industrial engineering department reported that these limits could not be increased without the purchase of additional equipment. Anticipated sales for 19x5 would require operating department 1 at 136 percent of capacity and department 2 at 121 percent. Standard costs data for the three products, each of which required activity in both departments, were based on the following production rates:

	A	B	C
Department 1	2 per hour	4 per hour	4 per hour
Department 2	4 per hour	8 per hour	1⅓ per hour

Four solutions to the problem of limited capacity were rejected. First, subcontracting the production out to other firms was considered to be unprofitable because of problems of maintaining quality. Second, operating a second shift was impossible because of shortage of labor. Third, operating overtime would have created problems because a large number of employees were "moonlighting" and would therefore have refused to work more than the normal 40-hour week. Finally, price increases were ruled out. Although they would result in higher profits in 19x5, the long-run competitive position of the firm would be weakened, resulting in lower profits in the future.

The treasurer then suggested that product C had been carried at a loss too long and that it was time to eliminate it from the product line. He argued that if all facilities were used to produce A and B, profits would be increased.

The sales manager objected to this solution because of the need to carry a full line. In addition he maintained that the firm's regular customers had provided and would continue to provide a solid base for the firm's activities and that these customers' needs must be met. He provided a list of these customers and their estimated purchases (in units) which totaled as follows:

Product A 80,000
Product B 32,000
Product C 12,000

It was impossible to verify these contentions, but they appeared to be reasonable, and therefore the president concurred.

The treasurer reluctantly acquiesced, but he maintained that the remaining capacity should be used to produce A and B. Because A produced four times as much profit as B, he suggested that the production of A (that is, the amount in excess of the 80,000 minimum set by the sales manager) be four times that of B (that is, the amount in excess of the 32,000 minimum set by the sales manager).

The production manager made some quick calculations and said that this would result in budgeted production and sales of:

Product A.................... 106,666 units
Product B.................... 38,667
Product C.................... 12,000

On this basis the treasurer made the following profit forecast:

Product A: 106,666 @ $4...................... $426,664
Product B: 38,667 @ $1......................   38,667
Product C: 12,000 @ —$4..................... (48,000)
Total.. $417,331

As this would represent an increase of more than 15 percent over the current year, there was a general feeling of self-satisfaction. Before final approval was given, however, the president said that he would like to have his new assistant check over the figures. Somewhat piqued, the treasurer agreed and at that point the group adjourned.

a) The president has just asked you to review the above information and report to him tomorrow. Prepare this report, using nontechnical language and indicating how much of each product should be produced and what the profit contribution is likely to be.

b) Formulate this as a linear programming problem.

c) What are the shadow prices? Prove your answer by finding the optimal product mix and profit if one hour is added to the capacity of each department, the capacity of the other being held constant. What would be the effect of adding one hour to the capacity of both departments at the same time?

d) How much profit, if any, is lost in the short run as a result of the imposition of the minimum sales constraints? Show your calculations.

Appendixes

appendix A

Compound Interest Tables for Present Value Calculations

Evaluation of capital expenditure proposals requires the translation of all cash flows into their equivalent values at a single point in time. This appendix provides an explanation of the translation process, together with a set of translation tables and instructions for using them.

If more extensive tables or specialized tables are needed, they can be found in readily available financial handbooks or derived from relatively simple computer programs.

THE CALCULATION OF PRESENT VALUE

Other things being equal, dollars expected to be available in the future are worth less than the same number of dollars now. One reason for this is that the future is uncertain. In most cases, the longer the wait, the greater the possibility that conditions will change and the dollar never will be received. The primary reason, however, is that the dollar received today can be invested to grow to more than a dollar a year from now. The amount now that will grow to a specified amount at a specified date in the future when invested at a specified interest rate is known as the present value of that future amount. Present value is always less than the future sum to which it is equivalent.

For example, suppose that an investor deposits $100 in a savings bank at the beginning of the year. The bank adds interest to this account every three months, the interest rate being 4 percent a year, or 1 percent each quarter. By the end of the year, the balance in the account will be not $100 but $104.06, computed in the following fashion:

727

Period	Beginning Balance	Quarterly Interest	Ending Balance
First quarter......................	$100.00	$1.00	$101.00
Second quarter....................	101.00	1.01	102.01
Third quarter.....................	102.01	1.02	103.03
Fourth quarter....................	103.03	1.03	104.06

The balance in the account has grown by the amount of interest on the sum originally deposited ($100 x 4% = $4), plus interest on the interest credited to the account during the first three quarters, in this case 6 cents. This crediting of interest on previously earned interest is known as *compounding*. In this case, interest has been compounded quarterly, meaning that interest is credited to the saver's account four times a year.

Exhibit A–1

FUTURE VALUES EQUIVALENT TO PRESENT VALUE OF $100
Interest Compounded Quarterly at 4 Percent

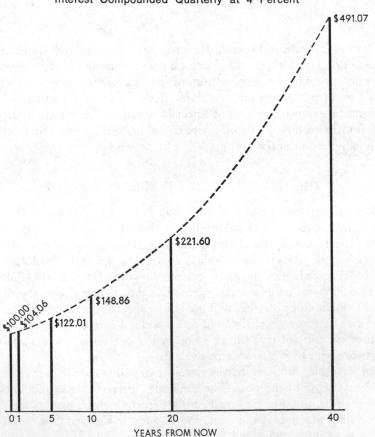

An investor who considers 4 percent compounded quarterly a satisfactory return on his money will regard $100 now as equivalent to $104.06 one year from now. That is, if someone promises to pay him $104.06 one year from now, the present value of that sum to him is $100. He will be unwilling to pay more than $100 for this promise.

Extending these calculations beyond one year reveals the relationships shown graphically in Exhibit A–1. The initial $100 will grow to $104.06 at the end of 1 year, $122.01 at the end of 5 years, $148.86 at the end of 10 years, and $491.07 when 40 years have passed, assuming interest compounded quarterly at 4 percent. At higher interest rates the growth would be even greater.

Another aspect of these relationships is that each of the future sums plotted on the chart in Exhibit A–1 has an identical present value, $100. In fact, every future amount that corresponds to a point on the dashed line has a present value of $100.

Applicability to Investment Problems

Knowledge of these relationships permits us to deal with problems in which differences in timing are important. The interest rate is, in a sense, the transfer price that would be applied to the exchange of cash at one point in time for cash at another. The use of this transfer price makes it possible to add or subtract sums that occur at different points in time.

For example, suppose that an investor decides that 4 percent compounded quarterly is an adequate return on any investments he may make. A promoter approaches him with a proposal to pay him $104.06 one year from now if he will invest $99.50 in the promoter's enterprise now. This proposal can be analyzed in the following fashion:

Date	Cash Inflow (+) or Outflow (−)	Present Value at 4%
Immediately.....................	−$ 99.50	−$ 99.50
One year later..................	+ 104.06	+ 100.00
Difference......................	+$ 4.56	+$ 0.50

Inasmuch as $100 is the time-adjusted equivalent of $104.06, the $99.50 and $100 can be added together algebraically. The amount to be received is worth more now than the amount that has to be paid to get it, so the proposal is a desirable one. To put it another way, investment of $99.50 in this proposal now will provide the investor with the same amount a year from now that he could get by investing $100 now in a savings account that compounds interest at 4 percent quarterly. He will have $0.50 more to spend or invest now if he accepts this proposal than if he rejects it and buys the same future cash flow from the savings bank—that is, he will be $0.50 better off.

Let us now suppose that the investor requires a 10 percent minimum return on investment. By repeating the calculations above, using quarterly compounding at a rate of 10 percent a year, we find that $100 now is equivalent to $110.38 one year later. Conversely, at this higher rate, $100 one year from now is equivalent to $90.60 now (0.906 being the ratio of $100 present value to the $110.38 future amount). Multiplying the anticipated $104.06 cash receipt by 0.906 (the "discount factor"), we obtain a present value of $94.28.

This process of multiplying a future sum by a discount factor is known as *discounting*. The discounted cash flows for this proposal are shown in the right-hand column of the following table:

Date	Cash Inflow (+) or Outflow (−)	Present Value at 10 Percent Factor	Amount
Immediately....................	−$ 99.50	1.000	−$99.50
One year later..................	+ 104.06	0.909	+ 94.28
Difference.....................	+$ 4.56	xxx	−$ 5.22

The investor would find this proposal unattractive because the present value of the cash he will receive from his investment is $5.22 less than the $99.50 he would have to pay now to receive the future benefit. Another way of saying this is that if the investor requires a 10 percent return on investment, the future cash receipt of $104.06 is inadequate to repay the original investment plus a return on investment at an annual rate of 10 percent.

The decision rule implicit in this discussion is to accept only those proposals that seem to promise a positive net present value—that is, those proposals for which the present value of the anticipated cash receipts exceeds the present value of the anticipated cash outlays. The higher the required rate of return on investment, the lower will be the present value of future receipts and the less attractive will be any proposal to invest funds now in anticipation of a future return.

Treatment of Depreciation

The amounts entered in the timetable above represented cash flows rather than the effects of the proposal on the company's annual net income. No deduction was made for the annual depreciation charges that would appear on the company's books. Explicit provisions for depreciation enter only into the calculation of the cash flows due to taxation, as described in Chapter 26.

This does not mean that the present value method ignores depreciation. Depreciation is deducted, but not at the time it is recognized for the calculation of net income. Depreciation of an investment over its life is measured by the difference between the initial outlay and the end-of-life salvage value, say $38,000 − $5,000 = $33,000. For income measurement, this is spread in some way over the life of the investment, perhaps $6,600 a year. For project evaluation, on the other hand, the deduction is made by subtracting the outlay ($38,000) and adding the salvage value ($5,000) at the times they will arise, at the zero date and five years later.

The comparison between the two approaches to depreciation is shown in the following table:

Years from Zero Date	Provisions for Depreciation	
	Income Measurement	Project Evaluation
0	...	−$38,000
1	−$ 6,600	...
2	− 6,600	...
3	− 6,600	...
4	− 6,600	...
5	− 6,600	5,000
Total	−$33,000	−$33,000

The net deduction is identical in both columns ($33,000); only the timing differs. Net present value will be negative unless the cash inflows are large enough to cover both lifetime depreciation and the company's minimum annual rate of return on investment.

The Compounding Interval

The present value of a cash flow is affected by the length of the compounding interval. In the example above, the compounding interval was three months—that is, interest was compounded quarterly.[1] We saw that at a 10 percent annual rate, $100 will grow through quarterly compounding to $110.38 at the end of one year. If interest is compounded only once a year (annual compounding) the future value will be only $110, because the interest earned in early months does not earn any interest at all during the first year.

---

[1] The term interest is often used to mean the lender's compensation for the use of his money. It is used here in a different sense, as an annual rate of return on capital. This capital may come from either lenders or owners. The available synonyms are to awkward to use in an introductory explanation.

If interest is compounded monthly, on the other hand, the future value of $100 now at 10 percent will be slightly greater than $110.38, because interest in the second month will be calculated not only on the original $100 but also on the first month's interest, and so on. The shorter the compounding interval (weekly, daily, hourly), the greater will be the amount of interest accumulated at a given interest rate. Continuous compounding is the limiting case, with the compounding interval at its shortest imaginable length. At a rate of 10 percent, $100 now is equivalent to $110.52 at the end of one year if interest is compounded continuously.

Strictly speaking, the compounding interval should correspond to the interval at which cash flows can be used. For example, if cash is reinvested monthly, then the compounding interval should be one month. Most companies use annual compounding, however, no matter what the investment interval.

USING THE INTEREST TABLES

Fortunately, the investor does not have to calculate interest multipliers every time he wishes to compute present value or future value. Present value multipliers or discount factors can be found in readily available tables or can be derived from simple computer programs.

A representative set of these interest tables is provided at the end of this appendix. The factors in these tables measure the present value of a dollar that is received or paid out at the end of the year indicated. (Since annual compounding is used, it must be assumed that all cash flows are concentrated at the end of each year.)

Arranging the Basic Data

The figures shown in these tables are the amounts or factors by which to multiply time-identified cash flow amounts to derive their present values. To facilitate the application of these tables, dollar figures relating to investment proposals should be arranged in the form of a timetable. Net cash outlays should be identified by a minus sign; net cash receipts should be identified by a plus sign.

Receipts or outlays should be identified as occurring a specified number of years subsequent to a reference date (zero date in the timetable). The reference date is usually selected as the date on which the first substantial outlays will be made. If a number of related or competing proposals are being studied, a single reference date or zero point should be selected for them all.

The net algebraic sum of all the cash flows indicates the net lifetime profit of the proposal at zero interest. Discounting these cash flows at some rate of interest serves to allow for the cost of capital.

Description of Tables

Tables 1 and 2 provide interest factors that will discount future cash flows to a common reference point or zero date. Table 1 shows the present value of $1 received or paid in a lump sum, discounted once each period. Table 2 shows the present value of an *annuity* of $1 received or paid as a series of lump sums at the end of individual periods, discounted once each period.

Table 1 is to be used for discounting receipts or outlays that occur a given number of years subsequent to the reference date. Table 2 is to be used for discounting receipts or outlays that are the same every year from the zero point to the end of the indicated time interval. The cash flow to be multiplied by the discount factor contained in Table 2 is the annual receipt or outlay—the annuity—rather than total receipts or outlays during the entire annuity period.

Calculation of Present Value

To compute present value at the reference date at a given rate of interest, simply multiply each item in the timetable by the applicable factor and find the discounted algebraic sum. The discounted value of each cash flow retains the sign of the corresponding undiscounted value.

Suppose that a proposed outlay of $38,000 is expected to yield operating cash receipts of $10,000 a year for five years, with a $5,000 salvage value at the end. The timetable would be as follows:

Years from Now	Cash Inflow (+) or Outflow (−)
0	−$38,000
1	+ 10,000
2	+ 10,000
3	+ 10,000
4	+ 10,000
5	+ 10,000
5	+ 5,000

Suppose that the company wishes to discover whether this proposal will earn at least 10 percent on the investment. The discount factor for the initial outlay is 1.000 because it takes place immediately. Present value of a present sum at any discount rate is equal to the outlay.

The discount factors for the future cash flows can be found in Table 1. The first figure in the 10 percent column is 0.909, which means that each dollar of cash received at the end of the first year is worth no more than 90.9 cents at the beginning of the year. A cash flow of $10,000 is thus worth 0.909 × $10,000 = $9,090.

Similarly, the second year's cash receipts are worth 0.826 × $10,000 =

$8,260, and so on for the next three years. The end-of-life salvage value is to be received at the end of the fifth year, and the appropriate multiplier therefore is the same as the one for the fifth annual operating cash flow.

The value of the proposal as a whole is summarized in Exhibit A–2. This shows that the cash flows anticipated from this proposal are more than adequate to recover the initial outlay of $38,000 plus interest compounded continuously at an annual rate of 10 percent. The present value of the cash flow is $3,005 in excess of interest and amortization requirements.

Exhibit A–2

USE OF INTEREST TABLES

Years from Now	Cash Inflow (+) or Outflow (−)	Present Value At 10 Percent	
		Multiplier	Amount
0.........................	− $38,000	1.000	− $38,000
1.........................	+ 10,000	0.909	+ 9,090
2.........................	+ 10,000	0.826	+ 8,260
3.........................	+ 10,000	0.751	+ 7,510
4.........................	+ 10,000	0.683	+ 6,830
5.........................	+ 10,000	0.621	+ 6,210
5.........................	+ 5,000	0.621	+ 3,105
Net present value...........			+ $ 3,005

Annuity Tables. The same answer can be reached in this case by a slightly different route. Because each year's operating cash flow is the same, $10,000, it is not necessary to multiply each one separately. Instead, the multipliers can be added together and then applied in a single multiplication.

This is the basis for the factors in the annuity table labeled Table 2. For example, the multiplier or annuity factor in the five-year row of the 10 percent column in Table 2 is 3.791. This is simply the sum of the first five multipliers in the 10 percent column of Table 1. Multiplying this by the annual cash flow of $10,000 yields a present value of $37,910, which differs by an insignificant rounding error from the sum of the first five positive figures in the right-hand column of Exhibit A–2.

COMPOUND INTEREST FORMULAS

The future value of a present sum one year later can be expressed mathematically as:

$$F_1 = P(1 + r) \tag{1}$$

where P is the present sum, r the rate of interest, and F_1 the value one year later.

The mathematical formula for the future value of this sum two years from now is:

$$F_2 = F_1(1 + r) = P(1 + r)(1 + r) = P(1 + r)^2 \qquad (2)$$

In general, it can be shown that if an amount P is put out at interest of r percent a year compounded annually, at the end of t years it will grow to:

$$F_t = P(1 + r)^t \qquad (3)$$

The formula for present value can be found by turning equation (3) around:

$$P = F_t(1 + r)^{-t} \qquad (4)$$

This is the formula underlying Table 1.

The formula for the present value of an annuity can be derived from equation (4). Using A to represent the annuity amount, the present value of the first payment (A_1), which is discounted for one period, is:

$$P = A_1(1 + r)^{-1}$$

The present value of the last, or tth, payment is:

$$P = A_t(1 + r)^{-t}$$

The sum of the present values (P_A) of all payments is:

$$P_A = A[(1 + r)^{-1} + (1 + r)^{-2} + \cdots + (1 + r)^{-t}] \qquad (5)$$

Multiplying equation (5) by $(1 + r)$ yields:

$$(1 + r)P_A = A[1 + (1 + r)^{-1} + \cdots + (1 + r)^{-(t-1)}] \qquad (6)$$

Subtracting equation (5) from equation (6) results in the formula for the present value of an annuity:

$$rP_A = A[1 - (1 + r)^{-t}]$$

$$P_A = A\left[\frac{1 - (1 + r)^{-t}}{r}\right] \qquad (7)$$

This is the formula underlying Table 2 where $A = \$1$.

Shortening the Compounding Interval

If interest is compounded more often than once each year, the interest rate per compounding interval is reduced proportionately. For example, if interest is compounded semiannually, equation (4) becomes:

$$P = F_t \frac{1}{\left(1 + \dfrac{r}{2}\right)^{2t}}$$

This can be restated in general terms by letting m represent the number of compounding intervals per year:

$$P = F_t \frac{1}{\left(1 + \dfrac{r}{m}\right)^{mt}}$$

If m/r is represented by the letter k, this becomes:

$$P = F_t \frac{1}{\left(\left(1 + \dfrac{1}{k}\right)^{k}\right)^{rt}}$$

As the length of the compounding interval $(1/m)$ becomes shorter, k becomes larger. As k approaches infinity, the quantity $[1 + (1/k)]^k$ approaches the limit e, which is the base of the so-called natural logarithms. In other words, with an infinitely short compounding interval, the present value formula becomes:

$$P = F_t \left(\frac{1}{e^{rt}}\right)$$

Table 1

PRESENT VALUE OF $1 RECEIVED OR PAID IN A LUMP SUM
Discounted Once Each Period for t Periods

t	5%	6%	7%	8%	9%	10%	11%	12%	13%	14%	15%	20%	25%	30%	40%
1	0.952	0.943	0.935	0.926	0.917	0.909	0.901	0.893	0.885	0.877	0.870	0.833	0.800	0.769	0.714
2	0.907	0.890	0.873	0.857	0.842	0.826	0.812	0.797	0.783	0.769	0.756	0.694	0.640	0.592	0.510
3	0.864	0.840	0.816	0.794	0.772	0.751	0.731	0.712	0.693	0.675	0.658	0.579	0.512	0.455	0.364
4	0.823	0.792	0.763	0.735	0.708	0.683	0.659	0.636	0.613	0.592	0.572	0.482	0.410	0.350	0.260
5	0.784	0.747	0.713	0.681	0.650	0.621	0.593	0.567	0.543	0.519	0.497	0.402	0.328	0.269	0.186
6	0.746	0.705	0.666	0.630	0.596	0.564	0.535	0.507	0.480	0.456	0.432	0.335	0.262	0.207	0.133
7	0.711	0.665	0.623	0.583	0.547	0.513	0.482	0.452	0.425	0.400	0.376	0.279	0.210	0.159	0.095
8	0.677	0.627	0.582	0.540	0.502	0.467	0.434	0.404	0.376	0.351	0.327	0.233	0.168	0.123	0.068
9	0.645	0.592	0.543	0.500	0.460	0.424	0.391	0.361	0.333	0.308	0.284	0.194	0.134	0.094	0.048
10	0.614	0.558	0.508	0.463	0.422	0.386	0.352	0.322	0.295	0.270	0.247	0.162	0.107	0.073	0.035
11	0.585	0.527	0.475	0.429	0.388	0.350	0.317	0.287	0.261	0.237	0.215	0.135	0.086	0.056	0.025
12	0.557	0.497	0.444	0.397	0.356	0.319	0.286	0.257	0.231	0.208	0.187	0.112	0.069	0.043	0.018
13	0.530	0.469	0.415	0.368	0.326	0.290	0.258	0.229	0.204	0.182	0.163	0.093	0.055	0.033	0.013
14	0.505	0.442	0.388	0.340	0.299	0.263	0.232	0.205	0.181	0.160	0.141	0.078	0.044	0.025	0.009
15	0.481	0.417	0.362	0.315	0.275	0.239	0.209	0.183	0.160	0.140	0.123	0.065	0.035	0.020	0.006
16	0.458	0.394	0.339	0.292	0.252	0.218	0.188	0.163	0.142	0.123	0.107	0.054	0.028	0.015	0.005
17	0.436	0.371	0.317	0.270	0.231	0.198	0.170	0.146	0.125	0.108	0.093	0.045	0.023	0.012	0.003
18	0.416	0.350	0.296	0.250	0.212	0.180	0.153	0.130	0.111	0.095	0.081	0.038	0.018	0.009	0.002
19	0.396	0.331	0.277	0.232	0.194	0.164	0.138	0.116	0.098	0.083	0.070	0.031	0.014	0.007	0.002
20	0.377	0.312	0.258	0.215	0.178	0.149	0.124	0.104	0.087	0.073	0.061	0.026	0.012	0.005	0.001
21	0.359	0.294	0.242	0.199	0.164	0.135	0.112	0.093	0.077	0.064	0.053	0.022	0.009	0.004	0.001
22	0.342	0.278	0.226	0.184	0.150	0.123	0.101	0.083	0.068	0.056	0.046	0.018	0.007	0.003	0.001
23	0.326	0.262	0.211	0.170	0.138	0.112	0.091	0.074	0.060	0.049	0.040	0.015	0.006	0.002	...
24	0.310	0.247	0.197	0.158	0.126	0.102	0.082	0.066	0.053	0.043	0.035	0.013	0.005	0.002	...
25	0.295	0.233	0.184	0.146	0.116	0.092	0.074	0.059	0.047	0.038	0.030	0.010	0.004	0.001	...
30	0.231	0.174	0.131	0.099	0.075	0.057	0.044	0.033	0.026	0.020	0.015	0.004	0.001	...	...
35	0.181	0.130	0.094	0.068	0.049	0.036	0.026	0.019	0.014	0.010	0.008	0.002	...	...	...
40	0.142	0.097	0.067	0.046	0.032	0.022	0.015	0.011	0.008	0.005	0.004	0.001	...	...	...
45	0.111	0.073	0.048	0.031	0.021	0.014	0.009	0.006	0.004	0.003	0.002	...	...	...	...
50	0.087	0.054	0.034	0.021	0.013	0.009	0.005	0.003	0.002	0.001	0.001	...	...	...	...

$$P = F_t(1 + r)^{-t}$$

Table 2

PRESENT VALUE OF AN ANNUITY OF $1 A PERIOD FOR *t* PERIODS
RECEIVED OR PAID AS A SERIES OF LUMP SUMS AT THE END
OF INDIVIDUAL PERIODS
Discounted Once Each Period for *t* Periods

t	5%	6%	7%	8%	9%	10%	11%	12%	13%	14%	15%	20%	25%	30%	40%
1..	0.952	0.943	0.935	0.926	0.917	0.909	0.901	0.893	0.885	0.877	0.870	0.833	0.800	0.769	0.714
2..	1.859	1.833	1.808	1.783	1.759	1.736	1.713	1.690	1.668	1.647	1.626	1.528	1.440	1.361	1.224
3..	2.723	2.673	2.624	2.577	2.531	2.487	2.444	2.402	2.361	2.322	2.283	2.106	1.952	1.816	1.589
4..	3.546	3.465	3.387	3.312	3.240	3.170	3.102	3.037	2.974	2.914	2.855	2.589	2.362	2.166	1.849
5..	4.329	4.212	4.100	3.993	3.890	3.791	3.696	3.605	3.517	3.433	3.352	2.991	2.689	2.436	2.035
6..	5.076	4.917	4.767	4.623	4.486	4.355	4.231	4.111	3.998	3.889	3.784	3.326	2.951	2.643	2.168
7..	5.786	5.582	5.389	5.206	5.033	4.868	4.712	4.564	4.423	4.288	4.160	3.605	3.161	2.802	2.263
8..	6.463	6.210	5.971	5.747	5.535	5.335	5.146	4.968	4.799	4.639	4.487	3.837	3.329	2.925	2.331
9..	7.108	6.802	6.515	6.247	5.995	5.759	5.537	5.328	5.132	4.946	4.772	4.031	3.463	3.019	2.379
10..	7.722	7.360	7.024	6.710	6.418	6.145	5.889	5.650	5.426	5.216	5.019	4.192	3.571	3.092	2.414
11..	8.306	7.887	7.499	7.139	6.805	6.495	6.207	5.938	5.687	5.453	5.234	4.327	3.656	3.147	2.438
12..	8.863	8.384	7.943	7.536	7.161	6.814	6.492	6.194	5.918	5.660	5.421	4.439	3.725	3.190	2.456
13..	9.394	8.853	8.358	7.904	7.487	7.103	6.750	6.424	6.122	5.842	5.583	4.533	3.780	3.223	2.468
14..	9.899	9.295	8.745	8.244	7.786	7.367	6.982	6.628	6.302	6.002	5.724	4.611	3.824	3.249	2.477
15..	10.380	9.712	9.108	8.559	8.061	7.606	7.191	6.811	6.462	6.142	5.847	4.675	3.859	3.268	2.484
16..	10.838	10.106	9.447	8.851	8.313	7.824	7.379	6.974	6.604	6.265	5.954	4.730	3.887	3.283	2.489
17..	11.274	10.477	9.763	9.122	8.544	8.022	7.549	7.120	6.729	6.373	6.047	4.775	3.910	3.295	2.492
18..	11.690	10.828	10.059	9.372	8.756	8.201	7.702	7.250	6.840	6.467	6.128	4.812	3.928	3.304	2.494
19..	12.085	11.158	10.336	9.604	8.950	8.365	7.839	7.366	6.938	6.550	6.198	4.844	3.942	3.311	2.496
20..	12.462	11.470	10.594	9.818	9.129	8.514	7.963	7.469	7.025	6.623	6.259	4.870	3.954	3.316	2.497
21..	12.821	11.764	10.836	10.017	9.292	8.649	8.075	7.562	7.102	6.687	6.312	4.891	3.963	3.320	2.498
22..	13.163	12.042	11.061	10.201	9.442	8.772	8.176	7.645	7.170	6.743	6.359	4.909	3.970	3.323	2.498
23..	13.489	12.303	11.272	10.371	9.580	8.883	8.266	7.718	7.230	6.792	6.399	4.925	3.976	3.325	2.499
24..	13.799	12.550	11.469	10.529	9.707	8.985	8.348	7.784	7.283	6.835	6.434	4.937	3.981	3.327	2.499
25..	14.094	12.783	11.654	10.675	9.823	9.077	8.422	7.843	7.330	6.873	6.464	4.948	3.985	3.329	2.499
30..	15.372	13.765	12.409	11.258	10.274	9.427	8.694	8.055	7.496	7.003	6.566	4.979	3.995	3.332	2.500
35..	16.374	14.498	12.948	11.655	10.567	9.644	8.855	8.176	7.586	7.070	6.617	4.992	3.998	3.333	2.500
40..	17.159	15.046	13.332	11.925	10.757	9.779	8.951	8.244	7.634	7.105	6.642	4.997	3.999	3.333	2.500
45..	17.774	15.456	13.606	12.108	10.881	9.863	9.008	8.283	7.661	7.123	6.654	4.999	4.000	3.333	2.500
50..	18.256	15.762	13.801	12.233	10.962	9.915	9.042	8.305	7.675	7.133	6.661	4.999	4.000	3.333	2.500

$$P = A\left[\frac{1 - (1 + r)^{-t}}{r}\right]$$

appendix B

Solutions to

Selected Problems

Chapter 2

2–3. *a*) Amounts in thousands:

	$p = 0.1$ State 1	$p = 0.2$ State 2	$p = 0.4$ State 3	$p = 0.2$ State 4	$p = 0.05$ State 5	$p = 0.05$ State 6
If spend....	−10	−5	0	+5	+10	+15
If don't spend....	0	0	0	0	0	0

b) Expected value:

	Spend	Don't Spend
0.1 × −10,000 =	−1,000	0
0.2 × − 5,000 =	−1,000	0
0.4 × 0 =	0	0
0.2 × + 5,000 =	+1,000	0
0.05 × +10,000 =	+ 500	0
0.05 × +15,000 =	+ 750	0
Total..........	+ 250	0

2–4.

		Revenue		Cost	Profit
At 75,000 units level	at $2.50	$187,500	at $2.00	$150,000	$37,500
At 50,000 units level	at $3.00	150,000	at $2.25	112,500	37,500
Incremental revenue		$ 37,500			
Incremental cost				$ 37,500	
Incremental profit					$ 0

Chapter 3

3–3.

Output Rate	Average Total Cost	Average Fixed Cost	Average Variable Cost	Marginal Cost
1..........	$11.00	$10.00	$1.00	$1.00
2..........	6.00	5.00	1.00	1.00
3..........	4.33	3.33	1.00	1.00
4..........	3.50	2.50	1.00	1.00
5..........	3.00	2.00	1.00	1.00
6..........	2.67	1.67	1.00	1.00
7..........	2.43	1.43	1.00	1.00
8..........	2.25	1.25	1.00	1.00
9..........	2.22	1.11	1.11	2.00
10..........	2.30	1.00	1.30	3.00

3–4.   *a*) $\text{Break-even volume} = \dfrac{\text{Total fixed costs}}{\text{Price} - \text{variable cost}} = \dfrac{\$320,000}{\$3.20}$

$\hspace{6cm} = 100,000 \text{ units}$

b)   Desired profit = $220,000 + $22,000 = $242,000

New P/V margin = $3.20/unit

$\text{Target sales volume} = \dfrac{\$242,000 + \$320,000}{\$3.20} = 175,625 \text{ units}$

3–5.   Average P/V ratio = 35%

Fixed costs + profit = $140,000

$\text{Desired sales} = \dfrac{\$140,000}{0.35} = \$400,000$

	A	B	Total
Sales.................	$200,000	$200,000	$400,000
Variable costs..........	120,000	140,000	260,000
Variable profit..........	$ 80,000	$ 60,000	$140,000
Fixed costs.............			100,000
Net profit.............			$ 40,000

Unit sales:

A.........40,000 units
B ....80,000 units

3–10.

	Product A	Product B
Price	$3.00	$5.00
Variable cost	1.78	2.65
Variable profit/unit	$1.22	$2.35
Total variable profit	$122,000	$282,000
Fixed costs	32,000	197,000
Profit Margin	$ 90,000	$ 85,000

The table above reflects the assumption that the averages given for fixed costs are correct—i.e., total fixed costs will change. On this basis, product A should be retained.

3–11. *a)* Costs for six-day operation:

	Total/Wk.	Average/Cwt.
Fixed: 6 × 2,100	$ 12,600	$0.35
Wheat: $2.17 × 2.35 × 6,000 × 6	183,582	5.10
Variable: $0.17 × 6,000 × 6	6,120	0.17
Total	$202,302	$5.62

Profit margin: $5.70 − $5.62 = $0.08/cwt.

b) Costs for seven-day operation:

	Total/Wk.	Average/Cwt.
Fixed	$ 12,810	$0.305
Wheat	214,179	5.100
Variable	8,100	0.193
Total	$235,089	$5.598

Increment in revenue: 6,000 × $5.70	$34,200
Increment in costs: $235,089 − $202,302	32,787
Increment in profit	$ 1,413/week

3–12. *a)* The first step in this problem is to adjust January–June power costs for the rate increase:

January:	$1,000 × 1.1	$1,100
February:	1,100 × 1.1	1,210
March:	1,300 × 1.1	1,430
April:	1,200 × 1.1	1,320
May:	1,200 × 1.1	1,320
June:	1,100 × 1.1	1,210

If you used the least-squares method, you found that the sum of the adjusted cost observations was $14,880, the sum of the volume observations was 48,000 machine-hours, the sum of the products was $60,204,000, and the sum of the squares of the volume observations was 195,420,000. This yields the following formula:

Power costs = $440 + $0.20 × machine-hours

b) The estimates are:

Machine-Hours	Power Costs
2,500	$ 940
5,500	1,540

The main question is whether good estimates for the 2,500 and 5,500 machine-hour levels can be derived by extrapolation from data that do not extend to or near these extremes. Another question on all the figures is whether enough observations are available for reliable estimates. This can be checked by statistical tests, but sometimes it is necessary to proceed with whatever data are available, even if statistical requirements are not met.

Chapter 5

5–1.

Job #7863			Quantity 100	
		Labor		
Date	Materials	Hours	Amount	Summary:
				Materials....... $6,300
8/4	$3,800			Labor.......... 2,090
8/8		200	$ 520	Overhead....... 1,275
8/9	1,700			Total......... $9,665
8/15		300	800	
8/20	800			
8/22		250	550	Unit cost: $96.65
8/25		100	220	
Total	$6,300	850	$2,090	

5–2.

Materials......................	$ 800
Labor.........................	200
Overhead ($9 × 60)............	540
Total........................	$1,540

Chapter 6

6–3. One alternative would be to credit department X with $20, but the answer in this particular case should be not to distribute the scrap credit at all on the ground that the amount is immaterial.

6–8. *a*) Normal working time:

(250 days − 3 days' sick leav) ` hours overtime = 2,026 hours

Overtime and Saturday houi. should be included in this total because these hours will have to be charged to jobs or overhead accounts in exactly the same manner as straight-time hours.

b) Straight-time wages: 2,026 × $4.................. $8,104.00
Extra pay:
  Vacation pay: 80 hours × $4.................. $320.00
  Holiday pay: 8 × 8 × $4...................... 256.00
  Sick pay: 3 × 8 × $4........................ 96.00   672.00
Payroll tax: 8% × $7,200......................   576.00
Pensions:
  Straight-time: 3% × 2,026 × $4............... $243.12
  Vacation, holiday, and sick pay: 3% × $672..... 20.16   263.28
Total....................................... $9,615.28

$$\text{Charging rate} = \frac{\$9,615.28}{2,026} = \$4.746 \text{ an hour}$$

c) (1) Vacation pay, holiday pay, and sick pay are not precisely proportional to hours worked, but there is probably enough proportionality to justify including them in the charging rate.

(2) Overtime and Saturday work premiums are excluded because they are not necessarily proportional to straight-time wages and because they are controllable separately.

(3) The cost of the employee recreation program might be included, but it is unlikely to have many variable cost elements and should be excluded.

(4) The cafeteria subsidy is a fixed cost and should be excluded on those grounds.

(5) Payroll taxes and pension contributions on overtime and Saturday work premiums should be added to those items rather than to the charging rate.

Chapter 7

7–1. *a*)   Materials (21,000 × $0.66)............. $13,860
Materials returned (800 × $0.66)....... (528)
Labor (2,000 × $2.15)................ 4,300
Overhead........................... 8,000
Total.............................. $25,632

$$\text{Unit cost} = \frac{\$25,632}{9,800} = \$2.62$$

b)   Work in Process.................... 26,160
  Materials Inventory.............   13,860
  Wages Payable................   4,300
  Factory Overhead..............   8,000

Materials Inventory................. 528
  Work in Process...............   528

Finished Goods.................... 25,632
  Work in Process...............   25,632

7–3. $$\text{Burden rate} = \frac{\$8,000 + 1.20 \times \$10,000}{\$10,000} = \$2/\text{DL\$}$$

Manufacturing Overhead			Manufacturing Overhead Absorbed		
(a)	21,700	(c) 18,800 Budget variance 2,900	(c)	18,800	(b) 18,000 Volume variance 800

Actual.............. 21,700
Budget.............. 18,800
   Spending variance..   2,900 Dr.
Absorbed........... 18,000
   Volume variance...   800 Dr.

Entry (c) is optional. It is introduced here as a means of isolating the variances directly in the accounts.

7–7. a)

ITEM: Material #1467A   UNIT: Each

Date	In			Out			Balance		
	Quantity	Price	Amount	Quantity	Price	Amount	Quantity	Price	Amount
April 1							200	$0 500	$100.00
2	500	$0.550	$275.00				700	0.536	375.00
4				50	$0.536	$ 26.80	650	0.536	348.20
8				200	0.536	107.20	450	0.536	241.00
12	500	.510	255.20				950	0.522	496.20
16				400	0.522	208.80	550	0.522	287.40
18				50	0.522	26.10	500	0.522	261.30
25				250	0.522	130.50	250	0.522	130.80
28	1,000	.501	500.60				1,250	0.505	631.40

b)

ITEM: Material #1467A   UNIT: Each

Date	In			Out			Balance		
	Quantity	Price	Amount	Quantity	Price	Amount	Quantity	Price	Amount
April 1							200	$0.500	$100.00
2	500	$0.550	$275.00				500	0.550	275.00
4				50	$0.500	$ 25.00	150	$0.500	$ 75.00
							500	0.550	275.00
8				150	0.500	75.00	450	$0.550	$247.50
				50	0.550	27.50			
12	500	0.510	255.20				500	0.510	255.20
16				400	0.550	220.00	50	$0.550	$ 27.50
							500	0.510	255.20
18				50	0.550	27.50	500	$0.510	255.20
25				250	0.510	127.50	250	$0.510	$127.70
28	1,000	0.501	500.60				1,000	0.501	500.60

7–8. $10,000 of the underabsorbed overhead came from the misclassification of the machinery cost and $3,000 from the misclassification of the president's salary. The entry to correct these two errors is:

Plant and Equipment.................. 10,000
Administrative Salaries................ 3,000
    Work in Process.................   1,560
    Finished Goods..................   2,600
    Cost of Goods Sold.............   8,840

No entry is required to correct the third error, although for data bank purposes the job order cost sheets should be corrected.

7–11. *a*)

Raw Material and Stores			
Bal.	12,650	(2)	7,250
(1)	4,500	Bal.	9,900
Bal.	9,900		

Work in Process			
Bal.	8,320	(6)	12,650
(2)	6,320		
(3)	3,300		
(5)	4,950	Bal.	10,240
Bal.	10,240		

Finished Goods			
Bal.	11,100	(8)	14,500
(6)	12,650	Bal.	9,250
Bal.	9,250		

Accounts Payable, Etc.			
		(1)	4,500
		(4)	2,700
		(7)	1,835

Accrued Payroll			
		(3)	7,780

Cost of Goods Sold			
(8)	14,500		
(11)	560		

Factory Overhead Summary			
(2)	930	(10)	5,510
(3)	1,880		
(4)	2,700		

Factory Overhead Absorbed			
(10)	5,510	(5)	4,950
		(11)	560

Selling and Admin. Expense			
(3)	2,600		
(7)	1,835		

Accounts Receivable			
(9)	19,350		

Sales Revenue			
		(9)	19,350

b)   ACE APPLIANCE COMPANY

Statement of Income for the Month Ending October 31

Sales......................................	$19,350
Cost of goods sold (Schedule A)...........	15,060
Gross margin.............................	$ 4,290
Selling and administrative expenses.........	4,435
Net Income (Loss)......................	$ (145)

Schedule A: Cost of Goods Sold

Direct materials.........................		$ 6,320
Direct labor............................		3,300
Factory overhead absorbed................		4,950
Total factory costs charged to production...		$14,570
Less: Increase in work in process:		
Work in process, October 31............	$10,240	
Work in process, October 1.............	8,320	(1,920)
Cost of goods finished...................		$12,650
Add: Decrease in finished goods:		
Finished goods, October 1..............	$11,100	
Finished goods, October 31.............	9,250	1,850
Cost of goods sold......................		$14,500
Add: Underabsorbed overhead............		560
Cost of goods sold (adjusted).............		$15,060

Chapter 8

8–2.   *a*)

	Materials	Labor
Units completed..................	9,000	9,000
Incomplete units, 5/31.............	800	480
Less: Incomplete units, 5/1.........	(1,000)	(400)
Output divisor...................	8,800	9,080

b)

Units completed..................	9,000	9,000
Incomplete units, 5/31.............	800	480
Output divisor...................	9,800	9,480

8–3.

	Mixing		Refining	
	Total	Per Unit	Total	Per Unit
Costs:				
Materials:				
Received..................	$ 49,500	$0.495	$138,000	$1.500
Lost unit adjustment........	xxx	0.005	xxx	0.033
Adjusted materials cost.....	$ 49,500	$0.500	$138,000	$1.533
Processing costs:				
Labor.....................	$ 57,300	$0.600	$ 42,500	$0.500
Other.....................	38,200	0.400	38,250	0.450
Total....................	$ 95,500	$1.000	$ 80,750	$0.950
Total costs....................	$145,000	$1.500	$218,750	$2.483
Cost distribution:				
Transferred..................	$138,000		$198,670*	
In process, 1/31..............	7,000		20,080	
Total costs distributed...........	$145,000		$218,750	

* Adjusted to absorb rounding error.

8–7. Dept. A:

	Materials		Processing Costs	
	Total	Per Unit	Total	Per Unit
Costs:				
In process, 6/1..................	$ 50		$ 50	
June costs......................	100		390	
Total costs...................	$150	$1.00	$440	$4.00
Cost distribution:				
To Dept. B (90 units).............	$ 90		$360	
In process, 6/30.................	60		80	
Total distributed..............	$150		$440	

Dept. B:

	Materials		Processing Costs	
Costs:				
In process, 6/1..................	$213		$150	
June costs......................	450		540	
Total costs...................	$663	$5.10	$690	$6.00
Cost distribution:				
To finished goods (85 units).......	$432.50		$510	
In process, 6/30.................	229.50		180	
Total distributed..............	$662.00		$690	

Chapter 9

9–3.

	Price	Direct Costs	Variable Overhead	Fixed Overhead
A.........	$20	$9	$1.00	$3.00
B.........	19	8	1.50	4.50
C.........	18	7	2.00	6.00
D.........	17	6	2.50	7.50

Profit margins:

	Full Costing		Variable Costing	
	Per Unit	Percent	Per Unit	Percent
A........	$7	35	$10.00	50
B........	5	26	9.50	50
C........	3	17	9.00	50
D........	1	6	8.50	50

9–4. *a*) Full costing:

	19 x 5	*19 x 6*
Cost of goods sold:		
Direct labor.....................	$ 50,000	$ 51,000
Direct materials..................	100,000	102,000
Fixed factory overhead............	60,000	61,200
Variable factory overhead........	40,000	40,800
Cost of goods sold, normal..........	$250,000	$255,000
Less: Overabsorbed overhead......	....	12,000
Cost of goods sold, net..............	$250,000	$243,000

    b) Variable costing:

Cost of goods sold:		
Direct labor.....................	$ 50,000	$ 51,000
Direct materials..................	100,000	102,000
Variable factory overhead........	40,000	40,800
Variable cost of goods sold......	$190,000	$193,800
Fixed factory overhead..............	60,000	60,000
Total charge to income..............	$250,000	$253,800

9–10. *a*)

	1st Quarter	*2nd Quarter*
Sales.....................................	$300,000	$450,000
Cost of goods sold...........................	220,000	330,000
Gross margin..............................	$ 80,000	$120,000
Less:		
Selling and administrative expenses............	$ 25,000	$ 27,000
Underabsorbed overhead......................	......	36,000
Total deductions....................	$ 25,000	$ 63,000
Profit.......................................	$ 55,000	$ 57,000
Ending inventory.............................	$110,000	$ 44,000

b)

	1st Quarter	2nd Quarter
Sales...	$300,000	$450,000
Cost of goods sold...........................	100,000	150,000
Gross margin..............................	$200,000	$300,000
Less:		
Selling and administrative expenses...........	$ 25,000	$ 27,000
Fixed overhead.............................	180,000	180,000
Total deductions......................	$205,000	$207,000
Profit (loss)...............................	$ (5,000)	$ 93,000
Ending inventory...........................	$ 50,000	$ 20,000

c)

	Full Cost	Direct Cost
Sales...	$450,000	$450,000
Cost of goods sold...........................	330,000	150,000
Gross margin..............................	$120,000	$300,000
Less:		
Selling and administrative expenses...........	$ 27,000	$ 27,000
Fixed costs................................	...	180,000
Total deductions......................	$ 27,000	$207,000
Profit.......................................	$ 93,000	$ 93,000
Ending inventory...........................	$110,000	$ 50,000

Chapter 10

10–1.

	Melting and Pouring	Molding	Core Making	Cleaning and Grinding
Indirect labor.................	$1,000	$300	$100	$300
Supplies used.................	50	50	200	100
Taxes:				
Machinery and equipment...	4	1	3	4
Building....................	3	12	3	6
Compensation insurance.......	20	15	6	24
Power......................	10	x	10	30
Heat and light...............	10	40	10	20
Depreciation:				
Building....................	8	32	8	16
Machinery.................	20	5	15	20
	$1,125	$455	$355	$520

10–2. *a*)   Dept. X charging rate $= \dfrac{\$2,000}{20,000} + \$0.20 = \$0.30/\text{service unit}$

Component of departmental burden rates:

Dept. 1: 1,000 × $0.30/10,000....... $0.03/direct labor hour
Dept. 2: 5,000 × $0.30/ 8,000....... $0.1875/direct labor hour
Dept. 3: 8,000 × $0.30/20,000....... $0.12/machine-hour
Dept. 4: 6,000 × $0.30/15,000....... $0.12/direct labor hour

Cost of S service included in cost of 1,000 units of product A:

Dept. 1: $0.03 × 10............................ $ 0.30
Dept. 2: $0.1875 × 20........................ 3.75
Dept. 3: $0.12 × 100........................ 12.00
Dept. 4: $0.12 × 5.......................... 0.60
Total.................................... $16.65

b) Cost of S service included in cost of 1,000 units of product A under variable costing:

Dept. 1: no department S cost because departmental
     consumption of S service is fixed............... ....
Dept. 2: $0.20 × ⅝ × 20.......................... $ 2.50
Dept. 3: $0.20 × ⁸⁄₂₀ × 100......................., 8.00
Dept. 4: $0.20 × ⁶⁄₁₅ × 5........................... 0.40
Total... $10.90

10–9. *a*) Dept. A: $\dfrac{\$12,000}{6,000 \text{ units}} = \$2/\text{unit}$

Dept. B: $\dfrac{\$18,000}{8,000 \text{ units}} = \$2.25/\text{unit}$

Dept. C: $\dfrac{\$20,000}{12,000 \text{ units}} = \$1.67/\text{unit}$

b)

	Dept. A	Dept. B	Dept. C	Production
Direct charges..........	$12,000	$18,000	$20,000	xxx
Allocations:				
Service dept. A.......	(12,000)	1,800	1,200	$ 9,000
Service dept. B........		(19,800)	2,949	16,851
Service dept. C........			(24,149)	24,149

Charging rates:
Department A: $12,000/8,000 = $1.50/service unit
Department B: $19,800/9,400 = $2.1064/service unit
Department C: $24,149/12,000 = $2.0124/service unit

c) Dept. A = $2.0788/unit
Dept. B = $2.2146/unit
Dept. C = $1.6510/unit

Computations:

$$\text{Rate}_A = \frac{\$12,000 + 600 \times \text{Rate}_B + 2,000 \times \text{Rate}_C}{8,000} \tag{1}$$

$$\text{Rate}_B = \frac{\$18,000 + 1,200 \times \text{Rate}_A + 1,000 \times \text{Rate}_C}{10,000} \tag{2}$$

$$\text{Rate}_C = \frac{\$20,000 + 800 \times \text{Rate}_A + 1,400 \times \text{Rate}_B}{15,000} \tag{3}$$

$$8{,}000 \ \text{Rate}_A = 12{,}000 + 600 \times \text{Rate}_B + 2{,}000 \times \text{Rate}_C \qquad (1)$$
$$\text{Rate}_A = 1.5 + 0.075 \ \text{Rate}_B + 0.25 \ \text{Rate}_C \qquad (1a)$$

Substituting this in equations (2) and (3):

$$10{,}000 \ \text{Rate}_B = 18{,}000 + (1{,}800 + 90 \ \text{Rate}_B + 300 \ \text{Rate}_C)$$
$$+1{,}000 \ \text{Rate}_C$$
$$9{,}910 \ \text{Rate}_B = 19{,}800 + 1{,}300 \ \text{Rate}_C \qquad (2a)$$
$$15{,}000 \ \text{Rate}_C = 20{,}000 + (1{,}200 + 60 \ \text{Rate}_B + 200 \ \text{Rate}_C)$$
$$+ 1{,}400 \ \text{Rate}_B$$
$$14{,}800 \ \text{Rate}_C = 21{,}200 + 1{,}460 \ \text{Rate}_B \qquad (3a)$$

Solving (2a) for Rate_B:

$$\text{Rate}_B = \frac{19{,}800}{9{,}910} + \frac{1{,}300}{9{,}910} \ \text{Rate}_C$$

Substituting in (3a):
$$14{,}800 \ \text{Rate}_C = \$21{,}200 + \frac{1{,}460 \times 19{,}800}{9{,}910} + \frac{1{,}460 \times 1{,}300}{9{,}910} \ \text{Rate}_C$$
$$\text{Rate}_C = \$1.6510/\text{unit}$$

Substituting this in (2a):
$$9{,}910 \ \text{Rate}_B = 19{,}800 + (1{,}300 \times \$1.6510)$$
$$\text{Rate}_B = \$2.2146/\text{unit}$$

Substituting in (1a):
$$\text{Rate}_A = \$1.5 + 0.075 \times \$2.2146 + 0.25 \times \$1.6510$$
$$\text{Rate}_A = \$2.0788/\text{unit}$$

Chapter 11

11–4. Aviation gasoline: $\left(\dfrac{\$ \ 50{,}000}{\$460{,}000} \times \$440{,}000\right) \div 8{,}000 \ \text{bbl.} = \$5.978$

Motor gasoline: $\left(\dfrac{\$210{,}000}{\$460{,}000} \times \$440{,}000\right) \div 42{,}000 \ \text{bbl.} = \$4.783$

Kerosene: $\left(\dfrac{\$ \ 44{,}000}{\$460{,}000} \times \$440{,}000\right) \div 10{,}000 \ \text{bbl.} = \$4.209$

Distillate fuels: $\left(\dfrac{\$ \ 80{,}000}{\$460{,}000} \times \$440{,}000\right) \div 20{,}000 \ \text{bbl.} = \$3.826$

Lubricants: $\left(\dfrac{\$ \ 50{,}000}{\$460{,}000} \times \$440{,}000\right) \div 5{,}000 \ \text{bbl.} = \$9.565$

Residual fuels: $\left(\dfrac{\$ \ 26{,}000}{\$460{,}000} \times \$440{,}000\right) \div 10{,}000 \ \text{bbl.} = \$2.487$

11–6. Total cost:

Material A	$12.00
Material B	7.50
Labor	6.00
Overhead	10.50
Total	$36.00

Product	Price	Value	% of Value	Allocation	Cost/Unit
I....................	$0.60	$18	37.5	$13.50	$0.45/lb.
II....................	0.40	24	50.0	18.00	0.30/lb.
III...................	0.30	6	12.5	4.50	0.225/gal.
Total...............		$48	100.0	$36.00	

11–11.

	Materials	Processing
Equivalent production:		
Finished output:		
Product A.........................	$ 8,000	$ 8,000
Product B.........................	12,000	12,000
Ending work in process:		
Product A: 2,000 × ½ × $0.80.......	800	400
Product B: 2,000 × ¼ × $2.40.......	1,200	600
Total...............................	$22,000	$21,000
Joint cost............................	$ 7,920	$ 9,240
Cost: Percent of market value............	36%	44% = 80% total

Unit cost:
Product A: 80% × $0.80 = $0.64
Product B: 80% × $2.40 = $1.92

Chapter 12

12–3.   Initial mix: Cost 80¢/gal.
After boiling: Cost 80¢/3/4 gal. = $1.067/gal.
Sugar   0.040/gal.
Total $1.107/gal.

After filling: $1.107/0.98 gal. = $1.129/gal. = $0.141/pint.

12–4. **a)** Average cost = $100 × (0.9)^3 = $72.90
Total cost = 800 × $72.90 = $58,320

b) Average cost = $72.90 × 0.9 = $65.61
Total cost = 1,600 × $65.61 = $104,976
Additional cost = $104,976 − $58,320 = $46,656 or $58.32/unit

c) Average cost = $10,000 × 9^s where $s = \dfrac{-0.0458}{0.301} = -0.15216$

Log av. cost = log 10,000 − 0.15216 log 9
= 4 − 0.1452 = 3.8548
Average cost = $71.5833/unit
Total cost = 900 × $71.5833 = $64,425
Incremental cost = $64,425 − $58,320 = $6,105 or $61.05/unit

12–6. There is room for legitimate differences of opinion as to the appropriate standard costs in this problem. This is typical of actual practice, however, and there is reason to be aware of this.

Wage rates: Although man-hours may be correlated with experience and therefore with wage rates, the evidence is not conclusive and thus the average wage rates, for each job category, are probably acceptable.

Crew composition: The composition of the breading crews has shown wide variation, although total man-hours per item seems to be relatively constant at all volumes. Furthermore, the 1-2-3 ratio of the three job categories held true exactly for the 2,000-item and 2,500-item batches. For the two smaller batches, the higher ratio of head cook hours to total hours probably indicates indivisibilities, in that the smaller the batch, the greater will be the proportion of the work performed by the head cook. Deviations of this kind represent higher cost operations and selection of 1-2-3 crew proportions will serve to emphasize these deviations. On these grounds, the man-hour data for the 2,000-item batch are probably reasonable.

Standard cost:

Head cooks:	3 hrs. at $3.80.........	$11.40
Assistant cooks:	6 hrs. at 3.15.........	18.90
Helpers:	9 hrs. at 1.80.........	16.20
Total	18 hrs................	$46.50 or 2.325¢/item and $2.583/man-hour

Chapter 13

13–1. *a*) Price = 1.4 × standard manufacturing cost

$$\text{Gross margin} = 0.4 \times \text{standard factory cost} = \frac{0.4}{1.4} \times \text{price}$$

$$\text{Break-even order size} = \frac{\$1.50}{0.4/1.4} = \$5.25$$

b) The main weakness in this analysis is that $1.50 may not be a good measure of the cost attributable to each order. For one thing, many of the fixed costs included in the averages used may be relatively indivisible. Second, costs of functions such as warehousing and shipping are likely to be less closely correlated with the number of orders than with other factors.

13–3.

	Bulk	Express
Variable cost (at actual):		
Loading-unloading..................................	$ 517	$ 517
Truck operation*:		
Labor..	2,250	1,440
Supplies and parts.............................	1,284	428
Employee benefits.............................	225	144
Truck repairs.................................	732	244
Total variable cost..................................	$5,008	$2,773

* Labor and employee benefits costs for truck operation distributed on basis of road time; supplies and parts costs distributed on basis of mileage.

The variable costs may also be computed on the basis of predetermined rates. In the case of truck repair costs, this may be a more accurate reflection of the costs than those actually recorded this month.

It makes little sense to allocate the undistributed fixed costs to the various functions and even less to divide these between bulk and express shipments. The fixed costs of truck operation probably should be allocated on the basis of total hours, including loading and unloading time as well as road time. The reason for this is that the company could probably use fewer trucks if one class of business or the other were to be discontinued, and that capacity is probably more a function of time than of miles. On this basis, the express deliveries should be assigned 520/1,220 of the fixed costs of truck operation, or $286, with the remaining $386 being assigned to bulk deliveries. The fixed costs of loading and unloading and of truck repairs are unlikely to be affected substantially by large changes in the volume of business in either type of delivery.

Chapter 14

14–2.

Material	Issued to Production (Units)		
	January	February	March
W	2,520	2,800	3,290
X	630	420	840
Y	10,000	9,920	11,060
Z	2,850	2,940	3,045

Material	January			February		
	Orders	Deliveries	EOM Inventory	Orders	Deliveries	EOM Inventory
W	....	4,000	5,480	4,000	....	2,680
X	1,000	....	1,370	....	1,000	1,950
Y	....	20,000	26,000	20,000	....	16,080
Z	....	....	4,150	5,000	....	1,210

	March		
	Orders	Deliveries	EOM Inventory
W	4,000	4,000	3,390
X	1,000	....	1,110
Y	....	20,000	25,020
Z	5,000	5,000	3,165

Material	January		February		March	
	Deliv. ($)	Payments	Deliv. ($)	Payments	Deliv. ($)	Payments
W	$ 800	$ 800		....	$ 800	$ 800
X	....	5,000	$5,000	....	....	5,000
Y	10,000	10,000	....	....	10,000	10,000
Z	....	....	....	....	10,000	10,000
Total	$10,800	$15,800	$5,000	....	$20,800	$25,800

Chapter 15

15–1.

Actual wages: 1,900 × $3.85	$7,315	
Actual hours × standard wage rate: 1,900 × $3.80. .	7,220	
Labor rate variance.		$(95)
Standard labor cost: 2 × 1,000 × $3.80	7,600	
Labor quantity variance.		380
Total labor variance.		$285

15–2.

Labor quantity variance:		
Standard labor quantity:		
1,500 units of A @ 2 hours × $4	$12,000	
4,000 units of B @ 3 hours × $4	48,000	
Total standard labor cost.	$60,000	
Actual labor quantity (14,500 hours @ $4)	58,000	
Favorable quantity variance.		$2,000
Labor rate variance, actual hours:		
Standard cost (14,500 @ $4)	$58,000	
Actual payroll.	59,000	
Unfavorable rate variance.		(1,000)
Net labor variance.		$1,000

15–3.

Units finished: 3,000 × $3	$9,000	
Ending inventory: 800 × ¼ × $3	600	
	$9,600	
Less: Beginning inventory: 500 × ½ × $3	750	
Standard direct labor cost of month's output.	$8,850	

15–6. Materials price variance:

Actual cost of materials purchased.	$110,000
Standard cost of materials purchased: 20,000 × $6	120,000
Materials price variance.	$ 10,000

Materials quantity variance:

Standard materials cost:	
Product A: 5,000 × 3 × $6	$ 90,000
Product B: 1,200 × 4 × $6	28,800
Total standard materials cost.	$118,800
Standard cost of materials used: 22,000 × $6	132,000
Materials quantity variance.	$(13,200)

Chapter 16

16–2. *a)*

Raw Material and Supplies				Material in Process			
Bal. 9/1	58,500	(5)	46,650	Bal. 9/1	6,700	(3)	40,350
(2)	44,620	Bal. 10/1	56,470	(5)	46,650	(6)	700
						Bal. 10/1	12,300
Bal. 10/1	56,470						
				Bal. 10/1	12,300		

Labor in Process				Accrued Wages			
Bal. 9/1	2,400	(3)	22,300	(8)	23,600	(4)	23,600
(4)	23,600						
(6)	1,000	Bal. 10/1	4,700				
Bal. 10/1	4,700						

		Control	
		Bal. 9/1	99,700
		(2)	42,380
		(8)	24,400

Finished Goods			
Bal. 9/1	32,100	(7)	63,500
(3)	62,650	Bal. 10/1	31,250
Bal. 10/1	31,250		

Cost of Goods Sold	
(7)	63,500

Material Price Variance		Labor Quantity Variance	
	(2) 2,240		(6) 1,000

Materials Quantity Variance		Wage Rate Variance	
(6) 700		(8) 800	

b)

Materials price variance.........	$2,240 Favorable
Wage rate variance.............	(800) Unfavorable
Materials quantity variance.......	(700) Unfavorable
Labor quantity variance..........	1,000 Favorable
Net variance..................	$1,740 Favorable

16–3. *a*) Materials costs earned = $30,000 − $5,000 = $25,000

Assuming that materials quantity variances are proportional to costs earned, the variance ratio is $5,000/$25,000 = 20 percent. Applying this ratio to ending work-in-process and finished goods inventories:

To work in process: $5,000 × 20%............. $ 1,000
To finished goods: 7,000 × 20%........... 1,400
                                              $ 2,400

Remainder, to cost of goods sold.............. $ 2,600

Cost of goods sold:
 Costs earned.............................. $25,000
 Decrease in work in process.................. 1,100
 Decrease in finished goods.................. 1,000
  Cost of goods sold at standard.............. $27,100
 Materials quantity variance:
  From prior year........................... (900)
  From this year............................ 2,600
 Adjusted cost of goods sold.................... $28,800

b) Materials Quantity Variances in Inventories........ 3,300
     Cost of Goods Sold............................ 1,700
          Materials Quantity Variances................   5,000

16–5.

(1) Materials............................... 123,000
     Purchase Price Variance.................... 8,000
          Accounts Payable....................   131,000

(2) Materials in Process...................... 140,000
          Materials...........................   140,000

(3) Materials Quantity Variance............... 12,000
          Materials...........................   12,000

(4) Materials............................... 8,000
          Materials Quantity Variance...........   8,000

(5) Labor in Process.......................... 80,000
     Labor Quantity Variance.................. 5,600
          Payroll Cost Summary.................   85,600

(6) Accrued Wages Payable.................... 8,200
          Payroll Cost Summary.................   8,200
     (Reversing entry.)

(7) Payroll Cost Summary...................... 79,500
          Cash...............................   79,500

(8) Payroll Cost Summary..................... 16,300
          Accrued Wages Payable...............   16,300

(9) Finished Goods........................... 198,900
          Materials in Process..................   122,400
          Labor in Process....................   76,500

(10) Labor Rate Variance....................... 2,000
          Payroll Cost Summary.................   2,000

Materials				Materials in Process		
(1)	123,000	(2)	140,000	(2)	140,000	(9)	122,400
(4)	8,000	(3)	12,000				

Labor in Process			Purchase Price Variance		
(5)	80,000	(9) 76,500	(1)	8,000	

Materials Quantity Variance			Labor Quantity Variance		
(3)	12,000	(4) 8,000	(5)	5,600	

Payroll Cost Summary			Accrued Wages Payable		
(7)	79,500	(5) 85,600	(6) 8,200	Bal.	8,200
(8)	16,300	(6) 8,200		(8)	16,300
		(10) 2,000			

Finished Goods		Labor Rate Variance	
(9)	198,900	(10)	2,000

Chapter 17

17–3. *a*) Only the first three overhead cost items listed are likely to be of any significance in evaluating the cost control performance of the department supervisor, and of these nonproductive time and other indirect labor have the greatest impact. Depreciation and building service charges are noncontrollable and have no bearing on managerial evaluation in this department.

b) Labor costs did not go down with decreasing volume. There are many possible reasons for this. This may merely be a time lag—management may have decided not to cut the labor force to meet the volume reduction in the hope that volume would recover quickly. This should be examined more critically if volume continues at these newer and lower levels. We cannot ignore any one month's reports, but we need to examine them in the context of a longer period of time. Even two months is likely to be too short a period for random forces to have averaged themselves out.

The other item in which the variance has increased is depreciation, and this should be labeled as noncontrollable.

Chapter 19

19–4. Charging rates:

$$\text{Plant operation} = \frac{\$22,110}{67,000 \text{ sq. ft.}} = 33\text{¢/sq. ft.}$$

$$\text{Factory office} = \frac{\$19,490 + 3,000 \times \$0.33}{64 \text{ employees}} = \$320/\text{employee}$$

$$\text{Storeroom} = \frac{\$24,460 + 10,000 \times \$0.33 + 2 \times \$320}{100 \text{ percent}}$$

$$= \$284/\text{percent}$$

Cost distribution sheet:

	Plant Operation	Factory Office	Storeroom	Milling	Machining	Painting	Assembly
Direct...........	$22,110	$19,490	$24,460	$40,000	$35,000	$42,000	$30,000
Allocations:							
Plant operation.	(22,110)	990	3,300	5,940	3,960	4,950	2,970
Factory office..		(20,480)	640	8,960	4,480	3,520	2,880
Storeroom.....			(28,400)	7,384	2,840	6,816	11,360
Total...........				$62,284	$46,280	$57,286	$47,210

19–7. *a)* Charge variable maintenance costs on the basis of $4.50 per maintenance labor hour. Charge the fixed component on the basis of normal monthly hours per production department. (Criteria of facilities provided and usage.)

Charge fixed finance department costs on the basis of each department's share of normal employment, the variable component at $1 per actual equivalent full-time employee. (Criteria of facilities provided and variability.) Actually, because costs are so nearly totally fixed, the entire charge might be predetermined on grounds of lower clerical cost.

Maintenance:

	Charged to Production	Actual	Variance
Fixed..................	$10,800	.....	....
Variable...............	59,850	.....	....
Total.................	$70,650	$72,900	$2,250

Finance:

Fixed..................	$18,000	.....	....
Variable...............	1,200	.....	....
Total.................	$19,200	$20,000	$ 800

b) The maintenance department variance reflects either poor cost control, rising wage rates, and so forth, or transitional effects of changing from one level of service volume to another. There is no volume variance as such, but it should be remembered that volume variances of a sort may arise when volume is changing rapidly and management either has not had time to adjust or has decided for other reasons not to adjust.

The finance department's variance may be interpreted in a similar fashion, except that it is not service provided but the number of employees that gives rise to transitional variances.

Chapter 20

20–1. *a*) $2 \times 30 + $3 \times 45 + $5 \times 25 = 320

b)

Product	Costs Earned		Mix Variance
	Actual Mix	Standard Mix	
A..........................	$ 3,200	$ 2,970	$ 230
B..........................	7,200	6,682	518
C..........................	4,750	6,188	(1,438)
Total......................	$15,150	$15,840	$ (690)
Actual cost.................	17,300	17,300	
Yield variance..............		$(1,460)	
Total variance.............	$(2,150)		

The yield variance can be further broken down into two parts:

Actual cost of processing 5,000 pounds..............	$17,300	
Standard cost of processing 5,000 pounds............	16,000	
Processing cost variance.......................		$(1,300)
Standard cost of lost units: 50 × $3.20..........		(160)
Total yield variance...........................		$(1,460)

20–2.

Actual labor cost............................	$30,000	
Actual labor hours at standard rates..............	29,000	
Labor rate variance.........................		$(1,000)
Actual labor hours at standard rates, standard mix (9,000 hours × $3.50).....................	31,500	
Labor mix variance..........................		2,500
Standard labor cost...........................	32,000	
Labor quantity variance......................		500
Total labor variance...........................		$ 2,000

20–5. Because overhead costs vary with *actual* machine-hours, a three-variance system should be used:

Actual.....................................	$21,750	
Budget at actual hours.......................	21,500	
Spending variance..........................		$ 250 unfavorable
Budget at standard hours.....................	22,000	
Machine efficiency variance.................		500 favorable
Earned.....................................	20,000	
Volume variance............................		2,000 unfavorable
Total variance.............................		$1,750 unfavorable

20–16.   *a)*

Materials Inventory				Purchase Price Variance		
Bal.	11,400	(3)	6,000	(2)	450	
(2)	5,400					
		Bal.	10,800			
Bal.	10,800					

Matls. in Process.—Dept. I				Payroll Cost Summary		
Bal.	2,400	(6a)	900	(4a)	14,200	(4b)	14,000
(3)	6,000	(6b)	3,000			
(8)	300	(6c)	3,600			
		Bal.	1,200			
Bal.	1,200					

Labor in Proc.—Dept. I				Overhead in Proc.—Dept. I		
Bal.	1,600	(6a)	2,400	Bal.	2,400	(6a)	3,600
(4b)	14,000	(6b)	6,000	(7)	18,300	(6b)	9,000
		(6c)	4,000			(6c)	6,000
		(9)	1,800			Bal.	2,100
		Bal.	1,400				
Bal.	1,400			Bal.	2,100		

Overhead Summary—Dept. I				Overhead Absorbed—Dept. I		
(5)	25,500	(10)	23,000*	(12)	22,100*	(7)	18,300
		(11)	2,500			(13)	3,800

Matls. Qty. Var.—Dept. I				Overhead Spending Var.—Dept. I		
		(8)	300	(11)	2,500		

Ov. Lab. Eff. Var.—Dept. I			
(10)	23,000*	(12)	22,100*

Labor Qty. Var.—Dept. I			
(9)	1,800		

Overhead Volume Var.—Dept. I			
(13)	3,800		

Matls. in Proc.—Dept. II				Payables, etc.		
(6a)	6,900				(2)	5,850
(6b)	18,000				(4)	14,200
(6c)	13,600				(5)	25,500

* Budget at actual hours: $16,000 + $2 \times 3,500 = $23,000$
Budget at standard hours: $16,000 + $2 \times 3,050 = $22,100$

Entries (10) and (12) may be omitted, but they facilitate the breakdown of the overhead variance. Entries (4a) and (4b) may be combined as a single entry.

b)

Materials price variance	$ (450)
Labor rate variance	(200)
Materials quantity variance	300
Labor quantity variance	(1,800)
Overhead spending variance	(2,500)
Overhead labor efficiency variance	(900)
Overhead volume variance	(3,800)
Total variance	$(9,350)

Chapter 21

21–2.

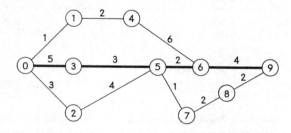

Critical path: 0–3–5–6–9 = 14 weeks.

Chapter 24

24–1. Budgeted profit margin per unit:

Sales		$6.00
Direct materials	$1.00	
Direct labor	1.30	
Variable overhead	0.52	
Fixed overhead	0.78	3.60
Profit margin		$2.40

Variance summary:

Increased sales volume: 1,000 × $2.40*	$ 2,400
Increased production volume*	780
Reduced selling price: 11,000 × $0.50	(5,500)
Materials quantity variance	(200)
Labor quantity variance	(400)
Overhead spending variance	(420)
Overhead labor efficiency variance	(160)
Selling and administrative expense variance	(500)
Total variance	$(4,000)

* These two figures would be combined in a variable costing system, and can be reported as a single figure if the change in production volume is assumed to be the effect of the change in sales volume.

24–6. On a product-by-product basis, two variances can be distinguished (numbers in the column headings refer to figures in the supporting calculations below):

	Sales Vol. Var. (1) – (3)	Sales Price Var. (3) – (4)	Total Variance (1) – (4)
Product X.........	$2,000	$1,200	$3,200
Product Y.........	(1,800)	(400)	(2,200)
Product Z.........	1,000	(500)	500
Total............	$1,200	$ 300	$1,500

The total of the sales volume variances can be further analyzed into mix and volume components, using figures from the calculations below:

Sales volume variance: (1) – (2)...... $1,200
Sales mix variance: (2) – (3)......... ...
　　Total............................. $1,200

These figures are based on the following calculations:

(1) Budgeted margin:

	Revenues	Costs	Margin	Unit Margin
Product X.......	$20,000	$12,000	$ 8,000	$0.80
Product Y.......	30,000	21,000	9,000	1.80
Product Z.......	20,000	16,000	4,000	1.00
Total..........	$70,000	$49,000	$21,000	30%

(2) Budgeted margin at actual volume and budgeted mix:

$74,000 \times 30\%$.......... $22,200

(3) Budgeted margin at actual volume and mix:

	Units Sold	Unit Margin	Total Margin
Product X..............	12,500	$0.80	$10,000
Product Y..............	4,000	1.80	7,200
Product Z..............	5,000	1.00	5,000
Total.................			$22,200

(4) Actual margin:

	Revenues	Costs	Margin
Product X...........	$26,200	$12,000	$11,200
Product Y...........	23,600	16,800	6,800
Product Z...........	24,500	20,000	4,500
Total..............	$74,300	$51,800	$22,500

Chapter 25

25–2. The memorandum should stress the following points:

If the alternative is idleness, the only incremental costs may be the variable costs of 90 cents a pound, and this is far less than the proposed transfer price. Hull's profit will be 70 cents greater for every pound of X it processes for the Hingham division. Without these 50,000 pounds, product X would show a loss of $20,000 after deducting its share of division fixed costs; with this production, the net profit figure would be $15,000.

If the Hull division will retain idle workers on the payroll in the absence of production to avoid losing a skilled work force, the incremental cost could be even less than 90 cents a pound because some labor costs would be sunk.

Even if the traceable fixed costs increase in steps, it is unlikely that these could be high enough to make an incremental loss. At the present volume they average only 27 cents a pound.

Divisional fixed costs may change with production, but not in the proportion indicated—variability tends to be small in these items.

Finally, the division manager should recognize a longer term problem—if cheaper substitutes are available, this may indicate a serious competitive weakness for the long run.

Chapter 26

26–1. *a)*

Time	Cash Flow	10 Per-cent Factor	PV at 10 Percent	PV at X Percent	Internal Rate of Return
				12%	
0............	−$10,000	1.000	−$10,000	−$10,000	
1–10.........	+ 1,750/yr.	6.145	+ 10,754	+ 9,888	
Net PV.......			+$ 754	−$ 112	11.7%

b)

				15%	
0............	−$10,000	1.000	−$10,000	−$10,000	
1–10.........	+ 1,500/yr.	6.145	+ 9,217	+ 7,529	
1–5..........	+ 500/yr.	3.791	+ 1,896	+ 1,676	
Net PV.......			+$ 1,113	−$ 795	12.9%

c)

				11%	
0............	−$10,000	1.000	−$10,000	−$10,000	
1–5..........	+ 1,500/yr.	3.791	+ 5,686	+ 5,544	
6–10.........	+ 2,000/yr.	2.354	+ 4,708	+ 4,386	
Net PV......			+$ 394	−$ 70	10.8%

d)

				9%	
0............	−$10,000	1.000	−$10,000	−$10,000	
1–10.........	+ 1,350/yr.	6.145	+ 8,296	+ 8,665	
10...........	+ 4,000	0.386	+ 1,544	+ 1,688	
Net PV......			−$ 160	+$ 352	9.7%

e)

				15%	
0............	−$10,000	1.000	−$10,000	−$10,000	
1–15.........	+ 1,750/yr.	7.606	+ 13,310	+ 10,232	
Net PV......			+$ 3,310	+$ 232	
				20%	
0............	−$10,000			−$10,000	
1–15.........	+ 1,750/yr.			+ 8,181	
Net PV.......				−$ 1,819	15.6%

26–6. *a)*

	Gross	Tax	Net
Purchase price.....................	$50,000	......	$ 50,000
Training..........................	10,000	$ (4,000)	6,000
Investment credit..................	......	(3,500)	(3,500)
Salvage (old machine)..............	(8,000)	(4,800)	(12,800)
Incremental outlay.................	$52,000	$(12,300)	$ 39,700

b) Gross cash savings before tax.................... $ 6,800
      Tax depreciation:
         New: 30% of $50,000....................... $15,000
         Old...................................... 3,000
            Increased depreciation...................... (12,000)
      Taxable saving................................ $ (5,200)
      Tax reduction at 40%.......................... (2,080)
      After-tax incremental cash savings................ $ 8,880

26–10. *a*) Initial outlay:
            Cost of machine............................ −$50,000
            Less: Sale value of old machine................ $10,000
               Tax reduction on retirement loss
                  on old machine...................... 10,000   + 20,000
            Net initial outlay............................ −$30,000
            Present value at 10% of after-tax future cash
               savings (see table below)...................... + 68,448
            Net present value............................ +$38,448

Calculation of discounted cash flows:

(1)	(2)	(3)	(4)	(5)	(6)	(7)	(8)	(9)
Years Hence	Net Book Value of New Machine	Tax Depreciation	Depreciation on old Machine	Increase in Depreciation	Taxable Income	Income Tax	After-Tax Cash Flow	Present Value at 10 Percent
1..........	$50,000	$10,000	$ 3,750	$ 6,250	$ 13,750	$ 6,875	$ 13,125	$11,931
2..........	40,000	8,000	3,750	4,250	15,750	7,875	12,125	10,015
3..........	32,000	6,400	3,750	2,650	17,350	8,675	11,325	8,505
4..........	25,600	5,120	3,750	1,370	18,630	9,315	10,685	7,298
5..........	20,480	4,096	3,750	346	19,654	9,827	10,173	6,317
6..........	16,384	3,277	3,750	− 473	20,473	10,237	9,763	5,506
7..........	13,107	2,621	3,750	− 1,129	21,129	10,564	9,436	4,841
8..........	10,486	2,097	3,750	− 1,653	21,653	10,826	9,174	4,284
9..........	8,389	1,678	—	1,678	18,322	9,161	10,839	4,596
10..........	{ 6,711 / 5,369	1,342 / 5,369	— / —	1,342 / 5,369	} 13,289	6,645	13,355	5,155
Total.......		$50,000	$30,000	$20,000	$180,000	$90,000	$110,000	$68,448

(3) 20% of (2).
(4) 12.5% of $30,000 (remaining book value).
(5) Col. 4 − Col. 3.
(6) $20,000 cash flow less increase in depreciation (col. 5).
(7) 50% of col. 6.
(8) $20,000 less col. 7.
(9) Col. 8 × Table 1, Appendix A.

b) The rate lies between 30 and 40 percent and must be approximated by interpolation. The calculations are:

Year	30% Factor	PV at 30%	40% Factor	PV at 40%
0.........	1.000	−$30,000	1.000	−$30,000
1.........	0.769	+ 10,093	0.714	+ 9,371
2.........	0.592	+ 7,178	0.510	+ 6,184
3.........	0.455	+ 5,153	0.364	+ 4,122
4.........	0.350	+ 3,740	0.260	+ 2,778
5.........	0.269	+ 2,737	0.186	+ 1,892
6.........	0.207	+ 2,021	0.133	+ 1,298
7.........	0.159	+ 1,500	0.095	+ 896
8.........	0.123	+ 1,128	0.068	+ 624
9.........	0.094	+ 1,019	0.048	+ 520
10.........	0.073	+ 975	0.035	+ 467
Net PV......		+$ 5,544		−$ 1,848

$$\text{Rate of return} = 30\% + \frac{5,544}{5,544 + 1,848} \times 10\% = 37.5\%$$

Chapter 27

27–3.

Price	Sales (Units)	Sales Revenues	Fixed Costs	Variable Costs	Total Costs	Profit Margin
$0.75......	100,000	$75,000	$11,000	$62,500	$73,500	$ 1,500
0.80......	90,000	72,000	11,000	55,400	66,400	5,600
0.85......	80,000	68,000	11,000	48,700	59,700	8,300
0.90......	70,000	63,000	10,000	42,300	52,300	10,700
0.95......	60,000	57,000	10,000	36,100	46,100	10,900
1.00......	50,000	50,000	10,000	30,000	40,000	10,000

The most profitable price is $0.95/unit.

27–4. *a*)

	West Coast	Midwest
Sales....................	$32.50	$44.00
Variable costs:		
Materials................	$18.70	$18.70
Labor...................	3.00	3.00
Variable burden..........	3.30	3.30
Freight.................	....	1.50
Commissions.............	....	2.20
Total variable cost.....	$25.00	$28.70
Variable profit.............	$ 7.50	$15.30

The indications are that the company could increase its profit by $7,500 − $1,500 a month, or $6,000. All present fixed costs can be charged against existing sales in making this decision.

b) One factor that definitely should be considered is whether the West Coast distributors would reship the products to distributors in the Midwest. The delivered cost in the Midwest would be $39.50. This is substantially less than the price now quoted to Midwest dealers, but whether it is low enough to tempt the West Coast distributors to set up a clandestine distribution outlet in the company's present market areas is not clear. The West Coast distributor would be unlikely to risk the loss of a franchise on which he has made a good deal of promotional effort, unless, of course, he is finding his West Coast operations unprofitable.

It is fairly certain that reshipment by West Coast dealers is unlikely, nor is it likely that ultimate industrial purchasers who having consuming plants in both areas would find it profitable to buy in the West and reship to the Midwest. There may be some questions on these points in the edges of the company's sales territory, but the issue is probably not serious.

Another problem is how to react to complaints by Midwest retailers when they hear of the lower West Coast retail price. There is probably no Robinson-Patman problem because this is in the nature of a trade discount and the areas are noncompeting, but dealers might exert pressure to get a reduction in the $44 price.

A more fundamental question, of course, is whether the company could go into the West Coast and perform the distribution function more economically—or whether the product would sell as well at $44 as at $42.50 on the West Coast.

Chapter 28

28–1. *a*) The objective function is:

$$\text{Profit} = \$5A + \$8B$$

The constraints are:

$$2A + B \leq 3{,}000$$
$$2A + 4B \leq 6{,}000$$
$$2{,}000 \geq A \geq 0$$
$$2{,}000 \geq B \geq 0$$

b) Construction of the departmental constraint lines:

$$A = 0, B = 3{,}000 \qquad B = 0, A = 1{,}500 \quad (\text{Dept. X})$$
$$A = 0, B = 1{,}500 \qquad B = 0, A = 3{,}000 \quad (\text{Dept. Y})$$

Slope of the isoprofit lines:

$$A = 0, B = 5 \qquad B = 0, A = 8$$

Drawing the graph:

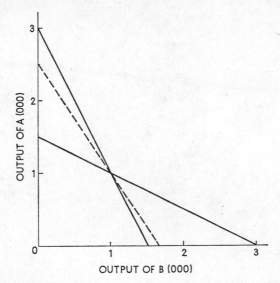

The optimal solution is to produce 1,000 units of each product, for a total profit contribution of $13,000.

An alternative approach is to start with a tentative solution (e.g., $B = O$, $A = 1,500$, using all the capacity of department X), and then see whether profit can be improved by substituting (e.g., one unit of B can be obtained by sacrificing half a unit of A, for a profit gain of $8 - $2.50). This substitution uses up three hours of department Y's idle time, and 1,000 of these substitutions are possible. The optimal solution is as computed above.

c) If the profit contribution of product A rises beyond $16, the optimal solution will be to manufacture no product B. If it falls below $4, the optimal solution will be to manufacture no product A. Between these two values, the optimal decision will be the same.

Index

Index